KT-838-181

Introduction to **Financial Accounting**

Eighth Edition

London Boston Burr Ridge, IL Dubuque, IA Madison, WI New York San Francisco
St. Louis Bangkok Bogotá Caracas Kuala Lumpur Lisbon Madrid Mexico City
Milan Montreal New Delhi Santiago Seoul Singapore Sydney Taipei Toronto

Introduction to Financial Accounting, Eighth Edition
Andrew Thomas & Anne Marie Ward

Published by McGraw-Hill Education
Shoppenhangers Road
Maidenhead
Berkshire
SL6 2QL
Telephone: 44 (0) 1628 502 500
Fax: 44 (0) 1628 770 224
Website: www.mheducation.co.uk

British Library Cataloguing in Publication Data
A catalogue record for this book is available from the British Library

Library of Congress Cataloguing in Publication Data
The Library of Congress data for this book has been applied for from the Library of Congress

Content Acquisitions Manager: Thomas Hill
Product Developer: Alice Aldous
Head of Production: Beverley Shields
Digital Controller: Sarah Fleming
Marketing Manager: Alexis Gibbs

Text Design by Hard Lines Studios
Cover design by Scott Poulson
Printed and bound in Singapore by Markono Print Media Pte Ltd

Published by McGraw-Hill Education. Copyright © 2015 by McGraw-Hill Education. All rights reserved. No part of this publication may be reproduced or distributed in any form or by any means, or stored in a database or retrieval system, without the prior written consent of McGraw-Hill Education, including, but not limited to, in any network or other electronic storage or transmission, or broadcast for distance learning.

Fictitious names of companies, products, people, characters and/or data that may be used herein (in case studies or in examples) are not intended to represent any real individual, company, product or event.

ISBN-13 9780077163884
ISBN-10 0077163885
© 2015. Exclusive rights by McGraw-Hill Education for manufacture and export. This book cannot be re-exported from the country to which it is sold by McGraw-Hill Education.

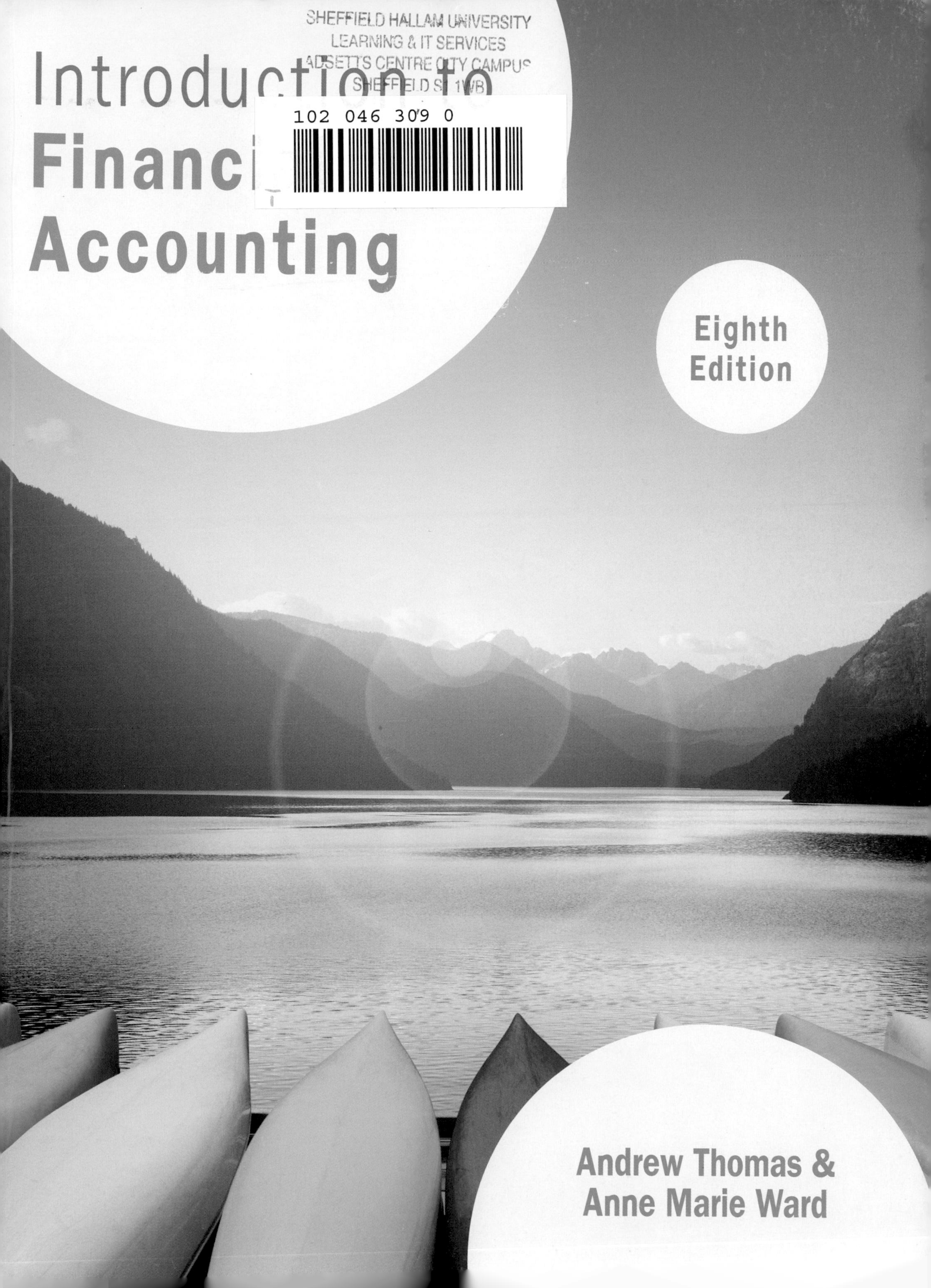

SHEFFIELD HALLAM UNIVERSITY
LEARNING & IT SERVICES
ADSETTS CENTRE CITY CAMPUS
SHEFFIELD S1 1WB
102 046 309 0

For my husband Martin and our kids – Thomas, Anna, Mary, Séamus and Barry

Anne Marie Ward

Brief Table of Contents

PART 1: The framework of accounting 1

1 Entities and financial reporting statements (including the nature and objectives of financial accounting) 3

2 Financial reporting: institutional framework and standards 23

3 The Conceptual Framework 1: objective of financial statements, stakeholders and other reports 43

4 The Conceptual Framework 2: concepts, principles and policies 65

5 The Conceptual Framework 3: the qualitative characteristics of financial information 87

6 Auditing, corporate governance and ethics 99

PART 2: Double-entry bookkeeping (recording transactions and the books of account) 119

7 The accounting equation and its components 121

8 Basic documentation and books of account 137

9 Double entry and the general ledger 149

10 The balancing of accounts and the trial balance 171

11 Day books and the journal 187

12 The cash book 201

13 The petty cash book 217

PART 3: Preparing final financial statements for sole traders 227

14 The final financial statements of sole traders (introductory) 229

15 Depreciation and non-current assets 249

16 Irrecoverable receivables and allowance for irrecoverable receivables 275

17 Accruals and prepayments 291

18 The extended trial balance and final financial statements (advanced) 309

PART 4: Internal control and check 327

19 The bank reconciliation statement 329

20 Control accounts 347

21 Errors and suspense accounts 367

22 Single entry and incomplete records 383

PART 5: Preparing final financial statements for manufacturing entities 409

23 Inventory valuation 411

24 Financial statements for manufacturing entities 429

PART 6: Partnerships 453

25 The final financial statements of partnerships 455

26 Changes in partnerships 485

27 Partnership dissolution and conversion to a limited company 521

PART 7: Companies 539

28 The nature of limited companies and their capital 541

29 The final financial statements of limited companies 557

30 Statement of cash flows 609

31 The appraisal of company financial statements using ratio analysis 647

Appendix 1: Case studies 683

Appendix 2: Solutions to Exercises 699

Index 799

The following chapters are available online at www.mheducation.co.uk/textbooks/thomas

32 The final financial statements of clubs

33 Changes in share capital

34 An introduction to consolidated financial statements

35 Value added tax, columnar books of prime entry and the payroll

36 Accounting for changing price levels

Detailed Table of Contents

About the Authors xv
Preface to Eighth Edition xvi
Acknowledgements xix
Guided Tour xx
Connect xxiii
Online Learning Centre xxvii

PART 1: The framework of accounting 1

1 Entities and financial reporting statements (including the nature and objectives of financial accounting) 3
Learning Objectives 3
1.1 Introduction and history of accounting 4
1.2 The nature and functions of financial accounting 4
1.3 The objectives of an appropriate accounting system 5
1.4 Accounting language 7
1.5 Financial statements 9
1.6 Types of entity 10
1.7 Sole traders 10
1.8 Partnerships 11
1.9 Member-governed bodies 13
1.10 Companies 15
1.11 The regulatory framework of accounting 17
Summary 18
Key terms and concepts 19
Review questions 20
Exercises 20
References 21

2 Financial reporting: institutional framework and standards 23
Learning Objectives 23
2.1 Introduction 24
2.2 The institutional framework for setting IFRSs 25
2.3 The International Accounting Standards Board (IASB) 26
2.4 SME Implementation Group 26
2.5 The IFRS Foundation Trustees 27
2.6 The Monitoring Board of Public Capital Market Authorities 27
2.7 The IFRS Interpretations Committee 27
2.8 The IFRS Advisory Council 28
2.9 IFRS Foundation Support Operations 28
2.10 The standard-setting process 28
2.11 UK Accounting Regulation (and the ROI) 30
2.12 Harmonization 33
2.13 International Financial Reporting Standards (IFRSs) 34
2.14 IAS 1 – Presentation of Financial Statements 34
2.15 IAS 2 – Inventories 35
2.16 IAS 7 – Statement of Cash Flows 35
2.17 IAS 8 – Accounting Policies, Changes in Accounting Estimates and Errors 35
2.18 IAS 10 – Events after the Reporting Period 36
2.19 IAS 16 – Property, Plant and Equipment 36
2.20 IAS 18 – Revenue 36
2.21 IAS 37 – Provisions, Contingent Liabilities and Contingent Assets 37
2.22 IAS 38 – Intangible Assets 37
2.23 IFRS 3 – Business Combinations 37
2.24 IFRS 5 – Non-current Assets Held for Sale and Discontinuing Operations 38

2.25 Current issues 38
Summary 39
Key terms and concepts 39
Review questions 40
Websites 41
References 41

3 The Conceptual Framework 1: objective of financial statements, stakeholders and other reports 43
Learning Objectives 43
3.1 Introduction 44
3.2 The conceptual framework of accounting 44
3.3 The objectives of general purpose financial reporting 47
3.4 The limitations of financial statements 48
3.5 Key users of annual reports and their information needs 50
3.6 Public accountability 51
3.7 Other users of annual reports and their information needs 53
3.8 Corporate social responsibility (CSR) 56
3.9 Environmental accounting (social accounting) 58
3.10 The conceptual framework debate, standardization and choice 59
Summary 60
Key terms and concepts 61
Review questions 62
Websites 62
References 62

4 The Conceptual Framework 2: concepts, principles and policies 65
Learning Objectives 65
4.1 Introduction 66
4.2 Key accounting concepts under the *Conceptual Framework* 66
4.3 Other concepts 69
4.4 Recognition 76
4.5 Measurement 77
4.6 Capital maintenance 78
4.7 Accounting policies 78
4.8 Selecting accounting policies 79
4.9 Changing accounting policies 80
4.10 The disclosure of accounting policies and estimation techniques 80
Summary 81
Key terms and concepts 82
Review questions 83
Exercises 84
References 86

5 The Conceptual Framework 3: the qualitative characteristics of financial information 87
Learning Objectives 87
5.1 The qualitative characteristics of financial information 88
5.2 Relevance 89
5.3 Faithful representation 90
5.4 Enhancing qualitative characteristics 91
5.5 Constraints on the qualitative characteristics 95
Summary 97
Key terms and concepts 97
Review questions 98
References 98

6 Auditing, corporate governance and ethics 99
Learning Objectives 99
6.1 Auditing 100
6.2 Corporate governance 107
6.3 Ethics 111
Summary 114
Key terms and concepts 115
Review questions 116
Exercises 116
References 116

PART 2: Double-entry bookkeeping (recording transactions and the books of account) 119

7 The accounting equation and its components 121
Learning Objectives 121
7.1 The accounting entity 122

7.2 The statement of financial position as an accounting equation 124
7.3 The accounting equation and profit reporting 127
7.4 The accounting period and profit reporting 129
7.5 Revenue expenditure versus capital expenditure 129
7.6 Measurement 132
7.7 Strengths and limitations of historical cost in accounting measurement 132
Summary 133
Key terms and concepts 134
Review questions 134
Exercises 135
References 136

8 Basic documentation and books of account 137
Learning Objectives 137
8.1 Introduction 138
8.2 Basic documentation for cash and credit transactions 138
8.3 Computerized accounting systems 144
Summary 147
Key terms and concepts 148
Review questions 148
Exercises 148

9 Double entry and the general ledger 149
Learning Objectives 149
9.1 The principles of double-entry bookkeeping 150
9.2 Cash and bank transactions 152
9.3 Ledger entries for credit transactions 155
9.4 Adjustments for drawings and capital introduced 161
9.5 Adjustments for goods on sale or return 162
9.6 Ledger account balances 163
Summary 164
Key terms and concepts 165
Exercises 166

10 The balancing of accounts and the trial balance 171
Learning Objectives 171
10.1 The balancing of accounts 172
10.2 The purposes and preparation of a trial balance 178
Summary 183
Key terms and concepts 183
Review question 184
Exercises 184

11 Day books and the journal 187
Learning Objectives 187
11.1 The contents of the day books and the journal 188
11.2 Opening entries/takeovers and the journal 194
Summary 196
Key terms and concepts 197
Review questions 197
Exercises 197

12 The cash book 201
Learning Objectives 201
12.1 Introduction 202
12.2 The two-column cash book 202
12.3 The three-column cash book 209
Summary 211
Key terms and concepts 212
Review questions 212
Exercises 212

13 The petty cash book 217
Learning Objectives 217
13.1 Introduction 218
13.2 The columnar petty cash book 218
13.3 The imprest system 218
Summary 222
Key terms and concepts 222
Review questions 222
Exercises 222

PART 3: Preparing final financial statements for sole traders **227**

14 The final financial statements of sole traders (introductory) 229
Learning Objectives 229
14.1 Introduction 230

14.2 The purpose and structure of statements of profit or loss 230
14.3 Gross profit: inventory and the cost of sales 231
14.4 The purpose and structure of a statement of financial position 234
14.5 Preparing financial statements from the trial balance 236
Summary 241
Key terms and concepts 242
Review questions 242
Exercises 243

15 Depreciation and non-current assets 249
Learning Objectives 249
15.1 The nature and types of non-current assets 250
15.2 The recognition and valuation of non-current assets 251
15.3 The nature of depreciation 253
15.4 Methods of depreciation 254
15.5 Accounting policy for depreciation 256
15.6 Accounting for depreciation 257
15.7 Profits and losses on the disposal of non-current assets 260
15.8 The depreciation charge on an asset in the years of acquisition and disposal: partial year depreciation 262
15.9 Creative accounting and depreciation 266
Summary 267
Key terms and concepts 268
Review questions 269
Exercises 270
References 273

16 Irrecoverable receivables and allowance for irrecoverable receivables 275
Learning Objectives 275
16.1 The nature of, and ledger entries for, irrecoverable receivables 276
16.2 The nature of, and ledger entries for, allowances for irrecoverable receivables 276
Summary 284
Key terms and concepts 284
Review questions 284
Exercises 285
References 288

17 Accruals and prepayments 291
Learning Objectives 291
17.1 The nature of, and ledger entries for, accrued expenses 292
17.2 The nature of, and ledger entries for, prepaid expenses 294
17.3 Accruals and prepayments and the preparation of final financial statements from the trial balance 296
17.4 Further year-end adjustment (inventories of tools, stationery and fuels) 298
17.5 Further year-end adjustment (company taxation) 300
Summary 301
Key terms and concepts 301
Review questions 301
Exercises 302

18 The extended trial balance and final financial statements (advanced) 309
Learning Objectives 309
18.1 Introduction 310
18.2 The extended trial balance 310
Summary 316
Key terms and concepts 317
Exercises 317

PART 4: Internal control and check 327

19 The bank reconciliation statement 329
Learning Objectives 329
19.1 The purpose and preparation of bank reconciliations 330
Summary 337
Key terms and concepts 337
Review questions 337
Exercises 338

20 Control accounts 347
Learning Objectives 347
20.1 The nature and preparation of control accounts 348

20.2 The purpose of control accounts 352
20.3 Alternative systems 355
Summary 356
Key terms and concepts 356
Review question 356
Exercises 356

21 Errors and suspense accounts 367
Learning Objectives 367
21.1 Introduction 368
21.2 Types of error that do not cause a trial balance to disagree 368
21.3 Types of error that cause a trial balance to disagree 370
21.4 Suspense accounts 371
Summary 374
Key terms and concepts 375
Review questions 375
Exercises 375

22 Single entry and incomplete records 383
Learning Objectives 383
22.1 Introduction 384
22.2 Incomplete records of revenue income and expenditure 384
22.3 Single entry 389
22.4 Record keeping for tax purposes 395
Summary 395
Key terms and concepts 396
Review question 396
Exercises 396

PART 5: Preparing final financial statements for manufacturing entities 409

23 Inventory valuation 411
Learning Objectives 411
23.1 Introduction 412
23.2 Monitoring inventory 412
23.3 The valuation of goods for sale and raw materials 412
23.4 The valuation of finished goods and work-in-progress 414
23.5 FIFO and LIFO compared 419
Summary 420
Key terms and concepts 420
Review questions 421
Exercises 421
References 428

24 Financial statements for manufacturing entities 429
Learning Objectives 429
24.1 Introduction 430
24.2 The classification of costs 430
24.3 Categories of inventory 430
24.4 Purposes and preparation of a manufacturing account 432
24.5 Manufacturing profits 437
24.6 The valuation of finished goods and work-in-progress 439
Summary 440
Key terms and concepts 441
Review questions 441
Exercises 441
Reference 451

PART 6: Partnerships 453

25 The final financial statements of partnerships 455
Learning Objectives 455
25.1 The law and characteristics of partnerships 456
25.2 The sharing of profits between the partners 457
25.3 Capital and current accounts 458
25.4 The appropriation account 459
25.5 Partners' commission 465
25.6 A guaranteed share of profit 465
25.7 Limited liability partnerships 465
Summary 466
Key terms and concepts 467
Appendix A: Departmental accounts 467
Review questions 468
Exercises 469

26 Changes in partnerships 485
Learning Objectives 485
26.1 Introduction 486
26.2 Retirement of a partner 486

26.3 Admission of a new partner 488
26.4 The revaluation of assets on changes in partners 492
26.5 The nature of goodwill 495
26.6 The recognition of goodwill in partnership financial statements 496
26.7 The valuation of goodwill 498
26.8 The admission of a new partner and the treatment of goodwill 498
26.9 An outgoing partner and the treatment of goodwill 502
26.10 Incoming and outgoing partners and goodwill 502
26.11 Changes in partners' profit-sharing ratio 504
Summary 509
Key terms and concepts 510
Review questions 510
Exercises 511
References 519

27 Partnership dissolution and conversion to a limited company 521
Learning Objectives 521
27.1 Introduction 522
27.2 Dissolution of partnerships 522
27.3 Conversion to a limited company 526
Summary 533
Key terms and concepts 533
Review questions 533
Exercises 533
Reference 538

PART 7: Companies 539

28 The nature of limited companies and their capital 541
Learning Objectives 541
28.1 Introduction 542
28.2 The characteristics of companies limited by shares 542
28.3 The classes of companies limited by shares 542
28.4 The legal powers and duties of limited companies 543
28.5 The nature and types of share and loan capital 544
28.6 The issue of shares and debentures 549
28.7 Interim and final dividends 550
28.8 The books of account and published financial statements 550
28.9 The auditors' report 551
28.10 Statutory books 551
28.11 The annual general meeting 551
Summary 553
Key terms and concepts 553
Review questions 554
Exercises 555
References 555

29 The final financial statements of limited companies 557
Learning Objectives 557
29.1 Introduction 558
29.2 Published financial statements 558
29.3 Determining the profit or loss for the period 558
29.4 The statement of financial position 560
29.5 Accounting for share issues (limited companies) 563
29.6 Accounting for share issues (public limited companies) 564
29.7 Other items in the statement of financial position 570
29.8 Statement of changes in equity 570
29.9 Notes to the financial statements 578
29.10 Reporting financial performance 583
29.11 Non-current assets held for sale and discontinued operations 583
29.12 Material/exceptional items 584
29.13 Prior period adjustments 585
29.14 Events after the reporting period 586
29.15 Provisions and contingencies 587
29.16 Accounting for debt 588
Summary 591
Key terms and concepts 592
Review questions 593
Exercises 594
References 608

30 Statement of cash flows 609
Learning Objectives 609
30.1 The nature and purpose of statements that analyse the cash flows of a business 610
30.2 Relationship between the statement of cash flows, the statement of profit or loss and the statement of financial position 610
30.3 Statements of cash flows – IAS 7 610
30.4 Presentation: statement of cash flows 615
30.5 IAS 7 – statement of cash flows: sole traders and partnerships 616
30.6 IAS 7 – statement of cash flows: companies 618
30.7 IAS 7 – statement of cash flows: notes 626
30.8 Purposes and uses of statements of cash flows revisited 626
30.9 Advantages and limitations of statements of cash flows 627
30.10 The purpose, uses and advantages of classified statements of cash flows 628
Summary 629
Key terms and concepts 629
Review questions 629
Exercises 630
Reference 645

31 The appraisal of company financial statements using ratio analysis 647
Learning Objectives 647
31.1 Introduction 648
31.2 Measures of a company's performance 650
31.3 Measures of solvency and liquidity 653
31.4 The appraisal of working capital 656
31.5 Measures of return on investment and risk 659
31.6 The limitations of ratio analysis 666
Summary 668
Key terms and concepts 669
Review questions 669
Exercises 670
References 682

Appendix 1: Case studies 683
Appendix 2: Solutions to Exercises 699
Index 799

The following chapters are available online at www.mheducation.co.uk/textbooks/thomas

32 The final financial statements of clubs
32.1 Introduction
32.2 Annual subscriptions
32.3 The preparation of final financial statements of clubs
32.4 Special items

33 Changes in share capital
33.1 Introduction
33.2 Share issues to the public
33.3 Purchase and redemption of shares

34 An introduction to consolidated financial statements
34.1 Introduction
34.2 Identifying business combinations
34.3 Goodwill on acquisition
34.4 The consolidated statement of financial position
34.5 Non-controlling interests (statement of financial position)
34.6 The consolidated statement of comprehensive income
34.7 Non-controlling interest (statement of comprehensive income)

35 Value added tax, columnar books of prime entry and the payroll
35.1 Value added tax
35.2 Columnar books of prime entry
35.3 Accounting for wages

36 Accounting for changing price levels
36.1 Recording transactions at historical cost in the measurement of income
36.2 Price change considerations and inflation accounting

About the Authors

Andrew Thomas is a former Senior Lecturer in the Accounting and Finance Group at the University of Birmingham Business School, UK

Dr Anne Marie Ward is a Professor of Accounting in the Department of Accounting, Finance and Economics at the University of Ulster at Jordanstown, Northern Ireland. She is also a qualified Chartered Accountant.

Preface to Eighth Edition

What's new

New material and structural changes

- The structure of topics covered in Part 1 has changed. Key changes include:
  - **(a)** Part 1 'The Framework of Accounting' has been restructured from seven to six chapters with a more succinct rewrite of several areas. The concept of capital maintenance is explained in Chapter 4 and the explanation of the other concepts restructured.
  - **(b)** Though Chapter 2 continues to consider the international institutional framework for accounting, more emphasis has been placed on the new institutional framework for accounting in the UK. The new UK financial reporting standards are outlined in brief, as are the conditions for their application.
- The chapter on the final financial statements of clubs has been updated and moved to the website as feedback from users indicated that this chapter was not widely used.
- The textbook has been updated in light of recent changes to relevant international financial reporting standards (IFRS) and the *Conceptual Framework*.
- Changes have been made to the chapter on ratio analysis. The worked examples, which are used as a teaching aid throughout the chapter, now include comparatives and suggested reasons for changes to the ratios. This introduces evaluating financial information over time.
- The chapter on the statement of cash flows has been rewritten. In the previous edition, the chapter started by examining sources and applications of funds. After consultation with reviewers and lecturers it was considered that this was an unnecessary step and now the chapter goes straight to cash flows from investing, financing and operating activities.
- The chapter 'The Final Financial Statements of Sole Traders (Advanced)' has been changed to 'The Extended Trial Balance and Final Financial Statements (Advanced)' as this new title is more reflective of the material being covered in the chapter.

New pedagogical features

- Adopting lecturers and students stated that they found the real world examples beneficial. Therefore, many of the examples have been updated (replaced with more recent examples) and some new ones added. The real world examples highlight the link between the topic being covered academically and the real business world.
- Again in response to positive feedback obtained on the last edition, additional diagrams have been introduced to several of the chapters, particularly chapters that are quite narrative in nature. This pictorial presentation of information should help student learning by breaking up the text and providing another vehicle to highlight key points and connections between them.

- Some new learning activities have been included in Part 1 to get students thinking about the practical application of the theory being covered. For instance, an example of a board of directors that has a weak structure under corporate governance recommendations is included in Chapter 6 and students are asked to advise on the structure.
- Solutions to some of the questions (those marked with an asterisk) are now included in Appendix 2.
- All references, key terms and learning objectives have also been updated as appropriate.

New and improved presentation

- The previous edition used a four-colour text design. This was received positively by students and lecturers. This edition continues with a full colour presentational approach and in addition uses graphics and pictures to represent some of the concepts being discussed. For example, balancing scales are used if double entry is being considered.

Aim of text

This book is primarily intended to be an introductory text for students taking a degree in accounting or business studies with a substantial element of accounting. It is IFRS compliant, though it also refers to UK terminology so that students are aware of the different accounting terms that are currently used in practice in the UK and Ireland. The new institutional framework for accounting in the UK is also outlined in Chapter 2.

The authors have tried to provide a textbook that deals with all the fundamental basic accounting techniques and practices required by the major accountancy bodies while at the same time going further to explain the reasons for accounting for transactions in a particular manner. The authors link the accounting techniques to the relevant International Financial Reporting Standard, the *Conceptual Framework* and real life examples where possible. In addition, in several of the chapters, the authors highlight how accounting can be used unethically, for example to smooth earnings. It is hoped that this deeper discussion will stimulate students to think strategically about the important influence that accounting can have on economic decision-making and hence society at large.

The book has been structured into seven parts for ease of reference. The first part covers the conceptual framework of accounting as the authors feel that students should be exposed to the most important issues underlying accounting at the start. It is not expected that students who are only starting to learn accounting, or who have a low level of accounting knowledge, will understand every aspect of these chapters; however, reading the chapters will make students aware of the language of accounting, how accounting information is communicated by companies and the regulation of world accounting. Students are unlikely to comprehend in full the conceptual framework of accounting at the start of any accounting course, but understanding of the conceptual framework should start to become clearer as the student progresses through their accounting studies.

Knowledge of Part 2 ('Double-entry Bookkeeping') is required before Part 3 ('Preparing Final Financial Statements for Sole Traders') can be fully appreciated and this section needs to be studied before Part 4 on internal controls and incomplete records is taught. However, the parts from then on, 'Preparing Final Financial Statements for Manufacturing Entities' (Part 5), 'Partnerships' (Part 6) and 'Companies' (Part 7) are stand-alone and can be approached in any order, so long as the first four parts have been studied.

The structure within each chapter also follows a deliberate pattern. These usually start by examining the purpose, theoretical foundation and practical relevance of the topic. This is followed by a description of the accounting methods and then a comprehensive example. A further unique feature of the book is that after most examples there is a series of notes. These are intended to explain the unfamiliar and more difficult aspects of the example in order that the reader is able to follow the example. The notes also provide guidance on further aspects of the topic that may be encountered in examination questions, such as alternative forms of wording.

Each chapter also contains a set of written review questions and numerical exercises designed by the authors to test whether the student has fulfilled the learning objectives set out in the chapter, as well as past questions from various examining bodies. The review questions and exercises are presented in a coherent progressive sequence designed to test understanding of terminology, legal requirements, theoretical foundations, etc. The exercises are categorized into three levels according to their level of difficulty. This is rather subjective for a book that focuses on the introductory level, but it is hoped that the following classification may be useful to students and lecturers:

- *Basic* questions are of a standard lower than those commonly found in the first year of an undergraduate degree in accounting or the professional accountancy bodies' examinations and can usually be completed in a relatively short time (i.e. less than about 35 minutes).
- *Intermediate* questions are of a standard commonly found in the first year of an undergraduate degree in accounting or the professional accountancy bodies' examinations and can usually be completed in about 35 minutes.
- *Advanced* questions are of a standard slightly higher than those commonly found in the first year of an undergraduate degree in accounting or the professional accountancy bodies' examinations, and/or more advanced in the depth of knowledge required to answer them, and can usually be completed in about 45 minutes.

All users, especially lecturers, should also be aware that some exercises are extensions of other exercises in previous chapters. This is intended to provide a more comprehensive understanding of the relationship between different topics in accounting, such as day books and cash books, and allowances for depreciation and irrecoverable receivables. Suggested solutions to some of the numerical exercises are included in Appendix 2 for student self-study. The answers to the rest of the numerical exercises are contained in a *Teachers' Solutions Manual* that is on the website for this book (page xxix).

Each chapter also includes learning objectives, learning activities, a summary, a list of key terms and concepts, and a real life example showing how a company is applying the topic or detailing a real life scenario. The learning objectives at the start of each chapter set out the abilities and skills that the student should be able to demonstrate after reading the chapter. Students should also refer back to these after reading each chapter. Similarly, students should satisfy themselves that they can explain the meaning of the key terms and concepts listed at the end of each chapter. The summaries provide a comprehensive but concise review of the contents of each chapter that students should find useful for revision purposes. The learning activities are mostly real-life activities of a project/case study type which require students to apply their knowledge to practical situations. They frequently necessitate students collecting publicly available data from actual companies, or their own financial affairs.

The authors are Anne Marie Ward (a Professor of Accounting at the University of Ulster at Jordanstown and a Chartered Accountant) and Andrew Thomas (who is a former Senior Lecturer in Accounting at the University of Birmingham). Anne Marie has taught the professional examinations of Chartered Accountants Ireland for their student services department for the past 16 years.

Anne Marie Ward and Andrew Thomas

Acknowledgements

Publisher's acknowledgements

Our thanks go to the following reviewers for their comments at various stages in the text's development:

Gloria Agyemang, Royal Holloway, University of London
M S Bashir, Sheffield Hallam University
David Bence, University of Bath
Tongyu Cao, University College Cork
Ian Crawford, University of Bath
Robert Jupe, University of Kent
David Mayston, University of York
Ian Money, University of York
Ying Ye, University of Leeds

We would also like to thank Susan Smith, University of Sussex and Kooi See Yeap, Middlesex University for their work on the online resources, as well as the LearnSmart authors and reviewers.

Author's acknowledgements

I would like to thank a number of people who, directly or indirectly, helped or contributed to the text, including:

My family, for being supportive

The lecturers who adopt the text

The reviewers as listed above, for their comments

Tom Hill, Beverley Shields, Alice Aldous and the production team at McGraw-Hill Education

Elaine Bingham, copy editor, and Gill Colver, proofreader

Sandra Brosnan and Robert Jupe for contributing case studies

The Association of Chartered Certified Accountants (ACCA), The Association of Accounting Technicians (AAT), The Associated Examining Board (AEB) and the Joint Matriculation Board (JMB) for allowing us to reproduce copies of their questions in the text

Every effort has been made to trace and acknowledge ownership of copyright and to clear permission for material reproduced in this book. The publishers will be pleased to make suitable arrangements to clear permission with any copyright holders whom it has not been possible to contact.

Guided Tour

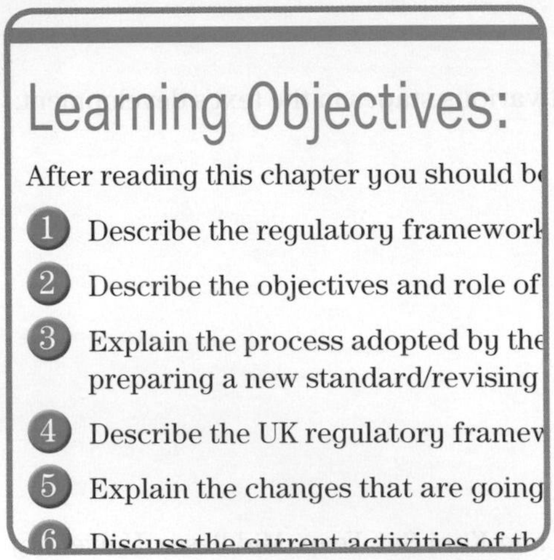

Learning Objectives:

After reading this chapter you should b

1 Describe the regulatory framework

2 Describe the objectives and role of

3 Explain the process adopted by the preparing a new standard/revising

4 Describe the UK regulatory framew

5 Explain the changes that are going

6 Discuss the current activities of th

Learning Objectives

Each chapter opens with a set of learning objectives, summarizing what you should learn from each chapter.

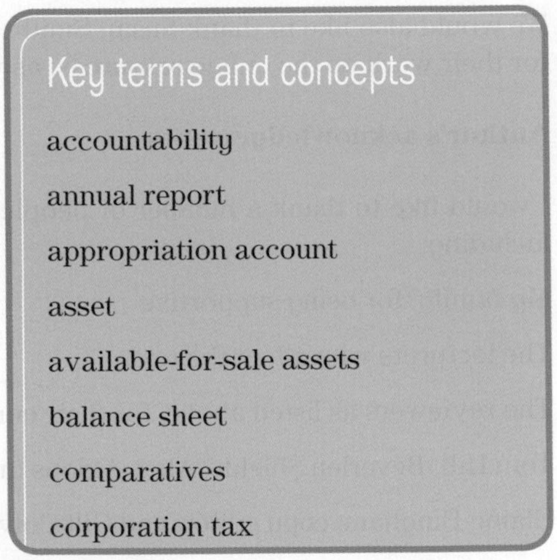

Key terms and concepts

accountability

annual report

appropriation account

asset

available-for-sale assets

balance sheet

comparatives

corporation tax

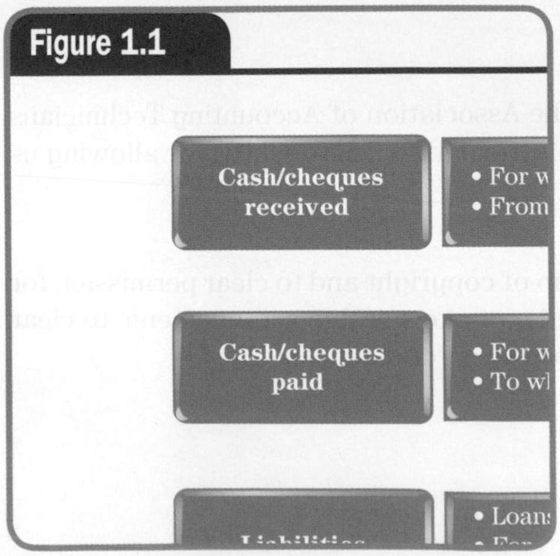

Key Terms and Concepts

These are highlighted throughout the chapter, with page number references at the end of each chapter so they can be found quickly and easily. A full glossary of definitions can be downloaded from the online learning centre.

Figure 1.1

Cash/cheques received

• For w
• From

Cash/cheques paid

• For w
• To wl

Liabilities

• Loan:

Figures and Tables

Figures and tables help you to visualize the various accounting documents, and to illustrate and summarize important concepts.

Learning Activity 1.2

Visit the Ryanair plc website and view a
with the reports provided by the directo
annual report extends to over 100 pag
statement, a separate statement of co
prefers to label this the statement of f
maintain the national terminology for t
the financial statements for the Group

1.6 Types of entity

Learning Activities

These quick activities give opportunities to test your learning and practise accountancy methods throughout the book.

REAL WORLD EXAMPLE 1.1

Structure, governance and managem

a) Constitution

The Union was first established in th
specifies that "there shall be a Unio
year, SUSU has significantly change
limited by guarantee and registering
these accounts, the Union operated a
aims, worked within a constitution co
structure of the organization and its

Real World Examples

The chapters contain many and varied examples, including real-life accounting situations and mini case studies which bring accounting to life.

WORKED EXAMPLE 10.1

Name of account
Bank
Capital introduced
Motor vehicles
Motor expense
Purchases
A. Brown (trade payable)
Sales revenue

Worked Examples

Examples of financial statements and worked problems will help you apply theory to practice.

Summary

The international framework of acco
is an independent board that aims to
role. Though reporting to the IFRS F
issuing IFRS and revising IAS. They ar
authoritative guidance on new issues,
SMEIG (monitors the implementation
issues raised by users, makes suggest
the issues raised and in light of change
major stakeholders of accounting info
the IFRS Foundation Support Operatio
and implementation of an IFRS Taxo
bodies that make up the institutional

Summary

These briefly review and reinforce the main topics covered in each chapter to ensure you have acquired a solid understanding of the key topics.

Review questions

International Framework

2.1* Describe the objectives of the Inte

2.2 Discuss the current activities of convergence/harmonization of acc

2.3 Explain the role of the IFRS Interp

2.4 Explain the role and objectives of

2.5 Describe the standard-setting proc

2.6 Describe the accounting treatment

Review Questions

These questions encourage you to review and apply the knowledge you have acquired from each chapter.

Exercises

10.2* Close off the ledger accounts in balances into the next period, th *account* where appropriate.

10.3* Prepare a trial balance for Worke

10.4* Close off the T accounts and prep

10.5* Close off the T accounts and prep

10.6 Close off the T accounts and prep

10.7 Close off the T accounts and prep

Exercises

This end-of-chapter feature is the perfect way to practise the techniques you have been taught and apply methodology to real-world situations. They are pitched at different levels to ensure all readers have questions appropriate to their stage of learning.

Case study 1

The following case study shows how to the preparation of final financial stateme to complete the relevant sections for Par Financial Statements for Sole Traders'.

Trading details and supporting doc

Mr O'Donnell, a sole trader, has owned an specializes in the purchase and sale of a number of reputable suppliers and reliab

You have been employed by Mr O'Donnel his financial statements. Following discu

Case Studies Appendix

The Appendix contains case studies designed to test how well you can apply the main techniques learned.

connect® ACCOUNTING

McGraw-Hill Connect Accounting is a learning and teaching environment that improves student performance and outcomes while promoting engagement and comprehension of content.

You can utilize publisher-provided materials, or add your own content to design a complete course to help your students achieve higher outcomes.

PROVEN EFFECTIVE

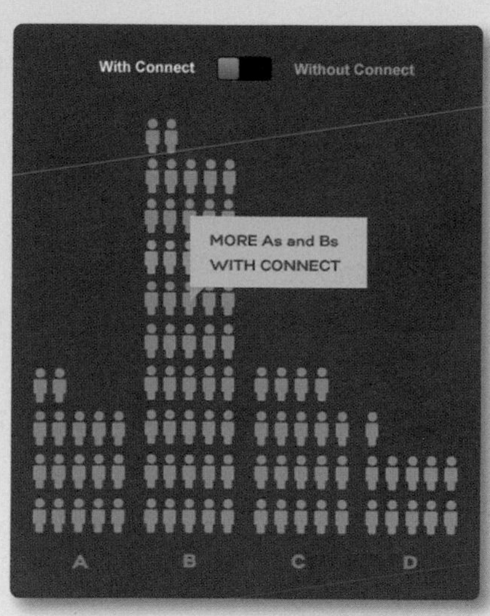

INSTRUCTORS

With McGraw-Hill Connect Plus Accounting, instructors get:

- Simple **assignment management**, allowing you to spend more time teaching.
- **Auto-graded** assignments, quizzes and tests.
- **Detailed visual reporting** where students' and section results can be viewed and analysed.
- Sophisticated **online testing** capability.
- A **filtering and reporting** function that allows you to easily assign and report on materials that are correlated to learning outcomes, topics, level of difficulty, and more. Reports can be accessed for individual students or the whole class, as well as offering the ability to drill into individual assignments, questions or categories.
- **Instructor materials** to help supplement your course.

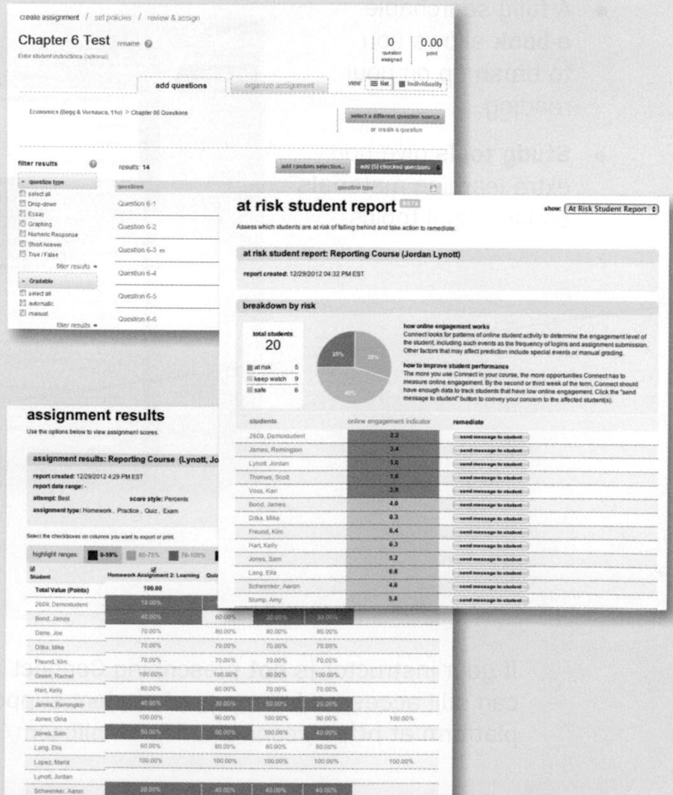

Get Connected. Get Results.

STUDENTS

With McGraw-Hill Connect Plus Accounting, students get:

Assigned content

- Easy **online access** to homework, tests and quizzes.
- **Immediate feedback** and 24-hour tech support.

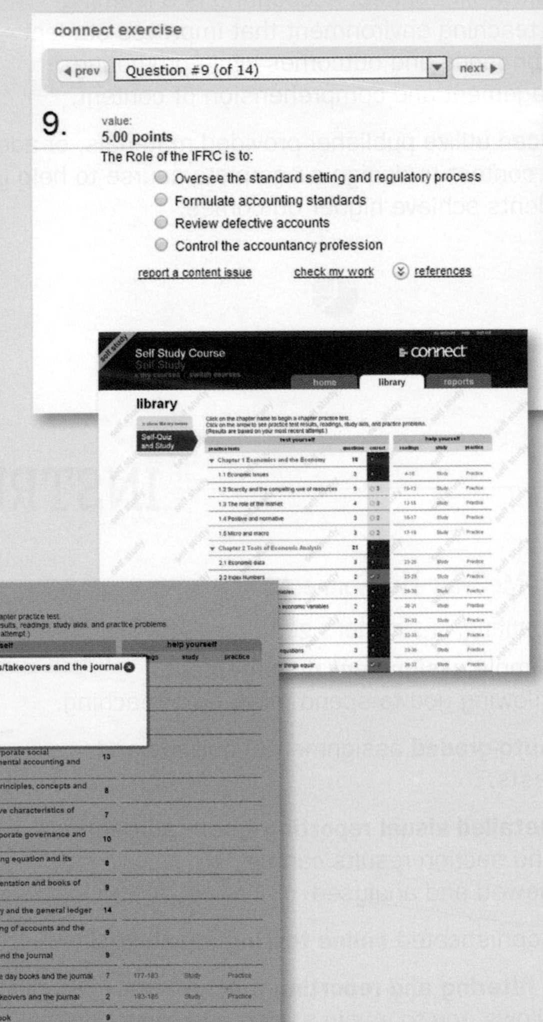

Self-Quiz and Study

- **Practice tests** help you to easily identify your strengths and weakness and create a clear revision plan.
- A fully searchable **e-book** allows you to brush up on your reading.
- **Study tools** give you extra learning materials on individual topics.

Self Study

If your instructor is **not** prescribing Connect as part of your course, you can still access a full range of student support resources on our Self Study platform at http://connect.mcgraw-hill.com/selfstudy

ACCESS OPTIONS

An online assignment and assessment solution that offers a number of powerful tools and features that make managing assignments easier, so faculty can spend more time teaching. With Connect Accounting, students can engage with their coursework anytime and anywhere, making the learning process more accessible and efficient.

Calculation questions

Test students' mathematical understanding, allowing them additional practice and further opportunity to develop their problem solving skills. The questions are auto-graded so faculty can spend more time teaching.

Required:
Prepare the relevant entries required for amending the statement of financial position to take account of the new up-to-date information and prepare the new updated statement of financial position. (Record the transactions in the given order. Be sure to list the assets in order of their liquidity. Input all amounts as positive values.Leave no cells blank - be certain to enter "0" wherever required. Omit the "£" sign in your response.)

Land a/c

Balance b/d		Balance c/d	
(Click to select)			
Balance b/d			

Plant and Equip a/c

Balance b/d		(Click to select)	
		Balance c/d	
Balance b/d			

P&E deprec a/c

(Click to select)		Balance b/d	
Balance c/d			
		Balance b/d	

Algorithmic problem sets

Provide repeated opportunities for students to practise and master concepts with multiple versions of each problem. Or use the algorithmic problems in class testing to provide each student with a different version than that seen by their peers.

library

» show library menu
assignments
my assignments
pre-built assignments

pre-built assignments
These assignments have been created to support the learning objectives of your course using the Connect question banks.

▾ **Instructor Library Content|Pre-built Assignments**

assignment name	type	# of questions	assign all
Mock Examination 1	homework	6	assign
Mock Examination 2	homework	6	assign
Mock Examination 3	homework	6	assign
Mock Examination 4	homework	30	assign
Mock Examination 5	homework	6	assign

▸ **Instructor Library Content|Pre-built Assignments|Chapter 01 - Entities and financial reporting statements**

▸ **Instructor Library Content|Pre-built Assignments|Chapter 02 - International financial reporting: institutional framework and standards**

▸ **Instructor Library Content|Pre-built Assignments|Chapter 03 - History and purpose of the conceptual framework**

▸ **Instructor Library Content|Pre-built Assignments|Chapter 04 - The nature and objectives of financial reporting**

Pre-built assignments

Assign all of the autogradable end of chapter material as a ready-made assignment with the simple click of a button.

Seamlessly integrates all of the Connect Accounting features with:

- An integrated e-book, allowing for anytime, anywhere access to the textbook.
- Dynamic links between assigned and self-study problems and the location in the e-book where that problem is covered.
- A powerful search function to pinpoint and connect key concepts.

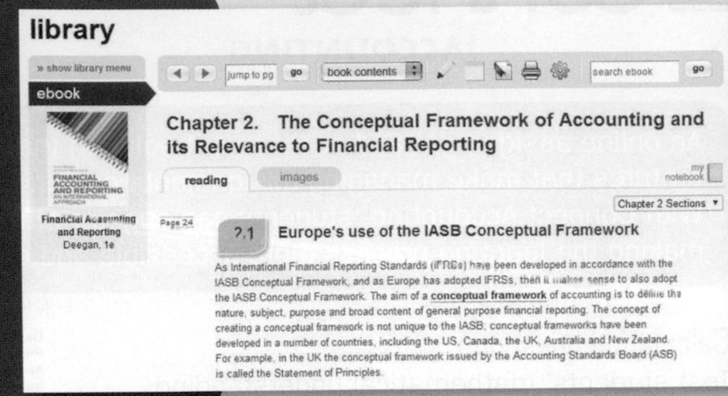

LearnSmart™

LearnSmart is the most widely used and intelligent adaptive learning resource that is proven to strengthen memory recall, improve course retention and boost grades. Distinguishing what students know from what they don't, and honing in on concepts they are most likely to forget, LearnSmart continuously adapts to each student's needs by building an individual learning path so students study smarter and retain more knowledge. Real-time reports provide valuable insight to instructors, so precious class time can be spent on higher-level concepts and discussion.

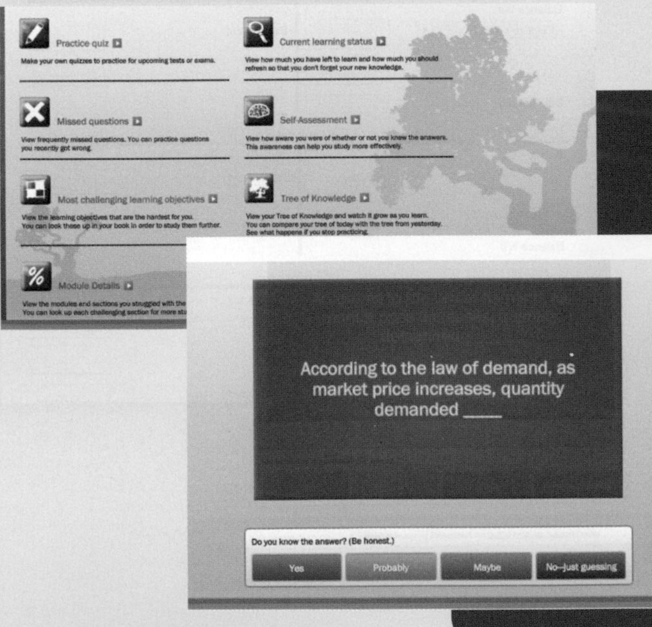

SmartBook™

Fuelled by LearnSmart—the most widely used and intelligent adaptive learning resource — SmartBook™ is the first and only adaptive reading experience designed to change the way students read and learn. It creates a personalized reading experience by highlighting the most impactful concepts a student needs to learn at that moment in time. As a student engages with SmartBook, the reading experience continuously adapts by highlighting content based on what the student knows and doesn't know. This ensures that the focus is on the content he or she needs to learn, while simultaneously promoting long-term retention of material. The result: better grades, more confidence, and greater success.

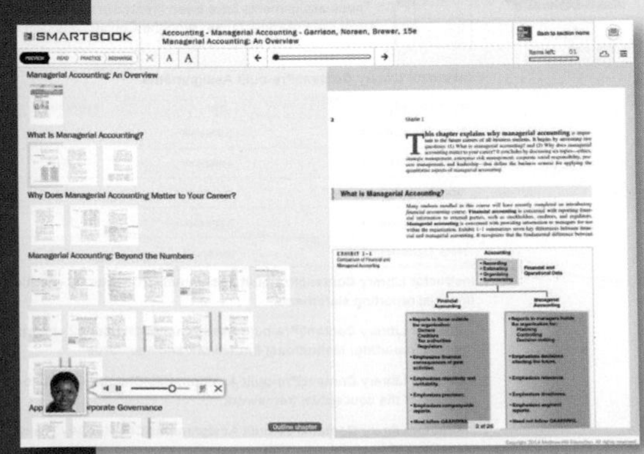

Online Learning Centre

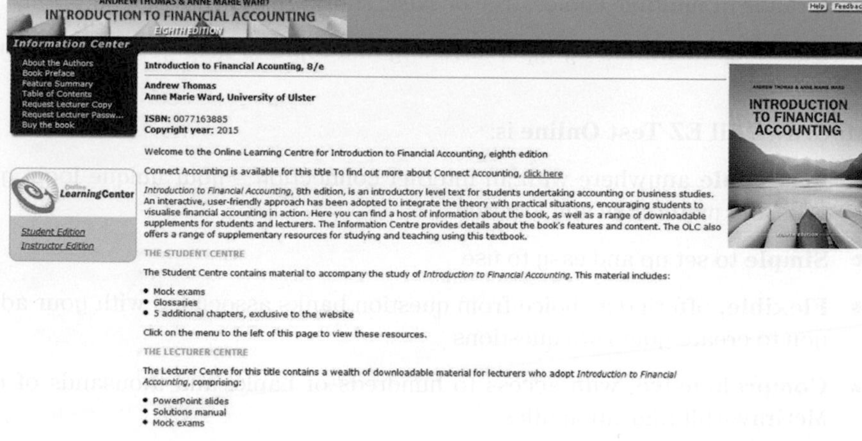

Lecturer support – Helping you to help your students

In addition to the assignments, questions, problems and activities McGraw-Hill Education provides within Connect, we also offer a host of resources to support your teaching.

- **Faster course preparation** – time-saving support for your module
- **High-calibre content to support your students** – resources written by your academic peers, who understand your need for rigorous and reliable content
- **Flexibility** – edit, adapt or repurpose; test in Connect or test through EZ Test. The choice is yours.

The materials created specifically for lecturers adopting this textbook include:

- PowerPoint slides
- Glossaries
- Solutions manual
- Mock exams
- Additional online chapters

To request your password to access these resources, contact your McGraw-Hill Education representative or visit:

www.mheducation-hill.co.uk/textbooks/thomas

Test Bank available in McGraw-Hill EZ Test Online

A test bank of hundreds of questions is available to lecturers adopting this book for their module. For flexibility, this is available for adopters of this book to use through Connect or through the EZ Test online website. For each chapter you will find:

- A range of multiple choice, true or false, short answer or essay questions
- Questions identified by type, difficulty and topic to help you to select questions that best suit your needs

McGraw-Hill EZ Test Online is:

- **Accessible** anywhere with an internet connection – your unique login gives you access to all your tests and material in any location
- **Simple** to set up and easy to use
- **Flexible,** offering a choice from question banks associated with your adopted textbook or allowing you to create your own questions
- **Comprehensive,** with access to hundreds of banks and thousands of questions created for other McGraw-Hill Education titles
- **Compatible** with Blackboard and other course management systems
- **Time-saving** – students' tests can be immediately marked and results and feedback delivered directly to your students to help them to monitor their progress.

To register for this FREE resource, visit www.eztestonline.com

Let us help make our content your solution

At McGraw-Hill Education our aim is to help lecturers to find the most suitable content for their needs delivered to their students in the most appropriate way. Our **custom publishing solutions** offer the ideal combination of content delivered in the way which best suits lecturer and students.

Our custom publishing programme offers lecturers the opportunity to select just the chapters or sections of material they wish to deliver to their students from a database called CREATE™ at

create.mheducation.com/uk

CREATE™ contains over two million pages of content from:

- textbooks
- professional books
- case books – Harvard Articles, Insead, Ivey, Darden, Thunderbird and BusinessWeek
- Taking Sides – debate materials

Across the following imprints:

- McGraw-Hill Education
- Open University Press
- Harvard Business Publishing
- US and European material

There is also the option to include additional material authored by lecturers in the custom product – this does not necessarily have to be in English.

We will take care of everything from start to finish in the process of developing and delivering a custom product to ensure that lecturers and students receive exactly the material needed in the most suitable way.

With a **Custom Publishing Solution**, students enjoy the best selection of material deemed to be the most suitable for learning everything they need for their courses – something of real value to support their learning. Teachers are able to use exactly the material they want, in the way they want, to support their teaching on the course.

Please contact your local McGraw-Hill Education representative with any questions or alternatively contact Warren Eels e: warren.eels@mheducation.com

Improve your grades!

20% off any Study Skills Book!

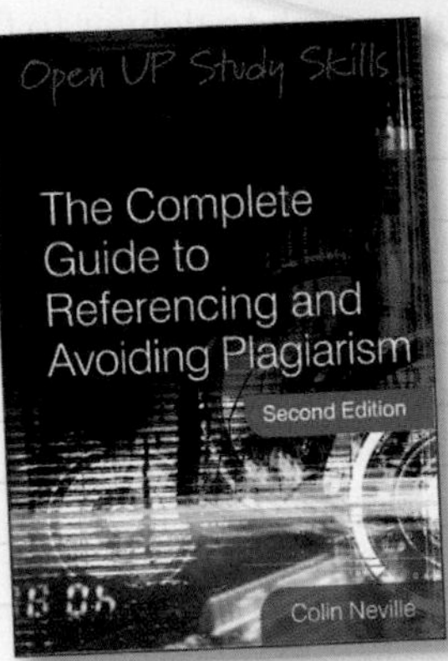

Our Study Skills books are packed with practical advice and tips that are easy to put into practice and will really improve the way you study.

Our books will help you:

- ✓ Improve your grades
- ✓ Avoid plagiarism
- ✓ Save time
- ✓ Develop new skills
- ✓ Write confidently
- ✓ Undertake research projects
- ✓ Sail through exams
- ✓ Find the perfect job

SPECIAL OFFER!

As a valued customer, buy online and receive 20% off any of our Study Skills books by entering the promo code **BRILLIANT**

www.openup.co.uk/studyskills

PART ONE
The framework of accounting

1. Entities and financial reporting statements (including the nature and objectives of financial reporting) 3
2. Financial reporting: institutional framework and standards 23
3. The Conceptual Framework 1: objective of financial statements, stakeholders and other reports 43
4. The Conceptual Framework 2: concepts, principles and policies 65
5. The Conceptual Framework 3: the qualitative characteristics of financial information 87
6. Auditing, corporate governance and ethics 99

Chapter 1

Entities and financial reporting statements (including the nature and objectives of financial accounting)

Learning Objectives:

After reading this chapter you should be able to do the following:

1. Discuss the nature and functions of financial accounting.
2. Outline the differences between a company, a member-governed body, a sole trader and a partnership.
3. Describe the financial statements for sole traders, partnerships and companies.
4. List the typical contents of a company's published annual report.
5. Describe the main regulatory influences on financial reporting.

—1.1 Introduction and history of accounting

Accounting is a necessity in every entity, regardless of type or size. It is so important that a full-time international body, the International Accounting Standards Board (IASB), representing accounting experts from several countries, exists to provide guidance on how to account for items and transactions and how to communicate (present) this information. This book is prepared using the most recent accounting guidance as produced by the IASB.

In its earliest form accounting involved keeping 'a count' of items. The first form of accounting was known as **stewardship accounting** as stewards were employed by wealthy individuals to keep 'a count' of items they owned (assets) and items they owed (liabilities). The difference between these two 'elements' represents the individuals' financial position (their net worth). Evidence from archaeological digs would suggest that this form of accounting might be 7,000 years old (stone tablets inscribed with hieroglyphic records of counts of assets were uncovered in Egypt). In Europe, archaeological evidence (wooden tally sticks which are argued to represent counts of assets and liabilities) from about 2000 BC were found and considered to be evidence of stewardship accounting. The information collected under this ancient form of accounting is still important today and is captured in one of the key statements provided in an entity's **annual report** – the **statement of financial position**. This statement is referred to as the '**balance sheet**' under UK accounting. The whole purpose of this statement is to identify the net worth of the entity. It provides information on what the entity owns (assets) and what the entity owes (liabilities). The difference represents 'equity capital' being the amount that the company owes the owners, or to consider it another way, it is the amount the owners have invested in the company either directly or indirectly.

The industrial revolution advanced the role and nature of accounting. For the first time the general public were able to purchase shares in companies. Before this time, most company managers were the company's owners. Accounting was more for internal control purposes. After the separation of ownership and control, accounting had to progress to provide information to people who were external to the company and who had little knowledge of what went on in the company. To help the external owners assess the performance of a company and the performance of management, legislation at this time required that companies provided their owners with statements of financial position and also required that they provide a statement detailing the performance of the company in the period. This statement is now called the **statement of profit or loss** or the **statement of comprehensive income**. In the UK this statement is also called the profit and loss account. This statement outlines the income for the period and the expenses incurred in the period. The difference between income and expenses is profit or loss. The requirement to produce the two statements is generally regarded as the start of financial accounting as we now know it. When the two statements are published together with other related information, the combined document is called the annual report.

Accounting is typically categorized into either financial accounting or management accounting. **Financial accounting** is concerned with the preparation of reports for external stakeholders and **management accounting** is concerned with the preparation of reports for internal management purposes. The role of the accountant has extended beyond recording transactions – accountants today have to have strong business acumen, to be good communicators, to provide advice and guidance to companies and people, to have an awareness of influences on a business and to predict the consequences of external changes in the economic environment on a business. They need to be able to provide consultancy services and general business advice, not just prepare financial statements. For example, accountants are typically used as expert witnesses in court cases when divorce matters are being settled or where there is a fraud case.

—1.2 The nature and functions of financial accounting

Financial accounting may be defined as the process of designing and operating an information system for collecting, measuring and recording an enterprise's transactions, and summarizing and communicating the results of these transactions to users to facilitate making financial/economic decisions.

The first part of this definition, relating to collecting and recording transactions, refers to the accounting system within an organization. This is typically a double-entry bookkeeping system, which consists of maintaining a record of the nature and money value of the transactions of an enterprise. In many businesses these records are maintained on computer systems. The second part of the definition, relating to communicating the results, refers to preparing final financial statements from the books of account (or any other system of recording) showing the profit earned during a given period (statement of profit or loss) and the financial position at the end of that period (statement of financial position). The two functions of financial accounting may be broken down further as described below.

1.3 The objectives of an appropriate accounting system

The recording and control of business transactions

Accounting systems need to keep a record of the cash in and out of the business and the assets and liabilities of the business as detailed in Figure 1.1.

The owners of a business wish to safeguard their assets and to ensure that they are being utilized efficiently to produce wealth. An appropriate accounting system should have controls in place to protect business assets and to determine how the company is performing. The control aspect of an accounting system includes ensuring that the correct amounts are paid to those entitled to them at the appropriate time, to ensure that the business's debts are paid when due, and to ensure that assets are safeguarded against fraud and misappropriation. For example, an appropriate accounting system will have an up-to-date list of all non-current assets (buildings, etc.), including their location and state of condition. These will be inspected periodically to verify that they have not been misappropriated. The latter function is often referred to as **internal control**. Control is considered further in Chapter 6, 'Auditing, Corporate Governance and Ethics'.

Figure 1.1

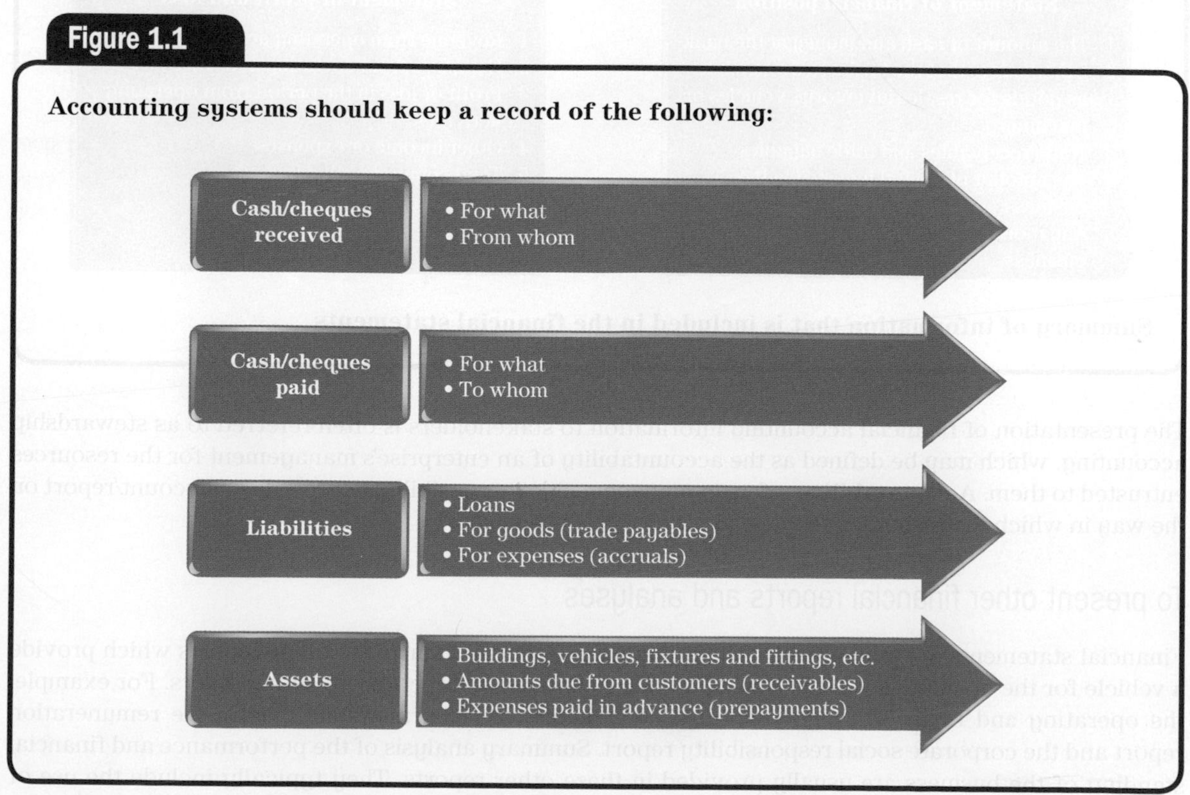

Accounting systems should keep a record of the following:
Cash/cheques received
• For what
• From whom
Cash/cheques paid
• For what
• To whom
Liabilities
• Loans
• For goods (trade payables)
• For expenses (accruals)
Assets
• Buildings, vehicles, fixtures and fittings, etc.
• Amounts due from customers (receivables)
• Expenses paid in advance (prepayments)

To maintain accuracy in recording

Transactions are usually recorded using 'double entry'. **Double-entry bookkeeping** is generally regarded as the most accurate method of bookkeeping, primarily because each transaction is entered in the books twice. This duplication, considered to be a form of **internal check**, highlights any errors.

To meet the requirements of the law

The law, in the form of the Companies Act 2006, states that companies must keep a proper record of their transactions. There is no legislation that specifically requires sole traders or partnerships to keep records of their transactions. However, HM Revenue and Customs expects financial statements to be prepared and proper accounting records to be kept for the purpose of determining the proprietor's income tax liability. In addition, any trader who does not keep proper records and goes bankrupt will find it more difficult to obtain discharge from bankruptcy.

To present final financial statements to the owners of the business

In summary, the financial statements will include the items detailed in Figure 1.2.

Figure 1.2

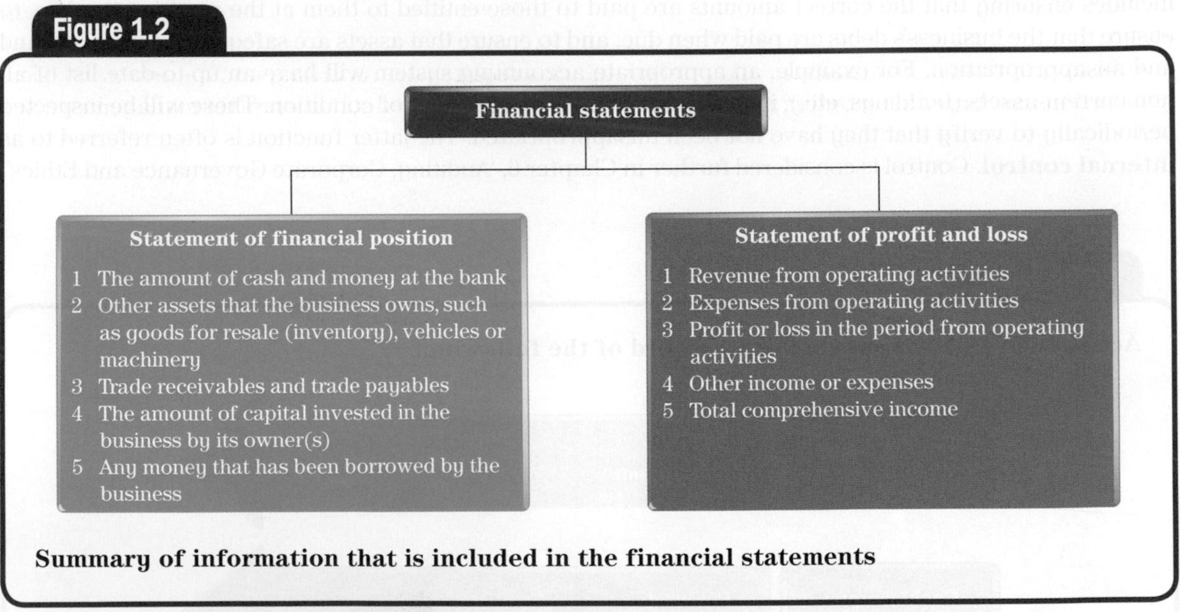

Financial statements
Statement of financial position
1 The amount of cash and money at the bank
2 Other assets that the business owns, such as goods for resale (inventory), vehicles or machinery
3 Trade receivables and trade payables
4 The amount of capital invested in the business by its owner(s)
5 Any money that has been borrowed by the business
Statement of profit and loss
1 Revenue from operating activities
2 Expenses from operating activities
3 Profit or loss in the period from operating activities
4 Other income or expenses
5 Total comprehensive income

Summary of information that is included in the financial statements

The presentation of financial accounting information to stakeholders is often referred to as stewardship accounting, which may be defined as the accountability of an enterprise's management for the resources entrusted to them. **Accountability** refers to management's responsibility to provide an account/report on the way in which the resources entrusted to them have been used.

To present other financial reports and analyses

Financial statements are contained within an annual report which includes other reports which provide a vehicle for the management team (directors) to communicate directly with stakeholders. For example, the operating and financial review, the directors' report, the chairman's statement, the remuneration report and the corporate social responsibility report. Summary analysis of the performance and financial standing of the business are usually provided in these other reports. They typically include the use of ratio analysis. Ratio analysis is examined in detail in Chapter 31, 'The Appraisal of Company Financial Statements Using Ratio Analysis'.

To facilitate the efficient allocation of resources

A view of the function of financial accounting is that it facilitates the efficient and effective allocation of resources (**economic decision-making**). At a macroeconomic level it enables investors to divert capital (funding) to the more efficient firms. By viewing financial statements investors can determine the companies that are efficient in the utilization of resources and which entities are not. More efficient firms will expand by more than less efficient firms and hence provide benefits for the economy and the population as a whole.

Employees can also make informed judgements about company efficiency and sustainability from the reports produced by accounting systems and are likely to seek employment from more efficient firms. The same interpretation could also be extended to other potential users of final financial statements and providers of resources in a broad sense that embraces quality of life and environmental considerations, and so on. This would include other stakeholders such as bank lenders, payables/suppliers, the government and the public in general. Therefore, everyone will be more interested in more efficient entities.

This function of financial accounting can also be viewed at a microeconomic or individual firm level. One of the main purposes of financial accounting may be said to be to enable an organization's management to operate the enterprise efficiently and effectively. This requires the recording and control of business transactions, accuracy in recording and the preparation of final financial statements (for management use). For example, by viewing financial information about internal departments or products, management can direct resources to those that are more profitable and may even close down those that are not providing appropriate returns. This will improve the performance of the entity overall. This 'internal' function of accounting is more commonly attributed to management accounting, particularly in larger organizations. Management accounting can be defined as the provision of information to an organization's management for the purposes of planning, control and decision-making. The latter includes production, marketing, investment and financing decisions.

Learning Activity 1.1

Imagine that you are in business in a small general store or as a plumber. Prepare a list of the financial information about the business that you would expect to be able to obtain from your records. Compare this with the items noted under Figure 1.2 and consider any differences.

1.4 Accounting language

Accounting has its own language and differences arise in the terminology used at national and international level. The key terms used in financial reports are now outlined in brief.

Statement of profit or loss terminology

Profit or loss is the total income made by the entity in the period less the total expenses incurred by the entity in the period. **Revenue** is income earned in the period from normal trading activities. When an entity has income from activities that are not its core business, such as receiving interest, then this is disclosed separately as '**other income**'. This is so the reader of the financial information can gauge management's performance in generating income from the business and income from investing activities. **Expenses** are yearly running costs. They are used up in the period being reported on. Examples include staff wages, electricity used to generate heat and light for the business and rent of the business premises for the period. The user is interested to see these costs as they can assess management's performance in their efficient use of resources. Information on expenses can enable the reader of the statement of profit or loss to determine how risky an entity's profits are.

Statement of financial position terminology

Assets

In simple terms, an asset is an item of value held by an entity that is going to generate income in the future. This income might, for example, come from the sale of an asset, or from its use. Assets are categorized into four types and have descriptions that signify how long the entity is likely to keep the asset. The four types of asset are detailed in Figure 1.3.

Assets are typically presented in the financial statements according to the length of time an entity expects to hold on to the asset. Cash and cash equivalents that are expected to be turned into cash within 12 months, other assets that are expected to be turned into cash within 12 months and all assets that are intended for sale or consumption as part of the entity's normal operating (trading) activities of the business are called

Figure 1.3

Tangible assets

- Referred to as **property, plant and equipment.**
- Can be seen and touched (they are tangible in nature); for example, a car, a house or a desk.

Intangible assets

- Cannot be seen or touched but have value.
- For example, your education. You are building up intellectual capital (your human value) as you progress through your studies. Companies will pay a premium to get access to your knowledge in the future.

Available-for-sale assets

- Investments that are denominated in money, or in paper.
- For example, shares and bonds that the entity holds for financial gain and which will be sold by the entity in the future.

Investments in associates

- Investments in paper shares.
- The intention is to retain this investment as part of the entity's normal activities.

The four types of asset commonly found in businesses

current assets. Other assets are called **non-current assets**. They typically are held for periods that extend beyond one year and include tangible, intangible and long-term financial assets.

Inventory (stock) is the name for goods that have been purchased as part of the operating activities for resale but are not yet sold. They are current assets. A **trade receivable** (debtor) is the term given to the money that is owed from a customer, to whom the entity has sold goods on credit as part of its operating activities (the goods were given in advance of the entity receiving money for the goods).

Liabilities

In simple terms, **liabilities** represent obligations that the entity has to meet in the future. For example, a loan from a bank is a liability because at some point in the future the entity has to pay this back. Getting goods on credit (in advance of having to pay for them) from a supplier is a liability because the supplier has to be paid in the future. A **trade payable** (creditor) is the term given to the money that is owed to a supplier who provided trade goods on credit. Liabilities that are due to be settled within 12 months or that are incurred as part of the firm's normal operating (trading) activities are called **current liabilities**. Other liabilities are called **non-current liabilities**. Non-current liabilities are typically due in periods that extend beyond one year, but not always.

Equity

Equity or **equity shareholder** is another name for owner. It is usually used in reference to limited companies to refer to the shareholders who own ordinary shares.

1.5 Financial statements

As mentioned in the introduction, all entities have to produce a document periodically (usually yearly), which details what has been made in the period (profit or loss) and the entity's financial position. The most up-to-date guidance on how to present company financial statements is provided in International Accounting Standard 1 *Presentation of Financial Statements* (IAS 1). This accounting standard recommends that accounting information is provided in a number of short statements. The first statement provides details on the profits/losses made by the entity in the period. There is choice in the way that this information can be presented. The information can either be presented in one statement called the statement of comprehensive income, which shows the **profits or losses for the period** from realized activities in the first section followed by a section providing information on **other comprehensive income** (typically unrealized gains/losses). The final line on this statement shows the total comprehensive income for the period. The second alternative splits the information into two consecutive statements the first of which is called the statement of profit or loss and the second the **statement of other comprehensive income**. An example format is provided in Figure 1.9 in section 1.10 'Companies'. The second statement provides information on the financial position of the entity at its reporting date and is called the statement of financial position. This lists the entity's assets, liabilities and capital on the reporting date. A **statement of changes in equity** is also required to show the changes in equity, such as dividends paid to owners, or new share issues (see Chapter 29, 'The Final Financial Statements of Limited Companies'). The three statements together are called **financial statements** (otherwise known as 'accounts'). Larger companies also have to provide a fourth statement, showing the source and use of cash in the period. This statement is called the **statement of cash flows** (see Chapter 30, 'Statement of Cash Flows'). As all the financial information about an entity is summarized in the four statements, which usually do not extend beyond one page each, more detail is provided in the **notes to the financial statements**. The financial statements and notes are included in an entity's 'annual report' along with reports from management telling the owners what they are doing and what they plan to do. The reports include: the operating and financial review, the directors' report, the chief executive's report, the chairman's statement and the corporate social responsibility report. They also provide information on how they govern themselves in a corporate governance report and remuneration report. The narrative part of the report also highlights key information about the company and outlines the principal risks that the company faces. A public limited company's annual report typically extends to over 100 pages.

Learning Activity 1.2

Visit the Ryanair plc website and view a copy of their most recent annual report. Familiarize yourself with the reports provided by the directors at the front of the annual report. Note that this part of the annual report extends to over 100 pages. The latter part of the annual report contains the income statement, a separate statement of comprehensive income, the balance sheet (as mentioned, IAS 1 prefers to label this the statement of financial position but many UK and Irish companies elect to maintain the national terminology for this statement), the statement of cash flows and the notes to the financial statements for the Group and separately for the company.

1.6 Types of entity

Changes in accounting practices and disclosures usually arise from the need to provide quality financial information that is regarded as useful for the external stakeholders of an entity. The stakeholders are discussed in detail in Chapter 3, 'The Conceptual Framework 1: Objective of Financial Statements, Stakeholders and Other Reports'. They include the owners of the company, investors, creditors, employees, customers, the government and the public. There are several types of entity, for example owner-managed entities (wherein the owners are the managers and there are no external owners) and publicly owned companies that are owned predominately by the public and are managed by paid employees (directors). Owner-managed entities include sole traders, partnerships and some limited companies. Publicly owned companies (plcs) include companies that are listed on stock exchanges.

The type of information required in financial statements depends on the type of entity and the information needs of its stakeholders (users). The main difference in the accounting requirements for each type of entity is in respect of presentation. Though most entities follow guidance provided by the accountancy bodies, which are geared towards companies with external owners, differences in presentation arise because the accounting information being prepared by different entities may be for different purposes. For example, owner-managed entities may have full knowledge of the performance of their business. They do not have to formalize this knowledge into a set of written financial statements. However, the tax authorities (HM Revenue and Customs) will require financial statements to determine the tax bill, or the bank which has given the entity a loan may require information to determine if the entity will be able to repay the loan. There are other differences in the information that an entity itself will wish to highlight for the benefit of its stakeholders. For example, a charity will wish to provide more information on the sources of its income and what it is doing with that income relative to a conventional business which will not wish such detail to be provided as this may give too much information to competitors. Therefore, different entities tend to present their financial information in slightly different ways.

1.7 Sole traders

Sole traders are individuals who have started a business on their own. In a sole-trader business there is only one owner, the 'sole' trader. Sole-trader businesses are **unincorporated businesses** – they are not separate legal entities, not companies. As such, the sole trader is responsible for the debts of the business. This means that creditors have a claim over the sole trader's personal wealth for unpaid debts when the business runs out of funds. There is no legal distinction between the assets of the business and the assets of the sole trader.

Profits made in sole trader businesses are regarded as the owner's by the tax authorities and are subject to income tax. Sole traders usually have to get financial statements prepared for the purposes of completing their self-assessment tax return for the taxation authorities. This return requires quite a bit of expense detail, therefore sole-trader statements of profit or loss are more detailed (have less aggregation of expenses) than company financial statements. Statement of financial position disclosures are similar to those required for companies; however, more detail is provided in this statement on non-current assets and on changes in the owner's capital.

Simple examples of a statement of profit or loss and a statement of financial position for a sole trader who operates a child-minding business are shown in Figures 1.4 and 1.5. Note the extensive detail provided on expenses. Many of the terms used have been explained earlier in this chapter and are not repeated here. The **cost of services** section includes those expenses that are directly related to the child-minding service that is being sold by the business. Typical costs might include food for the children, nappies and toiletries. In a business that sells goods, this description usually changes to **cost of goods sold**.

The format of sole trader financial statements is explained in more detail in Part 3.

Figure 1.4

T. Sole: Trading as T. Child Minding Services
Statement of profit or loss for the year ended 31 March 20X4

	£	£
Revenue		16,470
Less: cost of services		1,527
Gross profit		14,943
Other income		100
Less: expenses		
Travel and mileage	530	
Sundry expenses	33	
General running expenses	975	
Stationery	41	
Depreciation – toys	143	
Depreciation – equipment	67	
Depreciation – house fixtures	64	1,853
Profit for the year		13,190

A simple example of the layout of a statement of profit or loss for a sole trader

Note: Depreciation is an allocation of the cost, or value of tangible non-current asset, to the statement of profit or loss over the period the business expects to use and generate revenue from the asset. This is covered in detail in Chapter 15.

1.8 Partnerships

Partnerships are formed when two or more individuals get together to start a business. A partnership can be incorporated as a limited liability partnership or as an unincorporated business. If it is unincorporated then the same principles as outlined above for sole traders apply, except that the partners will be jointly

Figure 1.5

T. Sole: Trading as T. Child Minding Services Statement of financial position as at 31 March 20X4		
ASSETS	Note	£
Non-current assets		
Property, plant and equipment	2	824
Current assets		
Trade receivables		350
Bank		100
		450
Total assets		1,274
EQUITY AND LIABILITIES		
Owners' capital		
Opening capital		243
Capital introduced		0
Profit for the year		13,190
		13,433
Drawings		(12,609)
Closing capital		824
Current liabilities		
Trade and other payables		450
Total equity and liabilities		1,274
I approve these financial statements and confirm that all relevant information and explanations have been provided		
T. Sole	28th August 20X4	

A simple example of the layout of a statement of financial position for a sole trader

liable for the partnership's debts. In many instances the partnership will have a partnership agreement that may alter the profit-sharing ratios between the partners. The partners usually have to get financial statements prepared for the partnership for the purposes of completing a partnership return for the tax authorities, and for completing their personal self-assessment tax return, which has to be filed annually. The partners have to pay income tax on their share of the profits of the partnership. The partnership return requires quite a bit of expense detail; therefore, partnership statements of profit or loss are more detailed (have less aggregation of expenses) than company statements of profit or loss. If the partnership is limited, then the same principles as detailed under companies (discussed in Part 6) are relevant. A typical layout of a partnership statement of profit or loss can be seen in Figure 1.6.

The profit or loss for the period is apportioned between the partners using an **appropriation account** that is typically included at the base of the statement of profit or loss. This disclosure is unique to partnerships.

The statement of financial position is similar to that prepared for sole traders and companies, except the capital attributable to each owner is disclosed separately. Like sole traders, more detail on tangible non-current assets is also typically provided in the statement of financial position than is disclosed on the face of company financial statements, wherein the detail is provided in the notes (see Chapter 29). An example of a statement of financial position for a partnership can be seen in Figure 1.7.

Figure 1.6

X & Y: Trading as X & Y Hair Salon Statement of profit or loss for the year ended 31 March 20X4		
	£	£
Revenue		101,433
Less: cost of goods sold		
Opening inventory	200	
Purchases	15,836	
	16,036	
Less: closing inventory	500	15,536
Gross profit		85,897
Less: expenses		
Salaries	29,569	
Rent and rates	16,504	
Heat and light	2,386	
Telephone	200	
Advertising and stationery	817	
Laundry and cleaning	547	
Professional fees and insurance	1,600	
Bank interest and fees	2,144	
Accountancy fees	260	
Refreshments, papers, etc.	342	
Repairs	3,199	
Sundry expenses	544	
Travel	636	
Depreciation	33	58,781
Profit for the year		27,116
Apportioned between:		
X current account		13,558
Y current account		13,558
		27,116

An example of the layout of a statement of profit or loss for a partnership

It is also normal to provide some detail in partnership financial statements on the movements within owners' equity (see Figure 1.8).

The preparation of partnership financial statements is covered in detail in Part 6.

1.9 Member-governed bodies

Some entities are run by their members for the benefit of their members. Many are unincorporated (not established under law as a company). Some of these entities are large, formal and subject to their own legislation (not company legislation). However, their disclosure requirements usually follow those recommended by the accounting bodies. Examples of this type of organization include mutual building societies, sports clubs and life assurance companies. In many instances, to protect members' private

Figure 1.7

X & Y: Trading as X & Y Hair Salon Statement of financial position as at 31 March 20X4			
ASSETS			£
Non-current assets			
Equipment			100
Current assets			
Inventories			500
Trade and other receivables			7,743
Bank			7,095
Cash			200
			15,538
Total assets			15,638
OWNERS' EQUITY AND LIABILITIES			
Owners' equity:	Capital	Current	Total
	£	£	£
Partner X	3,000	500	3,500
Partner Y	2,500	791	3,291
	5,500	1,291	6,791
Non-current liabilities			
Loan			5,000
Current liabilities			
Trade and other payables			3,847
Total equity and liabilities			15,638

I approve these financial statements and confirm that all relevant information and explanations have been provided

X (Signature) Y (Signature)

31st May 20X4 31st May 20X4

An example of the layout of a statement of financial position for a partnership

Figure 1.8

Note: Statement of changes in owners' equity					
	Capital		Current		
	X	Y	X	Y	Total
	£	£	£	£	£
Opening capital	3,000	2,000	200	300	5,500
Capital introduced	–	500	–	–	500
Profit for the year	–	–	13,558	13,558	27,116
Drawings	–	–	(13,258)	(13,067)	(26,325)
Closing capital	3,000	2,500	500	791	6,791

An example of the layout of the statement of changes in owners' equity (capital and current accounts) for a partnership

wealth, these entities become incorporated; however, unlike normal companies, they are not limited by share, opting to become limited by guarantee instead. Therefore, they do not have a share capital or shareholders. The guarantor members agree to pay a fixed sum of money towards the debts of the entity in the event of the entity being unable to do so. The sums guaranteed by each member are small, typically £1. A real world example is now provided. In the year 2012 the University of Southampton Students' Union, an unincorporated entity, changed its constitution from an unincorporated entity to a company limited by guarantee and it registered as a charity. It is still governed for the benefit of its members; however, its legal structure has changed.

REAL WORLD EXAMPLE 1.1

Structure, governance and management

a) Constitution

The Union was first established in the Charter of the University of Southampton Charter which specifies that "there shall be a Union of Students of the University". During the course of the year, SUSU has significantly changed its governance structures; incorporating as a company limited by guarantee and registering as a charity. However, for the reporting period contained in these accounts, the Union operated as an unincorporated association and in order to pursue its aims, worked within a constitution comprising of Laws and Standing Orders which determine the structure of the organisation and its rules. The Laws can only be amended by Union Council and the University, and with effective from 1 August 2012 have been replaced by memorandum and articles of association

Source: http://www.susu.org/downloads/accounts/2012.pdf, accessed 15 August 2013.

This text does not consider the presentation requirements of all the different types of member organization; however, unincorporated clubs are covered online in Chapter 32 (www.mcgraw-hill.co.uk/textbooks/thomas).

1.10 Companies

Companies are incorporated by law as separate legal entities. Companies can own assets and take action in their own right. Companies have to pay **corporation tax** (company income tax). The two most common forms of company are **public limited companies** (plc) and **private limited companies** (Ltd). Under law incorporated companies have to include the abbreviation 'plc' or 'Ltd' in their name so that stakeholders (interested parties) are aware of their status. When a company is formed its ownership is split into shares. Plcs offer shares to the public on recognized share exchanges, such as the London Stock Exchange (LSE) or the Irish Stock Exchange (ISE). Plcs are commonly referred to as **listed companies** (because they are listed as members of a stock exchange). Limited companies are privately owned, usually by a family or a small group of investors. The owners in private companies also hold shares in the company. These shares may be sold privately but are not publicly sold on exchanges. In both public and private limited companies, owners' private wealth is protected from creditors by legislation. They have what is referred to as **limited liability** – owners will only lose their investment (represented by monies paid for shares held) in the company if it fails. Creditors cannot sue them for their private assets. Therefore, their liability is limited to the amount invested in the company.

The format of a company's financial statement is guided by IAS 1. IAS 1 states that companies should prepare a statement of comprehensive income. IAS 1 contains a disclosure example in its appendices, a simplified version is provided in Figure 1.9.

Figure 1.9

Milky Chocolate Ltd	
Statement of comprehensive income for the year ended 31 March 20X4	
	£'000
Revenue	101,433
Cost of sales	(25,537)
Gross profit	75,896
Other income	3,000
Distribution costs	(28,000)
Administration expenses	(41,285)
Other expenses	(895)
Finance costs	(2,514)
Profit before tax	6,202
Income tax expense	(2,850)
Profit for the year from continuing activities	3,352
Other comprehensive income	
Gains on property revaluation	1,500
Other comprehensive income net of tax	1,500
Total comprehensive income for the year	4,852

A simple example of the layout of a statement of comprehensive income for a company

A standard format for reporting a company's financial position (assets, liabilities and owners' capital) is also provided in the appendix to IAS 1. Figure 1.10 has been prepared in light of the example provided in IAS 1.

Total assets equals total equity and liabilities (both amount to £27,160,000). This balancing concept is explored fully in Chapter 7, 'The Accounting Equation and its Components' and forms the underlying principles behind double entry that is covered in Chapter 9, 'Double Entry and the General Ledger' and subsequent chapters. It is hoped that you will now be familiar with the consistencies and differences in the reporting between different types of entity.

The minimum contents of the statement of financial position specified in IAS 1 are also similar to that required by UK Generally Accepted Accounting Practice (GAAP), but the format and terminology are slightly different. In particular, under UK GAAP, the statement of financial position is called the balance sheet and the statement of profit or loss is referred to as the profit and loss account. The ordering of presentation is also quite different. In terms of terminology, non-current assets are referred to as **fixed assets** in UK legislation, non-current liabilities are referred to as **long-term liabilities**, trade receivables are referred to as **trade debtors**, and the trade and other payables are referred to as **trade creditors**. **Property, plant and equipment** is equivalent to the **tangible fixed assets** shown in the UK format and is made up of land and buildings, plant and machinery, and fixtures, fittings, tools and equipment. The retained earnings are equivalent to the balance on the profit and loss account as shown in the UK balance sheet format. The remaining items are self-explanatory.

Learning Activity 1.3

Access the financial statements of Morrison Supermarkets PLC for 2013. Note this company is adopting a UK GAAP format for its 'Balance Sheet'. Note the terminology and different presentation style.

http://www.morrisons-corporate.com/2013/annualreport/downloads/Default.aspx

Figure 1.10

Milky Chocolate Ltd Statement of financial position as at 31 March 20X4	
ASSETS	£'000
Non-current assets	
Property, plant and equipment	21,520
Goodwill	800
Other intangible assets	400
Available-for-sale investments	1,200
	23,920
Current assets	
Inventories	1,560
Trade receivables	1,480
Other current assets	120
Cash and cash equivalents	80
	3,240
Total assets	27,160
EQUITY AND LIABILITIES	
Capital and reserves	
Share capital	8,000
Retained earnings	6,528
Other components of equity	2,500
Total equity	17,028
Non-current liabilities	
Long-term borrowing	3,000
Long-term provisions	2,580
Total non-current liabilities	5,580
Current liabilities	
Trade and other payables	1,540
Short-term borrowing	520
Current portion of long-term borrowing	932
Current tax payable	980
Short-term provision	580
Total current liabilities	4,552
Total liabilities	10,132
Total equity and liabilities	27,160

A simple example of the layout of a statement of financial position for a company

In practice, prior year figures (called **comparatives**) are provided for nearly all financial information disclosed in financial statements regardless of entity type.

1.11 The regulatory framework of accounting

The **regulatory framework of accounting** is a general term used to describe the legislation and other rules that govern the content and format of company final financial statements. There is no legislation or other regulation covering the final financial statements of sole traders and partnerships. However, it is generally accepted that their financial statements should closely follow the rules and regulations relating to companies since these are regarded as 'best practice'. The main sources of regulation are presented in Figure 1.11.

Figure 1.11

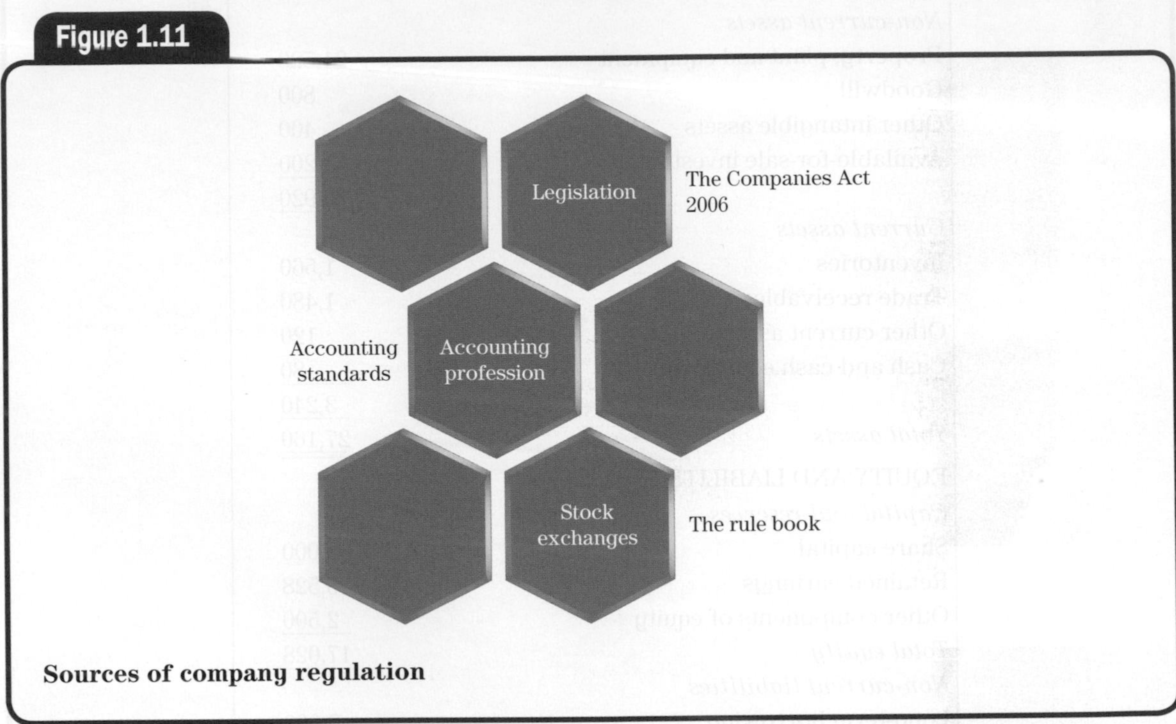

Sources of company regulation

Companies prepare financial statements under either International Financial Reporting Standards (IFRSs) or UK Financial Reporting Standards (FRSs). The regulatory framework for setting IFRS is described in Chapter 2, 'Financial Reporting: Institutional Framework and Standards'. IFRSs are compulsory for all publicly listed companies though can be adopted by all other types of entity also. UK FRSs cannot be applied by publicly listed companies though can be used for all other entities. In practice, the financial statements of unincorporated entities (e.g. sole traders and partnerships) are prepared using FRSs.

Summary

Financial accounting is the process of designing and operating an information system for collecting, measuring and recording business transactions, and summarizing and communicating the results of these transactions to users to facilitate the making of financial/economic decisions. The first part of this definition, relating to collecting and recording business transactions, is called double-entry bookkeeping. The purposes of financial accounting systems are to record and control business transactions, maintain accuracy in recording, meet the requirements of the law, present final financial statements and other financial reports to the owners of the enterprise, and facilitate the efficient allocation of resources.

Financial accounting emerged from demand for quality financial information about an entity's financial performance and financial position by stakeholders who are external to the entity. To provide information on performance, a statement of comprehensive income has evolved showing profit or loss from normal activities, other types of gains and the total comprehensive income (the sum of both these figures) for the period. To provide information on the state of a company's affairs, the statement of financial position has evolved. It shows the total assets of the entity split into non-current and current categories. The bottom half of the statement of financial position shows how the entity is financed. The amount of the owner's equity invested and the liabilities (split into non-current and current) are disclosed. The sum of the equity and liabilities should equal the total assets (it should balance).

Five types of business entity are covered in this book: sole traders, manufacturing entities, clubs, partnerships and companies. In this chapter, standard information is provided for sole traders, partnerships and companies, and differences between the standard proforma statements are outlined. For example, sole traders and partnerships have more detail on their expenses and assets in their reporting statements than companies do, as this information is required for an individual owner's self-assessment tax returns. These entities also provide more detail in the statement of financial position of movements in the owner's equity, whereas the detail of this is provided in the notes to company financial statements.

The contents of company financial statements are governed by a regulatory framework. In the UK this comprises the Companies Act 2006, London Stock Exchange regulations, and accounting standards as issued by the national and international accountancy bodies.

Key terms and concepts

accountability	6	expenses	8
annual report	4	financial accounting	4
appropriation account	12	financial statements	9
available-for-sale assets	8	fixed assets	16
balance sheet	4	intangible assets	8
comparatives	17	internal check	6
corporation tax	15	internal control	5
cost of goods sold	11	inventory	9
cost of services	11	investments in associates	8
current assets	9	liabilities	9
current liabilities	9	limited liability	15
double-entry bookkeeping	6	listed companies	15
economic decision-making	7	long-term liabilities	16
equity	9	management accounting	4
equity shareholder	9	non-current assets	9

non-current liabilities	9	statement of changes in equity	9
notes to the financial statements	9	statement of comprehensive income	4
other comprehensive income	9	statement of financial position	4
other income	7	statement of other comprehensive income	9
partnerships	11	statement of profit or loss	4
private limited companies	15	stewardship accounting	4
profit or loss for the period	9	tangible assets	8
property, plant and equipment	16	tangible fixed assets	16
public limited companies	15	trade creditors	16
regulatory framework of accounting	17	trade debtors	16
revenue	7	trade payable	9
sole traders	10	trade receivable	9
statement of cash flows	9	unincorporated businesses	10

An asterisk after the question number indicates that there is a suggested answer in Appendix 2.

Review questions

connect

1.1* Explain the nature and functions of financial accounting.

1.2 List the typical contents of an annual report for a public limited company.

1.3 Outline the differences between the information provided in the financial statements of sole traders and partnerships.

1.4 Outline the differences in the information provided in the financial statements of sole traders and companies.

1.5* a Describe the recording and control function of financial accounting.

b Explain the role of financial accounting with regard to the presentation of final financial statements.

Exercises

connect

BASIC

1.6* In which statement will the following appear, and under which heading will it be included:

a Furniture and fixtures;

b Rent;

c Wages;

d Amounts owing to a supplier;

e Amounts due from a customer.

1.7 Why are financial statements prepared by companies? BASIC

1.8 What do you think is the objective of financial statements? BASIC

1.9 Who do you think the stakeholders (users) of financial statement might be? BASIC

1.10* Explain briefly each of the following: internal control; internal check; stewardship accounting; and accountability. BASIC

References

International Accounting Standards Board (2014) *International Accounting Standard 1 – Presentation of Financial Statements* (IASB).

Ryanair Report and Financial Statements (2013) http://www.ryanair.com/doc/investor/2013/final_annual_report_2013_130731.pdf, accessed 14 August 2013.

Chapter 2

Financial reporting: institutional framework and standards

Learning Objectives:

After reading this chapter you should be able to do the following:

1. Describe the regulatory framework of international accounting.
2. Describe the objectives and role of the International Accounting Standards Board.
3. Explain the process adopted by the International Accounting Standards Board when preparing a new standard/revising an existing standard.
4. Describe the UK regulatory framework of accounting.
5. Explain the changes that are going to occur to the UK regulatory framework in 2015.
6. Discuss the current activities of the International Accounting Standards Board.
7. Describe in brief the main elements of each of the International Financial Reporting Standards that will be referred to in this book.

—2.1 Introduction

Accounting is not meant to be creative. It is meant to portray the economic substance of a transaction. This is not always as easy as it may seem. For example, in some instances it may be difficult to determine whether a transaction actually results in an asset. In other instances it is difficult to determine whether a liability should be created or not. Not all transactions are straightforward and there are incentives to account in a manner which best serves management (who are in charge of accounting). Guidance on how to account is required to protect stakeholders (users of accounting information) and to provide information that is useful for their economic decision-making.

Most countries have professional bodies or government departments that either provide national guidance on how to account for transactions or have adopted global accounting standards. The advantages and disadvantages of global accounting standards are summarized in Figure 2.1.

Global financial reporting standards are prepared by the **International Accounting Standards Board (IASB)**. The IASB is a worldwide umbrella accounting standards board which aims to issue one set of

Figure 2.1

Advantages	Disadvantages
• Having global financial reporting standards improves comparability of financial statements across countries • Global financial reporting standards provide a global business language which should lead to improvements in business communication • Businesses can more easily raise funds in other countries as their financial statements will be recognized by securities exchanges • Preparation of group accounts is simpler and less costly • Global financial reporting standards should lead to improved global decision-making that may lead to improved global growth • Global financial reporting standards should lead to increased levels of global investment as investors will be familiar with the financial statements • Having global finanical reporting standards reduces the cost of an entity starting a business in another country • When a country does not have the resources to create their own national framework, global financial reporting standards provide a high quality 'off-the-shelf' alternative • The use of global financial reporting standards provides legitimacy to businesses in countries that do not have their own financial reporting frameworks	• Using global financial reporting standards is argued to be a threat to national identity • The treatments recommended within global financial reporting standards may not reflect national culture • Global financial reporting standards may not be flexible enough to deal with unique transactions that are country specific • It is costly for entities to change from national financial reporting standards to global financial reporting standards • Global financial reporting standards are deemed to be inappropriate for small and medium-sized entities (this is one of the reasons that the UK did not fully converge with global standards)

The advantages and disadvantages of global financial reporting standards

accounting standards which are agreed upon and adopted in every country in the world. By 2014, 120 countries have required or permitted the use of IFRS, with Russia and Argentina being the most recent large nations requiring compliance (in 2012). This chapter examines the role of the IASB and describes in brief the 11 main **International Financial Reporting Standards** (IFRSs) that are referred to in this book. **International Accounting Standards** (IASs) is the name given to the standards that were issued by the International Accounting Standards Committee (IASC), the predecessor of the IASB. The IASB has adopted a number of the IASC's standards and the name (IAS) has not been changed, though new standards are called IFRSs.

2.2 The institutional framework for setting IFRSs

The institutional framework for setting IFRSs is shown in Figure 2.2.

According to the IFRS website the IASB is *'the independent standard-setting body of the IFRS Foundation'*. The IFRS Foundation is publicly accountable to the **Monitoring Board of Public Capital Market Authorities** (hereafter called the Monitoring Board). The IASB is supported by an external 'IFRS Advisory Council' and an 'IFRS Interpretations Committee' that offers guidance where divergence in practice occurs (IASB and the IFRS Foundation, 2013). Over the past few years it has also established an '**Accounting Standards Advisory Forum**' (ASAF), the 'Emerging Economies Group', a 'Financial Crisis Advisory Group' (work has concluded), an 'SME Implementation Group' and 'Consultative Groups'. Some brief detail is now provided on each of the main bodies involved.

Figure 2.2

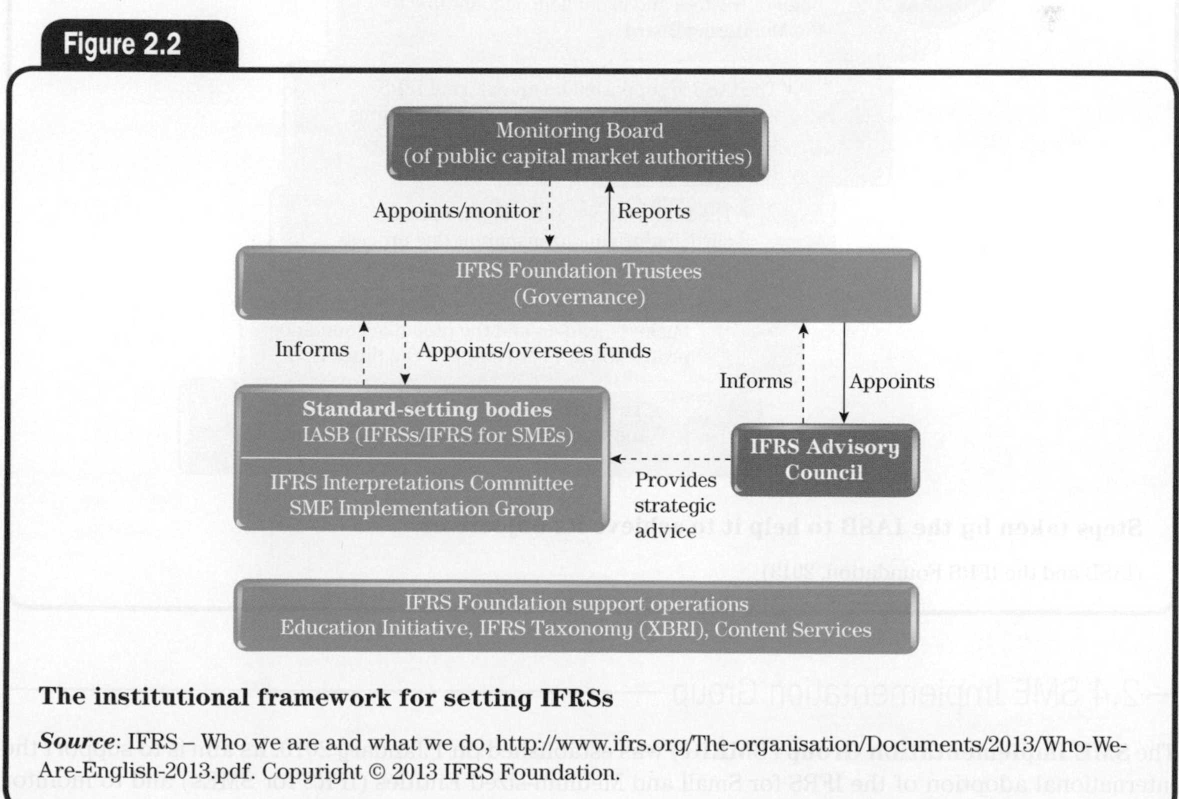

The institutional framework for setting IFRSs

Source: IFRS – Who we are and what we do, http://www.ifrs.org/The-organisation/Documents/2013/Who-We-Are-English-2013.pdf. Copyright © 2013 IFRS Foundation.

2.3 The International Accounting Standards Board (IASB)

The predecessor to the IASB, the **International Accounting Standards Committee (IASC)** was formed in 1973. Up until 2000 the IASC was governed by representatives from some of its member countries. In 2001 the IASC was renamed the IASB when it became governed by an independent board whose members are appointed by trustees. The members are drawn from the world's financial community, who represent the public interest. The IASB has 16 full-time members. These members have a variety of functional backgrounds – from academics, to former chief executives of financial institutions, to former partners in professional accounting firms. Each member has one vote. As mentioned previously, standards that are issued by the IASB are known as IFRSs. The IASC issued 41 IASs and a conceptual framework called *The Framework for the Preparation and Presentation of Financial Statements* (IASC, 1989). Currently, 28 IASs are still in existence and are promulgated by the IASB. Thirteen IFRSs have been produced by the IASB.

The main objective of the IASB is *'to develop a single set of high quality, understandable, enforceable and globally accepted financial reporting standards based upon clearly articulated principles'* (IASB and the IFRS Foundation, 2013). To achieve this, the IASB has detailed how it aims to achieve its objective. These are outlined in Figure 2.3.

Figure 2.3

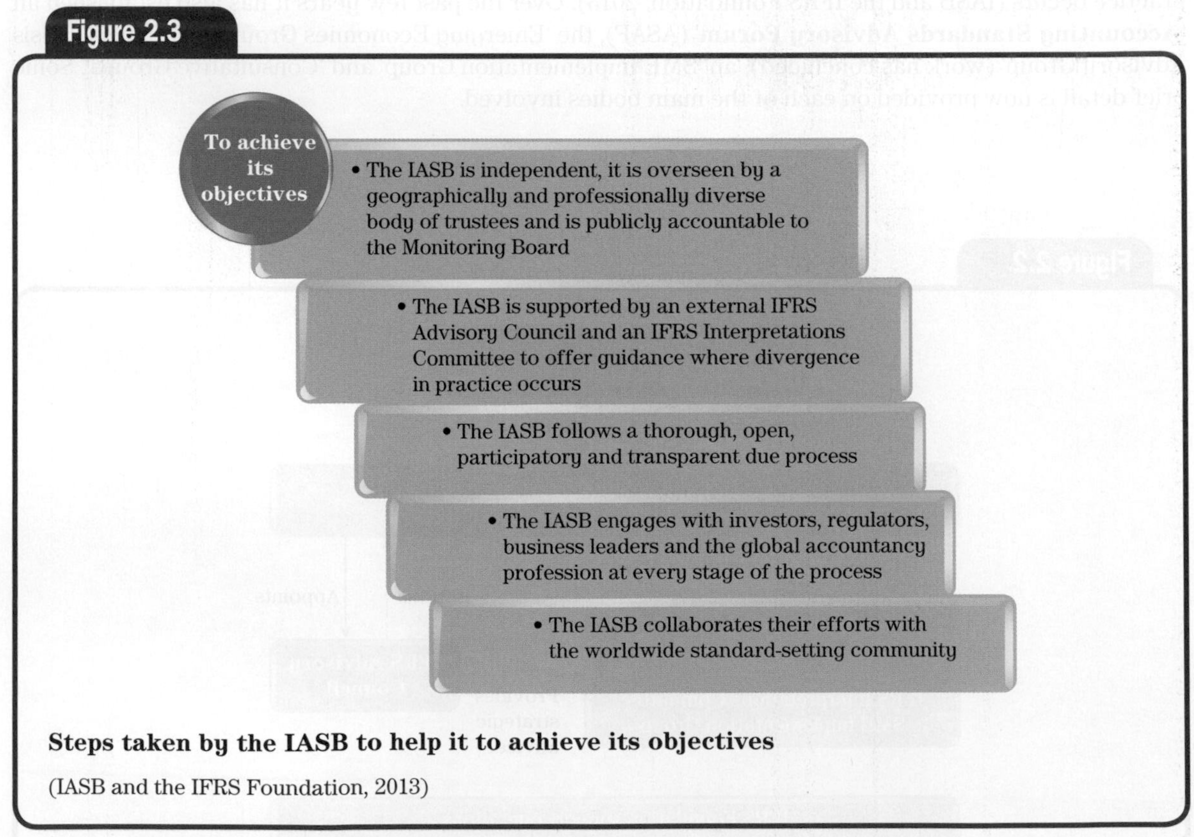

To achieve its objectives
• The IASB is independent, it is overseen by a geographically and professionally diverse body of trustees and is publicly accountable to the Monitoring Board
• The IASB is supported by an external IFRS Advisory Council and an IFRS Interpretations Committee to offer guidance where divergence in practice occurs
• The IASB follows a thorough, open, participatory and transparent due process
• The IASB engages with investors, regulators, business leaders and the global accountancy profession at every stage of the process
• The IASB collaborates their efforts with the worldwide standard-setting community

Steps taken by the IASB to help it to achieve its objectives

(IASB and the IFRS Foundation, 2013)

2.4 SME Implementation Group

The **SME Implementation Group (SMEIG)** was established on 1 January 2010. Its aim is to support the international adoption of the IFRS for Small and Medium-sized Entities (IFRS for SMEs) and to monitor its implementation. The **IFRS for SMEs** is a separate IFRS that was issued by the IASB in July 2009 to cater for the needs of smaller entities that deemed full IFRSs to be too onerous and inappropriate for their needs. It is based on the same principles as full IFRS but contains certain omissions, simplifications, and reduced disclosures, and has been written for clarity.

2.5 The IFRS Foundation Trustees

The **IFRS Foundation Trustees** was formed on 1 March 2012. The aim of the trustees is to promote the work of the IASB and the rigorous application of IFRSs. However, they are not involved in any technical matters relating to the standards. The trustees are accountable to an external body, the Monitoring Board. The Monitoring Board appoints the trustees. The objectives of the IFRS Foundation are:

> "1 *to develop, in the public interest, a single set of high-quality, understandable, enforceable and globally accepted IFRS through its standard-setting body, the IASB;*
>
> 2 *to promote the use and rigorous application of those standards;*
>
> 3 *to take account of the financial reporting needs of emerging economies and small and medium-sized entities (SMEs); and*
>
> 4 *to promote and facilitate adoption of IFRSs, being the standards and interpretations issued by the IASB, through the convergence of national accounting standards and IFRS.*"
>
> (IFRS website, 2013)

Ultimately the trustees are responsible for the governance of all the bodies that are directly involved in the development of international accounting standards. The IFRS website states that the responsibilities of the Foundation trustees include:

> "1 *appointing trustees, members of the IASB, the IFRS Interpretations Committee and the IFRS Advisory Council;*
>
> 2 *establishing and amending the operating procedures, consultative arrangements and due process for the IASB, the Interpretations Committee and the Advisory Council;*
>
> 3 *reviewing annually the strategy of the IASB and assessing its effectiveness;*
>
> 4 *ensuring the financing of the IFRS Foundation and approving annually its budget.*"
>
> (IFRS website, 2013)

2.6 The Monitoring Board of Public Capital Market Authorities

In 2009 the trustees of the IFRS Foundation established the Monitoring Board to enhance the public accountability of the IFRS Foundation whilst not impairing the independence of the standard-setting process. The Monitoring Board serves as a formal link and a forum for interaction between representatives of the main capital market authorities worldwide (nominated and appointed to the Board) and the IFRS Foundation. The aim of the Monitoring Board is to appoint members of the IFRS Foundation and to hold them accountable in their role.

2.7 The IFRS Interpretations Committee

The **IFRS Interpretations Committee (IFRIC)** is the interpretive body of the IFRS Foundation. The IFRS Interpretations Committee's mandate is to '*review on a timely basis widespread accounting issues that have arisen within the context of current IFRSs, to reach consensus on the appropriate accounting treatment and* *to provide authoritative guidance on those issues*' (IFRS website, 2013). The authoritative guidance is called 'IFRIC Interpretations' (these are published and have the same authority as IFRSs). They cover:

> "1 *newly identified financial reporting issues not specifically dealt with in IFRSs; and*
>
> 2 *issues where unsatisfactory or conflicting interpretations have developed or seem likely to develop in the absence of authoritative guidance.*"
>
> (IFRS website, 2013)

IFRIC Interpretations have to be approved by the IASB before publication.

—2.8 The IFRS Advisory Council

The **IFRS Advisory Council** is the formal advisory body to the IASB and the IFRS Foundation. The Advisory Council is '*made up of a wide range of representatives from user groups, preparers, financial analysts, academics, auditors, regulators, professional accounting bodies and investor groups that are affected by and interested in the IASB's work*' (IFRS, 2013). The primary objective of the Advisory Council is to give the IASB advice on issues including:

> "1 *input on the IASB's agenda;*
>
> 2 *input on the IASB's project timetable including project priorities, and consultation on any changes in agenda and priorities;*
>
> 3 *advice on projects, with particular emphasis on practical application and implementation issues, including matters relating to existing standards that may warrant consideration by the IFRS Interpretations Committee.*"
>
> (IFRS website, 2013)

The IFRS Advisory Council also supports the IASB in the promotion and adoption of IFRSs throughout the world.

—2.9 IFRS Foundation Support Operations

To promote and support the worldwide use of IFRS, the IFRS Foundation also has a number of supporting initiatives going on, including:

> "1 *the creation of an XBRL taxonomy for IFRSs and the IFRS for SMEs. The XBRL taxonomy is standardized formats and labels (called tags) which should enable the electronic use, exchange and comparability of financial data across countries;*
>
> 2 *the production of high-quality, understandable and up-to-date material (including training material) for the IFRS for SMEs and the organization of workshops and conferences on IFRSs;*
>
> 3 *promotion of the IFRS brand and the support of global adoption convergence. This involves dealing with translation and copyright issues;*
>
> 4 *providing day-to-day support and management of the IFRS Foundation.*"
>
> (IFRS website, 2013)

—2.10 The standard-setting process

The standard-setting process involves six stages. The first stage is 'setting the agenda'. This provides a timetable that highlights the various topic areas that the IASB are either working on or are planning to work on. The second stage is called 'planning the project'. This involves deciding on whether to progress with the standard on its own or with another standard-setter. The IASB may set up a working group at this stage to undertake research into the topic being considered. The standard-setting process formally starts with the publication of a **Discussion Paper (DP)** which is prepared by the IASB and distributed for public consultation to various interested parties. This discussion paper is prepared after the IASB has undertaken thorough research of the topic. The feedback received from the public consultation on the DP is incorporated into an **Exposure Draft (ED)** which is reissued to interested parties and the general public for comment. The IASB then reviews the comments/feedback received and may decide to revise and publish the ED again. After this a pre-ballot draft is prepared and subjected to external review, usually by the IFRIC, and shortly before the IASB ballots the standard a near-final draft is posted on eIFRS. Finally, when all outstanding issues are resolved and the IASB members vote in favour of the standard, a new IFRS is issued and is adopted by the various accounting bodies around the world who have signed up to IFRS. After two years the IASB reviews the IFRS and any communications/feedback that they have received in the intervening period. At this stage they may revise the IFRS or leave it as it is. The standard-setting process is captured diagrammatically in Figure 2.4.

Figure 2.4

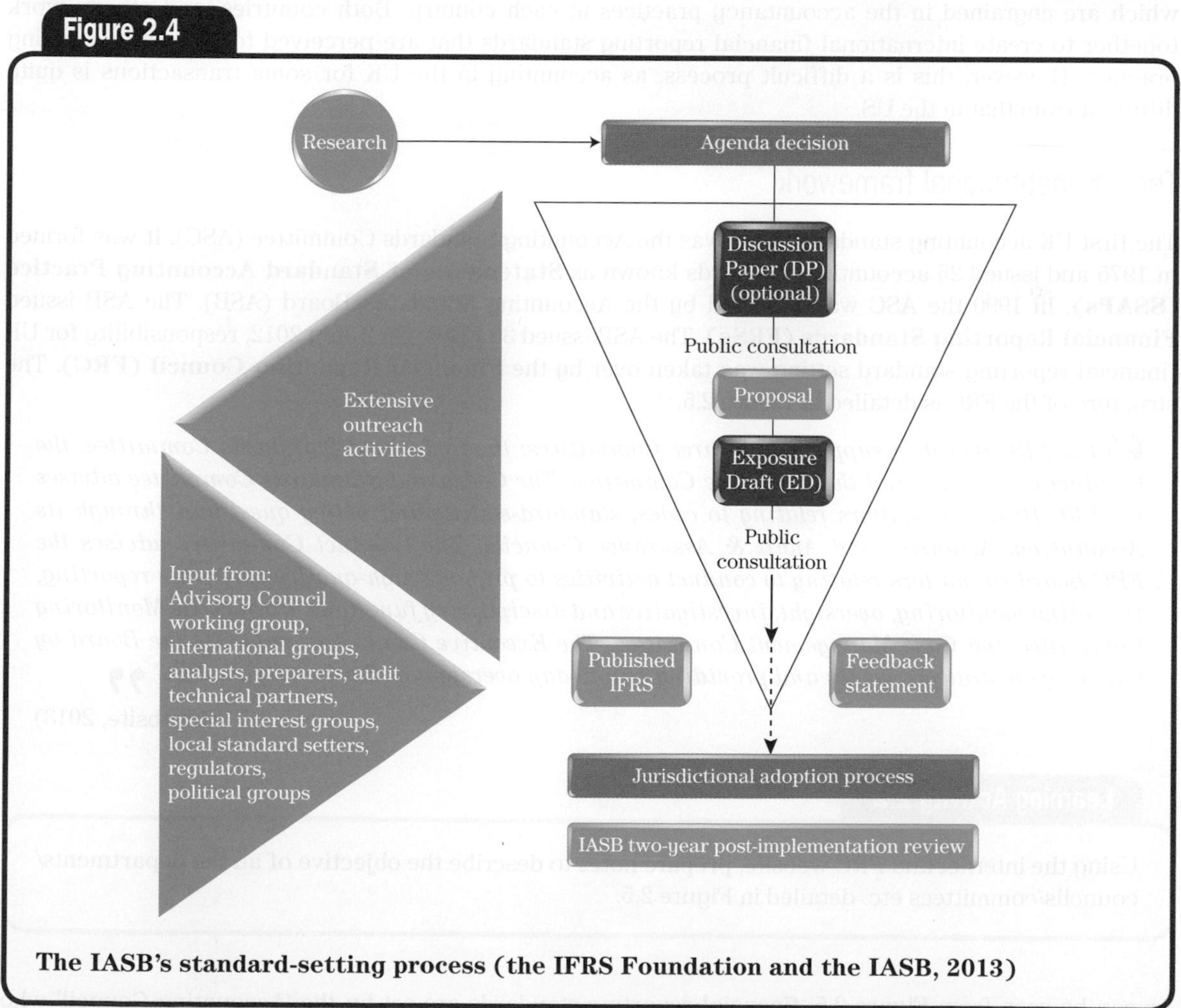

The IASB's standard-setting process (the IFRS Foundation and the IASB, 2013)

Learning Activity 2.1

Go to the IASB's website and read up on current proposed standards that the IASB are working on.

2.11 UK Accounting Regulation (and the ROI)

Introduction

This book focuses on accounting using international financial reporting standards. However, it would be remiss not to make students aware of the fact that the UK (and the ROI) has its own regulatory framework, with its own standards, which are still being used by most small, medium and some large-sized entities in the UK. One of the historic aims of the body responsible for UK accounting standard setting, the Financial Reporting Council (FRC), was to converge UK accounting standards with those of the IASB; however, convergence has not been popular with UK accountants and a framework that allows choice has been developed in response to consultation. This new framework is effective from 1 January 2015.

The UK and America were the first countries to have accounting standard-setting bodies and accounting standards. As a result the **Financial Accounting Standards Board (FASB)** (the American standard-setting body) and the FRC's predecessors (the **Accounting Standards Board (ASB)** and before them, the **Accounting Standards Committee (ASC)**) have established accounting practices and standards, which are engrained in the accountancy practices in each country. Both countries, and others, work together to create international financial reporting standards that are perceived to be best accounting practice. However, this is a difficult process, as accounting in the UK for some transactions is quite different from that in the US.

The UK institutional framework

The first UK accounting standard setter was the Accounting Standards Committee (ASC). It was formed in 1975 and issued 25 accounting standards known as **Statements of Standard Accounting Practice (SSAPs)**. In 1990 the ASC was replaced by the Accounting Standards Board (ASB). The ASB issued **Financial Reporting Standards (FRSs)**. The ASB issued 30 FRSs. On 2 July 2012, responsibility for UK financial reporting standard setting was taken over by the **Financial Reporting Council (FRC)**. The structure of the FRC is detailed in Figure 2.5.

> *The FRC Board is supported by three Committees: the Codes and Standards Committee, the Conduct Committee and the Executive Committee. The Codes and Standards Committee advises the FRC Board on matters relating to codes, standard-setting and policy questions, through its Accounting, Actuarial and Audit & Assurance Councils. The Conduct Committee advises the FRC Board in matters relating to conduct activities to promote high-quality corporate reporting, including monitoring, oversight, investigative and disciplinary functions, through its Monitoring Committee and Case Management Committee. The Executive Committee supports the Board by advising on strategic issues and providing day-to-day oversight of the work of the FRC.*
>
> (FRC website, 2013)

Learning Activity 2.2

Using the internet and FRC website, prepare notes to describe the objective of all the departments/councils/committees etc. detailed in Figure 2.5.

As can be seen from Figure 2.5, financial reporting standards are set by the 'Accounting Council' who report to the 'Codes and Standards Committee' who in turn report to the FRC Board. In 2012 the FRC adopted 29 of the FRSs that were issued by the ASB and 8 SSAPs that had not been superseded by FRSs. They also consider the Financial Reporting Standard for Smaller Entities (FRSSE) and the 31 Urgent Issues Taskforce (UITF) abstracts as accounting standards. However, major changes will become effective from

Figure 2.5

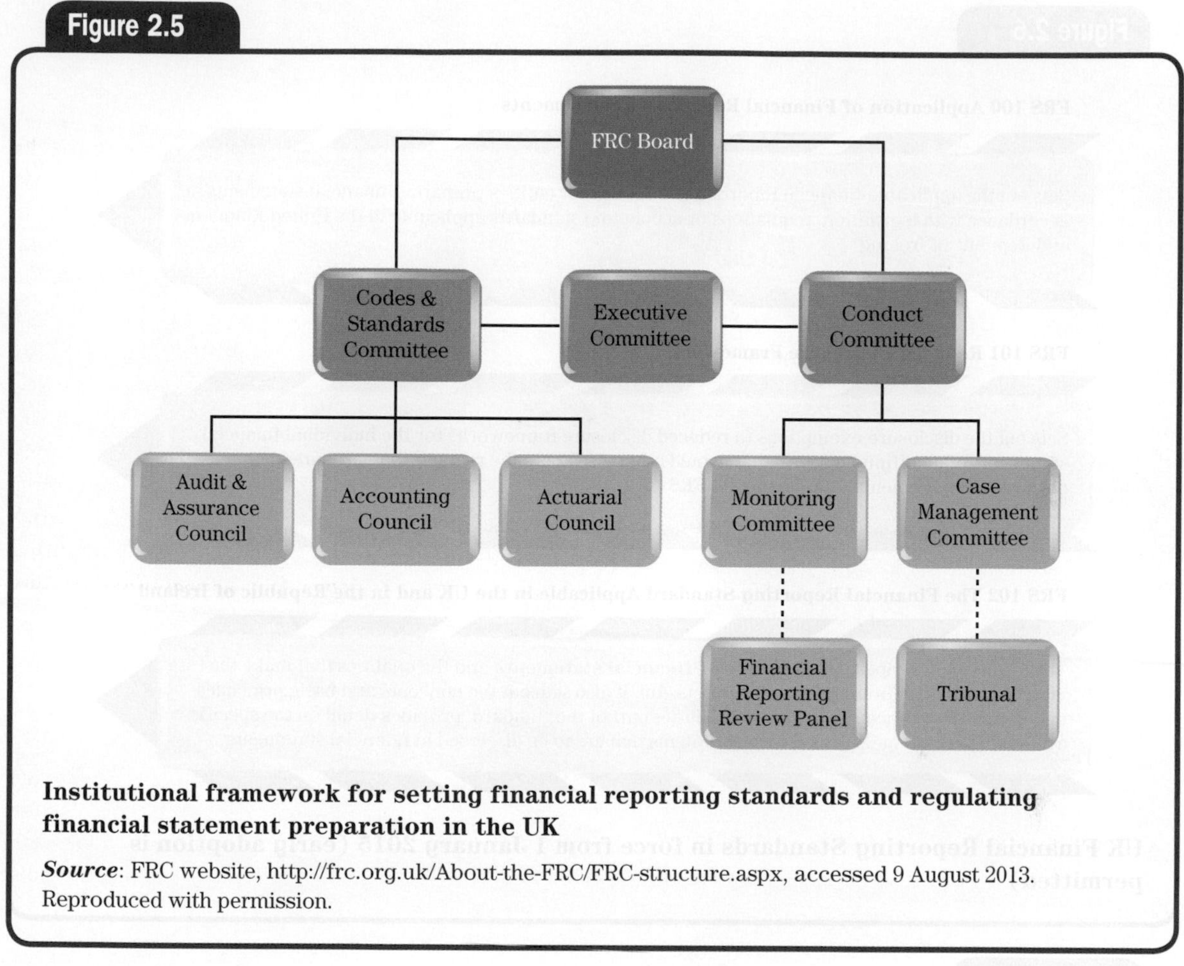

Institutional framework for setting financial reporting standards and regulating financial statement preparation in the UK

Source: FRC website, http://frc.org.uk/About-the-FRC/FRC-structure.aspx, accessed 9 August 2013. Reproduced with permission.

1 January 2015 when all SSAPs, FRSs and UITFs will be withdrawn and replaced by three standards. Details of the three standards are provided in Figure 2.6.

Qualifying entities under UK GAAP are entities that are included within published consolidated financial statements that have been prepared under EU-adopted IFRS.

The overriding objective of the FRC when setting accounting standards is to '*enable users of accounts to receive high-quality, understandable financial reporting proportionate to the size and complexity of the entity and users' information needs*' (FRS 100, paragraph 1). To this end they have shifted the choice of complexity in accounting treatment and disclosure to entities. As mentioned, all listed entities must prepare their financial statements under EU-adopted IFRS. Other entities, such as sole traders, partnerships, limited companies and charities have a choice under FRS 100. The possibilities are detailed in Figure 2.7.

Learning Activity 2.3

Visit the FRC website and familiarize yourself with the progress of the future of financial reporting in the UK.

Figure 2.6

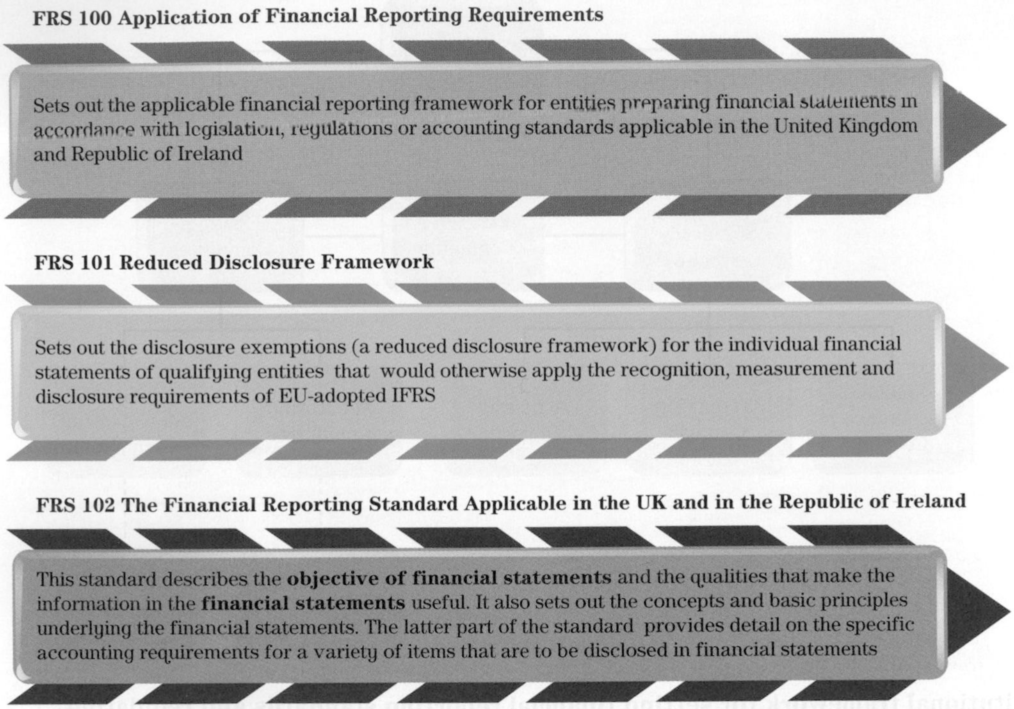

FRS 100 Application of Financial Reporting Requirements

Sets out the applicable financial reporting framework for entities preparing financial statements in accordance with legislation, regulations or accounting standards applicable in the United Kingdom and Republic of Ireland

FRS 101 Reduced Disclosure Framework

Sets out the disclosure exemptions (a reduced disclosure framework) for the individual financial statements of qualifying entities that would otherwise apply the recognition, measurement and disclosure requirements of EU-adopted IFRS

FRS 102 The Financial Reporting Standard Applicable in the UK and in the Republic of Ireland

This standard describes the **objective of financial statements** and the qualities that make the information in the **financial statements** useful. It also sets out the concepts and basic principles underlying the financial statements. The latter part of the standard provides detail on the specific accounting requirements for a variety of items that are to be disclosed in financial statements

UK Financial Reporting Standards in force from 1 January 2015 (early adoption is permitted)

Figure 2.7

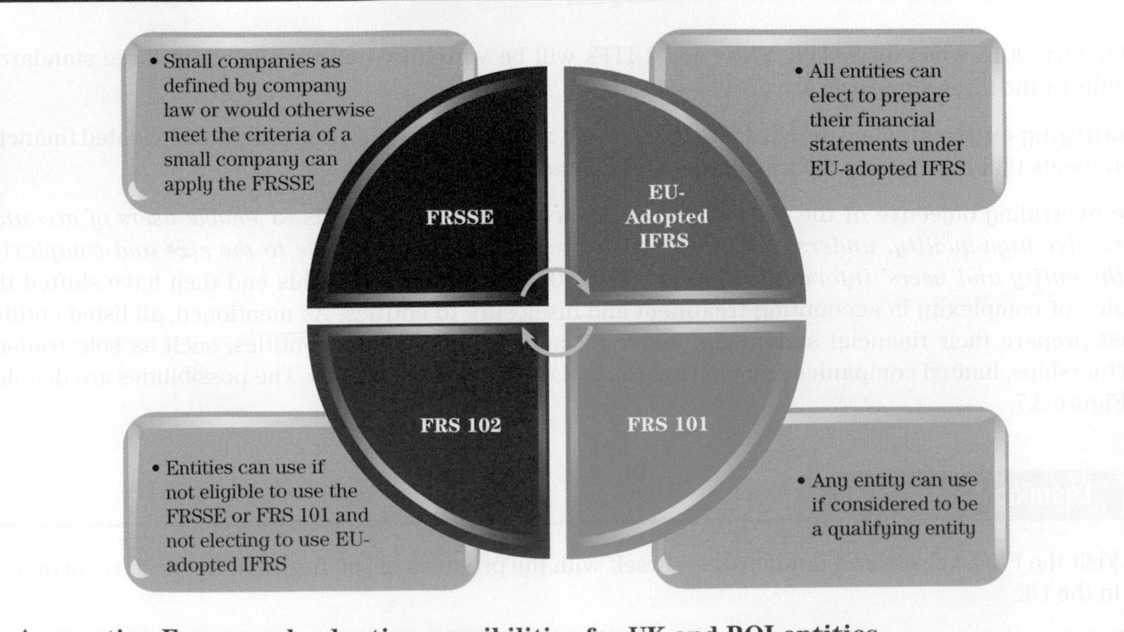
• Small companies as defined by company law or would otherwise meet the criteria of a small company can apply the FRSSE
• All entities can elect to prepare their financial statements under EU-adopted IFRS
FRSSE
EU-Adopted IFRS
FRS 102
FRS 101
• Entities can use if not eligible to use the FRSSE or FRS 101 and not electing to use EU-adopted IFRS
• Any entity can use if considered to be a qualifying entity

Accounting Framework adoption possibilities for UK and ROI entities

2.12 Harmonization

Many accountancy and standard-setting bodies throughout the world are involved in the work of the IASB, as are various government agencies and stock market regulators. For example, all the countries of the EU, Russia, the USA, Australia, China and many of the African countries require or permit the use of IFRSs. Indeed, 120 countries have required or permitted the use of IFRSs and in 2013 the G20 called for global adoption of a single set of high-quality financial reporting standards. The UK and the USA have a long tradition of standard setting and as a result these two countries have probably had the greatest influence on the development of IFRSs, especially given that the working language of the IASB is English.

From 2005 all EU listed companies have had to prepare their financial statements in accordance with EU-adopted IFRSs (Pope and McLeay, 2011). Since that date the IASB (International), FASB (USA) and the FRC (UK) have also been engaged in what is known as a 'convergence project' to harmonize international, US and UK accounting standards. It was hoped that full convergence would have occurred in 2012; however, stiff opposition from preparers in the UK resulted in the FRC continuing to issue national standards and in the US the Securities and Exchange Commission (SEC) has not yet backed full conversion. According to the FASB the project is still ongoing (see Real World Example 2.1). Hinks (2010) stated that the SEC's decision would be guided by an examination of six key areas: *'sufficient development and application of IFRS for the US; the independence of standard setting for the benefit of investors; investors' education and understanding; the regulatory systems that would be affected by adoption; the impact on public companies both large and small; human resource readiness'*. To aid globalization and harmonization the IFRS Foundation established the ASAF. Details of this new body are provided in Real World Example 2.1.

REAL WORLD EXAMPLE 2.1

International Convergence of Accounting Standards

The FASB and the IASB have been working together since 2002 to improve and converge US generally accepted accounting principles (GAAP) and IFRS. As of 2013, Japan and China were also working to converge their standards with IFRSs. The SEC consistently has supported convergence of global accounting standards. However, the SEC has not yet decided whether to incorporate IFRS into the US financial reporting system. The Commission staff issued its final report on the issue in July 2012 without making a recommendation . . .

. . . The IFRS Foundation in early 2013 established the Accounting Standards Advisory Forum (ASAF) to improve cooperation among worldwide standard setters and advise the IASB as it develops IFRS. The FASB was selected as one of the ASAF's twelve members. The FASB's membership on the ASAF is an opportunity to represent US interests in the IASB's standard-setting process and to continue the process of improving and converging US GAAP and IFRS.

Source: FASB website, http://www.fasb.org/jsp/FASB/Page/SectionPage&cid=1176156304264, accessed 9 August 2013. FASB material reproduced with permission.

The IASB clearly has enormous status and authority stemming from the impact of IFRSs worldwide and the focus of the global harmonization of national accounting standards. However, it is easy to overlook that unlike, for example, the FRC in the UK, the IASB really has no power to enforce IFRSs. Compliance depends on their adoption and enforcement by nation states and their respective stock market regulatory bodies such as the SEC and the London Stock Exchange (LSE).

2.13 International Financial Reporting Standards (IFRSs)

Figure 2.8 details the main IFRSs/IASs that are referred to in this book.

Figure 2.8

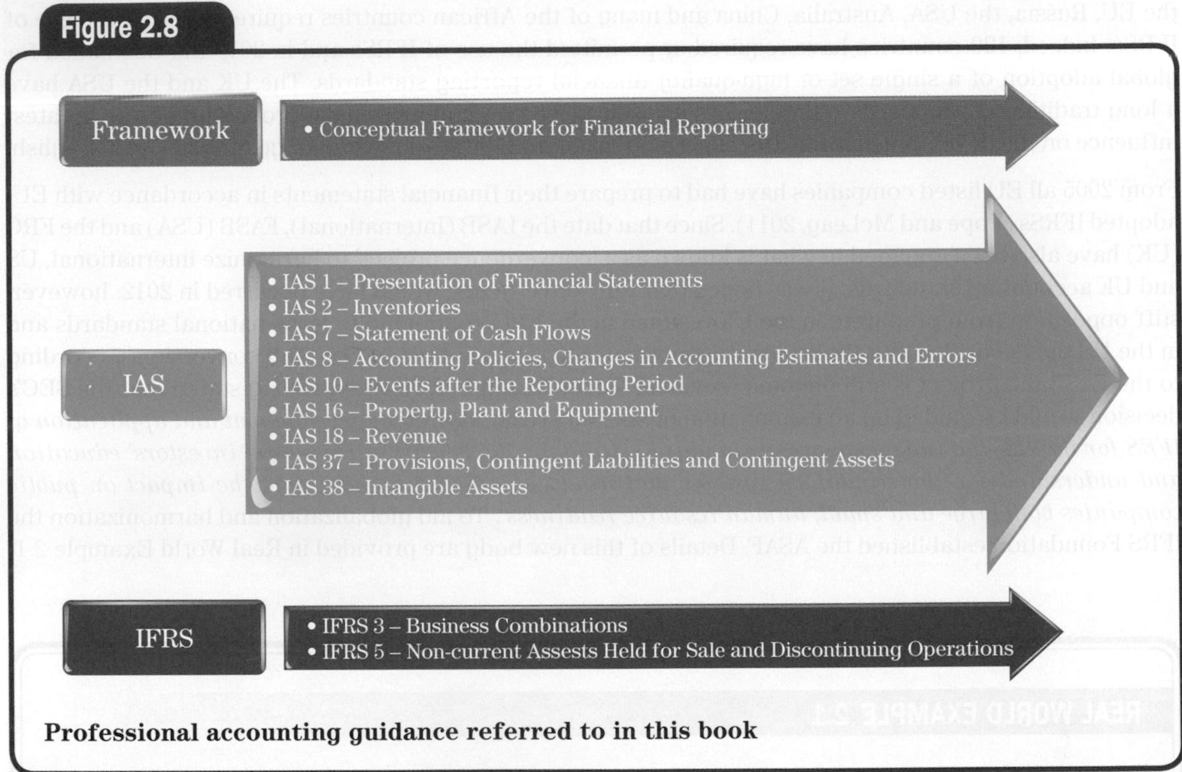

Framework
• Conceptual Framework for Financial Reporting
IAS
• IAS 1 – Presentation of Financial Statements
• IAS 2 – Inventories
• IAS 7 – Statement of Cash Flows
• IAS 8 – Accounting Policies, Changes in Accounting Estimates and Errors
• IAS 10 – Events after the Reporting Period
• IAS 16 – Property, Plant and Equipment
• IAS 18 – Revenue
• IAS 37 – Provisions, Contingent Liabilities and Contingent Assets
• IAS 38 – Intangible Assets
IFRS
• IFRS 3 – Business Combinations
• IFRS 5 – Non-current Assests Held for Sale and Discontinuing Operations

Professional accounting guidance referred to in this book

The remainder of this chapter outlines a brief summary of the international framework for accounting and each of the above IASs/IFRSs (the equivalent UK standard is identified as an endnote). At this stage these brief summaries are only intended to provide you with a sense of the type of information that is provided in IFRSs. You will have to return to study these summaries when you complete the book. They will be more understandable to you then.

Conceptual Framework for Financial Reporting[1]

The ***Conceptual Framework*** (IASB, 2011) sets out the concepts that underlie the preparation and presentation of financial statements. It provides guidance on the fundamentals of accounting. The key issues considered by the conceptual framework document are outlined in Figure 2.9.

The questions outlined in Figure 2.9 are examined in depth in Chapters 3, 4, 5 and 7.

2.14 IAS 1 – Presentation of Financial Statements[2]

IAS 1 (IASB, 2013a) was discussed in Chapter 1, 'Entities and Financial Reporting Statements'. It provides guidance on how to present financial information in the financial statements. It tries to promote standardization of accounting formats and terminology.

[1] The current UK equivalent is the Statement of Principles for Financial Reporting.

[2] The current UK equivalent is FRS 3 – Reporting Financial Performance.

Figure 2.9

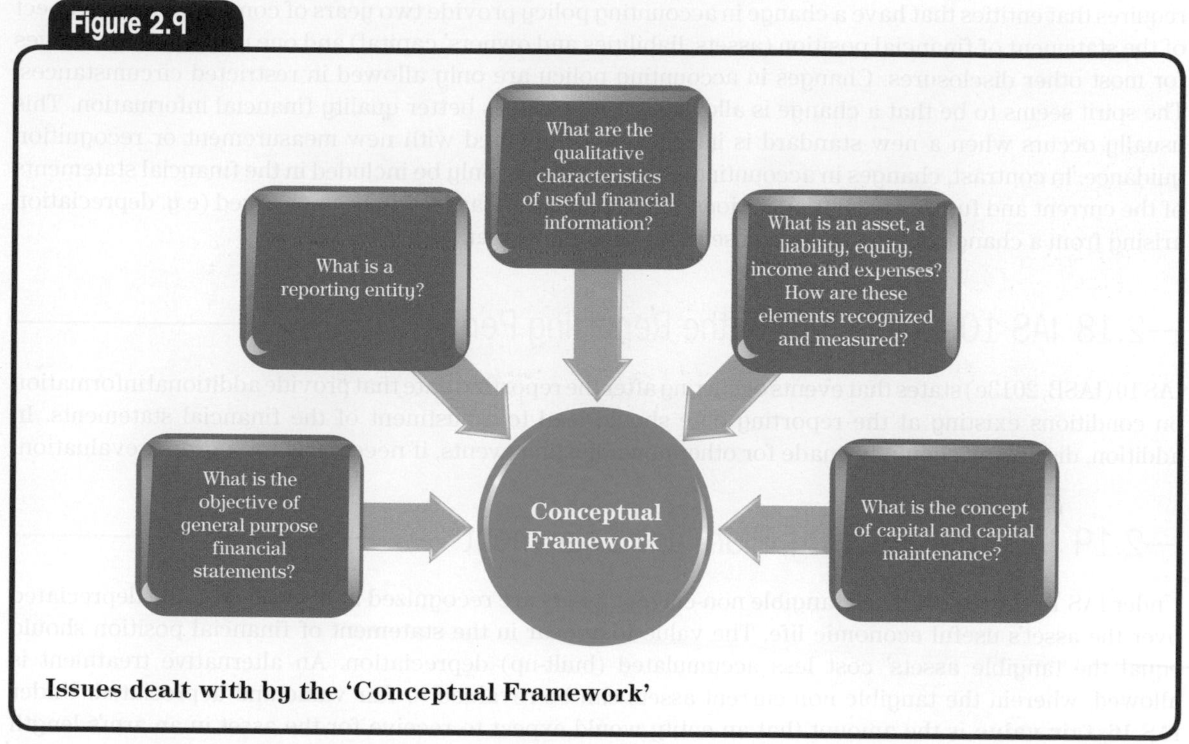

Issues dealt with by the 'Conceptual Framework'

—2.15 IAS 2 – Inventories[3]

IAS 2 (IASB, 2013b) requires that inventories should be measured at the lower of cost and net realizable value. Cost includes all expenditures required to transform inventories into a saleable condition. Where specific cost is not appropriate, the benchmark treatment is to use either the first-in-first-out (FIFO) or the weighted average cost (AVCO) methods for determining inventory value. Inventory valuation is covered in depth in Chapter 23.

—2.16 IAS 7 – Statement of Cash Flows[4]

In IAS 7 (IASB, 2013c) cash flows are classified under the headings of operating activities, investing activities and financing activities. Within the operating activities section of the statement of cash flows, a reconciliation of operation profit before tax from the statement of profit or loss to net cash inflows from operating activities is provided. Separate disclosure is required of the movement in cash equivalents and details should be provided for any significant non-cash transactions.

—2.17 IAS 8 – Accounting Policies, Changes in Accounting Estimates and Errors[5]

IAS 8 (IASB, 2013d) covers changes in accounting policies and the correction of errors. Changes in accounting policies and the correction of errors should be treated as prior year adjustments. This involves restating the **comparative figures** (previous year's figures) to take account of the adjustment. IAS 1

[3] The current UK equivalent is SSAP 9 – Stocks and Long-term Contracts.

[4] The current UK equivalent is FRS 1 – Cash Flow Statements.

[5] The current UK equivalent is SSAP 2 – Disclosure of Accounting Policies. Some of the issues are also covered in FRS 3 – Reporting Financial Performance and FRS 28 – Corresponding Amounts.

requires that entities that have a change in accounting policy provide two years of comparatives in respect of the statement of financial position (assets, liabilities and owners' capital) and one year of comparatives for most other disclosures. Changes in accounting policy are only allowed in restricted circumstances. The spirit seems to be that a change is allowable if it produces better quality financial information. This usually occurs when a new standard is introduced, or updated with new measurement or recognition guidance. In contrast, changes in accounting estimates should only be included in the financial statements of the current and future accounting periods, and their classification will be unchanged (e.g. depreciation arising from a change in the estimated useful life of a non-current asset).

2.18 IAS 10 – Events after the Reporting Period[6]

IAS 10 (IASB, 2013e) states that events occurring after the reporting date that provide additional information on conditions existing at the reporting date should lead to adjustment of the financial statements. In addition, disclosure should be made for other non-adjusting events, if necessary, for a proper evaluation.

2.19 IAS 16 – Property, Plant and Equipment[7]

Under IAS 16 (IASB, 2013f) all tangible non-current assets are recognized at historic cost and depreciated over the asset's useful economic life. The value to appear in the statement of financial position should equal the tangible assets' cost less accumulated (built-up) depreciation. An alternative treatment is allowed, wherein the tangible non-current assets can be revalued to fair value and depreciated. Under IAS 16, **fair value** is the amount that an entity would expect to receive for the asset in an arm's length transaction between two unconnected parties. This usually equates to market price, replacement cost or economic value. When an asset is revalued, the whole class of asset has to be revalued and the valuations have to be kept up to date.

2.20 IAS 18 – Revenue[8]

IAS 18 (IASB, 2013g) is concerned with revenue recognition. In particular, it sets out the following rules for determining the accounting year in which sales revenue should be included in the statement of profit or loss in the sale of goods:

> "*In a transaction involving the sale of goods, performance should be regarded as being achieved when the following conditions have been fulfilled:*
>
> **a** *the seller of the goods has transferred to the buyer the significant risks and rewards of ownership, in that all significant acts have been completed and the seller retains no continuing managerial involvement in, or effective control of, the goods transferred to a degree usually associated with ownership; and*
>
> **b** *no significant uncertainty exists regarding:*
>
> *i the consideration that will be derived from the sale of the goods;*
>
> *ii the associated costs incurred or to be incurred in producing or purchasing the goods;*
>
> *iii the extent to which the goods may be returned*"
>
> (IASB, 2013g)

[6] The current UK Equivalent is FRS 21 – Events after the Balance Sheet Date.

[7] The current UK standards dealing with this topic are FRS 15 – Tangible Fixed Assets and FRS 11 – Impairment of Fixed Assets and Goodwill.

[8] The current UK equivalent is FRS 5 – Reporting the Substance of Transactions.

Revenue from the rendering of services should be recognized by reference to the state of completion of the transaction at the reporting date (i.e. the percentage of completion).

2.21 IAS 37 – Provisions, Contingent Liabilities and Contingent Assets[9]

Under IAS 37 (IASB, 2013i) a provision has to be recognized when the enterprise has a present obligation to transfer economic benefits as a result of past events and it is probable (more likely than not) that such a transfer will be required and a reliable estimate of the obligation can be made. A present obligation exists when an entity has little or no discretion to avoid incurring the economic outflow. This means that the item comes into the statement of financial position as a liability and as an expense in the statement of profit or loss.

Contingent liabilities are liabilities whose outcome will be confirmed on the occurrence or non-occurrence of uncertain future events that are outside the entity's control. They are recognized in the financial statements (as a liability and an expense) if it is more likely than not (probable) that a transfer of economic benefits will result from past events and a reliable estimate of the amount can be made. When this condition cannot be fulfilled, disclosures of the nature and amount (if possible) should be provided in the notes to the financial statements.

Contingent assets should not be recognized unless they are reasonably certain, then they are treated as assets. If they are not reasonably certain they should be disclosed in the notes to the financial statements.

2.22 IAS 38 – Intangible Assets[10]

Under IAS 38 (IASB, 2013j) intangible assets can only be recognized if they meet the definition of an asset (i.e. if it is probable that future economic benefits attributable to the asset will flow to the enterprise and that cost of the asset can be measured reliably). Like IAS 16 an intangible asset can be carried at cost or at fair value. Fair value can only be determined in this instance with reference to an active market for the asset. Internally generated assets cannot be recognized unless they meet the recognition criteria for capitalizing development expenditure. The criteria are that the expenditure should be on a clearly defined product or process, capable of reliable measurement, technically feasible, there should be evidence of an intention to sell the product being developed for a profit (i.e. there should be evidence of the existence of a market in which to sell the product, or the product being developed should be demonstrated to be useful internally) and the entity should have the technical expertise and resources to complete the project. Intangible assets have to be amortized over their useful economic lives.

2.23 IFRS 3 – Business Combinations[11]

Under IFRS 3 (IASB, 2013k) any goodwill arising on a business combination (i.e. the excess amount given for a business over and above the value of its separately identifiable assets, liabilities and contingent liabilities) should be capitalized as an intangible non-current asset and impaired. This is covered in the section on partnerships and companies.

[9] The current UK equivalent is FRS 12 – Provisions, Contingent Liabilities and Contingent Assets.

[10] The current UK standards dealing with this topic are FRS 10 – Goodwill and Intangible Assets and FRS 11 – Impairment of Fixed Assets and Goodwill.

[11] The current UK standards dealing with this topic are FRS 2 – Accounting for Subsidiary Undertakings; FRS 6 – Acquisitions and Mergers; FRS 9 – Associates and Joint Ventures; FRS 7 – Fair Values in Acquisition Accounting.

2.24 IFRS 5 – Non-current Assets Held for Sale and Discontinuing Operations[12]

Under IFRS 5 (IASB, 2013h) discontinuing operations includes operations that actually discontinued in the reporting period and operations that are likely to be discontinued in the next reporting period. The assets, liabilities, revenue and expenses from those operations/assets should be presented separately from the assets, liabilities, revenues and expenses from continuing activities. All required disclosures in respect of these items should also be provided separately. In the statement of financial position, the assets and liabilities are disclosed separately for each main category (e.g. non-current assets). In the statement of profit or loss the approach is different, the revenue and expenses from the discontinuing activity are shown in a note to the financial statements, with the profit or loss for the period being added to the profit for the period from continuing operations. This is covered in Part 7, 'Companies'.

Learning Activity 2.4

Go to the UK FRC's website and read the summaries on each of the endnoted UK accounting standards. (After 1 January 2015, read the relevant parts of FRS 101 and FRS 102.) Note the similarities between these and the summaries provided in this chapter for the international equivalent.

2.25 Current issues

In response to criticism received after the financial crises, the IASB have been and are actively discussing current standards, or introducing new standards to deal with:

1 *Off-balance-sheet finance*: The IASB has issued three IFRSs to improve the quality of information being provided in consolidated financial statements (IFRS 10 Consolidated Financial Statements; IFRS 11 Joint Arrangements; IFRS 12 Disclosure of Interests in Other Entities) and is currently working on a standard to provide guidance on how to account for lease transactions. The IASB aims to issue an IFRS on leases in 2014.

2 *Fair value and financial instruments*: IFRS 13 Fair Value Measurement became effective on 1 January 2013. It provides general guidance on fair value measurement, which supports all other standards, rather than having all standards separately identifying how they measure fair value. In 2009, IFRS 9 Financial Instruments, was introduced. This standard deals with the classification and measurement of financial instruments and reduces the variety of accounting treatments that were available for financial instruments under IAS 39. Hedge accounting is currently under consultation and the final agreed approach will be published as a new IFRS.

3 *Disclosure*: The IASB implemented changes to the standard on disclosures on financial instruments (IFRS 7) and discussion on this area is still ongoing. IAS 1 is also undergoing scrutiny with an Exposure Draft expected on how to disclose information on the assessment of going concern.

4 The IASB is also currently revising the conceptual framework. The 'General Purpose Financial Reporting' chapter and the 'Qualitative Characteristics of Useful Financial Information' chapter have been changed. The IASB is currently working on the chapters that address the elements of financial statements, measurement, the reporting entity and presentation and disclosure. The comment period was scheduled to end on 14 January 2014.

5 The IASB continues to pursue globalization of its accounting standards. In 2013 they established the ASAF to focus on improving cooperation with national standard setters across the globe.

Source: IASB Work Plan – projected targets as at 29 July 2013, http://www.ifrs.org/Current-Projects/IASB-Projects/Pages/IASB-Work-Plan.aspx, accessed 9 August 2013.

---

[12] The current UK equivalent is FRS 3 – Reporting Financial Performance.

Summary

The international framework of accounting is made up of several bodies. The Monitoring Board is an independent board that aims to make the IFRS Foundation Trustees accountable in their role. Though reporting to the IFRS Foundation Trustees, the IASB has independent control over issuing IFRS and revising IAS. They are supported by the IFRS Interpretation Committee (publishes authoritative guidance on new issues, issues that are unclear or are omitted from an IFRS) and the SMEIG (monitors the implementation of the IFRS for SMEs, publishes questions and answers on issues raised by users, makes suggestions for changes to the IFRS for SMEs to the IASB in light of the issues raised and in light of changes to the full IFRS). The IFRS Advisory Council represents the major stakeholders of accounting information and provides strategic advice to the IASB. Finally, the IFRS Foundation Support Operations provides policy on education, champions the development and implementation of an IFRS Taxonomy (XBRL) and deals with the general running of all the bodies that make up the institutional international regulatory framework.

The objectives of the IASB are *'to develop a single set of high quality, understandable, enforceable and globally accepted financial reporting standards based on clearly articulated principles'*. At the time of writing 120 countries have either adopted IFRSs in their entirety, have converged national accounting standards with IFRSs, or allow IFRSs to be used. The IASB established the ASAF to improve cooperation among worldwide standard setters and to advise the IASB on issues relating to the development of IFRS. The G20 have also voiced support for the global adoption of a single set of high-quality financial reporting standards as has the SEC. It is therefore likely that convergence will continue, though cultural differences and cost will affect the rate of globalization.

The UK institutional framework was restructured in 2012 and the FRC is now responsible for accounting standards. After a period of consultation, complete harmonization has been rejected, with UK accounting stakeholders (preparers, auditors) electing to keep UK GAAP. The resultant framework will come into force on 1 January 2015 and it offers choice to the entities that have to prepare their accounts. In addition all UK accounting guidance is being consolidated into three accounting standards: the FRSSE, FRS 101 The Reduced Disclosure Framework and FRS 102 The Financial Reporting Standard Applicable in the UK and in the ROI. A further standard FRS 100 Application of Financial Reporting Requirements provides guidance on the choices open to entities when preparing financial statements. All UK-listed PLCs must prepare their financial statements using EU-adopted IFRS and other UK entities can also elect to prepare their financial statements under EU-adopted IFRS instead of using UK standards.

Key terms and concepts

Term	Page
Accounting Standards Advisory Forum (ASAF)	25
Accounting Standards Board (ASB)	30
Accounting Standards Committee (ASC)	30
comparative figures	35
Conceptual Framework	34
Discussion Paper (DP)	29
Exposure Draft (ED)	29
fair value	36
Financial Accounting Standards Board (FASB)	30
Financial Reporting Council (FRC)	30
Financial Reporting Standards (FRSs)	30
IFRS Advisory Council	28

IFRS for SMEs 26
IFRS Foundation Trustees 27
IFRS Interpretations Committee (IFRIC) 27
International Accounting Standards (IASs) 25
International Accounting Standards Board (IASB) 24
International Accounting Standards Committee (IASC) 26
International Financial Reporting Standards (IFRSs) 25
Monitoring Board of Public Capital Market Authorities 25
Qualifying entities 31
SME Implementation Group (SMEIG) 26
Statements of Standard Accounting Practice (SSAPs) 30

An asterisk after the question number indicates that there is a suggested answer in Appendix 2.

Review questions

connect

International Framework

2.1* Describe the objectives of the International Accounting Standards Board (IASB).

2.2 Discuss the current activities of the International Accounting Standards Board (IASB) in the convergence/harmonization of accounting standards.

2.3 Explain the role of the IFRS Interpretations Committee.

2.4 Explain the role and objectives of the IFRS Advisory Council.

2.5 Describe the standard-setting process for International Financial Reporting Standards (IFRSs).

2.6 Describe the accounting treatment for measuring the value of inventories under *IAS 2 – Inventories*.

2.7 Describe the rules relating to the recognition of product revenue set out in *IAS 18 – Revenue*.

2.8 State the two measurement methods recommended by *IAS 16 – Property, Plant and Equipment* for recording the value of tangible non-current assets.

UK Framework

2.9* Describe the sources of the rules and regulations that govern the content and format of company final financial statements in the UK (pre 1 January 2015).

2.10* Describe the current institutional framework concerned with the setting and enforcement of accounting standards in the UK.

2.11* Explain the accounting framework options open to the following types of UK entity from 1 January 2015:

a A subsidiary of a company that has prepared consolidated financial statements using EU-adopted IFRS

b A small limited company

c A public limited company

d A large limited company that is not listed on any exchange

Websites

For more information on topics covered in this chapter visit:

http://www.frc.org.uk/ Provides details on the UK framework and standards.

www.ifrs.org/ Provides guidance on the institutional framework underlying the production of IFRSs and new issues.

www.iasplus.com/ Provides a summary of IFRSs, the institutional framework and the objectives of all the bodies that are party to the framework.

References

Hinks, G. (2010) 'US Tests Standard Setter's Independence', *Accountancy Age*, 29 October, www.accountancyage.com.

International Accounting Standards Board (2011) *Conceptual Framework for Financial Reporting* (IASB), as at August 2013.

International Accounting Standards Board (2013a) *International Accounting Standard 1 – Presentation of Financial Statements* (IASB).

International Accounting Standards Board (2013b) *International Accounting Standard 2 – Inventories* (IASB).

International Accounting Standards Board (2013c) *International Accounting Standard 7 – Statement of Cash Flows* (IASB).

International Accounting Standards Board (2013d) *International Accounting Standard 8 – Accounting Policies, Changes in Accounting Estimates and Errors* (IASB).

International Accounting Standards Board (2013e) *International Accounting Standard 10 – Events after the Reporting Period* (IASB).

International Accounting Standards Board (2013f) *International Accounting Standard 16 – Property, Plant and Equipment* (IASB).

International Accounting Standards Board (2013g) *International Accounting Standard 18 – Revenue* (IASB).

International Accounting Standards Board (2013h) *International Financial Reporting Standard 5 – Non-current Assets Held for Sale and Discontinuing Operations* (IASB).

International Accounting Standards Board (2013i) *International Accounting Standard 37 – Provisions, Contingent Liabilities and Contingent Assets* (IASB).

International Accounting Standards Board (2013j) *International Accounting Standard 38 – Intangible Assets* (IASB).

International Accounting Standards Board (2013k) *International Financial Reporting Standard 3 – Business Combinations* (IASB).

International Accounting Standards Committee (1989) Adopted by the International Accounting Standards Board 2001, *Framework for the Preparation and Presentation of Financial Statements* (IASC).

International Accounting Standards Board and the IFRS Foundation (January 2013) *Who We Are and What We Do* (IFRS Foundation, 2013).

Pope, P. and McLeay, S. (2011) 'The European IFRS Experiment: Objectives, Research Challenges and Some Early Evidence', *Accounting and Business Research*, 41(3), 42–56.

Note: From 1 January 2015 all the recommended accounting practices will be contained in three standards: *FRSSE* (for SMEs), FRS 101 *The Reduced Disclosure Framework* (for qualifying entities) and FRS 102 *The Financial Reporting Standard Applicable in the UK and in the Republic of Ireland* (all other entities).

Chapter 3

The Conceptual Framework 1: objective of financial statements, stakeholders and other reports

Learning Objectives:

After reading this chapter you should be able to do the following:

1. Explain the nature, purpose and scope of the conceptual framework of accounting, including the main contents of the International Accounting Standards Board's *Conceptual Framework for Financial Reporting* (IASB, 2011).
2. Discuss the objectives of company financial statements.
3. Outline the limitations of financial statements.
4. Identify the users of annual reports and describe their information needs.
5. Explain corporate social responsibility and discuss the type of information included in a corporate social responsibility report.
6. Discuss the type of information a company includes under environmental reporting.
7. Describe the conceptual framework and standardization debates and discuss related issues.
8. Describe the main types of accounting theory and their implications for a conceptual framework of accounting.

3.1 Introduction

The nature of a conceptual framework – an analogy

At some point in their studies students may feel rather confused and frustrated by accounting theory. It is a hurdle that has to be overcome. On the one hand, students frequently have a perception of accounting as being definitive, because much of it is based on the law, and they have been taught a simplified set of rules about double-entry bookkeeping that is very systematic. On the other hand, they frequently think that accountants tend to bend the rules (or 'cook the books'), also known as **creative accounting**. Many of the later chapters of this book may reinforce this view because some transactions can be treated in different ways, thus giving possible alternative figures of profit.

It is important to appreciate the difference between 'cooking the books' and the professional judgement involved in decisions between alternative methods (bases) of accounting. An analogy may prove useful. Imagine you went to a private consultant because you had backache. In order to maximize his or her fee, the consultant might decide to operate on you. If this was the sole consideration, it would be unethical of the surgeon. Similarly, an accountant who chose a particular form of accounting treatment with the sole intention of reducing net profit would be acting unethically. However, an ethical physician or accountant is still faced with a number of possible forms of treatment. The physician might prescribe a number of different drugs, but needs to ascertain which is likely to be most appropriate for you. Similarly, the accountant has to choose which accounting treatment for, say, development costs is the most appropriate in the circumstances.

This analogy can be extended further to illustrate another very important relevant idea. The physician's judgement about your treatment for backache is guided by a body of expert knowledge and research, loosely known as 'medical science'. This includes such disciplines as anatomy and chemistry, which are based on generally accepted theories and concepts similar, in principle, to those discussed in this chapter relating to accounting. Similarly, the accountant's judgement about the most appropriate treatment of certain types of transaction is guided by a body of expert knowledge and research, which is loosely referred to as the theoretical or **conceptual framework of accounting**.

However, unlike medical science, the conceptual framework of accounting is not well developed and thus may contain apparent inconsistencies. It is also unlikely that a conceptual framework of accounting could be as definitive as, say, medical science in the foreseeable future since accounting theory, like other social sciences, is fundamentally different from natural sciences, such as medical science.

This tension between the need for a set of concepts/principles to guide the practice of accounting, and the awareness that these are unlikely to be conclusive/definitive, has given rise to an extensive debate over the past three decades about the development of a conceptual framework of accounting or what are sometimes called **generally accepted accounting principles (GAAP)**.

(*Note*: The abbreviation GAAP is commonly taken as referring to generally accepted accounting practice; that is, accounting standards.)

3.2 The conceptual framework of accounting

Definition and purpose

The definition and purpose of a conceptual framework of accounting is provided on the IFRS website (2013). It is presented diagrammatically in Figure 3.1.

Learning Activity 3.1

Visit the Financial Reporting Council (FRC) website (UK standard setters) and obtain a copy of their definition of a conceptual framework of accounting.

Figure 3.1

Definition
• Sets out the concepts that underlie the preparation and presentation of financial statements.
Purpose
• Practical tool to assist the IASB when developing and revising IFRSs.
• To improve financial reporting by providing the IASB with a complete and updated set of concepts to use when it develops or revises standards.

Definition and purpose of the *Conceptual Framework*

Source: IFRS website 2013, accessed 10 August 2013.

The definition highlights one of the main purposes of a conceptual framework; that is, to provide standard-setting bodies with a set of internally consistent definitions of accounting principles that can be used as a basis for setting accounting standards that are not contradictory or in conflict with each other. The other main purpose of a conceptual framework, explained earlier using the analogy with medicine, is to provide guidance to accountants in their day-to-day work of choosing appropriate forms of accounting treatments for various transactions and items. In addition, the *Conceptual Framework* provides a guide to resolving accounting issues that are not addressed directly in an IAS or an IFRS. When this happens judgement is required to develop and apply an accounting policy that results in information that is relevant, reliable and is a fair representation of the transaction.

The global financial crisis fuelled a debate on whether the international accounting framework (IFRS) is appropriate, as highlighted in Real World Example 3.1 which examines the role that the IFRS played in the financial crisis. The article is interesting because it distils the crisis into a simple accounting error caused by the introduction of the IFRS. It focuses on a key report by the Local Authority Pension Forum, which lays the blame squarely with the standards.

REAL WORLD EXAMPLE 3.1

'Accounting error' led to banks crisis

The financial crisis that left UK and Irish banks nursing losses of more than £150 billion has been blamed on a 'simple error' in accountancy standards backed by the EU. Changes to the system resulted in flawed accounting at banks, says a report by the Local Authority Pension Forum, whose 54 members have combined assets of £100 billion.

The introduction of International Financial Reporting Standards (IFRS) in 2005 caused banks to overstate their financial strength, it said. UK and Irish banks were most affected because they adopted IFRS more comprehensively than their EU counterparts.

In its report, the forum said failure to spot the new standards as a root cause of the initial phase of the crisis led to a 'misdiagnosis' of the problem. An error in IFRS meant accounts painted a false picture of banks' solvency so that some appeared to be flush with cash but within months faced collapse and taxpayer bailouts.

Forum Chairman Ian Greenwood said:

> *Our analysis clearly points to the fact that flawed IFRS played a significant contributory role.*
>
> *This implies that significant reform of both accounting standards and standard setters is required.*

(Express online, 1 December 2011, http://www.express.co.uk/finance/city/287060/Accounting-error-led-to-banks-crisis, accessed 10 August 2013).

The article highlights the view held by some that changes in accounting practices being recommended by the IASB actually contributed to the financial crisis. The IASB has been promoting a shift from financial statements providing reliable information to providing information that is relevant. To this end, the IASB has been promoting the use of Fair Value accounting, which in simple terms means valuing assets and liabilities at their market values. However, it is difficult to accurately value some assets, even when a market exists for the asset, as market sentiment will cause reported value to differ from underlying long-term value. For example, in the period up to the financial crisis it could be argued that the value of many of the assets that were reported in banks' financial statements was overstated, that the pursuit of fair value reduced the quality of the information being reported as the figures were less reliable and were not measured with a conservative approach. Then when the financial crisis occurred, the opposite occurred – the market for many of the banks' assets effectively froze, resulting in the assets having no market value. This meant that under fair value accounting rules banks had to write down their asset values to market value, resulting in breaches to their capital adequacy ratios and in addition their statements of profit or loss reported losses which undermined investors' and the public's confidence in banks. Yet in several instances the market value did not reflect the underlying value of the assets as they were still generating revenues (with the exception of assets based on subprime lending).

Since this time the IASB has undertaken a revision of several of the standards that were deemed to mislead stakeholders and they have also set about revising the conceptual framework.

One approach to determining the nature and scope of a conceptual framework of accounting is to answer questions in respect of information required from accounting (financial statements). Questions put forward in this respect include:

> - *For whom are financial statements to be prepared?*
> - *For what purposes do they want to use them?*
> - *What kind of accounting reports do they want?*
> - *How far are present financial statements suitable for these purposes? and*
> - *How could we improve accounting practice to make them more suitable?*

(ASC, 1978)

The scope of the international conceptual framework, as detailed in the *Conceptual Framework*, is to provide guidance in five areas represented by five chapters as outlined in Figure 3.2. These chapters are considered to represent different accounting principles.

Figure 3.2

Conceptual Framework
• Chapter 1: the objective of financial reporting
• Chapter 2: the reporting entity
• Chapter 3: the qualitative characteristics of useful financial information
• Chapter 4: the definition, recognition and measurement of the elements from which financial statements are constructed
• Chapter 5: concepts of capital and capital maintenance

Areas the IASB *Conceptual Framework* addresses

Note: This chapter discusses the issues covered in Chapters 1 and 2; Chapter 3 of the *Conceptual Framework* is covered in Chapter 5 of this textbook; and Chapters 4 and 5 are examined in the next chapter.

The international framework: scope restrictions

The guidance provided in the *Conceptual Framework* is restricted to accounting in general purpose financial statements only. **General purpose financial statements** are financial statements that comply with the conceptual framework requirements and accounting standards and meet the information needs common to users who are unable to command the preparation of financial statements tailored specifically to satisfy all their information needs. In addition, accounting is considered to provide information for a predefined group of users. Three types of user are mentioned in the *Conceptual Framework:*

- present and potential investors
- lenders
- other creditors

There is much controversy about this restriction as a variety of other stakeholders are argued to have a legitimate claim to information from companies. Other users include: employees, suppliers and other trade creditors, customers, governments and their agencies and the public.

3.3 The objectives of general purpose financial reporting

As explained above, one of the main functions of financial accounting is **financial reporting**, which involves the preparation of final financial statements, also referred to as **financial accounts**. These consist of a statement of comprehensive income, statement of changes in equity, a statement of financial position, a statement of cash flows and notes to the financial statements. In the case of companies, the final financial statements are often referred to as **published financial statements**. These are sent to equity shareholders in the form of a pamphlet known as the **annual or corporate report**. It is therefore usual to discuss the objectives of company final financial statements in terms of the functions of annual reports.

Chapter 1 of the *Conceptual Framework* states that general purpose financial reports should provide information that enables the primary users of general purpose financial reporting (present and potential investors, lenders and other creditors) to make decisions about buying, selling or holding equity or debt instruments and providing or settling loans or other forms of credit. This means that the financial statements should provide information on the economic resources of the entity not only to assess an entity's prospects for future net cash inflows but also how effectively and efficiently management has discharged their responsibilities to use the entity's existing resources (i.e., stewardship). The *Conceptual Framework* highlights that before making an economic decision, users will need to consider pertinent information from other sources as well.

3.4 The limitations of financial statements

This section provides a summary of the debate relating to whether financial statements achieve the objective of financial statements given in the *Conceptual Framework.* Four main themes are discussed here:

- The first is often referred to as the adequacy of financial statements in meeting users' information needs, and includes a debate about general-purpose versus specific-purpose financial reports (tailor-made financial reports).
- The second relates to problems of classification, aggregation and allocation.
- The third involves the lack of non-financial information in financial statements.
- The fourth theme in the debate concerns the use of largely historical information. This includes the use of historical cost accounting, which refers to recording transactions at cost price on the date the item is recognized in the financial statements – where the price reflects the price that has been agreed in an arm's-length transaction.

The limitations of historical cost accounting are discussed in depth in Chapter 4, 'The Conceptual Framework 2: Concepts, Principles and Policies'. Problems with classification, aggregation and allocation embrace a wide range of issues discussed throughout the book. For example, a classification problem might be the treatment of overdrafts. In most financial statements these are classified as current liabilities because they are repayable on demand. In practice the entity may be using an overdraft as a long-term source of funds and in practice the bank is not likely to ask for the overdraft to be repaid. In these circumstances the company might look as though it is having liquidity problems (problems paying its short-term commitments), when it does not. An example of how aggregation limits the quality of information is the disclosure on the face of the statement of financial position in company financial statements of trade receivables. One figure is provided, yet it represents two accounts: one shows the money owing to the company from trade customers (a positive account) and the other shows the amount of these trade customers who are not likely to pay (a negative account). Only the net amount is disclosed, yet information on potential bad debts is vital for highlighting the efficiency of the credit control policies of the entity. Finally, an example of the limitations associated with allocation can be found in the treatment of non-current tangible assets. The cost of these assets is allocated to the statement of profit or loss in the years that the assets help to generate revenue. This is a process called 'depreciation'. The concept is simple, yet in practice there are a variety of methods used to allocate this cost, all ending up with different profit or loss figures.

Some companies voluntarily publish specific-purpose financial reports, each of which is aimed at a particular class or classes of users of financial statements. These include a statement of value added, an employee report, an environmental report and simplified financial statements. Some of these are included in the annual report with the financial statements, and others are published as separate documents. However, there is a fundamental presumption underlying most of the authoritative pronouncements on financial reporting that financial statements should be general purpose documents. This is based on the premise that the main information needs of users other than investors are similar to those of investors. That is, they all need information about the financial performance and financial position of the reporting entity in order to assess its ability to provide rewards (dividends, wages, etc.) and the likelihood of its continued existence, respectively. This is explained by the IASB as follows:

> *While all of the information needs of these users cannot be met by financial statements, there are needs which are common to all users. As investors are providers of risk capital to the entity, the provision of financial statements that meet their needs will also meet most of the needs of other users that financial statements can satisfy.*

Financial statements have several other limitations (see Figure 3.3) that suggest they do not reflect the full impact of transactions or events on an entity's financial position or performance.

Figure 3.3

Other limitations of financial statements

- There is a substantial degree of classification and aggregation of items.
- Transactions are allocated to discrete reporting periods but they are continuous events.
- The non-financial effects of an event are ignored or no non-financial information is provided at all.
- The information is historical and therefore does not reflect future events or transactions that may enhance or impair the entity's operations, nor do they anticipate the impact of potential changes in the economic environment

Limitations of financial statements prepared under IFRS

Learning Activity 3.2

Download Ryanair plc's annual report and financial statements.

Read through the financial statements (statement of profit or loss, balance sheet (statement of financial position), statement of cash flows and the related notes) and make a list of whatever information you find that is likely to be useful to a potential investor. Draw up a different list of any other information that is missing and that you think would be useful to a potential investor. Then read the narrative reports at the start of the annual report.

Do these reports provide the information you listed as being useful for investors, but not present in the financial statements?

3.5 Key users of annual reports and their information needs

The users of annual reports identified in the *Conceptual Framework* are described below.

Investors

Investors are providers of risk capital. They are concerned with evaluating the 'risk in, and return provided by their investment'. A basic premise in the *Conceptual Framework* is that *'investors require information to help them determine whether they should buy, hold or sell. Shareholders are also interested in information which enables them to assess the ability of the entity to pay dividends'*. Though the *Conceptual Framework* does not explicitly refer to investors being interested in the stewardship of management, this is implicit in the decision on whether to retain, buy or sell shares. More explicit information needs are set out in the *The Corporate Report* (ASSC, 1975, p. 20) – investors require information for five purposes:

1 To evaluate the performance of the entity and its management, and assess the effectiveness of the entity in achieving its objectives.

2 To assess the economic stability and vulnerability of the reporting entity including its liquidity (i.e. whether it will have enough money to pay its debts), its present or future requirements for additional capital, and its ability to raise long- and short-term finance.

3 To estimate the value of users' own or other users' present or prospective interests in, or claims on, the entity.

4 To ascertain the ownership and control of the entity.

5 To estimate the future prospects of the entity, including its capacity to pay dividends and to predict future levels of investment.

Accountants have traditionally regarded published financial statements as fulfilling two main functions: (1) stewardship, and (2) facilitating share trading and lending decisions. The concept of stewardship roughly corresponds with everyday usage of the word and refers to the directors' responsibility to account for the uses to which they have put the equity shareholders' investment. This is the one function of published financial statements on which most accountants agree. However, it is debatable whether past data is likely to be useful in predicting future profits, dividends or share prices. The literature on efficient market theory suggests that the content of annual reports has little, if any, predictive value. Published financial statements may therefore only perform a stewardship and feedback function.

Lenders

According to the *Conceptual Framework*, lenders are interested in information that enables them to determine whether their loans, and the interest attached to them, will be paid when due. Lenders encapsulate entities like the bank and investors in debt capital (bonds). Holders of debt capital that is traded on a recognized stock exchange will have similar information requirements to equity investors as they will also have to decide whether to hold, buy or sell their bonds. Certain information will be of particular relevance, such as that relating to:

1 The present and likely future cash position, since this will determine whether the company will be able to pay the annual interest on loans and repay the money borrowed as and when it becomes due (liquidity and solvency).

2 The economic stability and vulnerability of the company in so far as this reflects the risk of possible default in repayment of money borrowed by the company (risk).

3 Prior claims on the company's assets in the event of its going into liquidation (security).

Suppliers and other creditors

Suppliers and other creditors will have similar interests to lenders. When a supplier provides goods in advance of receiving payment, this is like giving a loan. Therefore, they will be interested to determine at the outset whether to trade with the entity or not, and will want to make judgements on the length of credit period to give and the amount of credit to allow. Suppliers and other creditors are interested in information that enables them to determine whether amounts owing to them will be paid when due. Credit suppliers are likely to be interested in an entity over a shorter period than lenders unless they are dependent upon the continuation of the entity as a major customer. Therefore, they are most interested in liquidity and changes in liquidity. A supplier may be interested in determining whether the company is growing as they may have to decide whether to increase their production capacity in order to meet the reporting entity's future demands.

How financial reporting is meeting the needs of the primary users

Information about the nature and amounts of a reporting entity's economic resources and claims is provided in the statement of financial position. The objective of this statement is to assist users when assessing an entity's financial strengths and weaknesses; when assessing the entity's liquidity and solvency; and the entity's need and ability to obtain financing. Information about the claims and payment requirements assists users to predict how future cash flows will be distributed among those with a claim on the reporting entity.

Changes in a reporting entity's economic resources and claims that result from that entity's performance are included in the statement of comprehensive income; and changes in a reporting entity's economic resources from other events or transactions, such as issuing debt or equity instruments, are disclosed in the statement of changes in equity. The separation of these changes in economic resources and claims into two different accounting reports helps users to distinguish between both types of change.

Information about a reporting entity's cash flows during the reporting period is disclosed in the statement of cash flows. The aim of the statement of cash flows is to assist users when assessing an entity's ability to generate future net cash inflows from different sources. This information indicates how the entity obtains and spends cash, including information about its borrowing and repayment of debt, cash dividends to shareholders, etc.

An underlying assumption of the *Conceptual Framework* is that to meet the objective of financial reporting the financial statements should be prepared using the accruals and going concern concept (discussed in Chapter 4).

3.6 Public accountability

The basic philosophy of *The Corporate Report* (ASSC, 1975) is reflected in the need for what is called **public accountability**:

> “*there is an implicit responsibility to report publicly . . . incumbent on every entity whose size or format renders it significant; . . . we consider the responsibility to report publicly (referred to . . . as public accountability) is separate from and broader than the legal obligation to report and arises from the custodial role played in the community by economic entities; . . . they are involved in the maintenance of standards of life and the creation of wealth for and on behalf of the community.*”

The ‘custodial role’ of business enterprises refers to their responsibility to use the assets with which they have been entrusted to create wealth and maintain the standard of living, and other considerations such as the quality of the environment. It follows from this notion of public accountability that the objective or function of annual reports is: ‘*to communicate economic measurements of and information about the resources and performance of the reporting entity useful to those having reasonable rights to such information.*' 'Reasonable rights' is defined as follows: '*A reasonable right to information exists where the activities of an organisation impinge or may impinge on the interest of a user group.*'

There is widespread support for the notion that companies have responsibility for and are accountable to a wider range of stakeholders than the three user types referred to in the *Conceptual Framework*. Indeed, a cursory search through company annual reports and websites will highlight the fact that companies recognize their duty to other stakeholders. Real World Example 3.2 is an extract from Tesco Plc's website which has a whole section devoted to 'Tesco and Society'. Tesco have identified key stakeholders and highlighted the steps that they have taken to improve/strengthen links with the stakeholders.

REAL WORLD EXAMPLE 3.2

Tesco: Listening to and working with our stakeholders

Through our scale for good strategy we are working to tackle big challenges facing society. We are well placed to make a positive difference, but we can't do it alone.

We need to listen to experts, build strong partnerships and consider the views of all groups who are influenced by or are interested in our business.

Customers

Our success as a business is built on working hard for our customers and making what matters better, together.

We have a range of channels through which we engage with our customers. @Tesco was ranked as the number one customer service Twitter account in 2013 for its responsiveness and speed of response. Each year we run thousands of focus groups (called Customer Question Time) and we have ongoing customer research trackers.

Colleagues

Our dedicated colleague viewpoint survey is an important tool that we use to listen and respond to our colleagues' views, concerns and ideas and to make sure that Tesco is a great place to work. We have a dedicated Yammer network which helps our colleagues to stay connected. We also have a scale for good website where colleagues can submit ideas on how we can become a better business.

Our scale for good ambitions are shared across the business. To achieve our goals it is essential that our colleagues are engaged. Many are already making a difference and are leading on important initiatives. You can see a selection by watching our video.

Investors

Our dedicated investor relations team meets with investors regularly. In February we ran an investor and analyst day to share our business vision with the investment community. We also have a colleague who is dedicated to working with the responsible investment community.

Industry

We have sought specific feedback from experts and campaigners who lead the way on reducing food waste, helping young people into work and tackling obesity.

On issues where industry collaboration is required, such as deforestation, we seek to engage with partners and other retailers to bring about long-term positive change. We also continue to work with wider industry bodies such as the British Retail Consortium.

Local communities

We have over 300 Community Champions working in our stores. They identify initiatives and causes in the local community that we can support, for example charity events and career fairs.

We have also launched regional Twitter accounts in the UK so that people can stay up to date with news in their area.

Suppliers

We have a global team of commercial, technical and ethical managers with local expertise who work directly with suppliers to make sure we provide our customers with high quality products that are responsibly produced. Our online communities, The Knowledge Hub and Producer Network, now have over 1,000 and 2,000 members respectively. Suppliers can also give us feedback through an anonymous partner viewpoint questionnaire.

Other groups

We regularly respond to Government consultations on a wide range of topics and we have given expert evidence to public working groups and inquiries. We also seek the expertise of academics from many of the world's leading universities.

Source: Tesco website (2013), http://www.tescoplc.com/index.asp?pageid=86, accessed August 2014.
© Tesco Stores Limited, reproduced with permission.

3.7 Other users of annual reports and their information needs

Employees

Employees and their representative groups are typically interested in information about the stability and profitability of their employers. They are also interested in information which enables them to assess the ability of the entity to provide remuneration, retirement benefits and employment opportunities. It is considered that entities have a responsibility for the future livelihood and prospects of their employees (*Corporate Report*, p. 21). Employee representatives (trade unions) will be interested in information for the purpose of wage bargaining. According to *The Corporate Report* such information may relate to

> *"the ability of the employer to meet wage demands, management's intentions regarding employment levels, locations and working conditions, the pay, conditions and terms of employment of various groups of employees and the contributions made by employees in different divisions. In addition, employees are likely to be interested in indications of the position, progress and prospects of the employing enterprise as a whole and about individual establishments and bargaining units."*

Some companies produce employee reports that usually contain a summary of the year's trading results in a simplified form. In its financial statements Ryanair emphasizes growth in employees, training, pilot licensing, flight attendant training, engineers' training, pilot compensation, pay increases (or not) to the different types of employee, possible changes to the working hours of pilots, the Employment Representation Committee, information on unsuccessful attempts to form a pilot union and share option plans. The report extends to two pages – a small extract has been included in Real World Example 3.3.

REAL WORLD EXAMPLE 3.3

Ryanair

Ryanair's pilots, flight attendants and maintenance and ground operations personnel undergo training, both initial and recurrent. A substantial portion of the initial training for Ryanair's flight attendants is devoted to safety procedures, and cabin crew are required to undergo annual evacuation and fire drill training during their tenure with the airline. Ryanair also provides salary increases to its engineers who complete advanced training in certain fields of aircraft maintenance. Ryanair utilizes its own Boeing 737-800 aircraft simulators for pilot training …

… On June 19, 2009, BALPA (the UK pilots union) made a request for voluntary recognition under applicable UK legislation, which Ryanair rejected. BALPA had the option of applying to the UK's Central Arbitration Committee (CAC) to organize a vote on union recognition by Ryanair's pilots in relevant bargaining units, as determined by the CAC but BALPA decided not to proceed with an application at that time. The option to apply for a ballot remains open to BALPA and if it were to seek and be successful in such a ballot, it would be able to represent the UK pilots in negotiations over salaries and working conditions.

Ryanair Holdings' shareholders have approved a number of share option plans for employees and directors. Ryanair Holdings has also issued share options to certain of its senior managers. For details of all outstanding share options, see Item 10. Additional Information – Options to Purchase Securities from Registrant or Subsidiaries.

Source: Ryanair plc (2013), Annual Report 2013, http://www.ryanair.com/doc/investor/2013/final_annual_report_2013_130731.pdf, accessed August 2013.

Customers

Customers have an interest in information about the continuance of an entity. Therefore, going concern will be of particular interest, especially when the customer has a long-term involvement with, or is dependent on, the entity. For example, if the reporting entity is engaged in construction work, customers will wish to assess the likelihood of its being able to complete long-term contracts. In the case of manufactured goods, such as computers and vehicles, customers will be concerned about the reporting entity's continued existence because of its warranty obligations and the need for spare parts. Annual reports may thus be useful to customers in assessing the likelihood of a reporting entity's continued existence.

Governments and their agencies

Governments and their agencies are interested in the allocation of resources and, therefore, the activities of entities. They also require information in order to regulate the activities of entities and determine taxation policies, and as the basis for national income and similar statistics. For example HM Revenue and Customs have a statutory right to information about the reporting entity for the purpose of assessing its liability to taxation. The Department of Trade and Industry require industry sector statistics to determine how sectors are performing. The government can utilize this information to provide assistance to particular sectors (e.g. grants and subsidies are awarded to the farming sector) and to penalize other sectors (e.g. a windfall tax was charged on utility companies in 1997). The government also needs to estimate economic trends, including balance of payments figures (imports versus exports), employment figures and inflation levels. In the UK most of this information is collected through special government returns. However, in some other countries corporate reports perform this function.

The public

Entities affect members of the public in a variety of ways. For example, entities may make a substantial contribution to a local economy in many ways including the number of people they employ and their patronage of local suppliers. Financial statements may assist the public by providing information about the trends and recent developments in the prosperity of the entity and its range of activities. The public has a right to information about a local entity as most entities use community-owned assets such as roads and car parks. Their employment requirements may bring an influx of people to the area. More people means more places required in schools, longer waits for the doctor, and so on.

Some members of the public may be concerned about the employment policies of the reporting entity and therefore want information relating to local employment levels or discrimination in employment, for example. Other members of the public may be interested in any plans that the reporting entity has that affect the environment, including issues relating to conservation, pollution and congestion. Other matters of a political or ethical nature may also be of particular concern to some sections of the community, such as contributions to political organizations, pressure groups or charities, and whether the reporting entity is trading with countries having repressive political regimes. Some of this information must be disclosed under the Companies Act 2006 (e.g. donations to political parties and charities). Most companies provide information that is relevant for the public and the local community in their CSR report, others provide it in the directors' report. Wm Morrison Supermarket plc provided information on what they do for local communities within their annual report (see Real World Example 3.4).

REAL WORLD EXAMPLE 3.4

Wm Morrison Supermarket plc providing information for the local community

Heart of the community

At Morrisons, we want our stores to be truly part of the communities they serve. We are committed to growing our people to build a loyal and committed workforce, which provides the basis of a strong Morrisons culture and increased social mobility.

We also want our communities to benefit from our growth plans by creating opportunities. We continue to open new stores and, on average, 75% of colleagues in our new stores are recruited from the local area. We are committed to paying our colleagues fairly and all our apprentices earn at least twice the apprentice minimum wage.

Each of our stores has a community champion interacting with and benefiting our local communities. In particular, through our Raise a Smile scheme, we have worked with Save the Children and since April 2011 raised £4.5 m.

This year we launched the Feeding Britain's Future scheme to help young people (16 to 24) get first-hand experience of working in retail. The participants spent three days in-store, visiting a number of different departments. We also provided skills training, including CV writing, interviewing skills and marketing experience. The scheme received excellent feedback and we are pleased to have had more than 100 placement candidates join us as permanent colleagues.

Source: Wm Morrison Supermarket plc (2013) Annual Report 2012/13, http://www.morrisons-corporate.com/Investor-centre/Financial-reports/#, accessed August 2013.

Other users

Three further categories of user have also been mentioned in previous conceptual framework documents – the analyst–adviser group, competitor and takeover bidders, and management. These are described next.

The analyst–adviser group

This group's information needs are satisfied by financial statements that have been prepared for the three key user groups identified in the *Conceptual Framework*. This grouping is explicitly referred to in *The Corporate Report*, which states that *'the information needs of the analyst–adviser group are likely to be similar to the needs of the users who are being advised. For example, the information needs of stockbrokers are likely to be similar to the needs of investors and those of trade unions are likely to be similar to the needs of employees'*. *The Corporate Report* makes the point that this group, because of their expertise, will tend to demand more elaborate information than other groups.

Competitors and takeover bidders

This grouping comes under 'the business contact group' in *The Corporate Report*. The rationale for competitors having a right to information is a little vague but seems to rest on the premise that inter-firm comparisons of performance and costs can facilitate improvements in efficiency. Similarly, given that mergers and takeovers of less efficient firms are in the public interest, a case can be made for the disclosure of information to potential bidders.

Management

One of the duties required of management is to prepare financial statements that give a true and fair view of the state of the company's affairs for the period and its financial position at the end of the period. This involves ensuring that they comply with the *Conceptual Framework*, the accounting standards and legislation. The IASB recognizes that management are users of financial statements. However, it takes the view that financial statements should not be prepared with management's information needs in mind. Management have access to information which can be, and is, tailored to their information needs. As their needs are varied and bespoke given the decision being made, it is considered that the *Conceptual Framework* and the information included in financial statements should ignore their needs. Regardless, management usually find the information useful as they use it to assess their performance in the past and to determine if their projections of what will happen in the future are realistic or not.

Though there is no formal legislative rule or accounting standard requiring companies to provide information to a wider range of stakeholder, it is clear that companies have accepted that they are accountable to a number of different groups (employees, the public, etc.) and that the function of annual reports is also to provide each of them with information. Two topical reports that are typically disclosed in annual reports are corporate social responsibility reports and environmental reports.

3.8 Corporate social responsibility (CSR)

Over the past twenty years there has been an increase in the level of disclosures provided by companies on how they interact with society, stakeholders and the environment. The increased focus on a wide range of users has been supplemented by some regulatory requirements, for example, EU Directives on company law and other matters (e.g. employee participation) require greater disclosure of information that is primarily for the benefit of employees, potential employees and trade unions in the annual report. Furthermore, the privatization of government-owned enterprises and greater environmental awareness has resulted in more demand from members of the public, such as small investors and environmental activist groups, for tailored annual reports. To cater for these wider interests directors in publicly listed companies prepare a *corporate social responsibility report* which can be issued as a document in its own right or as part of the company's annual report.

Corporate social responsibility (CSR) describes how entities adopt policies of their own free will which benefit stakeholders. Figure 3.4 outlines some of the different types of stakeholder and potential action taken by companies that may be reported in a CSR report.

Figure 3.4

Steps taken by companies as part of their CSR might include:

Local communities	• Purchasing produce from the locality, volunteering in local schools, providing money donations to local charities, sponsoring prizes for educational programmes, etc.
Employees	• Health and safety, fair wages, pensions, training, promotion, share options, etc.
Customers	• Warranties, customer support, guarantees, etc.
The environment	• Pollution, recycling, energy saving
In general	• Conducting business in an ethical manner (ethical code of practice)

The function of the CSR report is to communicate social and environmental effects of a company's actions to interested parties within society and to society at large (Gray et al., 1987). CSR activities are mooted to bring benefits to an organization. Bhattacharya et al. (2008) argue that CSR can help with the recruitment and retention of employees, as they have a better perception of the company if they have policies such as payroll giving, active fundraising or releasing staff to do community volunteering (on full pay). It is also argued that CSR is good risk management. Promoting a culture of doing good means that, when deviant behaviour does occur, the markets and public will react less negatively as the behaviour will be seen as being out of character. CSR activities also lead to brand enhancement and a stronger brand reputation; this can lead to investor loyalty and customer loyalty, which is beneficial for the organization. A real life example detailing how Tesco views its corporate social responsibilities and the link between CSR and company success is provided in Real World Example 3.5.

REAL WORLD EXAMPLE 3.5

Tesco CSR: objectives and areas of focus

We are a major global business and we want to keep growing and being successful. But we can only succeed if we meet the expectations of our customers and colleagues and make a positive contribution to wider society.

A key part of this is about getting the essentials right – the core activities we need to carry out every day in line with our new value: we use our scale for good. All these activities are closely connected to the way we run our business, day by day, and affect the way we are valued and appreciated by wider society.

Businesses that are liked by customers and respected by society tend to have a strong culture of ethics and compliance. They act ahead of the curve in dealing with emerging issues; they develop a culture of openness to talk about challenges and they build up a reserve of trust to be drawn on during a crisis.

That is why our aim as a company is to act responsibly and fairly in everything we do.

We will focus our energy and resources on the four areas that matter most to our customers, colleagues and people from across society.

- Trading responsibly
- Reducing our impact on the environment
- Being a great employer
- Supporting local communities

Source: Tesco website (2013) http://www.tescoplc.com/index.asp?pageid=83, accessed August 2013.

Tesco go on to state that they raised £70 million for charities by colleagues and customers since 2000, made £290 million annual savings on energy and fuel costs since 2006 and made a 32.5 per cent reduction in carbon intensity of stores and distribution centres since 2006. In addition, they highlight that 31 per cent of senior management positions are held by women and 77 per cent of senior executives have worked their way up through the company.

On the downside, some environmentalists argue that UK companies 'greenwash' their annual reports, highlighting what they do for the environment and the community; however, they do not identify the environmental risks that their entity creates for the community/environment, nor the steps taken to hedge against these risks. BP is one example of a company that champions CSR, even changing its brand name to 'BP – beyond petroleum' to emphasize its environmental objectives. However, the environmental catastrophe that occurred in 2010 in the Gulf of Mexico (the Deepwater oil leak) was caused by reckless practice that had not been identified as a potential environmental risk (Thornton, 2010).

3.9 Environmental accounting (social accounting)

Sometimes referred to as 'green accounting' or 'social accounting', environmental accounting has many aims. At government level it tries to highlight the contribution that the natural environment makes to the economy both in terms of the economic contribution earned from the environment's resources and the impact that a clean economy has on social well-being. In addition, it tries to determine the expenditure that is incurred in ensuring that the environment is protected (for example, expenditure on controlling pollution or controlling resource depletion such as the destruction of the Amazon forest).

At company level environmental reporting is used to raise public/stakeholder awareness about the steps that an entity is taking to protect the environment. It typically identifies the costs incurred in, for example, reducing pollution, protecting wildlife and wildlife habitats. The impact that a company's actions have on society and the environment is difficult to ascertain as many of the benefits and costs are intangible, are difficult to identify, and when identified are difficult to quantify as the values may be very subjective. Nonetheless, many companies make reference to environment management in their annual report and prepare a separate report providing details of all their activities that impact on society and the environment. An example of the type of information that is provided and the problems with separately identifying the relevant costs can be seen from the following excerpt from the sustainability part of BP's website.

REAL WORLD EXAMPLE 3.6

BP: Environmental expenditure

	$ million	$ million	$ million
Environmental expenditure relating to the Gulf of Mexico oil spill	2010	2011	2012
Spill response	13,628	671	118
Additions to environmental remediation provision	929	1,167	801
Other environmental expenditure			
Operating expenditure	716	704	742
Capital expenditure	911	819	1,207
Clean-ups	55	53	46
Additions to environmental remediation provision	361	510	549
Additions to decommissioning provision	1,800	4,596	3,756

BP continues to incur significant costs related to the 2010 Gulf of Mexico oil spill. The spill response cost incurred during the year is $118 million (2011 $671 million), and $345 million (2011 $336 million) remains as a provision at 31 December 2012.

The environmental remediation provision includes amounts for BP's commitment to fund the Gulf of Mexico Research Initiative, estimated natural resource damage (NRD) assessment costs, emergency NRD restoration projects and early NRD restoration projects under the $1-billion framework agreement. The provision for NRD assessment costs was increased during the year.

Further amounts for spill response costs were provided during the year, primarily to reflect increased costs for patrolling and maintenance and shoreline treatment projects. The majority of the active clean-up of the shorelines was completed in 2011.

Details on the other environmental expenditure can be obtained from the website link.

Source: BP website (2013) http://www.bp.com/en/global/corporate/sustainability/environment/managing-our-impact-on-the-environment/environmental-expenditure.html, accessed 10 August 2013.

3.10 The conceptual framework debate, standardization and choice

Much controversy has surrounded the idea of developing a conceptual framework of accounting, particularly in the UK where the self-regulatory standard-setting institutions have limited resources. There are two main related issues. The first is whether the cost of preparing a conceptual framework is justified in terms of its benefits, including the questions of whether it is possible to develop a set of consistent fundamentals and whether these will lead to improvements in accounting standard setting. The second issue concerns whether accounting standards just make published financial statements more consistent rather than comparable, or alternatively whether more meaningful comparisons would result from allowing companies to choose those accounting policies that are appropriate to their individual circumstances. This has always been an issue in standard setting, but the development of a conceptual framework accentuates the debate because it will presumably lead to greater standardization.

There is a wide variety of schools of thought on the conceptual framework debate, but for the sake of structuring and simplifying the discussion, these can be grouped into two extremes comprising the normative/deductive approach and the positive/empiricist approach.

The normative/deductive approach regards a conceptual framework as absolutely essential. **Normative theories** view accounting as a technical process that is capable of measuring the 'true income' of a business given a set of theories that specify how this should be done (e.g. Hicks, 1946). They often use the analogy that financial statements are like maps, which have the potential to provide a **faithful representation** of reality given a set of underlying consistent rules (i.e. a conceptual framework). Similarly, **deductive theories** view accounting as a technical process but advocates a user needs' approach based on identifying the objectives of financial statements similar to that taken in all the conceptual framework projects to date.

In contrast, the positive/empiricist approach regards a conceptual framework as at best unnecessary, and at worst positively dysfunctional. **Empirical theories** view accounting as an economic process, and the objective of financial statements as being to facilitate predictions (of profits, insolvency, etc.). Thus, accounting methods should be selected on the basis of which give the best predictions – that is, not according to some conceptual framework. Many **positive theories** view accounting, and particularly standard setting, as a political process that may be used to provide information for some stakeholders (equity shareholders) to the detriment of other stakeholders (employees, creditors). They maintain that standard setting should be as a result of consensus and not dictatorial pronouncements based on a conceptual framework which, itself, is the product of a particular set of class interests (e.g. equity shareholders' interests).

At present the international accounting standard setters seem to have taken a deductive view – emphasizing the need for accounting information to satisfy user information needs. However, standards are created after an extensive consultation period wherein all stakeholders are encouraged to contribute their view.

It is difficult to determine if the monetary cost of preparing a conceptual framework is justified in terms of the benefits (in the form of improvements in standard setting). In recent years some of the standards have been considered to have been poor (for example, the standard on accounting for derivative transactions). Furthermore, the development of a conceptual framework is unlikely to quieten those who argue that accounting standards may promote more consistency of accounting policies between companies but this does not necessarily result in greater comparability. There are said to be 'circumstantial variables' or 'differences in circumstances' between companies that necessitate the exercise of managerial discretion in the choice of accounting methods. It is argued that standardization forces companies to use the same accounting policies, but it does not necessarily mean that they are the most appropriate accounting policies for each company and thus comparisons may be misleading. The existence of a conceptual framework is likely to lead to greater standardization and, it is said, more rigidity, a lack of flexibility, and thus less innovation. It is easy to be cynical about innovation when it takes the form of creative accounting, but it must be recognized that standardization taken to the extreme (as uniformity) would probably reduce innovation, which is said to be the case in some countries with uniform national accounting systems specified solely by law.

Summary

All professions need a body of theological, empirical and/or theoretical knowledge to guide the actions of their practitioners. In accounting this is not as well developed as in some other professions, such as medicine, nor is it likely to be in the foreseeable future. The tension between this need for a set of rules to guide practice, and the awareness that these are unlikely to be definitive, has given rise to extensive debate about the current development of a conceptual framework of accounting, also known as generally accepted accounting principles (GAAP).

The FASB, IASC/IASB and ASC/ASB have all published conceptual frameworks of accounting. The main purposes of a conceptual framework of accounting are to provide a basis for the development and review of accounting standards, and to assist preparers, users and auditors of financial statements. This takes the form of an internally consistent set of interrelated objectives and fundamentals that prescribe the nature, function and limits of financial statements.

The IASB conceptual framework is contained in its *Conceptual Framework for Financial Reporting* (2011). This sets out the objective of financial statements, the reporting entity (not yet available), the qualitative characteristics of useful financial information, the definition, recognition and measurement of the elements from which financial statements are constructed, and concepts of capital and capital maintenance.

The IASB's *Conceptual Framework* views the role of accounting as providing information to potential and existing investors, loan providers and other creditors to assist their economic decision-making. This accountability is discharged through financial reports (the statement of comprehensive income, the statement of changes in equity, the statement of financial position and the statement of cash flows). However, in practice, it is recognized that businesses have accountability responsibilities that go beyond providing information for investors, loan and other creditors. They have a responsibility to a wider range of users including employees, suppliers, customers, governments and their agencies, and the public. Each of these will have particular information needs.

Therefore, most plc companies provide information for employees and on their activities towards the local community and the environment within a CSR report. The CSR report can form part of the annual report or can be a separate report

Key terms and concepts

Term	Page
annual or corporate report	47
conceptual framework of accounting	44
corporate social responsibility	56
creative accounting	44
deductive theories	60
empirical theories	60
faithful representation	60
financial accounts	47
financial reporting	47
general purpose financial statements	47
generally accepted accounting principles (GAAP)	44
normative theories	60
positive theories	60
public accountability	51
published financial statements	47

An asterisk after the question number indicates that there is a suggested answer in Appendix 2.

Review questions

connect

3.1* Provide two definitions for the 'conceptual framework of accounting'.

3.2 Describe the purposes of a conceptual framework of accounting.

3.3 What is the difference in role between the IASB *Conceptual Framework* and IFRSs?

3.4 Describe the nature and contents of a conceptual framework of accounting.

3.5 'A conceptual framework of accounting is likely to lead to greater standardization, less choice, less innovation and thus reduced comparability because of the existence of fundamental differences between companies in the way they conduct their activities.' Discuss.

3.6 What is a general purpose financial statement?

3.7 a Outline the objective of financial statements as set out in the IASB's *Conceptual Framework for Financial Reporting* (2011).

b Identify the users of financial statements and briefly describe their information needs.

3.8* The *Conceptual Framework* states that general purpose financial reports should provide information that enables the primary users of general purpose financial reporting (present and potential investors, lenders and other creditors) to make decisions about buying, selling or holding equity or debt instruments and providing or settling loans or other forms of credit.

Required

a State five potential users of company published financial statements, briefly explaining for each one their likely information needs from those statements.

b Briefly discuss whether you think UK company published financial statements achieve the objective stated above, giving your reasons. Include in your answer two ways in which you think the quality of the information disclosed in financial statements could be improved.

(ACCA)

Websites

For more information on topics covered in this chapter visit:

http://www.frc.org.uk/ Provides details on the UK *Conceptual Framework*.

www.ifrs.org/ Provides guidance on the development of the *Conceptual Framework* underlying the production of IFRSs and new issues.

www.iasplus.com/ Provides a summary of the *Conceptual Framework*.

References

Accounting Standards Board (1999) *Statement of Principles for Financial Reporting* (ASB).

Accounting Standards Committee (1978) *Setting Accounting Standards: A Consultative Document* (ASC).

Accounting Standards Steering Committee (ASSC) (1975) *The Corporate Report* (ICAEW).

Bhattacharya, C.B., Sen, S. and Korschun, D. (2008) 'Using Corporate Social Responsibility to Win the War for Talent', *Sloan Management Review*, 49(2), 37–44.

Gray, R.H., Owen, D.L. and Maunders, K.T. (1987) *Corporate Social Responsibility: Accounting and Accountability*, Prentice Hall, Hemel Hempstead.

Hicks, J.R. (1946) *Value and Capital* (2nd edn), Clarendon Press, Oxford.

International Accounting Standards Board (2011), *Conceptual Framework for Financial Reporting* (IASB).

Thornton, J. (2010) 'Companies Put on Notice to Report Environmental Impact of their Work', *Guardian*, Thursday, 4 November, www.guardian.co.uk.

Chapter 4

The Conceptual Framework 2: concepts, principles and policies

Learning Objectives:

After reading this chapter you should be able to do the following:

1. Explain the nature of accounting principles, accounting concepts, measurement bases, accounting policies and estimation techniques.
2. Explain the nature of the going concern concept, the accruals concept, the matching concept, the prudence concept, the entity concept, the materiality concept, the time period concept, the cost concept, the money measurement concept, the duality concept, the substance over form concept, the consistency concept and the separate determination concept, including their implications for the preparation of financial statements.
3. Outline the recognition criteria required before transactions can be included in financial statements.
4. Describe the objectives against which an entity should judge the appropriateness of accounting policies, that is, relevance and faithful representation.
5. Describe the constraints that an entity should take into account in judging the appropriateness of accounting policies.
6. Describe the requirements of *IAS 8 – Accounting Policies, Changes in Accounting Estimates and Errors* (IASB, 2013a) with regard to the selection, review, change in and disclosure of accounting policies, estimation techniques and errors.

4.1 Introduction

An appreciation of the conceptual and theoretical foundations of financial accounting is fundamental to the preparation, understanding and interpretation of financial statements. The conceptual and theoretical foundations can be described as a set of rules, **accounting principles**, postulates, conventions and methods. As mentioned in Chapter 3, the IASB has put more emphasis on providing information that is relevant over information that is reliable, arguing that reliable information is of limited use to economic decision-makers if it does not also influence their economic decision-making. Therefore, the IASB promotes fair value (market value) accounting. Traditional accounting practices focus more on reliability and as such argue for the use of historical cost accounting. As a result of this change in focus, the concepts pursued under each approach differ in terms of prominence.

The first part of this chapter provides a general overview of the nature of the underlying concepts of accounting. Then, the concepts that are deemed to be fundamental under fair value accounting and that are referred to explicitly in the *Conceptual Framework for Financial Reporting* (the *Conceptual Framework*) (IASB, 2011) are discussed (i.e. the going concern and accruals concept). The prudence concept is a fundamental concept under historic cost accounting and it and other concepts not explicitly referred to in the *Conceptual Framework* are also explained. Then the recognition and measurement principle are examined in brief. The latter part of the chapter considers accounting policies and provides a summary of the relevant parts of IAS 8. The *Conceptual Framework* is supported by *IAS 1 – Presentation of Financial Statements* (IASB, 2013d) and by IAS 8. IAS 8 focuses on the selection, change in and disclosure of accounting policies, accounting estimates and errors.

4.2 Key accounting concepts under the *Conceptual Framework*

Accounting concepts were defined in the UK standard *SSAP 2 – Disclosure of Accounting Policies* (ASSC, 1971) as '*broad basic assumptions that underlie the periodic financial statements of business enterprises*'. There are several, though one is specifically singled out for explicit mention in the *Conceptual Framework*, the going concern concept, as it is regarded as being fundamental for ensuring that financial statements meet their objective (i.e. providing useful information). In addition, the accruals concept is discussed under the chapter on general purpose financial reporting.

Going concern

The **going concern** concept is the assumption that an entity will continue in operational existence for the foreseeable future. Any user when looking at an entity's financial statements has the right to assume that the company is not going to liquidate or curtail materially the scale of its operations. Users should be able to look at the financial implications of prior activity as captured in the financial statements and use this as an indication of future activity.

Learning Activity 4.1

Consider, from a company's viewpoint, why it is important to be regarded as a going concern. List three potential consequences of not being regarded as a going concern.

Compare your suggestions to those set out in Figure 4.1.

The implication of the going concern assumption is that assets are valued at an appropriate measurement basis, such as historical cost, fair value or value-in-use, not their scrap value. It is assumed that the entity will continue to operate for the remaining useful life of the non-current assets; hence, the asset's cost

Figure 4.1

The damaging effects of a going concern disclosure could include:

A modified audit opinion being interpreted as a business having broken the terms of its loan agreement with the bank
A bank refusing to lend a company the money it needs to run its business and pay staff wages
Going concern disclosure consequences
Suppliers deciding to withdraw credit facilities (time to pay) to a business, disrupting its trading activities
Landlords enforcing break clauses on rented business premises

Source: Izza, M. (2009) 'The Importance of a "Going Concern"', BBC News, http://news.bbc.co.uk/1/hi/business/7875661.stm, accessed September 2013.

will be allocated to the statement of profit and loss over the useful life of the asset to match against the revenues that the asset helps to generate. If, however, the entity were going to close, the asset cost would have to be written down to the net revenue that it is expected to generate on sale; that is, the sales price less any costs associated with the sale. This may be significantly lower than the book value recorded in the statement of financial position, particularly where the asset is unique, bespoke or specialized, as there will be a limited second-hand market for the sale of the asset.

If there is reason to believe that the entity will not be able to continue in business, then the going concern principle no longer holds and the assets should be valued on a cessation basis; that is, at their **net realizable value**. For example, a £10,000 machine, which can easily generate output for the next 10 years, would be recognized in the statement of financial position at cost price less depreciation, if the company is a going concern. However, if the company decides to go into voluntary liquidation, then this machine is not going to produce revenue for the next 10 years, hence should be written down to the value expected to be received on its sale (its net realizable value). This may be zero.

In terms of disclosures, IAS 1 states that '*when an entity does not prepare financial statements on a going concern basis, it shall disclose that fact, together with the basis on which it prepared the financial statements and the reasons why the entity is not regarded as a going concern*'. There are real economic consequences of this disclosure as highlighted in the following real world example.

REAL WORLD EXAMPLE 4.1

Harvest Natural Drops After 'Going Concern' Warning

Harvest Natural Resources Inc. fell the most ever after reporting a 2012 loss and disclosing a 'going concern qualification' by auditors because of its liquidity.

Harvest declined 33 percent to $3.69 at 10:16 a.m. in New York. Earlier the shares fell 47 percent, the biggest intraday drop since the company began trading publicly in 1989, according to data compiled by Bloomberg. It had fallen 60 percent in 2013 by March.

Source: Adapted from Polson, J. (2013) Bloomberg, http://www.bloomberg.com/news/2013-03-19/harvest-natural-auditors-to-give-going-concern-warning.html

Accruals concept

According to IAS 1, to meet their objectives, financial statements should be prepared on the accruals basis of accounting.

The **accruals concept** is concerned with allocating expenses and income to the periods to which they relate (when the **expenses** were used by the entity or when the income was earned, as distinctly different to when cash is paid out for expenses and when cash is received from a sale). The *Conceptual Framework* states that *'accrual accounting depicts the effects of transactions and other events and circumstances on a reporting entity's economic resources and claims in the periods in which those effects occur, even if the resulting cash receipts and payments occur in a different period'*. In most instances transactions will be recorded in the accounting period in which the goods or services physically pass from the seller to the buyer. The accounting terms for different types of accrual transaction are presented in Figure 4.2.

Figure 4.2

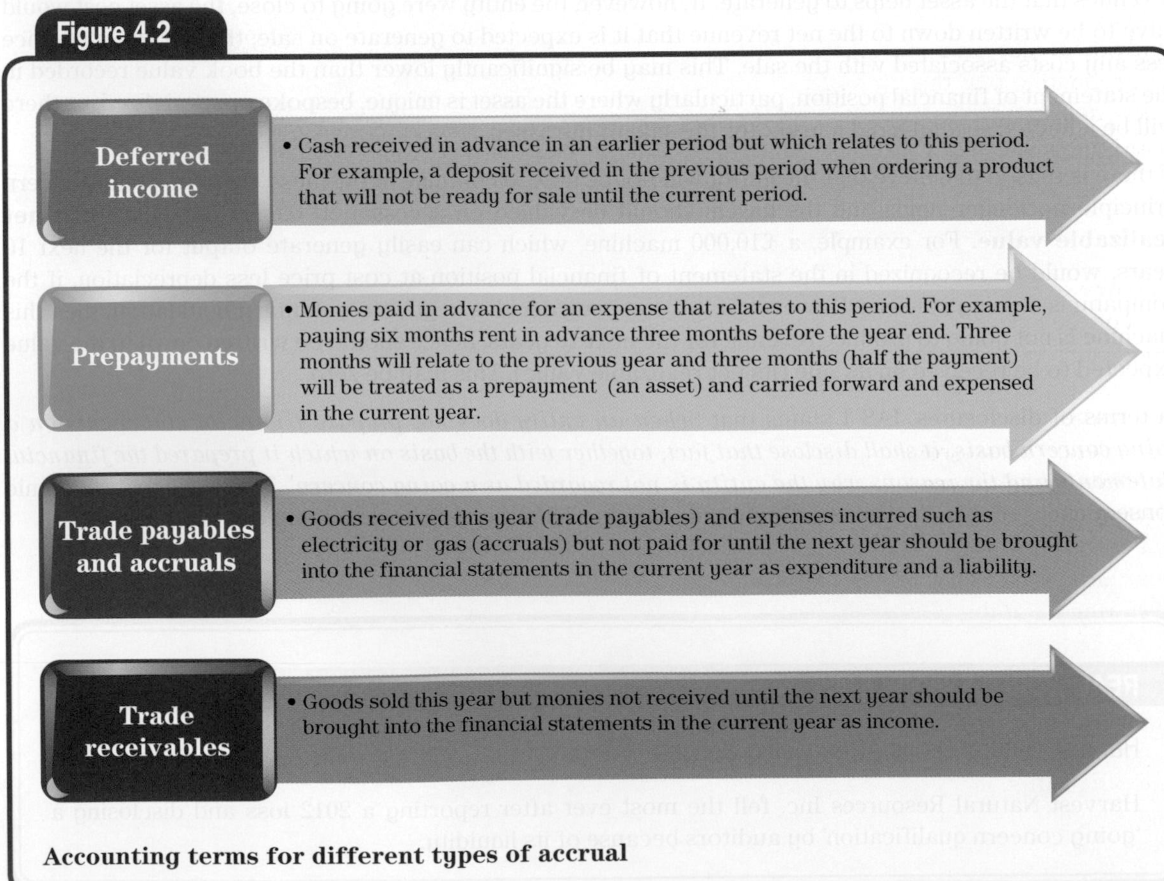

Deferred income
• Cash received in advance in an earlier period but which relates to this period. For example, a deposit received in the previous period when ordering a product that will not be ready for sale until the current period.
Prepayments
• Monies paid in advance for an expense that relates to this period. For example, paying six months rent in advance three months before the year end. Three months will relate to the previous year and three months (half the payment) will be treated as a prepayment (an asset) and carried forward and expensed in the current year.
Trade payables and accruals
• Goods received this year (trade payables) and expenses incurred such as electricity or gas (accruals) but not paid for until the next year should be brought into the financial statements in the current year as expenditure and a liability.
Trade receivables
• Goods sold this year but monies not received until the next year should be brought into the financial statements in the current year as income.

Accounting terms for different types of accrual

Accrued and prepaid expenses are dealt with in more depth in Chapter 17, 'Accruals and **Prepayments**'.

In the case of sales revenue, application of the accruals principle has traditionally been referred to as **revenue recognition**. It relates to the assumption that a sale is deemed to have taken place at the time at which the goods are delivered or services provided (i.e. when the revenue is earned), and not when the proceeds of sale are received. In practice this is normally also the date of the invoice. However, where the invoice is rendered some time after the date of delivery, the sale is deemed to have taken place on the date of delivery and not the date of the invoice. Though coming under the remit of the accruals concept, revenue recognition is such an important principle that a whole standard has been dedicated to provide guidance on the accounting for certain types of revenue: *IAS 18 – Revenue* (IASB, 2013b). This standard applies to the accounting for revenue arising from the sale of goods, the rendering of services and the use by others of entity assets yielding interest, royalties and dividends.

Legislation has also impacted on the interpretation of the accruals concept. Companies legislation requires that only profits realized at the period end should be included in the statement of profit and loss. '*It is generally accepted that profits shall be treated as realized, for these purposes, only when realized in the form either of cash or of other assets, the ultimate cash realization of which can be assessed with reasonable certainty.*' This is known as the **realization concept**. Unrealized profits are shown in the statement of comprehensive income for the year net of tax.

4.3 Other concepts

Under the *Conceptual Framework*, going concern is the fundamental concept and the accruals concept with its related concepts (revenue recognition and realization) are also discussed. There are a number of other concepts that had more prominence under traditional accounting practices (the prudence concept) and others that are implicit in the preparation of financial statements and are so engrained in the process of accounting that they are not explicitly mentioned in the *Conceptual Framework*. Some have already been mentioned in earlier chapters and some will be focused on in later chapters. To be comprehensive, a short explanation of each is given in this chapter.

Prudence concept

The **prudence concept**, as the name implies, assumes that the financial statements have been prepared on a prudent basis. This allows the user to have confidence that no profits are included that are not earned and, if not yet received, are reasonably certain to be received. The user can also be confident that expenses are complete and are not understated, that assets are not overstated and liabilities are complete and are not understated. At one time this concept was deemed to be fundamental to the objective of financial statements (i.e. to provide relevant information to a wide range of users for economic decision-making). However, it was abused by some companies. When companies did well they tended to overstate expenses (by creating provisions for expenditure) and understate revenue. Then, in years when performance was not strong, the companies reversed the adjustments – reducing the provisions and the expenses in the year and increasing revenue. The result was that users could not quite work out how the company really performed. For this reason prudence was downgraded and provisions and manipulations that were based on the prudence concept are no longer allowed.

These transactions did not follow the spirit of this concept. They manipulated it for earnings management purposes. **Earnings management** is where the preparers of financial statements use accounting adjustments to alter the reported performance of the reporting entity. They usually try to smooth profits, that is, to show steady profits. The concept still is applicable; however, it cannot be used as a defence for earnings management or earnings manipulation. An example of where prudence was used inappropriately to the extent that it undermined the reliability of the financial statements is now provided.

REAL WORLD EXAMPLE 4.2

Nortel – accounting irregularities involving the manipulation of reserves to obtain bonuses

In November 2002, three senior managers of Nortel – Dunn, Beatty and Gollogly – learned that Nortel was carrying over $300 million in excess reserves. Dunn, Beatty and Gollogly did not release these excess reserves into income as required under US GAAP. Instead, they concealed their existence and maintained them for later use. Further, in early January 2003, Beatty, Dunn and Gollogly directed the establishment of yet another $151 million in unnecessary reserves during the 2002 year-end closing process to avoid posting a profit and paying bonuses earlier than Dunn had predicted publicly. These reserve manipulations erased Nortel's *pro forma* profit for the fourth quarter of 2002 and caused it to report a loss instead.

In the first and second quarters of 2003 Dunn, Beatty and Gollogly directed the release of at least $490 million of excess reserves specifically to boost earnings, fabricate profits and pay bonuses. These efforts turned Nortel's first quarter 2003 loss into a reported profit under US GAAP, which allowed Dunn to claim that he had brought Nortel to profitability a quarter ahead of schedule. In the second quarter of 2003, their efforts largely erased Nortel's quarterly loss and generated a *pro forma* profit. In both quarters, Nortel posted sufficient earnings to pay tens of millions of dollars in so-called 'return to profitability' bonuses, largely to a select group of senior managers.

Source: USSEC Press Release, http://www.sec.gov/news/press/2007/2007-39.htm, November 2010.

Prudence is deeply embedded in accounting and possibly even in the personality of many accountants. It is one of the main reasons why accountants are often described as conservative, prudent, cautious, pessimistic, and so on. Correctly applied, prudence refers to not overstating the profit in the statement of profit and loss and the financial position in the statement of financial position. This is achieved by making cautious estimates of items such as the amount of potential irrecoverable receivables and the depreciation of non-current assets; that is, where the estimate is a range of amounts, prudence dictates that the amount entered in the financial statements will be the highest figure of a probable loss or liability, and the lowest figure of a gain or asset.

Matching concept

The **matching concept/principle** refers to the assumption that in the measurement of profit, costs should be set against the revenue that they generate at the time when this arises. A classic example of the application of the matching principle is inventory. Where goods are bought in one accounting year but sold in the next, their cost is carried forward as inventory at the end of the year and set against the proceeds of sale in the accounting year in which it occurs. This is expounded in *IAS 2 – Inventories* (IASB, 2013c) as follows: *'When inventories are sold, the carrying amount of those inventories shall be recognised as an expense in the period in which the related revenue is recognised.'*

In terms of the calculation of the gross profit in the statement of profit and loss, this process of carrying forward costs takes the form of the computation of the cost of sales. The cost is carried forward by being deducted from purchases in the form of the inventory at the end of the year. It is brought forward to the following year in the form of the opening inventory, which is matched against the proceeds of sale by virtue of its being included in the cost of sales.

A more theoretical view of the matching principle is that it refers to ascertaining profit on the basis of a cause and effect relationship. Costs cause or give rise to certain effects that take the form of revenue.

Matching is thus the determination of profit by attributing specific causes to particular effects at the time at which the effects occur.

The accruals concept and matching principle can be illustrated by a simplified example (see Worked Example 4.1).

WORKED EXAMPLE 4.1

Suppose a business only had the following transactions:

15 Jan	Purchased goods costing £100 on credit
15 Feb	Paid for the goods purchased on 15 January
15 Mar	Sold on credit for £150 the goods purchased on 15 January
15 Apr	Received payment for the goods sold on 15 March

The accruals (and matching) concept dictates that:

1 The cost of the goods was *incurred* in January.

2 The sales revenue was *earned* in March.

3 There was no profit or loss in January, February or April. The profit of £50 arose in March, the cost of the goods being carried forward as inventory at the end of January and February.

Unfortunately, the application of the accruals concept in general, and the revenue recognition concept and matching principle in particular, is not always as simple as implied above. Although the contents of this section thus far would usually be sufficient to answer most examination questions at this level, students might be expected to demonstrate an awareness of its relevance to current issues. There have recently been several high-profile cases of large companies throughout the world where abuses of the revenue recognition and the matching principle have resulted in the overstatement of profits, and in some cases, corporate bankruptcy. Many of the issues concerning revenue recognition arise where the revenue received in one accounting year relates to goods or services that the business will provide in the next, or future, accounting year(s).

As noted in the next Real World Example, use of the accruals concept and revenue classification type can have serious consequences on reported profit figures.

REAL WORLD EXAMPLE 4.3

Hewlett-Packard's Autonomy Allegations: A Material Write Down Puts All Four Audit Firms on the Spot

Deloitte was the auditor of Autonomy, a UK software firm acquired by HP in 2011 for $11.1 billion. HP announced today it is writing down more than $5 billion, or almost half of the acquisition price, because of 'serious accounting improprieties, misrepresentation and disclosure failures'.

HP, in the understatement of the year, says it is 'extremely disappointed' to find out some former members of Autonomy's management team inflated Autonomy's underlying financial metrics – GAAP and non-GAAP. HP boldly called it a 'willful effort to mislead investors and potential buyers'.

That's PR-speak for fraud.

The *Wall Street Journal*'s All Things D blog has a good summary of all the revenue recognition related allegations that HP is making against Autonomy.

'So what is alleged to have happened? For one thing, Autonomy, as HP tells it, was selling some hardware at a loss. During a period of about eight quarters prior to HP's acquisition, Autonomy sold some hardware products that had a very low margin or on which it may have even taken a loss. It then allegedly turned around and booked those hardware sales as high-margin software sales. At least some portion of the cost on these products, Whitman said, was booked as a marketing expense, not as cost of goods sold.

There's a second piece of the puzzle, where HP says that Autonomy was selling software to value-added resellers – the middlemen in so many technology transactions – in which there are ultimately no end users. That, too, inflated apparent revenue.

Third, there were some long-term hosting deals – essentially, Autonomy hosting applications for its customers on a subscription basis – that were converted to short-term licensing deals. Future revenue for software subscriptions – that should have been deferred or recorded as coming in the future but not yet booked – were stripped out and booked all at once.'

Source: McKenna, F. (2012) Forbes website, www.forbes.com/sites/francinemckenna/2012/11/20/hewlett-packards-autonomy-allegations-a-material-writedown-puts-all-four-audit-firms-on-the-spot/, accessed September 2013; and Hesseldahl, A. (2012) 'What Exactly Happened at Autonomy?', All Things D website, http://allthingsd.com/20121120/what-exactly-happened-at-autonomy/, accessed September 2013.

An example of a complex revenue issue is now examined. When consumers purchase electrical goods they are often encouraged to buy an extended warranty. The consumer pays a one-off premium at the time of purchase, and the seller undertakes to maintain and/or repair the item for some fixed future period of often three to five years. The customer is invoiced at the time of sale. Thus, applying the revenue recognition concept might suggest that the premium would be treated as earned/realized in the statement of profit and loss in the year of sale, which is a practice that some companies have sought to adopt in their financial statements. However, this does not accord with the matching principle. The costs of the repairs that the seller is obliged to make under the extended warranty will be incurred over several future accounting years, and thus the matching principle dictates that the premium received should be spread over this period. This is referred to as **deferred income**.

This is not the end of the problem. The issue now arises as to how much of the premium should be recognized as revenue in each of the future accounting years. The repairs to the item in question are likely to be more common and more costly as the item becomes older. A proper matching would thus require a higher proportion of the premium to be recognized in each of the later years. The precise proportion to be recognized in each year will thus be highly subjective/arbitrary, which is where the further possibility of abuse arises (allocation limitation). Furthermore, the extended warranty illustration does not highlight another very subjective decision. Extended warranties cover a fixed number of years, whereas other goods and services of a similar nature often do not relate to a given period (for example, the warranty may cover parts for the first 60,000 miles on a motor vehicle). In applying the matching principle it will thus be necessary to determine over how many years the income should be recognized. This again gives scope for revenue manipulation.

Similar issues arise in deciding whether expenditure should be treated as capital (i.e. on non-current assets) or revenue (i.e. expenses), and in the case of capital expenditure, over what period to write off the asset and how much should be charged to each year (classification and allocation limitations). This is discussed further in Chapter 15, 'Depreciation and Non-current Assets'.

Entity concept

The **entity concept** is otherwise known as the **accounting entity** or the **business entity** concept. This concept is discussed in detail in Chapter 1, 'Entities and Financial Reporting Statements'. In simple terms this concept allows the user to look at a reporting entity's financial statements and to know that these represent the performance and financial position of the business unit and do not include any assets, liabilities, income or expenditure that are not related to the business. Therefore, when a sole trader uses the business cheque book to buy a car for personal use, this car will not form part of the business's assets; it will be treated as the owner withdrawing equity capital. This is called a 'drawing'.

Materiality concept

The **materiality concept** affects every transaction and every set of financial statements. This concept affects two main areas: presentation and application of accounting standards. This concept is discussed in full in Chapter 5, 'The Conceptual Framework 3: The Qualitative Characteristics of Financial Information' as materiality is considered to be an attribute of relevant information.

Time period concept

Another concept, the **time period concept**, otherwise known as the **time interval** or periodicity concept, refers to the practice of dividing the life of an entity into discrete periods for the purpose of preparing financial statements. The norm, as required by company law, is one year. Therefore, a user has the right to assume that the figures shown in a set of financial statements refer to a one-year period. When the period is different to one year, the financial statements need to make it clear that this is the case. Indeed, company law limits the ability of companies to change their accounting year-end date. Entities can of course elect to report for different time periods; however, to comply with law and the tax authorities they will also need to prepare financial statements every 12 months.

The time period concept causes issues as allocating an item either side of the reporting date can have a direct impact on, for example, revenues, profits and consequentially share price. Real World Example 4.4 highlights the importance of allocating items to the correct time period.

REAL WORLD EXAMPLE 4.4

Transat forced to restate 2011 earnings over 'recurring accounting error' in U.K. unit

... Denis Pétrin, Transat chief financial officer, said the company decided to release its yearend results a day earlier than expected alongside an admission about the financial irregularities after a newspaper report said a group of employees were alleging a potential fraud had taken place at the company.

'This, of course, is very serious and potentially damaging to our reputation. So the best way to manage the situation was to go ahead with the facts,' he said on a conference call. 'I can tell you there is no fraud, and the allegations in the article are without merit.' But Mr. Pétrin did say the company had identified an issue that its U.K. subsidiary was not following Transat's methodology for how customer deposits were recorded between 2006 and 2011. In the course of its yearend process, he said, Transat discovered the U.K. unit had been recording revenue from future departures in its results when they should have been accounted for in the following year.

'As a consequence, we were then underestimating our deferred income and overestimating our yearly results,' he said. As a result, Transat said it reduced its earnings as of Nov. 1, 2010, by $11.7-million, which was the sum of the variance between 2006 and 2010.

For the year ended Oct. 31, 2011, the company increased its net loss by $2.9-million, or 8¢ a share, to $14.7-million, as well . . .

. . . Mr. Tyerman said it appeared someone had been borrowing from the next year's deposits to make budget in the current year, and the irregularities only grew over time.

'It looks like somebody got caught with their hand in the cookie jar,' he said. 'It certainly gave me pause when I saw it.'

Source: Scott Deveau, S. (2012) 'Transat Forced to Restate 2011 Earnings over "Recurring Accounting Error" in U.K. Unit,' *Financial Post*, http://business.financialpost.com/2012/12/19/transat-forced-to-restate-2011-earnings-over-recurring-accounting-error-in-u-k-unit/, accessed September 2013.
Material reprinted with the express permission of: **National Post**, a division of Postmedia Network Inc.

Historical cost concept/fair value

The **historical cost concept** allows a user to assume that all the transactions in an entity's financial statements reflect the actual cost price billed or revenue charged for items. In addition, it allows the reader to see the history of the management team's investment decision-making from the statement of financial position. This concept is becoming less relevant now as it is widely believed that historical cost information does not support financial statements in their aim of producing information that is useful for economic decision-making. In particular the impact of inflation means that many of the items recorded at historic cost, do not reflect current value. The ASC tried to introduce a standard (*SSAP 16 current cost accounting*) to enable entities to incorporate inflation into their financial statements; however, this standard had to be withdrawn due to lack of support from the business community. Measuring items at fair value is deemed to provide more relevant information. **Fair value** is defined by the IASB in paragraph 9 of IFRS 13 'Fair Value Measurement' as *'the price that would be received to sell an asset or paid to transfer a liability in an orderly transaction between market participants at the measurement date'*.

Money measurement concept

The **money measurement concept** allows the user to assume that the performance and financial position of a reporting entity will be expressed in monetary amounts (usually in the currency of the country where the business is registered). In this book it is assumed that the relevant currency is the sterling pound (£).

Duality concept

The **duality concept**, otherwise known as the **dual aspect** concept or **double entry**, assumes that every transaction has two aspects. Every transaction affects two accounts in a set of financial statements in such a manner as to keep the accounting equation in balance (i.e. assets will always equal liabilities plus owners' capital). This is discussed in detail in Chapter 7, 'The Accounting Equation and its Components'.

Substance over form concept

The **substance over form concept** was formally introduced in the UK with the implementation of *FRS 5 – Substance Over Form* (ASB, 1994). This concept involves identifying all the rights and obligations arising from a transaction or event, and accounting for the transaction or event in a way that reflects its economic substance. Information must be accounted for and presented with regard for the economic **substance of a transaction** and not merely its **legal form** (although the effects of the legal characteristics of a transaction or other event are themselves a part of its substance and commercial effect). The legal form of a transaction or event is not always consistent with the economic reality of the transaction. This was a reactive concept/standard that was introduced to try to stop the accounting practices that had emerged of creating complicated legal transactions which, because of their legal form, allowed transactions to be omitted from the financial statements. In particular, debts/liabilities were arranged in such a manner as to enable them to be left off the statement of financial position. This would make the company look stronger, healthier and in general masked the real debt commitment that the entity had, from the users. This is no longer allowed. Regardless of the legal contract underlying a transaction, the preparer of the financial statements has to determine whether the transaction creates an asset or a liability as defined by the *Conceptual Framework* (IASB, 2011). If the transaction does, then the preparer has to account for it as such. For example, an entity may pass legal ownership of an item of property to another party, yet, when the circumstances are looked into in full, it may be that the entity continues to have access to all the future economic benefits of the item of property. In such circumstances, the reporting of a sale of the property would not represent faithfully the transaction entered into. In this instance it might be more appropriate to account for this as obtaining a loan using the property as security.

The classic example of the relevance of substance relates to certain types of lease, such as where a company has contracted to lease a motor vehicle at a given monthly rental for a period of, say, three years, at the end of which it has the option to purchase the vehicle for a nominal/small amount. The legal form of this transaction is a rental agreement. If the legal form were to dictate the accounting entries, the rental payments would appear as an expense in the statement of comprehensive income and the vehicle would not be included in the non-current assets on the statement of financial position. This is why such transactions are referred to as a form of **off-balance-sheet finance**. However, the economic substance of this transaction is the purchase of a vehicle payable by instalments, very similar to a hire purchase transaction. Thus, the substance characteristic dictates that the rental payments are not treated as an expense; instead, they are capitalized. This means that the vehicle is recorded as the purchase of a non-current asset and the total rental payments for the three years are shown as a finance lease liability.

Consistency concept

The **consistency concept** allows the user to look at a set of financial statements over a number of years for an entity and to assume that the same methods, policies and **estimation techniques** have been used from year to year. This allows the user to compare the performance of the entity over time. Financial information should allow users to determine trends in the performance of an entity over time. If accounting policies, techniques and methods used were allowed to vary from year to year, this would make comparisons meaningless. Similarly, users should be able to look at the financial statements of several entities within the same industry and make informed comparisons in the performance and financial standing of each entity, relative to each other. If consistent accounting policies and practices are not adopted, this process would be very difficult. Consistency is one of the qualities that financial information should have, as detailed in the *Conceptual Framework*. As such, it is discussed later in this chapter.

Separate determination concept

The **separate determination concept** also protects the user. IAS 1 states that *'an entity shall not offset assets and liabilities or income and expenses, unless required or permitted by an IFRS'*. Company law does not allow netting, except in some limited instances. For example, netting is allowed in the disclosure of hedged derivative products, which is beyond the scope of this book. Under this concept, netting transactions is only allowed when offsetting reflects the substance of the transactions or other event. For example, trade discounts and volume rebates can be offset against sales revenue under *IAS 18 – Revenue* as this net amount reflects the fair value of the consideration to be received.

This concept allows the user to look at the **assets**, **liabilities**, **income** and expenditure and to know that the reported figure is the total value for each of these elements. The entity should have a separate record of every asset held. The asset category in the financial statement should not be just a big bath that includes a whole host of untraceable past transactions. This concept also does not allow a company to net one element against another. This is important as netting can mislead users. For example, if a company were able to net its debt against some assets so that less debt is shown in the statement of financial position, then the user would be unable to make a proper assessment of the entity's ability to pay back its the debt as the user would assume the repayments required to clear it were less than they actually were.

4.4 Recognition

Recognition is the process of including an item in either the statement of financial position or in the statement of comprehensive income. To be included two conditions must be met: the item must meet the definition of one of the elements as set out in the *Conceptual Framework* and must also meet the criteria for recognition as detailed by the *Conceptual Framework* (IASB, 2011) – summarized in Figure 4.3.

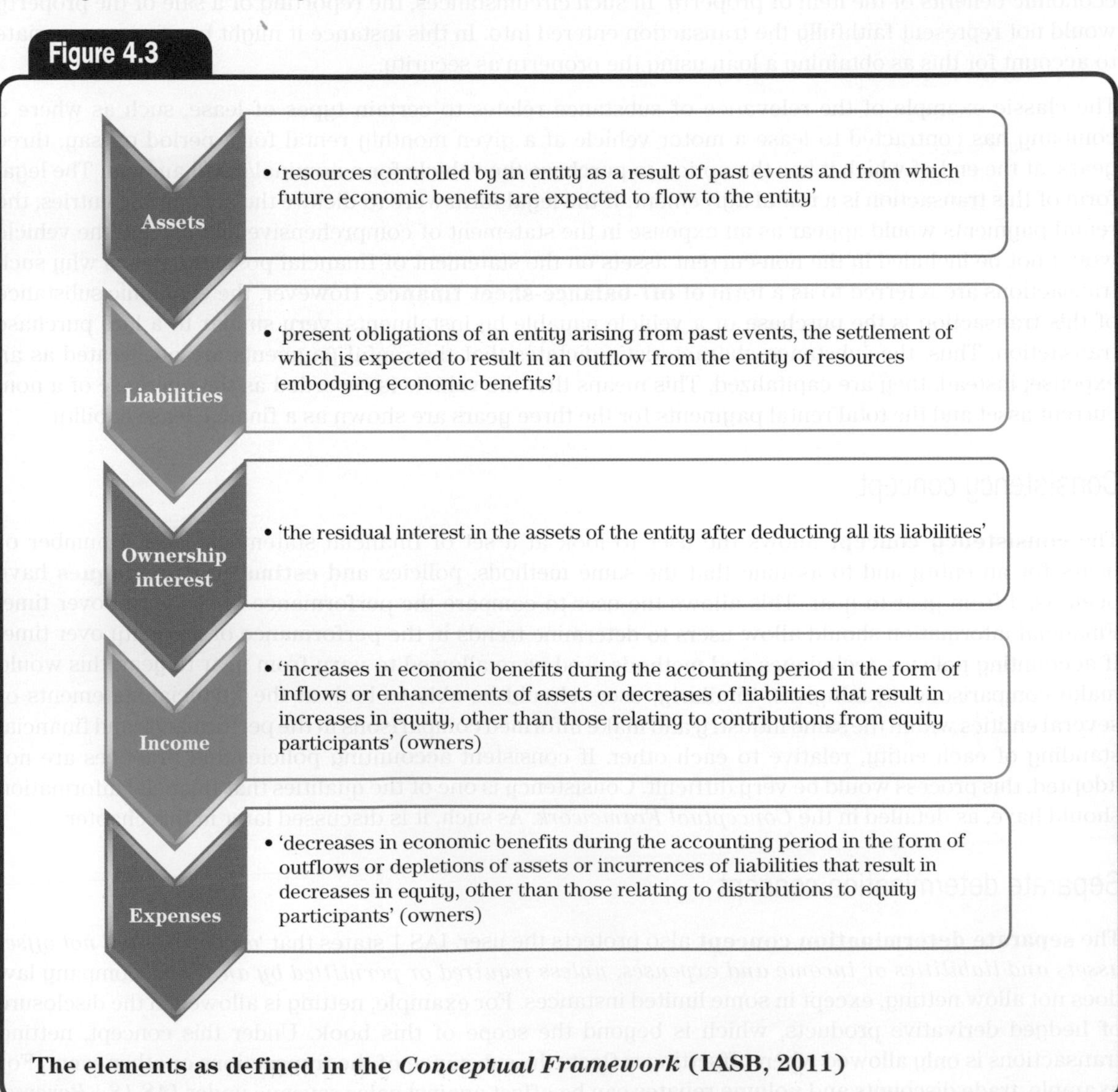

Figure 4.3
Assets
• 'resources controlled by an entity as a result of past events and from which future economic benefits are expected to flow to the entity'
Liabilities
• 'present obligations of an entity arising from past events, the settlement of which is expected to result in an outflow from the entity of resources embodying economic benefits'
Ownership interest
• 'the residual interest in the assets of the entity after deducting all its liabilities'
Income
• 'increases in economic benefits during the accounting period in the form of inflows or enhancements of assets or decreases of liabilities that result in increases in equity, other than those relating to contributions from equity participants' (owners)
Expenses
• 'decreases in economic benefits during the accounting period in the form of outflows or depletions of assets or incurrences of liabilities that result in decreases in equity, other than those relating to distributions to equity participants' (owners)

The elements as defined in the *Conceptual Framework* (IASB, 2011)

In addition to meeting the definition of an element, the transaction can only be recognized if it is *'probable that any future economic benefit associated with the item will flow to, or from the entity; and the item has a cost or value that can be measured with reliability'*.

4.5 Measurement

Measurement is defined in the *Conceptual Framework* as: *'the process of determining the monetary amounts at which the elements of the financial statements are to be recognised and carried in the statement of financial position and the statement of comprehensive income'*.

Measurement bases are the methods used to determine the monetary value. The main bases are outlined in Figure 4.4.

Figure 4.4

Measurement bases

1 ***Historical cost***: *Assets are recorded at the amount of cash or cash equivalents paid or the fair value of the consideration given to acquire them, at the time of their acquisition. Liabilities are recorded at the amount of proceeds received in exchange for the obligation, or in some circumstances (for example, income taxes) at the amounts of cash or cash equivalents expected to be paid.*

2 ***Current cost***: *Assets are carried at the amount of cash or cash equivalents that would have to be paid if the same or an equivalent asset was acquired currently. Liabilities are carried at the undiscounted amount of cash or cash equivalents that would be required to settle the obligation currently.*

3 ***Realizable (settlement) value***: *Assets are carried at the amount of cash or cash equivalents that could currently be obtained by selling the asset in an orderly disposal. Liabilities are carried at their settlement values; that is, the undiscounted amounts of cash or cash equivalents expected to be paid to satisfy the liabilities.*

4 ***Present value***: *Assets are carried at the present discounted value of the future net cash inflows that the item is expected to generate in the normal course of business. Liabilities are carried at the present discounted value of the future net cash outflows that are expected to be required to settle the liabilities.*

The four main measurement bases as provided in the *Conceptual Framework* (IASB, 2011)

Many entities use a combination of these measurement bases for measuring the value of different items, deeming that some of the bases are better for some items than others. For example, inventory is commonly recorded at the lower of historic cost or net realizable value. Many oil companies use **current cost** techniques to value their cost of goods sold. Lease liabilities or pension liabilities are usually measured at the **present value** of the future expected economic outflows.

The historical cost concept is revisited again in more depth in Chapter 7, 'The Accounting Equation and its Components'.

4.6 Capital maintenance

Capital maintenance is explained in Chapter 5 of the *Conceptual Framework* (2011). It is concerned with how an entity measures profit. It takes the view that only surpluses made after capital value has been maintained should be regarded as profit. Hence, when calculating profit, expenses and a charge for the maintenance of capital value should be deducted from income to determine the true profit for the period. The concept is not straightforward as capital value is constantly changing due to inflation and the higher the inflation, the greater the charge required against income in order to maintain capital value. This is explained using a simple example – assume a company's capital had a reported value of £1 million at the start of the year and inflation over the year was 10 per cent. In this scenario a capital maintenance charge of £100,000 would be required against income as the reported value of assets at the end of the year would need to equate to £1,100,000 if it were to have the same real value as the assets at the start of the year.

This concept is controversial and will be considered by the IASB over the next few years.

4.7 Accounting policies

Accounting policies are defined in IAS 8 as: '*the specific principles, bases, conventions, rules and practices applied by an entity in preparing and presenting financial statements. An accounting policy will deal with three issues, recognising, selecting measurement bases for, and presenting assets, liabilities, income, expenses and changes to owners' funds*' (IASB, 2013a).

Some simple examples of accounting policies are the choice between treating expenditure on items such as tools and equipment, or development expenditure, as expenses in the statement of profit or loss, or as non-current assets in the statement of financial position. A real world example of three accounting policies currently being followed by Tesco plc is given below.

REAL WORLD EXAMPLE 4.5

Tesco Plc

Inventories

Inventories comprise goods and properties held for resale and properties held for, or in the course of, development with a view to sell. Inventories are valued at the lower of cost and fair value less costs to sell using the weighted average cost basis.

Revenue (Small Extract)

Revenue comprises the fair value of consideration received or receivable for the sale of goods and services in the ordinary course of the Group's activities.

Sale of goods

Revenue is recognised when the significant risks and rewards of ownership of the goods have transferred to the buyer and the amount of revenue can be measured reliably.

Revenue is recorded net of returns, discounts/offers and value added taxes.

Trade payables

Trade payables are non-interest bearing and are recognised initially at fair value and subsequently measured at amortised cost using the effective interest method.

Source: Annual Report and Financial Statements, 2013, Accounting policies extract, http://files.the-group.net/library/tesco/annualreport2013/pdfs/tesco_annual_report_2013.pdf

As is notable from Tesco plc's accounting policies, the measurement bases and recognition criteria are detailed where relevant. For example, lower of cost and fair value are two measurement bases. This is an example of the prudence concept in practice. The revenue accounting policy focuses on detailing the recognition criteria (i.e. Revenue is recorded . . . when the significant risks and rewards of ownership have been transferred to the buyer) which corresponds exactly with the criteria laid down in the *Conceptual Framework*. The policy also details the measurement bases (Revenue is recorded net of returns, relevant vouchers/offers and value added taxes). Accounting policies are dealt with in more detail later.

Estimation techniques

Estimation techniques are the methods that are used to apply accounting policies. They are not measurement bases. For example, methods of depreciation, such as straight line, reducing balance and sum of digits, are different estimation techniques that can be used to allocate the cost of a non-current asset that has been recorded using the measurement basis – historical cost – to the statement of profit and loss in each accounting period. In the Real World Example 4.5 on Tesco plc's accounting policies, inventory is valued using the weighted average cost method of valuation. This is the estimation technique used.

4.8 Selecting accounting policies

According to IAS 8,

❝*management should develop and apply an accounting policy that results in information that is:*

a *relevant to the economic decision-making needs of users; and*

b *reliable, in that the financial statements:*

i *represent faithfully the financial position, financial performance and cash flows of the entity;*

ii *reflect the economic substance of transactions, other events and conditions, and not merely their legal form;*

iii *are neutral, i.e. free from bias;*

iv *are prudent; and*

v *are complete in all material respects.*❞

(IASB, 2013a)

These attributes are the qualities that financial information included in financial statements should have. They are discussed in depth in the next chapter. In addition, IAS 8 explicitly refers to the consistency concept, recommending that entities '*select and apply its accounting policies consistently for similar transactions, other events and conditions, unless a standard or an interpretation specifically requires or permits categorisation of items for which different policies may be appropriate'.* In these circumstances *'an appropriate accounting policy needs to be selected and applied consistently to each category'.* IAS 8 also reminds management not to forget that the recognition criteria as detailed in the *Conceptual Framework* and guidance given in IASs is also influential. Selecting the most appropriate policy is important; IAS 1 highlights this by stating that *'inappropriate accounting policies are not rectified either by disclosure of the accounting policies used or by notes or explanatory material'.*

4.9 Changing accounting policies

As mentioned in the previous paragraph consistency in the application of accounting policies is very important. Changes in accounting policy can impact on profit or loss and on the values presented in the statement of financial position. The result of this is that users are unable to assess trends in the performance of an entity over time as they are not comparing like with like. Therefore, IAS 8 sets out limits on what is deemed to be acceptable reasons for changing an accounting policy:

> "*An entity shall change an accounting policy only if the change:*
>
> **a** *is required by a Standard or an Interpretation; or*
>
> **b** *results in the financial statements providing reliable and more relevant information about the effects of transactions, other events or conditions on the entity's financial position, financial performance or cash flows.*"
>
> (IASB, 2013a)

When a change in accounting policy is permitted, the financial statements of the previous period (the comparatives), which are included in a set of financial statements, and the opening balances are amended to take account of the cumulative change and a specific disclosure on the reason for the change and the impact of the change on profit or loss is disclosed. IAS 1 requires that two years' comparative figures for the statement of financial position be provided, amended to reflect application of the new accounting policy. This helps the user to compare the results of the current year with previous years.

> "*IAS 8 outlines two occasions that involve adopting a new approach, which are not considered to be changes in accounting policy:*
>
> **a** *the application of an accounting policy for transactions, other events or conditions that differ in substance from those previously occurring: and*
>
> **b** *the application of a new accounting policy for transactions, other events or conditions that did not occur previously or were immaterial.*"
>
> (IASB, 2013a)

4.10 The disclosure of accounting policies and estimation techniques

To achieve fair presentation of accounting information, IAS 1 states that an entity has to *'select and apply accounting policies in accordance with IAS 8 and to present information, including accounting policies, in a manner that provides relevant, reliable, comparable and understandable information'.* IAS 1 recommends that an entity has a section in its financial statements called the '**summary of significant accounting policies**', which should highlight *'the measurement basis (or bases) used in preparing the financial statements and the other accounting policies used that are relevant to an understanding of the financial statements'.* The disclosure should also include any judgements (not judgements in respect of estimations as these are included in the note, not the accounting policy) made by management when applying accounting policies within the accounting policy note. Not all accounting policies need to be disclosed, only those that management consider to be material. An accounting policy is deemed to be material when it is considered that disclosing details of the policy will *'assist users in understanding how transactions, other events and conditions are reflected in the reported financial performance and financial position'* (IAS 8).

When the disclosures in relation to any change made in accounting policies as a result of the implementation of a new standard have material consequences on the reported performance and/or reported financial position of an entity, then IAS 8 requires that additional information is provided in the year of the change to explain the nature of the change, the transitional arrangements (if any), the impact of these transitional arrangements on future performance, the change made to the figures reported in the financial statements (on a line-by-line basis), the cumulative impact on previous years' results and financial position and limits on the ability to determine the cumulative impact of the change where it has been impractical to determine the cumulative impact.

In terms of accounting estimates used as part of an accounting policy, such as the level of irrecoverable receivables written off or inventory obsolescence, IAS 8 recommends that an entity should *'disclose the nature and amount of a change in an accounting estimate that has an effect in the current period or is expected to have an effect in future periods, except for the disclosure of the effect on future periods when it is impracticable to estimate that effect'*. Changes in accounting estimate are not changes in accounting policy; therefore, changes should be included in the current period only.

Summary

The IASB's *Conceptual Framework* of accounting may be described as a set of accounting principles. These are said to comprise the objective of general purpose financial statements, the reporting entity, the qualitative characteristics of financial information, the elements of financial statements, recognition in financial statements, measurement in financial statements and concepts of capital maintenance. Knowledge of accounting concepts is also important when studying financial accounting. Accounting concepts are defined as broad basic assumptions that underlie the accounting for transactions or events in the periodic financial statements of business enterprises.

Recognition and measurement in financial statements include two accounting concepts that have been described as 'part of the bedrock of accounting': namely, the accruals concept and the going concern assumption, respectively. The going concern assumption is that the information provided in financial statements is most relevant if prepared on the hypothesis that the entity is to continue in operational existence for the foreseeable future. The implication of this is that assets will normally be valued, and shown in the statement of financial position at their historical cost or if more appropriate, fair value. The accruals concept requires that transactions and other events should be reflected in the financial statements for the accounting period in which they occur and not, for example, in the period in which any cash involved is received or paid. In most instances this refers to the accounting period in which the goods or services physically pass from the seller to the buyer. The accruals concept has traditionally been taken to include the matching principle. This refers to the assumption that in the measurement of profit, costs should be set against the revenue that they generate at the time when this arises. A classic example of the application of the matching principle is inventory.

In addition, there are a number of other accepted accounting concepts that are not explicitly referred to in the *Conceptual Framework*. These include the prudence concept, matching concept, entity concept, materiality concept, time period concept, historical cost concept, fair value concept, money measurement concept, duality concept, substance over form concept, consistency concept and the separate determination concept.

The preparation of financial statements involves selecting measurement bases, accounting policies and estimation techniques. Measurement bases are defined as the monetary attributes of the elements of financial statements – assets, liabilities, income, expenses and changes to owners' funds – that are reflected in financial statements. Accounting policies are defined as those principles, bases, conventions, rules and practices applied by an entity that specify how the effects of transactions and other events are to be reflected in its financial statements through recognizing, selecting measurement bases for, and presenting assets, liabilities, income, expenditure and changes to owners' funds. Estimation techniques are defined as the methods adopted by an entity to arrive at estimated monetary amounts, corresponding to the measurement bases selected, for assets, liabilities, income, expenses and changes to owners' funds.

The objectives against which an entity should judge the appropriateness of accounting policies to its particular circumstances are relevance and faithful representation. These are discussed in the next chapter. IAS 8 provides detailed guidance relating to the selection, review, change in and disclosure of accounting policies and estimation techniques.

There are two constraints that an entity should take into account in judging the appropriateness of accounting policies to its particular circumstances, which are the need to balance the different objectives set out above, and the need to balance the cost of providing information with the likely benefit of such information to users of the entity's financial statements.

Key terms and concepts

accounting concepts	66	expenses	68
accounting entity	73	fair value	74
accounting policies	78	going concern	66
accounting principles	66	historical cost concept	74
accruals concept	68	income	76
assets	76	legal form	75
business entity	73	liabilities	76
capital maintenance	78	matching concept/principle	70
consistency concept	75	materiality concept	73
current cost	77	measurement	77
deferred income	72	measurement bases	77
double entry	74	money measurement concept	74
dual aspect	74	net realizable value	67
duality concept	74	off-balance-sheet finance	75
earnings management	69	prepayments	69
entity concept	73	present value	77
estimation techniques	75	prudence concept	69

realization concept	69	summary of significant accounting policies	80
revenue recognition	69	time interval	73
separate determination concept	75	time period concept	73
substance of a transaction	75		
substance over form concept	74		

An asterisk after the question number indicates that there is a suggested answer in Appendix 2.

Review questions

connect

4.1* Describe the accounting concept that would be relevant when deciding on how to account for a transaction, which involves an owner of a business taking inventory for his own use.

4.2 Describe the nature of accounting principles.

4.3* a Define each of the following elements:

i assets

ii liabilities

iii ownership interest

iv income

v expenses

b Define each of the following terms:

i off-balance sheet finance

ii substance over form

iii threshold quality.

4.4 Explain the nature of the going concern assumption and its implications for the preparation of financial statements.

4.5 Explain the nature of the accruals concept and the matching concept. Give an example of the application of each.

4.6 Describe the nature of each of the following:

a measurement bases

b accounting policies

c estimation techniques.

Give one example of each.

4.7 According to *IAS 8 – Accounting Policies, Changes in Accounting Estimates and Errors* (IASB, 2013a) management should develop and apply an accounting policy that provides quality information that will be of benefit to users. Outline the main attributes that information resulting from the application of an accounting policy should have.

4.8 Explain the relevance of prudence to the appropriateness of accounting policies.

4.9 Outline the circumstances that must be prevalent before a change in accounting policy is permitted under *IAS 8 – Accounting Policies, Changes in Accounting Estimates and Errors* (IASB, 2013a).

4.10 Describe the information that should be disclosed in financial statements relating to an entity's accounting policies and estimation techniques.

4.11 Describe the nature of any adjustments required and the information that should be disclosed when an entity changes an accounting policy.

4.12 Describe the nature of any adjustments required and the information that should be disclosed when an entity changes an accounting estimate.

Exercises

connect

BASIC

4.13 An acquaintance of yours, H. Gee, has recently set up in business for the first time as a general dealer. The majority of his sales will be on credit to trade buyers but he will sell some goods to the public for cash. He is not sure at which point of the business cycle he can regard his cash and credit sales to have taken place.

After seeking guidance on this matter from his friends, he is thoroughly confused by the conflicting advice he has received. Samples of the advice he has been given include:

The sale takes place when:

1 you have bought goods which you know you should be able to sell easily;

2 the customer places the order;

3 you deliver the goods to the customer;

4 you invoice the goods to the customer;

5 the customer pays for the goods;

6 the customer's cheque has been cleared by the bank.

He now asks you to clarify the position for him.

Required

a Write notes for Gee setting out, in as easily understood a manner as possible, the accounting conventions and principles that should generally be followed when recognizing sales revenue.

b Examine each of the statements 1–6 above and advise Gee (stating your reasons) whether the method advocated is appropriate to the particular circumstances of his business.

(ACCA)

INTERMEDIATE

4.14 On 20 December 20X3 your client paid £10,000 for an advertising campaign. The advertisements will be heard on local radio stations between 1 January and 31 January 20X4. Your client believes that as a result sales will increase by 60 per cent in 20X4 (over 20X3 levels) and by 40 per cent in 20X5 (over 20X3 levels). There will be no further benefits.

Required

Write a memorandum to your client explaining your views on how this item should be treated in the financial statements for the three years, 20X3 to 20X5. Your answer should include explicit reference to at least *three* relevant traditional accounting conventions, and to the requirements of *two* classes of user of published financial statements.

(ACCA)

4.15* 'If a business invests in shares, and the market value of the shares increases above cost then, until and unless the business sells them, no profit is made. If the business invests in inventory for resale, and the market value of the inventory falls below cost then the loss is recognized even though no sale has taken place.' INTERMEDIATE

'If a business undertakes an intensive advertising campaign which will probably result in increased sales (and profit) in succeeding years it will nevertheless usually write off the cost of the campaign in the year in which it is incurred.'

Required

Explain the reasoning behind the application of accounting principles in situations such as these and discuss the effect on the usefulness of accounting information in relation to users' needs.

(ACCA)

4.16 Classify each of the following as either a measurement basis, an accounting policy or an estimation technique, and explain your reasons: INTERMEDIATE

a Advertising expenditure that has been treated as a non-current asset rather than an expense.

b The use of the straight-line method of depreciation.

c The valuation of an asset at the lower of cost or net realizable value.

d Allowance for irrecoverable receivables of 5 per cent of the amount of trade receivables at the end of the accounting period.

e Land and buildings have been shown on the statement of financial position at their current replacement cost.

f Listed investments have been shown on the statement of financial position as a current asset.

g The historical cost of inventory has been ascertained by taking a weighted average of the prices paid during the accounting period.

4.17 One of your clients is a beef farmer. She informs you that the price of beef has fallen dramatically over the past few months and that she expects it to fall even further over the next three months. She therefore argues that the prudence principle should be applied to the valuation of her beef herd, stating that it should be valued at the lower of cost or net realizable value; in this case at the latter value. She further asserts that this treatment is reasonable on the grounds that it will reduce her profit for tax purposes by the loss in value of her herd. INTERMEDIATE

One of your colleagues has advised you that this may be a misinterpretation of the prudence principle and could contravene the neutrality principle. Discuss.

4.18 Nesales plc, a large food manufacturer, has purchased the brand name of a chocolate bar from one of its competitors for £5 million. It proposes to include this on its statement of financial position as a non-current asset. INTERMEDIATE

Cadberry plc, another large food and soft drinks manufacturer, has spent £5 million this year on promoting a new brand of chocolate bar. It proposes to include this on its statement of financial position as a non-current asset.

You are required to discuss whether the proposed accounting treatment of these two items is likely to achieve quality financial information, as outlined in the IASB's *Conceptual Framework for Financial Reporting* (IASB, 2011).

INTERMEDIATE

4.19 Minisoft plc, a manufacturer of computer software, has spent £10 million in the current accounting year on staff recruitment, training and development. It proposes to include this on its statement of financial position as a non-current asset. Discuss.

References

Accounting Standards Board (1994) *Financial Reporting Standard 5 – Substance Over Form* (ASB).

Accounting Standards Steering Committee (1971) *Statement of Standard Accounting Practice 2 – Disclosure of Accounting Policies* (ASSC).

Hesseldahl, A. (2012) 'What Exactly Happened at Autonomy?', All Things D website, http://allthingsd.com/20121120/what-exactly-happened-at-autonomy/, accessed September 2013.

International Accounting Standards Board (2011) *Conceptual Framework for Financial Reporting* (IASB).

International Accounting Standards Board (2013a), *International Accounting Standard 8 – Accounting Policies, Changes in Accounting Estimates and Errors* (IASB).

International Accounting Standards Board (2013b) *International Accounting Standard 18 – Revenue* (IASB).

International Accounting Standards Board (2013c) *International Accounting Standard 2 – Inventories* (IASB).

International Accounting Standards Board (2013d) *International Accounting Standard 1 – Presentation of Financial Statements* (IASB).

International Accounting Standards Board (2013e) *International Financial Reporting Standard 13 – Fair Value Measurement* (IASB).

Chapter 5

The Conceptual Framework 3: the qualitative characteristics of financial information

Learning Objectives:

After reading this chapter you should be able to do the following:

1. Describe the qualitative characteristics of financial information contained in the IASB's *Conceptual Framework for Financial Reporting* (IASB, 2011).
2. Discuss the two fundamental qualitative characteristics – relevance and faithful presentation.
3. Discuss the enhancing qualitative characteristics – comparability, verifiability, timeliness and understandability.
4. Evaluate the conflict that can arise between the qualitative characteristics of financial information.

5.1 The qualitative characteristics of financial information

According to the *Conceptual Framework* 'qualitative characteristics are attributes that make the information provided in financial statements useful to users'. Try Learning Activity 5.1 to determine if you can identify information that is useful for decision-making.

Learning Activity 5.1

You are an investor who is considering investing in two companies. You have £750,000 to invest and are only going to select one company. Both companies had similar results in the previous year.

You have already spent 4 hours and £400 investigating whether company A has potential and you have been able to obtain audited financial statements for company A for three years ago and for last year.

The other alternative is company B. You were able to obtain a set of this company's audited financial statements from the past year at no cost and you also found published projections on their website in respect of what they plan to do in the next five years and the expected economic consequences.

As you have spent money on investigating company A you would be inclined to invest in that company – to recoup the funds spent. In addition, you have two sets of financial statements that are audited so this gives you confidence in the information on which to base your decision.

Of the limited information that is available, which types of information do you think would be more relevant to your decision?

The IASB's *Conceptual Framework* identifies two principal **qualitative characteristics**, **relevance** and faithful representation. To be useful, information must be relevant and faithfully represented. Decision-making is not assisted by a faithful representation of an irrelevant phenomenon or by an unfaithful representation of a relevant phenomenon. Information on the two required characteristics is summarized in Figure 5.1.

Figure 5.1

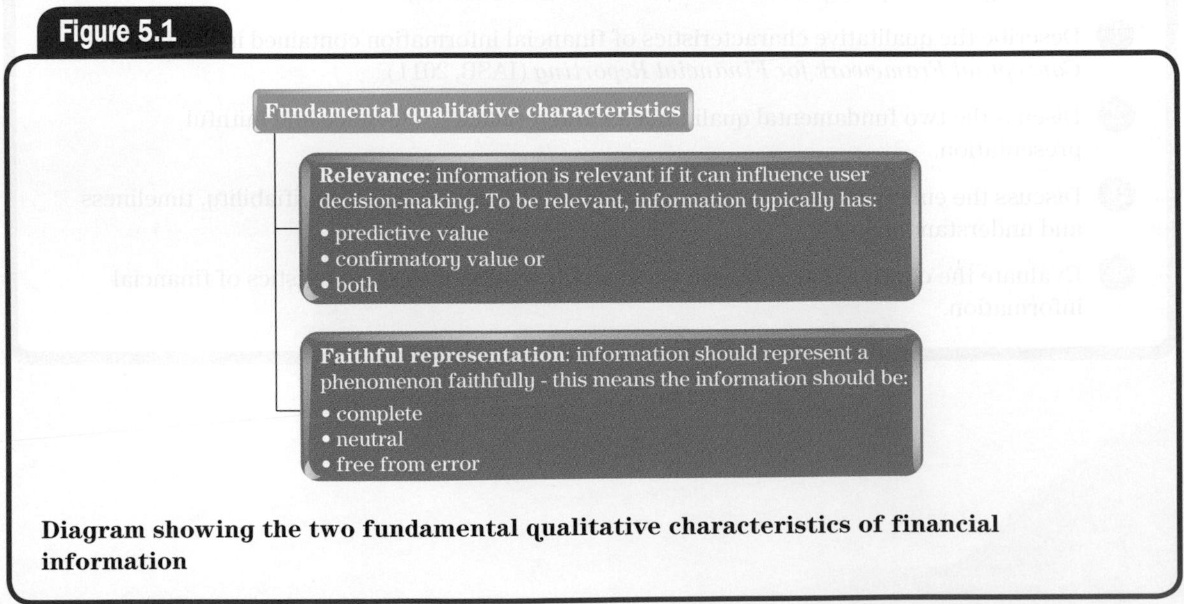

Fundamental qualitative characteristics
Relevance: information is relevant if it can influence user decision-making. To be relevant, information typically has:
• predictive value
• confirmatory value or
• both
Faithful representation: information should represent a phenomenon faithfully - this means the information should be:
• complete
• neutral
• free from error

Diagram showing the two fundamental qualitative characteristics of financial information

These characteristics are now discussed in turn.

5.2 Relevance

According to the *Conceptual Framework* information is relevant if it is capable of making a difference to the decisions made by users. This is the case even if the user elects not to use the information. The *Conceptual Framework* explains that relevant information typically has predictive value, confirmatory value or both. Information has **predictive value** if it can be used to help users to evaluate or assess past, present or future events. To have predictive value, information need not be in the form of an explicit forecast or prediction. However, the ability to make predictions from financial statements is enhanced by the manner in which the information on the past is presented. For this reason, comparatives are provided and exceptional, one-off and abnormal items are identified separately in the financial statements from normal activities. In addition, transactions involving newly acquired businesses or businesses that are being disposed of, are separately disclosed from transactions from continuing operations. Therefore, a diligent user can determine changes in the performance and financial position of the entity that resulted from normal activities that are expected to continue into the future.

Information has **confirmatory value** if it helps users to confirm or change their past evaluations and assessments. Information may have both predictive and confirmatory value.

Materiality

According to the *Conceptual Framework* the relevance of information is affected by its nature and **materiality**. Information is deemed material if its omission or misstatement could influence decisions that users make on the basis of financial information about a specific reporting entity. Use of the words 'specific reporting entity' is important as this highlights that materiality is entity specific. Materiality affects two main areas: presentation of financial information and application of accounting standards.

There are numerous references to materiality in the Companies Act 2006 and in IFRSs. They typically require separate disclosure of certain items, such as plant hire charges and rents receivable, *where the amounts are material*. Materiality provides guidance as to how a transaction or item of information should be classified in financial statements and/or whether it should be disclosed separately rather than being aggregated with other similar items. This is important as attention being afforded to immaterial items can mislead the user. The user should be able to look at a set of financial statements and focus on the important figures, not see a mass of information, much of which is of no use for economic decision-making. For example, it is irrelevant to disclose a yearly spend on stationery of £100 and a yearly spend on coffee of £75, if the company has a turnover of £10 million and total expenditure of £8 million. The immaterial items need to be grouped together, or aggregated into categories that are material. For example, the stationery and coffee could be combined into administration expenses that might have a total of £2.5 million. Knowing about the £100 spend on stationery, or the £75 spend on coffee, will not influence users' economic decision-making. Indeed, if such detail was provided, the user might not easily see that total expenses are £8 million. However, where an individual item that is normally aggregated with other similar items is expected to influence decision-making, then the item is said to be material and should be disclosed separately from the other similar items. For example, redundancy payments made to employees.

The second area of relevance is when deciding whether to comply with guidance given in accounting standards. As a general rule of thumb, accounting standards only apply to material items. Therefore, a company that spends £2,000 per year on heating oil (with other expenditure of £8 million) does not have to apply the cost flow inventory valuation techniques as detailed in *IAS 2 Inventories* (see Chapter 23, 'Inventory Valuation') when valuing its oil inventories. This saves the company time, hence money. Whether the final value for the year ended up as £2,000 or £2,100 would not affect users' economic decision-making. Another common application of materiality concerns whether an item of expenditure is to be regarded as a non-current asset and capitalized under *IAS 16 Property, Plant and Equipment* or treated as an expense. Where the amount is not material, the item would be treated as an expense even though it would be regarded as a non-current asset. Examples include relatively inexpensive tools (a spanner), sundry items of office equipment/stationery (hole punch, stapler) and sundry fixtures and fittings (picture hooks).

The only time that immaterial-sized items become 'material' is when the *nature* of the item makes them so. For example, when an entity experiences theft by staff or the directors have borrowed money from the entity, then even though the amounts may be small relative to the entity's overall performance and financial position, they indicate weaknesses that users should be aware of. Theft by staff indicates weak internal controls and directors borrowing money may highlight fiduciary problems.

Methods of determining materiality levels

Whether or not a transaction or item is material or significant is generally taken to be a matter of professional judgement. The *Conceptual Framework* states that materiality depends on the nature or magnitude, or both, of the items to which the information relates in the context of an individual entity's financial report. Therefore, materiality provides a **threshold** or cut-off point rather than being a primary qualitative characteristic which information must have if it is to be useful.

The principal factors to be taken into account when determining if information is material are set out below. It will usually be a combination of these factors, rather than any one in particular, that will determine materiality.

a An item's size is judged in the context both of the financial statements as a whole and of the other information available to users that would affect their evaluation of the financial statements. If the item is likely to influence users' perceptions of the trends in the performance and financial position of the entity, then it is material. For example, if the item were to cause a profit to turn to a loss, then it is more likely to be material. If there are two or more similar items, the materiality of the items in aggregate as well as the materiality of the items individually needs to be considered.

b Consideration should also be given to the item's nature. In particular, in relation to:

i what gave rise to the item;

ii how legal, sensitive and normal the transaction is;

iii the potential consequences of the event or transaction underlying the item;

iv the identity of the parties involved;

v the particular headings and disclosures that are affected.

An example is that of the reporting of a new segment. This may affect the assessment of the risks and opportunities facing the entity irrespective of the materiality of the results achieved by the new segment in the reporting period. This would be particularly important if the new segment were located in a country such as Afghanistan or Iraq (given the current unstable economic climates in both countries).

5.3 Faithful representation

The 2011 *Conceptual Framework* removed the characteristic called 'Reliability' and replaced it with 'Faithful Representation' (see Figure 5.1). According to the *Conceptual Framework, to be useful, information must also faithfully represent the phenomenon that it purports to represent'*. A phenomenon is **faithfully represented** when:

1 it is complete;

2 it is free from deliberate or systematic bias (i.e. it is neutral);

3 it is free from error.

Information that faithfully represents an underlying transaction or event will also reflect the substance of the underlying transaction or event.

Completeness

According to the *Conceptual Framework*, to be complete all information necessary for a user to understand the phenomena being depicted, including all necessary descriptions and explanations, is required. For example, if the phenomena being depicted is assets, to be **complete** the information should describe the nature of the assets (buildings, motor vehicles etc.), provide numerical information about the assets and information on what the numerical information represents (for example, historical cost, fair value, etc.). Disclosure on the quality of the items and circumstances that impacts on the financial information and the process used for reporting the items is also required. This may involve disclosing the use to which the assets are put and the depreciation policy used to allocate the cost of the assets to the statement of profit and loss.

Complete information also means no omissions. An omission can cause the financial statements to be false or misleading and thus unreliable and deficient in terms of its relevance.

Neutrality

According to the *Conceptual Framework*, financial information that is faithfully represented in financial statements needs to be **neutral** – in other words, free from bias. Relevant financial information is information that can influence user decision-making. However, information that is slanted, weighted, emphasized, de-emphasized or otherwise manipulated to portray information in a more favourable or less favourable light that may impact on user decision-making is not neutral. Financial statements are not neutral if, by the selection or presentation of information, they influence the making of a decision or judgement in order to achieve a predetermined result or outcome.

Free from error

Faithful representation does not mean that the information is 100% accurate. The *Conceptual Framework* states that information faithfully represents what it purports to, when it is **free from error**. According to the *Conceptual Framework* free from error means *'there are no errors or omissions in the description of the phenomenon, and the process used to produce the reported information has been selected and applied with no error in the process'*. This new definition is important due to the increase in use of estimates that are consistent with using measurement approaches such as fair value or value-in-use. Faithful representation of the phenomenon that is considered free from error would include providing clear and accurate information on estimated prices or estimated interest rates used, including the fact that the information is estimates, justification for the estimates and any limitations with the estimating process. The estimating process should be appropriate and applied without error.

To sum up, a statement of financial position should represent faithfully the transactions and other events that give rise to assets, liabilities and owners' equity and the statement of profit or loss should represent faithfully the transactions that give rise to income and expenditure in the period. A transaction or other event is faithfully represented in the financial statements if the way in which it is recognized, measured and presented in those statements corresponds closely to the economic effect of that transaction or event.

5.4 Enhancing qualitative characteristics

The *Conceptual Framework* identifies four qualitative characteristics that enhance the usefulness of information that is relevant and faithfully represented. These are summarized in Figure 5.2.

Figure 5.2

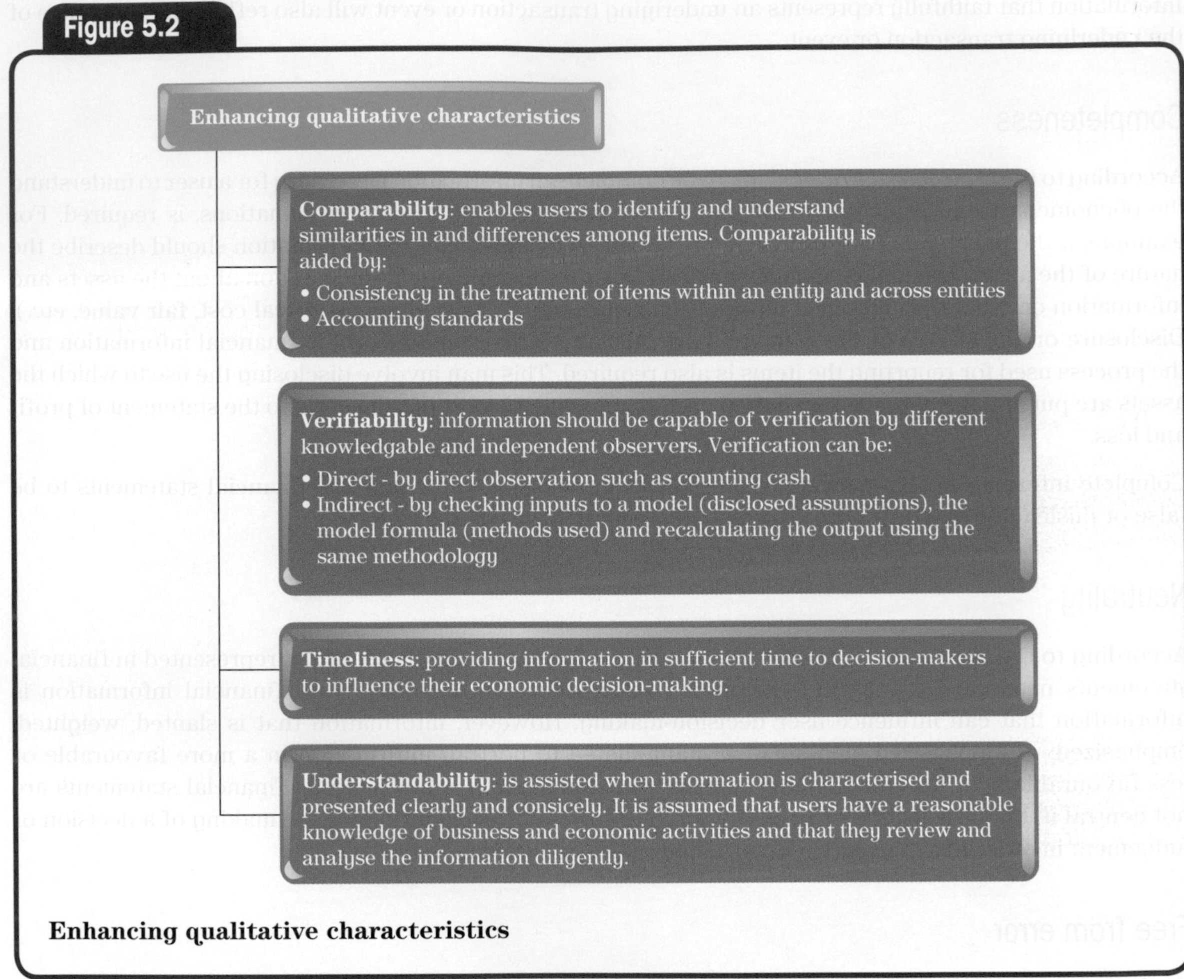

Enhancing qualitative characteristics
Comparability: enables users to identify and understand similarities in and differences among items. Comparability is aided by:
• Consistency in the treatment of items within an entity and across entities
• Accounting standards
Verifiability: information should be capable of verification by different knowledgable and independent observers. Verification can be:
• Direct - by direct observation such as counting cash
• Indirect - by checking inputs to a model (disclosed assumptions), the model formula (methods used) and recalculating the output using the same methodology
Timeliness: providing information in sufficient time to decision-makers to influence their economic decision-making.
Understandability: is assisted when information is characterised and presented clearly and consicely. It is assumed that users have a reasonable knowledge of business and economic activities and that they review and analyse the information diligently.

Enhancing qualitative characteristics

According to the *Conceptual Framework* enhancing qualitative characteristics should be maximized when possible; however, they cannot make information useful if the information is irrelevant or not faithfully presented.

Comparability

Users must be able to compare items within financial statements of an entity: (1) within one time period, (2) over time and (3) relative to other entities, in order to properly assess the entity's relative financial position, performance and changes in financial position. Several attributes of information are considered to be related to comparability including consistency, uniformity, accounting policies and comparative disclosures. These are now discussed in turn.

Consistency: Consistency is not the same as comparability. According to the *Conceptual Framework*, **consistency** refers to the use of the same methods for the same items, from period to period or across entities in a single period. On its own consistency is not an enhancing qualitative characteristic; however, consistency can help to achieve comparability. Consistency in the application of appropriate accounting policies is important for producing comparable information. Any changes to the accounting policies and the impact of these changes should be disclosed (discussed in detail in Chapter 4, 'The Conceptual Framework 2: Concepts, Principles and Policies').

Uniformity: Comparability is NOT uniformity. Some items should be similar and treated with consistency but other items should be treated differently to be faithfully represented. Comparability does not mean treating different items in the same manner just for the sake of uniformity.

Accounting standards and accounting policies: When accounting standards allow different accounting methods to be used to account for the same economic phenomena then comparability is diminished. Even so, accounting standards typically allow a limited number of accounting methods to be used and require disclosure of the methods being used as 'accounting policies'. Therefore, compliance with IFRSs, including disclosure of the accounting policies adopted by the entity, helps to achieve **comparability**. To assist in the making of comparisons despite inconsistencies, users need to be able to identify any differences between:

1 the accounting policies adopted by an entity to account for some transactions relative to others;

2 the accounting policies adopted from period to period by an entity;

3 the accounting policies adopted by different entities.

Users also need to be able to assess the impact of changes in the accounting policies of the entity. Therefore, disclosures are required detailing the reason for the change, the impact and cumulative impact on two years' statements of financial position and the opening balances.

Learning Activity 5.2

Go to the website of the following companies – Tesco plc, Ryanair plc, Diageo plc and Morrison Supermarkets plc. You already have copies of their most recent financial statements. For each company access the financial statements for the preceding two years. Go to the pages showing the accounting policies. Select two items (for example, turnover or inventory) and read the accounting policy being adopted. Note the consistency in application of accounting treatments across the three years.

Comparatives: To aid comparability financial statements should include the current year statements, the statement of comprehensive income and statement of financial position, presented beside the prior year statements (called **comparatives**). In Real World Example 5.1, Tesco plc provide their previous year's income and expense figures alongside the current year's items to aid comparison.

To be able to view similarly prepared financial statements over time allows users to make judgements about trends in performance and in changes in financial position and to use this information to predict into the future. This is required for economic decision-making, such as deciding whether to buy, sell or retain a holding of equity shares in the entity. As well as providing a copy of the previous period's statement of profit and loss and statement of financial position, the user needs to be able to ascertain if the figures have been prepared using the same methods of recognition and measurement; therefore, the material accounting policies should be disclosed and consistently applied.

Verifiability

When information is **verifiable** this does not mean that different knowledgeable and independent observers will agree with the exact amount being depicted in the financial statements; it does however mean that they should be able to reach a consensus that the information provided faithfully represents the underlying transaction/phenomenon. Some items can be verified quite easily, such as inventory values – wherein the number, cost price and valuation method (under IAS 2) of the inventory is known. In this instance the observer has just to recalculate the inventory amount and agree it to that disclosed in the financial statements. In other instances, verification is more difficult, as the financial information disclosed may be based on estimates that can only be directly verified in the future when an event happens. In

REAL WORLD EXAMPLE 5.1

Tesco plc

Group income statement

Year ended 23 February 2013	Points	52 weeks 2013 £m	52 weeks 2012 £m
Continuing operations			
Revenue (sales excluding VAT)	2	64,826	63,916
Cost of sales		(60,737)	(58,519)
Gross profit		4,089	5,397
Administrative expenses		(1,562)	(1,612)
Profit/losses arising on property-related items	3	(339)	397
Operating profit		2,188	4,182
Share of post-tax profits of joint ventures and associates	13	54	91
Finance income	5	177	176
Finance costs	5	(459)	(411)
Profit before tax	3	1,960	4,038
Taxation	6	(574)	(874)
Profit for the year		1,386	3,164
Loss for the year from discontinued operations	7	(1,266)	(350)
Profit for the year		120	2,814

Source: Tesco plc (2013) *Annual Report 2013*, p. 72, http://files.the-group.net/library/tesco/annualreport2013/pdfs/tesco_annual_report_2013.pdf, accessed September 2013.

these instances to assist verifiability the preparer must disclose sufficient information on the underlying assumptions with supporting information.

Timeliness

Timeliness is particular to the information being depicted. In some instances, the older the information the less relevant it becomes; in other instances older information becomes more relevant as it enables the user to better assess trends or improves the verifiability and hence faithful representation of the information.

Understandability

Understandability includes **users' abilities** and **aggregation and classification**. For information to be useful, users need to be able to perceive its significance. The *Conceptual Framework* states that those preparing financial statements are entitled to assume that users have a reasonable knowledge of business and economic activities and a willingness to study with reasonable diligence the information provided. However, this does not mean that anyone studying business or accounting is equipped fully to understand financial information. This is not possible as some transactions are very complex. In this regard, the *Conceptual Framework* states that in some instances even well-informed and diligent users may require the assistance of an adviser where there are complex economic phenomena.

To aid understandability, financial information is aggregated and classified according to standard **disclosure** formats (the statement of profit and loss and the statement of financial position are examples of this). As was explained earlier under 'Materiality', too much detail in financial statements can actually camouflage the real information that should be portrayed by the financial statements. The adage 'one cannot see the wood for the trees' captures this issue. Each entity has numerous different ledger accounts; indeed, large companies will have thousands of these. To provide a list of all the balances would be meaningless to users. For example, the benefit of providing a list of all the credit customer balances at the year end is limited, whereas a total figure for all the trade receivables does provide information that can be of use to users. They can compare the trade receivables this year to those last year. This will give some indication as to how credit management has changed over time.

Learning Activity 5.3

Obtain the financial statements for Tesco plc, Ryanair plc, Diageo plc and Morrison Supermarkets plc. Go to the pages showing the statement of comprehensive income and statement of financial position. Note the standardized presentation adopted by all of the companies. They are following the presentation rules set out in IAS 1. This consistent format aids understandability.

5.5 Constraints on the qualitative characteristics

Some underlying constraints on relevant and reliable information (timeliness, balance between benefit and cost, and balance between qualitative characteristics) are now outlined.

Timeliness

Conflict between relevance and faithful representation can arise over the timeliness of information. If there is undue delay in the reporting of information making it out of date, then this will affect its relevance. On the other hand, reporting on transactions and other events before all the uncertainties involved are resolved may affect the information's verifiability. This information cannot be omitted as omitting information from the financial statements because of verifiability concerns may affect the completeness, and therefore faithful representation of the information provided. If reporting is delayed until the underlying information is verifiable, it may be of little use to users who have economic decisions to make in the interim. In achieving a balance between timeliness and relevance and verifiability, the entity should take all steps possible to produce verifiable information in a timely manner. The overriding consideration affecting the timing of reporting should be '*how best to satisfy the information needs of users for economic decision-making*'.

Balance between benefit and cost

The general rule laid down in the *Conceptual Framework* is that '*the benefits derived from information should exceed the cost of providing that information*'. The evaluation of the benefits and costs is regarded as judgemental. A summary of some of the possible benefits and costs outlined in the *Conceptual Framework* is portrayed in Figure 5.3.

It is difficult to undertake a practical cost–benefit study on the provision of a particular type of information; nevertheless, the *Conceptual Framework* states that the preparers and standard setters should be aware of this general constraint. When preparing a standard the IASB seek information on the nature and quantity of expected costs and benefits from providers of financial information, users, auditors, academics and others.

Figure 5.3

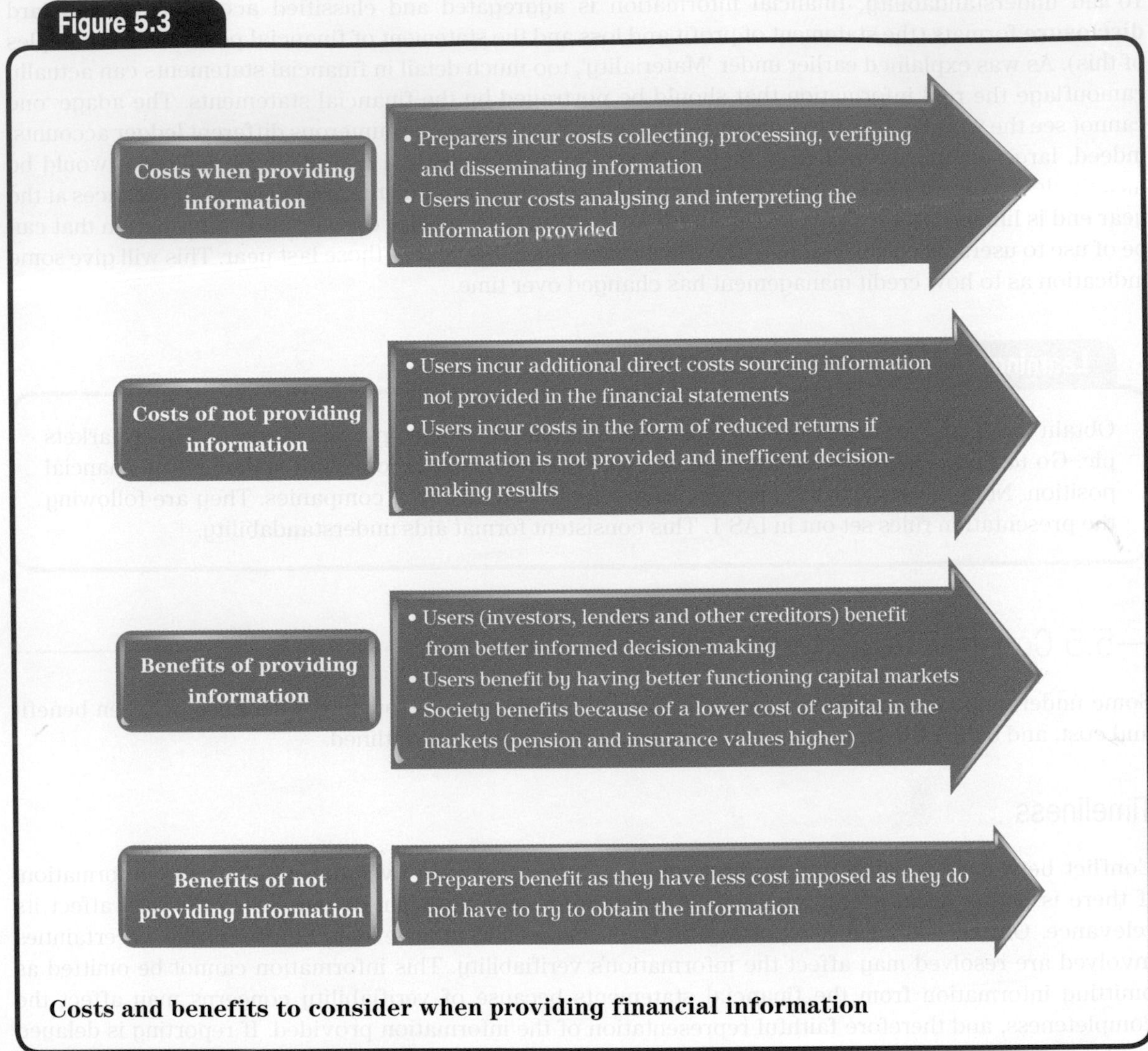

Costs when providing information
• Preparers incur costs collecting, processing, verifying and disseminating information
• Users incur costs analysing and interpreting the information provided
Costs of not providing information
• Users incur additional direct costs sourcing information not provided in the financial statements
• Users incur costs in the form of reduced returns if information is not provided and inefficent decision-making results
Benefits of providing information
• Users (investors, lenders and other creditors) benefit from better informed decision-making
• Users benefit by having better functioning capital markets
• Society benefits because of a lower cost of capital in the markets (pension and insurance values higher)
Benefits of not providing information
• Preparers benefit as they have less cost imposed as they do not have to try to obtain the information

Costs and benefits to consider when providing financial information

Balance between qualitative characteristics

In some instances, conflict may arise between the characteristics of relevance, faithful representation, comparability and understandability. In such circumstances, a trade-off needs to be found that still enables the objective of financial statements to be met. The relative importance of some of the characteristics in different instances is a matter for professional judgement. Some examples include the following:

1 *Relevance and verifiability.* Sometimes information that is the most relevant is not the most verifiable and vice versa. Choosing the amount at which to measure an asset or liability will sometimes involve such a conflict. In such circumstances, it will usually be appropriate to use the information that is the most relevant of whichever information is verifiable. For example, when a realistic estimate of the impact of a transaction or an event (such as the potential damages to be paid on a legal claim) cannot be made, that fact and details of the transaction or event should be disclosed.

2 *Understandability.* It may not always be possible to present a piece of relevant, faithfully represented and comparable information in a way that can be understood by all users. However, information that

is relevant and faithfully represented should not be excluded from the financial statements simply because it is too difficult for some users to understand as this would make the financial statements misleading.

3 *Consistency and faithful representation.* Consistency should not be confused with mere uniformity. It is not an end in itself and it should not be allowed to become an impediment to the introduction of improved accounting practices and accounting standards. It is not appropriate to keep accounting for an item in the same manner as before, when a new treatment emerges that provides information that is more relevant and provides a better faithful representation of the phenomena.

Summary

Qualitative characteristics are the attributes that make the information provided in financial statements useful to users. According to the *Conceptual Framework* the qualitative characteristics of financial information comprise two fundamental characteristics that make financial information useful – relevance and faithful representation. Relevant attributes include materiality, predictive value and confirmatory value. Information that is faithfully represented will be complete, neutral and free from error. The *Conceptual Framework* also refers to four enhancing qualitative characteristics. These comprise comparability, verifiability (direct and indirect), timeliness and understandability. Comparability includes consistency, uniformity and accounting standards, policies and disclosures. Understandability includes users' abilities, and aggregation and classification. Conflict can arise between the qualitative characteristics. For example, conflict can arise between relevance versus timeliness, costs versus benefits, relevance versus verifiability, understandability versus consistency and consistency versus faithful representation.

Key terms and concepts

aggregation and classification	94	materiality	89
comparability	93	neutral	91
comparatives	93	predictive value	89
complete	91	qualitative characteristics	88
confirmatory value	89	relevance	88
consistency	92	threshold	90
disclosure	95	understandability	94
faithful representation	90	users' abilities	94
free from error	91	verifiable	93

An asterisk after the question number indicates that there is a suggested answer in Appendix 2.

Review questions

connect

5.1 a Briefly explain the nature of a qualitative characteristic of financial information.

b Prepare a diagram showing the qualitative characteristics of financial information and the relationship between each of them.

5.2* Define and explain the qualitative characteristic of relevance, including its predictive value and confirmatory value.

5.3 Define and explain the qualitative characteristic of faithful representation, including the attributes of completeness, neutrality, and being free from error.

5.4 Define and explain the qualitative characteristics of comparability and understandability.

5.5 Define and explain materiality.

5.6 Describe the constraints on the qualitative characteristics of financial information.

5.7 According to the *Conceptual Framework* there is a potential conflict between the characteristics of relevance and verifiability. There can also be tension between two aspects of reliability – consistency and faithful representation. Explain the nature of these conflicts/tensions and how they can be reconciled.

5.8 'It is unrealistic to expect a conceptual framework of accounting to provide a basis for definitive or even generally accepted accounting standards in the foreseeable future because of inherent conflicts and inconsistencies between, for example, the qualitative characteristics of accounting information as well as the differing information needs and abilities of users.' Discuss.

References

Accounting Standards Board (1999) *Statement of Principles for Financial Reporting* (ASB).

International Accounting Standards Committee (2011) *Conceptual Framework for Financial Reporting* (IASB).

Chapter 6

Auditing, corporate governance and ethics

Learning Objectives:

After reading this chapter you should be able to do the following:

1. Explain the objective and principles of auditing as identified in *International Standard on Auditing 200 – Overall Objectives of the Independent Auditor and the Conduct of an Audit in Accordance with International Standards on Auditing* (IAASB, 2013a).
2. Describe the auditing assertions.
3. Describe the audit process.
4. Outline the content of a typical 'clean' audit report.
5. Explain the term *audit risk*.
6. Explain the expectations gap.
7. Define corporate governance and outline the reasons for the growth in its importance over the past few decades.
8. Describe some of the ethical conflicts facing management in the UK.
9. Explain auditor ethics and the importance of an auditor being ethical.

6.1 Auditing

An **audit** is an independent check on reported financial statements that are produced from an entity's accounting system. Therefore, an audit has to determine whether an entity's accounting system is appropriate or not. In 1973 the American Accounting Association (AAA), in a statement of basic auditing concepts, defined auditing as:

> *a systematic process of objectively obtaining and evaluating evidence regarding assertions about economic actions and events, to ascertain the degree of correspondence between those assertions and established criteria and communicating the results to interested users.*

Auditing assertions are indications that information is complete, accurate, properly prepared, applied in the correct period (cut-off), classified correctly, exists, is correctly valued, treated and disclosed in an understandable manner, and in accordance with accounting standards and applicable law. An auditor typically performs an audit on behalf of the members or equity shareholders of an entity.

International guidance on auditing and the conduct of an audit is provided by the International Auditing and Assurance Standards Board (IAASB). According to their website the IAASB is

> *an independent standard-setting body that serves the public interest by setting high-quality international standards for auditing, assurance, and other related standards, and by facilitating the convergence of international and national auditing and assurance standards. In doing so, the IAASB enhances the quality and consistency of practice throughout the world and strengthens public confidence in the global auditing and assurance profession.*

The IAASB supports 36 International Standards on Auditing and an International Standard or Quality Control. The UK Financial Reporting Council (FRC) has adopted all but one IAASB ISA, electing to revise and publish its own version of ISA 700, called *ISA (UK and Ireland) 700: The Independent Auditors Report on Financial Statements (Revised June 2013).*

Objective, scope and principles of auditing

ISA 200 – Overall Objectives of the Independent Auditor and the Conduct of an Audit in Accordance with International Standards on Auditing (IAASB, 2013a) states that:

> *The purpose of an audit is to enhance the degree of confidence of intended users in the financial statements. This is achieved by the expression of an opinion by the auditor on whether the financial statements are prepared, in all material respects, in accordance with an applicable financial reporting framework.*

The financial statements of limited companies are required by the Companies Act 2006 to give a true and fair view of the company's financial position at the reporting period date and of its profit or loss for the reporting period. Financial statements provide a **true and fair view** if they contain sufficient information (in quantity and quality) to satisfy the reasonable expectations of the users of financial statements. Auditors provide an informed professional independent *opinion* on this, and that is all. This opinion is based on the company's compliance with accounting practices, principles and norms. These are captured in accounting standards. Therefore, it is assumed that financial statements that are properly prepared in accordance with the *Conceptual Framework* and IFRS will show a true and fair view of the financial performance for the period being reported on and state of a company's affairs at the period end.

Guidance is provided in the APB's *Ethical Standards for Auditors* (APB, 2013) on what is required when undertaking an audit in order to properly form an opinion on the financial statements. This is summarized in Figure 6.1.

Figure 6.1

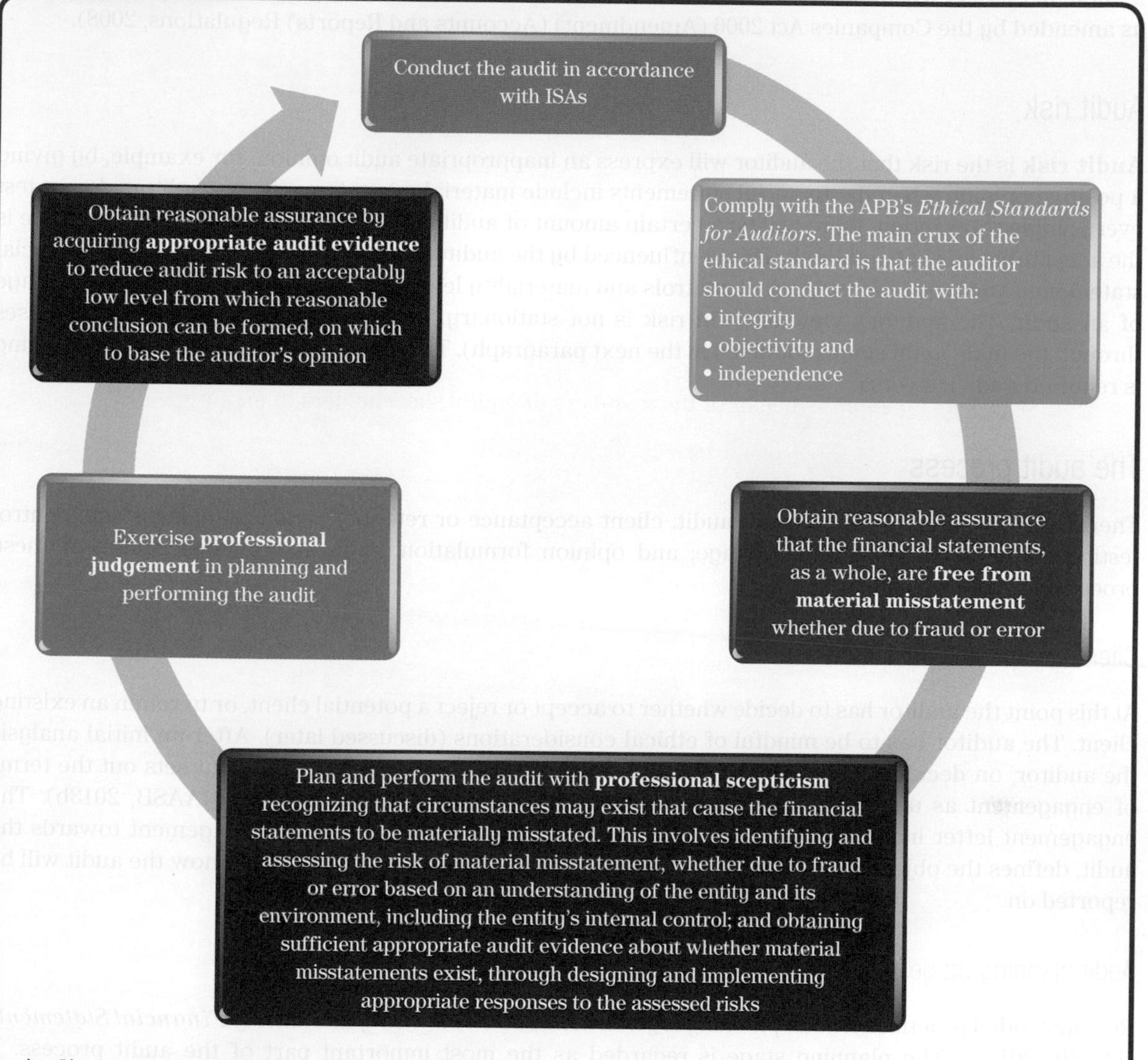

Conduct the audit in accordance with ISAs

Comply with the APB's *Ethical Standards for Auditors.* The main crux of the ethical standard is that the auditor should conduct the audit with:
- integrity
- objectivity and
- independence

Obtain reasonable assurance that the financial statements, as a whole, are **free from material misstatement** whether due to fraud or error

Plan and perform the audit with **professional scepticism** recognizing that circumstances may exist that cause the financial statements to be materially misstated. This involves identifying and assessing the risk of material misstatement, whether due to fraud or error based on an understanding of the entity and its environment, including the entity's internal control; and obtaining sufficient appropriate audit evidence about whether material misstatements exist, through designing and implementing appropriate responses to the assessed risks

Exercise **professional judgement** in planning and performing the audit

Obtain reasonable assurance by acquiring **appropriate audit evidence** to reduce audit risk to an acceptably low level from which reasonable conclusion can be formed, on which to base the auditor's opinion

Auditor requirements

The scope of an audit is not only restricted to providing an opinion on financial statements; some companies have to get grant applications verified, hospitals have to have their systems for processing patients checked, and so on.

Why is a statutory external audit required?

All the companies that are listed on stock exchanges are publicly owned. Indeed, many limited companies have owners who are not involved in the management of the company. Companies produce financial statements that portray the performance and financial position of an entity. However, these are open to manipulation by management, so owners require an independent audit to assess if management are discharging their stewardship function appropriately (i.e. looking after the owner's assets). A statutory audit is required for all listed companies and larger companies. Private limited companies may be exempt from needing an audit where they meet two of the following three criteria – turnover of no more than £6.5 million; net assets worth no more than £3.26 million; and fewer than 50 employees (Companies Act 2006 as amended by the Companies Act 2006 (Amendment) (Accounts and Reports) Regulations, 2008).

Audit risk

Audit risk is the risk that the auditor will express an inappropriate audit opinion: for example, by giving a positive opinion when the financial statements include material misstatements. As auditors do not test every single transaction, there will be a certain amount of audit risk. What the auditor has to evaluate is the acceptable level of audit risk. This is influenced by the auditor's knowledge of the entity, the financial statements, audit assertions, internal controls and materiality level. Audit risk is prevalent at every stage of an audit. The auditor's view of audit risk is not stationary. It may change as the audit progresses through the main audit stages (outlined in the next paragraph). The higher the audit risk, the more testing is required and vice versa.

The audit process

There are five main stages to every audit: client acceptance or retention; audit planning stage; control testing stage; substantive testing stage; and opinion formulation stage. A brief description of these processes is now provided.

Client acceptance or retention

At this point the auditor has to decide whether to accept or reject a potential client, or to retain an existing client. The auditor has to be mindful of ethical considerations (discussed later). After an initial analysis the auditor, on deciding to accept the client, will issue a **letter of engagement** that sets out the terms of engagement as under *ISA 210 – Agreeing the Terms of Audit Engagements* (IAASB, 2013b). The engagement letter includes a summary of responsibilities of the auditor and management towards the audit, defines the objective of the audit, the scope of the work to be carried out and how the audit will be reported on.

Audit planning stage

Recommended practice on audit planning is given in *ISA 300 – Planning an Audit of Financial Statements* (IAASB, 2013c). The planning stage is regarded as the most important part of the audit process. It determines the audit approach to take. The plan will be influenced by the auditors' knowledge of the business, risk assessment of the entity's controls and records, the risk of fraud and an analytical review of the financial statements and other provided information at the planning stage. Effective audit planning should result in a more focused, prompt, efficient, cost-effective and higher quality audit for the client. It should result in the focus on risky areas; that is, **auditing by exception**. The **audit plan** is detailed in the **audit planning memorandum**. The auditor will have to complete an audit plan for every type of item being audited, such as inventories, trade receivables, income, and so on.

Control testing stage

The planning stage will detail the extent of testing required on information systems controls (**compliance testing**). At this stage the systems will be thoroughly recorded and controls noted. *ISA 330 – The Auditor's Responses to Assessed Risks* (IAASB, 2013d) requires that the auditor should carry out tests of controls when the risk assessment relies on those controls (both when the operating effectiveness of the controls is relied on and when it is believed that the controls reduce the potential for material misstatement) and when substantive tests alone do not provide sufficient appropriate audit evidence at assertion level.

Substantive testing stage

Substantive testing involves testing in detail individual transactions that have been selected using statistical techniques to ensure that they have been properly authorized, processed and accounted for correctly. They focus on ensuring that audit assertions can be made (see Figure 6.2).

Figure 6.2

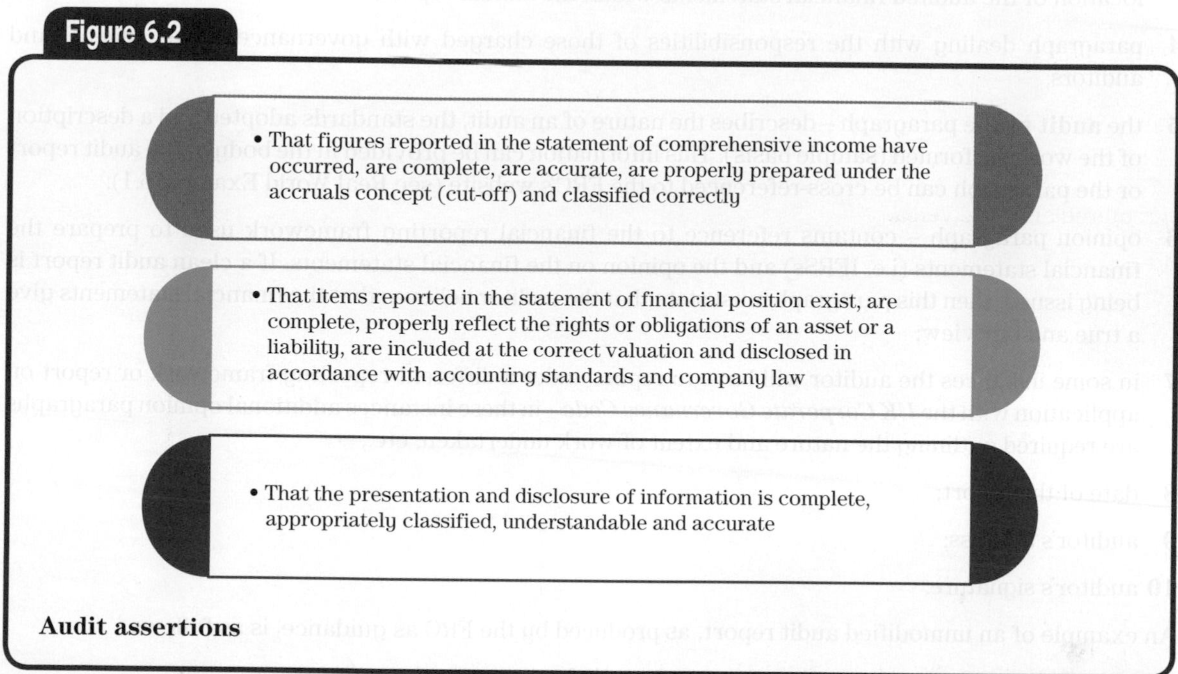

• That figures reported in the statement of comprehensive income have occurred, are complete, are accurate, are properly prepared under the accruals concept (cut-off) and classified correctly
• That items reported in the statement of financial position exist, are complete, properly reflect the rights or obligations of an asset or a liability, are included at the correct valuation and disclosed in accordance with accounting standards and company law
• That the presentation and disclosure of information is complete, appropriately classified, understandable and accurate

Audit assertions

Opinion formulation stage

This involves determining whether, based on the risk assessment, based on the results of tests completed and based on management assertions, the auditor believes that the financial statements show a true and fair view of the entity's financial performance and financial position. Before the opinion is provided, the audit work will be reviewed by an audit manager, then by an audit partner and management will have been asked to formally provide assertions about the completeness, validity and accuracy of the information provided in the financial statements. This is important as an audit is provided on a test basis. In general, an assertion about **completeness** is management stating that all items that should be included are included. An assertion about **validity** is management stating that the financial statements do not include any information that should not be included and an assertion about **accuracy** is management confirming that items that are included are included correctly.

The audit report

An audit opinion is provided in an **audit report**. The audit report is included with a company's financial statements in a company's annual return. Indeed, the financial statements cannot be issued without it. The form and content of an audit report is provided in *ISA (UK and Ireland) 700 (Revised) – The Independent Auditors Report on Financial Statements* (FRC, 2013). The audit report has standard form and content – it is argued that this helps to promote users' understandability and highlights variations/problems when they occur. An audit report with a positive opinion on a company's financial statements is called an **unmodified, unqualified** or a **clean audit report**. The main contents of a clean audit report include:

1 title (independent audit report);

2 addressee (typically to the shareholders of company name);

3 introductory paragraph – provides the date of the financial statements, the period covered and the location of the audited financial statements within the annual report;

4 paragraph dealing with the responsibilities of those charged with governance (management) and auditors;

5 the **audit scope** paragraph – describes the nature of an audit, the standards adopted and a description of the work performed (sample basis). This information can be provided in the body of the audit report or the paragraph can be cross-referenced to the FRC's website (see Real World Example 6.1);

6 opinion paragraph – contains reference to the financial reporting framework used to prepare the financial statements (i.e. IFRSs) and the opinion on the financial statements. If a clean audit report is being issued, then this paragraph must state that the auditor believes that the financial statements give a true and fair view;

7 in some instances the auditor will have to report under a different reporting framework or report on application with the *UK Corporate Governance Code* – in these instances additional opinion paragraphs are required outlining the nature and extent of work undertaken, etc.;

8 date of the report;

9 auditor's address;

10 auditor's signature.

An example of an unmodified audit report, as produced by the FRC as guidance, is as follows.

REAL WORLD EXAMPLE 6.1

Independent Auditor's Report to the Members of XYZ PLC

We have audited the group financial statements of XYZ PLC for the year ended 31 December 2014 which comprise the Group Statement of Financial Position, the Group Statement of Comprehensive Income, the Group Statement of Cash Flows, the Group Statement of Changes in Equity and the related notes on pages 25 to 114. The financial reporting framework that has been applied in their preparation is applicable law and International Financial Reporting Standards (IFRSs) as adopted by the European Union.

Respective responsibilities of directors and auditor

As explained more fully in the Directors' Responsibilities Statement set out on page 24 the directors are responsible for the preparation of the group financial statements and for being satisfied that they give a true and fair view. Our responsibility is to audit and express an opinion on the group financial statements in accordance with applicable law and International Standards on Auditing (UK and Ireland). Those standards require us to comply with the Auditing Practices Board's (APB's) Ethical Standards for Auditors.

Scope of the audit of the financial statements

Either:

A description of the scope of an audit of financial statements is [provided on the FRC's website at www.frc.uk/apb/scope/private.cfm]/[set out on page 23 of the Annual Report].

Or:

An audit involves obtaining evidence about the amounts and disclosures in the financial statements sufficient to give reasonable assurance that the financial statements are free from material misstatement, whether caused by fraud or error. This includes an assessment of: whether the accounting policies are appropriate to the group's circumstances and have been consistently applied and adequately disclosed; the reasonableness of significant accounting estimates made by the directors; and the overall presentation of the financial statements. In addition, we read all the financial and non-financial information in the [*describe the annual report*] to identify material inconsistencies with the audited financial statements and to identify any information that is apparently materially incorrect based on, or materially inconsistent with, the knowledge acquired by us in the course of performing the audit. If we become aware of any apparent material misstatements or inconsistencies we consider the implications for our report.

Opinion on financial statements

In our opinion the group financial statements:

- give a true and fair view of the state of the group's affairs as at 31 December 2014 and of its profit for the year then ended;
- have been properly prepared in accordance with IFRSs as adopted by the European Union; and
- have been prepared in accordance with the requirements of the Companies Act 2006 and Article 4 of the IAS Regulation.

Our assessment of risks of material misstatement

[*Insert a description of those specific assessed risks of material misstatement that were identified by the auditor and which had the greatest effect on the audit strategy; the allocation of resources in the audit; and directing the efforts of the engagement team.*]

Our application of materiality

[*Insert an explanation of how the auditor applied the concept of materiality in planning and performing the audit. Such explanation shall specify the threshold used by the auditor as being materiality for the financial statements as a whole.*]

An overview of the scope of our audit

[*Insert an overview of the scope of the audit, including an explanation of how the scope addressed the assessed risks of material misstatement and was influenced by the auditor's application of materiality.*]

[*The disclosures about the above three matters are made in a manner that complements the description of significant issues relating to the financial statements required to be set out in the separate section of the annual report describing the work of the audit committee in discharging its responsibilities.*]

Opinion on other matter prescribed by the Companies Act 2006

In our opinion the information given in the Directors' Report for the financial year for which the group financial statements are prepared is consistent with the group financial statements.

Matters on which we are required to report by exception

We have nothing to report in respect of the following:

Under the ISAs (UK and Ireland), we are required to report to you if, in our opinion, information in the annual report is:

- materially inconsistent with the information in the audited financial statements; or
- apparently materially incorrect based on, or materially inconsistent with, our knowledge of the Group acquired in the course of performing our audit; or
- is otherwise misleading.

In particular, we are required to consider whether we have identified any inconsistencies between our knowledge acquired during the audit and the directors' statement that they consider the annual report is fair, balanced and understandable and whether the annual report appropriately discloses those matters that we communicated to the audit committee which we consider should have been disclosed.

Under the Companies Act 2006 we are required to report to you if, in our opinion:

- certain disclosures of directors' remuneration specified by law are not made; or
- we have not received all the information and explanations we require for our audit.

Under the Listing Rules we are required to review:

- the directors' statement, set out on page 21, in relation to going concern; and
- the part of the Corporate Governance Statement relating to the company's compliance with the nine provisions of the UK Corporate Governance Code specified for our review; and
- certain elements of the report to shareholders by the Board on directors' remuneration.

Other matter

We have reported separately on the parent company financial statements of XYZ PLC for the year ended 31 December 2013 and on the information in the Directors' Remuneration Report that is described as having been audited. [That report includes an emphasis of matter] [The opinion in that report is (qualified)/(an adverse opinion)/(a disclaimer of opinion)].

[***Signature***] Address

John Smith (Senior statutory auditor) *Date*

for and on behalf of ABC LLP, Statutory Auditor

Source: FRC, 2013, Illustrative Example of a UK auditor's report reflecting the requirements of ISA (UK and Ireland) 700 (Revised June 2013), http://www.frc.org.uk/Our-Work/Publications/Audit-and-Assurance-Team/ISA-700-(UK-and-Ireland)-700-(Revised)/Illustrative-example-of-a-UK-auditor-s-report.aspx, accessed September 2013. Reproduced with permission.

There are two types of **modified audit report** (also called **adverse opinion**, or **qualified audit report**): those where (1) matters arise that do not affect the auditor's opinion; and (2) matters arise that do affect the auditor's opinion.

There is only one type of modified audit report that can also be regarded as clean (i.e. not affecting the audit opinion) and that is when the auditor wants to emphasize some matter to the reader of the financial statements. In this instance the auditor includes an **'emphasis of matter paragraph'** usually after the opinion paragraph so the reader is in no doubt that the financial statements are 'clean'. This paragraph refers to the issue briefly and usually cross-references the audit report to a note in the financial statements where more detail is provided.

Expectations gap

The **expectations gap** is the gap between the auditors' role and opinion and the public's perception of the auditors' role. Many members of the public believe that auditors are looking for fraud when they undertake an audit, that auditors say the financial statements are accurate (many believe the financial statements to be 100 per cent accurate if audited), that auditors certify financial statements, that a 'clean' audit report is stating the financial statements are accurate, that the auditors are responsible for the financial statements and that auditors should give warnings about the future of the entity when they suspect it is going to fail.

However, in practice auditors argue that managers prepare the financial statements; therefore they are responsible for them. Auditors are quick to argue that an audit report is only an opinion that at best provides reasonable assurance that the financial statements are free from **material misstatement**. The audit report does not say the financial statements are correct. Auditors only check a sample of transactions, not every transaction; therefore, they cannot guarantee that fraud will be detected, though they plan their tests so as to uncover any fraud that may cause material misstatement in the financial statements. An audit does not guarantee that a company will succeed in the future.

As is noted in this section and highlighted in previous paragraphs, management are responsible for the financial statements that they prepare or that are prepared on their behalf. Management are also fully responsible for the running of the company. The next section 'Corporate governance' outlines in brief the responsibility that management have for the proper conduct of their management of affairs on behalf of a company's equity shareholders.

6.2 Corporate governance

Corporate governance has been defined in the Cadbury Report (1992) as:

> *the system by which companies are directed and controlled.*

Agency theory (the equity holder and director conflict)

Corporate governance is important because of the conflict that arises between owners and management. Management are employed by a company's owners (its equity shareholders) to manage the company on their behalf; therefore, they are agents for the equity shareholders (who are the principals). However, management have difficulty making decisions which, though in shareholders' best interests, may damage their own interests. For example, equity shareholder value is typically enhanced by taking decisions that maximize the long-run earnings of a company. However, these decisions may result in the rejection of other investments that provide higher short-term returns. Directors' bonus packages may be tied into short-term profitability. This conflict is discussed in the relevant literature under **'agency theory'**.

A commonly used method to encourage congruence between the aims of directors and equity shareholders is to align the financial rewards available to the board of directors with those of the equity shareholders. This may involve setting bonuses and rewards for meeting long-term performance targets or to award share options to directors as part of their salary package. **Share options** allow the holder to purchase shares at a set price on a future date – usually in 3–10 years' time. If management has performed well and taken decisions that maximize equity holder value, then the share price on the exercise date will exceed the target exercise price when the options were first issued. Management can then purchase the shares at the lower exercise price and can either sell them immediately, realizing a financial gain, or retain the shares and benefit from future capital value increases.

Every company incurs a considerable amount of expenditure in trying to reduce/monitor the agency problem. These costs are termed '**agency costs**' and include audit fees, costs associated with the remuneration committee and costs of aligning salaries with equity holder objectives. The costs of policing corporate governance are agency costs. Ensuring that a company has strong corporate governance is the responsibility of company directors, not the equity shareholders – though they suffer the cost of it. Good corporate governance practices help to reduce agency conflicts.

The rise in the importance of corporate governance

A number of high-profile company scandals and collapses in Britain (Robert Maxwell, Mint and Boxed, Levitt, Polly Peck, Barings Bank, Royal Bank of Scotland (RBS)), in Ireland (Powerscreen, Allied Irish Banks) and in the US (WorldCom, Enron, Lehman Bros) have increased the attention afforded by regulators to the corporate governance of companies. The scandals reduced public confidence in financial reporting, the audit process and the worth of regulatory watchdogs (e.g. the London Stock Exchange, auditors and the government). To build confidence, the London Stock Exchange set up a committee in 1991, to investigate the responsibilities of executive and non-executive directors, to determine whether an audit committee is required, to clarify the principal responsibilities of auditors and to consider the responsibilities the board of directors has to other stakeholders. This committee issued a report in 1992: the first '*code of best practices*' for the governance of a company. This report is known as the ***Cadbury Report*** (Cadbury, 1992) after Sir Adrian Cadbury, the lead investigator.

The *Cadbury Report* detailed the composition of a typical board of directors in a company with good corporate governance practices and outlined the board's recommended responsibilities. It suggested that the board of directors meet regularly, take steps to ensure that they have control of the company at all times and ensure that the board has sufficient segregation of duties so that no one director has ultimate control. The report recommended conditions to ensure the independence of non-executive directors (they should not be awarded share options as remuneration, have no dealings with the company and be able to obtain independent advice at the company's expense). The report recommended that executive directors (and non-executive directors) hold office for only three years, though they could be reappointed by equity holders. The report also recommended the establishment of two committees: a remuneration committee to deal with remuneration packages, and an audit committee to control the internal audit within a company. Companies listed on the London Stock Exchange had to disclose the extent of compliance with the *Cadbury Report*. Non-public limited companies were not required to disclose the extent of their compliance; however, it was recommended by professional accounting bodies that it be included.

The ***Greenbury Report*** (Greenbury, 1995) strengthened some of the suggestions made in the *Cadbury Report* by recommending that all members of the remuneration committee be non-executive directors, and a remuneration report setting out all the remuneration details for each director (executive and non-executive) should be made available in the annual report of a company. A further report, the ***Hampel Report*** (Hampel, 1998), recommended that the role of the chairman and chief executive be segregated and that directors receive training on corporate governance. This report recommends that directors narrow their responsibilities to their primary duty – the enhancement of equity holders' value. These reports were integrated to form the ***Combined Code*** in 1999 (FRC, 1999).

Learning Activity 6.1

Visit the Ryanair plc website and view a copy of their annual report. The qualitative reports at the front of the annual report will contain information on the company's corporate governance. Make a list (in bullet point form) of the corporate governance procedures/structures in place for the company.

Corporate governance, risk and strategic management

Risk identification, evaluation and management have become more important over the past two decades. After the establishment of the *Combined Code* of practice for corporate governance (FRC, 1999), a working party was established to provide best practice guidance on how to comply with the *Combined Code*. This group was led by Nigel Turnbull and their recommendations were published in 1999, in a report called *Internal Control: Guidance for Directors on the Combined Code* (referred to as the ***Turnbull Report***) (LSE, 1999). The report suggests that a risk-based approach should be taken when establishing internal controls and when reviewing their effectiveness. The ethos of the report is not that a company should undertake a box-ticking exercise to ensure compliance, but should embrace the principles of risk-based management as a means of increasing company value. This approach is captured by Sir Brian Jenkins, the Chairman of the Corporate Governance Group of the ICAEW, in the preface to the guidance report: *Implementing Turnbull: A Board Room Briefing*, 1999 (LSE, 1999) when he stated:

> “*for directors the task ahead is to implement control over the wider aspects of business risk in such a way as to add value rather than merely go through a compliance exercise. There is also a need to get the buy-in of people at all levels of the organisation and to focus on risk management and internal controls in such a way as to improve the business.*”

The *Combined Code* (1999) was updated in 2003 to include the *Turnbull Report* (LSE, 1999) and the ***Smith Report*** (FRC, 2005a) and updated again in 2005 (FRC, 2005b) by a working party led by Douglas Flint. The findings of this review were that there is widespread support for the recommendations of Turnbull, with most companies adopting a risk-based approach to their strategic management. Indeed, the US Securities and Exchange Commission (SEC) identified the Turnbull guidance as a suitable framework for reporting on a company's internal controls for financial reporting. The US legal requirements for disclosures in relation to internal controls are set out in section 404(a) of the Sarbanes–Oxley Act (2002) and the SEC's rules. In contrast to the US's 'rule-based' approach, in the UK the approach is 'principle-based', with Flint recommending that this approach remain.

The financial crises stimulated a further review of the corporate governance of companies by the FRC and resulted in new corporate governance guidance for UK entities called *The UK Corporate Governance Code* (FRC, 2012). The main changes to the *Combined Code* are that it is now recommended that all directors of FTSE 350 companies be subject to re-election yearly and that directors disclose how they have complied with the code and explain reasons for non-compliance if relevant. In addition the report suggests that: '*More attention be afforded to the spirit of the code as well as its letter. Secondly that the impact of shareholders in monitoring the code could and should be enhanced by better interaction between the boards of listed companies and their shareholders.*' To this end the FRC published *The UK Stewardship Code* in July 2010 to encourage engagement between investors and investees (Hamill et al., 2010). There is also a requirement that a greater emphasis be placed on risk identification and management.

An example of the risk-based approach to governance can be found in Diageo. Diageo, a large drinks company which owns brand names such as Guinness, Baileys, Smirnoff and Johnny Walker, has dedicated pages of information on risk factors in its 2013 Annual Report (pages 39 to 42). In the business description its identifies 17 potential risks categorized into themes including: risks relating to the global economy, risks related to the industry, risks related to regulation, risks related to Diageo's business, and risks related to its securities. In the business review section (page 79), which forms part of the audited part of the financial statements, Diageo provides specific information on the identification and management of funding risk, currency risk, interest rate risk, liquidity risk, credit risk, commodity price risk and insurance, and refers to more detail being provided in the notes to the financial statements (see Real World Example 6.2).

REAL WORLD EXAMPLE 6.2

Diageo Annual Report 2013

The group's funding, liquidity and exposure to foreign currency, interest rate risks, financial credit risk and commodity price risk are conducted within a framework of board-approved policies and guidelines, which are recommended and subsequently monitored by the finance committee. This committee is described in the corporate governance report. The finance committee receives monthly reports on the activities of the treasury department, including any exposures that differ from the defined benchmarks.

The group purchases insurance for commercial or, where required, for legal or contractual reasons. In addition, the group retains some insurable risk where external insurance is not considered to be an economic means of mitigating this risk. Loan, trade and other receivables exposures are managed locally in the operating units where they arise and credit limits are established as deemed appropriate for the customer.

For a detailed analysis of the group's exposure to foreign exchange, interest rate, commodity price, credit and liquidity risks see note 19 to the consolidated financial statements.

Source: Diageo Annual Report (2013), http://www.diageoreports.com/, accessed September 2013.

Learning Activity 6.2 encourages students to read the most recent Code and to apply their knowledge to a practical example.

Learning Activity 6.2

Download and read the UK Corporate Governance Code (https://www.frc.org.uk/Our-Work/Publications/Corporate-Governance/UK-Corporate-Governance-Code-September-2012.pdf). Then put the theoretical guidance into practice by trying this short question. The following information provides details of the board of directors and their salaries for a fictitious UK quoted company. This information is included in their financial statements.

Board of directors (20X5)		***Basic Salary (£)***	***Outstanding share options (No.)***
Chairman and chief executive	R.A. Gilway	410,000	1,000,000
Finance director	Ms I.M. Smyth (CA)	240,000	200,000
Production director	K.L. Mindfield	170,000	200,000
Other executive directors	S.R. Winery	150,000	100,000
	Lord Give	200,000	200,000
	G.H. Jazz	160,000	100,000
Non-executive directors	Dr A.D. Hald	40,000	120,000
	Mrs R.T. Gilway	50,000	200,000

Dr A.D. Hald has plenty of experience of being a director. He is currently also a non-executive director of seven other quoted companies.

Mrs Gilway was recommended for the post by R.A. Gilway, her brother-in-law.

The agenda for the forthcoming Annual General Meeting (AGM) of the company is as follows:

1. Apologies
2. Minutes of the last meeting
3. Matters arising from the last meeting
4. Consideration of the remuneration of board members for 20X6
5. Proposal for the formation of an audit committee, with Ms I.M. Smyth, Lord Give and Dr A.D. Hald as nominated committee members.
6. Any other business including other potential committees.

What steps do you think the company should take to ensure that it complies with current corporate governance guidance in Britain and Ireland?

A number of practical issues arise from Learning Activity 6.2 and the main issues are now outlined, in brief. R.A. Gilway should not hold both the posts of chairman and chief executive. Current guidance specifically suggests that these two posts be held by separate individuals. It is also deemed to be good practice to have more non-executive directors on the board than executive directors as this gives them power over certain decision-making. Therefore it may be in the company's interest to replace some of the executive directors with non-executives. The remuneration disclosures just include basic salary details. Full details of all remuneration should be included – including pension contributions, car benefits, option values (not just numbers) and details thereof. The number of directors on the board should be odd. It is currently even. This is to enable decision-making to take place and not to have a deadlock situation. Non-executive directors should not participate in share options as this may undermine their independence. Therefore the two non-executives should give up their options. A remuneration committee should be established to determine the remuneration of the board. It should be made up of non-executive directors, preferably three. The audit committee should also be made up of non-executive directors who can contact the external auditors. The non-executive directors should not be related to the executive directors, even if an in-law. Mrs R.T. Gilway should resign and be replaced by a suitably qualified independent director. The non-executive directors should not have more than one other non-executive directorship. They should be encouraged to give up some of their other appointments. Otherwise it could be argued that they are too busy to fully challenge the executive board. They should also set up a risk committee to highlight risks facing the company and to determine the impact of the risk and to come up with ways to manage that risk. Finally, all directors should be subject to re-election at the AGM and this should be part of the agenda. The appointment and role of the external auditors and other expert consultants should be affirmed at the meeting.

6.3 Ethics

This text will deal with two streams of ethics: **management ethics** and **auditor ethics**.

Management ethics

As a country the UK has some of the highest ethical business standards in the world. Indeed, in many instances, having regard to ethical practices might restrict the profitability of a company. For example, in a global economy, there is much to be gained by companies that have products that can be made in countries that have no employment laws. For example, profits and company value will increase if a company is able to access cheap labour, or even child labour, for next to nothing (so long as the company does not advertise its policy in this area, as this may cause an adverse reaction in the stock market, as equity holders are likely to react irrationally). In these circumstances, companies justify their actions by arguing that some income to a family is better than none, or by highlighting the fact that, though the salaries paid are low, they are higher than those paid by indigenous companies. Many companies also use some of their profits for social purposes in the communities that they are located in, by for example, building schools, building churches, building hospitals or getting running water. These are deemed to be signs of these companies acting ethically.

The use of bribery or corruption may be seen as part and parcel of normal trade within certain countries, but not in the UK. In a global economy, when there is so much pressure to perform, directors may consider using unethical approaches to secure a contract. However, unethical behaviour cannot be defended on the

Figure 6.3

Threat	Guidance
Business relationships	• Allowed only if the transactions are in the normal course of business, are at arm's length and are immaterial to both parties.
Financial interests	• An auditor should not have any direct financial interest in an audit client or any indirect material financial interest that may question their independence.
Employment relationships	• An audit member of staff can only work on a part-time basis for a client and must not hold a management role nor make management decisions and should not direct the audit client into a particular position or accounting treatment.
Family and other personal relationships	• Should be reported immediately and a decision taken as to whether this reduces independence. It may be necessary to select an audit team that has no links with the client.
Length of service	• The audit firm should rotate the engagement partner on audit engagements, as close relationships between the client and individual auditor may foster over time, reducing perceived independence. In plcs, rotation should be at least every five years.
Fees, remuneration, litigation, gifts and hospitality	• The fee from a non-listed audit client should not exceed 15 per cent of the audit firm's total fee income and the fee from a listed audit client should not exceed 10 per cent. In these instances the auditors should resign as they are not deemed to be independent. Auditors, or their family, should not accept gifts from audit clients unless the amount is insignificant. The provision of non-audit services, such as tax advice, is also severely restricted.

Threats to auditor independence

grounds of it being normal practice in a country, nor can it be defended by the argument 'if I did not do it, someone else would' or 'we would lose the business to a competitor who does it'.

Acting unethically does not have to be as dramatic as the examples provided in the previous two paragraphs. A company should also act ethically in relation to company stakeholders because doing so is in a company's long-term interest. By treating customers and suppliers correctly, future sales and supplies will be secured. Paying loan creditors on time the interest and capital repayments they are due will ensure that this source of finance can be used again in the future. Avoiding the practice of gearing the company unnecessarily just to make returns to equity holders builds confidence in the management of the company, from the creditors' perspective. Showing concern for employee welfare (and acting on it) will ensure loyalty and increased effort from employees. By taking steps to reduce pollution, the health of employees will not deteriorate, which will reduce staff absenteeism. In addition, thc company's image will be improved and future sales may result. Equity shareholders should also be treated fairly; they should be kept well informed about a company's performance, future developments and strategies. Equity shareholders should not be surprised by the dividend that they are paid. If equity holders feel that they are being treated fairly, then the market will value the company higher and the equity holder body is more likely to support director decisions in the future.

Auditor ethics

To be an auditor, an accounting practice must be registered under law with a Recognized Supervisory Body (RSB) and be eligible for appointment as an auditor under the rules of that Body. Under law auditors should be independent, carry out their work with integrity, be technically up to date, be competent and maintain competence and be able to defend their audit work. Most accounting institutes are RSBs who apply the ethical standards as set out by the APB's *Ethical Standards for Auditors* (APB, 2013). These standards are concerned with ensuring the integrity, objectivity and independence of auditors.

An auditor's **integrity** is supported when they are fit and proper persons. This means being sufficiently competent as verified by being appropriately qualified with an up-to-date record of continuing professional development and when they are visibly independent from the audit client.

The *Ethical Standards for Auditors* (APB, 2013) outlines guidance on circumstances that may be considered to breach an auditor's **independence**. These are outlined briefly in Figure 6.3.

REAL WORLD EXAMPLE 6.3

The fall of Arthur Andersen

The fee Enron paid Arthur Andersen was $25 million for audit work the year before it collapsed. In addition to this, Enron paid Arthur Andersen a further $27 million in consultancy fees. The level of fees paid was commonly cited afterwards as an indicator that Arthur Andersen was not independent. The outcome of Arthur Andersen's behaviour in the Enron debacle meant that the public lost confidence in Arthur Andersen as auditors and this huge international audit firm collapsed.

Arthur Andersen's problems started at least a decade earlier, when the audit firm focused on securing lucrative consultancy work with many of their audit firms, which downgraded the less profitable audit work and brought Andersen's independence into question. The seeds of their demise is captured by the following quote from the *Chicago Tribune* (1 September 2002):

> *"Through the 1990s, Andersen aggressively sold lucrative consulting services to those who relied on them for audits in what turned out to be a profitable strategy. Andersen's*

top partners tripled their earnings in the '90s, a feat that put them on a par with their Andersen consulting siblings, who had split into their own division in 1989. But the new strategy also planted the seeds of the firm's downfall. Suddenly, partners who faced accounting dilemmas with clients had a lot more at stake when deciding whether to reject questionable practices uncovered in audits. The fallout from those decisions has unfolded in the headlines about shredded documents, restated earnings, shady loans and financial sleight of hand at Enron, WorldCom Inc., and Waste Management Inc., all Andersen clients beset by accounting scandals."

Source: http://www.chicagotribune.com/news/chi-0209010315sep01,0,538751.story?page = 1, accessed November 2010.

Not only has the auditor to be seen to be acting ethically but the auditor also has to prove (using documentation) that they have conducted the audit ethically (independently, objectively and with integrity) and have acted with confidentiality. Part of being ethical is the need to conduct the audit and to treat the financial information obtained about the client with **confidentiality**. This involves not telling anyone outside the audit firm who the audit firm clients are and taking steps to ensure that client audit records are secure.

Summary

Auditing is defined as an evaluation of an organization, system, process or product. It is performed by a competent, objective and unbiased person or persons who are known as auditors. The purpose of an audit of an entity's financial statements is to verify that the financial statements were completed according to approved and accepted standards, statutes, regulations or practices. An audit also usually evaluates the entity's controls to determine if it is likely that the entity will continue to conform with these standards, and so on. Auditing involves collecting evidence to support auditing assertions. Auditing assertions are indications that information is complete, accurate, properly prepared, applied in the correct period (cut-off), classified correctly, exists, is correctly valued, treated and disclosed in an understandable manner in accordance with accounting standards and applicable law.

According to ISA 200 (IFAC, 2013a), the objective of an audit of financial statements is *'to enable auditors to give an opinion on whether the financial statements are prepared, in all material respects, in accordance with an applicable financial reporting framework'*. An audit typically has five main stages: client acceptance or retention (this involves assessing independence and audit risk and preparing a terms of engagement); audit planning stage (reviewing audit risk, knowledge of the entity, systems, controls, financial statement information, risk of fraud and other material errors and preparing audit planning schedules detailing the work to be performed); control testing stage (this involves undertaking compliance tests of controls to determine if they work properly); substantive testing (sample testing of individual transactions or balances); and opinion formulation stage (taking into account all the evidence obtained during the audit and management assertions). The result of the audit is reported in an independent audit report.

The expectations gap is the difference that exists between the public's perception of what an auditor does and what audited financial statements mean, relative to the auditor's perception of what these mean. The audit report is one step that has been taken by auditors to try to reduce the expectations gap as this report explicitly refers to auditor and management responsibility and details out the restricted nature of audit tests that had been performed. The audit report also provides an opinion only, not a certification.

Corporate governance is the system by which companies are directed and controlled. Corporate governance has become more important over the past two decades when it became clear that a number of large, seemingly successful companies failed unexpectedly (Polly Peck, WorldCom, Enron). Though auditing firms suffered some of the blame, and agency problems were apparent, the corporate world also considered that the systems of ensuring good corporate governance required strengthening. A number of changes to corporate governance have occurred over the past two decades and at present the approach is a risk-based approach. Underlying all the high-profile corporate collapses was a breakdown in ethics, both in terms of management's governance of the respective entities and in terms of auditors exercising due diligence in their auditing work and adhering to independence principles.

Key terms and concepts

accuracy 103
adverse opinion 107
agency costs 108
agency theory 107
audit 100
audit assertions 100
audit plan 102
audit planning memorandum 102
audit report 103
audit risk 102
audit scope 104
auditing by exception 102
auditor ethics 111
Cadbury Report 108
clean audit report 104
Combined Code 108
completeness 103
compliance testing 102
confidentiality 114
corporate governance 107
emphasis of matter paragraph 107
expectations gap 107
Greenbury Report 108
Hampel Report 108
independence 113
integrity 113
letter of engagement 102
management ethics 111
material misstatement 107
modified audit report 107
qualified audit report 107
share options 108
Smith Report 109
substantive testing 103
true and fair view 100
Turnbull Report 109
unmodified audit report 104
unqualified audit report 104
validity 103

An asterisk after the question number indicates that there is a suggested answer in Appendix 2.

Review questions

connect

6.1 What is the objective of an audit?

6.2 Explain the term 'audit risk'.

6.3 Describe the five main stages of an audit briefly.

6.4 Explain the audit expectations gap to a new trainee auditor.

6.5 Explain the term 'corporate governance'.

6.6 Why does corporate governance influence company value?

6.7 Outline six characteristics of good corporate governance, detailing how each can influence company value.

6.8 Explain the role of a non-executive director to a company and outline possible benefits of such an appointment to the company.

Exercises

connect

INTERMEDIATE

6.9* Zonton, a UK public limited company, has been experiencing a downturn in its fortunes. The company's performance in the past seems to have moved in line with the performance of the UK economy. The directors of the company are concerned about the current economic climate in the UK and are looking for suggestions to reduce their risk to the UK economy and to boost profits. Cara Van informed the board at a brainstorming session that a way to alleviate the impact of the expected downturn in the economy would be to open a factory in Tomarat (a fictional emerging economy). She suggests that with a couple of small bribes – to the right people – a suitable factory can be obtained and that the local indigenous population (from the age of 5 upwards) would be delighted to work for a mere fraction of the wages being paid in this country. This would reduce costs and increase profit margins, which would more than outweigh the expected reduction in sales units.

Required

Your father sits on the board of this company and he asks you as an accounting student for advice on the appropriateness of this proposal.

References

Auditing Practice Board (2013) *Ethical Standards for Auditors* (APB).

Cadbury, Sir A. (1992) *Report of the Committee on the Financial Aspects of Corporate Governance (Cadbury Committee Report)*, Gee Publishing.

Department of Trade and Industry (2003) *Review of the Role and Effectiveness of Non-executive Directors*, DTI, The Stationery Office.

Financial Reporting Council (1999) *Committee on Corporate Governance: The Combined Code* (FRC), Gee Publishing.

Financial Reporting Council (2005a) *Guidance on Audit Committees (Smith Report)*, FRC.

Financial Reporting Council (2005b) *Committee on Corporate Governance: The Combined Code (Revised)* (FRC), Gee Publishing.

Financial Reporting Council (2010) *The UK Stewardship Code* (FRC).

Financial Reporting Council (2012) *The UK Corporate Governance Code* (FRC), http://www.slc.co.uk/media/78872/uk-corporate-governance-code-september-2012.pdf

Financial Reporting Council (2013) *International Standard on Auditing (UK and Ireland) 700 (Revised) – The Independent Auditors Report on Financial Statements* (FRC).

Greenbury, Sir R. (1995) *Directors' Remuneration: Report of a Study Group Chaired by Sir Richard Greenbury (Greenbury Committee Report)*, Gee Publishing.

Hamill, P., Ward, A.M. and Wylie, J. (2010) 'Corporate Governance Policy: New Dawn in Ireland and the UK', *Accountancy Ireland*, December, 42(6), 56–59.

Hampel, Sir R. (1998) *Committee on Corporate Governance: Final Report (Hampel Committee Report)*, Gee Publishing.

International Accounting Standards Board (2011) *Conceptual Framework for Financial Reporting* (IASB).

International Auditing and Assurance Standards Board (2013a) *International Standard on Auditing (UK and Ireland) 200 – Overall Objectives of the Independent Auditor and the Conduct of an Audit in Accordance with International Standards on Auditing* (IFAC).

International Auditing and Assurance Standards Board (2013b) *International Standard on Auditing (UK and Ireland) 210 – Agreeing the Terms of Audit Engagements* (IFAC).

International Auditing and Assurance Standards Board (2013c) *International Standard on Auditing (UK and Ireland) 300 – Planning an Audit of Financial Statements* (IFAC).

International Auditing and Assurance Standards Board (2013d) *International Standard on Auditing (UK and Ireland) 330 – The Auditor's Responses to Assessed Risks* (IFAC).

London Stock Exchange (1999) *Internal Control: Guidance for Directors on the Combined Code (Turnbull Report)*, LSE.

McRoberts, F. (2002) 'The Fall of Andersen', *Chicago Tribune*, 1 September 2002, http://www.chicagotribune.com/news/chi-0209010315sep01,0,538751.story?page = 1, accessed November 2010.

PART TWO
Double-entry bookkeeping (recording transactions and the books of account)

7	The accounting equation and its components	121
8	Basic documentation and books of account	137
9	Double entry and the general ledger	149
10	The balancing of accounts and the trial balance	171
11	Day books and the journal	187
12	The cash book	201
13	The petty cash book	217

Chapter 7

The accounting equation and its components

Learning Objectives:

After reading this chapter you should be able to do the following:

1. Explain the relevance of the accounting entity concept in financial accounting.
2. Describe the accounting equation, including how it is reflected in the statement of financial position.
3. Explain the nature of assets, liabilities and capital.
4. Prepare simple statements of financial position and compute the profit from these.
5. Explain the nature of profit and capital maintenance, including their interrelationship.
6. Explain the relevance of the accounting period concept in financial accounting.
7. Distinguish between revenue expenditure and capital expenditure, including their effects on the statement of financial position.
8. Discuss the relevance and limitations of the historical cost concept in financial accounting.

7.1 The accounting entity

A **reporting entity** is defined in the *Statement of Principles for Financial Reporting* (ASB, 1999) as '*an entity for which there are users who rely on the financial statements as their major source of financial information about the entity*'. Accounting for a reporting entity focuses on setting up a means of recording all accounting information in relation to that entity, as distinct from information that does not relate to the entity. The reporting entity may be, for example, a particular company, club or business partnership. We are used to hearing that a financial report relates to a specific organization, but now the organization is called an 'entity'. The use of the word 'entity' emphasizes the properties of being separate and discrete. Greater precision is demanded by accounting in deciding what is, and is not, part of the entity. Boundaries are created to separate out the **accounting entity** (the entity concept). Realizing that these boundaries are necessary, even though they may be artificial, is the key to the entity concept. It becomes possible to accept that a business may be separate from its sole proprietor. Worked Example 7.1 provides examples of the entity concept operating in practice, wherein only business expenses are included in the business accounting records.

WORKED EXAMPLE 7.1

A trainee accountant is starting to prepare the financial statements for a sole proprietor who has a retail shop as his business. The following items appear in the list of cheques written by the businessman. The trainee accountant has been asked to state whether or not the items of expenditure below should be included in the financial statements of the retail shop.

1 Cheque paying the shop's rates.
2 Cheque paying the sole proprietor's house rates.
3 Cheque paying for a new cash till.
4 Cheque paying for a new washing machine for the proprietor's wife's birthday.
5 Cheque for stationery (90 per cent is for the shop, 10 per cent is for his kids).
6 Cheque purchasing overalls for himself for cleaning the shop.
7 Cheque paying for a new outfit, which he can wear to work.

Required

Complete a table detailing whether the items should enter the accounting system of the reporting entity or not.

Solution

	Yes	No
1. Shop rates	√	
2. House rates		√
3. Till	√	
4. Washing machine		√
5. Stationery	√ (90%)	√ (10%)
6. Overalls	√	
7. New outfit		√

By defining the boundaries of the organizational unit, the accounting entity concept determines the transactions that will be recorded in the financial statements. For example, when a local plumber buys tools to carry out his work, that action can be regarded as a purchase by the business, while when the same man buys a cinema ticket this would be seen as a personal purchase. In the same way, the salary paid to a company director is treated not as some internal transfer within a company but as a payment to an officer as a separate individual. In general, accounting sets up 'the business', 'the company' or 'the club' as entities that are artificial constructs, separate from their owners and employees as individuals.

In some instances the boundary between business and private expenditure is difficult to determine, particularly where an expense is incurred for both business and private purposes. It is normal to estimate the portion that is business and to allocate that portion to the business entity. This adjustment provides the potential for manipulating an entity's reported performance. Where private expenses are treated as business expenditure, a lower profit results, which can have detrimental consequences for users, particularly the tax man and a divorcee (assuming they are making a claim for a share of the value of the business). The taxation authorities have identified that treating private expenses as business expenses is 'tax evasion' and hence a crime, as explained in Real World Example 7.1.

REAL WORLD EXAMPLE 7.1

Tax Avoidance is Legal; Tax Evasion is Criminal

Although they sound similar 'tax avoidance' and 'tax evasion' are radically different. **Tax avoidance** lowers your tax bill by structuring your transactions so that you reap the largest tax benefits. Tax avoidance is completely legal – and extremely wise.

Tax evasion, on the other hand, is an attempt to reduce your tax liability by deceit, subterfuge, or concealment. Tax evasion is a crime. How do you know when shrewd planning – tax avoidance – goes too far and crosses the line to become illegal tax evasion? Often the distinction turns upon whether actions were taken with fraudulent intent.

The IRS notes that the following are some of the most common criminal activities in violations of the tax law:

- **Claiming personal expenses as business expenses**. This is an easy trap for a sole practitioner to fall into because often assets, such as a car or a computer, will have both business and personal use. Proper record-keeping will go a long way in preventing a finding of tax fraud.

Source: BizFilings (2013) Tax Avoidance is Legal; Tax Evasion is Criminal, http://www.bizfilings.com/toolkit/sbg/tax-info/fed-taxes/tax-avoidance-and-tax-evasion.aspx, accessed September 2013.

The consequence of not respecting the entity concept when accounting for private transactions can be great as highlighted in Real World Example 7.2. In this example two individuals set up a company separate from the real business and then paid funds to the 'fake company' as consultancy. They then used the funds in the fake company to pay their personal expenses.

REAL WORLD EXAMPLE 7.2

Former Illinois Business Owners Sentenced for Filing False Tax Returns

On August 6, 2013, in Chicago, Ill., Michael H. Martorano, of Ft. Atkinson, Wis., and William S. Sefton, of Scottsdale, Ariz., were sentenced to 42 months and 48 months in prison, respectively. Both defendants were also fined $12,500 and ordered to pay the mandatory court costs. In addition,

Martorano paid approximately $1.494 million in restitution and Sefton paid approximately $1.441 million in restitution for individual income taxes they owed the IRS, and together they paid approximately $7.308 million in corporate taxes owed by their business. Each defendant pleaded guilty in March 2013 to three counts of filing false income tax returns. According to court documents, Martorano was president and Sefton was vice president/secretary of the former Consumer Benefit Service, Inc., or Cbsi, a Naperville business that provided membership and consumer discount programs to businesses and associations worldwide. Martorano and Sefton admitted that on a number of occasions between December 2005 and December 2009, they caused Cbsi to transfer more than $21.656 million into bank accounts in the name of a consulting firm they controlled. Both defendants used some of this money to pay personal expenses and moved other amounts in approximately equal portions into other accounts they controlled individually. As a result, they each obtained approximately $10.828 million. Neither defendant disclosed the receipt of any of this money to their individual tax return preparer.

Source: IRS (2013) 'Examples of Fraud Investigations in 2013', http://www.irs.gov/uac/Examples-of-General-Fraud-Investigations-Fiscal-Year-2013

As will be seen in later chapters, one accounting entity can be a part of another accounting entity. For example, a branch of a retail chain store (such as Marks & Spencer plc) may be treated as a separate accounting entity for internal reporting purposes. However, the branch will also be a part of the business as a whole, which would be treated as another accounting entity for external reporting purposes. Similarly, one company may be a subsidiary of (i.e. owned by) another (holding) company. In this case the subsidiary will be one accounting entity, and its final financial statements must also be consolidated with those of the holding (owner) company into group final financial statements, representing another accounting entity.

In summary, an accounting entity can be a legal entity, part of a legal entity, a combination of several legal entities, part of another accounting entity, or a combination of accounting entities.

7.2 The statement of financial position as an accounting equation

An accounting entity may also be viewed as a set of assets and liabilities. Perhaps the most familiar form this takes is the **statement of financial position**. As an equation this would appear as follows:

Proprietor's ownership interest in the business = Net resources of the business

The ownership interest or claims are called owner's **equity** or owner's **capital**. The net resources are analysed into assets and liabilities.

In relatively simple terms, an **asset** can be defined as a tangible or intangible resource that is owned or controlled by an accounting entity and which is expected to generate future economic benefits. Examples of assets include land and buildings, motor vehicles, plant and machinery, tools, office furniture, fixtures and fittings, office equipment, goods for resale (known as inventory), amounts owed to the accounting entity by its customers (i.e. trade receivables), money in a bank cheque account and cash in hand.

The use of the word 'net' to describe the resources possessed by the business recognizes that there are some amounts set against or to be deducted from the assets; these are called liabilities. In relatively simple terms, a **liability** can be defined as a legal obligation to transfer assets or provide services to another entity that arises from some past transaction or event. Liabilities represent claims by outsiders (compared to the owners, whose claims are equity or capital) and may include such items as loans made to the business and amounts owed for goods supplied (i.e. trade payables).

Given that liabilities can be regarded as being negative in relation to assets, the **accounting equation** can now be stated in the form:

$$\boxed{\text{Assets} - \text{Liabilities} = \text{Owners' capital}}$$

Or alternatively:

$$\boxed{\text{Assets} = \text{Owners' capital} + \text{Liabilities}}$$

This equation is based on what is sometimes referred to as the '**duality**' or 'dual aspect concept' (explained in Chapter 4 'The Conceptual Framework 2: Concepts, Principles and Policies'). This concept purports that every transaction has two aspects: one represented by an asset and the other a liability, or two changes in either the assets or the liabilities. For example, the purchase of an asset on credit will increase the assets and the liabilities by the same amount. The purchase of a vehicle for cash will increase the value of the vehicle asset but decrease the amount of the cash asset.

The accounting equation is a valuable basis from which to begin understanding the whole process of accounting. It sets out the financial position of the owners at any point in time, although in practice a complete and detailed statement of financial position may only be produced periodically, such as monthly or yearly. Most accounting activity is concerned with individual transactions. For now we will examine accounting simply in terms of statements of financial position. Let us trace how this approach reflects the setting-up of a plumbing business (see Worked Example 7.2).

WORKED EXAMPLE 7.2

Adam Bridgewater decided to start his business by opening a bank account for business transactions and depositing £2,000 into it on 1 July 20X4. This transaction involves a flow of value from Adam Bridgewater to his business and will affect two parts of the accounting equation: owner's capital and assets. Owner's capital will increase by £2,000 as the business is now indebted to Adam for the £2,000 that he provided to the business and cash at the business bank will have increased by £2,000. There are several ways of presenting this. In practice companies usually adopt a vertical approach, placing capital vertically below net assets in the form:

Bridgewater (Plumber) Statement of financial position as at 1 July 20X4	
	£
Assets	
Cash at bank	2,000
Equity	
Owner's capital	2,000

However, a side-by-side or horizontal presentation may illustrate more clearly the accounting equation format. A question arises: on which side should assets be included? There is considerable variation and it is a matter of convention. The most useful convention at this stage is to put assets on the left-hand side, as shown below. However, there is a long, well-established tradition in accounting of putting assets on the right-hand side, and liabilities and capital on the left-hand side. The lack of consistency may seem unnecessarily confusing, but students need to be prepared to encounter either convention.

Bridgewater (Plumber) Statement of financial position as at 1 July 20X4			
Assets	£	*Equity*	£
Cash at bank	2,000	Owner's capital	2,000

WORKED EXAMPLE 7.3

Following on from Worked Example 7.2, if on 2 July 20X4 Adam draws out £800 cash and spends it all on purchasing tools, then cash at bank will be decreased by £800 and a new asset, tools, is introduced on the statement of financial position with a balance of £800.

Bridgewater (Plumber) Statement of financial position as at 2 July 20X4			
Assets	£	*Equity*	£
Tools	800	Owner's capital	2,000
Cash at bank	1,200		
	2,000		2,000

In this case one asset is increased by exactly the same amount as another is decreased (£800), so that the accounting equation, assets equals capital plus liabilities, continues to balance.

WORKED EXAMPLE 7.4

Following on from Worked Example 7.3, on 3 July Adam buys a range of plumbing accessories for £300 from the local storekeeper, but arranges to pay in the next few days. The arrangement is described as 'on credit'. The credit transaction with the storekeeper becomes a trade payable since he is now owed a debt of £300. There is no problem in maintaining the balance of the equation when including the effects of this transaction in the business statement of financial position, since the new liability of £300 owed to the store exactly complements the £300 increase in assets represented by the inventory of accessories:

Bridgewater (Plumber) Statement of financial position as at 3 July 20X4			
Assets	£	*Equity and liabilities*	£
Tools	800	Owner's capital	2,000
Inventory	300	*Liability*	
Cash at bank	1,200	Trade payable	300
	2,300		2,300

As mentioned, the horizontal approach adopted to portray the outcome of the last three transactions reflects the accounting equation (assets = liabilities + equity). However, in practice this is rarely utilized; therefore, the vertical approach is used throughout the remainder of this book.

WORKED EXAMPLE 7.5

Following on from Worked Example 7.4, if on the next day, Bridgewater pays the store the £300 to clear the outstanding debt, this will decrease both the cash (from £1,200 to £900) and the trade payable (from £300 to £0) – an asset and a liability – by the same amount, giving:

Bridgewater (Plumber) Statement of financial position as at 4 July 20X4	
	£
Assets	
Tools	800
Inventory	300
Cash at bank	900
	2,000
Equity and liabilities	£
Owner's capital	2,000
	2,000

Learning Activity 7.1

Prepare a statement of financial position listing your assets, liabilities and resultant capital, or those of your family. Use the original purchase price of the assets.

7.3 The accounting equation and profit reporting

Drawing up a statement of financial position after each of the enormous number of transactions carried out every day or week in large corporations would be very time consuming and inefficient, and a business cannot be expected to do so. However, it is normal for even small businesses to produce a statement of financial position once a year as shown in Worked Example 7.6 (follows on from Worked Example 7.5).

WORKED EXAMPLE 7.6

Bridgewater may be interested to see how his business has progressed in its first year. For him to be able to draw up a statement of financial position he needs to know the amounts to include for assets and liabilities at that date. Suppose he has the following amounts relating to his financial position at the end of the day's trading on 30 June 20X5:

Assets of business: Building £5,000; tools £1,100; inventory of accessories £500; trade receivables £350; cash at bank £200.

Liabilities: Bank loan £3,500; trade payables £450.

Many changes and transactions are likely to have taken place during the year to reach this position, but these have not been tracked from statement of financial position to statement of financial position. The absence of a figure for capital will not prevent the statement of financial position being drawn up, given that it is the only missing figure in the accounting equation as the accounting equation rule will apply – the debits will equal the credits. As the assets and liabilities are known then the difference will be the capital. So the statement of financial position becomes:

Bridgewater (Plumber) Statement of financial position as at 30 June 20X5	
	£
ASSETS (DEBITS)	
Building	5,000
Tools	1,100
Inventory	500
Trade receivables	350
Cash	200
Total assets	7,150
EQUITY AND LIABILITIES (CREDITS)	£
Equity	
Owners' capital (to balance)	3,200
Non-current liabilities	
Bank loan	3,500
Trade payables	450
Total non-current liabilities	3,950
Total equity and liabilities	7,150

Capital is the balancing item. Note that the capital figure at the end of the year is different to that at the beginning, and analysis and explanation of that change is needed to provide a more complete picture. In this case we see that the balance on the capital account has increased by £1,200 being the closing capital balance (£3,200) less the opening capital balance (£2,000). How could this have arisen?

One possible explanation is that Bridgewater paid some more money into the business. In this case let us decide that we know that he paid in a further £1,000. Of course, the opposite of paying in would be taking money out, so let us say that he also took out £750 for personal use. The net effect will produce an increase of £1,000 – £750 = £250. The rest of the increase in capital (i.e. £1,200 – £250 = £950) would be profit – that is, increased capital generated by the business itself.

A simple example will illustrate how profit is able to generate increases in capital. A trader is able to start a small venture with £30 in cash, equivalent to £30 capital. She uses the money to buy a bath. When she sells the bath for £40 she now has £40 cash and has increased capital by £10 (profit).

To provide a more useful definition of profit as increased capital, accounting has made use of explanations given by the economist Hicks (1946) who defines **profit** as the maximum amount that could be withdrawn in a period from the business while leaving the capital intact. In the case of Bridgewater's business, the capital that is kept intact is the £2,000 figure at the start of the period. Therefore the profit is £1,200 being the increase in capital (assuming no capital is introduced or withdrawn by the owner). Measuring profit in relation to capital that is kept intact is commonly described as a **capital maintenance** approach, which forms one of the major pillars of profit measurement theory (see Chapter 4, 'The Conceptual

Framework 2: Concepts, Principles and Policies'). It is implicit in all profit measurement approaches that will be drawn upon in this book.

7.4 The accounting period and profit reporting

The **accounting period concept** (sometimes called **periodicity concept**) is a means of dividing up the life of an accounting entity into discrete periods for the purpose of reporting performance for a period of time (in a statement of profit or loss) and showing its financial position at a point in time (in a statement of financial position). The period of time is usually one year and is often referred to as the **accounting year**, **financial year** or **reporting period**. Each accounting year of an entity's life normally ends on the anniversary of its formation, and therefore does not necessarily coincide with the calendar year. It could thus end on any day of the calendar year, but for convenience the accounting year is nearly always taken to be the end of a calendar month, and sometimes adjusted to the end of the calendar year or to the end of a particular month (e.g. for tax reasons). Some companies report on their financial position half-yearly or even quarterly. Thus, the accounting period can be less than one year.

The accounting period concept is also sometimes referred to as the **time interval** or **time period** concept (discussed briefly in Chapter 4 'The Conceptual Framework 2: Concepts, Principles and Policies').

The previous section commenced by recognizing the significance of annual reporting in assessing business performance. Profit is defined in terms of potential consumption 'in a period'. Although the use of a period of a year is no more than a convention – albeit a very useful one – the idea of periodic reporting is fundamental to present-day accounting. The approach adopted in accounting is an extension of the use of the entity concept. For accounting purposes, each complete period, usually of a year, is treated as a separate entity. It inherits as its opening statement of financial position the closing statement of financial position of the previous period. Therefore, at each year end items need to be classified into two types: those that will be included in the closing statement of financial position to be properly carried forward as part of the opening position of the new entity commencing next period, and those that are properly attributable to the period just finished. An aspect of this has already been seen in the simple illustration of buying and selling a bath to make a profit. The transactions involved are all treated as being complete by the time the profit figure for the year is calculated. Details of the buying and selling transactions are not part of the next year's position except to the extent that they form an element contained within the total capital figure (i.e. the profit part of £10).

The matching concept, as discussed in Chapter 4, 'The Conceptual Framework 2: Concepts, Principles and Policies', helps to determine in which period to classify an item in profit or loss. In brief, sales associated with a particular period are recognized as the revenue of that period. The expenditures used up in that period in creating those sales are matched against them. The aggregate sales less the aggregate expenditures matched against them gives the profit for the year. Before analysing this in depth, it is necessary to be able to identify period expenditure (called 'revenue expenditure') and statement of financial position expenditure (capital expenditure).

7.5 Revenue expenditure versus capital expenditure

The word 'capital' is associated with items that appear in the statement of financial position (e.g. owners' capital), whereas the word 'revenue' encapsulates items that appear in the statement of profit or loss (comprehensive income). Expenditure of the type that is to be matched against the period's revenue and is used up in the period is called **revenue expenditure**. Revenue expenditure accounts will have no value at the end of the period to which they relate. Revenue expenditure is distinguished from **capital expenditure** – amounts that are to be carried forward into the next period as part of the next year's opening statement of financial position. Capital expenditure is carried forward because it will be used over a number of periods and contributes to several periods' revenues. Examples of both types of expenditure are provided in Worked Example 7.7.

WORKED EXAMPLE 7.7

A trainee accountant who has been given the task of listing items of expenditure as being either capital or revenue expenditure approaches you for advice. She specifically wants to know whether the following expenditures (which relate to a builder's yard) should be classed as capital or revenue items:

1 rates charge for the year;

2 a new delivery van;

3 rent for the building;

4 sand that is not yet sold;

5 stationery;

6 telephone bills for the year;

7 a new telephone;

8 a new fence surrounding the yard (this is expected to reduce theft);

9 wages;

10 electricity bills;

11 timber in the yard that is not yet sold.

Required

Complete a table detailing whether the items are capital or revenue in nature.

Solution

	Capital	Revenue
1. Rates		√
2. Delivery van (motor vehicle)	√	
3. Rent		√
4. Sand (inventory)	√	
5. Stationery		√
6. Telephone bill		√
7. New telephone (office equipment)	√	
8. Fence (fixtures and fittings)	√	
9. Wages		√
10. Electricity		√
11. Timber (inventory)	√	

Note

To improve the presentation of financial information, it is common practice to categorize items into accounts that have generic names. These are provided in brackets where they differ to the exact name of the expense. For example, electricity, oil, gas, etc. are commonly grouped into the account named 'heat and light'.

Capital expenditure typically includes the cost of purchasing a non-current asset (including the costs of getting the non-current asset operational at the outset) and the cost of improvements to a non-current asset that lead to increased revenue, or sustained revenue. Expenditure on tools, which represent the long-term equipment of the business, is capital expenditure and is carried forward from statement of financial position to statement of financial position. Rental expenditure on a building used during the year is revenue expenditure – what it provides is used up in the period. The purchase of the building, however, would be capital expenditure, as it is entirely appropriate to represent ownership being carried forward from period to period. More complex aspects of revenue and capital expenditure are considered in Worked Example 7.8.

WORKED EXAMPLE 7.8

A trainee accountant who has been given the task of analysing items of expenditure in respect of the motor vehicles of the business in the year approaches you for advice. She specifically wants to know whether the following expenditures should be classed as capital or revenue items:

1 repair of a lorry (the lorry is already included in the opening statement of financial position);

2 purchase of a new van;

3 motor tax on the van and lorry;

4 cost of removing seats in the van to create more room for transporting goods for the business;

5 new tyres for the lorry;

6 advertising painted on the side of both the lorry and the van.

Required

Complete a table detailing whether the items are capital or revenue in nature.

Solution

	Capital	Revenue
1. Repair of a lorry		√
2. Purchase of new van	√	
3. Motor tax		√
4. Cost of removing seats – more storage	√	
5. New tyres		√
6. Advertising	√	

Allocating expenditure to the incorrect type of account has a major impact on an entity's reported performance and financial position. Revenue expenditure reduces profitability, whereas capital expenditure ends up in the statement of financial position with a portion of the expenditure being allocated to the statement of profit or loss in line with the use of the asset (the reduction in the useful economic life of the asset). The latter is discussed in depth in Chapter 15, 'Depreciation and Non-Current Assets'. To allocate capital expenditure as revenue expenditure will cause profitability to fall, and vice versa. To knowingly allocate expenditure to the incorrect type of account is fraud, as users (particularly investors, lenders and the tax authorities) are misled and can suffer a loss. A high-profile example of accounting fraud which used this technique is now outlined.

REAL WORLD EXAMPLE 7.3

WorldCom plc

WorldCom was one of the largest telecommunications companies in the world. In the late 1990s it came under increasing pressure to maintain reported cash flow and earnings before interest and taxation levels. However, orders for new telecommunication equipment were declining. This environment led the management of the company to commit one of the largest accounting frauds in world history. The overall reporting irregularities amounted to about $11 billion. The SEC (2003) found four major areas of fraud, one of which was 'the unauthorized movement of line costs to capital as prepaid. Line costs are paid to local telephone companies for originating and terminating long-distance calls and account for the largest single expense for long-distance companies. By moving these costs to capital, the costs could be depreciated over time thereby increasing the current year's earnings before interest and tax.'

Source: Scharff, M.M. (2005) 'Understanding WorldCom's Accounting Fraud: Did Groupthink Play a Role?', *Journal of Leadership and Organizational Studies*, 11(3), 109–118.

7.6 Measurement

For accounting statements to represent the various values of assets and liabilities and to be able to aggregate these, it is necessary for a **measurement unit** to be established and a **valuation model** to be adopted. We have already been using a measurement unit, the sterling £. Providing this represents a stable unit for expressing economic values, **money measurement** is appropriate to accounting statements intended to reflect the performance and financial position of business entities. Money provides a common denominator for measuring, aggregating and reporting the performance of an accounting entity and the attributes of transactions and items. Examples of other less plausible alternatives might include the amount of energy (e.g. electrical) or labour hours consumed in creating an asset.

As regards a valuation model, the price that is agreed in an arm's-length transaction when an asset or liability is originally acquired provides a readily available objective valuation expressed in terms of monetary units of measurement. This is the major source of valuation used by **historical cost accounting**. Sales are recorded at the contracted sales value and purchases at the agreed purchase price.

Over the past decade a change in emphasis has occurred in terms of measurement basis, with the standard setters putting more emphasis on **fair value accounting** (at present this change is mostly targeted at listed companies and larger limited companies). The underlying principle behind the fair value measurement basis is the view that items stated in the financial statements should reflect their economic value, whether this is market value, or the present value of the expected future revenues expected from the item. In many instances fair value equates to historical cost values. As the focus of this book is accounting for small entities, the historical cost approach is utilized.

7.7 Strengths and limitations of historical cost in accounting measurement

Historical cost accounting has many strengths. It permits financial statements to be produced by collecting information about business transactions. This is particularly useful not only for preparing financial statements but also commercially for managing an entity's finances, as it can assist in tracking down what amounts have to be paid and collected and in determining the cash balances that remain after making payments and collections. Amounts are determined 'automatically' by the transactions themselves rather than being left to the judgement and possible abuse of individuals. For these and other reasons historical cost continues to be the predominant basis for accounting record keeping and reporting in non-plc entities.

However, the historical cost approach is not without disadvantages. These arise largely because there is change over time in prices (both of individual items and because of inflation). As a result, accounting reports based on historical costs may become unrealistic and those based on fair value more relevant. Statements of financial position prepared under the historic cost will contain values for assets that are out of date, being based on prices when they were originally purchased, which may be several years ago; capital, which is being maintained in the profit measurement process, represents a value that is also out of date, in terms of both its value to the owners, and the capacity of the facilities that it could provide for the business. The matching process becomes debased to the extent that sales may be made at prices which, although above the original purchase price of the items being sold, are below the current replacement price. This would mean that a business might be reporting a profit on a sale even though this put it in the position where it was no longer able to buy the goods it owned prior to the sale. Current policy as promoted by the IASB is that fair value accounting is more appropriate than historic cost accounting as it provides information that is up-to-date, that fairly represents the economic reality and that is more relevant for economic decision-making.

Learning Activity 7.2

As far as is possible, repeat Learning Activity 7.1 for one year ago. Calculate the change in the value of your capital over the year and list the main reasons for the change. What do these tell you about the nature of the profit, capital maintenance and the effect of valuing assets at their historical cost?

Summary

The accounting entity concept defines the boundaries of the organizational unit that is the focus of the accounting process, and thus the transactions that will be recorded. An accounting entity may also be viewed as a set of assets and liabilities, the difference between the money values of these being capital. This is referred to as the accounting equation, and can be presented in the form of a statement of financial position in which the assets and liabilities are valued at their historical cost (or fair value if a listed entity).

The accounting period concept divides up the life of an entity into discrete periods (usually of one year) for the purpose of reporting profit and its financial state of affairs. The profit for an accounting year can be measured either in terms of the change in the value of the capital over this period, or by a process of matching sales revenue with the expenditure incurred in generating that revenue. This involves distinguishing between revenue expenditure and capital expenditure. Knowingly allocating a capital transaction as revenue and vice versa is fraud, as this can lead to tax evasion, or to losses being incurred by other users, such as investors or loan creditors. This is a criminal offence that can result in a fine, jail or both!

Key terms and concepts

accounting entity	122	measurement unit	132
accounting equation	125	money measurement	132
accounting period concept	129	periodicity concept	129
accounting year	129	profit	128
asset	124	reporting entity	122
capital (ownership)	124	reporting period	129
capital expenditure	129	revenue expenditure	129
capital maintenance	128	statement of financial position	124
duality concept	125	tax avoidance	123
equity	124	tax evasion	123
fair value accounting	132	time interval	129
financial year	129	time period	129
historical cost accounting	132	valuation model	132
liability	124		

An asterisk after the question number indicates that there is a suggested answer in Appendix 2.

Review questions

connect

7.1* Explain the relevance of the entity concept in accounting.

7.2 Define and distinguish between the following:

a assets and liabilities;

b capital and revenue expenditure.

7.3 a State the accounting equation and explain its components.

b The financial position of a business at any time is represented in the statement of financial position. Why is it that every business entity's position should 'balance'?

7.4 Explain briefly what is meant by the following terms: profit; capital; and capital maintenance.

7.5 Explain the relevance of the accounting period concept in accounting.

7.6 Discuss the relevance and limitations of the historical cost concept in accounting.

Exercises

connect

7.7* J. Frank commenced business on 1 January 20X4. His position was: BASIC

Assets: land and buildings, £7,500; fixtures, £560; balance at bank, £1,740.

Liabilities: mortgage on land and buildings, £4,000.

He traded for a year, withdrawing £500 for his personal use and paying in no additional capital. His position on 31 December 20X4 was:

Assets: land and buildings, £7,500; fixtures, £560; delivery van, £650; sundry receivables, £470; inventory, £940; balance at bank, £1,050; cash in hand, £80.

Liabilities: mortgage on land and buildings, £5,000; sundry payables, £800.

Required

Calculate Frank's profit or loss for 20X4.

7.8 Prepare J. Magee's statement of financial position (vertical format as utilized in the chapter) as at 31 December 20X4 from the following: BASIC

	£
Office machinery	18,000
Trade payables	1,000
Sundry payables	800
Inventory of goods	2,900
Stationery inventory	200
Cash at bank	550
Trade receivables	8,150
Sundry receivables	2,000

Note: You have to determine J. Magee's equity capital balance.

7.9 Using the information from question 7.8, re-prepare J. Magee's statement of financial position, using the horizontal format, as at 31 December 20X4. BASIC

7.10 State whether the following expenditures for a local school are revenue or capital in nature. In addition, state the name of the classification (current asset, non-current asset, etc.) and the generic account name that the item would appear in within the financial statements. BASIC

For example: tins of beans on the shelf of a grocery store are a type of current asset called 'inventory'.

1 A filing cabinet

2 Replacement pitched roof (the old roof was a flat roof)

3 Rates bill for the year

4 Insurance paid for the premises

5 Cleaners' wages

6 A till

7 A chair

8 A blackboard in the school

9 Chalk used on the blackboard in the year

10 Oil

11 Double-glazed windows (replaced single-glazed windows)

12 Repainting the classrooms

13 Painting the extension for the first time

14 Teachers' wages

References

Accounting Standards Board (1999) *Statement of Principles for Financial Reporting* (ASB).

Hicks, J.R. (1946) *Value and Capital* (2nd edn), Clarendon Press, Oxford.

Chapter 8

Basic documentation and books of account

Learning Objectives:

After reading this chapter you should be able to do the following:

1. Distinguish between cash transactions and credit transactions.
2. Describe the nature of trade discount and cash discount.
3. List the documents and describe the procedure relating to credit transactions.
4. Describe the contents of those documents that are entered in the books of account.
5. Explain the purpose of books of prime entry.
6. List the books of prime entry and state what each is used to record.
7. Explain the role of computerization in accounting systems

8.1 Introduction

No two businesses are exactly the same and the same can be said of the accounting systems used by firms. Most firms have their own particular ways of doing things. Some use manual record-keeping, others use off-the-shelf accounting software packages such as Sage, while others create their own bespoke accounting systems. However, there is a certain degree of homogeneity in keeping accounting records that is prevalent among the great majority of firms. This chapter focuses on providing background information on the typical documentation and books of account that are used by most firms.

8.2 Basic documentation for cash and credit transactions

In accounting, a **cash transaction** is one where goods or services are paid for in cash or by cheque when they are received or delivered. A **credit transaction** is one where payment is made or received some time after delivery (normally in one instalment). This should not be confused with hire purchase or credit card transactions. Credit transactions are extremely common in many industries. The credit terms of most UK businesses are that goods which are delivered at any time during a given calendar month should be paid for by the end of the following calendar month.

Credit transactions often involve **trade discount**. This is a discount given by one trader to another. It is usually expressed as a percentage reduction of the recommended retail price of the goods, and is deducted in arriving at the amount the buyer is charged for the goods.

A large number of businesses also allow their customers **cash discounts**. This is a reduction in the amount that the customer has to pay, provided payment is made within a given period stipulated by the seller at the time of sale (e.g. 5 per cent if paid within 10 days).

A cash transaction is recorded in the books of account from the receipt received if paid in cash, or from the cheque book stub if paid by cheque. A credit transaction, in contrast, involves a number of documents, not all of which are recorded in the books of account. Figure 8.1 shows, in chronological order, the documents and procedures relating to a business transaction on credit, including who originates each document. Note that only the invoice, debit note, credit note and cheque are recorded in the books of account. The main documents involved in a credit transaction are now discussed.

The invoice

The purpose of the **invoice**, which is sent by the seller, is primarily to inform the buyer how much is owed for the goods supplied. It is *not* a demand for payment. A specimen invoice is shown in Figure 8.2.

The information shown on an invoice is detailed in Figure 8.3.

The buyer checks the invoice against the order and the delivery note (or more usually with a goods received note prepared by the receiving department). If correct, the invoice is then entered in the buyer's books. Similarly, a copy of the invoice would have been entered in the seller's books.

The debit note

A **debit note** is sent by the seller if the buyer has been undercharged on the invoice. It has basically the same layout and information as the invoice except that instead of details of the goods, it shows details of the undercharge. It is recorded in the books of the seller and buyer in the same way as an invoice.

The credit note

A **credit note** may be sent by the seller for a number of reasons. These include:

- The buyer has returned goods because they were not ordered, or they were the wrong type, quantity or quality, or are defective.

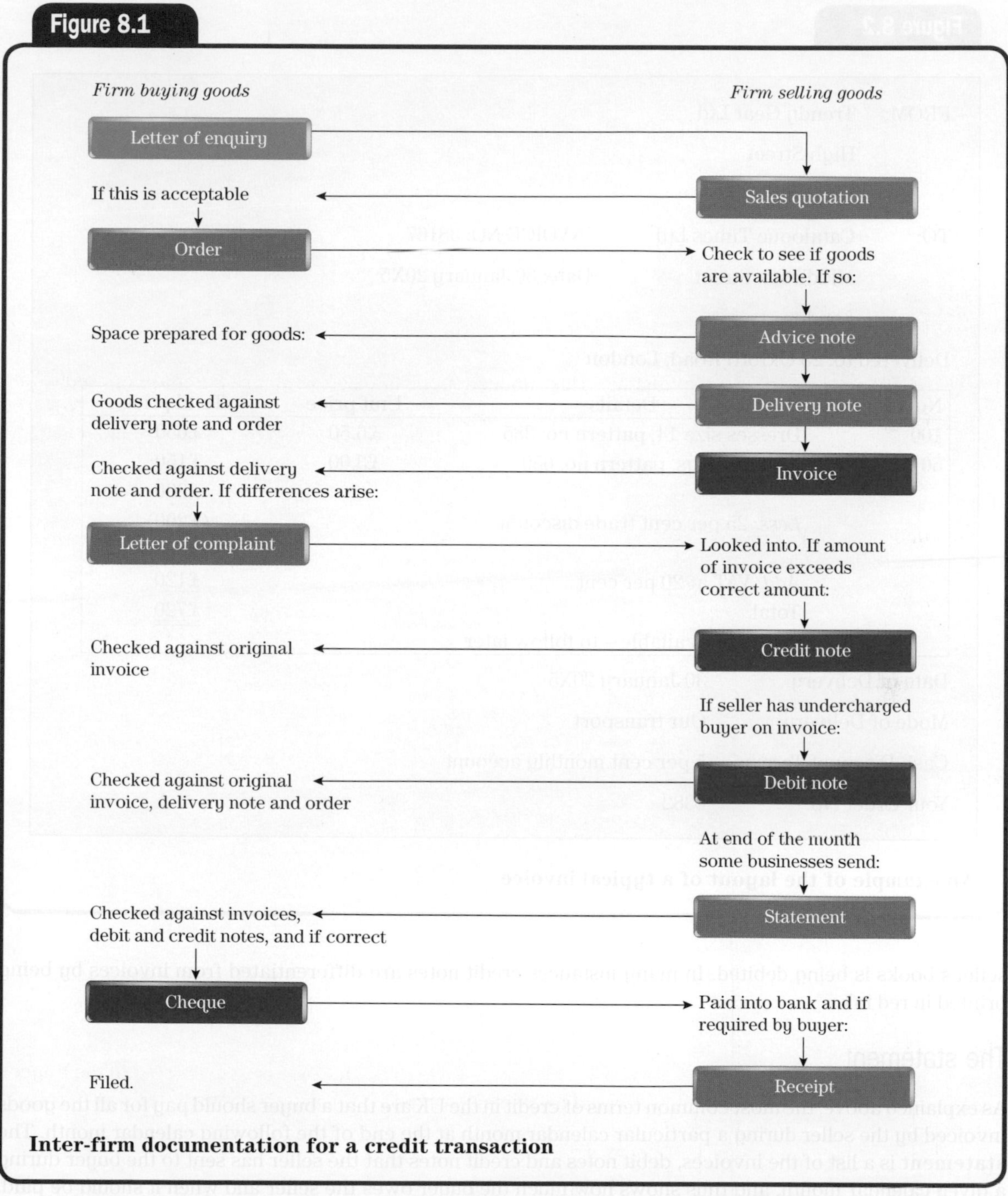

Inter-firm documentation for a credit transaction

- The seller has overcharged the buyer on the invoice. This may be due to an error in the unit price or calculations.

A credit note has basically the same layout and information as an invoice, except that instead of the details of the goods, it will show the reason why it has been issued.

A credit note will be recorded in the books of the seller and buyer in a similar way to the invoice, except that the entries are the reverse. It is called a credit note because it informs the buyer that the account in the books of the seller is being credited. Conversely, a debit note informs the buyer that the account in the

Figure 8.2

FROM: Trendy Gear Ltd
High Street
London

TO: Catalogue Times Ltd
Middlesex Street
London

INVOICE NO: 38167
Date: 30 January 20X5

Delivered to: 23 Oxford Road, London

No. of units	Details	Unit price	Total price
100	Dresses size 14, pattern no. 385	£6.50	£650
50	Leather bags, pattern no. 650	£3.00	£150
			£800
	Less: 25 per cent trade discount		(£200)
			£600
	Add: VAT at 20 per cent		£120
	Total		£720
	Tights unavailable – to follow later		

Date of Delivery: 30 January 20X5

Mode of Delivery: Our transport

Cash Discount Terms: 5 per cent monthly account

Your Order No: 6382

An example of the layout of a typical invoice

seller's books is being debited. In many instances credit notes are differentiated from invoices by being printed in red ink.

The statement

As explained above, the most common terms of credit in the UK are that a buyer should pay for all the goods invoiced by the seller during a particular calendar month at the end of the following calendar month. The **statement** is a list of the invoices, debit notes and credit notes that the seller has sent to the buyer during a given calendar month, and thus shows how much the buyer owes the seller and when it should be paid. The statement is often a copy of the buyer's account in the seller's books. This is illustrated in Figure 8.4.

The statement may be kept by the buyer for reference purposes or returned to the seller with the buyer's cheque. In either case neither the buyer nor the seller records the statement in the books. Not all businesses use statements.

The cheque

A **cheque** is the most common form of payment in business because of its convenience and safety. Most cheques are crossed and therefore have to be paid into a bank account. This makes it possible to trace

Figure 8.3

Invoice

- the name and address of the seller **and** the buyer;
- the invoice and delivery note number of the seller (usually the same);
- the date of the invoice;
- the address to which the goods were delivered;
- the buyer's order number;
- the quantity of goods supplied;
- details of the goods supplied;
- the price per unit of each of the goods;
- the total value of the invoice before value added tax (VAT)*;
- the trade and cash discount;
- VAT payable and the total value of the invoice including VAT;
- when payment should be made;
- the seller's terms of trade.

* *VAT affects a large number of sales and purchase transactions which, in turn, must be incorporated in the recording of those transactions. Including VAT introduces little in the way of principles but some additional detail. In order to concentrate on the subject matter developed in this book, VAT is recognized here but its treatment is covered in depth in a separate chapter on the OLC – Chapter 35, 'Value Added Tax, Columnar Books of Prime Entry and the Payroll'* (**www.mcgraw-hill.co.uk/textbooks/thomas**).

The information provided on an invoice

Figure 8.4

Seller's name and address

Buyer's name and address — Month: January 20X5

Date of invoice	Invoice/Credit note no.	Debits (amount of invoices and debit notes)	Credits (amount of credit notes and payments)	Balance
2 Jan	In426	£23.12		£23.12
9 Jan	In489	£16.24		£39.36
16 Jan	In563	£52.91		£92.27
22 Jan	Cheque		£25.14	£67.13
25 Jan	Cr1326		£6.00	£61.13

Amount due on 28 February: £61.13

Cash discount terms: 5 per cent monthly

An example of the layout of a typical statement

the cheque if it is stolen and fraudulently passed on to someone else. A crossed cheque may be paid into anyone's bank account if the payee endorses (i.e. signs) the back of the cheque. However, if the words 'account payee only' are written between the crossings it must be paid into the account of the person named on the cheque. The information that must be shown on a cheque is provided in Figure 8.5.

Figure 8.5

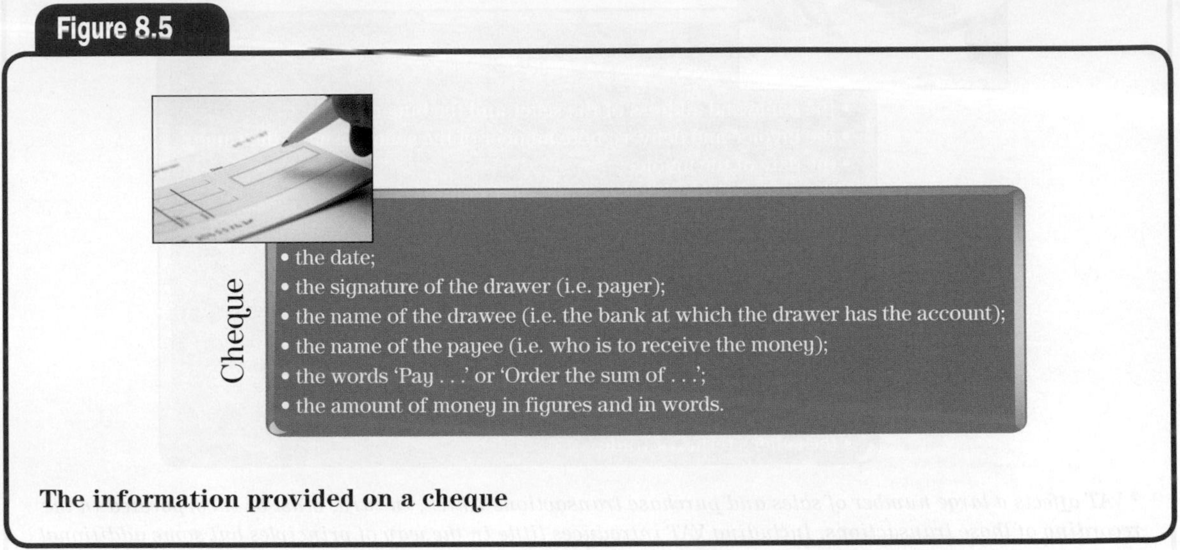

Cheque
• the date;
• the signature of the drawer (i.e. payer);
• the name of the drawee (i.e. the bank at which the drawer has the account);
• the name of the payee (i.e. who is to receive the money);
• the words 'Pay . . .' or 'Order the sum of . . .';
• the amount of money in figures and in words.

The information provided on a cheque

The bank account number of the drawer, and the cheque and bank number are also shown on preprinted cheques.

Since there is only one copy of a cheque, it is essential to write on the cheque stub or counterfoil to whom the cheque was paid (i.e. the payee), the amount and what the payment was for. Without this information the books of account cannot be written up.

The bank paying-in book

The **bank paying-in book** provides a record of the cash and cheques received that have been paid into the business's bank account. The information shown on the bank paying-in book stub consists of:

- the date;
- the amounts paid in, from whom they were received, and to what they relate.

Cash and cheques received paid into the business's bank account are recorded in the books of account from the information on the bank paying-in book stub or counterfoil, which must therefore be accurate and complete.

The receipt

The law requires the seller to give the buyer a **receipt** for goods or services that have been paid for in cash. However, there is no legal requirement to do so in the case of payments by cheque.

A receipt must contain the following information:

- the name of the payer;
- the signature of the recipient;

- the amount of money in figures and in words;
- the date.

A receipt is only recorded in the books of account when it relates to cash receipts and payments.

Books of account

The main book of account in which all transactions are recorded is called the **ledger** (otherwise known as the **general ledger** or the **nominal ledger**). However, before a transaction is recorded in the ledger, it must first be entered in a **book of prime entry**. These books are designed to show more detail relating to each transaction than appears in the ledger. They also facilitate making entries in the ledger, in that transactions of the same type can be posted periodically in total rather than one at a time. Sometimes, there are analysis columns in each book of prime entry in which are collected all those transactions relating to the same type of expenditure or income. For example, the cheque journal may record payments made for credit purchases in one column, for motor expenses in another column and for stationery in a further column. A business may use up to nine books of prime entry, which consist of the following:

1 The **sales day book**, in which is recorded the sale on credit of those goods bought specifically for resale. It is written up from copies of sales invoices and debit notes retained by the seller. The amount entered in the sales day book is after deducting trade discount (but before deducting cash discount).

2 The **purchases day book**, in which is recorded the purchase on credit of goods intended for resale. It is written up from the invoices and debit notes received from suppliers. The amount entered in the purchases day book is after deducting trade discount (but before deducting cash discount).

3 The **sales returns day book**, in which is recorded the goods sold on credit that are returned by customers. It is written up from copies of credit notes retained by the seller.

4 The **purchases returns day book**, in which is recorded the goods purchased on credit that are returned to suppliers. It is written up from the credit notes received from suppliers.

5 The **petty cash book**, in which is recorded cash received and cash paid. This is written up from receipts (or petty cash vouchers where employees are reimbursed expenses).

6 The **cash book**, in which are recorded cheques received (and cash paid into the bank) and payments made by cheque (and cash withdrawn from the bank). This is written up from the bank paying-in book stub and cheque book stubs.

7 The **bills receivable book**, in which are recorded bills of exchange received by the business from customers. A **bill of exchange** can best be described as being similar to a post-dated cheque, except that instead of being written out by the person paying the money, it is prepared by the business to whom the money is owed (the seller) and then signed by the entity/person paying the money (customer) as agreed and returned to the seller. When the period of credit given by the bill of exchange has expired, which is usually 30, 60 or 90 days, the entity in possession of the bill (seller) presents the bill to the customer and receives payment.

8 The **bills payable book**, in which are recorded bills of exchange given to creditors as payment.

9 The **journal**, in which are recorded any transactions that are not included in any of the other books of prime entry. At one time all entries passed through the journal, but now it is primarily used to record the purchase and sale of non-current assets on credit, the correction of errors, opening entries in a new set of books and any remaining transfers. Non-current assets are items not bought specifically for resale, such as land and buildings, machinery or vehicles. The journal is written up from copies of invoices and adjustments requested by the accountant.

Figure 8.6 provides a summary of the seven main books of prime entry, including the documents from which each is written up. Each of these books of prime entry is discussed in depth in later chapters.

Figure 8.6

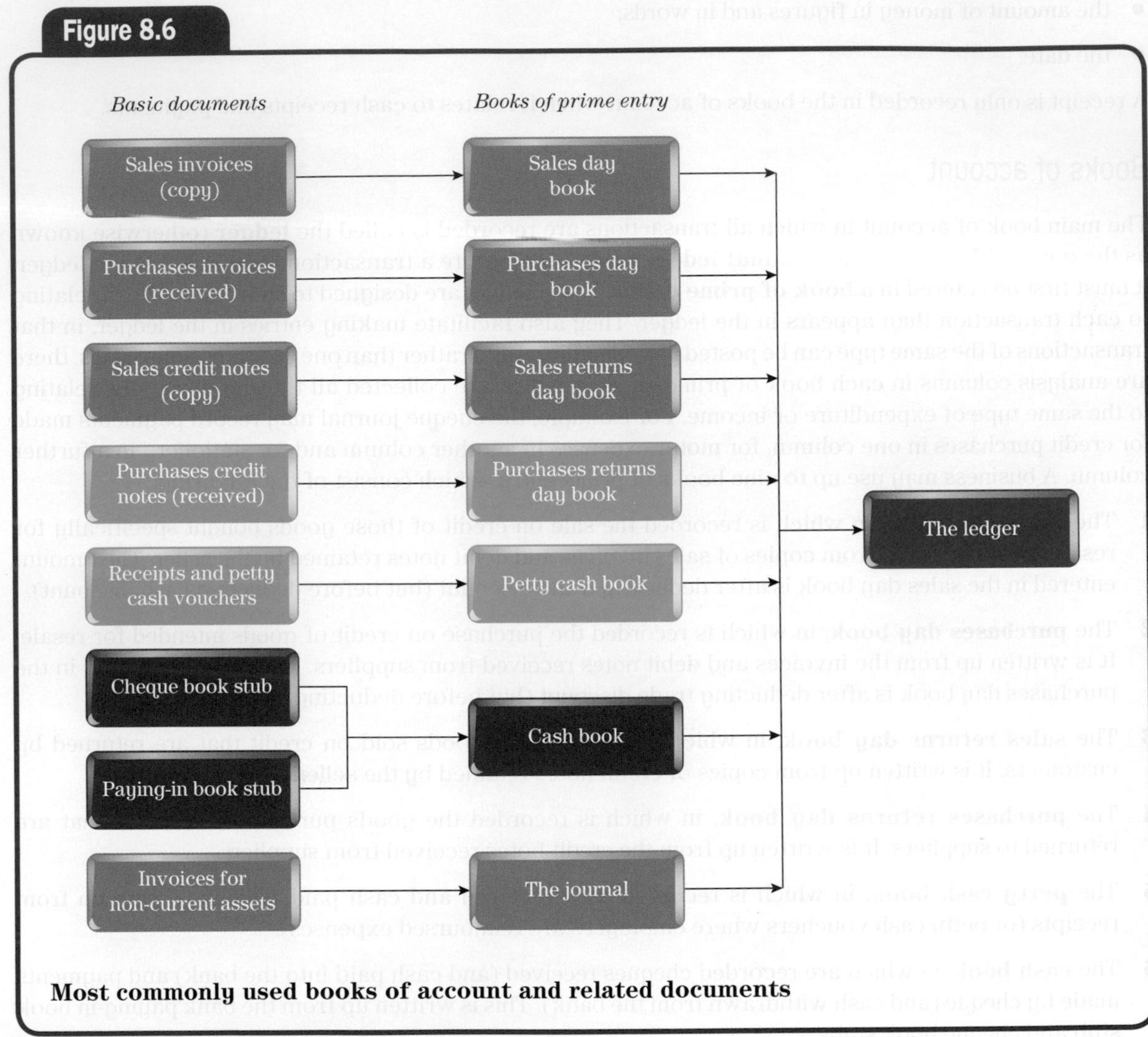

Most commonly used books of account and related documents

8.3 Computerized accounting systems

In the majority of firms accounting systems are computerized. The systems are either purchased off-the-shelf (standard product such as SAGE) or are bespoke (written to suit the specific company's requirements). In all instances the systems have computerized versions (called modules) of each of the books mentioned in Figure 8.6. There are several advantages to computerization. These are listed in Figure 8.7.

Learning Activity 8.1

Consider, from a company's viewpoint, what disadvantages may arise from having a computerized accounting system.

Though there are reported benefits from computerization, problems have also occurred as outlined in an extract from a BBC article reproduced in Real World Example 8.1. An over-reliance on computerized accounting systems combined with a view that they cannot be incorrect may not reflect reality as all computerized systems are written by humans, hence are prone to having 'bugs'.

Figure 8.7

Cost savings	• Fewer administration staff required as information only has to be input once to the system • Similar tasks can be automated including double entry
Timely information	• Most accounting systems work in real time and across the globe so someone in the US can input information as well as someone in the UK • Once entered the information is available immediately to report and reports are updated automatically
Simultaneous access to data	• Large numbers of users can have access to the same information
Improved accuracy of data	• The accounting system can do numerous checks; for example, to prevent a key item of data from being omitted by mistake, or to ensure that the amount received in a payment matches the amount due
Improved detail	• More information on a transaction can be stored in a computer package and then used afterwards for analysis
Improved reporting	• The production of reports is automated and predefined formats are included in the software such as the format of the statement of profit or loss • Reports can highlight problems which can assist in decision-making by focusing management attention in problem areas

Advantages of computerization of accounting systems

REAL WORLD EXAMPLE 8.1

Bug identified in Post Office software

A report by forensic accountants that found computer bugs in the Post Office's computer system has underlined the importance of basic bookkeeping and staff training, experts say.

The report by Second Sight comes after UK sub-postmasters said they had been wrongly accused of theft, fraud and false accounting. Some lost their homes and a few went to prison.

Second Sight was hired by the Post Office to investigate a handful of the sub-postmasters' claims. Although the accountants' interim report found no evidence of systemic problems with the core software, it did find bugs in it.

It found two occasions, in 2011 and 2012, when the Post Office identified 'defects' in Horizon, its computer system that resulted in a shortfall of about £9,000 at 76 branches. The Post Office took a year to realise that the second computer defect had happened.

The Post Office later made good those losses and the sub-postmasters were not held liable.

Sub-postmasters criticised Horizon for being too complex, having unreliable hardware and having inadequate helpdesk support, the report found.

The Post Office said the report showed its system was effective but said it would improve training and support…

It's still unclear whether accounting errors were caused by computer error, poor working practices or lax safeguards against fraud.

As Second Sight's report notes: "Our experience over many years, shows that even apparently robust controls sometimes fail to work, or can be circumvented by a determined and skilful person."

Source: Accounting Web, http://www.accountingweb.co.uk/article/bug-found-post-office-computer-system-after-losses/544264, accessed July 2014

In addition, unless proper internal controls are established and maintained, computer systems can actually assist fraud. An example is provided in Real World Example 8.2, wherein HM Treasury report on a fraud that occurred within a government department.

REAL WORLD EXAMPLE 8.2

Bill Paying Fraud

…A junior member of staff over a period of two years was able to defraud a department of over £100,000 by exploiting weaknesses in purchasing and payments systems.

The junior clerk had been employed by the department for six years in the purchasing directorate. He showed an aptitude for computers and as well as the normal duties associated with his position he was also asked to carry out tasks such as setting up and maintaining computer records. He would also fill in for colleagues who were ill or on annual leave and so built up an extensive knowledge of how the purchasing directorate operated.

Two years after the junior clerk joined the department there was an upgrade to the computer system. As part of this process the purchasing directorate updated its supplier records and moved them onto a database. The junior clerk was involved in setting up the database and cleaning up individual records to be moved on to the database. He was given a password which enabled him to create and edit records. On completion of this task the junior clerk moved to a purchasing team where he was involved in the processing of purchase orders and the information needed to enable payments to be made to suppliers.

Security over the computer system was lax and the junior clerk realized that the password previously given to him to carry out specific tasks still allowed him access. In particular, he was able to access the supplier database and create false supplier records. He was aware that only a minimal check of the database was carried out by management and that generally there was very little checking and monitoring of the work of the procurement teams.

Having created bogus suppliers, he opened bank accounts in their names. Through his position in the purchasing team he was able to introduce fictitious invoices from these suppliers, designed on his computer at home, into the payment system. He easily obtained and signed the purchase orders and authorization forms necessary to support the invoices for payment. The finance section accepted his signature as authorization for payment. The finance section had in fact built up a practice of accepting any purchasing staff signature as payment authorization. There was no effective budgetary control over purchases and little monitoring of actual expenditure against budgets. The junior clerk was in fact responsible for what little monitoring there was and he was able to satisfy his managers that where there had been an overspend this was a result of operational demands. No further checking was carried out by management.

The fictitious invoices were paid by payable orders in the normal manner. These were sent to accommodation addresses arranged by the junior clerk who visited these regularly and banked the orders.

***Source*:** HM Treasury, 'Bill Paying Fraud, Fraud Case Notes', pp. 1–45 http://www.xact.org.uk/information/downloads/Fraud/Fraud_case_notes.pdf, accessed September 2013.

Summary

In accounting a distinction is made between cash and credit transactions. A cash transaction is one where goods or services are paid for in cash or by cheque when they are received or delivered. A credit transaction is one where payment is made or received some time after delivery. Credit transactions often involve trade discounts and cash discounts. Trade discount is a discount given by one trader to another in arriving at the price of the goods. Cash discount is a reduction in the amount that the customer has to pay provided payment is made within a given period which is stipulated by the seller.

Cash transactions are recorded in the books of account from the receipt, if paid or received in cash, or from the cheque book and bank paying-in book, if paid or received by cheque. Cash receipts and payments are entered in a book of prime entry known as the 'petty cash book'. Cheque receipts and payments are entered in the 'cash book'.

Credit transactions involve a number of different documents, but those which are recorded in the books of account comprise invoices, debit notes and credit notes. These arise in connection with both purchases and sales, and are entered in a set of books of prime entry commonly known as 'day books'. Purchase invoices and debit notes are entered in the 'purchases day book', and purchase credit notes in the 'purchases returns day book'. Sales invoices and debit notes are entered in the 'sales day book', and sales credit notes in the 'sales returns day book'.

A further book of prime entry known as the 'journal' is used to record all other transactions, particularly the purchase and sale of non-current assets on credit.

Key terms and concepts

bank paying-in book	142	invoice	138
bill of exchange	143	journal	143
bills payable book	143	ledger	143
bills receivable book	143	nominal ledger	143
book of prime entry	143	petty cash book	143
cash book	143	purchases day book	143
cash discounts	138	purchases returns day book	143
cash transaction	138	receipt	142
cheque	140	sales day book	143
credit note	138	sales returns day book	143
credit transaction	138	statement	140
debit note	138	trade discount	138
general ledger	143		

An asterisk after the question number indicates that there is a suggested answer in Appendix 2.

Review questions

connect

8.1 Explain the difference between a cash transaction and a credit transaction.

8.2 Explain the difference between trade discount and cash discount.

8.3 Outline the purpose and content of (a) an invoice; (b) a debit note; and (c) a credit note.

8.4 Explain the difference between an invoice and (a) a statement; (b) a receipt.

8.5 List the books of prime entry with which you are familiar and briefly describe what each is intended to record, including the documents used to write them up.

8.6 Briefly describe the nature of a bill of exchange.

8.7 Explain the purpose of books of prime entry.

Exercises

connect

BASIC

8.8 You have received goods from trader X who invoiced you and delivered the invoice with the goods. You have just received a debit note for £100.

a What is a debit note?

b How should the £100 be accounted for?

BASIC

8.9* List the four books of prime entry that are used to record inventory movements.

BASIC

8.10* What do you have to do to a cheque to make it safe when sending it to a supplier using the postal system?

Chapter 9

Double entry and the general ledger

Learning Objectives:

After reading this chapter you should be able to do the following:

1. Explain the principles of double-entry bookkeeping, including the purpose of having different ledger accounts.
2. List the three steps to take when performing double entry.
3. Describe the format and contents of the general ledger and ledger accounts.
4. Distinguish between asset and expense accounts, and between capital, liability and income accounts.
5. Enter cash (including cheque) transactions and credit transactions in the ledger.

9.1 The principles of double-entry bookkeeping

Bookkeeping versus accounting

As mentioned earlier, financial accounting is all about providing useful information in the financial statements to users to enable them to make economic decisions. It is all about communicating information. Recording transactions in the books of an entity is not accounting, it is bookkeeping. Accountants usually come in after the bookkeeper has finished and use the information supplied by the bookkeeper to prepare financial statements. However, to be able to account properly, accountants need to understand bookkeeping. Therefore this section of the book focuses on bookkeeping. There are two approaches to recording entities transactions: single-entry bookkeeping or double-entry bookkeeping. **Single-entry bookkeeping** focuses on recording the income and expenses of a business. It usually does not provide sufficient information to enable the preparation of the statement of financial position. It is a simple system that is not costly to operate; however, it can be costly in the long run as errors are less likely to be detected than if the system were double entry and the information being prepared from the resulting data is less likely to be relied on for decision-making. For example, if a bank were considering whether to offer a business a loan, they would likely require accounting information that is prepared from a double-entry bookkeeping system. **Double-entry bookkeeping** involves recording each transaction twice. One entry is positive (inflow of value) the other negative (an outflow of value) and overall the positive entries should equal the negative entries hence errors are more likely to be noted. It is a systematic method of recording an enterprise's transactions and uses a book (or module if the system is computerized) called the **general ledger**, **nominal ledger** or simply the '**ledger**'. Each page of the ledger is split into two halves: the left half is called the **debit side** and the right half is called the **credit side**. The ledger is divided into sections called **accounts**. In practice, each of these accounts is on a separate page. There is usually an 'account' for every class of expenditure, income, asset and liability. Separate accounts are created to record transactions into and out of the business by its owner(s). For example, there are typically separate accounts for wages expenses, for stationery, for heat and light, for motor vehicles, loans, drawings, capital introduced by the owner, and so on. There could be 1,000 accounts, depending on the detail required by management. Each of these 'accounts' can be traced to the financial statements. More detail is provided in the ledger than is provided in the statement of profit or loss and in the statement of financial position, as too much detail would reduce the understandability of the information being presented (i.e. the user would not see the wood for the trees).

Indeed, many of the transactions that enter the ledger are summarized in other bookkeeping books beforehand to reduce the entries to the ledger. In this chapter it is assumed that all transactions are posted directly to the ledger (in practice transactions are entered into a day book before entry to the ledger, for example, sales are recorded in the sales day book, of which the daily/weekly total is entered into the general ledger).

Double-entry bookkeeping

Double-entry bookkeeping is an application of the dual aspect concept. Under this concept each transaction affects two accounts (hence the name 'double-entry') and records a flow of value between the accounts. In accounting, a language has developed to indicate the direction of the flow: to debit an account means to have value flow into that account, whereas to credit an account means to have value flow out of that account. Convention has it that a debit always means an adjustment to the left-hand side of the ledger account, whereas a credit means an adjustment to the right-hand side of the ledger account. Some people find it easier to think of debits as being a ' + ' and a credit as being a ' – '.

The money value of each transaction is entered once on each side of the general ledger in different accounts. The actual process of placing the bookkeeping entry in each account is called '**posting the transaction**' or simply '**posting**'. For example, if we take one transaction such as the sale of goods for cash of £100 on 6 January, this would be recorded (posted) as follows:

Ledger

Debit				Credit			
Date	**Details**	**Folio**	**Amount**	**Date**	**Details**	**Folio**	**Amount**
Cash account (page 1)							
6 Jan	Sales	p. 2	100				

Debit				Credit			
Date	**Details**	**Folio**	**Amount**	**Date**	**Details**	**Folio**	**Amount**
Sales account (page 2)							
				6 Jan	Cash	p. 1	100

The cash account on page 1 is debited with £100 and the sales account on page 2 is credited with £100.

T accounts

Many academics and textbooks create a simplified version of a ledger account called a 'T' account to teach bookkeeping to students. A T account leaves out some of the detail that is given in ledger accounts, such as the reference to the folio page (the pages in a ledger are typically called folios) and contains fewer lines. A typical T account has the following headings:

Debit		*Account name*			Credit
Date	**Details**	**£**	**Date**	**Details**	**£**

The date column is the date of the transaction, the details column outlines the other account being posted to (so that the transaction can be traced) and the £ column records the amount that is being posted. Just like the ledger, flows of value to the account will be debited to the left-hand side, and flows of value from the account are recorded on the right-hand side (credited). A separate T account is opened for every type of expense, asset, liability, income and transaction with the owner (capital introduced and separately, drawings).

The three steps required for every double-entry transaction are outlined in Figure 9.1.

Figure 9.1

Double entry

- Determine the two accounts to be adjusted
- Consider the flow of value (which account does it go to? Which account does it leave?)
- Identify the money value that is being transferred

Steps to take when performing double entry (posting)

The transaction noted previously was the sale of goods for cash of £100 on 6 January.

1 The two accounts affected are the *sales account* and the *cash account*.

2 Cash comes in (debit); therefore, the value must leave the *sales account* (credit).

3 The value transferring is £100.

In accounting language this translates as:

Debit:	*Cash account*	£100	
Credit:	*Sales account*		£100

and is shown in the two T accounts as follows:

Cash account						*Sales account*					
Date	**Details**	**£**	**Date**	**Details**	**£**	**Date**	**Details**	**£**	**Date**	**Details**	**£**
6 Jan	Sales	100							6 Jan	Cash	100

9.2 Cash and bank transactions

When cash is received, it is entered on the debit side of the **cash account** (as the flow of value is to cash) and credited to the account to which the transaction relates. When cash is paid out, it is entered on the credit side of the *cash account* (an outflow of value from cash) and on the debit side of the account to which the transaction relates. The same occurs with cheques received and paid, except that they are entered in an account called the **bank account** instead of the *cash account*.

When someone starts a business they usually put money into the business. This is debited to the *cash* or *bank account* (depending on whether it is cash or a cheque) and credited to a **capital introduced account**. Money introduced at a later date by the proprietor as additional capital is treated in the same way. Any money withdrawn by the proprietor is credited in the *cash* or *bank account* (depending on whether it is cash or a cheque) and debited to a **drawings account**. These accounts are never netted against each other.

Sometimes businesses also borrow money. The amount received is debited to the *cash* or *bank account* (depending on whether it is cash or a cheque) and credited to an account in the name of the lender, who is referred to as a **loan creditor**. Examples of double entry are covered in Worked Example 9.1.

Learning Activity 9.1

Prepare a *cash account* for your cash transactions over the forthcoming week or month. Make the necessary double-entry in the other ledger accounts.

Double entry is now taken a step further by introducing monetary values and T account entries. The entries for various cash transactions are illustrated in Worked Example 9.2.

WORKED EXAMPLE 9.1

Complete the following table showing which accounts are to be debited and which are to be credited in the spaces provided:

	Debit	Credit
a) Bought office machinery in cash		
b) Bought lorry for cash		

c) A loan of £200 is received by cheque from Earls		
d) Paid stationery by cheque		
e) Paid rates by cash		
f) Owner wrote a cheque to himself		
g) Owner put cash into the business		
h) Owner buys a washing machine for his home and pays by cheque		

Solution

	Debit	Credit
a) Bought office machinery in cash	Office machinery a/c	Cash a/c
b) Bought lorry for cash	Motor vehicles a/c	Cash a/c
c) A loan of £200 is received by cheque from Earls	Bank a/c	Earls a/c (loan creditor)
d) Paid stationery by cheque	Stationery a/c	Bank a/c
e) Paid rates by cash	Rates a/c	Cash a/c
f) Owner wrote a cheque to himself	Drawings a/c	Bank a/c
g) Owner put cash into the business	Cash a/c	Capital introduced a/c
h) Owner buys a washing machine for his home and pays by cheque	Drawings a/c	Bank a/c

WORKED EXAMPLE 9.2

S. Baker started business on 1 January 20X5 as a grocer with capital (in cash) of £1,000. She also borrowed £500 in cash from London Bank Ltd. Her transactions during January, which are all in cash, were as follows:

1 Jan Paid one month's rent for the shop: £100

2 Jan Bought fixtures and fittings for the shop: £300

8 Jan Purchased goods for resale: £400

9 Jan Paid £25 carriage inwards

10 Jan Bought stationery for £50

15 Jan Paid £200 in wages for shop assistant

20 Jan Cash taken by S. Baker for her private use: £150

31 Jan Cash takings for the month: £600

You are required to write up the accounts in the general ledger.

Solution

Cash account					
20X5	**Details**	**£**	**20X5**	**Details**	**£**
1 Jan	Capital	1,000	1 Jan	Rent	100
1 Jan	Loan – London Bank Ltd	500	2 Jan	Fixtures and fittings	300
31 Jan	Sales revenue	600	8 Jan	Purchases	400
			9 Jan	Carriage inwards	25
			10 Jan	Stationery	50
			15 Jan	Wages	200
			20 Jan	Drawings	150

Capital introduced account					
20X5	**Details**	**£**	**20X5**	**Details**	**£**
			1 Jan	Cash	1,000

Loan – London Bank account					
20X5	**Details**	**£**	**20X5**	**Details**	**£**
			1 Jan	Cash	500

Rent account					
20X5	**Details**	**£**	**20X5**	**Details**	**£**
1 Jan	Cash	100			

Fixtures and fittings account					
20X5	**Details**	**£**	**20X5**	**Details**	**£**
2 Jan	Cash	300			

Purchases account					
20X5	**Details**	**£**	**20X5**	**Details**	**£**
8 Jan	Cash	400			

Carriage inwards account					
20X5	**Details**	**£**	**20X5**	**Details**	**£**
9 Jan	Cash	25			

Stationery account					
20X5	**Details**	**£**	**20X5**	**Details**	**£**
10 Jan	Cash	50			

Wages account					
20X5	**Details**	**£**	**20X5**	**Details**	**£**
15 Jan	Cash	200			

Drawings account

20X5	Details	£	20X5	Details	£
20 Jan	Cash	150			

Sales revenue account

20X5	Details	£	20X5	Details	£
			31 Jan	Cash	600

Notes

1 The narrative in the details column of an account specifies the name of the account that contains the other entry for each transaction.

2 **Carriage inwards** refers to haulage costs relating to goods that this business has purchased and is responsible for transporting from the seller's premises.

9.3 Ledger entries for credit transactions

The entries in the ledger for credit transactions are more complicated than those for cash transactions. This is because a credit transaction involves at least two (and sometimes three) events, each of which is recorded in double-entry form. In this section, credit bookkeeping is explained using the most common types of credit transactions – the purchase and sale of inventory. Movements in inventory are not recorded in an *inventory account* because the value moving out of the account (sale) is different to the value moving into the account (the purchase). Putting the two transactions in the one account would be an example of netting (off-set), which is not allowed under law. Users are interested in knowing sales figures; it is one of the growth indicators. They are also interested in knowing how much the items cost that were sold. Therefore, they want to see purchases. The difference between the sales value and the purchase value of the item(s) sold is the **gross profit** on the item(s) and this information is disclosed separately in the statement of profit or loss (covered later). In addition to sales and purchases, there are two other types of inventory movement that have to be recorded separately: purchase returns and sales returns. The level of sales returns gives an indication of the quality of the entity's products and the level of purchase returns provides information on the entity's purchasing policy. Therefore, inventory movements are recorded in four separate accounts (see Figure 9.2).

Figure 9.2

Movements inwards	*Posting*	*Movements outwards*	*Posting*
Purchases account	*Debit*	Sales account	*Credit*
Sales returns account (returns inward)	*Debit*	Purchase returns account (returns outward)	*Credit*

The recording of purchase and sales returns inventory

Postings to the *purchases* and *sales returns* ledger accounts will always be on the debit side and these accounts will always have a debit balance, and postings to the *sales* and *purchase returns* ledger accounts will always be on the credit side and these accounts will always have a credit balance. A walked-through example of the double-entry posting to the appropriate T accounts is now provided. At this stage it is assumed that the sales ledger and the purchase ledger are not kept separate from the general ledger, so each credit customer and credit supplier has their own account in the general ledger. These accounts are typically recorded in separate day books with only the total 'trade receivables' and total 'trade payables' entering the general ledger. This is not covered in this chapter but will be examined in depth in Chapter 11, 'Day Books and the Journal'.

Credit sales

The first event consists of the purchase or sale of goods on credit as evidenced by an invoice. The invoice is recorded in the ledger as follows:

1 Feb	Sold goods on credit to AB Ltd for £500

The first step is to identify the two accounts affected: The *sales account* and *AB Ltd account (trade receivable)*.

The next step is to identify the flow of value: The goods represent the value and the goods physically go to AB Ltd (so the value leaves the *sales account* (credit) and flows to *AB Ltd's account* (debit)).

The next step is to identify the monetary value flowing between the accounts: In this case it is £500.

Sales account						*AB Ltd account*					
20X5	**Details**	**£**	**20X5**	**Details**	**£**	**20X5**	**Details**	**£**	**20X5**	**Details**	**£**
			1 Feb	AB Ltd	500	1 Feb	Sales	500			

The amount outstanding on credit from a credit customer is referred to as a **trade receivable**. In the above example, the balance owing from AB Ltd is a trade receivable of the business whose books are being prepared. In the UK, trade receivables are commonly called 'debtors'. The term '**debtor**' arises from the existence of an account in the seller's books that contains more on the debit side than on the credit side. International Financial Reporting Standards (IFRSs) do not use the term 'debtor'.

Credit purchases

2 Feb	Purchased goods on credit from CD Ltd for £250

Identify the two accounts affected: The *purchases account* and *CD Ltd account (trade payable)*.

Identify the flow of value: The goods represent the value and they physically come from CD Ltd (so the value flows to the *purchases account* (debit) and from *CD Ltd's account* (credit)).

Identify the monetary value flowing between the accounts: In this case it is £250.

CD Ltd account						*Purchases account*					
20X5	**Details**	**£**	**20X5**	**Details**	**£**	**20X5**	**Details**	**£**	**20X5**	**Details**	**£**
			2 Feb	Purchases	250	2 Feb	CD Ltd	250			

The amount owing to a business or person from whom goods are purchased on credit is referred to as a **trade payable**. In the above example, the balance owing to CD Ltd is a trade payable of the business whose books are being prepared. In the UK, trade payables are commonly called 'creditors'. The term '**creditor**' arises from the existence of an account in the purchaser's books which contains more on the credit side than on the debit side. IFRSs do not use the term 'creditor'.

Sales returns

A second event that may occur when goods are bought and sold on credit is the return of goods. This can arise, for example, when some of the goods delivered were not ordered, or are defective. When goods are returned the seller sends the buyer a credit note. This is recorded in the ledger as follows:

3 Feb	AB Ltd returned goods invoiced for £100

Identify the two accounts affected: The *returns inward account* and *AB Ltd account (trade receivable).*

Identify the flow of value: The goods represent the value and they come from AB Ltd (so the value flows to the *returns inward account* (debit) and comes from *AB Ltd's account* (credit)).

Identify the monetary value flowing between the accounts: In this case it is £100.

Returns inward account						*AB Ltd Account*					
20X5	**Details**	**£**	**20X5**	**Details**	**£**	**20X5**	**Details**	**£**	**20X5**	**Details**	**£**
3 Feb	AB Ltd	100				1 Feb	Sales	500	3 Feb	Returns inward	100

Purchase returns

Similarly, goods received may be defective, or not fit for purpose. These will be returned to the supplier. They are not treated as a reduction in purchases, but are recorded in a separate account, the *returns outward account.*

Then on 4 Feb	The entity returned goods to CD Ltd invoiced for £50

Identify the two accounts affected: The *returns outward account* and *CD Ltd account (trade payable).*

Identify the flow of value: The goods represent the value and they go to CD Ltd (so the value flows to *CD Ltd's account* (debit) and comes from the *returns outward account* (credit)).

Identify the monetary value flowing between the accounts: In this case it is £50.

CD Ltd account						*Returns outwards account*					
20X5	**Details**	**£**	**20X5**	**Details**	**£**	**20X5**	**Details**	**£**	**20X5**	**Details**	**£**
4 Feb	Returns outwards	50	2 Feb	Purchases	250				4 Feb	CD Ltd	50

The balance on the customer's (AB Ltd) and supplier's (CD Ltd) accounts thus show the amounts of money owed at any point in time net of returns.

Receiving funds from credit customers

The third event that occurs when goods are bought and sold on credit is the transfer of money in settlement of the debt. The entries on settlement of a trade receivable account by a credit customer are recorded in the ledger as follows:

5 Feb	Received from AB Ltd cash of £400

Identify the two accounts affected: The *cash account* and *AB Ltd account (trade receivable)*.

Identify the flow of value: Money is the value and it flows to the *cash account* (debit) and flows from *AB Ltd's account* (credit).

Identify the monetary value flowing between the accounts: In this case it is £400.

Cash account						*AB Ltd account*					
20X5	**Details**	**£**	**20X5**	**Details**	**£**	**20X5**	**Details**	**£**	**20X5**	**Details**	**£**
5 Feb	AB Ltd	400				1 Feb	Sales	500	3 Feb	Returns inward	100
									5 Feb	Cash	400

Paying credit suppliers

The entries on settlement of a trade payable account by the business are recorded in the ledger as follows:

6 Feb	Paid CD Ltd £200 in cash

Identify the two accounts affected: The *cash account* and *CD Ltd account (trade payable)*.

Identify the flow of value: Money is the value and it flows from the *cash account* (credit) and flows to *CD Ltd's account* (debit).

Identify the monetary value flowing between the accounts: In this case it is £200.

CD Ltd account						*Cash account*					
20X5	**Details**	**£**	**20X5**	**Details**	**£**	**20X5**	**Details**	**£**	**20X5**	**Details**	**£**
4 Feb	Returns outwards	50	2 Feb	Purchases	250	5 Feb	AB Ltd	400	6 Feb	CD Ltd	200
6 Feb	Cash	200									

An illustration of both a credit and cheque transaction is shown in Worked Example 9.3. The three steps are not shown in each instance. This is something that is done subconsciously and is not recorded.

A further related complication occurs where a business pays cash sales into its bank account. This can be treated as two transactions. The first transaction is cash sales that are recorded as a debit in the *cash account* and a credit in the *sales account*. The second is the payment of this money into the bank that is recorded as in Worked Example 9.3, note 5a. Alternatively, where cash sales are banked on a regular basis, such as daily, the more common method of recording this is simply to debit the *bank account* and credit the *sales account*. There are thus no entries in the cash account.

WORKED EXAMPLE 9.3

E. Blue commenced business in 1 July 20X4 as a wholesale greengrocer with capital in the bank of £2,000. His transactions during July were as follows:

1 July Bought a second-hand van by cheque for £800

3 July Paid insurance on the van by cheque for £150

7 July Purchased goods costing £250 on credit from A. Brown

11 July	Sold goods on credit to B. Green amounting to £450
14 July	Paid carriage outwards by cheque amounting to £20
16 July	Returned goods to A. Brown of £50
18 July	Repairs to van paid by cheque: £30
20 July	B. Green returned goods of £75
23 July	Sent A. Brown a cheque for £140
26 July	Received a cheque from B. Green for £240
31 July	Paid telephone bill by cheque: £65
31 July	Paid electric bill by cheque: £45

You are required to write up the accounts in the general ledger.

Solution

Bank account

20X4	**Details**	**£**	**20X4**	**Details**	**£**
1 July	Capital	2,000	1 July	Vehicles	800
26 July	B. Green	240	3 July	Motor expenses	150
			14 July	Carriage outwards	20
			18 July	Motor expenses	30
			23 July	A. Brown	140
			31 July	Telephone and postage	65
			31 July	Light and heat	45

Capital account

20X4	**Details**	**£**	**20X4**	**Details**	**£**
			1 July	Bank	2,000

Motor vehicles account

20X4	**Details**	**£**	**20X4**	**Details**	**£**
1 July	Bank	800			

Motor expenses account

20X4	**Details**	**£**	**20X4**	**Details**	**£**
3 July	Bank	150			
18 July	Bank	30			

Purchases account

20X4	**Details**	**£**	**20X4**	**Details**	**£**
7 July	A. Brown	250			

A. Brown account (trade payable)					
20X4	**Details**	**£**	**20X4**	**Details**	**£**
16 July	Returns	50	7 July	Purchases	250
23 July	Bank	140			

Sales account					
20X4	**Details**	**£**	**20X4**	**Details**	**£**
			11 July	B. Green	450

B. Green account (trade receivable)					
20X4	**Details**	**£**	**20X4**	**Details**	**£**
11 July	Sales	450	20 July	Returns	75
			26 July	Bank	240

Purchase returns (outwards) account					
20X4	**Details**	**£**	**20X4**	**Details**	**£**
			16 July	A. Brown	50

Sales returns (inwards) account					
20X4	**Details**	**£**	**20X4**	**Details**	**£**
20 July	B. Green	75			

Carriage outwards account					
20X4	**Details**	**£**	**20X4**	**Details**	**£**
14 July	Bank	20			

Telephone and postage account					
20X4	**Details**	**£**	**20X4**	**Details**	**£**
31 July	Bank	65			

Light and heat account					
20X4	**Details**	**£**	**20X4**	**Details**	**£**
31 July	Bank	45			

Notes

1 The narrative in the details column of the expense accounts is 'bank' because the other side of the double entry is in the *bank account*.

2 Where there is more than one transaction relating to the same type of expenditure these are all entered in the same account (e.g. *motor expenses*). However, the purchase of a vehicle (capital expenditure) is shown in a different account from the running costs, referred to as an **asset account**.

3 Lighting and heating expenses, such as coal, electricity, gas and heating oil, are usually all entered in an account called *light and heat.* The same principle is applied in the case of the *telephone and postage account,* the *rent and rates account* and the *printing and stationery account.*

4 **Carriage outwards** refers to haulage costs relating to goods that this business has sold and is responsible for delivering.

5 A business sometimes pays cash into its bank account and at other times withdraws cash from its bank account. The ledger entries for these transactions are as follows:

(a) Paying cash into the bank:

Debit:	*Bank account*	£'XXX	
Credit:	*Cash account*		£'XXX

(b) Withdrawing cash from a bank account:

Debit:	*Cash account*	£'XXX	
Credit:	*Bank account*		£'XXX

Learning Activity 9.2

Prepare a bank account for your cheque transactions over the forthcoming week or month. Make the necessary double-entry in ledger accounts.

9.4 Adjustments for drawings and capital introduced

Drawings may take a number of forms in addition to cash. For example, it is common for the owner to take goods out of the business for his or her personal consumption. This requires an adjustment that may be done by either of two entries:

1 debit *drawings* and credit *purchases* with the *cost* of the goods to the business; or

2 debit *drawings* and credit *sales* where the goods are deemed to be taken at some other value such as the normal selling price.

Another form of drawings occurs where the business pays the owner's personal debts. A common example of this is taxation on the business profits. Sole traders and partnerships are not liable to taxation as such. It is the owner's personal liability and not that of the business; therefore, if taxation is paid by the business, it must be treated as drawings. The ledger entry is to debit *drawings* and credit the *cash account.*

A similar form of drawings occurs when the business has paid expenses, some of which relate to the owner's private activities. The most common example is where the business has paid motor expenses, some of which relate to the owner's private vehicle or the use of a business asset for domestic or social purposes. The ledger entry in this case is to debit *drawings* and credit the relevant expense account. The principle is exactly the same where the owner takes a non-current asset out of the business for his or her permanent private use.

WORKED EXAMPLE 9.4

6 Feb	Owner took £50 worth of vegetables for private use

Identify the two accounts affected: The *drawings account* and the *purchases account.*

Identify the flow of value: The goods are the value and the flow is from the *purchases account* (credit) to the *drawings account* (debit).

Identify the monetary value flowing between the accounts: In this case it is £50.

Purchases a/c						*Drawings account*					
20X5	**Details**	**£**	**20X5**	**Details**	**£**	**20X5**	**Details**	**£**	**20X5**	**Details**	**£**
			6 Feb	Drawings – vegetables	50	6 Feb	Purchases	50			

Some other examples of drawings occasionally found in examination questions include where the owner buys a private asset (e.g. a car, holiday, groceries) for himself or herself, or for a friend or relative (e.g. spouse), and pays for it from the business cash or bank account. The ledger entry is to debit *drawings* and credit the *cash book (cash account)*. A similar but more complicated example is where a credit customer of the business pays their debt to the owner (who pays the money into his or her private bank account) or alternatively the owner accepts some private service (repairs to his or her private assets, a holiday, and so on) in lieu of payment. In this case the ledger entry is to debit *drawings* and credit the *credit customer's trade receivables account.*

After all the drawings for the accounting year have been entered in the *drawings account*, this account must be closed by transferring the balance to the *capital account*. The entry is to credit the *drawings account* and debit the *capital account.*

Capital introduced after the start of a business usually takes the form of either cash/cheques or other assets (e.g. a vehicle). The ledger entry is to credit the *capital introduced account* and debit the appropriate asset account (e.g. *cash book, motor vehicles*). A slight variation on this occurs when the owner buys a business asset (e.g. vehicle or goods for resale) or pays a business expense or liability from his or her private cash/bank account. In this case the ledger entry is to credit the *capital introduced account* and debit the relevant asset (e.g. *motor vehicles*), *liability*, *expense* or *purchases account*. A more complicated version of the same principle is where the owner privately provides some service to a supplier of the business in lieu of payment. The ledger entry for this will be to credit the *capital introduced account* and debit the *credit suppliers' account.*

Some of these examples of drawings and capital introduced are quite common in small businesses, and particularly important in the context of partnerships, as will be seen in Part 7, 'Partnerships'.

9.5 Adjustments for goods on sale or return

Goods that have been sent to potential customers on sale or return or on approval must not be recorded as sales until actually sold. In the ledger, **goods on sale or return** at the end of an accounting year are included in inventories at cost. In many instances it is difficult to determine the exact number of sales that have been made (the cost of finding this out may outweigh the benefits) and an estimate of expected returns is used instead. This approach is evident in the following real world example.

REAL WORLD EXAMPLE 9.1

Bloomsbury Publishing accounting policy

v) Critical accounting estimates and judgments…

…Book returns

As books are returnable by customers, the Group makes a provision against books sold in the accounting period which is then carried forward and offset against trade receivables in the statement of financial position in anticipation of book returns received subsequent to the reporting period end. The provision is calculated by reference to historical returns rates and expected future returns.

Source: extract from Bloomsbury Publishing Annual Report, 2013, http://www.bloomsbury-ir.co.uk/annual_reports/2013/085.asp#, accessed September 2013.

9.6 Ledger account balances

Each account can be totalled to give a balance that represents all the transactions affecting that account in the period. This balance can then be transferred to the statement of profit or loss or the statement of financial position. The main purposes of the ledger accounting system are to provide a means of ascertaining the total amount of each type of income and expenditure, the total value of the assets owned by the business (e.g. cash), and how much is owed to and by the business. For example, the *cash account* shows how much money the business has at any time. Also, when there are several transactions, the *sales account* will contain all the sales made during a period and thus it is possible to see at a glance the total sales for that period. Similarly, other accounts, such as *wages* and *postage*, will show the total amount spent on each of these types of expense for the period. These are referred to as **nominal accounts** (also called general ledger or simply ledger accounts). The information extracted from the totals of the nominal accounts is used to ascertain the profit or loss for a given period.

When the total amount of money on the debit side of an account is greater than that on the credit side, the account is said to have a **debit balance**. When the reverse is the case, the account is said to have a **credit balance**. An account that contains a debit balance represents either an asset (such as cash) or an expense or loss. An account with a credit balance represents capital, a liability, income (such as sales) or a gain.

Summary of expected balances on particular types of account Statement of profit or loss account	
Debit balances	*Credit balances*
Expenses	Income

Therefore, a profit is a credit balance (as a profit results when income exceeds expenditure) and a loss is a debit balance. The income and expense nominal account balances do not carry forward into the next year (as discussed in Chapter 7, 'The Accounting Equation and its Components') but are all transferred to the statement of profit or loss account where they are netted against each other to form either a profit or a loss. This can be regarded as being a statement of financial position account. The statement of financial position accounts are carried into the next year. A summary of the expected balances on nominal accounts in the statement of financial position is as follows:

Statement of financial position	
Debit balances	*Credit balances*
Assets	Liabilities
Drawings	Capital (opening balance)
Losses	Capital introduced
	Profits

The **capital account** can be regarded as the owner's investment in the entity. From the entity's perspective, the *capital account* is the liability of the entity to the owner. Hence the *capital account* usually has a credit balance. Having knowledge of what the owner withdraws and introduces to the business is deemed to be of relevance for users. Hence, the movements in the owner's *capital account* are recorded in three accounts – *drawings, capital introduced* and the *statement of profit or loss account.*

As mentioned, the statement of profit or loss is an account that takes the balances of all the revenue type accounts (income and **expense accounts**), summarizes them and presents them in a manner that is deemed to be of use to users and then transfers the balance (profit or loss) to the owner's *capital account.* In the context of the *capital account*, it can be assumed that every sale is made on behalf of the owners and increases the liability to them (hence is a credit) and every expense reduces the amount that is due to the owners (hence is a debit).

Therefore, profits and capital introduced will increase the balance on the capital account and drawings and losses will reduce the balance on the capital account.

Owners' capital movement accounts	
Debit balances	*Credit balances*
Drawings	Capital introduced
Losses	Profits

At the end of each reporting period the balances on each of these accounts are cleared to the *capital account*, to either increase or decrease the capital balance that has been carried forward from the previous statement of financial position. The closing balance of this account is then carried forward into the statement of financial position in the next period.

Summary

After being recorded in a book of prime entry, all business transactions are entered in another book called the 'ledger'. This is based on the double-entry principle and comprises various accounts. Each account is divided into two halves; the left half is called the debit side and the right half is called the credit side. The money value of every transaction is recorded once on each side of the ledger in different accounts. The main purposes of this system are to provide a means of ascertaining the total amount of each type of income and expenditure for a period, and the value of the assets and liabilities at a point in time. When the total amount on the debit side of an account is greater than that on the credit side, the account is said to have a debit balance. When the reverse is the case, the account is said to have a credit balance. An account that contains a debit balance represents an asset, a drawing, an expense or a loss. An account with a credit balance represents capital, capital introduced, a liability, income or a gain.

The ledger entries for cash transactions are made in a *cash account* (if in cash) or a *bank account* (if by cheque). These are then posted to the opposite side of another account representing the nature of the transaction. The ledger entries for credit transactions are more complicated because these are treated in accounting as comprising at least two separate transactions: the purchase (or sale) of goods on credit, and the settlement of the debt. The purchase of goods is debited to the *purchases account* and credited to the *supplier's trade payables account*. The sale of goods is credited to the *sales account* and debited to the *customer's trade receivables account*. When the supplier is paid this is credited to the *cash* (or *bank) account* and debited to the *supplier's trade payables account*. When money is received from a customer, this is debited to the *cash* (or *bank) account* and credited to the *customer's trade receivables account*.

Key terms and concepts

accounts	150	drawings	161
asset account	160	drawings account	152
bank account	152	expense account	164
capital account	164	general ledger	150
capital introduced	162	goods on sale or return	162
capital introduced account	152	gross profit	155
carriage inwards	155	ledger	150
carriage outwards	161	loan creditor	152
cash account	152	nominal account	163
credit balance	163	nominal ledger	150
credit side	150	posting	150
creditor	157	posting the transaction	150
debit balance	163	single entry bookkeeping	150
debit side	150	trade payable	156
debtor	156	trade receivable	156
double-entry bookkeeping	150		

An asterisk after the question number indicates that there is a suggested answer in Appendix 2.

Exercises

connect

BASIC

9.1 (Statement of profit or loss double-entry)

Complete the following table showing which ledger account is to be debited and which is to be credited:

	Debit	Credit
a) Stationery purchased on credit from Gormley		
b) Rates paid by direct debit		
c) Telephone bill paid by cash		
d) Stationery returned to Gormley		
e) Insurance paid by direct debit		
f) Cash sales		
g) Cheques received for sales		
h) Cash wages		
i) Wages paid by BACS		

BASIC

9.2 (Inventory movements)

Complete the following table showing which ledger accounts are to be debited and which are to be credited:

	Debit	Credit
a) Goods sold on credit to Gormley		
b) Goods bought on credit from Morgan		
c) Goods bought for cash		
d) Goods bought by cheque		
e) Goods sold for cash		
f) Goods sold on credit to Earls		
g) Goods bought on credit from McAfee		

BASIC

9.3* H. George commenced business as a butcher on 1 October 20X4 introducing cash of £5,000 from her personal bank account to the newly opened business bank account. Her transactions during October 20X4, which were all in cash, are as follows:

1 Oct	Rent of shop: £200
2 Oct	Purchases of goods: £970
4 Oct	Bought fixtures and fittings: £1,250
6 Oct	Borrowed £3,500 from S. Ring
9 Oct	Purchased delivery van: £2,650
12 Oct	Sold goods for £1,810
15 Oct	Paid wages of £150

18 Oct	Purchases: £630
19 Oct	Drawings: £350
21 Oct	Petrol for van: £25
22 Oct	Printing costs: £65
24 Oct	Sales: £1,320
25 Oct	Repairs to van: £45
27 Oct	Wages: £250
28 Oct	Purchased stationery costing £35
30 Oct	Rates on shop: £400
31 Oct	Drawings: £175

You are required to record the above transactions in the ledger (use T accounts).

9.4* L. Johnson started business on 1 March 20X5 with capital of £10,000 in a bank current/cheque account. During March 20X5 he made the following transactions: BASIC

1 Mar	Paid £5,000 by cheque for a 10-year lease on a shop
2 Mar	Bought office equipment by cheque at a cost of £1,400
4 Mar	Bought goods costing £630 from E. Lamb on credit
6 Mar	Paid postage of £35 by cheque
9 Mar	Purchases by cheque: £420
11 Mar	Sold goods on credit to G. Lion for £880
13 Mar	Drawings by cheque: £250
16 Mar	Returned goods costing £180 to E. Lamb
18 Mar	Sold goods and received a cheque for £540 in payment
20 Mar	Paid telephone bill by cheque: £120
22 Mar	G. Lion returned goods invoiced at £310
24 Mar	Paid gas bill by cheque: £65
26 Mar	Sent E. Lamb a cheque for £230
28 Mar	Received a cheque for £280 from G. Lion
30 Mar	Paid electricity bill of £85 by cheque
31 Mar	Paid bank charges of £45

You are required to enter the above transactions in the ledger (use T accounts).

9.5 N. Moss commenced business on 1 May 20X5 with a capital of £5,000 of which £1,000 was in cash and £4,000 was in a bank current/cheque account. Her transactions during May were as follows: BASIC

1 May	Borrowed £2,000 from Birmingham Bank Ltd in the form of a cheque
2 May	Paid rent of £750 by cheque
5 May	Paid wages of £120 in cash
8 May	Purchased goods for £1,380 by cheque

10 May	Sold goods for £650 cash
12 May	Withdrew £200 in cash for personal use
15 May	Bought goods on credit for £830 from S. Oak
18 May	Sold goods on credit for £1,250 to K. Heath
20 May	Bought shop fittings of £2,500 by cheque
23 May	Paid water rates of £325 in cash
25 May	Paid gas bill of £230 by cheque
27 May	Returned goods costing £310 to S. Oak
28 May	K. Heath returned goods with an invoice value of £480
29 May	N. Moss introduced further capital by cheque: £3,000
30 May	Bought stationery of £90 in cash
31 May	Sent S. Oak a cheque for £300
31 May	Received a cheque for £500 from K. Heath.

You are required to show the above transactions in the ledger (use T accounts).

BASIC

9.6 Enter the following transactions in the books of 'Seamus McKee' for November (use T accounts).

1 Nov	Started business with £10,000 in the bank
2 Nov	Paid for advertising by cheque: £130
3 Nov	Paid for stationery by cheque: £50
5 Nov	Bought goods on credit from Red: £900
5 Nov	Sold goods for cash: £300
6 Nov	Paid for insurance in cash: £8
8 Nov	Bought machinery on credit from Black: £700
9 Nov	Paid for machinery expenses in cash: £150
10 Nov	Sold goods on credit to Flanagan: £800
11 Nov	Returned goods to Red: £200
12 Nov	Paid wages in cash: £20
13 Nov	Received cheque from Flanagan: £500
15 Nov	Paid rent by cheque: £200
20 Nov	Bought stationery on credit for £60 from Hutchinson
21 Nov	Paid Black £700 by cheque
30 Nov	Paid Hutchinson £60 by cheque
30 Nov	Sold goods on credit to Flanagan: £500

BASIC

9.7 Enter the following transactions in the books of 'Mary Ward' for December (use T accounts).

1 Dec	Introduced a motor vehicle to the new business worth £8,000
1 Dec	Transferred a computer from home to the business: £500

1 Dec	Withdrew £200 cash from her personal account to cover the cash expenses of the business
1 Dec	Put a cheque in the business bank account to cover business start-up costs: £10,000
1 Dec	Purchased goods for sale by cheque: £4,000
2 Dec	Bought a van using a loan from the bank: £15,000
2 Dec	Bought office equipment using a loan from the bank: £5,000
3 Dec	Received cheques amounting to £5,000 for sales made
4 Dec	Purchased stationery for £450
5 Dec	Purchased envelopes for £25 using cash
6 Dec	Paid wages by cheque: £400
9 Dec	Purchased goods for sale for £2,000 by cheque
10 Dec	Sales lodged: £3,000
10 Dec	Cash sales: £1,000
12 Dec	Cash lodged: £800
14 Dec	Pens purchased in cash: £20
15 Dec	Loan instalment transferred by direct debit (DD): £1,000
18 Dec	Mary wrote a business cheque to her personal account: £2,000
21 Dec	Petrol paid by cheque: £280
22 Dec	Petrol for vehicles paid by cash: £40
23 Dec	Wages paid by cheque: £400
24 Dec	Second loan instalment DD from bank: £1,000

Chapter 10

The balancing of accounts and the trial balance

Learning Objectives:

After reading this chapter you should be able to do the following:

1. Balance and close ledger accounts (T accounts).
2. Describe the nature and purposes of a trial balance.
3. Prepare a trial balance from the ledger or list of ledger account balances (T accounts).

10.1 The balancing of accounts

At the end of every accounting period it is necessary to balance each account in the ledger. This has to be done at least annually, and more likely monthly.

The procedure for balancing an account is as follows:

1 Leave one blank line under the last entry in the ledger account and draw parallel lines on the top and bottom of the next line in the amounts column on each side. When this happens it marks the end of the period. All the transactions before the totalling lines represent the period that has just ended and the area after the totalling lines represents the new period.

2 Add up each side of the ledger account and calculate the difference using a separate piece of paper (when you become familiar with balancing off accounts you will no longer need to use a separate piece of paper, except perhaps for the bank account).

3 If the amount of the debit side exceeds that on the credit side, enter the difference on the credit side immediately after the last entry on that side (in step one you left a blank line for this purpose). This is the closing balance on the account. Similarly where the amount on the credit side exceeds that on the debit side, the difference should be entered on the debit side immediately after the last entry on that side. The result is that with the entered closing balance, both sides will total exactly.

4 Enter the total of each side of the ledger account between the parallel lines. These two figures should now be the same.

5 There are three descriptions used to close off accounts. These descriptions identify where the closing balance will end up in the new period.

   a When the ledger account is a statement of financial position account (an asset, capital or liability account, for example the motor vehicles account, bank account, loan account, etc.), the closing balance within the period (before the parallel lines) should be described as the '**balance carried down**' (Bal. c/d). Enter the same figure on the opposite side below the parallel lines. This should be described as the '**balance brought down**' (Bal. b/d). This is double-entry in practice – the closing balance from one period is being carried forward as the opening balance in the next period. For example, this may involve debiting the current period with the closing balance and crediting the new period with the same amount (the opening balance). Statement of financial position accounts typically have opening balances.

   b When the account is a statement of profit or loss account (income or expense accounts, for example sales, wages, purchases, heat and light, etc.) the closing balance transfers to the *statement of profit or loss account* and should be described as such (shortened sometimes to P/L a/c). This is a T account that is set up to determine the profit or loss made in the period. These ledger accounts will typically not have opening balances in the next period as the balance from the previous period has been transferred somewhere else (the statement of profit or loss account); however, whenever there are accruals or adjustments (Chapter 17) these accruals will be carried forward into the ledger T accounts in the next period. The accrual entries are statement of financial position items; however, they typically remain within the statement of profit or loss account. The *statement of profit or loss account* should be the second last account to be closed.

   c Finally, any account that represents a movement in owners' capital (drawings, capital introduced and the statement of profit or loss account) will be balanced off to the *owners' capital account*. Therefore, the description showing the destination of the closing balance on these accounts will be 'owners' capital'. The *owners' capital account* is a statement of financial position account. As all movements take place in the latter-mentioned accounts, this account will only have the opening balance. When all the movement accounts are closed and the balances transferred to this account, it will be closed and the balance carried down to the next period. This is the last account to be closed off.

This is illustrated below using the ledger accounts from the answer to Worked Example 9.3 (Chapter 9). It is the period end (31 July) and the ledger accounts are being closed for the purposes of preparing the financial statements. This illustration will take you step by step through the stages of closing off an entity's books. An example of the three different types of account and the different way of closing them off is highlighted by shading.

Closing a statement of financial position account – the *bank account*

Step one – identify the type of account it is (*Bank* is a statement of position account. It is the least predictable account as the bank can be either a current asset or a current liability, if in overdraft).

Step two – leave a gap below the longest column of figures (shaded below) and put totals' lines on both the credit and debit sides of the account. Leave room below the totals' lines for the opening balance. In practice, in a ledger there would be enough room after the total rows for several periods' transactions after July.

Bank account

20X4	Details	£	20X4	Details	£
1 July	Capital	2,000	1 July	Vehicles	800
26 July	B. Green	240	3 July	Motor expenses	150
			14 July	Carriage outwards	20
			18 July	Motor expenses	30
			23 July	A. Brown	140
			31 July	Telephone and postage	65
			31 July	Light and heat	45

Step three – add up each side of the ledger account and calculate the difference using a separate piece of paper. In this instance the debit side totals £2,240 and the credit side totals £1,250. As the debit side has a larger balance, this will be the expected sign of the opening balance in the next period. This account will be regarded as having a debit balance (debits > credits). The larger of the sides will be the amount that goes in the totals' column (£2,240), as follows.

Bank account

20X4	Details	£	20X4	Details	£
1 July	Capital	2,000	1 July	Vehicles	800
26 July	B. Green	240	3 July	Motor expenses	150
			14 July	Carriage outwards	20
			18 July	Motor expenses	30
			23 July	A. Brown	140
			31 July	Telephone and postage	65
			31 July	Light and heat	45
		2,240			2,240

Step four – work out the closing balance and put it in the correct side. In this instance, the closing balance is £990 (£2,240 – £1,250) and the balance will have to go on the credit side of the account, otherwise the numbers on the credit side will not add up to £2,240. This is shown as follows:

Bank account

20X4	Details	£	20X4	Details	£
1 July	Capital	2,000	1 July	Vehicles	800
26 July	B. Green	240	3 July	Motor expenses	150
			14 July	Carriage outwards	20
			18 July	Motor expenses	30
			23 July	A. Brown	140
			31 July	Telephone and postage	65
			31 July	Light and heat	45
					990
		2,240			2,240

Step five – complete the double entry (otherwise the books will not balance). If you make an entry into an account, you must carry the value to another account, or in this case to the next period of the same account. At this stage the correct date and description need to be entered beside the closing balance. As a statement of position account, this period will be closed off and the balance carried into the next period (which starts on 1 August).

Bank account

20X4	Details	£	20X4	Details	£
1 July	Capital	2,000	1 July	Vehicles	800
26 July	B. Green	240	3 July	Motor expenses	150
			14 July	Carriage outwards	20
			18 July	Motor expenses	30
			23 July	A. Brown	140
			31 July	Telephone and postage	65
			31 July	Light and heat	45
			31 July	Balance c/d	990
		2,240			2,240
1 Aug	Balance b/d	990			

Closing a movement in capital account – the *capital introduced account*

This account is a movement in capital account and the balance on it will be transferred to the *capital account* at the period end (as this is a new business, this *capital account* will have to be opened).

Capital introduced account

20X4	Details	£	20X4	Details	£
			1 July	Bank	2,000
31 July	Capital a/c	2,000			
		2,000			2,000

The double-entry to close the *capital introduced account* is provided in journal form to assist student understanding. This is not required to be produced in exams and is not reproduced in the examples from now on. Instead (just in the case of this example), the relevant entries are shaded to highlight the debit–credit relationship.

Debit:	*Capital introduced account* (to close)	£2,000	
Credit:	*Capital account*		£2,000

The *capital introduced account* is now closed and has no opening balance in the new period. This makes sense as users will want to see what the owner has introduced in each period. This information would be difficult to obtain if all the items affecting owners were just pooled into the *capital account.*

Capital account

20X4	Details	£	20X4	Details	£
			31 July	Capital introduced a/c	2,000

The *capital account* is not closed yet; it is the last ledger account to close as the *statement of profit or loss account* is closed off to this account.

The next account to close is the motor vehicles account.

Motor vehicles account

20X4	Details	£	20X4	Details	£
1 July	Bank	800			
			31 July	Balance c/d	800
		800			800
1 Aug	Balance b/d	800			

As an asset, the *motor vehicles account* is a statement of financial position account; therefore, the closing balance is carried into the next period.

Closing a revenue type account – the *motor expenses account*

As a revenue expense, this account will balance into the *statement of profit or loss ledger account* and will have no opening balance in the next period. The *statement of profit or loss ledger account* for this period has to be opened to receive this expense.

Motor expenses account

20X4	Details	£	20X4	Details	£
3 July	Bank	150			
18 July	Bank	30			
			31 July	Statement of P&L a/c	180
		180			180

The *motor expenses account* is described as having a debit balance as the debit side is greatest and the balance is carried into the debit side of the *statement of profit or loss ledger account.* The *statement of profit or loss ledger account* is not closed at this time. It is the second last ledger account to be closed.

Statement of profit or loss account

20X4	Details	£	20X4	Details	£
31 July	Motor expenses	180			

The next account to be closed is the *purchases account.* As a revenue expense, this is a statement of profit or loss account, hence will be closed off in the same manner as the *motor vehicles account.*

Purchases account					
20X4	**Details**	**£**	**20X4**	**Details**	**£**
7 July	A. Brown	250			
			31 July	Statement of P&L a/c	250
		250			250

Statement of profit or loss account					
20X4	**Details**	**£**	**20X4**	**Details**	**£**
31 July	Motor expenses	180			
31 July	Purchases	250			

The next account to be closed is *A. Brown's trade payable account*. As a liability, this account is a statement of financial position account; hence the balance will be carried into the next period.

A. Brown account (trade payable)					
20X4	**Details**	**£**	**20X4**	**Details**	**£**
16 July	Returns	50	7 July	Purchases	250
23 July	Bank	140			
31 July	Balance c/d	60			
		250			250
			1 Aug	Balance b/d	60

The *sales revenue account* is a revenue account; as such it will be closed off to the *statement of profit or loss ledger account*.

Sales revenue account					
20X4	**Details**	**£**	**20X4**	**Details**	**£**
			11 July	B. Green	450
31 July	Statement of profit or loss a/c	450			
		450			450

Statement of profit or loss account					
20X4	**Details**	**£**	**20X4**	**Details**	**£**
31 July	Motor expenses	180	31 July	Sales revenue	450
31 July	Purchases	250			

B. Green's account is a trade receivable. Trade receivables are current assets, which are statements of financial position ledger accounts; therefore, the closing balance will be carried forward into the next period.

B. Green account (trade receivable)					
20X4	**Details**	**£**	**20X4**	**Details**	**£**
11 July	Sales revenue	450	20 July	Returns	75
			26 July	Bank	240
			31 July	Balance c/d	135
		450			450
1 Aug	Balance b/d	135			

The *purchase returns account* is a revenue account; as such the balance is transferred to the *statement of profit or loss ledger account.*

Purchase returns (outwards) account					
20X4	**Details**	**£**	**20X4**	**Details**	**£**
			16 July	A. Brown	50
31 July	Statement of P&L a/c	50			
		50			50

Statement of profit or loss account					
20X4	**Details**	**£**	**20X4**	**Details**	**£**
31 July	Motor expenses	180	31 July	Sales revenue	450
31 July	Purchases	250	31 July	Purchase returns	50

Likewise, the *sales returns account* is a revenue account; as such the balance is transferred to the *statement of profit or loss ledger account.*

Sales returns (inwards) account					
20X4	**Details**	**£**	**20X4**	**Details**	**£**
20 July	B. Green	75			
			31 July	Statement of P&L a/c	75
		75			75

Statement of profit or loss account					
20X4	**Details**	**£**	**20X4**	**Details**	**£**
31 July	Motor expenses	180	31 July	Sales revenue	450
31 July	Purchases	250	31 July	Purchases returns	50
31 July	Sales returns	75			

Carriage outwards, telephone and postage, and heat and light are revenue expenses; therefore, the balances will be transferred to the *statement of profit or loss ledger account.*

Carriage outwards account					
20X4	**Details**	**£**	**20X4**	**Details**	**£**
14 July	Bank	20			
			31 July	Statement of P&L a/c	20
		20			20

Telephone and postage account					
20X4	**Details**	**£**	**20X4**	**Details**	**£**
31 July	Bank	65			
			31 July	Statement of P&L a/c	65
		65			65

Heat and light account					
20X4	**Details**	**£**	**20X4**	**Details**	**£**
31 July	Bank	45			
			31 July	Statement of P&L a/c	45
		45			45

At this stage all the ledger accounts (except the *capital account*) have been closed; therefore, the *statement of profit or loss ledger account* can be closed. The balance represents the period's profit or loss. If the sum of the debit side (expenses) is greater than the sum of the credit entries then the entity has made a loss in the period; if the credit side (income) is greater, then the entity has made a profit in the period. Either way the balance is transferred to the *owners' capital account*. No balance will appear in the next period. Like the bank, the balance on this account can be either a debit or a credit, so it is good practice to add up each side and determine the largest before proceeding with the closure. In this instance the debit side is larger at £635, whereas the credit side adds to £500. Therefore the balance is a loss.

Statement of profit or loss account

20X4	Details	£	20X4	Details	£
31 July	Motor expenses	180	31 July	Sales revenue	450
31 July	Purchases	250	31 July	Purchase returns	50
31 July	Sales returns	75			
31 July	Carriage outwards	20			
31 July	Telephone and postage	65			
31 July	Heat and light	45			
			31 July	Capital a/c	135
		635			635

At this stage the *capital ledger account* (a statement of financial position account) can be closed with the balance carried forward into the next period to reflect the owner's investment in the business on that date. This becomes the opening capital balance in the new period.

Capital account

20X4	Details	£	20X4	Details	£
31 July	Loss from P/L a/c	135	31 July	Capital introduced a/c	2,000
31 July	Balance c/d	1,865			
		2,000			2,000
			31 July	Balance b/d	1,865

The ledger accounts are now fully closed for the period.

By now you should have noticed some of the rules outlined in the last chapter happening in practice. Expense accounts always have debit balances. Income accounts have credit balances. Asset accounts have debit balances. Liability accounts have credit balances. The *capital account* mostly has a credit balance (though in rare instances an owner may withdraw more than he or she is entitled to, in which case the capital account balance becomes a debit – because the owner owes the business money).

If the total of each side of an account is the same there will be a nil balance.

10.2 The purposes and preparation of a trial balance

The **trial balance** is neither part of the general ledger nor is it a book of prime entry (although it is often prepared on paper with the same ruling as the journal). It is a list of the balances in the general ledger (nominal ledger, ledger) at the end of an accounting period, divided between those ledger accounts with debit balances and those with credit balances. Since every transaction recorded in the ledger consists of both a debit and a credit entry, the total of the balances on each side should be the same. This is checked by entering on the trial balance the balance of each account in the ledger, and adding up each side. The purposes of the trial balance are summarized in Figure 10.1.

Figure 10.1

To ascertain whether the total of the ledger accounts with debit balances equals the total of the ledger accounts with credit balances	• This proves that the same money value of each transaction has been entered on both sides of the general ledger. • It proves the arithmetic accuracy of the ledger accounts. However, a trial balance can agree but there may still be errors in the ledger. For example, an amount may have been entered on the correct side but in the wrong account, or a transaction could have been completely omitted.
To assist in the preparation of the financial statements	• To easily identify the totals on the revenue accounts for the period for inclusion in the statement of profit or loss. • To easily identify the assets and liabilities at the end of that period for inclusion in the statement of financial position. • In practice this is done in the form of an extended trial balance (see Chapter 18, 'The Extended Trial Balance and Final Financial Statements (Advanced)').

Purposes of a trial balance

All the ledger accounts end up in two reports in the financial statements: the statement of profit or loss and the statement of financial position. Because the ledger accounts making up the statement of profit or loss are disclosed separately for users' benefits they are separately listed in the trial balance and the *statement of profit or loss ledger account* is not created until after the trial balance has been prepared. As noted, the trial balance does not form part of the double-entry process. The trial balance is just a memorandum that is used to check that the ledger accounts balance and to assist in preparing the financial statements for disclosure purposes. As mentioned, it is expected that expenses, returns inward and assets will have debit balances and income, returns outward, capital and liabilities will have credit balances. An illustration of the preparation of a trial balance is given in Worked Example 10.1. The amounts are taken from the closed ledger accounts noted in the last section of this chapter. *Note*: the *capital account* and the *statement of profit or loss account* are not listed as these accounts only include the closing balances of other ledger accounts. To include them in the trial balance would be to account for all their component accounts twice.

WORKED EXAMPLE 10.1

E. Blue

Trial balance as at 31 July 20X4

Name of account	Debit £	Credit £
Bank	990	
Capital introduced		2,000
Motor vehicles	800	
Motor expense	180	
Purchases	250	
A. Brown (trade payable)		60
Sales revenue		450
B. Green (trade receivable)	135	
Purchase returns		50
Sales returns	75	
Carriage outwards	20	
Telephone and postage	65	
Heat and light	45	
	2,560	2,560

If a trial balance does not agree, students often fail to take a systematic approach to ascertaining the reason. It is therefore suggested that the following procedure be adopted, which will minimize effort and time spent looking for the errors.

1 Recast the trial balance.

2 Check that no ledger account has been omitted from the trial balance. This sometimes happens with the *cash* and *bank account* balances as they are usually in separate books.

3 Check that each amount entered in the trial balance is on the correct side. This is quick to do once you become familiar with the nature of different ledger accounts.

4 Check to see that the amounts entered in the trial balance are the same as those shown in the ledger accounts.

5 If the error has still not been found, it will then be necessary to check all the entries in the general ledger.

6 If the difference between the totals of the trial balance is divisible by nine, then it is likely that a ledger account balance or a transaction has been transposed incorrectly – for example, if the heat and light account had been recorded as £54 instead of £45, or the account B. Green had been recorded as £315 instead of £135.

It is also worth noting that often in examinations no marks are given for correct trial balance totals. The student will therefore only lose marks for the error that caused it to disagree. Thus, do not spend more than a few minutes trying to make a trial balance agree.

A further illustration of the preparation of a trial balance is given in Worked Example 10.2. The data in the question would not be presented in this manner in practice, but the question is a useful way of testing your knowledge of which ledger accounts contain debit balances and which contain credit balances.

WORKED EXAMPLE 10.2

The following is a list of the balances appearing in the general ledger of T. Wall at 30 September 20X4:

	£		£
Capital	32,890	Trade payables	4,620
Drawings	5,200	Land and buildings	26,000
Loan from M. Head	10,000	Plant and machinery	13,500
Cash	510	Listed investments	4,800
Bank overdraft	1,720	Interest paid	1,200
Sales revenue	45,600	Interest received	450
Purchases	29,300	Rent received	630
Returns inwards	3,800	Salaries	3,720
Returns outwards	2,700	Repairs to buildings	810
Carriage inwards	960	Plant hire charges	360
Carriage outwards	820	Bank charges	240
Trade receivables	7,390		

You are required to prepare a trial balance.

Solution

T. Wall ***Trial balance as at 30 September 20X4***		
Name of account	**Debit**	**Credit**
Capital		32,890
Drawings	5,200	
Loan from M. Head		10,000
Cash	510	
Bank overdraft		1,720
Sales revenue		45,600
Purchases	29,300	
Returns inwards	3,800	
Returns outwards		2,700
Carriage inwards	960	
Carriage outwards	820	
Trade receivables	7,390	
Trade payables		4,620
Land and buildings	26,000	
Plant and machinery	13,500	
Listed investments	4,800	
Interest paid	1,200	
Interest received		450
Rent received		630
Salaries	3,720	
Repairs to buildings	810	
Plant hire charges	360	
Bank charges	240	
	98,610	98,610

Notes

1 As mentioned before, the *cash account* can only have a debit balance. However, the *bank account* may contain either a debit or a credit balance. A credit balance occurs where the business is overdrawn at the bank.

2 The items 'Trade receivables' and 'Trade payables' are common in trial balances. These are the totals of the individual personal accounts of credit customers and suppliers, respectively.

3 The account *'Listed investments'* refers to money invested in equity stocks and shares that are listed/quoted on the London Stock Exchange/Irish Stock Exchange.

Learning Activity 10.1

Prepare a trial balance for the ledger entries made for Learning Activities 9.1 and 9.2.

At this point in your studies of accounting you have covered the core systems (accounts, ledgers, posting and the trial balance) that underpin the accounting system in any entity. This knowledge is valued by businesses as highlighted by the following example recruitment advertisement from late 2013.

REAL WORLD EXAMPLE 10.1

Reed Accountancy

Bookkeeper

Job type: Permanent, full-time £17,000 – £18,000 per annum

Organisation Description

My client is looking for a bookkeeper to join its small but busy team.

Job Description

Main responsibilities include:

– All aspects of sales/purchase ledger

– Accruals, prepayments

– Accounts to trial balance

– VAT returns

– Intrastat/Sales EC reporting

– Month end reporting

– Ad-hoc duties

Person Specification

Ideally you will have good knowledge of all round accounting and strong experience of Sage Line 50.

Reed Specialist Recruitment Limited is an employment agency and employment business

Source: Adapted from http://www.reed.co.uk/jobs/bookkeeper/23442925#/jobs/accountancy/bookkeeper, accessed September 2013.

Errors that cause the trial balance to disagree are covered in section 21.2 of Chapter 21 'Errors and Suspense Accounts'. You may wish to cover this topic at this point.

Summary

At the end of each accounting period every account in the ledger must be balanced. The balance is the difference between the monetary amounts on the two sides of an account. There are three ways to close off ledger accounts depending on the nature of the account. If the ledger account is a movement in the *owners' capital account*, then it is balanced off to the *capital account* (a statement of financial position account). If the account is a revenue ledger account (income or expense), the balance is transferred to the *statement of profit or loss ledger account*. Finally, if the ledger account is an asset, liability or capital account, then the balance carries forward into the new period. The closing balance is entered in the ledger account as a balance carried down at the end of the period, and as a balance brought down at the start of the following period.

The balances on all the ledger accounts are used to prepare a trial balance on a loose sheet of paper. A trial balance is a list of the balances in a general ledger at a specific time, divided into those with debit balances and those with credit balances. Since every transaction is recorded in the general ledger on both the debit and credit sides, the total of the ledger accounts with debits should equal the total of the ledger accounts with credit balances. The main purpose of the trial balance is to ascertain whether this is the case, and thus to check the accuracy of the ledger. Another function of the trial balance is to facilitate the preparation of final financial statements.

Key terms and concepts

balance brought down	172	trial balance	178
balance carried down	172		

An asterisk after the question number indicates that there is a suggested answer in Appendix 2.

Review question

connect

10.1 Explain the main purposes of a trial balance.

Exercises

connect

BASIC **10.2*** Close off the ledger accounts in Worked Example 9.2 (Chapter 9) fully transferring the ledger balances into the next period, the *capital ledger account* or the *statement of profit or loss ledger account* where appropriate.

BASIC **10.3*** Prepare a trial balance for Worked Example 9.2 (Chapter 9).

BASIC **10.4*** Close off the T accounts and prepare a trial balance from your answer to Question 9.3 in Chapter 9.

BASIC **10.5*** Close off the T accounts and prepare a trial balance from your answer to Question 9.4 in Chapter 9.

BASIC **10.6** Close off the T accounts and prepare a trial balance from your answer to Question 9.5 in Chapter 9.

BASIC **10.7** Close off the T accounts and prepare a trial balance from your answer to Question 9.6 in Chapter 9.

BASIC **10.8** Close off the T accounts and prepare a trial balance from your answer to Question 9.7 in Chapter 9.

BASIC **10.9** The following is a list of balances in the ledger of C. Rick at 31 May 20X5:

	£
Cash at bank	2,368
Purchases	12,389
Sales revenue	18,922
Wages and salaries	3,862
Rent and rates	504
Insurance	78
Motor expenses	664
Printing and stationery	216
Light and heat	166
General expenses	314
Premises	10,000
Motor vehicles	3,800
Fixtures and fittings	1,350
Trade receivables	3,896
Trade payables	1,731
Cash in hand	482
Drawings	1,200
Capital	12,636
Bank loan	8,000

Required

Prepare a trial balance.

10.10 The following is a list of balances in the general ledger of R. Keith at 30 June 20X4:

	£
Capital	39,980
Drawings	14,760
Loan – Bromsgrove Bank	20,000
Leasehold premises	52,500
Motor vehicles	13,650
Investment	4,980
Trade receivables	2,630
Trade payables	1,910
Cash	460
Bank overdraft	3,620
Sales revenue	81,640
Purchases	49,870
Returns outwards	960
Returns inwards	840
Carriage	390
Wages and salaries	5,610
Rent and rates	1,420
Light and heat	710
Telephone and postage	540
Printing and stationery	230
Bank interest	140
Interest received	620

Required

Prepare a trial balance.

10.11 The following is a list of balances in the general ledger of J. McKee at 30 June 20X5: BASIC

	£'000
Drawings	50
Loan – Mainstreet Bank	500
Freehold premises	1,000
Vans	250
Fixtures and fittings	35
Trade receivables	650
Sundry tools	20
Sundry tools returned	5
Trade payables	500
Cash	2
Bank overdraft	56
Deposit account	100
Sales revenue	3,300
Purchases	1,800
Returns outwards	150
Returns inwards	100
Carriage inwards	80
Carriage outwards	10
Wages and salaries	850

	£'000
Rent and rates	58
Light and heat	45
Telephone and postage	18
Printing and stationery	25
Bank interest	5
Interest received	6
Rent received	23
Commission received	12

Required

a Prepare a trial balance.

b The trial balance does not balance (on purpose). Which account is missing? How much is the balance on this account (the accounting equation will help you answer this question)?

Chapter 11

Day books and the journal

Learning Objectives:

After reading this chapter you should be able to do the following:

1. List the books of prime entry for credit transactions.
2. Describe the purpose of each of the books of prime entry that are used to record credit transactions.
3. Describe the transactions and documents that are recorded in each of the day books and the journal.
4. Enter credit transactions in the appropriate day books or journal and post these to the relevant ledger accounts.
5. Prepare opening journal entries to record capital introduced other than cash, and the takeover of another sole trader.

11.1 The contents of the day books and the journal

Before a transaction is recorded in the general ledger, it must first be entered in a book of prime entry. These are intended to facilitate the posting of the general ledger, in that transactions of the same type are entered in the same book of prime entry, which is periodically posted to the general ledger in total (rather than one transaction at a time). These initial entries do not form part of double-entry bookkeeping.

There are several books of prime entry. This chapter examines only those that are used to record credit transactions as highlighted in Figure 11.1.

Figure 11.1

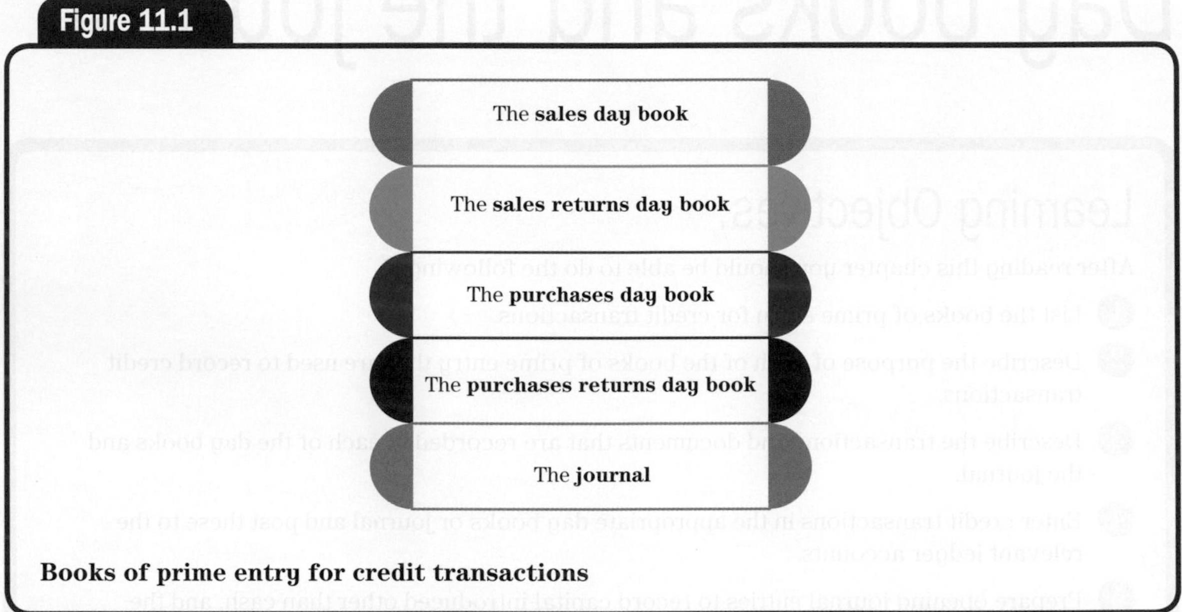

Books of prime entry for credit transactions

The transactions recorded in these books are as follows.

The sales day book

The **sales day book** is used to record the sale on credit of those goods bought specifically for resale. It is written up from copies of the sales invoices and debit notes retained by the seller. The amount entered in the sales day book is after deducting **trade discount**. At the end of each period, say calendar month, the total of the sales day book is credited to the *sales account* in the general ledger and the amount of each invoice and debit note is debited to the *individual credit customer's trade receivable account* in the sales ledger. Most entities have several credit customers. Keeping separate ledger accounts for each credit customer in the general ledger and recording these in the trial balance would be cumbersome. Therefore, to reduce clutter in the general ledger and the trial balance and to serve as a control (the latter point is dealt with in Chapter 20, 'Control Accounts') individual credit customers are maintained in a separate ledger called the **sales ledger**. The total of the balances on this ledger becomes the trade receivables amount. This total should agree to the balance on the *trade receivables account* in the general ledger. This balance is included in the statement of financial position.

The purchases day book

The **purchases day book** is used to record the purchase on credit of those goods bought specifically for resale. It is written up from the invoices and debit notes received from suppliers. The amount entered in the purchases day book is after deducting any trade discount received. At the end of each period, say calendar month, the total of the purchases day book is debited to the *purchases account* in the general ledger and the amount of each invoice and debit note received is credited to the *individual credit supplier's trade payable account* in the purchase ledger. Like credit customers, most entities also have several suppliers who provide goods on credit. Keeping separate ledger accounts for each credit supplier in the general ledger and recording these in the trial balance would be cumbersome. Therefore, to reduce clutter in the general ledger and the trial balance and to serve as a control, individual credit suppliers ledger accounts are maintained in a separate ledger called the **purchases ledger**. The total of the balances on this ledger becomes the trade payables amount. This total should agree to the balance on the *trade payables account* in the general ledger. The balance of this account is included in the statement of financial position.

The sales returns day book

The **sales returns day book** is used to record the credit notes sent to customers relating to goods they have returned or where they have been overcharged on an invoice. Note that the entry is made when a credit note has been issued, and not when the goods are returned or the amount of the invoice is queried. The sales returns day book is written up from copies of the credit notes retained by the seller. The amount shown in the sales returns day book is after deducting trade discount. At the end of each period (for example, calendar month) the total of the sales returns day book is debited to the *sales returns account* in the general ledger and the amount of each credit note credited to the *individual credit customer's trade receivable account* in the sales ledger.

The purchases returns day book

The **purchases returns day book** is used to record the credit notes received from suppliers relating to goods returned or where there has been an overcharge on the invoice. Note that the entry is made when a credit note is received and not when the goods are returned or the amount of the invoice is queried. The purchases returns day book is written up from the credit notes received from suppliers. The amount entered in the purchases returns day book is after deducting trade discount. At the end of each period (for example, calendar month) the total of the purchases returns day book is credited to the *purchases returns account* in the general ledger and the amount of each credit note received is debited to the *individual credit supplier's trade payable account* in the purchases ledger.

The journal

The **journal** is used to record a variety of things, most of which consist of accounting adjustments, such as the correction of errors, rather than transactions. However, the journal is also used to record transactions that are not appropriate to any other book of prime entry, the most common being the purchase and sale of **non-current assets** on credit. These are items not specifically bought for resale but to be used in the production and distribution of those goods normally sold by the business. Non-current assets are durable goods that usually last for several years and are normally kept by the business for more than one year. Examples include land and buildings, plant and machinery, motor vehicles, furniture, fixtures and fittings, and office equipment.

Unlike the sales, purchases and returns day books, the journal has debit and credit columns. These are not a part of the double entry in the ledger. They are used to indicate what entries are going to be made in the general ledger accounts in respect of a given transaction or adjustment. Each entry in the journal consists of the name of the ledger account that is to be debited (and the amount) and the name of the ledger account that is to be credited (and the amount). The nature of the entry must also be explained in a narrative that commonly starts with the word 'being'. Use of the word 'being' is considered to be old-fashioned and is not as strictly used. However, because it is still commonly used by many firms in practice, we have decided to continue to use it in this book. Having a description is of particular importance because of the variety of entries that are made in the journal. In addition, journals are usually used to record the posting of unusual transactions that may take quite a bit of explaining. Indeed, I recall at one time writing 10 lines of description to explain a complicated adjusting entry made to a client's records when I was a practising accountant.

An illustration of the entries in the above five books of prime entry (sales day book, purchases day book, sales return day book, purchases return day book and the journal) and the three ledgers (general ledger, sales ledger and purchase ledger) is given in Worked Example 11.1.

WORKED EXAMPLE 11.1

Bright Spark is an electrical goods wholesaler. The transactions during June 20X5, which are all on credit, were as follows:

1 June Bought on credit from Lights Ltd various bulbs with a retail price of £1,000 and received 20 per cent trade discount

4 June Sold goods on credit to Electrical Retailers Ltd for £500 and allowed them 10 per cent trade discount on this amount

8 June Sent Electrical Retailers Ltd a credit note for goods returned that had a retail value of £300

10 June Sold goods on credit to Smith Retailers Ltd for £600 after deducting 40 per cent trade discount

12 June Purchased goods with a retail value of £1,000 from Switches Ltd who allowed us 30 per cent trade discount

15 June Purchases on credit from Cables Ltd goods costing £550

16 June Sent Smith Retailers Ltd a credit note for goods returned that had a retail value of £100

18 June Switches Ltd sent us a credit note for £300 in respect of goods returned

19 June Received a credit note for goods returned to Lights Ltd that had a retail value of £250

25 June Sold goods to General Retailers Ltd on credit for £250

27 June Sent General Retailers Ltd a credit note for £50 to rectify an overcharge on their invoice

28 June Sold goods on credit to Electrical Retailers Ltd at a price of £560

29 June Purchased on credit a motor van from Brown Ltd that cost £800

30 June Sold on credit to London Trading Co. some fixtures and fittings no longer required in the shop for £350. (Prior to this the business owned fixtures costing £1,000.)

Required

Make the necessary entries in the books of prime entry and general ledger.

Before starting to undertake double entry, the first step is to summarize the transactions in the day books. The first part of this solution deals with the transactions that do not impact on the journal.

The entries are as follows:

Sales day book

Date	Name of credit customer	Our invoice number	Folio	Amount
20X5				**£**
4 June	Electrical Retailers Ltd	I00446	F34	450
10 June	Smith Retailers Ltd	I00447	F8	600
25 June	General Retailers Ltd	I00448	F45	250
28 June	Electrical Retailers Ltd	I00449	F15	560
				1,860

Sales returns day book

Date	Name of credit customer	Our credit note number	Folio	Amount
20X5				**£**
8 June	Electrical Retailers Ltd	CRN06	F34	270
16 June	Smith Retailers Ltd	CRN07	F8	60
27 June	General Retailers Ltd	CRN08	F45	50
				380

Purchases day book

Date	Name of credit supplier	Our ref no for supplier's invoice	Folio	Amount
20X5				**£**
1 June	Lights Ltd	Inv460	T23	800
12 June	Switches Ltd	I000672	T5	700
15 June	Cables Ltd	S0056932	T10	550
				2,050

Purchases returns day book

Date	Name of supplier	Our ref no for supplier's invoice	Folio	Amount
20X5				**£**
18 June	Switches Ltd	C00569	T5	300
19 June	Lights Ltd	SC452	T23	200
				500

The next step is to take the day books and to use them to enter the information into the main double-entry bookkeeping system (the general ledger, sales ledger and purchase ledger). These ledger accounts are shown in T account format. In practice they would enter a ledger (which has a similar format).

The first two day books to be closed off and posted are those involving customers (sales day book and the sales return day book). The sales day book is totalled and the total entered into the credit side of the *sales account* in the general ledger. The corresponding credit entry will be to the four *credit customer accounts* in the sales ledger (entries highlighted by shading). Similarly, the sales returns day book is totalled and the total entered into the debit side of the *sales return general ledger account*, with the corresponding credit entry being posted to the three *credit customers' accounts* in the sales ledger who returned goods (entries highlighted in bold). Note the normal double-entry rules in respect of recording the flow of value are being applied.

General ledger entries

Sales account

20X5	Details	£	20X5	Details	£
			30 June	Total per sales day book	1,860

Sales returns account

20X5	Details	£	20X5	Details	£
30 June	Total per sales returns day book	380			

Sales ledger entries

Electrical Retailers Ltd

20X5	Details	£	20X5	Details	£
4 June	Sales	450	8 June	Returns	**270**
28 June	Sales	560			

Smith Retailers Ltd

20X5	Details	£	20X5	Details	£
10 June	Sales	600	16 June	Returns	**60**

General Retailers Ltd

20X5	Details	£	20X5	Details	£
25 June	Sales	250	27 June	Returns	**50**

Next, the two day books involving suppliers (purchases day book and the purchases returns day book) are closed and posted. The purchases day book is totalled and the total entered into the debit side of the *purchases account* in the general ledger. The corresponding credit entry will be to the three *credit suppliers' accounts* in the purchases ledger (entries highlighted by shading). Similarly, the purchases returns day book is totalled and the total entered into the credit side of the *purchases return general ledger account*, with the corresponding credit entry being posted to the two *credit suppliers' accounts* in the purchases ledger who we returned goods to (entries highlighted in bold).

General ledger entries

Purchases account

20X5	Details	£	20X5	Details	£
30 June	Total per purchases day book	2,050			

Purchases returns account

20X5	Details	£	20X5	Details	£
			30 June	Total per purchases returns day book	**500**

Purchases ledger entries

Lights Ltd

20X5	Details	£	20X5	Details	£
19 June	Returns	**200**	1 June	Purchases	800

Switches Ltd					
20X5	**Details**	**£**	**20X5**	**Details**	**£**
18 June	Returns	**300**	12 June	Purchases	700

Cables Ltd					
20X5	**Details**	**£**	**20X5**	**Details**	**£**
			15 June	Purchases	550

The journal

The entries required to post the motor van on credit and the sale of fixtures and fittings are first recorded in the journal before they enter the general ledger bookkeeping system as follows:

Date	Details (account in which the ledger entry is to be made)	Folio	Debit amount	Credit amount
20X5				
29 June	*Motor vehicles*	Dr	800	
	To: Brown Ltd	Cr		800
	Being purchase on credit of motor van reg no ABC123.			
29 June	*London Trading Co*	Dr	350	
	To: fixtures and fittings	Cr		350
	Being sale on credit of shop fittings.			

Second, the journal is taken and its entries are posted to the individual ledger accounts in the general ledger as follows:

General ledger entries

Motor vehicles account					
20X5	**Details**	**£**	**20X5**	**Details**	**£**
29 June	Brown Ltd	800			

Brown Ltd account (sundry payable)					
20X5	**Details**	**£**	**20X5**	**Details**	**£**
			29 June	Motor vehicles	800

Fixtures and fittings account					
20X5	**Details**	**£**	**20X5**	**Details**	**£**
1 June	Balance b/d	1,000	30 June	London Trading Co	350
			30 June	Balance c/d	650
		1,000			1,000
1 July	Balance b/d	650			

London Trading Co account (sundry receivable)					
20X5	**Details**	**£**	**20X5**	**Details**	**£**
30 June	Fixtures and fittings	350			

Notes

1 The fixtures and fittings that were sold must obviously have already been owned by the business. Their cost is therefore included in the balance brought down on the debit side of the fixtures and fittings account along with the cost of other fixtures and fittings owned at that date.

2 The London Trading Co. is referred to as a sundry receivable and Brown Ltd as a sundry payable.

11.2 Opening entries/takeovers and the journal

Another use of the journal is to record and post **opening entries** as part of the double-entry bookkeeping system. An opening entry is an entry to record the capital introduced into the business by the owner when it consists of assets in addition to cash and, possibly, liabilities. As the name implies, this entry usually occurs when the business is formed and the books are being opened. However, it is also used to record the takeover of another business. This is illustrated in Worked Example 11.2.

WORKED EXAMPLE 11.2

A. King went into business on 1 March 20X5 by taking over a firm owned by B. Wright. The purchase consideration was £47,500, which had been computed by valuing the assets and liabilities that were taken over as follows:

	£
Shop	30,000
Fixtures and fittings	12,500
Inventories	4,600
Trade receivables	3,100
Trade payables	2,700

Required

Show the opening entries in the journal of A. King.

The journal

Date	Details/account		Debit	Credit
20X5				
1 Mar	*Land and buildings*	Dr	30,000	
	Fixtures and fittings	Dr	12,500	
	Inventories	Dr	4,600	
	Trade receivables	Dr	3,100	
	To: Trade payables	Cr		2,700
	To: Capital	Cr		47,500
			50,200	50,200
	Being assets and liabilities introduced into business by owner from takeover of an existing business			

Notes

1 The ledger entries will consist of debiting and crediting the ledger accounts shown above in the details column. In the case of trade receivables and trade payables the amounts will be entered in the personal accounts of the individuals/firms concerned in the sales ledger and the purchases ledger.

2 The capital of £47,500 is the difference between the total assets and liabilities brought into the business. This will be credited to the *capital introduced account.*

Learning Activity 11.1

Where possible, approach a local business or a family member who works in the administration function of a business and ask them about the books of account of the business. Ask them to explain the transactions that they record in each type of book. Different names to those used in this chapter may exist; however, they will typically perform the same function.

The bookkeeping system described in this chapter is manual. In practice most companies use computerized bespoke packages with different modules for each book which are automatically linked into the general nominal ledger. Examples include Sage (caters for all the different books), Dosh Cash book (focuses on recording cash transactions) or Microsoft (caters for all the different books). Some packages are freely downloadable. In an article by Williams (2013) the benefits of a number of 'free' packages are outlined. An excerpt is provided in Real World Example 11.1.

REAL WORLD EXAMPLE 11.1

Best free accounting software: 8 programs we recommend

1. TurboCASH 5

TurboCash is an open source small business accounting package, which the developers say has more than 80,000 users worldwide.

It has all the usual standard functions – stock control, invoicing, debtors, creditors, general ledger, VAT accounting, balance sheet and income statements, and plenty of reports – and also supports multiple users, and even multiple companies.

As with any similar package, if you're new to accounting in general then there's a great deal to learn. TurboCASH does make things easier with example books, though, and a detailed online manual helps you to get started.

The program is also highly configurable, and it's also a relief to use a free accounting tool which isn't always demanding that you 'upgrade'.

(*Other packages described in the article include*)

2. TAS Basics

3. GnuCash

4. NCH Express Invoice

5. xTuple PostBooks

6. VT Cash Book

7. Invoice Expert XE

8. Adminsoft Accounts

Source: Williams, M. (2013) http://www.techradar.com/news/software/applications/best-free-accounting-software-8-programs-we-recommend-1136684

Summary

Before a transaction is recorded in the ledger, it must first be entered in a book of prime entry. These are intended to facilitate the posting of the general ledger, in that transactions of the same type are entered in the same book of prime entry, the totals of which are periodically posted to the general ledger rather than one transaction at a time.

Credit transactions are recorded in a set of books of prime entry known as day books. The sales day book is used to record the sale of goods on credit of those goods specifically bought for resale, and is written up from copies of the sales invoices. The purchases day book is used to record the purchase on credit of those goods intended for resale, and is written up from the invoices received from suppliers. The sales returns and purchases returns day books are used to record returns, and are written up from the credit notes.

The posting of day books to the general ledger follows a common principle. The total of the day book is entered in the relevant general account (i.e. *sales, purchases, sales returns* or *purchases returns*), and the individual invoices or credit notes shown in the day book are posted to the *customers'* or *suppliers' personal trade credit accounts*, which are held separately from the general ledger in two ledgers called the 'sales ledger' and the 'purchases ledger'. The total of the balances on these ledgers represents the balance on the *trade receivables* (sales ledger) and *trade payables* (purchases ledger) *ledger accounts* in the trial balance. These balances are used to prepare the subsequent statement of financial position.

Credit transactions not relating to goods for resale (or services), such as the purchase and sale of non-current assets, are recorded in another book of prime entry known as the 'journal'. This is also used to record transactions that are not appropriate to any other book of prime entry, and various accounting adjustments that are not the subject of a transaction such as the correction of errors. The format of the journal includes a details column and two money columns labelled 'debit' and 'credit'. The narrative in the details column and amounts in the money columns indicate the entries that will be made in the ledger in respect of a given transaction or item.

Key terms and concepts

journal	189	purchases returns day book	189
non-current assets	189	sales day book	188
opening entries	194	sales ledger	188
purchases day book	188	sales returns day book	189
purchases ledger	189	trade discount	188

An asterisk after the question number indicates that there is a suggested answer in Appendix 2.

Review questions

connect

11.1 a Outline the purposes of those books of prime entry referred to as day books.

b Describe the contents, and state which documents are used to write up each of the following:

- **i** the sales day book;
- **ii** the purchases day book;
- **iii** the sales returns day book;
- **iv** the purchases returns day book.

11.2 a State two fundamentally different types of transactions/items that are recorded in the journal.

b Describe how these two transactions are recorded in the journal.

Exercises

connect

BASIC

11.3 B. Jones is in business as a builders' merchant. The following credit transactions took place during April 20X5:

1 Apr	Bought goods on credit from Brick Ltd for £725
2 Apr	Sold goods on credit to Oak Ltd for £410
4 Apr	Bought goods costing £315 from Stone Ltd on credit
7 Apr	Sold goods on credit to Pine Ltd for £870
11 Apr	Bought goods costing £250 from Slate Ltd on credit
15 Apr	Sold goods to Lime Ltd for £630 on credit
17 Apr	Bought goods on credit from Brick Ltd for £290
19 Apr	Received a credit note for £120 from Brick Ltd

22 Apr Sent Oak Ltd a credit note for £220

24 Apr Stone Ltd sent us a credit note for £75 in respect of goods returned

27 Apr Sent Pine Ltd a credit note for £360

Required

You are required to make the necessary entries in the books of prime entry and the general ledger.

BASIC

11.4 Veronica Reichester owns a shop. The following transactions happened in November.

1 Nov Credit sales: C. Flanagan £456, S. Morgan £300, F. Hutchinson £645, A. Adair £987

2 Nov Credit purchases: N. Ward £123, F. Wood £465, S. Duffy £786, N. Hynd £56

5 Nov Credit sales: C. Flanagan £560, S. Ruddle £560

6 Nov Credit purchases: F. Wood £79, N. Hynd £560

7 Nov Goods returned to Veronica by: F. Hutchinson £45, S. Ruddle £60

10 Nov Veronica returned goods to: N. Ward £19, N. Hynd £60

25 Nov Veronica sold goods on credit to: C. Flanagan £50, S. Morgan £45

28 Nov Veronica returned goods to: N. Ward £4

Required

a You are required to show the above transactions in the day books of Veronica's shop.

b Using this information post the transactions to the general ledger, sales ledger and purchase ledger.

c Close the ledger accounts and extract the trial balance.

BASIC

11.5* B. Player buys and sells soft furnishings and office equipment. During August 20X5 she had the following credit transactions:

1 Aug Bought goods on credit from Desks Ltd which had a retail price of £1,000 and trade discount of 25 per cent

3 Aug Purchased goods with a retail price of £500 from Chairs Ltd who allowed 30 per cent trade discount

6 Aug Sold goods on credit to British Cars Ltd for £700 less 10 per cent trade discount

10 Aug Received a credit note from Desks Ltd in respect of goods returned that had a retail price of £300 and trade discount of 25 per cent

13 Aug Sold goods to London Beds Ltd on credit. These had a retail value of £800 and trade discount of 15 per cent

16 Aug Sent British Cars Ltd a credit note in respect of goods returned that were invoiced at a retail price of £300 less 10 per cent trade discount

18 Aug Purchased goods on credit from Cabinets Ltd that had a retail value of £900 and trade discount of 20 per cent

21 Aug Received a credit note from Chairs Ltd for goods returned that had a retail price of £200 and 30 per cent trade discount

23 Aug Sold goods on credit to English Carpets Ltd for £1,300 less 10 per cent trade discount

25 Aug Sent London Beds Ltd a credit note relating to an overcharge of £100 in the retail value of those goods delivered on 13 August that carried trade discount of 15 per cent

Required

You are required to make the necessary entries in the books of prime entry and the general ledger.

11.6* Show the journal and ledger entries in respect of the following: BASIC

a On 20 April 20X5 purchased on credit a machine (not for resale) from Black Ltd at a cost of £5,300.

b On 23 April 20X5 sold on credit a motor vehicle for £3,600 to White Ltd. This had previously been used to deliver goods sold.

c On 26 April 20X5 purchased some shop fittings for £480 on credit from Grey Ltd. These were not for resale.

d On 28 April 20X5 sold on credit to Yellow Ltd for £270 a typewriter that had previously been used in the sales office.

11.7* W. Green decided to go into business on 1 August 20X4 by purchasing a firm owned by L. House. The purchase consideration was £96,000, which had been computed by valuing the assets and liabilities that were taken over as follows: BASIC

	£
Premises	55,000
Plant and machinery	23,000
Goods for resale	14,600
Trade receivables	6,300
Trade payables	2,900

Required

You are required to show the opening entries in the journal and ledger of W. Green.

11.8 You are provided with the following details about a company's credit customers for the month of November. BASIC

Balances in sales ledger

		£
1 November 20X4	Boycey	200
	Del Boy	100
	Rachel	100
	Rodney	150
		550

Credit sales

		£
8 Nov	Boycey	320
11 Nov	Rodney	250
14 Nov	Del Boy	80
		650

Sales returns

		£
16 Nov	Boycey	70

Required

You are required to update the sales ledger accounts (individual trade receivable accounts) highlighting the balances to be carried down on 1 December and prepare the general ledger accounts to reflect November's transactions.

BASIC

11.9 You are supplied with the following information in respect of B. Score's transactions in September with its suppliers.

The list of opening balances per the purchases ledger is as follows:

J. Smith & Co	£378	
A. Brown	£459	
C. Jones	£235	
M. Mann	£684	
Payne & Co	£245	
		£2,001
Less Debit – J. Cann & Co		£18
		£1,983

The following are the transactions relating to the suppliers' accounts in September:

		£	£
4 Sept	J. Cann & Co – goods purchased from B. Score		48
	A. Gray – Goods		30
11 Sept	C. Jones – goods		39
	A. Brown – goods		75
18 Sept	Goods returned to A. Brown		10
	M. Mann contra for goods purchased by him		90
	Payne & Co – goods		83
25 Sept	A. Read – goods		120
30 Sept	Allowance by Gray for soiled goods		4
	Trade discount allowed by A. Read		24
	(Not previously deducted from the invoice)		

Required

a Prepare the entries to the purchases day book and the purchases returns book.

b Open up ledger accounts for all the other transactions.

c Update the suppliers' accounts in the purchases ledger.

Chapter 12

The cash book

Learning Objectives:

After reading this chapter you should be able to do the following:

1. Describe the format of a two-column cash book.
2. Describe the format of a three-column cash book.
3. Explain the relationship between a cash book and the *cash* and *bank accounts* in the ledger, including the implications of its being a book of prime entry as well as a part of the double-entry system.
4. Explain the function of the cash discount columns in cash books.
5. Enter transactions in a two- or three-column cash book and post these to the appropriate ledger accounts.

—12.1 Introduction

The **cash book** is a book of prime entry. It contains a record of cheques received (and cash paid into the bank) and payments made by cheque (and cash withdrawn from the bank). In a manual accounting system the entries to the cash book originate from bank paying-in book and cheque book stubs. In a computerized system the cash book is automatically updated when the entity generates a payment from the bank or records a receipt into the bank. Where an entity operates a single entry accounting system then this is typically the only/main book to be used to record transactions. The pages of the cash book, like the general ledger, are divided into two halves; the debit side is on the left and the credit side is on the right. A cash book can take one of two forms as outlined in Figure 12.1 – a **two-column cashbook** that only deals with bank transactions or a **three-column cashbook** that deals will all bank and cash transactions.

In practice, cash received and paid is usually recorded in a separate petty cash book. Thus, the cash book normally consists of a two-column cash book of the type shown in Figure 12.1.

Figure 12.1

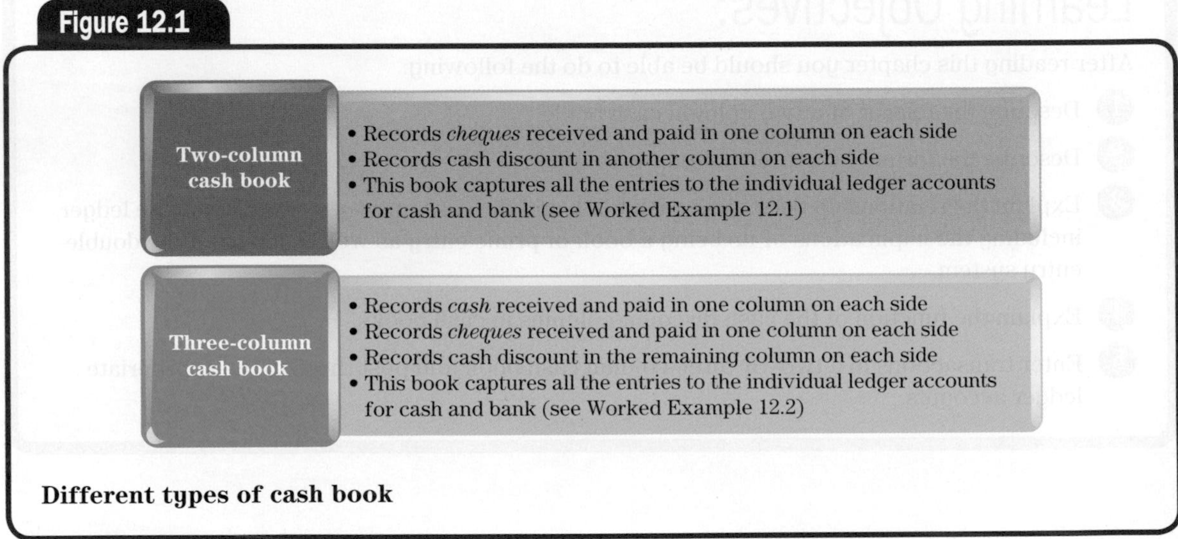

Two-column cash book
• Records *cheques* received and paid in one column on each side
• Records cash discount in another column on each side
• This book captures all the entries to the individual ledger accounts for cash and bank (see Worked Example 12.1)
Three-column cash book
• Records *cash* received and paid in one column on each side
• Records *cheques* received and paid in one column on each side
• Records cash discount in the remaining column on each side
• This book captures all the entries to the individual ledger accounts for cash and bank (see Worked Example 12.2)

Different types of cash book

—12.2 The two-column cash book

The two-column cash book is used to record receipts and payments by cheque. It is written up from the bank paying-in book and cheque book stubs. The cash book is used instead of a *bank account* in the ledger. This is because there are usually a large number of transactions involving the receipt and payment of cheques, and if these were recorded in a *bank account* in the ledger it would become cumbersome. Moreover, it permits a division of labour in that one person can write up the cash book while another is working on the general ledger. This also reduces the possibility of errors and provides a check on the work of the person who writes up the cash book where it is posted to the general ledger by someone else.

In addition to being a book of prime entry, the cash book is part of the double-entry system. Thus, debits in this book are credited to a ledger account in the general ledger and no further entries are necessary. Similarly, credits in this book are debited to an account in the ledger and no further entries are necessary.

The two-column cash book gets its name from the existence of two money columns on the debit side and two on the credit side. The additional column on the debit side is used to record the cash **discount allowed** to credit customers and the extra column on the credit side is used to record the cash **discount**

received from credit suppliers. Both of these additional columns are, like the day books, memorandum columns in that each item entered in these columns requires both a debit and a credit in the general ledger.

Cash discount is a reduction given (in addition to trade discount) by the supplier of goods to a buyer if the latter pays for them within a period stipulated by the seller at the time of sale. Often in practice all goods supplied during a particular calendar month must be paid for by the end of the following calendar month if cash discount is to be obtained. Note that cash discount is not deducted on the invoice but is calculated from the amount shown on the invoice, and deducted at the time of payment.

Apart from the entries in these two additional columns, the cash book is written up in the same way as the *bank account*. A debit balance on the cash book represents the amount of money the business has in the bank. Unlike the *cash account* the cash book may have a credit balance, which means that the business has an overdraft at the bank.

An illustration of the entries in the two-column cash book is given in Worked Example 12.1. The question and that part of the answer relating to the entries in the cash book should be read now.

WORKED EXAMPLE 12.1

In an extension to Worked Example 11.1, enter the following transactions in a two-column cash book and write up the ledger accounts in the general ledger:

Capital at 1 July 20X5	£5,750
Bank balance at 1 July 20X5	£4,750

Bright Spark has the following cheque receipts and payments during July 20X5:

1	**1 July**	Cash sales paid into the bank: £625
2	**3 July**	Received a cheque for £70 for goods sold
3	**4 July**	Paid rent by cheque: £200
4	**6 July**	Received a cheque from the London Trading Co. for £350
5	**8 July**	Paid an electricity bill by cheque: £50
6	**11 July**	Sent Brown Ltd a cheque for £800
7	**13 July**	Bought a car that cost £1,000 and paid by cheque
8	**16 July**	The owner of Bright Spark paid into the business a cheque for £900 as additional capital
9	**20 July**	Paid wages of £150 by cheque
10	**23 July**	Purchases paid for by cheque: £670
11	**24 July**	The proprietor withdrew a cheque for £100
12	**31 July**	Paid Lights Ltd a cheque for their June account (balance £600) and they allowed us 5 per cent cash discount
13	**31 July**	Sent Switches Ltd a cheque for their June account of £400 and deducted $2\frac{1}{2}$ per cent cash discount
14	**31 July**	Paid Cables Ltd a cheque for £300 on account

15 31 July Received from Smith Retailers Ltd a cheque for £525 after allowing them £15 cash discount

16 31 July Received a cheque for £720 from Electrical Retailers Ltd in full settlement of their account, which amounted to £740

17 31 July General Retailers Ltd paid £190 by cheque after deducting cash discount of £10, which was not allowed by us

As explained above, the cheques received and paid shown in the debit and credit amount columns respectively are posted to the relevant ledger accounts in the normal manner. However, the amounts shown in the memorandum columns relating to the discount allowed and received require both a debit and a credit entry in the general ledger. In simple terms, the entry for discount allowed is:

Debit:	*Discount allowed account*	£'XXX	
Credit:	*Customer's personal account (trade receivable)*		£'XXX

Similarly, the entry for discount received is:

Debit:	*Supplier's personal account (trade payable)*	£'XXX	
Credit:	*Discount received account*		£'XXX

This can be illustrated using just two of the personal accounts that were created for Worked Example 11.1 and transactions 15 and 12 as follows (double entry is highlighted by shading):

Smith Retailers Ltd

20X5	**Details**	**£**	**20X5**	**Details**	**£**
10 June	Sales	600	16 June	Returns	60
			31 July	Bank	525
			31 July	Discount allowed	15
		600			600

Discount allowed

20X5	**Details**	**£**	**20X5**	**Details**	**£**
31 July	Smith Retailers	15			

Lights Ltd

20X5	**Details**	**£**	**20X5**	**Details**	**£**
9 June	Returns	200	1 June	Purchases	800
31 July	Bank	570			
31 July	Discount received	30			
		800			800

Discount received

20X5	**Details**	**£**	**20X5**	**Details**	**£**
			31 July	Lights Ltd	30

However, entering each item of discount in the *discount allowed* and *discount received accounts* individually is inefficient, and defeats the main objective of the two-column cash book. The memorandum columns in the two-column cash book are intended to provide a means of ascertaining the total discount allowed and discount received for the period. The total of the memorandum discount allowed column is debited to the *discount allowed account* and the amount of each item of discount allowed is credited to the *individual customers' accounts* in the sales ledger. Similarly, the total of the memorandum discount received column is credited to the *discount received account* and the amount of each item of discount received is debited to the *individual suppliers' accounts* in the purchase ledger.

Therefore, the memorandum discount columns in the cash book operate on the same principle, and perform the same function, as day books. That is, they facilitate the bulk posting of transactions to the general ledger by aggregating items of the same type. However, since they are not a part of the double-entry system, each item requires both a debit and a credit entry in the general ledger.

The proper ledger entries for discount allowed and discount received can now be illustrated by using the answer to Worked Example 11.1 as follows:

Cash book

Date	Details	Folio	Memo: Discount allowed	Debit amount	Date	Details	Folio	Cheque number	Memo: Discount received	Credit amount
20X5					**20X5**					
1 July	Balance	b/d		4,750	4 July	Rent and rates		54301		200
1 July	Sales			625	8 July	Light and heat		2		50
3 July	Sales			70	11 July	Brown Ltd		3		800
6 July	London Trad. Co.			350	13 July	Motor vehicles		4		1,000
16 July	Capital			900	20 July	Wages		5		150
31 July	Smith Ret. Ltd		15	525	23 July	Purchases		6		670
31 July	Electrical Ret's		20	720	24 July	Drawings		7		100
31 July	General Ret's Ltd			190	31 July	Lights Ltd		8	30	570
					31 July	Switches Ltd		9	10	390
					31 July	Cables Ltd		10		300
					31 July	Balance c/d			40	3,900
			35	8,130					40	8,130
1 Aug	Balance	b/d		3,900						

The general ledger accounts

Sales returns

20X5	Details	£	20X5	Details	£
30 June	Total per sales returns day book	380			

Sales revenue

20X5	Details	£	20X5	Details	£
			30 June	Total per sales day book	1,860
			1 July	Bank	625
			3 July	Bank	70

London Trading Co. (other payable)					
20X5	**Details**	**£**	**20X5**	**Details**	**£**
30 June	Fixtures and fittings	350	6 July	Bank	350

Fixtures and fittings					
20X5	**Details**	**£**	**20X5**	**Details**	**£**
1 June	Balance b/d	1,000	30 June	London Trading Co	350
			31 July	Balance b/d	650
		1,000			1,000
1 Aug	Balance b/d	650			

Capital introduced					
20X5	**Details**	**£**	**20X5**	**Details**	**£**
31 July	Capital a/c	900	16 July	Bank – capital introduced	900

Drawings					
20X5	**Details**	**£**	**20X5**	**Details**	**£**
24 July	Bank – drawings	100	31 July	Capital a/c	100
		100			100

Capital					
20X5	**Details**	**£**	**20X5**	**Details**	**£**
31 July	Drawings a/c	100	1 July	Balance b/d	5,750
31 July	Balance c/d	6,550	31 July	Capital introduced a/c	900
		6,650			6,650
			1 Aug	Balance b/d	6,650

Discount allowed					
20X5	**Details**	**£**	**20X5**	**Details**	**£**
31 July	Total per cash book	35			

Smith Retailers Ltd (trade receivable)					
20X5	**Details**	**£**	**20X5**	**Details**	**£**
10 June	Sales revenue	600	16 June	Returns	60
			31 July	Bank	525
			31 July	Discount allowed	15
		600			600

Electrical Retailers Ltd (trade receivable)					
20X5	**Details**	**£**	**20X5**	**Details**	**£**
4 June	Sales revenue	450	8 June	Returns	270
28 June	Sales revenue	560	31 July	Bank	720
			31 July	Discount allowed	20
		1,010			1,010

General Retailers Ltd (trade receivable)					
20X5	**Details**	**£**	**20X5**	**Details**	**£**
25 June	Sales revenue	250	27 June	Returns	50
			31 July	Bank	190
			31 July	Balance c/d	10
		250			250
1 Aug	Balance c/d	10			

Rent and rates					
20X5	**Details**	**£**	**20X5**	**Details**	**£**
4 July	Bank	200			

Light and heat					
20X5	**Details**	**£**	**20X5**	**Details**	**£**
8 July	Bank	50			

Brown Ltd (other payable)					
20X5	**Details**	**£**	**20X5**	**Details**	**£**
11 July	Bank	800	29 June	Motor vehicles	800

Motor vehicles					
20X5	**Details**	**£**	**20X5**	**Details**	**£**
29 June	Brown Ltd	800	31 July	Balance c/d	1,800
13 July	Bank	1,000			
		1,800			1,800
1 Aug	Balance b/d	1,800			

Wages					
20X5	**Details**	**£**	**20X5**	**Details**	**£**
20 July	Bank	150			

Purchase returns					
20X5	**Details**	**£**	**20X5**	**Details**	**£**
			30 June	Total per purchases returns day book	500

Purchases					
20X5	**Details**	**£**	**20X5**	**Details**	**£**
30 June	Total: purchases day book	2,050			
23 July	Bank	670			

Discount received					
20X5	**Details**	**£**	**20X5**	**Details**	**£**
			31 July	Total per cash book	40

Lights Ltd (trade payable)					
20X5	**Details**	**£**	**20X5**	**Details**	**£**
19 June	Returns	200	1 June	Purchases	800
31 July	Bank	570			
31 July	Discount received	30			
		800			800

Switches Ltd (trade payable)					
20X5	**Details**	**£**	**20X5**	**Details**	**£**
18 June	Returns	300	12 June	Purchases	700
31 July	Bank	390			
31 July	Discount received	10			
		700			700

Cables Ltd (trade payable)					
20X5	**Details**	**£**	**20X5**	**Details**	**£**
31 July	Bank	300	15 June	Purchases	550
31 July	Balance c/d	250			
		550			550
			1 Aug	Balance b/d	250

Note

1 The personal accounts are usually balanced at the end of each month.

12.3 The three-column cash book

The three-column cash book is an extension of the two-column cash book described above. The additional column on each side is used to record cash received (debit side) and cash payments (credit side). These columns are intended to replace the *cash account* in the ledger. Thus, the three-column cash book is used instead of the *cash account* and *bank account* in the general ledger.

In addition to being a book of prime entry, the three-column cash book is part of the double-entry system. Thus, entries in either the cash or bank columns require only one further entry in another ledger account on the opposite side.

The only additional complication that arises in the case of the three-column cash book concerns cash paid into the bank and cash withdrawn from the bank. At this point the reader may find it useful to refer back to Chapter 9 (Worked Example 9.3, Note 5) which explains the double entry for these items. The form that this takes in the three-column cash book is as follows:

a Paying cash into the bank:

Debit:	*Bank account column*	£'XXX	
Credit:	*Cash account column*		£'XXX

b Withdrawing cash from the bank:

Debit:	*Cash account column*	£'XXX	
Credit:	*Bank account column*		£'XXX

The three-column cash book is not common in practice because in most businesses cash received and paid is usually recorded in a separate petty cash book instead of a *cash account*. This is discussed further in the next chapter.

An illustration of the three-column cash book is given in Worked Example 12.2.

WORKED EXAMPLE 12.2

B. Andrews is in business as a motor factor and parts agent. The balances shown in her cash book at 1 December 20X5 were: bank, £1,630 and cash, £820. The following receipts and payments occurred during December 20X5:

2 Dec	Received a cheque for £1,000 from J. Sutcliffe as a loan repayable in five years
3 Dec	Purchased a personal computer for £1,210 and paid by cheque
4 Dec	Purchased in cash goods for resale costing £340
5 Dec	Paid wages of £150 in cash
6 Dec	Cash sales paid into bank: £480
8 Dec	Purchases by cheque: £370
9 Dec	Cash sales of £160
11 Dec	Cheque sales: £280

12 Dec Paid telephone bill of £320 by cheque

15 Dec Paid cash of £200 into bank

17 Dec Drawings by cheque: £250

18 Dec Bought stationery of £80 in cash

20 Dec Introduced additional capital in the form of a cheque for £500

21 Dec Paid water rates of £430 by cheque

23 Dec Withdrew cash of £100 from the bank

24 Dec Sent K. Vale a cheque for £530 after deducting cash discount of £40

24 Dec Received a cheque for £640 from A. Green who deducted £35 cash discount

27 Dec Paid M. Fenton £720 by cheque after deducting £25 cash discount

28 Dec J. Evans sent us a cheque for £860 after deducting £45 cash discount

29 Dec Received a cheque from B. Court for £920 who deducted £50 cash discount which we did not allow

Required

Enter the above transactions in a three-column cash book.

Cash book

Date	Details	Memo: Discount allowed	Bank	Cash	Date	Details	Memo: Discount received	Bank	Cash
20X5					**20X5**				
1 Dec	Balance b/d	—	1,630	820	3 Dec	Office equipment		1,210	
2 Dec	J. Sutcliffe – loan		1,000		4 Dec	Purchases			340
6 Dec	Sales revenue		480		5 Dec	Wages			150
9 Dec	Sales revenue			160	8 Dec	Purchases		370	
11 Dec	Sales revenue		280		12 Dec	Telephone		320	
15 Dec	Cash		200		15 Dec	Bank			200
20 Dec	Capital		500		17 Dec	Drawings		250	
23 Dec	Bank			100	18 Dec	Stationery			80
24 Dec	A. Green	35	640		21 Dec	Rates		430	
28 Dec	J. Evans	45	860		23 Dec	Cash		100	
29 Dec	B. Court		920		24 Dec	K. Vale	40	530	
					27 Dec	M. Fenton	25	720	
					31 Dec	Balance c/d		2,580	310
		80	6,510	1,080			65	6,510	1,080
1 Aug	Balance b/d	—	2,580	310					

Learning Activity 12.1

Prepare a two-column cash book with cash and bank columns to record your cash and cheque transactions over the forthcoming week or month. Make the necessary double entry in the other general ledger accounts.

Having appropriate internal controls over the handling and recording of cash and bank transactions is vital as it is the area that is most likely to be subject to fraud. An example of the type of fraud that can occur is reproduced in Real World Example 12.1.

REAL WORLD EXAMPLE 12.1

Breckman and Company: Chartered Certified Accountants

Personal and company cheques

There are numerous fraudulent schemes involving personal or company cheques.

For example, an employee writes a cheque payable to cash and posts the debit to an expense account that will be written off at the year end. He or she then discards the cancelled cheque when it arrives with the bank statement and reconciles the statements.

Another example might be an employee taking money from the petty cash and replacing it with a personal cheque. The cash box is always balanced, but the cheque is not deposited into the company bank account.

To prevent these kinds of fraud:

- Examine bank reconciliations thoroughly
- Scrutinize bank statements and cancelled cheques for cheques made out to cash, employees, or unusual suppliers
- Instruct the bank to send company statements to your home address for your attention.

Source: http://www.breckmanandcompany.co.uk/business/business-finance/dealing-fraud/identify-and-prevent-fraud-your-business, accessed September 2013.

Summary

The cash book is both a book of prime entry and part of the double-entry system in the general ledger, and thus has the same format as a general ledger account. It usually takes one of two forms: a two- or a three-column cash book. The two-column cash book has two money columns on each side. One column on each side is used to record cheques received and paid. The other column on each side is used to record cash discount allowed and cash discount received. The two-column cash book replaces the *bank account* in the general ledger, and is written up from the bank paying-in book and cheque book stubs. The three-column cash book has three money columns on each side. Two of these are the same as the two-column cash book. The third is used to record cash receipts and payments, and is written up from copies of the receipts. The three-column cash book replaces the *bank* and *cash ledger accounts* in the general ledger.

Because the cash book is a part of the double-entry system, entries in the cash book in respect of cash and cheque transactions need only to be posted to the opposite side of the relevant general ledger account. However, this is not the case with regard to the entries in the cash discount columns. These columns are memoranda, and essentially intended to serve the same purpose as day books: namely to facilitate the periodic bulk posting of items of the same type. Thus, the total of the memo discount allowed column is debited to the *discount allowed account* in the ledger, and the individual amounts are credited to the relevant *credit customers' personal accounts* (sales ledger). Similarly, the total of the memo discount received column of the cash book is credited to the *discount received account*, and the individual amounts are debited to the relevant *credit suppliers' personal accounts* (purchase ledger).

Key terms and concepts

cash book	202	discount received	202
cash discount	203	three-column cash book	202
discount allowed	202	two-column cash book	202

An asterisk after the question number indicates that there is a suggested answer in Appendix 2.

Review questions

connect

12.1 Describe the different forms of two- and three-column cash books with which you are familiar.

12.2 Describe the entries in the cash book and general ledger in respect of discount allowed and discount received.

Exercises

connect

BASIC

12.3* B. Jones is in business as a builders' merchant. He had £3,680 in the bank on 1 May 20X5. The following receipts and payments by cheque took place during May 20X5:

3 May Introduced additional capital: £2,000

4 May Sales by cheque: £840

7 May Purchases by cheque: £510

10 May Paid wages by cheque: £200

13 May Paid rent by cheque: £360

15 May Cash sales paid into bank: £490

18 May Purchased shopfittings for £2,450

20 May Paid gas bill of £180

23 May Bought stationery by cheque: £70

26 May Drawings by cheque: £250

31 May Sent Brick Ltd a cheque for £850 after deducting £45 cash discount

31 May Received a cheque from Oak Ltd for £160 after deducting £30 cash discount

31 May Paid Stone Ltd £220 after deducting cash discount of £20

31 May Pine Ltd sent us a cheque for £485 after deducting £25 cash discount

31 May Sent Slate Ltd a cheque for £480 after deducting cash discount of £40. However, Slate Ltd did not allow the discount

31 May Lime Ltd sent us a cheque for £575

Required

Show the entries in respect of the above in a two-column cash book.

12.4* Using your answers to Question 11.3 in Chapter 11 and Question 12.3 above: BASIC

a make the necessary entries in the general ledger given a balance on the capital account at 1 May 20X5 of £3,680;

b prepare a trial balance at 31 May 20X5.

12.5* B. Player buys and sells soft furnishings and office equipment. On 1 September 20X5 the bank balance per the cash book was £1,950 and the cash balance per the cash book was £860. During September 20X5 the following receipts and payments occurred: BASIC

3 Sep Cash sales paid into bank: £470

4 Sep Cash purchases: £230

6 Sep Paid electricity bill of £510 (paid by cheque)

9 Sep Sales by cheque: £380

10 Sep Drew a cheque for £250 in respect of wages

12 Sep Cash sales: £290

15 Sep Paid £40 in cash for travelling expenses

16 Sep Paid water rates by cheque: £410

19 Sep Drawings in cash: £150

20 Sep Purchases by cheque: £320

21 Sep Paid postage of £30 in cash

22 Sep Paid cash of £350 into the bank

24 Sep Introduced further capital of £500 by cheque

25 Sep Purchased a delivery vehicle for £2,500 and paid by cheque

26 Sep Received a cheque for £1,000 from B. Jones as a three-year loan

27 Sep Returned goods costing £170 and received a cash refund

28 Sep Paid tax and insurance on delivery vehicle of £280 in cash

29 Sep Withdrew cash of £180 from bank

30 Sep Received a cheque from British Cars Ltd for £350 after deducting £10 cash discount

30 Sep Received a cheque from London Beds Ltd for £580 after deducting £15 cash discount

30 Sep Paid Desks Ltd a cheque for £500 after deducting £25 cash discount

30 Sep Paid Chairs Ltd a cheque for £190 after deducting £20 cash discount

30 Sep Received a cheque from English Carpets Ltd for £1,100 after deducting £70 cash discount. However, this cash discount was not allowed

30 Sep Paid Cabinets Ltd a cheque for £500 on account

Required

Enter the above in a three-column cash book.

BASIC **12.6*** Using your answers to Question 11.5 in Chapter 11 and Question 12.5 above:

a make the necessary entries in the ledger given a balance on the capital account at 1 September 20X5 of £2,810; and

b prepare a trial balance at 30 September 20X5.

BASIC **12.7** The following information is an extension to Question 11.4 in Chapter 11.

a Enter the following transactions using a three-column cash book.

The following cash transactions happened in November:

9 Nov Cash paid to: Veronica by A. Adair £900, S. Ruddle £500

12 Nov Veronica received cheques from: F. Hutchinson £600, C. Flanagan £456

26 Nov Veronica paid by cheque the following: N. Ward £100, F. Wood £465, N. Hynd £56

b Make the necessary entries in the ledgers using your answers to Question 11.4 in Chapter 11.

c Prepare the trial balance at 30 November.

BASIC **12.8** The following information is an extension to Question 11.8 in Chapter 11:

Cash book (receipts side)		Discount allowed £	Amount received from customers £
7 Nov	Boycey	20	180
9 Nov	Rodney	15	135
12 Nov	Del Boy	10	90
		45	405

Required

a Make the necessary entries in the ledgers using your answers to Question 11.8 in Chapter 11.

b Close the suppliers' accounts at 30 September.

BASIC **12.9** The following information is an extension to Question 11.9 in Chapter 11.

a Enter the following transactions relating to the suppliers' accounts in September using a three-column cash book:

			£	£
4 Sept	Paid	J Smith & Co		150
	Paid	A. Brown	268	
		Discount	7	275
11 Sept	Paid	C. Jones	169	
		Discount	6	175
18 Sept	Paid	M. Mann		300
	Paid	Payne & Co	164	
		Discount	5	169

b Make the necessary entries in the ledgers using your answers to Question 11.9 in Chapter 11.

c Close the suppliers' accounts at 30 September.

12.10 Enter the following transactions in ledger accounts of ABC (including a two-column cash book), balance off and extract the trial balance. BASIC

1 Jan ABC started business and put £1,000 in the business bank account

2 Jan Bought £200 worth of inventory on credit from Brown

3 Jan Purchased a van by cheque for £300

3 Jan Got a logo painted on the side of the van for £100 paid by cheque

4 Jan Sold goods to Yellow on credit worth £300

8 Jan Purchased pencils by cheque for £50

9 Jan Yellow paid his account in full by cheque

10 Jan Paid Brown his account in full by cheque

12 Jan Purchased more inventory on credit from Brown for £300

14 Jan Sold goods to Yellow on credit for £500

15 Jan Purchased a lorry for £100 paying by cheque

20 Jan ABC put another £100 in the business bank account from his own personal account

Chapter 13

The petty cash book

Learning Objectives:

After reading this chapter you should be able to do the following:

1. Explain the relationship between a petty cash book and the *cash account* in the general ledger, including the implications of the petty cash book being a book of prime entry as well as being a part of the double-entry system.
2. Explain the differences between a petty cash book and a cash book.
3. Describe the format of a columnar petty cash book.
4. Explain the function of the analysis columns in a columnar petty cash book.
5. Describe the petty cash imprest system and its advantages.
6. Enter transactions in a columnar petty cash book using the imprest system, and post these to the appropriate ledger accounts.

13.1 Introduction

The **petty cash book** is different to the cash book. It is used to record the receipt and payment of small amounts of cash. Any large amounts of cash received and cash takings are usually paid into the bank and thus recorded in the cash book. The petty cash book is written up from receipts and petty cash vouchers (where employees are reimbursed expenses).

The petty cash book is used instead of a *cash ledger account* in the general ledger. This is because there usually are a large number of transactions in cash, and if these were recorded in a *cash ledger account* in the general ledger it would become cumbersome. Like the cash book, it also permits a division of labour and facilitates improved control. In addition to being a book of prime entry, the petty cash book is part of the double-entry system. Thus, debits in this book are credited to a ledger account in the general ledger and no further entries are necessary. Similarly, credits in this book are debited to a ledger account in the general ledger and no further entries are necessary.

13.2 The columnar petty cash book

It is usual for a **(columnar) petty cash book** to have analysis columns on the credit side. Each column relates to a particular type of expenditure, such as postage, stationery or travelling expenses. These are intended to facilitate the posting of entries to the general ledger. Every item of expenditure is entered in both the credit column and an appropriate analysis column. At the end of each calendar week or month the total of each analysis column is debited to the relevant ledger account in the general ledger. Thus, instead of posting each transaction to the general ledger separately, expenditure of the same type is collected together in each analysis column and the total for the period posted to the relevant ledger account.

13.3 The imprest system

Many firms also operate their petty cash on an **imprest system**. At the beginning of each period (week or month) the petty cashier has a fixed amount of cash referred to as a **float**. At the end of each period (or the start of the next) the petty cashier is reimbursed the exact amount spent during the period, thus making the float up to its original amount. The reimbursement usually takes the form of a cheque drawn for cash. The amount of the petty cash float is determined by reference to the normal level of petty cash expenditure in each period. The advantages of the imprest system are outlined in Figure 13.1.

An illustration of a columnar petty cash book and the imprest system is shown in Worked Example 13.1.

WORKED EXAMPLE 13.1

A. Stone uses a columnar petty cash book to record his cash payments. He also operates an imprest system with a float of £150. During August 20X4 the cash transactions were as follows:

1 Aug Postage stamps: £5

2 Aug Cleaning materials: £13

4 Aug Recorded delivery: £2

5 Aug Gratuity to delivery man: £4

7 Aug Tea, milk, etc.: £1

9 Aug Rail fare: £11

10 Aug Paper clips and pens: £6

13 Aug Window cleaner: £10

18 Aug Travelling expenses: £7

21 Aug Envelopes: £3

22 Aug Postage stamps: £9

24 Aug Stationery: £14

27 Aug Taxi fare: £12

28 Aug Office cleaning: £8

31 Aug Received reimbursement to make float up to £150

You are required to make the necessary entries in the petty cash book using appropriate analysis columns, and show the relevant general ledger account entries.

The petty cash book

Debit	**Credit**								
Amount	Date	Details	Amount	Telephone and postage	Cleaning	Printing and stationery	Travelling expenses	Miscellaneous expenses
£			£	£	£	£	£	£
	20X4							
b/d 150	1 Aug	Stamps	5	5				
	2 Aug	Materials	13		13			
	4 Aug	Recorded delivery	2	2				
	5 Aug	Gratuity	4					4
	7 Aug	Tea and milk	1					1
	9 Aug	Rail fare	11				11	
	10 Aug	Clips and pens	6			6		
	13 Aug	Windows	10		10			
	18 Aug	Travelling	7				7	
	21 Aug	Envelopes	3			3		
	22 Aug	Stamps	9	9				
	24 Aug	Stationery	14			14		
	27 Aug	Taxi	12				12	
	28 Aug	Office	8		8			
105	31 Aug	Reimbursement	105	16	31	23	30	5
	31 Aug	Balance c/d	150					
255			255					
b/d 150	1 Sep							

In some firms the cash reimbursement is made at the beginning of the next period, in which case the entries are as follows (highlighted by shading):

Debit	Credit								
Amount	Date	Details	Amount	Telephone and postage	Cleaning	Printing and stationery	Travelling expenses	Miscellaneous expenses
£			£	£	£	£	£	£
	31 Aug	Totals	105	16	31	23	30	5
	31 Aug	Balance c/d	45					
150			150					
b/d 45								
105	1 Sep	Reimbursement						
150								

Ledger entries

Telephone and postage

20X4	Details	£	
31 Aug	Total per PCB	16	

Cleaning

20X4	Details	£	
31 Aug	Total per PCB	31	

Printing and stationery

20X4	Details	£	
31 Aug	Total per PCB	23	

Travelling expenses

20X4	Details	£	
31 Aug	Total per PCB	30	

Miscellaneous expenses

20X4	Details	£	
31 Aug	Total per PCB	5	

Cash book (bank account)

20X4	Details	£	20X4	Details	£
31 Aug	Balance b/d	150	31 Aug	Total per PCB	105

Notes

1 When designing a columnar petty cash book it is necessary first to decide on the appropriate number of analysis columns. This is done by identifying the number of different types of

expenditure for which there is more than one transaction. In Worked Example 13.1 there are four different types, namely postage, cleaning, stationery and travelling expenses. These four, plus a column for miscellaneous expenses, give five columns. The headings for each of these columns should be the same as the name of the general ledger account to which the total of the column will be posted.

2 The details column of the petty cash book is used to describe the nature of each transaction, rather than the name of the general ledger account containing the double entry, since this is given at the head of the analysis column in which the item is entered.

3 The items entered in the miscellaneous expenses column sometimes have to be posted to several different ledger accounts according to the nature of each transaction.

4 When cash is withdrawn from the bank to restore the float to its original amount the ledger entry consists of:

Debit:	*Petty cash book*	£'XXX	
Credit:	*Cash book (bank account)*		£'XXX

Figure 13.1

Imprest system

- Facilitates control of the total petty cash expenditure in each period as the petty cashier cannot spend more than the amount of the float, except by applying to the management for an increase.
- Deters theft of cash by the petty cashier since a large cash balance cannot be accumulated by drawing cash from the bank at irregular intervals.
- The entries in the petty cash book are kept up to date because the cash expenditure is not reimbursed until the petty cash book is written up and the total amount of expenditure for the period is known.
- Discourages the practice of loans and subs from petty cash since these would have to be accounted for at the end of the period, and in addition may result in insufficient cash to meet the necessary expenditure.

Advantages of an imprest system

Learning Activity 13.1

Prepare a columnar petty cash book for your cash transactions over the forthcoming week or month. Make the necessary double entry in the other ledger accounts.

Summary

The petty cash book is both a book of prime entry and a part of the double-entry system in the ledger, and thus has the same format as a ledger account. It is used to record cash receipts and payments, and is written up from copies of the receipts and petty cash vouchers. The petty cash book replaces the *cash ledger account* in the general ledger, and thus entries in this book need only to be posted to the opposite side of the relevant ledger accounts.

The most common form of petty cash book is a columnar petty cash book. This has several analysis columns on the credit side, each relating to a particular type of expenditure. These columns are memoranda, and essentially intended to serve the same purpose as day books; namely, to facilitate the periodic bulk posting of transactions of the same type.

Many organizations also operate their petty cash on an imprest system. This essentially comprises a fixed cash float that is replenished at the end of each period by an amount equal to that period's cash expenditure. The imprest system has several very important advantages including facilitating control of the total cash expenditure for a period, deterring the theft of cash, discouraging cash loans/subs, and ensuring that the entries in the petty cash book are kept up to date.

Key terms and concepts

(columnar) petty cash book	218	imprest system	218
float	218	petty cash book	218

An asterisk after the question number indicates that there is a suggested answer in Appendix 2.

Review questions

connect

13.1 a Describe the purpose and format of a columnar petty cash book.

b Explain how you would determine the appropriate number of analysis columns.

13.2 a Describe how a petty cash imprest system operates.

b Explain how such a system facilitates control.

Exercises

connect

BASIC

13.3* C. Harlow has a petty cash book that is used to record his cash receipts and payments. This also incorporates an imprest system that has a float of £400. During February 20X5 the following cash transactions took place:

1 Feb	Purchases: £31
3 Feb	Wages: £28
6 Feb	Petrol for delivery van: £9
8 Feb	Bus fares: £3
11 Feb	Pens and pencils: £8
12 Feb	Payments for casual labour: £25
14 Feb	Repairs to delivery van: £17
16 Feb	Copying paper: £15
19 Feb	Goods for resale: £22
20 Feb	Train fares: £12
21 Feb	Repairs to premises: £35
22 Feb	Postage stamps: £6
23 Feb	Drawings: £20
24 Feb	Taxi fares: £7
25 Feb	Envelopes: £4
26 Feb	Purchases: £18
27 Feb	Wages: £30
28 Feb	Petrol for delivery van: £14

On 28 February 20X5 the cash float was restored to £400.

Record the above in the petty cash book using appropriate analysis columns and make the necessary entries in the ledger.

13.4 The Oakhill Printing Co. Ltd operates its petty cash account on the imprest system. It is maintained at a figure of £80 on the first day of each month. At 30 April 20X5 the petty cash box held £19.37 in cash. During May 20X5, the following petty cash transactions arose: BASIC

		£
1 May	Cash received to restore imprest	to be derived
1 May	Bus fares	0.41
2 May	Stationery	2.35
4 May	Bus fares	0.30
7 May	Postage stamps	1.70
7 May	Trade journal	0.95
8 May	Bus fares	0.64
11 May	Correcting fluid	1.29
12 May	Printer ink cartridge	5.42
14 May	Parcel postage	3.45
15 May	Paper clips	0.42
15 May	Newspapers	2.00
16 May	Photocopier repair	16.80
19 May	Postage stamps	1.50

20 May	Drawing pins	0.38
21 May	Train fare	5.40
22 May	Photocopier paper	5.63
23 May	Display decorations	3.07
23 May	Correcting fluid	1.14
25 May	Wrapping paper	0.78
27 May	String	0.61
27 May	Sellotape	0.75
27 May	Biro pens	0.46
28 May	Replacement laser mouse	13.66
30 May	Bus fares	2.09
1 June	Cash received to restore imprest	to be derived

Required

Open and post the company's petty cash account for the period 1 May to 1 June 20X5 inclusive and balance the account at 30 May 20X5.

In order to facilitate the subsequent double-entry postings, all items of expense appearing in the 'payments' column should then be analysed individually into suitably labelled expense columns.

(ACCA)

BASIC

13.5 Belfast cleaning company operates its petty cash account using an imprest system. It is maintained at a figure of £100 on the first day of each month. At 31 December 20X4 £21.48 was held in the petty cash box. During January 20X5, the following petty cash transactions arose:

		£
1 Jan	Cash received to restore imprest	to be derived
1 Jan	Postage	0.63
2 Jan	Taxi	4.25
4 Jan	Pens	8.56
7 Jan	Bus fare	1.90
8 Jan	Paper clips	3.56
9 Jan	Brown envelopes	5.68
11 Jan	Bus fare	1.90
12 Jan	Taxi fare	5.00
12 Jan	Coffee	8.25
13 Jan	Rulers	6.50
15 Jan	Taxi fare	4.50
17 Jan	Box of envelopes	12.80
19 Jan	Sandwiches for guests	15.60
20 Jan	Toilet roll	4.59
21 Jan	Taxi	5.25
25 Jan	Stamps	1.31
28 Jan	Recorded delivery	2.49
31 Jan	Bus fare	1.45
1 Feb	Cash received to restore imprest	to be derived

Required

Open and post the company's petty cash account for the period 1 January to 1 February 20X5 inclusive and balance the account at 31 January 20X5.

All items of expense appearing in the 'payments' column should be analysed and posted to the respective ledger accounts.

BASIC

13.6 London Printing Co. has an opening balance on its cash account on 1 January of £20.00. A cheque for £100 is cashed on the first of each month to cover that month's potential petty cash requirements. The secretary records the expenses manually for the month in a cash journal which analyses the transactions according to the ledger accounts utilised in the trial balance. The company does not operate an imprest system.

The total petty cash spend for January, February and March is as follows:

January totals					
Stationery	**Postage**	**Travel**	**Sundries**	**Cleaning wages**	**Drawings**
£15.68	£25.36	£32.00	£16.58	£36.00	£10.00

February totals					
Stationery	**Postage**	**Travel**	**Sundries**	**Cleaning wages**	**Drawings**
£14.50	£3.50	£45.00	£25.00	£36.00	—

March totals					
Stationery	**Postage**	**Travel**	**Sundries**	**Cleaning wages**	**Drawings**
£8.56	£5.60	£28.00	£31.50	£36.00	£20.00

Required

Write up the general ledger accounts for the three months January to March.

PART THREE
Preparing final financial statements for sole traders

14 The final financial statements of sole traders (introductory) 229

15 Depreciation and non-current assets 249

16 Irrecoverable receivables and allowance for irrecoverable receivables 275

17 Accruals and prepayments 291

18 The extended trial balance and final financial statements (advanced) 309

Chapter 14

The final financial statements of sole traders (introductory)

Learning Objectives:

After reading this chapter you should be able to do the following:

1. Explain the purpose and structure of the statement of profit or loss and the statement of financial position.
2. Describe the nature of administrative expenses, selling and distribution expenses, non-current assets, current assets, current liabilities, non-current liabilities and capital.
3. Explain the relevance of inventory and the cost of sales in the determination of gross profit.
4. Prepare a simple statement of profit or loss and statement of financial position from a trial balance using either an account/horizontal format or a vertical format.
5. Make general ledger account and journal entries relating to the *profit or loss account* and the resulting statement of profit or loss.

—14.1 Introduction

Final financial statements consist of a **statement of comprehensive income** (or statement of profit or loss) and a **statement of financial position**. These are prepared at the end of a business's accounting period after the trial balance has been completed. Some businesses also produce final financial statements half yearly, quarterly or even monthly. This chapter focuses on the preparation of financial statements for sole traders. The purpose, structure and preparation of the statement of profit or loss and statement of financial position are discussed below. Sole traders rarely have unrealized gains or losses; therefore, a full statement of comprehensive income is not prepared.

—14.2 The purpose and structure of statements of profit or loss

The **statement of profit or loss** provides a summary of the results of a business's trading activities during a given accounting year. It shows the profit or loss for the year. The purpose of a statement of profit or loss is to enable users of financial statements, such as the owner, to evaluate the financial performance of a business for a given accounting year. It may be used to determine the amount of taxation on the profit.

Chapter 7, 'The Accounting Equation and its Components', explained that **profit** can be defined as the amount that could be taken out of a business as drawings in the case of a sole trader or partnership, or is available for distribution as dividends to shareholders in the case of a company, after maintaining the value of the **capital** of a business. Profit is not the same as an increase in the amount of money the business possesses. It is the result of applying certain accounting principles to the transactions of the business. These were described in detail in Chapter 4, 'The Conceptual Framework 2: Concepts, Principles and Policies'.

The basic format of the statement of profit or loss is shown in Figure 14.1.

Figure 14.1

ABC
Statement of profit or loss for the year ended . . .

	£	£
Revenue		X
Cost of sales		(X)
Gross profit		X
Other income		X
Distribution costs		(X)
Administrative expenses		(X)
Finance costs		(X)
Profit/(Loss) for the period		X

An example of the layout of a statement of profit or loss for a sole trader

In the financial statements of sole traders and partnerships, the actual composition of each of the above groupings of costs would be shown in detail. Selling and distribution costs include advertising expenditure, the wages of delivery-van drivers, motor expenses including petrol and repairs, and so on. Administrative expenses usually comprise the salaries of office staff, rent and rates, light and heat, printing and stationery, telephone and postage, and so on. The published final financial statements of companies contain a classification of costs similar to that shown above.

14.3 Gross profit: inventory and the cost of sales

The first stage in the determination of the profit for the year involves calculating gross profit. It is usually carried out in the statement of profit or loss. However, this part of the statement of profit or loss is sometimes presented as a separate account referred to as the *trading account*.

The **gross profit** for a given period is computed by subtracting the cost of goods sold/cost of sales from sales revenue. It is important to appreciate that the cost of goods sold is not usually the same as the amount of purchases. This is because most businesses will have purchased goods that are unsold at the end of the accounting period. These goods are referred to as **inventory**. The cost of inventory unsold is carried forward into the next accounting period to be matched against the income that it generates (matching concept), by being transferred to the statement of financial position at the end of the year.

A manufacturing business will have a number of different types of inventory. However, for simplicity, the following exposition is confined to non-manufacturing businesses whose inventory consists of goods purchased for resale that have not undergone any further processing by the entity.

The **cost of sales** is determined by taking the cost of goods in inventory at the start of the period, adding to this the cost of goods purchased during the period, and subtracting the cost of goods unsold at the end of the period. The cost of sales is then deducted from the sales revenue to give the gross profit. This is illustrated in Worked Example 14.1.

WORKED EXAMPLE 14.1

S. Mann, whose accounting year ends on 30 April, buys and sells one type of product. On 1 May 20X4 there were 50 units in inventory that had cost £100 each. During the subsequent accounting year he purchased a further 500 units at a cost of £100 each and sold 450 units at a price of £150 each. There were 100 units that cost £100 each that had not been sold at 30 April 20X5. You are required to compute the gross profit for the year.

S. Mann
Trading account for the year ended 30 April 20X5

Units		£	£
450	Sales revenue		67,500
	Less: Cost of goods sold:		
50	Inventory of goods at 1 May 20X4	5,000	
500	*Add:* Goods purchased during the year	50,000	
550	Cost of goods available for sale	55,000	
100	*Less:* Inventory of goods at 30 April 20X5	10,000	
450	Cost of sales		45,000
	Gross profit for the year		22,500

Note

1 The number of units is not usually shown in a trading account. They have been included in the above to demonstrate that the cost of sales relates to the number of units that were sold.

The trading account

The **trading account** is an account in the general ledger and is thus a part of the double-entry system. It is used to ascertain the gross profit and is prepared by transferring the balances on the *sales revenue*, *purchases* and *returns ledger accounts* to the *trading ledger account*. In addition, certain entries are required in respect of inventory. These are as follows:

1 Inventory at the start of the period:

Debit:	*Trading account*	£'XXX	
Credit:	*Inventory account*		£'XXX

2 Inventory at the end of the period:

Debit:	*Inventory account*	£'XXX	
Credit:	*Trading account*		£'XXX

Note that the inventory at the start of the period will be the inventory at the end of the previous period. This is a statement of financial position account. The ledger entries in respect of inventories are illustrated in Worked Example 14.2 using the data in Worked Example 14.1.

WORKED EXAMPLE 14.2

Prior to the preparation of the trading account the ledger will appear as follows:

Sales revenue

20X5	Details	£	20X5	Details	£
			30 Apr	Balance b/d	67,500

Purchases

20X5	Details	£			
30 Apr	Balance b/d	50,000			

Inventory

20X4	Details	£			
30 Apr	Balance b/d	5,000			

The trading income account will then be prepared as follows:

Sales revenue

20X5	Details	£	20X5	Details	£
30 Apr	Trading account	67,500	30 Apr	Balance b/d	67,500

Purchases

20X5	Details	£	20X5	Details	£
30 Apr	Balance b/d	50,000	30 Apr	Trading account	50,000

Inventory					
20X4	**Details**	**£**	**20X5**	**Details**	**£**
1 May	Balance b/d	5,000	30 Apr	Trading account	5,000
20X5					
30 Apr	Trading account	10,000			

S. Mann ***Trading income account for year ending 30 April 20X5***			
	£		**£**
Inventory at 1 May 20X4	5,000	Sales revenue	67,500
Purchases	50,000	Inventory at 30 April 20X5	10,000
Gross profit c/d	22,500		
	77,500		77,500
		Gross profit b/d	22,500

Notes

1 The gross profit is the difference between the two sides of the trading account and must be brought down to the opposite side of the account.

2 No date columns are shown in the trading account since the date appears as part of the heading of the account.

3 When the trading account is prepared in account-form the inventory at the end of the year may be shown as either a credit entry or deducted on the debit side as shown below. This has the advantage of showing the cost of sales.

S. Mann ***Trading account for the year ended 30 April 20X5***			
	£		**£**
Opening inventory	5,000	Sales revenue	67,500
Add: Purchases	50,000		
	55,000		
Less: Closing inventory	10,000		
Cost of sales	45,000		
Gross profit c/d	22,500		
	67,500		67,500
		Gross profit b/d	22,500

4 The trading income account is a ledger account in the general ledger and thus part of the double-entry system. However, when it is prepared for submission to the management, the owner(s) of a business or Revenue and Customs, it is often presented vertically as shown at the start of Worked Example 14.1.

5 No entries other than those shown above (and the correction of errors) should be made in an inventory account. It is not a continuous record of the value of inventory.

6 The inventory shown in a trial balance will always be that at the end of the previous year (and thus the opening inventory of the year to which the trial balance relates).

The statement of profit or loss

The statement of profit or loss is taken from a ledger account in the general ledger (called the *profit or loss account*) and thus is part of the double-entry system. It is used to ascertain the **profit** (or **loss**) **for the period** and is prepared in the same way as the *trading account*. That is, the balances on the income and expense ledger accounts in the general ledger are transferred to the *profit or loss account* by means of double entry.

14.4 The purpose and structure of a statement of financial position

The statement of financial position is a list of the assets, liabilities and capital of a business at the end of a given accounting period. It therefore provides information about the resources and debts of the reporting entity. The statement of financial position enables users of financial statements to evaluate the entity's financial position, in particular whether the business is likely to be able to pay its debts. The statement of financial position is like a photograph of the financial state of affairs of a business at a specific time.

Statements of financial position contain five groups of items, as follows.

1 **Non-current assets**. These are items not specifically bought for resale but to be used in the production or distribution of those goods normally sold by the business. They are utilized to generate economic inflows to the entity. Non-current assets are durable goods that usually last for several years, and are normally kept by a business for more than one accounting year. Examples of non-current assets include land and buildings, plant and machinery, motor vehicles, office equipment, furniture, fixtures and fittings. These are tangible assets. The different types are recorded in separate ledger accounts with the balances on each account being disclosed in the statement of financial position.

   In company financial statements tangible non-current assets are collectively referred to as '*property, plant and equipment*' – only one combined figure would be disclosed in a company's statement of financial position.

2 **Current assets**. These are items that are normally kept by a business for less than one accounting year and/or support the operating activities of the entity. Indeed, the composition of each type of current asset is usually continually changing. Examples include inventories, trade receivables, short-term investments, money in a bank account and cash.

3 **Equity capital**. This refers to the amount of money invested in the business by the owner(s). This can take the form of cash introduced or profits not withdrawn.

4 **Non-current liabilities**. These are debts owed by a business that are not due until after one year (often much longer) from the date of the statement of financial position. Examples include loans and mortgages.

5 **Current liabilities**. These are debts owed by a business that are payable within one year (often considerably less) from the date of the statement of financial position. Examples include trade payables and bank overdrafts.

Learning Activity 14.1

Prepare a statement of financial position listing your assets and liabilities, or those of your family. Use an appropriate method of classifying the assets and liabilities and show the relevant totals and subtotals.

The structure of a statement of financial position is shown in Figure 14.2. Note that the items shown in bold are subtotals or totals that should be shown on the statement of financial position.

Figure 14.2

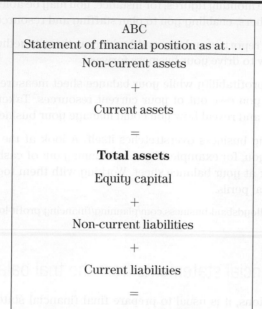

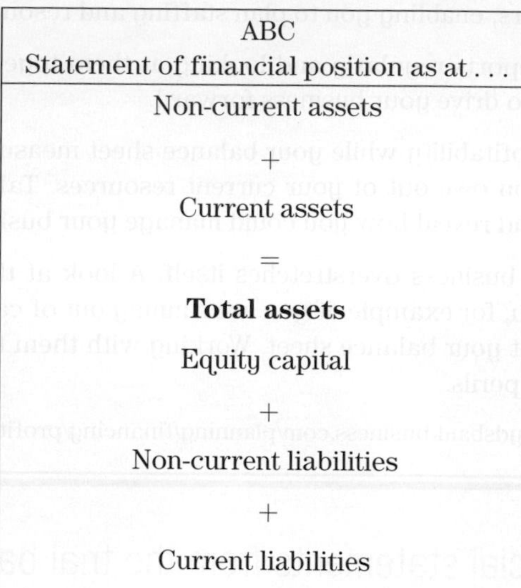

ABC
Statement of financial position as at . . .
Non-current assets
+
Current assets
=
Total assets
Equity capital
+
Non-current liabilities
+
Current liabilities
=
Total equity and liabilities

An example of the key areas covered in a statement of financial position for a sole trader

The benefits of preparing a statement of profit or loss and a statement of financial position are highlighted in advice provided to businesses on the Lloyds Bank website. An extract is reproduced in Real World Example 14.1.

REAL WORLD EXAMPLE 14.1

Lloyds Bank: The benefits of producing accurate profit & loss accounts and balance sheets

Your profit and loss account (P&L) shows business performance. It measures how much money you have made, and how you made it, over a given period. Typically, this period is a month or consolidated months over a year.

Your balance sheet shows the value of your business, at a specific point in time (for example, the last day of the month or the end of your financial year). It shows how the profits shown in the P&L have been used.

These records are valuable for many reasons.

- Your bank manager, financiers and prospective partners will want to see clear records of the business' profitability.
- You get a clear view of patterns emerging in the way you do business.

- By examining accurate monthly figures, for instance, you may be able to identify months when you are busier than others, enabling you to plan staffing and resource levels more efficiently.
- Producing both these reports regularly and looking at them together gives you a wealth of information about how to drive your business forward.

The P&L measures your profitability while your balance sheet measures your financial health – your ability to pay what you owe out of your current resources. Taken together, they indicate your long-term prospects and reveal how you could manage your business better.

It could be that a growing business overstretches itself. A look at the P&L will reveal healthy profit, but will not show you, for example, if you are running out of cash, as you build stock. For this you will need to look at your balance sheet. Working with them together allows you to plot growth and avoid financial perils.

Source: http://businesshelp.lloydsbankbusiness.com/planning/financing/profit-loss/, accessed August 2014.

14.5 Preparing financial statements from the trial balance

In practice, and in examinations, it is usual to prepare final financial statements from the information given in the trial balance. However, it is important to appreciate that the general ledger entries described in earlier chapters to close the income and expenditure ledger accounts also have to be done, for adjustments.

An illustration of the preparation of final financial statements, including the required ledger entries, is shown in Worked Example 14.3.

WORKED EXAMPLE 14.3

The following is the trial balance of A. Dillon at 31 March 20X5:

	Debit	*Credit*
	£	£
Capital		42,140
Drawings	13,600	
Loan from S. Rodd		10,000
Bank	5,800	
Cash	460	
Sales revenue		88,400
Purchases	46,300	
Sales returns	5,700	
Purchases returns		3,100
Inventory at 1 Apr 20X4	8,500	
Carriage inwards	2,400	
Carriage outwards	1,600	
Trade receivables	15,300	
Trade payables		7,200

	Debit £	Credit £
Motor vehicles	23,100	
Fixtures and fittings	12,400	
Wages and salaries	6,800	
Rent	4,100	
Light and heat	3,200	
Telephone and postage	1,700	
Discount allowed	830	
Discount received		950
	151,790	151,790

The inventory at 31 March 20X5 was valued at £9,800. The loan from S. Rodd is repayable on 1 January 20X7.

Required

Prepare the statement of profit or loss and statement of financial position (horizontal format) for A. Dillon from the trial balance provided.

Sales revenue			
Trading a/c	88,400	Balance b/d	88,400

Sales returns			
Balance b/d	5,700	Trading a/c	5,700

Purchases			
Balance b/d	46,300	Trading a/c	46,300

Purchases returns			
Trading a/c	3,100	Balance b/d	3,100

Inventories			
Balance b/d	8,500	Trading a/c	8,500
Trading a/c	9,800		

Carriage inwards			
Balance b/d	2,400	Trading a/c	2,400

Wages and salaries			
Balance b/d	6,800	Profit or loss a/c	6,800

Rent			
Balance b/d	4,100	Profit or loss a/c	4,100

Light and heat			
Balance b/d	3,200	Profit or loss a/c	3,200

Telephone and postage			
Balance b/d	1,700	Profit or loss a/c	1,700

Discount allowed			
Balance b/d	830	Profit or loss a/c	830

Discount received			
Profit or loss a/c	950	Balance b/d	950

Drawings			
Balance b/d	13,600	Capital a/c	13,600

All other accounts contain only the balances shown in the trial balance.

A. Dillon

Trading and profit or loss account for the year ended 31 March 20X5

	£	£		£
Inventory at 1 Apr 20X4		8,500	Sales revenue	88,400
Purchases	46,300		*Less:* returns	5,700
Less: Returns	3,100			82,700
	43,200			
Add: Carriage inwards	2,400	45,600		
		54,100		
Less: Inventory at 31 Mar 20X5		9,800		
Cost of sales		44,300		
Gross profit c/d to P/L a/c		38,400		
		82,700		82,700
Carriage outwards		1,600	*Gross profit b/d from trading a/c*	38,400
Wages and salaries		6,800	Discount received	950
Rent		4,100		
Light and heat		3,200		
Telephone and postage		1,700		
Discount allowed		830		
Profit for the period c/d		21,120		
		39,350		39,350
Capital a/c (Profit transferred)		21,120	*Profit for the year b/d*	21,120

Capital			
Drawings	13,600	Balance b/d	42,140
Balance b/d	49,660	Profit or loss a/c	21,120
	63,260		63,260
		Balance b/d	49,660

Notes

1 The *trading account* is combined with the *profit or loss account* (top half) in this example. The gross profit is the difference between the two sides of the *trading account* and must be brought down to the opposite side of the *profit or loss account.*

2 The profit for the period is the difference between the two sides of the *profit or loss account.* This is brought down to the credit side of the *profit or loss account* and then transferred to the *capital account* by debiting the *profit or loss account* and crediting the *capital account.* The reason for this transfer is because the profit belongs to the owner and it increases the amount of capital he or she is entitled to withdraw from the business.

3 If the debit side of the *profit or loss account* exceeds the credit side, this is shown as a net loss (carried down) on the credit side and debited to the *capital account.*

4 The balance on the *drawings account* at the end of the period must be transferred to the *capital account.*

5 Each of the transfers from the ledger accounts to the *trading income and profit or loss ledger account* should also be entered in the journal.

A. Dillon				
Statement of financial position as at 31 March 20X5				
Credit (see note 6)	£	**Debit** (see note 6)	£	£
EQUITY AND LIABILITIES		**ASSETS**		
Equity capital		*Non-current assets*		
Balance at 1 Apr 20X4	42,140	Motor vehicles		23,100
Add: Profit for year	21,120	Fixtures and fittings		12,400
	63,260			35,500
Less: Drawings	13,600	*Current assets*		
Balance at 31 Mar 20X5	49,660	Inventories	9,800	
Non-current liabilities		Trade receivables	15,300	
Loan from S. Rodd	10,000	Bank	5,800	
Current liabilities		Cash	460	
Trade payables	7,200			31,360
	66,860			66,860

6 Note that the debit balances remaining in the ledger after the *profit or loss account* has been prepared are shown on the right-hand side of the statement of financial position and the credit balances on the left-hand side. This may seem inconsistent with the debit and credit sides of the ledger being on the left and right, respectively. However, it is a common form of presentation in accounting.

7 Like the trial balance, the total of each side of the statement of financial position should be the same. That is, the total of the ledger accounts with debit balances should equal the total of the ledger accounts with credit balances. If this is not the case, it indicates that an error has occurred in the preparation of the *trading income, profit or loss account* or the statement of financial position.

8 The current assets in the statement of financial position are shown in what is called their 'reverse order of liquidity'. The latter refers to how easily assets can be turned into cash.

9 The entries on the statement of financial position in respect of capital are a summary of the movements in the *capital account* in the ledger.

10 Carriage inwards is added to the cost of purchases because it relates to the haulage costs of goods purchased. Carriage outwards is shown in the statement of *profit or loss account* because it relates to the haulage costs of goods sold and is thus a selling and distribution expense.

When the statement of profit or loss and statement of financial position are presented to the owner(s) of a business and HM Revenue and Customs, it is common to use a vertical format. This is illustrated next using the data in this worked example. This format is adapted from the suggested formats for statements of profit or loss under the IFRS (2013) – *Taxonomy 2013 – Illustrative Examples* as it is deemed to provide the most useful information to the users; therefore, it is utilized in this book from now on. If you do not use the words 'Less' then the number should be in brackets. More columns are used as this is common practice in the UK for sole traders and partnerships.

A. Dillon
Statement of profit or loss for the year ending 31 March 20X5

	£	£	£
Revenue			88,400
Less: Returns			5,700
			82,700
Less: Cost of sales:			
Inventory at 1 Apr 20X4		8,500	
Add: Purchases	46,300		
Less: Returns	3,100		
		43,200	
Add: Carriage inwards		2,400	
		54,100	
Less: Inventory at 31 Mar 20X5		9,800	
			44,300
Gross profit			38,400
Add: Discount received			950
			39,350
Less: Expenditure:			
Carriage outwards		1,600	
Wages and salaries		6,800	
Rent		4,100	
Light and heat		3,200	
Telephone and postage		1,700	
Discount allowed		830	18,230
Profit for the year			21,120

A. Dillon *Statement of financial position as at 31 March 20X5*	
ASSETS	£
Non-current assets	
Motor vehicles	23,100
Fixtures and fittings	12,400
	35,500
Current assets	
Inventories	9,800
Trade receivables	15,300
Bank	5,800
Cash	460
	31,360
Total assets	66,860
OWNER'S EQUITY AND LIABILITIES	
Owner's capital	
Balance at 1 Apr 20X4	42,140
Add: Profit for year	21,120
	63,260
Less: Drawings	13,600
Balance at 31 Mar 20X5	49,660
Non-current liabilities	
Loan from S. Rodd	10,000
Current liabilities	
Trade payables	7,200
Total liabilities	17,200
Total equity and liabilities	66,860

Summary

Final financial statements comprise a statement of profit or loss and a statement of financial position. These are prepared at the end of the accounting year after the trial balance has been completed. The statement of comprehensive income can be split into three parts: the first focuses on calculating the gross profit for the period and is commonly referred to as the 'trading account'; the next part includes all the other realized income and expenditure for the period and determines the profit/loss for the period; and the final part considers other unrealized gains or losses in the period, such as asset revaluation increases. Sole traders prepare a statement of profit or loss because they rarely disclose unrealized gains or losses. The statement of profit or loss enables users to evaluate the performance of the enterprise. The statement of financial position is a list of the assets and liabilities (and capital) of a business at the end of a given accounting year. It enables users to evaluate the financial position of the enterprise, including whether it is likely to be able to pay its debts. In the statement of financial position, assets are classified as either non-current or current, and liabilities as either current or non-current.

The gross profit is the difference between the sales revenue and the cost of sales. The cost of sales is the amount of purchases as adjusted for the opening and closing inventories. The inventory at the end of an accounting year has to be entered in the general ledger by debiting an inventory account and crediting the trading income account. The *trading income* and *profit or loss accounts* are then prepared by transferring the balances on the income and expense accounts in the general ledger to these ledger accounts.

The statement of financial position is a list of the balances remaining in the ledger after the *trading income* and *profit or loss ledger accounts* have been prepared. It is extracted in essentially the same way as a trial balance, but presented using a more formal layout to show the two groups of both assets and liabilities, and pertinent subtotals.

Key terms and concepts

capital (equity)	230	non-current assets	234
cost of sales	231	non-current liabilities	234
current assets	234	profit	230
current liabilities	234	profit for the period	234
equity capital	234	statement of comprehensive income	230
final financial statements	230	statement of financial position	230
gross profit	231	statement of profit or loss	230
inventory	231	trading account	232
loss for the period	234		

An asterisk after the question number indicates that there is a suggested answer in Appendix 2.

Review questions

connect

14.1 a Explain the purposes of a statement of profit or loss and a statement of financial position.

b Describe the structure of each.

14.2 Explain the relevance of inventory in the determination of gross profit.

14.3 Explain each of the entries in the following inventory account:

Inventory			
Trading a/c	4,600	Trading a/c	4,600
Trading a/c	6,300		

Exercises

connect

BASIC

14.4 A company has 100 units in inventory at the start of the year valued at £1,000. During the year it purchases a further 500 units for £5,000 and sells 400 units for £8,000.

Required

a What is the quantity and value of the closing inventories?

b What is the gross profit for the year?

c Prepare the trading account for the year.

BASIC

14.5 Balances on the main inventory accounts are as follows:

– sales revenue	£18,000
– purchases	£12,000
– opening inventory	£1,000
– returns inward	£1,500
– returns outward	£500
– carriage outward	£200
– carriage inward	£900
– discount received	£1,000

The closing inventory count reveals inventory of £1,500.

Required

Determine the gross profit.

BASIC

14.6 Extract the statement of profit or loss for the year ended 31 December 20X4 for M. McKee and the statement of financial position as at 31 December 20X4 from the following.

M. McKee
Trial balance at 31 December 20X4

	Dr £	Cr £
Capital		66,405
Drawings	5,258	
Cash at bank	4,200	
Buildings	30,000	
Fixtures	18,750	
Trade receivables and payables	15,250	8,750
Motor vans	2,500	
Purchases and revenue	86,452	109,250
General expenses	5,250	
Salaries	13,560	
Motor expenses	1,365	
Lighting and heating	890	
Insurance	550	
Rent	380	
	184,405	184,405

Additional information

Inventory at the year end was £11,000.

BASIC

14.7* The following is the trial balance of R. Woods as at 30 September 20X5:

	Debit	Credit
	£	£
Inventory 1 Oct 20X4	2,368	
Purchases	12,389	
Revenue		18,922
Salaries and wages	3,862	
Rent and rates	504	
Insurance	78	
Motor expenses	664	
Printing and stationery	216	
Light and heat	166	
General expenses	314	
Premises	5,000	
Motor vehicles	1,800	
Fixtures and fittings	350	
Trade receivables	3,896	
Trade payables		1,731
Cash at bank	482	
Drawings	1,200	
Capital		12,636
	33,289	33,289

The inventory at 30 September 20X5 is valued at £2,946.

Required

Prepare a statement of profit or loss for the year ended 30 September 20X5 and a statement of financial position at that date (publishable format).

BASIC

14.8 On 31 December 20X5, the trial balance of Joytoys showed the following chart of accounts and balances:

	Debit	Credit
	£	£
Bank	500	
Capital		75,000
Bank loan		22,000
Inventory	12,000	
Purchases	108,000	
Sales revenue		167,000
Rent, rates and insurance	15,000	
Plant and machinery at cost	70,000	
Office furniture and fittings at cost	24,000	
Discount allowed	1,600	
Bank interest	400	
Discount received		3,000

Cont'd	Debit	Credit
Wages and salaries	13,000	
Light and heat	9,000	
Drawings	10,000	
Returns outwards		4,000
Returns inwards	1,000	
Trade payables		16,000
Trade receivables	22,500	
	287,000	287,000

Additional information

1 The inventory at 31 December 20X5 was valued at £19,500.

2 The bank loan is repayable in five years' time.

Required

Prepare a statement of profit or loss for the year ended 31 December 20X5 and a statement of financial position at that date (publishable format).

14.9* The following is the trial balance of A. Evans as at 30 June 20X5: BASIC

	Debit	Credit
	£	£
Capital		39,980
Drawings	14,760	
Loan – Solihull Bank		20,000
Leasehold premises	52,500	
Motor vehicles	13,650	
Investments	4,980	
Trade receivables	2,630	
Trade payables		1,910
Cash	460	
Bank overdraft		3,620
Sales revenue		81,640
Purchases	49,870	
Returns outwards		960
Returns inwards	840	
Carriage outwards	390	
Inventory	5,610	
Rent and rates	1,420	
Light and heat	710	
Telephone and postage	540	
Printing and stationery	230	
Bank interest	140	
Interest received		620
	148,730	148,730

Additional information

1 The inventory at 30 June 20X5 has been valued at £4,920.

2 The bank loan is repayable on 1 June 20X8.

Required

Prepare a statement of profit or loss for the year ended 30 June 20X5 and a statement of financial position as at that date (publishable format).

BASIC

14.10 The following is the trial balance of J. Peters as at 30 September 20X5:

	Debit	*Credit*
	£	£
Capital		32,890
Drawings	5,200	
Loan from A. Drew		10,000
Cash	510	
Bank overdraft		1,720
Purchases and revenue	29,300	45,600
Returns inwards	3,800	
Returns outwards		2,700
Carriage inwards	960	
Carriage outwards	820	
Trade receivables	7,390	
Trade payables		4,620
Land and buildings	26,000	
Plant and machinery	13,500	
Listed investments	4,800	
Interest paid	1,200	
Interest received		450
Rent received		630
Inventory	3,720	
Repairs to buildings	810	
Plant hire charges	360	
Bank charges	240	
	98,610	98,610

Additional information

1 The inventory at 30 September 20X5 was valued at £4,580.

2 The loan from A. Drew is repayable on 1 January 20Y1.

Required

Prepare a statement of profit or loss for the year ended 30 September 20X5 and a statement of financial position as at that date.

BASIC

14.11 B. Good drew up the following trial balance as at 31 March 20X5. Extract the statement of profit or loss for the year ended 31 March 20X5 and statement of financial position as at that date.

	Debit	***Credit***
	£	**£**
Sundry expenses	1,090	
Rent received		200
Office expenses	560	
Insurance	525	
Wages and expenses	4,580	
Telephone	1,250	
Purchases and sales revenue	125,560	189,560
Motor expenses	569	
Rent	2,500	
Rates	1,250	
Carriage outwards	546	
Carriage inwards	200	
Returns outwards		302
Returns inwards	560	
Building	230,000	
Motor vehicle	12,500	
Fixtures	5,365	
Trade receivables and payables	28,560	48,560
Cash	12	
Bank		32,250
Drawings	5,562	
Capital		178,907
Opening inventory	28,590	
	449,779	449,779

Additional information

Inventory at the year-end was £35,650.

BASIC

14.12 The balances extracted from the books of G. Ryan at 31 December 20X4 are given below:

	£
Drawings	7,180
Heating and lighting	1,234
Stationery and postage	268
Carriage outwards	1,446
Insurance	1,818
Wages and salaries	18,910
Inventory at 1 January 20X4	42,120
Purchases	74,700
Sales revenue	131,040
Rent and rates	2,990
General expenses	1,460
Discount received	426
Plant and machinery	9,060
Cash at bank	3,222
Cash in hand	65
Trade receivables	1,920
Trade payables	630
Sales returns	1,310
Purchases returns	747

Additional information

At 31 December 20X4 inventory was valued at £33,990.

Required

a Prepare the statement of profit or loss for the year ended 31 December 20X4.

b Prepare the statement of financial position as at 31 December 20X4.

When you have completed this chapter you are encouraged to try Case Study 1 and Case Study 4 in Appendix 1 of this book.

Chapter 15

Depreciation and non-current assets

Learning Objectives:

After reading this chapter you should be able to do the following:

1. Distinguish between capital expenditure and revenue expenditure.
2. Describe the nature, recognition and valuation of non-current assets including intangible non-current assets such as goodwill and development expenditure.
3. Discuss the nature of depreciation.
4. Describe the straight-line, reducing balance and sum of the years' digits methods of depreciating assets including the resulting pattern of charges to the statement of profit or loss over an asset's useful life, and the circumstances in which each might be the most appropriate.
5. Compute the amount of depreciation using the methods in the point above, and show the relevant entries in the journal, general ledger, statement of profit or loss and statement of financial position.
6. Compute the depreciation on an asset in the years of acquisition and disposal, and the profit or loss on disposal; and show the relevant entries in the journal, general ledger, statement of profit or loss and statement of financial position.

15.1 The nature and types of non-current assets

At the time of writing the *Conceptual Framework* (IASB, 2011) defines an asset as '*a resource controlled by the enterprise as a result of past events and from which future economic benefits are expected to flow to the enterprise*'. This definition is currently being reviewed and a suggestion is that the definition change to '*a present economic resource*' (IASplus, 2013). The ability to generate future economic benefits is arguably the most important criterion in determining whether expenditure is to be classified as an asset or not, and the current discussion is that this should not form part of the definition but part of the recognition criteria. Assets are categorized as being either current or non-current in the statement of financial position as outlined in Figure 15.1.

Figure 15.1

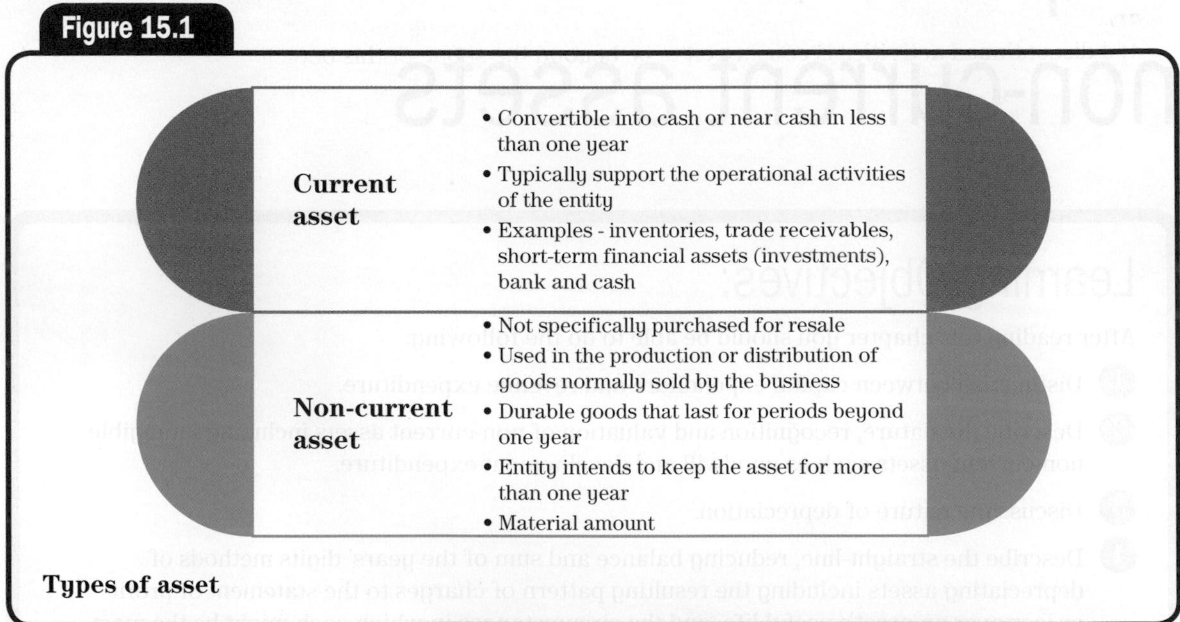

Current asset
• Convertible into cash or near cash in less than one year
• Typically support the operational activities of the entity
• Examples - inventories, trade receivables, short-term financial assets (investments), bank and cash
Non-current asset
• Not specifically purchased for resale
• Used in the production or distribution of goods normally sold by the business
• Durable goods that last for periods beyond one year
• Entity intends to keep the asset for more than one year
• Material amount

Types of asset

Money spent on non-current assets is referred to as **capital expenditure**. All other costs and expenses are referred to as **revenue expenditure**. The latter are entered in the statement of profit or loss for the year in which the costs are incurred.

Non-current assets are classified as either tangible or intangible.

Tangible assets

Tangible assets are assets that have physical substance. The accounting for tangible assets can be found in four standards:

1 *International Accounting Standard (IAS) 16 – Property, Plant and Equipment* (IASB, 2013a) is the most relevant when it comes to accounting for sole traders. It outlines the accounting recommended for tangible assets that are most likely to be held by sole traders, such as property, plant and equipment, fixtures and fittings, motor vehicles, office equipment (such as computers) and loose tools. Tools that are only expected to last for less than one year are referred to as 'consumable tools', and treated as revenue expenditure. **Tangible non-current assets** include assets that are held for use in the production or supply of goods or services, or for administrative purposes and are expected to be used during more than one period. This chapter concentrates predominately on the accounting practices suggested in this standard. The other types of tangible asset are now mentioned in brief.

2 *IAS 40 – Investment Property* (IASB, 2013b) provides guidance on accounting for investment properties.

3 *IAS 17 – Leases* (IASB, 2013d) provides guidance on the accounting for leased assets. In brief, capitalized leased assets are depreciated in the same manner as assets that are subject to the recommended practices outlined in IAS 16. Leases and accounting for leases is considered to be beyond the scope of this book.

4 *International Financial Reporting Standard 5 – Non-current Assets Held for Sale and Discontinued Operations* (IASB, 2013e) provides guidance on the accounting treatment for assets that are no longer held with long-term prospects in mind. They no longer form part of the business's operational activities. In brief, the standard recommends that these assets be disclosed separately and labelled as being 'held for sale', or 'discontinued', and should be carried at fair value. **Fair value** is defined in the standard as '*the amount for which an asset could be exchanged between knowledgeable, willing parties in an arm's length transaction*' – that is, market value. The accounting for non-current assets held for sale and discontinued activities is considered to be beyond the scope of this book.

Intangible assets

Intangible assets are defined in *IAS 38 – Intangible Assets* (IASB, 2013f) as '*identifiable non-monetary assets without physical substance*'. Examples include goodwill, patents, trademarks, copyrights, fishing licences, milk quota, franchises, customer or supplier relationships, mortgage servicing rights, customer loyalty, market share, brand name and development expenditure such as expenditure creating computer software.

Goodwill usually arises in the statement of financial position because at some time in the past the business has taken over, or been formed from, another business. Recommended accounting for goodwill is provided in *IFRS 3 – Business Combinations* (IASB, 2013 g). The figure shown in the statement of financial position for goodwill is the difference between the amount paid for that business and the value of its net assets. Goodwill is sometimes said to represent the potential future profits or sales arising from a business's reputation and the continuing patronage of existing customers. However, it is much more than this, in that it represents the advantages that are gained from taking over an existing business rather than building up a new business from scratch (e.g. not having to recruit staff, find premises or identify suppliers). Goodwill is discussed in Chapter 26 'Changes in Partnerships'.

Non-financial assets, also called **non-monetary assets**, are assets other than cash, money in a bank cheque or deposit account, investments, and amounts receivable such as trade receivables (these are examples of financial assets). An example of a non-financial asset is gold or property.

Financial assets are assets that derive value from a potential claim. They are also frequently included under the heading of non-current assets. These may consist of shares and/or debentures that are listed (quoted) on a stock exchange and unlisted securities. Investments should only be classified as a non-current asset where they are held on a long-term basis for the purpose of generating income. If this is not the case, investments should be treated as a current asset (available-for-sale).

15.2 The recognition and valuation of non-current assets

The term 'valuation' refers to the amount at which assets are shown in the statement of financial position. IAS 16 allows non-current tangible assets to be valued using two approaches: historical cost and the alternative treatment, revalued amount.

Historical cost

In historical cost accounting, non-current assets are valued at their historical cost less the **aggregate/accumulated depreciation** from the date of acquisition to the date of the statement of financial position. The resulting figure is known as the **written-down value** (WDV), **net book value** (NBV) or **net carrying amount**. Depreciation is discussed later in this chapter.

Historical cost refers to the purchase price. Where the business is value added tax (VAT) registered, the cost excludes VAT (as the business can claim this back). Where the business is not VAT registered, the cost includes VAT as this is a cost of the asset to the business which cannot be reclaimed. The historical cost of a non-current asset may also include a number of additional costs. The cost of land and buildings, for example, may include legal expenses and stamp duty, and the cost of any subsequent extensions and improvements (but not repairs and renewals). Similarly, the cost of machinery is taken to include delivery charges and installation expenses. However, the costs of any extended warranty, maintenance agreement and replacement/spare parts (for future use) that have been included in the purchase price must be removed from the capital account and treated as revenue expenses. Similarly, the cost of vehicles must exclude the first year's road tax and fuel where these have been included in the purchase price.

Revalued amount

The Companies Act 2006 and IAS 16 allow companies to revalue their tangible non-current assets and show them in the statement of financial position at fair value rather than historical cost. This is known as the alternative treatment.

- The carrying value for an asset accounted for under historical cost is its net book value.
- The **carrying amount** for a revalued asset is its fair value at the date of the revaluation less any subsequent accumulated depreciation and subsequent accumulated impairment losses.

Revaluations are most commonly used in the case of land and buildings that were acquired several years previously, and thus their current market value can exceed the historical cost, unless of course the property was purchased in the period before the financial crises of 2007. If it were purchased in this period then is it likely that the asset's fair value is actually below its **book value**, in which case, regardless of the valuation method adopted, the asset will have to be written down to its net realizable value. This represents a diminution in value (discussed in the next section). The **current value** of a tangible non-current asset to the business is the lower of replacement cost and recoverable amount. The **recoverable amount** is the higher of fair value and value-in-use.

Where a tangible non-current asset is revalued, all tangible non-current assets of the same class should be revalued. If a company revalues one or more classes of tangible non-current assets, it should continue to adopt the same policy in future years: that is, IAS 16 does not allow one-off revaluations. There must be regular revaluations. In the case of land and buildings, IAS 16 requires that revaluations be made with sufficient regularity to ensure that *'the carrying amount does not differ materially from that which would be determined using fair value at the statement of financial position date'*.

The IASB promotes the use of fair value accounting. Recording assets at fair value is considered to provide more relevant information to stakeholders as the true wealth of the entity is disclosed. This will enable investors to make more informed decisions. Other stakeholders will also benefit, for example, when a lender uses the assets as security for a loan provided to the company – they will be able to determine the strength of that security by examining the financial statements. A disadvantage is the additional cost involved in determining up-to-date fair values.

Impairment of assets

Non-current assets should also be reviewed for impairment under *IAS 36 – Impairment of Assets* (IASB, 2013c). As mentioned, the recoverable amount is *'the higher of fair value (less costs to sell) and value in use'*. If the carrying amount of the asset exceeds the recoverable amount, the asset is impaired and should be written down to its recoverable amount.

For the sake of simplicity the remainder of this chapter assumes that non-current assets are valued at historical cost. Revaluations are discussed further in Chapter 26, 'Changes in Partnerships' and Chapter 29, 'The Final Financial Statements of Limited Companies'.

15.3 The nature of depreciation

The purchase of a non-current asset occurs in one year but the revenue generated from its use normally arises over a number of years. This is referred to as its **useful (economic) life**. In IAS 16 the useful life of an asset is defined as *'the period over which an asset is expected to be available for use by an entity; or the number of production or similar units expected to be obtained from the asset by an entity'*.

If the cost of non-current assets were treated as an expense in the statement of profit or loss in the year of purchase, this would probably result in an excessive loss in that year, and excessive profits in the years in which the revenue arose. This gives a misleading view of the profits and losses of each year and distorts comparisons over time. Thus, the cost of a non-current asset is not treated as an expense in the year of purchase but rather carried forward and written off to the statement of profit and loss over the useful economic life of the asset in the form of depreciation. The part of the cost of an asset that is 'used up' or 'consumed' in each year of the asset's useful economic life must be set against the revenue that this generates (in conjunction with other factors of production). That part of the cost of a non-current asset, which is 'used up' or 'consumed' during an accounting period, is referred to as 'depreciation'. IAS 16 defines **depreciation** as *'the systematic allocation of the depreciable amount of an asset over its useful life'* where the **depreciable amount** is *'the cost of the asset, or other amount attributed to that asset, less its residual value'*.

The allocation tries to measure the reduction in or consumption of the economic benefits available from the tangible non-current asset. **Consumption** is generally considered to include the wearing-out, using-up or other reduction in the useful economic life of a tangible non-current asset. The reduction can be caused by wear and tear as a result of use, the passing of time or obsolescence through either changes in technology or demand for the goods and services produced by the asset.

Obsolescence through technological change refers to the situation where a new model of the asset, which is significantly more efficient or performs additional functions, comes on to the market. **Obsolescence through demand changes** occurs when there is a substantial reduction in demand for the firm's product because of, for example, technological advances in competitors' products. Both of these causes of obsolescence usually result in a sudden, relatively large decrease in value of the asset, particularly where it cannot be used for any other purpose.

A misconception when defining depreciation is that it represents a loss in an asset's value. This misconception is widespread and is what a typical non-accounting individual would define depreciation as. This misconception is not helped by the use of the term 'depreciation' by some companies to indicate a loss in value as portrayed in Real World Example 15.1.

REAL WORLD EXAMPLE 15.1

What Car?

'What Car?' have a 'depreciation index' on their website so that users of the site can see in advance the potential loss in value of each model of car. For example, the depreciation index returned the following values for the expected future value of a Volkswagon Caddy Maxi MPV 1.6 TDI 102 5 dr:

Yr0	Yr1	Yr2	Yr3	Yr4
£20,332	£12,106	£9,940	£8,153	£6,972

This is the expected future sale price of the vehicle.

Source: http://www.whatcar.com/car-depreciation-calculator/results?makeId = 25321&modelVersionId = 35877&editionId = 35879, accessed September 2013.

Accountants typically deny that the amount of depreciation shown in final financial statements is a reflection of the loss in value of a non-current asset. They argue that accountants are not valuers, and that depreciation is simply the allocation of the cost of a non-current asset over its useful economic life to the business, and that permanent diminutions in value are a separate issue, and are dealt with by a separate standard. They would consider a loss in value to be a diminution in value. The Companies Act 2006 requires that *'provisions for diminution in value shall be made in respect of any non-current asset which has diminished in value, if the reduction in its value is expected to be permanent'*. Depreciation is a provision. However, under accounting standards where an asset suffers diminution in value, then the asset's value is reduced. A provision is not created.

A further misconception about depreciation is that it represents a build-up of funds (through the provision) for the replacement of non-current assets. The view is that the annual charge for depreciation in the statement of profit or loss represents a setting-aside of some of the income so that over the useful life of the asset sufficient 'funds' are retained in the business to replace the asset. However, it must be emphasized that no money is specifically set aside. Thus, when the time comes to replace the asset, the money needed to do so will not automatically be available. Furthermore, where depreciation is based on the historical cost of the asset, the amount of funds set aside will be insufficient to provide for any increase in the replacement cost of the asset.

Finally, it should be noted that IAS 16 requires that all tangible non-current assets except land are depreciated. This includes depreciating buildings. The reason is that although the market value of buildings at any point in time may exceed their historical cost, they nevertheless have a finite life and thus should be depreciated over their useful economic life. However, some businesses do not depreciate their buildings on the grounds that the market value at the end of the year, and/or the estimated residual value at the end of their expected useful life, is not less than the original cost. It is also sometimes argued that since repairs and maintenance costs on buildings are charged to the statement of profit or loss, to also charge depreciation on an asset, the useful life of which is being effectively maintained into perpetuity, would amount to a double expense charge and the creation of secret reserves. However, these arguments ignore that depreciation is not a method of valuation of assets but rather a process of allocation of the cost over the asset's useful life which, however long, must still be finite. Buildings, for example, can be entered in the statement of financial position at a revalued amount in excess of their cost, but this revalued amount should still be depreciated. Revaluations are discussed further in Chapter 26, 'Changes in Partnerships' and Chapter 29, 'The Final Financial Statements of Limited Companies'. The accounting for buildings under IAS 16 is different from the accounting for investment properties under IAS 40. IAS 40 allows investment properties not to be depreciated, but to be revalued yearly to fair value, with the movement in value being charged/credited to the statement of profit or loss. IFRS 5 (IASB, 2013e) also allows assets that are held for sale, or discontinued, not to be depreciated but to be revalued at fair value each year with the change in value being charged/credited to the statement of profit or loss. The reason for the different treatment is that the latter are considered to be investments, not tangible non-current assets that are being consumed by the business.

15.4 Methods of depreciation

A number of different methods have been developed for measuring depreciation, each of which will give a different annual charge to the statement of profit or loss. There is no one method of depreciation that is superior to all others in all circumstances. The most appropriate method will depend on the type of asset and the extent to which it is used in each period. Whichever method is used to calculate depreciation, at least three pieces of data relating to the asset in question are needed, as outlined in Figure 15.2.

The useful life of an asset refers to the period that the business regards as being the most economical length of time to keep the particular asset. This will depend on a number of factors, such as the pattern of repair costs. The useful life of an asset may well be considerably shorter than its total life. **Residual value** refers to the estimated proceeds of sale at the end of the asset's useful life to the business. This is usually considerably more than its scrap value. It should be noted that both the useful life and the residual value have to be estimated when the asset is purchased.

Figure 15.2

Depreciation determinants

- Historical cost of the asset
- Expected useful economic life to the business
- Estimated residual value of the asset at the end of its useful economic life

Determinants of depreciation

As mentioned earlier, the difference between the historical cost of a tangible non-current asset and its residual value is referred to in IAS 16 as the 'depreciable amount'. According to IAS 16, the depreciable amount of a tangible non-current asset should be allocated to reflect the pattern in which the economic benefits are expected to be consumed by the entity. The two most common methods of depreciation in the UK are the **straight-line/fixed instalment method** and **reducing balance method**. Another method more common in the USA is the **sum of the years' digits method (sum of digits)**. These are described below.

The straight-line/fixed instalment method

Under this method the annual amount of depreciation that will be charged to the statement of profit or loss, referred to as the **depreciation expense**, is computed as follows:

$$\text{Depreciation} = \frac{\text{Cost} - \text{Estimated Residual value}}{\text{Estimated useful life in years}}$$

Alternatively the annual rate of depreciation can be expressed as a percentage. The annual amount of depreciation is then calculated by applying this percentage to the cost of the asset.

$$\text{Depreciation} = \text{Rate of depreciation (\%)} \times \text{Cost of asset}$$

This method gives the same charge for depreciation in each year of the asset's useful life. It is therefore most appropriate for assets that are depleted as a result of the passage of time (e.g. buildings, leases, pipelines, storage tanks, patents and trademarks). The method may also be suitable where the utilization of an asset is the same in each year.

The main advantages of the straight-line method are that it is easy to understand and the computations are simple. The main disadvantage is that it may not give an accurate measure of the reduction in the useful life of an asset.

The diminishing/reducing balance method

Under the **diminishing/reducing balance** method it is necessary first to compute the annual rate of depreciation as a percentage, as follows:

$$\text{Rate of depreciation} = 100 - \left(\text{ul}\sqrt{\frac{\text{Residual value}}{\text{Cost}}} \times 100\right)$$

where *ul* refers to the estimated useful life.

The annual amount of depreciation that will be charged to the statement of profit or loss is then computed as:

$$\boxed{\text{Depreciation} = \text{Rate of depreciation (\%)} \times \text{WDV of asset (at start of year)}}$$

The WDV of the asset refers to its cost less the aggregate depreciation of the asset since the date of acquisition. This method gives a decreasing annual charge for depreciation over the useful life of the asset. It is therefore most appropriate for non-current assets that deteriorate primarily as a result of usage where this is greater in the earlier years of their life (e.g. plant and machinery, motor vehicles, furniture and fittings, office equipment). However, this method may also be suitable even if the utilization is the same in each year. The logic behind this apparently contradictory assertion involves taking into consideration the pattern of repair costs. These will be low in the earlier years of the asset's life and high in later years. Thus, the decreasing annual amount of depreciation combined with the increasing repair costs will give a relatively constant combined annual charge in each year of the asset's useful life that is said to reflect the constant annual usage.

The main criticisms of this method relate to its complexity, and there is an arbitrary assumption about the rate of decline built into the formula.

The sum of the years' digits method

Under this method the annual amount of depreciation that will be expensed in the statement of profit or loss is computed by multiplying the depreciable amount by a fraction. The denominator in this fraction is the same each year, and is the sum of a decreasing arithmetic progression, the first number of which is the useful life of the asset and the last is one. For example, where an asset has a useful life of three years, the denominator is calculated as follows ($3 + 2 + 1 = 6$), with the numerator in the fraction being the number of years of the asset's remaining useful life at the start of the accounting year in question (e.g. 3 years, 2 years, 1 year). Therefore, in year one the depreciable amount will be multiplied by $\frac{3}{6}$, in year two the depreciable amount will be multiplied by $\frac{2}{6}$ and so on.

This method gives a decreasing annual charge for depreciation over the useful life of the asset that is similar to, but not the same amount as, the reducing balance method. The arguments for and against the sum of the years' digits method are thus the same as those relating to the reducing balance method except that the former is simpler. Moreover, the difference in the annual depreciation expense highlights the arbitrary nature of the different assumptions about the rates of decline that are built into the two methods.

A numerical example of the above methods of depreciation is given in Worked Example 15.1, which follows after the section on explaining the accounting entries for depreciation.

15.5 Accounting policy for depreciation

Most entities provide details of how they value their assets and how they calculate depreciation in their accounting policies. An example can be found in the financial statements of Viridian Group as follows:

REAL WORLD EXAMPLE 15.2

Viridian Group

Tangible fixed assets and depreciation

Tangible fixed assets are included in the balance sheet at cost, less accumulated depreciation and any recognized impairment loss. The cost of self-constructed assets includes the cost of materials, direct labour and an appropriate portion of overheads.

> Interest on funding attributable to significant capital projects is capitalized during the period of construction and written off as part of the total cost of the asset.
>
> Freehold land is not depreciated. Other tangible fixed assets are depreciated on a straight-line basis so as to write off the cost, less estimated residual value, over their estimated useful economic lives as follows:
>
> - Generation assets – 12 to 30 years
> - Freehold operational land – nil
> - Fixtures and equipment – up to 25 years
>
> The carrying values of tangible fixed assets are reviewed for impairment when events or changes in circumstances indicate the carrying values may not be recoverable. Where the carrying values exceed the estimated recoverable amount, the assets are written down to their recoverable amount.
>
> ***Source***: Viridian Group Holdings Limited, 2013, Annual Report and Accounts 2013, http://www.viridiangroup.co.uk/Site/10/Documents/VGIL%20FY2013%20annual%20report.pdf, accessed September 2013.

As can be seen, this comprehensive accounting policy covers how the company defines cost for purchased assets and internally generated assets, the method of accounting for depreciation, how impairments are determined and when the company no longer recognizes an asset. Viridian use UK GAAP terminology not IFRS terminology.

Learning Activity 15.1

Using the financial statements of any plc for guidance (use the Web to locate a company with tangible assets), draft a pro forma note on tangible non-current assets. This should show the typical movements in a cost account and in a provision for depreciation account with the resultant opening and closing written-down values being highlighted.

Note how the property, plant and equipment note in the company's financial statements reconciles with the figure that is disclosed on the face of the company's statement of financial position.

15.6 Accounting for depreciation

The accounting entries in respect of the annual charge for depreciation are made after the trial balance has been extracted when the statement of profit or loss is being prepared. These consist of the following:

Debit:	*Depreciation expense account*	£'XXX	
Credit:	*Provision for depreciation account*		£'XXX

The depreciation expense account is transferred to the *profit or loss account* thus:

Debit:	*Profit or loss account*	£'XXX	
Credit:	*Depreciation expense account*		£'XXX

The effect is to accumulate the provision while making a charge in the statement of profit or loss each year.

WORKED EXAMPLE 15.1

D. McDonald has an accounting year ending on 31 December. On 1 January 20X4 he purchased a machine for £1,000, which has an expected useful life of three years and an estimated residual value of £343.

Required

a Calculate the amount of depreciation in each year of the asset's useful life using: (i) the straight-line method; (ii) the reducing balance method; and (iii) the sum of the years' digits method.

b Show the journal and ledger entries relating to the purchase and the provision for depreciation in each year (using the amounts calculated from the straight-line method).

c Show the relevant entries on the statement of financial position for 20X5 (using the amounts calculated from the straight-line method).

Solution

a *The calculation of depreciation*

i The straight-line method:

$$\text{Annual depreciation} = \frac{£1{,}000 - £343}{3} = £219 \text{ per annum}$$

ii The reducing balance method:

$$\text{Depreciation rate} = 100 - \left(\sqrt[3]{\frac{343}{1000}} \times 100 \right) = 100 - (0.7 \times 100) = 30 \text{ per cent}$$

The annual amount of depreciation is calculated by applying this rate to the cost of the asset minus the aggregate depreciation of previous years (i.e. the WDV at the start of each year) as follows:

For 20X4: 30% of £1,000 = £300
For 20X5: 30% of (£1,000 – £300) = £210
For 20X6: 30% of [£1,000 – (£300 + £210)] = £147

iii The sum of the years' digits method:

Depreciable amount = £1,000 – £343 = £657
Sum of the years' digits = 3 + 2 + 1 = 6

Annual depreciation:

For 20X4 : $\frac{3}{6} \times £657 = £329$
For 20X5 : $\frac{2}{6} \times £657 = £219$
For 20X6 : $\frac{1}{6} \times £657 = £109$

b *The ledger entries (straight line only)*

The journal

20X4				
31 Dec	*Depreciation expense*	Dr	219	
	Provision for depreciation	Cr		219
	Being the charge for depreciation on plant for 20X4			
31 Dec	*Statement of profit or loss*	Dr	219	
	Depreciation expense	Cr		219
	Being the entry to close the depreciation expense account at the year end			

The entries for 20X5 and 20X6 would be exactly the same.

Plant and machinery

20X4	Details	£			
1 Jan	Bank	1,000			

Depreciation expense account

20X4	Details	£	20X4	Details	£
31 Dec	Provision for depreciation A/C	219	31 Dec	P/L A/C (depreciation charge)	219
20X5			**20X5**		
31 Dec	Provision for depreciation A/C	219	31 Dec	P/L A/C (depreciation charge)	219
20X6			**20X6**		
31 Dec	Provision for depreciation A/C	219	31 Dec	P/L A/C (depreciation charge)	219

Provision for depreciation on plant and machinery

20X4	Details	£	20X4	Details	£
31 Dec	Balance c/d	219	31 Dec	Depreciation expense a/c	219
20X5			**20X5**		
			1 Jan	Balance b/d	219
31 Dec	Balance c/d	438	31 Dec	Depreciation expense a/c	219
		438			438
20X6			**20X6**		
			1 Jan	Balance b/d	438
31 Dec	Balance c/d	657	31 Dec	Depreciation expense a/c	219
		657			657
			20X7		
			1 Jan	Balance b/d	657

c *The statement of financial position at 31 December 20X5* would appear as follows:

Non-current assets	£
Plant and machinery at cost	1,000
Less: provision for depreciation	438
Written down value (WDV)	562

Alternatively, where there are several types of non-current asset, it is easier to present the non-current assets in columnar form as follows:

Non-current assets			
	Cost	**Provision for depreciation**	**WDV**
	£	**£**	**£**
Plant and machinery	1,000	438	562

Notes

1 The entries in the statement of financial position comprise the balance on the *non-current asset ledger account* at the end of the year and the balance on the *provision for depreciation ledger account* at the end of the year. The latter is referred to as the **provision for, aggregate** or **accumulated depreciation** and is deducted from the historical cost to give the WDV. In sole trader and partnership financial statements both the cost and provision accounts are disclosed on the face of the statement of financial position, with the WDV also being provided.

2 Because the entries in the *depreciation expense account* only ever consist of a single debit and credit of the same amount, most people do not use this ledger account. Instead, the annual charge is credited to the *provision for depreciation ledger account* and debited directly to the *profit or loss ledger account*. This practice will be adopted in future examples and answers to exercises.

15.7 Profits and losses on the disposal of non-current assets

Almost without exception, when an asset is sold at the end of (or during) its useful life the proceeds of sale differ from the estimated residual value (or WDV if sold during its useful life). Where the proceeds are less than the WDV, this is referred to as a **loss on sale**. Where the proceeds are greater than the WDV, this is referred to as a **profit on sale**. This can be illustrated using Worked Example 15.1. Suppose the asset was sold on 31 December 20X6 for £400. The WDV is the difference between the cost of the asset and the aggregate depreciation up to the date of disposal; that is, £1,000 – £657 = £343. The profit (or loss) on sale is the difference between the proceeds of sale and the WDV of the asset. There is thus a profit on sale of £400 – £343 = £57.

When a non-current asset is sold the cost of the asset is transferred from the *non-current asset account* to an *asset disposals account*. This is sometimes referred to as an '*asset realization account*'. The aggregate depreciation on the asset that has been sold, the proceeds of sale, and the cost of the asset are all entered in the disposals account. The balance on this account is either a profit or a loss on sale. This will be transferred to the *profit or loss account*.

Profit and losses on the disposal of non-current assets

The steps taken when posting the entries to record the disposal of an asset are outlined in Figure 15.3.

Figure 15.3

Asset disposal

- Credit the proceeds of sale to the *asset disposals account.*
- Transfer the aggregate depreciation for the asset sold up to the date of disposal from the *provision for depreciation account* to the *asset disposals account.*
- Transfer the cost of the asset from the *cost account* to the *disposals account.*
- Calculate the loss or profit on sale. A loss on sale should then be credited to the *asset disposals account* and debited to the *profit and loss account.* A profit on sale would be debited to the *asset disposals account* and credited to the *profit or loss account.*

Posting entries on the disposal of an asset

This is illustrated with the continuation of Worked Example 15.1 and the additional data above in Worked Example 15.1.

WORKED EXAMPLE 15.1 CONTINUED

The journal

20X6				
31 Dec	*Provision for depreciation*	Dr	657	
	Asset disposals account	Cr		657
	Being the aggregate depreciation at the date of sale of the asset removed from the ledger account.			
31 Dec	*Asset disposals account*	Dr	1,000	
	Plant and machinery	Cr		1,000
	Being the cost of the asset at the date of sale removed from the ledger account			
31 Dec	*Asset disposals account*	Dr	57	
	Profit or loss account	Cr		57
	Being the profit on sale of plant and machinery to P/L A/C			

The ledger entries

Plant and machinery					
20X6	**Details**	**£**	**20X6**	**Details**	**£**
1 Jan	Balance b/d	1,000	31 Dec	Asset disposals a/c	1,000
		1,000			1,000

Provision for depreciation					
20X6	**Details**	**£**	**20X6**	**Details**	**£**
31 Dec	Asset disposals	657	31 Dec	Balance b/d	657

Asset disposals account (Plant and machinery)					
20X6	**Details**	**£**	**20X6**	**Details**	**£**
31 Dec	Plant and machinery	1,000	31 Dec	Bank – proceeds of sale	400
			31 Dec	Provision for depreciation	657
31 Dec	Profit or loss a/c (profit on sale)	57			
		1,057			1,057

Profit or loss account			
	£		£
Loss on sale of non-current assets	–	Profit on sale of plant and machinery	57

15.8 The depreciation charge on an asset in the years of acquisition and disposal: partial year depreciation

The previous example dealt with the highly unlikely situation of an asset being purchased and sold on the first day and last day of an accounting year, respectively. In practice, these transactions could occur on any day of the year. The way in which depreciation would then be computed depends on the usual practice of the business, or in examinations on what you are explicitly or implicitly instructed to do. Unless the question states otherwise, the depreciation must be calculated on a strict time basis for the period the asset is owned. In examination questions, assets tend to be purchased and sold on the first or last day of a calendar month for simplicity of calculation. It can be argued that in practice one should also calculate depreciation on a strict time basis. The charge for depreciation in the *year of purchase* would be as follows:

$$\text{Rate of depreciation} \times \text{Cost of asset} \times \frac{\text{Number of months (or days) between the date of purchase and the end of the accounting year in which the asset is purchased}}{12 \text{ (or } 365)}$$

The charge for depreciation in the *year of sale* would be as follows:

$$\text{Rate of depreciation} \times \text{Cost of asset (or WDV)} \times \frac{\text{Number of months (or days) between the start of the accounting year in which the asset is sold and the date of sale}}{12 \text{ (or 365)}}$$

In practice, to avoid these tedious calculations, some firms have a policy of charging a full year's depreciation in the year of purchase and none in the year of sale. There is little theoretical justification for this. Also, in examination questions, where the date of purchase or sale is not given, this is usually an indication to adopt this policy.

The accounting entries in respect of depreciation on acquisitions and disposals are illustrated in Worked Example 15.2.

WORKED EXAMPLE 15.2

P. Smith has an accounting year ending on 31 December. On 31 December 20X4 her ledger contained the following accounts:

	£
Motor vehicles	50,000
Provision for depreciation on vehicles	23,000

Vehicles are depreciated using the straight-line method at a rate of 20 per cent per annum on a strict time basis.

The following transactions occurred during 20X5:

1 Apr Purchased a van for £5,000.

31 Aug Sold a vehicle for £4,700. This cost £7,500 when it was bought on 31 July 20X3.

30 Sep Used one car as part exchange for another. The part exchange allowance on the old car was £4,100 and the balance of £3,900 was paid by cheque. The old car cost £10,000 when it was bought on 1 January 20X3.

You are required to show the entries in the motor vehicles and provision for depreciation accounts in respect of the above for 20X5.

Date of acquisitions and disposals	Details	Total depreciation on disposals	Depreciation charge for year ending 31 Dec 20X5
		£	£
	Depreciation on disposals		
31 July 20X3	For year ending 31/12/X3: 20% × £7,500 × $\frac{5}{12}$	625	
	For year ending 31/12/X4: 20% × £7,500	1,500	
31 Aug 20X5	For year ending 31/12/X5: 20% × £7,500 × $\frac{8}{12}$	1,000	1,000
		3,125	

	Book value at 31/8/X5: £7,500 – £3,125 = £4,375		
	Profit on sale £4,700 – £4,375 = £325		
1 Jan 20X3	For year ending 31/12/X3: 20% × £10,000	2,000	
	For year ending 31/12/X4	2,000	
30 Sept 20X5	For year ending 31/12/X5: 20% × £10,000 × $\frac{9}{12}$	1,500	1,500
		5,500	
	Book value at 30/9/X5: £10,000 – £5,500 = £4,500		
	Loss on sale £4,500 – £4,100 = £400		
	Depreciation on acquisitions		
1 Apr 20X5	20% × £5,000 × $\frac{9}{12}$		750
30 Sept 20X5	20% × (£3,900 + £4,100) × $\frac{3}{12}$		400
	Depreciation on remainder 20% × (£50,000 – £7,500 – £10,000)		6,500
			10,150

Note

1 The 'depreciation on the remainder' of the vehicles is calculated on the vehicles owned at the start of the year that were not disposed off during the current year. Those items that were bought and sold during the year have already been depreciated in the previous calculations.

The ledger

Motor vehicles

20X5	Details	£	20X5	Details	£
1 Jan	Balance b/d	50,000	31 Aug	Disposals account	7,500
1 Apr	Bank	5,000	31 Sep	Disposals account	10,000
30 Sep	Bank	3,900	31 Dec	Balance c/d	45,500
30 Sep	Disposals account – part exchange	4,100			
		63,000			63,000
20X6					
1 Jan	Balance b/d	45,500			

Motor vehicles disposals

20X5	Details	£	20X5	Details	£
31 Aug	Motor vehicles	7,500	31 Aug	Bank	4,700
31 Aug	Profit or loss a/c		31 Aug	Provision for depreciation	3,125
	– profit on sale	325	30 Sep	Motor vehicles	
30 Sep	Motor vehicles	10,000		– part exchange	4,100
			30 Sep	Provision for depreciation	5,500
			30 Sep	Profit or loss a/c	
				– loss on sale	400
		17,825			17,825

Provision for depreciation

20X5	Details	£	20X5	Details	£
31 Aug	Vehicles	3,125	1 Jan	Balance b/d	23,000
30 Sep	Vehicles	5,500	31 Dec	Profit or loss a/c	10,150
31 Dec	Balance c/d	24,525			
		33,150			33,150
			20X6		
			1 Jan	Balance b/d	24,525

There should never be a balance on the *disposals account* at the end of the year after the statement of profit or loss has been prepared.

Notes

1 When one asset is used as part exchange for another, the part exchange allowance is debited to the *asset cost account* and credited to the *asset disposals account* and referred to as a 'contra'. The credit entry represents the proceeds of sale of the old asset, and the debit entry represents a part payment for the new asset. The balance that has to be paid for the new asset in cash is debited to the *asset account* in the normal way. This, together with the debit contra, represents the total cost of the new asset.

2 The transfer from the *provision for depreciation account* to the *non-current asset account* relating to the aggregate depreciation on disposals must include the depreciation on disposals in respect of the current year. This therefore cannot be done until the total depreciation for the current year has been ascertained. Thus, all the entries in the *provision for depreciation account* are usually made at the end of the year after the trial balance has been prepared. It is important to note that this also means that any balance on a *provision for depreciation account* shown in a trial balance must relate to the balance at the end of the previous year.

15.9 Creative accounting and depreciation

As an accounting adjustment that is subjective, depreciation can be used to manipulate profit. For example, selecting a short useful economic life and a lower expected residual value will result in a larger depreciation charge and lower reported profits. This may be attractive to a business that is doing well now but is uncertain about how its performance will be in the future as it involves allocating higher amounts of the cost in the earlier years when profits are strong. Alternatively, selecting a long useful economic life and a high residual value will result in a lower deprecation charge and will be attractive when a business is not performing very well. This variation is highlighted in Real World Example 15.3.

REAL WORLD EXAMPLE 15.3

Tesco

In 2010 a Citigroup analyst accused Tesco of using aggressive accounting methods for revenue recognition, depreciation, the allocation of profits from property, capitalized interest expense and pension accounting. The methods used are reported to be very different from those used by its competitors. The analyst suggests that the outcome of this is that Tesco's profit cannot be compared with other companies in the industry. Indeed, the analyst reported that Tesco's increase in profit in the year of £3.4 billion would have been £800,000 less had similar methods to those used by its competitors been used. For example, if Tesco had used the same period to depreciate their buildings and fittings, their depreciation charge would have been 15 per cent higher to that reported.

Source: Adapted from Finch (2010) www.guardian.co.uk/business/2010/jun/30/tesco-accounting-comment, accessed September 2013.

Smith (1992) commented that 'one popular choice of creative bookkeeping is altering the calculation of depreciation'. In a research study on creative accounting, Phillips and Drew (1992) reported that depreciation was used by 9 per cent (17 out of the 185 companies investigated) of major UK companies to manipulate profit figures. Details of a famous US fraud case that involved accounting manipulations including depreciation are provided in Real World Example 15.4.

REAL WORLD EXAMPLE 15.4

Waste Management – Distorted Accounting Methods for Depreciation and Amortization Expenses

Even before Enron and WorldCom, there was Waste Management (WM) Inc. whose financial statements were considered by the SEC as part of the garbage that the company was managing . . .

. . . Waste Management's accounting manipulations are summarized as follows:

- Depreciation expenses on garbage trucks were distorted by assigning large amounts of residual or salvage values, while useful lives were extended beyond what was prescribed by industry standards.
- Other fixed assets, which previously had no salvage values, were recomputed by assigning arbitrary salvage values.

- The value of the landfill sites were assigned with book values that did not conform to their reduced or degraded values as land filled with wastes.
- Various expenses were capitalized in order to allocate the impact of WM's wrong accounting practices for a period of 10 years. These were orchestrated and directed by the CEO and chairman of WM's Board of Directors, Dean Buntrock, President; Phillip Rooney, COO; and James Koenig, EVP and Chief Financial Officer.
- Based on the inflated revenues, top officials of Waste Management earned for themselves hefty amounts of compensation packages comprising substantial profit share bonuses, basic salaries, enhanced retirement benefits, and stock options, which were all practically derived from money infused by investors.
- While formal investigations were going on in 2002, top officials of WM started cashing in on their stock options, which started the downward trend of WM's stock price to more than 33%. In addition, the CFO ordered the destruction of important documents to obstruct investigations.
- The company's shareholders reportedly lost over $6 billion after the final accounting of the Waste Management fraud was completed.

Source: Adapted from Richter, L. (2010) 'Unraveling the Details of 10 High-Profile Accounting Scandals', http://www.brighthub.com/office/finance/articles/101200.aspx, accessed September 2013.

Summary

A non-current asset is an asset that: is held by an enterprise for use in the production or supply of goods and services; has been acquired with the intention of being used on a continuing basis; and is not intended for sale in the ordinary course of business. It is also usually expected to generate revenue over more than one accounting year. Non-current assets are classified as either tangible (land and buildings), intangible (such as goodwill) or financial assets (investments). Money spent on non-current assets is referred to as 'capital expenditure'. All other costs are referred to as 'revenue expenditure'. Non-current assets in sole trader and partnership financial statements are normally valued in the statement of financial position at historical cost, which refers to their purchase price.

All non-current assets except for land and investment properties must be depreciated in the final financial statements. Depreciation is *'the systematic allocation of the depreciable amount of an asset over its useful life'* where the depreciable amount is *'the cost of the asset, or other amount attributed to that asset less its residual value'*.

There is a range of acceptable depreciation methods. Management should select the method regarded as most appropriate to the type of asset and its use in the business so as to allocate depreciation as fairly as possible to the periods expected to benefit from the asset's use. The depreciation method adopted should reflect the consumption, wearing-out, using-up or other reduction in the useful economic life of a non-current asset whether arising from use, effluxion of time or obsolescence. The two most common methods are the straight-line/fixed instalment method and diminishing/reducing balance method. The former gives the same charge for depreciation in each year of the asset's useful life. The latter results in a decreasing annual charge over the useful life of the asset.

Where an asset is acquired or disposed of during the accounting year, it is normal to compute the depreciation for that year according to the period over which the asset was owned. When an asset is disposed of during the accounting year, this usually also gives rise to profit or loss on sale. This is the difference between the proceeds of sale and the written-down or book value of the asset. The WDV is the difference between the historical cost and the accumulated/aggregate depreciation from the date of acquisition to the date of disposal.

The ledger entries for depreciation are to credit a *provision for depreciation ledger account* and debit a *depreciation expense ledger account* with the annual amount of depreciation. The balance on the *depreciation expense ledger account* is transferred to the *profit or loss ledger account* representing the charge for the year. The balance on the *provision for depreciation account* is shown on the statement of financial position as a deduction from the cost of the non-current asset to give the WDV, which enters into the total of the statement of financial position. When an asset is sold, all the original entries relating to that asset are reversed to an *asset disposals account*. The cost and any adjustments to cost and the aggregate depreciation on non-current assets disposed of during the year must be transferred from *the cost ledger account* and from the *provision for depreciation ledger account* to a *disposals account*. The receipt (or trade-in value) for the asset is credited to the *disposals account* also. The balance on this account will represent either a profit or a loss on disposal. This is transferred to the *profit or loss ledger account*.

Key terms and concepts

aggregate/accumulated depreciation 251
book value 252
capital expenditure 250
carrying amount 252
consumption 253
current assets 250
current value 252
depreciable amount 253
depreciation 253
depreciation expense 255
diminishing balance method 255
fair value 251
financial assets 251
intangible assets 251
loss on sale 260
net book value 251
net carrying amount 251
non-current asset 250
non-financial assets 251
non-monetary assets 251
obsolescence through demand changes 253
obsolescence through technological change 253
profit on sale 260
provision for, aggregate or accumulated depreciation 260
recoverable amount 252
reducing balance method 255
residual value 254
revenue expenditure 250
straight-line/fixed instalment method 255
sum of the years' digits method (sum of digits) 255
tangible assets 250
tangible non-current assets 250
useful (economic) life 253
written-down value 251

An asterisk after the question number indicates that there is a suggested answer in Appendix 2.

Review questions

connect

15.1 Explain the nature of non-current assets.

15.2 a Explain the difference between capital expenditure and revenue expenditure.

b What criteria would you use to decide whether expenditure should be classified as relating to a non-current asset?

15.3 Briefly explain the circumstances in which each of the following would be regarded as a non-current asset: (a) tools; (b) investments; and (c) advertising expenditure.

15.4 a Explain the difference between tangible and intangible non-current assets.

b What is goodwill and how does it usually arise in a statement of financial position?

15.5 a Describe how non-current assets are valued under historical cost accounting.

b How would you account for expenditure on double-glazing? Explain your reasons.

15.6 Explain fully the nature of depreciation.

15.7* 'Depreciation is the loss in value of a non-current asset.' Discuss.

15.8 Describe the data needed in order to compute depreciation.

15.9 Describe two common methods of depreciation including the resulting pattern of charges to the statement of profit or loss for depreciation expense over an asset's useful economic life. In what circumstances might each of these be the most appropriate method and why?

15.10 'Although the straight-line method of depreciation is the simplest to apply, it may not always be the most appropriate.' Explain and discuss.

15.11 In the year to 31 December 20X5, Amy bought a new non-current asset and made the following payments in relation to it:

	£	£
Cost as per supplier's list	12,000	
Less: agreed discount	1,000	11,000
Delivery charge		100
Erection charge		200
Maintenance charge		300
Additional component to increase capacity		400
Replacement parts		250

Required

a State and justify the cost figure that should be used as the basis for depreciation.

b What does depreciation do, and why is it necessary?

c Briefly explain, without numerical illustration, how the straight-line and reducing balance methods of depreciation work. What different assumptions does each method make?

d It is common practice in published financial statements in Germany to use the reducing balance method for a non-current asset in the early years of its life, and then to change to the straight-line method as soon as this would give a higher annual charge. What do you think of this practice? Refer to relevant accounting conventions in your answer.

(ACCA)

Exercises

connect

BASIC

15.12 You bought a lorry for £5,000.

Its useful life is estimated at four years.

The residual value is expected to be £1,000 after the four years.

Required

Calculate the depreciation charge for each of the four years using the straight line, reducing balance and the sum of digits methods.

BASIC

15.13 On 31 December 20X4, plant and machinery acquired at a cost of £200,000 in 20X1 was sold for £30,000. The accumulated depreciation to date was £130,000.

Required

Calculate the profit or loss on disposal (show all ledger account entries).

BASIC

15.14 Plant was purchased in the year for £10,000. It has been decided to provide for depreciation on a reducing balance basis (25 per cent). A full year's depreciation is charged in the year of purchase.

Required

a Show the entries in the ledgers for the first two years.

b Provide extracts to show the disclosures in the statement of profit or loss and in the statement of financial position for both years.

BASIC

15.15 An item of plant and machinery was sold within the year for £5,000.

The asset cost the company £10,000 over two years ago.

The balances on the cost account and accumulated depreciation account were £118,000 and £18,000.

It is company policy to provide for depreciation in the year of purchase but not in the year of sale. (Two years' depreciation charged at 20 per cent straight line per year had been expensed in relation to this asset.)

Required

Calculate the profit or loss on disposal (show all ledger account entries).

BASIC

15.16 Pusher commenced business on 1 January 20X2 with two lorries – A and B. A cost £1,000 and B cost £1,600. On 3 March 20X3, A was written off in an accident and Pusher received £750 from the insurance company. This vehicle was replaced on 10 March 20X3 by C which cost £2,000.

A full year's depreciation is charged in the year of acquisition and no depreciation is charged in the year of disposal.

a You are required to show the appropriate extracts from Pusher's statement of financial position and statement of profit or loss for the three years to 31/12/X2, 31/12/X3 and 31/12/X4 assuming that:

i the vehicles are depreciated at 20 per cent on the straight-line method.

ii the vehicles are depreciated at 25 per cent on the reducing balance method.

b Comment briefly on the pros and cons of using the straight line and reducing balance methods of depreciation.

(ACCA)

15.17* A. Black & Co. Ltd owned two machines that had been purchased on 1 October 20X4 at a combined cost of £3,100 ex works. They were identical as regards size and capacity and had been erected and brought into use on 1 April 20X5. The cost of transporting the two machines to the factory of A. Black & Co. Ltd was £130 and further expenditure for the installation of the two machines had been incurred totalling £590 for the foundations, and £180 for erection. INTERMEDIATE

Provision for depreciation using the straight-line method has been calculated from the date on which the machines started work, assuming a life of 10 years for the machines. The first charge against profits was made at the end of the financial year, 30 September 20X5.

One of the machines was sold on 31 March 20Y3 for £800 ex factory to H. Johnson. The work of dismantling the machine was undertaken by the staff of A. Black & Co. Ltd at a labour cost of £100. This machine was replaced on 1 May 20Y3, by one exactly similar in every way, which was purchased from R. Adams at a cost of £2,800, which covered delivery, erection on the site of the old machine, and the provision of adequate foundations. This new machine was brought into general operation on 1 July 20Y3.

Required

a Show the journal entries that should be made on 31 March and 1 May 20Y3.

b Show how you would arrive at the amount of the provision for depreciation as regards the three machines for the year ended 30 September 20Y3.

Note: It is the practice of the company to charge depreciation on a pro rata time basis each year, and to operate a machinery disposal account where necessary.

15.18 Makers and Co. is a partnership with a small factory on the outskirts of London. They decide to erect an extension to their factory. INTERMEDIATE

The following items appear in the trial balance of the firm, as at 31 December 20X4:

	Debit	Credit
	£	£
Purchases	12,800	
Wages	16,400	
Hire of machinery	520	
Plant and machinery at cost to 31 December 20X3	5,900	
Plant and machinery purchased during the year	2,540	
Plant and machinery sold during the year (cost in 20W6 £900; depreciation to 31 December 20X3 £540)		160
Freehold premises at cost to 31 December 20X3 (Land £3,000; Buildings £4,000)	7,000	
Freehold land purchased during the year for a factory extension	2,800	
Provision for depreciation of plant and machinery at 31 December 20X3		2,400
Legal charges	280	

In the course of your examination of the books you ascertain that:

1 building materials used in building the extension and costing £1,800 had been charged to the purchases account;

2 wages paid to men engaged in building the extension amounted to £1,500 and had been charged to the wages account;

3 the hire charge was in respect of machinery used exclusively in the construction of the extension;

4 the legal charges, apart from £50 relating to debt collecting, were incurred in the purchase of the land.

It is decided that depreciation on plant and machinery is to be provided at $12\frac{1}{2}$ per cent on the closing book value.

Required

a Write up the following ledger accounts:

Factory extensions, freehold premises, plant and machinery, and provision for depreciation of plant and machinery.

b Show the particulars that should appear on the firm's statement of financial position at 31 December 20X4.

(ACCA)

INTERMEDIATE

15.19* Wexford Ltd, who prepare their financial statements on 31 December each year, provide for depreciation of their vehicles by a reducing balance method, calculated as 25 per cent on the balance at the end of the year. Depreciation of plant is calculated on a straight line basis at 10 per cent per annum on cost; a full year's depreciation is charged in the year in which plant is acquired and none in the year of sale.

The statement of financial position for 31 December 20X3 showed:

	Vehicles	Plant
	£	£
Original cost	25,060	96,920
Accumulated depreciation	(14,560)	(50,120)
Net book value	10,500	46,800

During the year ended 31 December 20X4, the following transactions took place:

Purchase of vehicles	£4,750
Purchases of plant	£33,080

	Year of purchase	Original cost	Proceeds of sale
		£	£
Sale of vehicle 1	20X0	3,200	1,300
Sale of vehicle 2	20X2	4,800	2,960
Sale of plant	20W8	40,000	15,000

Required

a Present the ledger accounts relating to the purchases and sales of vehicles and plant for the year ended 31 December 20X4.

b Show the journal entries for depreciation for the year.

INTERMEDIATE

15.20 The statement of financial position of Beta Ltd as at 30 June 20X4 shows motor vehicles as follows:

	£
Motor vehicles at cost	61,850
Accumulated depreciation	(32,426)
Net book value	29,424

Vehicles are depreciated on the straight line basis over a five-year life. Depreciation is charged pro rata to time in the year of acquisition but no charge is made in the year of disposal. The disposal account is written up on the last day of each year.

During 20X4–X5 the following vehicle transactions took place:

30 Sep	Purchased delivery van: £8,600
31 Oct	Purchased sales manager's car: £10,700
28 Feb	Purchased lorry: £4,000

The lorry was second-hand and originally cost £9,600.

Sales of vehicles:

31 Oct	Car	£300 originally cost £2,800
31 Dec	Tractor	£540 originally cost £2,400
31 Mar	Van	£420 originally cost £1,900

The car was originally purchased on 1 July 20X0, the tractor on 30 November 20X1 and the van on 1 April 20X2.

You are required to write up the accounts for vehicles, vehicle depreciation and vehicle disposals.

(ACCA)

References

IASplus (2013) Conceptual Framework – Definition of Elements (IASB), http://www.iasplus.com/en/meeting-notes/iasb/2013/iasb-february-2013/cf-elements, accessed September 2013.

International Accounting Standards Board (2011), *Conceptual Framework for Financial Reporting* (IASB).

International Accounting Standards Board (2013a) *International Accounting Standard 16 – Property, Plant and Equipment* (IASB).

International Accounting Standards Board (2013b) *International Accounting Standard 40 – Investment Property* (IASB).

International Accounting Standards Board (2013c) *International Accounting Standard 36 – Impairment of Assets* (IASB).

International Accounting Standards Board (2013d) *International Accounting Standard 17 – Leases* (IASB).

International Accounting Standards Board (2013e) *International Financial Reporting Standard 5 – Non-current Assets Held for Sale and Discontinued Operations* (IASB).

International Accounting Standards Board (2013f) *International Accounting Standard 38 – Intangible Assets* (IASB).

International Accounting Standards Board (2013 g) *International Financial Reporting Standard 3 – Business Combinations* (IASB).

Phillips and Drew (1992) *Ranking of Creative Accounting Practices used by 185 Major UK Companies*, cited by Mike Jones in his slide show on 'Creative Accounting, Fraud and Accounting Scandals', http://www.docstoc.com/docs/3414029/Creative-Accounting-Fraud-and-Accounting-Scandals

Smith, T. (1992) *Accounting for Growth: Stripping the Camouflage from Company Accounts*, Century Business Publications, London.

Chapter 16

Irrecoverable receivables and allowance for irrecoverable receivables

Learning Objectives:

After reading this chapter you should be able to do the following:

1. Explain the nature of irrecoverable receivables and allowances for irrecoverable receivables.
2. Distinguish between specific and general allowances for irrecoverable receivables.
3. Explain when a general allowance should be prepared.
4. Explain how a general allowance estimate is determined.
5. Show the entries for irrecoverable receivables and allowances for irrecoverable receivables in the journal, general ledger, statement of profit or loss and statement of financial position.

16.1 The nature of, and ledger entries for, irrecoverable receivables

When goods are sold on credit, it sometimes transpires that the customer is unwilling or unable to pay the amount owed. This is referred to as a **bad debt** or **irrecoverable receivable**. The decision to treat a debt as irrecoverable is a matter of judgement. A debt may be regarded as irrecoverable for a number of reasons, such as being unable to trace the credit customer, it not being worthwhile financially to take the credit customer to court, or the credit customer being bankrupt. However, if a credit customer is bankrupt, this does not necessarily mean that the whole of the debt is irrecoverable. When a person is bankrupt, his or her possessions are seized and sold in order to pay the creditors. Such payments are often made in instalments known as 'dividends'. Frequently, the dividends do not consist of the repayment of the whole of the debt. Thus, when the 'final dividend' is received, the remainder of the debt is irrecoverable. When a debt is regarded as irrecoverable the entries in the ledger are as follows:

Debit:	*Irrecoverable receivables ledger account*	£'XXX	
Credit:	*Trade receivables account* (the individual credit customer's account would be amended in the sales ledger)		£'XXX

Occasionally, debts previously written off as bad are subsequently paid. When this happens, the ledger entries are the reverse of the above, and the *trade receivables ledger account* is credited with the money received in the normal way.

Debit:	*Trade receivables account* (the individual credit customer's account would be amended in the sales ledger)	£'XXX	
Credit:	*Irrecoverable receivables ledger account*		£'XXX

At the end of the accounting year the balance on the *irrecoverable receivables account* is transferred to the *statement of profit or loss account.*

16.2 The nature of, and ledger entries for, allowances for irrecoverable receivables

The need for an **allowance for irrecoverable/doubtful receivables** essentially arises because goods sold and recognized as sales revenue in one accounting year may not become known to be irrecoverable until the following accounting year. Thus, the profit of the year in which the goods are sold would be overstated by the amount of the irrecoverable receivable. In order to adjust for this, an allowance in respect of probable irrecoverable receivable is created in the year of sale (matching concept).

An allowance for irrecoverable receivables may consist of either a **specific allowance** or a **general allowance**, or both. A specific allowance involves ascertaining which particular credit customers at the year-end are unlikely to pay their debts. A general allowance is an estimate of the total amount of irrecoverable receivables computed using a percentage (based on previous years' figures) of the trade receivables at the end of the current year. Where both specific and general allowances are made, the two amounts are added together and the total is entered in the general ledger.

The accounting entries in respect of an allowance for irrecoverable receivables are made after the trial balance has been extracted when the statement of profit or loss is being prepared. It is important to appreciate that any balance on an *allowance for irrecoverable receivables account* shown in a trial balance must therefore relate to the balance at the end of the previous year. A charge (or credit) is made to the *statement of profit or loss* in each year that consists of an amount necessary to increase (or decrease) the allowance at the end of the previous year to the amount required at the end of the current year.

An increase in an allowance always consists of:

Debit:	*Profit or loss account* (increase in allowance for irrecoverable receivables)	£'XXX	
Credit:	*Allowance for irrecoverable receivables account*		£'XXX

A decrease in an allowance is entered thus:

Debit:	*Allowance for irrecoverable receivables account*	£'XXX	
Credit:	*Profit or loss account* (decrease in allowance for irrecoverable receivables)		£'XXX

The balance on the *allowance for irrecoverable receivables account* at the end of the year is deducted from trade receivables in the statement of financial position to give the net amount that is expected to be received from credit customers – that is, their net realizable value. The treatment of irrecoverable receivables and allowances for irrecoverable receivables is illustrated in Worked Examples 16.1 and 16.2.

WORKED EXAMPLE 16.1

A. Jones has an accounting year ending on 30 November. At 30 November 20X4 his ledger contained the following accounts:

	£
Trade receivables	20,000
Allowance for irrecoverable receivables	1,000

The trade receivables at 30 November 20X5 were £18,900. This includes an amount of £300 owed by F. Simons that was thought to be irrecoverable. It also includes amounts of £240 owed by C. Steven, £150 owed by M. Evans and £210 owed by A. Mitchell, all of which are regarded as doubtful receivables.

You have been instructed to make an allowance for irrecoverable receivables at 30 November 20X5. This should include a specific allowance for debts regarded as irrecoverable and a general allowance of 5 per cent of trade receivables.

Show the ledger entries in respect of the above and the relevant statement of financial position extract.

Allowance for irrecoverable receivables at 30 November 20X5	£
Specific allowance – C. Steven	240
M. Evans	150
A. Mitchell	210
	600
General allowance – 5% × (£18,900 – £300 – £600)	900
	1,500

The ledger

(*Note*: Assume the individual customer accounts are maintained in the general ledger; A. Jones does not keep a sales ledger.) The individual balances add to £20,000.

F. Simons (trade receivable)

20X5	Details	£	20X5	Details	£
30 Nov	Balance b/d	300	30 Nov	Irrecoverable receivables	300

Irrecoverable receivables

20X5	Details	£	20X5	Details	£
30 Nov	F. Simons	300	30 Nov	Profit or loss a/c	300

Allowance for irrecoverable receivables

20X5	Details	£	20X4	Details	£
30 Nov	Balance c/d	1,500	1 Dec	Balance b/d	1,000
			20X5		
			30 Nov	Profit or loss a/c	500
		1,500			1,500
			20X5		
			1 Dec	Balance b/d	1,500

Profit or loss account

20X5	Details	£			
30 Nov	Irrecoverable receivables	300			
30 Nov	Allowance for irrecoverable receivables	500			

Statement of financial position (extract)

Current assets	£
Trade receivables (£18,900 – £300)	18,600
Less: Allowance for irrecoverable receivables	1,500
	17,100

Notes

1 No entries are made in the accounts of those credit customers that comprise the specific allowance, since these are only doubtful receivables and thus not yet regarded as irrecoverable.

2 The balance carried down on the allowance for irrecoverable receivables account at the end of the year is always the amount of the new allowance. The amount charged to the *profit or loss account* is the difference between the allowance at the end of the current year and that at the end of the previous year. In this example the allowance is increased from £1,000 to £1,500 by means of a credit to the *allowance for irrecoverable receivables account* of £500 and a corresponding debit to the *profit or loss account.*

3 In computing the amount of the general allowance, any irrecoverable receivables and specific allowances must be deducted from trade receivables. Otherwise, the specific allowance would be duplicated and an allowance would be made for debts already written off as irrecoverable.

4 The irrecoverable receivables written off must also be removed from trade receivables in preparing the statement of financial position.

5 There is another method of accounting for irrecoverable receivables and allowances for irrecoverable receivables that essentially involves combining these two accounts. This is shown below.

(Allowance for) irrecoverable receivables

20X5	**Details**	**£**	**20X4**	**Details**	**£**
30 Nov	F Simons	300	1 Dec	Balance b/d	1,000
30 Nov	Balance c/d	1,500	**20X5**		
			30 Nov	Profit or loss a/c	800
		1,800			1,800
			20X5		
			1 Dec	Balance b/d	1,500

Profit or loss account

20X5	**Details**	**£**	
30 Nov	Irrecoverable receivables	800	

The combined charge to the *statement of profit or loss* for the year in respect of irrecoverable receivables and the allowance for irrecoverable receivables is the difference between the two sides of the *(allowance for) irrecoverable receivables account* after inserting the amount of the allowance at 30 November 20X5 as a balance carried down. The charge to the *statement of profit or loss* under both methods is always the same in total.

WORKED EXAMPLE 16.2

This is a continuation of Worked Example 16.1.

During the year ended 30 November 20X6 C. Steven was declared bankrupt and a first dividend of £140 was received from the trustee. M. Evans was also declared bankrupt and a first and final dividend of £30 was received from the trustee. A. Mitchell paid his debt in full. A further debt of £350 owed by R. Jackson that is included in trade receivables at 30 November 20X5 proved to be irrecoverable.

The trade receivables at 30 November 20X6 were £24,570. This figure is after recording all money received but does not take into account irrecoverable receivables.

You have been instructed to make an allowance for irrecoverable receivables at 30 November 20X6. This should include a specific allowance for irrecoverable receivables and a general allowance of 5 per cent of trade receivables.

Show the ledger entries in respect of the above and the relevant statement of financial position extract.

Allowance for irrecoverable receivables at 30 November 20X6	
	£
Specific allowance – C. Steven (£240 – £140)	100
General allowance – 5% × (£24,570 – £120 – £350 – £100)	1,200
	1,300

The ledger

(*Note*: Assume the *individual customer accounts* are maintained in the general ledger, i.e., A. Jones does not keep a sales ledger.) The individual balances add to £24,570.

C. Steven (trade receivable)

20X5	Details	£	20X6	Details	£
1 Dec	Balance b/d	240	30 Nov	Bank	140
			30 Nov	Balance c/d	100
		240			240
20X6					
1 Dec	Balance b/d	100			

M. Evans (trade receivable)

20X5	Details	£	20X6	Details	£
1 Dec	Balance b/d	150	30 Nov	Bank	30
			30 Nov	Irrecoverable receivables	120
		150			150

R. Jackson (trade receivable)

20X5	Details	£	20X6	Details	£
1 Dec	Balance b/d	350	30 Nov	Irrecoverable receivables	350

Irrecoverable receivables

20X6	Details	£	20X6	Details	£
30 Nov	M. Evans	120	30 Nov	Profit or loss a/c	470
30 Nov	R. Jackson	350			
		470			470

Allowance for irrecoverable receivables

20X6	Details	£	20X5	Details	£
30 Nov	Profit or loss a/c	200	1 Dec	Balance b/d	1,500
30 Nov	Balance c/d	1,300			
		1,500			1,500
			20X6		
			1 Dec	Balance b/d	1,300

Profit or loss account					
20X6	**Details**	**£**	**20X6**	**Details**	**£**
30 Nov	Irrecoverable receivables	470	30 Nov	Allowance for irrecoverable receivables	200

Statement of financial position	
Current assets	**£**
Trade receivables (£24,570 – £120 – £350)	24,100
Less: Allowance for irrecoverable receivables	1,300
	22,800

Alternative method

(Allowance for) irrecoverable receivables					
20X6	**Details**	**£**	**20X5**	**Details**	**£**
30 Nov	M. Evans	120	1 Dec	Balance b/d	1,500
30 Nov	R. Jackson	350	**20X6**		
30 Nov	Balance c/d	1,300	30 Nov	Profit or loss a/c	270
		1,770			1,770
			20X6		
			1 Dec	Balance b/d	1,300

Notes

1 The amount due from M. Evans is written off as an irrecoverable receivable because the final dividend in bankruptcy was declared, which means that no more money will be received in respect of this debt. However, the amount due from C. Steven is not written off as an irrecoverable receivable, despite the fact that he was declared bankrupt, because further dividends are expected. Thus, this debt is the subject of a specific allowance in respect of the amount still outstanding.

2 No entries are required where a debt that was previously treated as a specific allowance is subsequently paid, as in the case of A. Mitchell.

3 The main method shown above (that has separate *irrecoverable receivables* and *allowance for irrecoverable receivables accounts*) is the most common in practice. However, this tends to obscure the logic behind allowances for irrecoverable receivables, because it accounts for the allowance separately from the irrecoverable receivables. The 'alternative method' shown above allows the logic to be demonstrated as follows. The irrecoverable receivables for the year (£120 + £350 = £470) are set against the allowance at the end of the previous year (£1,500). Any under- or over-allowance (£1,500 – £470 = over-allowance of £1,030) is written back to the *profit or loss account*. The amount of the allowance required at the end of the current year (£1,300) is then created in full by debiting the *profit or loss account* with this amount. This can be illustrated as follows.

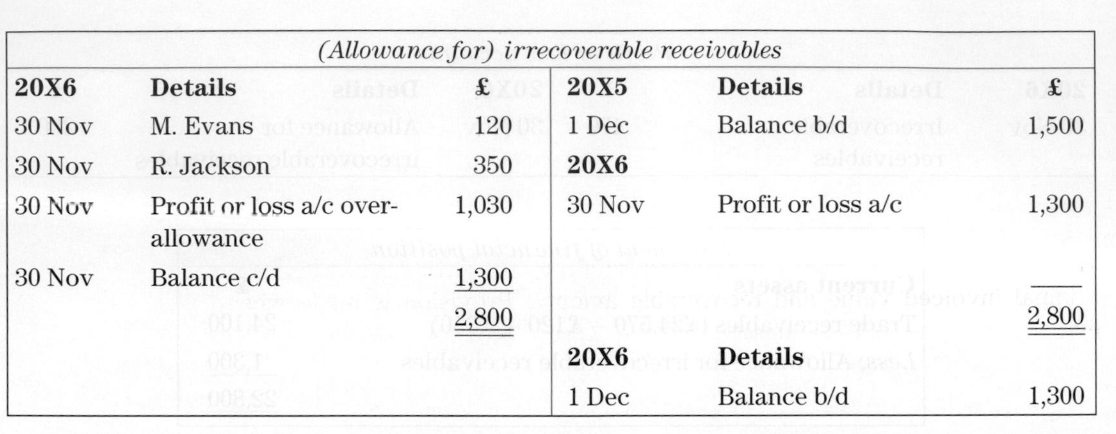

(Allowance for) irrecoverable receivables					
20X6	**Details**	**£**	**20X5**	**Details**	**£**
30 Nov	M. Evans	120	1 Dec	Balance b/d	1,500
30 Nov	R. Jackson	350	**20X6**		
30 Nov	Profit or loss a/c over-allowance	1,030	30 Nov	Profit or loss a/c	1,300
30 Nov	Balance c/d	1,300			
		2,800			2,800
			20X6	**Details**	
			1 Dec	Balance b/d	1,300

The debit entry of £1,030 is the reversal of the over-allowance. The credit entry of £1,300 is the creation of the new allowance. The net effect is the same as in the previous answer – a debit to the *profit or loss account* of £270 and a balance on the *(allowance for) irrecoverable receivables account* of £1,300. However, it should be observed that the over-allowance of £1,030 as calculated above is an oversimplification. This is not usually readily identifiable, since the irrecoverable receivables normally comprise not only those relating to sales in the previous year for which an allowance was created, but also irrecoverable receivables arising from sales in the current year. The charge to the *profit or loss account* shown in the 'alternative method' therefore usually comprises:

1 a reversal of the under- or over-allowance;

2 the irrecoverable receivables arising from sales in the current year;

3 the amount of the new allowance at the end of the current year.

Furthermore, it should be stressed that nobody would prepare an *(allowance) for irrecoverable receivables account* in the manner shown immediately above since it involves the unnecessary calculation of the under- or over-allowance. However, the illustration serves to demonstrate that:

1 the underlying logic behind the allowance for irrecoverable receivables is essentially to shift the irrecoverable receivables back into the year in which the goods were sold;

2 this requires an estimate of the allowance;

3 the estimate usually gives rise to an under- or over-allowance that has to be reversed. However, this can be done without identifying the under- or over-allowance separately by means of a single charge to the *statement of profit or loss* when the new allowance for irrecoverable receivables at the end of the current year has been created.

Accounting policy for allowance for irrecoverable receivables

Most entities provide details of how they value their trade receivables and how they calculate the allowance for irrecoverable receivables in their accounting policies. An example can be found in the financial statements of Viridian Group as follows:

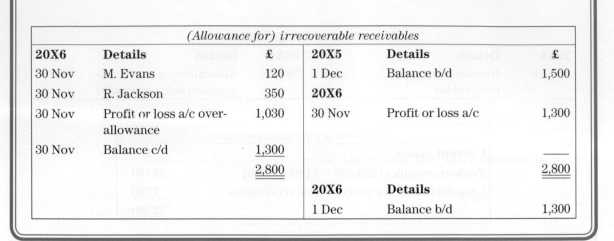

REAL WORLD EXAMPLE 16.1

Viridian Group

Extract from the accounting policies note

Trade debtors

Trade debtors do not carry any interest and are recognised and carried at the lower of their original invoiced value and recoverable amount. Provision is made when there is objective evidence that the asset is impaired. Balances are written off when the probability of recovery is assessed as being remote.

Source: Viridian Group Ltd (2013) Viridian Group Holdings Limited Annual Report and Accounts 2013, http://www.viridiangroup.co.uk/Site/10/Documents/VGIL%20FY2013%20annual%20report.pdf, accessed September 2013.

Learning Activity 16.1

Using a plc's financial statements (search the Web) for guidance, draft a pro forma note on the allowance for irrecoverable receivables. This should show the typical movements to be expected in an *allowance* and a *trade receivables account*.

Note how the company you have selected provides details on the age of their outstanding debts. This can be used to determine if the allowance is realistic, or not.

Accounting manipulation and allowances for irrecoverable receivables

Like most accounting adjustments there is an element of subjectivity about estimating the extent of general allowance that is required. Research has found that movements in the allowance for irrecoverable receivables are used to manipulate accounting profits (see Smith, 1992 and Phillips and Drew, 1992). An example is provided in Real World Example 16.2.

REAL WORLD EXAMPLE 16.2

Accounting irregularities – the provision for bad debts

In 2009 the UK sub-prime lending company 'Cattle' sacked six executives after an under-provision for bad debts was uncovered amounting to £700,000. The outcome of this revelation was that Cattle's future was called into question, trading in the company's shares was suspended by the stock market and publication of the company's accounts was delayed, pending investigation (Bowers and Durrani, 2009). Hyde's Brewery, a Manchester-based firm, was also found to have accounting irregularities which included under-providing for bad debts. It had to restate its financial statements in 2008 to include an increase in the provision for bad debts of £675,000 and in the year to 2009 a further provision of £369,000 was required (Gerrard, 2010).

Summary

A receivable is treated as irrecoverable if a credit customer is unwilling or unable to pay, and the enterprise decides it is uneconomical to pursue the matter further. The ledger entry for irrecoverable debts is to credit the credit customers' *trade receivable personal account* and debit an *irrecoverable receivables account*. The balance on the *irrecoverable receivables account* is transferred to the *statement of profit or loss account* at the end of the accounting year.

An allowance for irrecoverable receivables may consist of a specific allowance and/or a general allowance. The accounting entries in respect of an allowance for irrecoverable receivables are made after the trial balance has been extracted when the statement of profit or loss and statement of financial position are being prepared. A charge (or credit) is made to the *statement of profit or loss* that consists of an amount necessary to increase (or decrease) the allowance at the end of the previous year to the amount required at the end of the current year. The ledger entries are to debit (or credit) the *profit or loss account* and credit (or debit) an *allowance for irrecoverable receivables account*. The latter is shown on the statement of financial position as a deduction from trade receivables to give a net figure representing the amount that the enterprise expects to receive from these credit customers during the forthcoming accounting year.

Key terms and concepts

allowance for irrecoverable/doubtful receivables 276

bad debt 276

general allowance 276

irrecoverable receivable 276

specific allowance 276

An asterisk after the question number indicates that there is a suggested answer in Appendix 2.

Review questions

connect

16.1 What do you understand by the term 'irrecoverable receivables'? In what circumstances might a debt be treated as irrecoverable?

16.2 a Explain the nature of an allowance for irrecoverable receivables.

b Explain the difference between a specific and general allowance for irrecoverable receivables.

16.3 Examine the purpose and logic behind an allowance for irrecoverable receivables, with particular reference to the timing of profits and losses arising from credit sales.

16.4 a Which accounting concepts directly influence the creation of an allowance for irrecoverable receivables?

b Explain your reasoning.

16.5 **a** Businesses often create an allowance for irrecoverable receivables.

i Of which concept is this an example? Explain.

ii What is the purpose for creating an allowance for irrecoverable receivables?

iii How might the amount of an allowance for irrecoverable receivables be calculated?

b What is the difference between irrecoverable receivables and an allowance for irrecoverable receivables?

Exercises

connect

16.6* A business has an accounting year ending on 31 July. It sells goods on credit and on 31 July 20X5 had trade receivables of £15,680. This includes debts of £410 due from A. Wall and £270 from B. Wood, both of which were regarded as irrecoverable.

BASIC

The business has decided to create an allowance for irrecoverable receivables at 31 July 20X5 of 4 per cent of trade receivables. Previously there was no allowance for irrecoverable receivables.

You are required to show the ledger entries in respect of the above irrecoverable receivables and allowance for irrecoverable receivables.

16.7* B. Summers has an accounting year ending on 30 April. At 30 April 20X4 his ledger contained the following accounts:

BASIC

	£
Trade receivables	25,000
Allowance for irrecoverable receivables	750

The trade receivables at 30 April 20X5 were £19,500. This includes £620 due from A. Winters and £880 from D. Spring, both of which are thought to be irrecoverable.

You have been instructed to make an allowance for irrecoverable receivables at 30 April 20X5 of 3 per cent of trade receivables.

Show the ledger entries in respect of the irrecoverable receivables and allowance for irrecoverable receivables.

16.8 YEAR 1

BASIC

1 The balance on trade receivables at the year-end is £110,000.

2 Two of the balances in the sales ledger have to be written off. One is £4,500, the other is £5,500.

3 The company is to provide 5 per cent for an allowance for irrecoverable receivables and 5 per cent for an allowance for discounts.

YEAR 2

The sales in the year were £10,000 lower than the cash received in the year (consider the impact of this on the closing balance).

1 One of the debts that had been written off last year (£5,500) is now recoverable.

2 At the end of this year the auditor has identified £500 of the sales ledger balances as irrecoverable receivables. These should be written off.

3 The allowance for discounts should be increased to 10 per cent.

4 The allowance for irrecoverable receivables should be adjusted to 2 per cent.

Required

Show the transactions in the sales ledger and the general ledger accounts and the extract entries from the statement of profit or loss and statement of financial position for the two years.

INTERMEDIATE

16.9 The financial statements for the year ended 30 November 20X5 of Springboard Ltd included an allowance for irrecoverable receivables at that date of £900.

During the year ended 30 November 20X6, the company received £500 from Peter Lyon towards the settlement of a debt of £700 that had been written off as irrecoverable by the company in 20X3. There is no evidence that Peter Lyon will be able to make any further payments to the company.

Trade receivables at 30 November 20X6 amounted to £22,000, which includes the following balances:

	£
Mary Leaf	800
Angus Way	300

It has now been decided to write off these debts as irrecoverable.

In its financial statements for the year ended 30 November 20X6, the company is to continue its policy of maintaining an allowance for irrecoverable receivables of 5 per cent of trade receivables at the year end.

(***Note***: Irrecoverable receivables written off or recovered are not to be recorded in the allowance for irrecoverable receivables account.)

Required

a Prepare the journal entry (or entries) in the books of the company necessitated by the receipt from Peter Lyon.

Note:

1 Journal entries should include narratives.

2 For the purposes of this question, assume that cash receipts are journalised.

b Prepare the *allowance for irrecoverable receivables account* in the books of the company for the year ended 30 November 20X6.

c Show the entry for trade receivables which will be included in the statement of financial position as at 30 November 20X6 of the company.

(AAT, adapted)

INTERMEDIATE

16.10 The following transactions are to be recorded. At the beginning of year 1 an allowance for irrecoverable receivables account is to be opened. It should show an allowance of 2 per cent against trade receivables of £50,000. During the year irrecoverable receivables of £2,345 are to be charged to the allowance account. At the end of year 1 the irrecoverable receivables allowance is required to be 2 per cent against trade receivables of £60,000.

In year 2 irrecoverable receivables of £37 are to be charged against the account. At the end of year 2 an allowance of 1 per cent against trade receivables of £70,000 is required.

Required

Prepare an allowance for irrecoverable receivables account for the two years. Show in the account the double entry for each item, and carry down the balance at the end of each year.

(ACCA, adapted)

INTERMEDIATE

16.11 The statement of financial position as at 31 December 20X4 of Zoom Products Ltd included:

	£
Trade receivables	85,360

The financial statements for the year ended 31 December 20X4 included an allowance for irrecoverable receivables at 31 December 20X4 of 3 per cent of the balance outstanding from credit customers. During 20X4, the company's sales totalled £568,000, of which 90 per cent, in value, was on credit and £510,150 was received from credit customers in settlement of debts totalling £515,000. In addition, £3,000 was received from J. Dodds in a settlement of a debt that had been written off as irrecoverable in 20X4; this receipt has been credited to J. Dodds' account in the sales ledger.

On 30 December 20X5, the following outstanding debts were written off as irrecoverable:

	£
J. White	£600
K. Black	£2,000

Entries relating to irrecoverable receivables are passed through the *allowance for irrecoverable receivables account*. The balance at 31 December 20X5 on the allowance for irrecoverable receivables account is to be 3 per cent of the amount due to the company from credit customers at that date.

Required

a Write up the allowance for irrecoverable receivables account for the year ended 31 December 20X5, bringing down the balance at 1 January 20X6.

b Prepare a computation of the amount to be shown as trade receivables in the company's statement of financial position at 31 December 20X5.

(AAT, adapted)

INTERMEDIATE

16.12 Because of the doubtful nature of some debts, P. Rudent instructed his accountants to make a specific allowance in the financial statements for the year ended 30 June 20X5 against the following debts:

	£
J. Black	28
C. Green	6
B. Grey	24
Fawn Ltd	204

He also instructed that a general allowance of 5 per cent for irrecoverable receivables should be created on the other trade receivables, which at 30 June 20X5 amounted to £8,000.

No further business transactions were entered into with any of these credit customers during the year ended 30 June 20X6, but an amount of £9 was received from J. Black's trustee in bankruptcy by way of a first dividend; a first and final dividend of £70 was received from the liquidator of Fawn Ltd and B. Grey paid his debt in full. A further debt of £95 due from S. White proved to be irrecoverable.

On 30 June 20X6 P. Rudent instructed his accountants to maintain the allowance existing against C. Green's debt and to provide for the balance owing by J. Black, and to make further allowance for debts owing by J. Blue £19 and R. Brown £15. The other trade receivables amounted to £7,500 and the accountants were instructed to make the allowance for irrecoverable receivables equal to 5 per cent of these debts.

Show what entries should be made in P. Rudent's nominal ledger to record these facts.

INTERMEDIATE **16.13*** M. Shaft has an accounting year ending on 31 December. At 31 December 20X4 the ledger contained the following balances:

	£
Plant and machinery	30,000
Provision for depreciation on plant and machinery	12,500
Trade receivables	10,760
Allowance for irrecoverable receivables	1,260

The allowance for irrecoverable receivables consisted of a general allowance of £500 and specific allowances comprising: A. Bee £320; C. Dee £180; and F. Gee £260.

The following transactions occurred during 20X5:

31 Mar	Part exchanged one piece of plant for another. The part exchange allowance on the old plant was £4,000 and the balance of £1,000 was paid by cheque. The old plant cost £8,000 when it was purchased on 1 July 20X3.
30 Apr	A. Bee was declared bankrupt and a first dividend of £70 was received from the trustee.
15 June	A debt of £210 owed by J. Kay that is included in trade receivables at 31 December 20X4 was found to be irrecoverable.
3 Aug	C. Dee paid his debt in full.
7 Oct	F. Gee was declared bankrupt and a first and final dividend at £110 was received from the trustee.

Plant and machinery is depreciated using the reducing balance method at a rate of 25 per cent per annum on a strict time basis. The trade receivables at 31 December 20X5 were £12,610. This figure is after recording all money received but does not take into account any of the above irrecoverable receivables. The relevant specific allowances and a general allowance for irrecoverable receivables of 5 per cent should be maintained at 31 December 20X5.

Required

a Show the ledger entries in respect of the above, including the charges to the statement of profit or loss and the balances at 31 December 20X5. Show your workings clearly and take all calculations to the nearest £.

b Briefly discuss the similarities between allowances for irrecoverable receivables and depreciation.

References

Bowers, S. and Durrani, A. (2009) 'Sub-prime Lender Cattles Faces £850m Write-down in Risk Management Scandal', *Guardian*, 1 July, http://www.theguardian.com/business/2009/apr/02/cattles-mortgages, accessed September 2013.

Gerrard, N. (2010) 'Hyde's Brewery Reports £1.3m Annual Pre-tax Loss', http://www.catererandhotelkeeper.co.uk/Articles/2010/01/26/331868/Hydes-Brewery-reports-1631.3m-annualpre-tax-loss.htm, accessed September 2013.

Phillips and Drew (1992) *Ranking of Creative Accounting Practices used by 185 Major UK Companies*, cited by Mike Jones in his slide show on 'Creative Accounting, Fraud and Accounting Scandals', http://www.docstoc.com/docs/3414029/Creative-Accounting-Fraud-and-Accounting-Scandals

Smith, T. (1992) *Accounting for Growth: Stripping the Camouflage from Company Accounts*, Century Business Publications, London.

Chapter 17

Accruals and prepayments

Learning Objectives:

After reading this chapter you should be able to do the following:

1. Explain the conceptual foundation of accruals and prepayments.
2. Ascertain how accrual and prepayment amounts can be determined in practice.
3. Show the entries for accruals and prepayments in the journal, general ledger, statement of profit or loss and statement of financial position.
4. Prepare simple final financial statements from a trial balance making the required adjustments for accruals and prepayments.
5. Prepare the ledger entries for common year-end adjustments such as inventory of tools, inventory of stationery and inventory of fuel.
6. Prepare final financial statements after adjustments for expense related inventories have been posted.

17.1 The nature of, and ledger entries for, accrued expenses

As discussed in Chapter 4, 'Conceptual Framework 2: Concepts, Principles and Policies', the accruals concept dictates that costs are recognized as they are incurred, not when money is paid. That is, goods and services are deemed to have been purchased on the date they are received. This gives rise to **accrued expenses/accruals**. Accruals are 'payables' in respect of services received that have not been paid for at the end of the accounting year. Accrued expenses can obviously only occur where services are paid for in arrears, such as electricity or gas.

An accrual may comprise either or both of the following:

1 Invoices received (for expenses) that have not been paid at the end of the accounting year.

2 The value of services received for which an invoice has not been rendered at the end of the accounting year.

In the case of the latter, this requires an estimate to be made of the amount of the services consumed during the period between the date of the last invoice and the end of the accounting year. The estimate may be based on any one of the following:

1 A meter reading taken at the end of the accounting year (electricity).

2 The amount consumed over a corresponding period during the current year.

3 The amount consumed during the same period of the previous year as adjusted for any change in the unit price.

However, in practice, final financial statements are often not prepared until some time after the end of the accounting year. By that time the invoice covering the period in question is likely to have been received and can thus be used to ascertain the value of the services consumed during the relevant period. The accrual convention has been used in the past to manipulate reported earnings (profits) in a fraudulent manner. It is for this reason that auditors afford special attention to the determination of accrual amounts and cut-off periods. An example is now provided.

REAL WORLD EXAMPLE 17.1

Diamond Foods Accounting Scandal Seeds Sown Years Ago

The historic business practices of Diamond Foods, the largest walnut processor in the U.S. and maker of Emerald nuts, show a number of warning signs, including unusual timing of payments to growers, a leap in profit margins, and volatile inventories and cash flows.

According to a Huffington Post article published in May 2012, the suspicions of Douglas Barnhill, an accountant who is also a farmer of 75 acres of California walnut groves, were raised when he received an unexpected cheque for nearly $46,000 from Diamond in September 2011. Barnhill was still waiting for full payment for the walnuts he had sent Diamond in 2010, and twice talked to Eric Heidman, Diamond's director of field operations, on whether the cheque was a final payment for his 2010 crop or pre-payment for the 2011 harvest.

Not long after he received the cheque, Barnhill saw news reporting of the company saying the payments were an advance payment for the next crop. But according to Barnhill, Heidman told him the opposite, indicating that the payment was for the 2010 crop, part of fiscal 2011, but that it would be "budgeted into the next year". Barnhill knew that, under accounting rules, you cannot legitimately pay in a future fiscal year for a prior year's crop, and informed Heidman of this.

As the Huffington Post article explains, following an investigation Diamond's audit committee found payments of $20 million to walnut growers in August 2010 and $60 million in September 2011 that were not booked in the correct periods. A delay in booking payments from one fiscal year to the next could artificially reduce the company's costs and boost earnings in that period.

Source: Adapted from http://www.huffingtonpost.com/2012/03/19/diamond-foods-accounting-scandal_n_1361234.html, 19 March 2012, accessed August 2014.

Although accrued expenses are essentially payables, rather than have a separate accruals account it is usual to enter accruals in the relevant expense account. This consists of debiting the amount owing at the end of the year to the expense account as a balance *carried down* and crediting the same account as a balance *brought down* in the next period. Thus, the amount that will be transferred to the profit or loss account consists of the amount paid during the year plus the accrual at the end of the year (less the accrual at the start of the year). This will reflect the total value of the services that have been received during the current accounting year. The balance brought down is entered on the statement of financial position as a current liability. A pro forma ledger account showing typical entries is now provided (see Figure 17.1). This can be used to check that entries have been correctly posted.

Figure 17.1

Light and heat

20X4	Details	£	20X4	Details	£
	Bank	XX	1 Jan	Opening accrual b/d	X
31 Dec	Closing accrual c/d	X	31 Dec	Profit or loss a/c	XX
		XX			XX
			20X5		
			1 Jan	Opening accrual b/d	X

A pro forma expense ledger account showing typical entries for expense accruals

The shaded entry is the entry that is derived when the account is closed. This is the charge for the year. The opening accrual on 1 January 20X5 is the amount that will be disclosed under current liabilities in the statement of financial position. The journal to record (post) the year end accrual shown in Figure 17.1 is as follows:

Debit:	*Light and heat account current period* (this will end up in the current year profit or loss charge)	£'XXX	
Credit:	*Light and heat account new period* (opening accrual in the next period – this balance will form part of the profit or loss charge in the next period)		£'XXX

The mechanics of calculating the yearly charge are illustrated in Worked Example 17.1.

WORKED EXAMPLE 17.1

D. Spring has an accounting year ending on 31 December. The following amounts have been paid for electricity:

Date paid	Quarter ended	£
29 Mar 20X4	28 Feb 20X4	96
7 July 20X4	31 May 20X4	68
2 Oct 20X4	31 Aug 20X4	73
5 Jan 20X5	30 Nov 20X4	82
3 Apr 20X5	28 Feb 20X5	105

You are required to show the entries in the *light and heat account* for the year ended 31 December 20X4 and the relevant statement of financial position extract.

Workings

$$\text{Accrual at 1 Jan 20X4} = \tfrac{1}{3} \times £96 = £32$$

$$\text{Accrual at 31 Dec 20X4} = £82 + \left(\tfrac{1}{3} \times £105\right) = £117$$

Light and heat

20X4	Details	£	20X4	Details	£
29 Mar	Bank	96	1 Jan	Accrual b/d	32
7 July	Bank	68	31 Dec	Profit or loss a/c	322
2 Oct	Bank	73			
31 Dec	Accrual c/d	117			
		354			354
			20X5		
			1 Jan	Accrual b/d	117

Statement of financial position as at 31 December 20X4 (extract)	£
Current liabilities	
Accrued expenses	117

Note: The amount transferred to the statement of profit or loss is the difference between the two sides of the *light and heat account* after entering the accrual at the end of the year.

17.2 The nature of, and ledger entries for, prepaid expenses

The accruals concept also gives rise to **prepaid expenses/prepayments**. Prepayments are 'receivables' in respect of services that have been paid for but not received at the end of the accounting year. Prepayments can obviously only occur where services are paid for in advance, such as rent, local government taxes, road tax and insurance.

The amount of the prepayment is ascertained by determining on a time basis how much of the last payment made during the accounting year relates to the services that will be received in the following accounting year.

Although prepaid expenses are essentially receivables, rather than have a separate prepayment account, it is usual to enter the prepayment in the relevant expense account. This consists of crediting the amount of the prepayment to the expense account as a balance *carried down* and debiting the same account as a balance *brought down*. Thus, the amount that will be transferred to the *profit or loss account* consists of the amount paid during the year minus the prepayment at the end of the year (plus the prepayment at the start of the year). This will reflect the total value of the services that have been received during the current accounting year. The balance brought down is entered on the statement of financial position as a current asset. A pro forma ledger account showing the relevant entries is provided in Figure 17.2. This can be used to check entries.

Figure 17.2

Rent

20X4	Details	£	20X5	Details	£
1 July	Opening prepayment b/d	X	30 June	Profit or loss a/c	XX
1 Sep	Bank	XX	30 June	Closing prepayment c/d	X
		XX			XX
20X5					
1 July	Opening prepayment b/d	X			

A pro forma expense ledger account showing typical entries for expense prepayments

The shaded entry is the entry that is derived when the account is closed. This is the charge for the year. The opening prepayment on 1 July 20X5 is the receivable that will be disclosed under current assets in the statement of financial position. The mechanics of calculating the yearly charge are illustrated in Worked Example 17.2.

WORKED EXAMPLE 17.2

M. Waters has an accounting year ending on 30 June. The following amounts have been paid as rent:

Date paid	Quarter ended	£
2 Jun 20X4	31 Aug 20X4	600
1 Sep 20X4	30 Nov 20X4	600
3 Dec 20X4	28 Feb 20X5	660
5 Mar 20X5	31 May 20X5	660
4 Jun 20X5	31 Aug 20X5	720

You are required to show the entries in the rent account for the year ended 30 June 20X5 and the relevant statement of financial position extract.

Workings

$$\text{Prepaid at 1 July 20X4} = \tfrac{2}{3} \times £600 = £400$$
$$\text{Prepaid at 30 June 20X5} = \tfrac{2}{3} \times £720 = £480$$

Rent

20X4	Details	£	20X5	Details	£
1 Jul	Prepayment b/d	400	30 Jun	Profit or loss a/c	2,560
1 Sep	Bank	600			
3 Dec	Bank	660			
20X5					
5 Mar	Bank	660			
4 Jun	Bank	720	30 Jun	Prepayment c/d	480
		3,040			3,040
20X5					
1 Jul	Prepayment b/d	480			

Statement of financial position as at 30 June 20X5 (extract)	**£**
Current assets	
Prepayments	480

Note: The amount transferred to the *statement of profit or loss* is the difference between the two sides of the *rent account* after entering the prepayment at the end of the year.

Learning Activity 17.1

Obtain copies of the electricity bills for the house in which you live. From these prepare a light and heat account relating to the last complete calendar year. Repeat this exercise for insurance.

17.3 Accruals and prepayments and the preparation of final financial statements from the trial balance

The statement of profit or loss is usually prepared from the trial balance. This involves adjusting the amounts shown for any accruals and prepayments at the end of the accounting year. It is important to appreciate that, because the trial balance is taken out at the end of the accounting year, the amounts shown in it include any accruals and prepayments at the start of the year. Thus, when preparing a statement of profit or loss from the trial balance, it is only necessary to add to the amount shown in the trial balance any accrual at the end of the accounting year and to subtract any prepayment.

WORKED EXAMPLE 17.3

Extract from the trial balance of A. Trader at the year end:

	Debit £	Credit £
Trade receivables	20,000	
Trade payables		6,000
Heat and light	4,000	
Rent	6,000	
	XXXX	XXXX

Additional information

1 There is an accrual at the year end of £200 for heat and light.

2 Rent amounting to £1,000 was prepaid at the reporting period end.

Required

a Prepare the ledger accounts showing the year-end adjustments.

b Show the adjusted trial balance.

c Provide extracts from the statement of financial position to show the relevant disclosures for the accrual and the prepayment.

Heat and light

	£		£
Balance b/d from TB	4,000		
Closing accrual c/d	200	Profit or loss a/c	4,200
	4,200		4,200
		Opening accrual b/d	200

Rent

	£		£
Balance b/d from TB	6,000	Profit or loss a/c	5,000
		Closing prepayment c/d	1,000
	6,000		6,000
Opening prepayment b/d	1,000		

Amended trial balance

	Debit (£)	Credit (£)
Trade receivables	20,000	
Trade payables		6,000
Heat and light	4,200	
Rent	5,000	
Accruals		200
Prepayments	1,000	
	XXXX	XXXX

The shaded area shows the accounts that have changed.

Extract from the statement of financial position as at XX	
ASSETS	£
Current assets	
Inventories	XX
Trade receivables	20,000
Prepayments	1,000
Bank	XX
Cash	XX
	X
Total assets	XXX
OWNER'S EQUITY AND LIABILITIES	
Owner's capital	XXX
Current liabilities	
Trade payables	6,000
Accruals	200
	6,200
Total equity and liabilities	XXX

17.4 Further year-end adjustment (inventories of tools, stationery and fuels)

As explained in Chapter 15, 'Depreciation and Non-current Assets', **loose tools** are regarded as non-current assets, whereas **consumable tools** are designated as revenue expenditure. Thus, any inventories of consumable tools, such as inventories of stationery and fuel, are treated as current assets. However, irrespective of their classification, the accounting adjustments in respect of these items are essentially the same. That is, the value of the items in inventories at the end of the accounting year is entered in the relevant ledger account as a balance *carried down* on the credit side and as a balance *brought down* on the debit side (in exactly the same way as with prepaid expenses). The difference between the two sides of the ledger account is then transferred to the profit or loss account. In the case of loose tools this is described as 'depreciation', which is referred to as having been computed using the revaluation method.

The principle that is applied to each of these items is as follows:

Inventory at end of previous year at valuation
Add: Purchases during the year
Less: Inventory at end of current year at valuation
= Charge to statement of profit or loss

In the ledger this will be presented as follows:

Stationery/oil/tools					
20X4	**Details**	**£**	**20X4**	**Details**	**£**
1 Jan	Opening inventory b/d	XX	30 Nov	Profit or loss a/c	XXX
	Payments mid-year	XXX	31 Dec	Closing inventory c/d	XX
		XXX			XXX
20X5					
1 Jan	Opening inventory b/d	XX			

The charge to the *profit or loss account* represents the value of stationery, fuel or tools that has been consumed during the year. The same principle is also applied in the financial statements of farming businesses with respect to livestock and growing crops, and in retailing businesses when accounting for containers and packing materials.

WORKED EXAMPLE 17.4

Extract from the trial balance of A. Trader at the year end:

	Debit €	Credit €
Trade receivables	20,000	
Trade payables		6,000
Opening balance of heating oil (500 litres)	250	
Heat and light	4,000	
Rent	6,000	
	XXXX	XXXX

Additional information

1 There is an accrual at the year end of €200 for heat and light.

2 At the end of the year, A. Trader had 600 litres of heating oil in the oil tank. This had cost 60c per litre.

Required

Prepare the ledger account showing the adjustments to the 'Heat and Light' account.

Heat and light account			
	€		€
Opening inventory of oil b/d	250		
Balance b/d from TB	4,000	Profit or loss a/c	4,090
Closing accrual c/d	200	Closing inventory of oil c/d	360
	4,450		4,450
Opening inventory of oil b/d	360	Opening accrual b/d	200

17.5 Further year-end adjustment (company taxation)

Under IAS 12 Taxation, company tax is called 'income tax', though in the UK and Ireland it is termed 'corporate tax'. Sole trader and partnerships do not have to account for tax as they are not separate legal entities. Under law, the tax due on sole trader and partnership profits is due by the individual(s) who own them; therefore are not business expenses. It is different for companies; they are legally responsible for any tax due on profits made, therefore tax must be included in the financial statements of companies. Tax is typically due within nine months and one day of the year end; therefore if a company's year-end is 31 December 20X4, taxation will have to be paid to the Inland Revenue by 1 December 20X5. The expected taxation charge for the year ended 31 December 20X4 will have to be accrued in that year. The following journal reflects the typical entry that is required:

Debit:	*Income tax account current period* (with the expected tax charge for the year)	£'XXX	
Credit:	*Income tax account new period* (opening accrual in the next period – this balance will form part of the profit or loss charge in the next period)		£'XXX

The actual amount that is paid may differ from the amount accrued at the end of the previous year as Revenue & Customs may not agree with the tax calculation. For example, some expenses may not be allowable for tax purposes and Revenue & Customs will have to investigate this so it is not uncommon for a balance to be carried forward in the income tax expense account that relates to the previous year. If the amount is not material it is normally released to the current period. This, and accounting for the year-end accrual, are covered in Worked Example 17.5.

WORKED EXAMPLE 17.5

ABC Limited incurred the following transactions in relation to company income tax for the year ended 31 December 20X4. The materiality threshold is £5,000.

At 31 December 20X3 £15,000 was accrued for taxation for that year.

On 30 June 20X4 the company paid £14,500 to the revenue in respect of taxation for the year to 31 December 20X3. This was the final agreed taxation computation.

At the end of 31 December 20X4 the company estimates that they will have to pay £12,000 for taxation for the year.

Required

Prepare the ledger account for income tax for the year ended 31 December 20X4.

Income tax

20X4	Details	£	20X4	Details	£
30 Jun	Bank	14,500	1 Jan	Op accrual	15,000
31 Dec	Cl accrual c/d	12,000	31 Dec	Profit or loss a/c	11,500
		26,500			26,500
			20X5		
			1 Jan	Opening accrual b/d	12,000

The current period charge is £12,000 less the £500 over-accrual from the previous period. This accrual is deemed to be immaterial and hence is not separately disclosed.

Note: If the amount were material then it would be a fundamental error and the prior period financial statement would have needed to have been restated to reflect a reduced accrual of £14,500 and a reduced taxation charge in that period.

Summary

The accruals concept dictates that costs are recognized as they are incurred, not as money is paid. That is, goods and services are deemed to have been purchased on the date they are received. This gives rise to accrued and prepaid expenses. Accrued expenses are payables in respect of services received that have not been paid for at the end of an accounting year. Prepaid expenses are receivables in respect of services that have been paid for, but not received, at the end of an accounting year.

After a trial balance has been extracted, the final financial statements are prepared, which necessitates adjustments relating to accrued and prepaid expenses. These adjustments are made in the relevant expense accounts in the form of a balance at the end of the year. The remaining difference between the two sides of the expense account is transferred to the *profit or loss account*, and represents the cost of services received during the year. The balance on the expense account is shown on the statement of financial position as a current liability in the case of accruals, or as a current asset in the case of prepayments.

Key terms and concepts

accrued expenses/accruals 292
consumable tools 298
loose tools 298
prepaid expenses 294
prepayments 294

An asterisk after the question number indicates that there is a suggested answer in Appendix 2.

Review questions

connect

17.1 a Explain the nature of accrued and prepaid expenses.

b Describe how the amount of each may be ascertained.

Exercises

connect

BASIC

17.2* K. Wills has an accounting year ending on 31 December. The following amounts were paid in respect of rent and gas:

Expense	Date paid	Quarter ended	£
Rent	1 Nov 20X3	31 Jan 20X4	900
Rent	29 Jan 20X4	30 Apr 20X4	930
Gas	6 Mar 20X4	28 Feb 20X4	420
Rent	2 May 20X4	31 July 20X4	930
Gas	4 Jun 20X4	31 May 20X4	360
Rent	30 Jul 20X4	31 Oct 20X4	930
Gas	3 Sep 20X4	31 Aug 20X4	270
Rent	5 Nov 20X4	31 Jan 20X5	960
Gas	7 Dec 20X4	30 Nov 20X4	390
Gas	8 Mar 20X5	28 Feb 20X5	450

You are required to show the ledger entries in the *rent* and *light and heat accounts* for the year ended 31 December 20X4.

BASIC

17.3 Oriel Ltd, whose financial year runs from 1 June to the following 31 May, maintains a combined rent and rates account in its ledger.

Rent is fixed on a calendar year basis and is payable quarterly in advance. Rent was £2,400 for the year ended 31 December 20X4 and is £3,000 for the year ending 31 December 20X5.

Oriel Ltd has made the following payments of rent by cheque:

Date	Amount	Details
20X4	£	
3 Jan	600	Quarter to 31 Mar 20X4
1 Apr	600	Quarter to 30 Jun 20X4
1 July	600	Quarter to 30 Sep 20X4
1 Oct	600	Quarter to 31 Dec 20X4
20X5		
3 Jan	750	Quarter to 31 Mar 20X5
1 Apr	750	Quarter to 30 Jun 20X5

Rates are assessed annually for the year from 1 April to the following 31 March and are payable in one lump sum by 30 September. The rates assessment was £2,040 for the year ended 31 March 20X5 and £2,280 for the year ending 31 March 20X6.

Oriel Ltd paid the rates for the year ended 31 March 20X5 by cheque on 30 September 20X4 and intends to pay the rates for the year ended 31 March 20X6 on 30 September 20X5.

Required

a Prepare the *rent and rates account* for the year ended 31 May 20X5 only as it would appear in the ledger of Oriel Ltd.

b Explain with particular reference to your answer to (a) the meaning of the term 'matching'.

(AAT, adapted)

BASIC

17.4 Munch Catering Ltd, whose financial year runs from 1 December to the following 30 November, maintains a 'Building occupancy costs' account in its general ledger. This account is used to record all payments in respect of rent, insurance and property taxes on the company's business premises.

Rent is fixed on a calendar year basis and is payable quarterly in advance. Rent was £1,800 for the year ended 31 December 20X4 and is £2,100 for the year ended 31 December 20X5.

Munch Catering Ltd has made the following payments of rent by cheque:

Date	Amount	Details
20X4	**£**	
29 Sep	450	Quarter to 31 Dec 20X4
29 Dec	525	Quarter to 31 Mar 20X5
20X5		
30 Mar	525	Quarter to 30 Jun 20X5
29 Jun	525	Quarter to 30 Sep 20X5
28 Sep	525	Quarter to 31 Dec 20X5

Munch Catering Ltd paid its building contents insurance premium of £547 for the year to 30 November 20X5 on 17 November 20X4. This policy was cancelled as from 31 May 20X5 and Munch Catering Ltd received a cheque for £150 as a rebate of premium on 21 June 20X5. A new buildings contents insurance policy was taken out with a different insurance company with effect from 1 June 20X5. The premium on this policy was £400 and this was paid in full by cheque by Munch Catering Ltd on 18 May 20X5.

Property taxes are assessed annually for the year from 1 April to the following 31 March and are payable in one lump sum by 30 September. Munch Catering Ltd's assessment was £840 for the year to 31 March 20X5 and £1,680 for the year to 31 March 20X6. Munch Catering Ltd paid the assessment for the year ended 31 March 20X5 by cheque on 2 October 20X4 and the assessment for the year ended 31 March 20X6 by cheque on 26 September 20X5.

Required

Prepare the *Building occupancy costs account* for the year ended 30 November 20X5 only as it would appear in the general ledger of Munch Catering Ltd.

(AAT)

BASIC

17.5 **a** Commission: received in advance at the start of the year £50; received in the year £5,600; receivable at the year end £250.

b Rates: paid in the year £950; prepaid at the start of the year £220; prepaid at the year end £290.

c Motor insurance: prepaid at the start of the year £75; paid in the year £744; owing at the year end £100.

d Stationery: paid in the year £1,800; owing at the start of the year £250; owing at the end of the year £490.

e Rent income: receives £550 for rent in the year. Tenant owed £180 at the start of the year and £210 at the end of the year.

f Insurance: paid in the year £420; prepaid at the year end £35.

Required

Prepare the ledger account for the above transactions.

BASIC

17.6 **a** Stationery: During the year to 31 December 20X4 £1,300 was paid in respect of stationery. The amount owing at 31 December 20X3 was £140 and the amount owing at 31 December 20X4 was £200.

b Rent: Kristal received rent of £3,000 during the year ended 31 December 20X4. The tenant owed Kristal £210 on 31 December 20X3 and owed her £340 on 31 December 20X4.

Required

Draft 'T' accounts for the above transactions including the balances transferred to the *statement of profit or loss account* for 20X4 and the balances brought down to 20X5

BASIC

17.7 The company's year end is 31 December 20X5. Prepare ledger accounts for the following accounts showing the adjustments that are necessary for the year-end accruals and prepayments and the balances that would appear in the financial statements.

a The opening accrual for heat and light was £100. The company paid £4,500 in the year. The last payment was in December for the period 1 September to 30 November. This amounted to £1,500.

b The inventory of toiletries on 1 January 20X5 was £250. An additional £580 was purchased in the year. At the year end there were 10 packets of toilet rolls left costing £20 each.

c The rates bill paid last year was £1,200. It was accounted for correctly using the accruals concept. The rates bill paid this year in April amounted to £1,800 (rates bills cover the period 1 April to 31 March in the next year).

d In December 20X4 our tenant paid us £1,200 for the period 1 December to 28 February. During the year we received another £5,000, including £1,500 in December for the three months to 29 February 20X6.

e At the start of the year an agent for a product owed us £400 commission for sales targets we met last year. This year we made the target sales again. They paid us £6,000 but still owe us £900 at the year end.

BASIC

17.8* The ledger of RBD & Co. included the following account balances:

	At 1 June 20X4	At 31 May 20X5
	£	£
Rents receivable: prepayments	463	517
Rent and rates payable:		
prepayments	1,246	1,509
accruals	315	382
Trade payables	5,258	4,720

During the year ended 31 May 20X5 the following transactions had arisen:

	£
Rents received by cheque	4,058
Rent paid by cheque	7,491
Rates paid by cheque	2,805
Credit suppliers paid by cheque	75,181
Discounts received from credit creditors	1,043
Purchases on credit	to be derived

Required

Post and balance the appropriate accounts for the year ended 31 May 20X5, deriving the transfer entries to the statement of profit or loss, where applicable.

(ACCA, adapted)

17.9 The balances on certain accounts of Foster Hardware Co. as at 1 April 20X5 were: INTERMEDIATE

	£
Rent and rates payable – accruals	2,200
– prepayments	1,940
Rent receivable – prepayments	625
Vehicles (at cost)	10,540
Provision for depreciation of vehicles	4,720
During the financial year the business:	
Paid rent by cheque	5,200
Paid rates by cheque	3,050
Received cheque for rent of sublet premises	960
Traded in vehicle – original cost	4,710
– accumulated depreciation	3,080
– part exchange allowance	1,100
Paid balance of price of new vehicle by cheque	5,280
Closing balances as at 31 March 20X6 were:	
Rent and rates payable – accruals	2,370
– prepayments	1,880
Rent receivable – prepayments	680
Vehicles (at cost)	to be derived
Provision for depreciation of vehicles	3,890

Required

Post and balance the appropriate accounts for the year ended 31 March 20X6, deriving the transfer entries to the statement of profit or loss where applicable.

(ACCA, adapted)

17.10 The trial balance of Snodgrass, a sole trader, at 1 January 20X5 is as follows: INTERMEDIATE

	Debit £'000	Credit £'000
Capital		600
Non-current assets (net)	350	
Trade receivables	200	
Prepayments – rent	8	
– insurance	12	
Trade payables		180
Accruals – electricity		9
– telephone		1
Inventories	200	
Bank	20	
	790	790

The following information is given for the year:

	£'000
Receipts from credit customers	1,000
Payments to credit suppliers	700
Payments for: rent	30
insurance	20
electricity	25
telephone	10
wages	100
Proprietor's personal expenses	50
Discounts allowed	8
Irrecoverable receivables written off	3
Depreciation	50

At 31 December 20X5 the following balances are given:

	£'000
Trade receivables	250
Prepayments – rent	10
– telephone	2
Trade payables	160
Accruals – electricity	7
– insurance	6
Inventories	230

Required

Prepare a statement of profit or loss for the year, and a statement of financial position as at 31 December 20X5.

(ACCA, adapted)

INTERMEDIATE **17.11** Bush, a sole trader, commenced trading on 1 January 20X4.

a *Telephone expense details*

The quarterly rental payable in advance on 1 January, 1 April, 1 July and 1 October is £30. Telephone calls are payable in arrears: January to March 20X4 paid 1 April 20X4 £318; April to June 20X4 paid 1 July 20X4 £422; and July to September 20X4 paid 1 October 20X4 £172.

He is to prepare his first financial statements to 31 October 20X4 and estimates that the cost of his calls for October 20X4 will be £44.

Rent expense details

Bush also pays rent quarterly in advance for his premises and has made payments as follows:

1 January 20X4	£800
1 April 20X4	£950
1 July 20X4	£950
1 October 20X4	£950

Required

Prepare Bush's ledger accounts for telephone and rent for the period from 1 January 20X4 to 31 October 20X4, showing clearly the amounts to be transferred to his statement of profit or loss for the period together with any balances carried forward on 31 October 20X4.

b At 1 November 20X4, the following balances were brought forward in the ledger accounts of Bush:

Rates payable account	Dr	£1,500
Electricity account	Cr	£800
Interest receivable account	Dr	£300
Allowance for irrecoverable receivables account	Cr	£4,800

You are told the following:

Rates are payable quarterly in advance on the last day of December, March, June and September, at the rate of £4,000 per annum.

Interest was received during the year as follows:

2 November 20X4	£250 (for the six months to 30 October 20X4)
3 May 20X5	£600 (for the six months to 30 April 20X5)

You estimate that interest of £300 is accrued at 31 October 20X5.

Electricity is paid as follows:

5 December 20X4	£1,000 (for the period to 30 November 20X4)
10 March 20X5	£1,300 (for the period to 28 February 20X5)
8 June 20X5	£1,500 (for the period to 31 May 20X5)
7 September 20X5	£1,100 (for the period to 31 August 20X5)

At 30 October 20X5, the electricity meter shows that £900 has been consumed since the last bill was received.

At 30 October 20X5, the balance of trade receivables amounts to £250,000. The allowance for irrecoverable receivables is to be amended to 10 per cent of trade receivables.

Required

Write up the ledger accounts for:

1 rates payable;

2 electricity;

3 interest receivable;

4 allowance for irrecoverable receivables.

and bring down the balances at 31 October 20X5.

c Explain two accounting concepts that govern the treatment of the above items in the financial statements of Bush.

Chapter 18

The extended trial balance and final financial statements (advanced)

Learning Objectives:

After reading this chapter you should be able to do the following:

1. Prepare an extended trial balance taking into account adjustments for inventories, depreciation, allowance for irrecoverable receivables, accruals, prepayments.
2. Prepare a statement of profit or loss and a statement of financial position from an extended trial balance.

—18.1 Introduction

As explained in Chapter 14, 'The Final Financial Statements of Sole Traders (Introductory)', final financial statements are prepared after the trial balance has been produced and this involves transferring the balances on various income and expense accounts to the statement of profit or loss. In addition, the process of preparing final financial statements involves a number of **adjustments**, some of which have been described in Chapters 15–17. These are summarized in Figure 18.1.

This chapter brings together all the information/adjustments that typically impact on an entity's financial statements post-trial balance stage.

Figure 18.1

Accounting adjustments

- Year-end inventories and work-in-progress;
- Provisions for depreciation;
- Provision for irrecoverable receivables;
- Accruals and prepayments;
- Taxation;
- The correction of omissions and errors such as irrecoverable receivables not written off during the year.

Common accounting adjustments post trial balance

—18.2 The extended trial balance

As explained above, the preparation of final financial statements involves various adjustments. In the preceding three chapters these were described mainly in terms of the necessary ledger entries. However, in practice and in examinations, final financial statements are usually prepared from the trial balance, the ledger entries being done at some later date when the final financial statements are completed.

Because the preparation of final financial statements from the trial balance involves a large number of adjustments, in practice it is usual to make these adjustments using an **extended trial balance**. This may take a number of forms, but a useful approach is to set it up to comprise eight columns made up of four pairs as follows:

1 **The trial balance debit side**

2 **The trial balance credit side**

3 *Adjustments to the debit side*

4 *Adjustments to the credit side*

5 **The profit or loss account debit side**

6 **The profit or loss account credit side**

7 *The statement of financial position debit side*

8 *The statement of financial position credit side*

The first two columns are the normal trial balance. Columns 3 and 4 are used to make adjustments to the figures in the trial balance in respect of provisions for depreciation and irrecoverable receivables, accruals and prepayments, and so on. The adjustments in these two columns need to be made to the individual ledger accounts in the nominal ledger. Columns 5 and 6 are used to compute the amounts that will be entered in the statement of profit or loss. The entries in these columns also need to be made to the individual ledger accounts. Columns 7 and 8 are used to ascertain the amounts that will be shown in the statement of financial position.

No adjustments must be entered in the statement of financial position columns because the statement of financial position does not involve entries in the ledger.

To recap, the double entry and positioning of the most common adjustments found in the extended trial balance are as follows:

1 *Depreciation*:

Debit:	*Depreciation expense* (in the statement of profit or loss column)	£'XXX	
Credit:	*Provision for depreciation account* (in the adjustment column)		£'XXX

2 *Allowance for irrecoverable receivables*:

Debit:	*Increase in the allowance for irrecoverable receivables expense* (in the statement of profit or loss column)	£'XXX	
Credit:	*Allowance for irrecoverable receivables account* (in the adjustment column)		£'XXX

The opposite double entry is required when there is a decrease.

3 *Accruals and prepayments*:

The example used here is a rent accrual at the year end.

Debit:	*Rent* (in the adjustment column)	£'XXX	
Credit:	*Rent* (in the adjustment column)		£'XXX

The accrual will also be recorded in the statement of financial position column on the credit side.

4 *Inventory at the end of the year*:

Debit:	*Year-end Inventory* (in the adjustment column)	£'XXX	
Credit:	*Year-end inventory* (in the statement of profit or loss column)		£'XXX

See Worked Example 18.1 for examples of all these adjustments in a practical setting.

After all the necessary adjustments have been made in the adjustment and profit or loss account columns, the amounts that will be entered in the statement of profit or loss and statement of financial position columns can be ascertained. These are found by cross-casting the amounts relating to each ledger account shown in the original trial balance. For example, if the original trial balance contained a rent account with a debit balance, any prepayment shown in the credit adjustment column would be deducted from this and the difference entered in the statement of profit or loss debit column. The prepayment shown in the debit adjustment column would also be extended across and entered in the statement of financial position debit column. Expenses with accrued charges are treated in a similar way.

When all the amounts have been entered in the statement of profit or loss and statement of financial position columns, the profit (or loss) can be computed in the normal manner as the difference between the two statements of profit or loss columns. The profit is entered in the statement of profit or loss debit column and the credit adjustment column. The latter is then extended into the statement of financial position credit column and eventually added to the capital account balance.

When all the items in the trial balance have been extended across into the statement of profit or loss and statement of financial position columns and the profit has been ascertained, the amounts in these columns are entered in the final version of the statement of profit or loss and statement of financial position. An illustration of the use of the extended trial balance is given in Worked Example 18.1.

WORKED EXAMPLE 18.1

T. King has an accounting year ending on 30 April. The following trial balance was prepared for the year ended 30 April 20X5:

	Debit	Credit
	£	£
Capital		59,640
Drawings	7,600	
Bank overdraft		1,540
Cash	1,170	
Plant and machinery	87,000	
Provision for depreciation on plant		27,000
Sales revenue		68,200
Purchases	42,160	
Trade receivables	15,200	
Trade payables		12,700
Allowance for irrecoverable receivables		890
Irrecoverable receivables	610	
Rent	4,200	
Light and heat	3,700	
Stationery	2,430	
Inventories	5,900	
	169,970	169,970

Additional information

1 Plant and machinery is depreciated using the reducing balance method at a rate of 10 per cent per annum.

2 The allowance for irrecoverable receivables at 30 April 20X5 should be 5 per cent of trade receivables.

3 There is an accrual at 30 April 20X5 in respect of gas amounting to £580, and rent prepaid of £600.

4 Inventory at 30 April 20X5 was £7,220.

You are required to prepare an extended trial balance at 30 April 20X5 and final financial statements in vertical form.

Workings

1 Depreciation = 10% × (£87,000 − £27,000) = £6,000

2 Allowance for irrecoverable receivables = (5% × £15,200) − £890 = £130 decrease.

The journal to post these two adjustments is as follows:

Date	Details (account in which the ledger entry is to be made)	Folio	Debit amount	Credit amount
20X5		**£**	**£**	
30 April	*Profit or loss a/c – Depreciation*	Dr	6,000	
	Provision for depreciation	Cr		6,000
	Being the depreciation on plant and machinery for the year now posted.			
30 April	*Allowance for irrecoverable receivables account*	Dr	130	
	Profit or loss a/c – Decrease in allowance for irrecoverable receivables	Cr		130
	Being the decrease in the allowance for irrecoverable receivables at the year end now posted.			

The extended trial balance is as follows:

T. King: Extended trial balance as at 30 April 20X5								
	Trial balance		*Adjustments*		*Profit or loss a/c*		*Statement of financial position*	
	Dr	**Cr**	**Dr**	**Cr**	**Dr**	**Cr**	**Dr**	**Cr**
	£	**£**	**£**	**£**	**£**	**£**	**£**	**£**
Capital		59,640	7,600					52,040
Drawings	7,600			7,600				
Bank overdraft		1,540						1,540
Cash	1,170						1,170	
Plant and machinery	87,000						87,000	
Provision for depreciation on plant		27,000		6,000	6,000			33,000
Sales revenue		68,200				68,200		
Purchases	42,160				42,160			
Trade receivables	15,200						15,200	
Trade payables		12,700						12,700
Allowance for irrecoverable receivables		890	130			130		760
Irrecoverable receivables	610				610			
Rent	4,200		600	600	3,600		600	
Light and heat	3,700		580	580	4,280			580
Stationery	2,430				2,430			
Inventories at 1 May 20X4	5,900				5,900			
Inventories at 30 April 20X5			7,220			7,220	7,220	
Profit for the period				10,570	10,570			10,570
	169,970	169,970			75,550	75,550	111,190	111,190

T. King: Statement of profit or loss for the year ended 30 April 20X5		
	£	£
Sales revenue		68,200
Less: Cost of sales:		
Inventories at 1 May 20X4	5,900	
Add: Purchases	42,160	
	48,060	
Less: Inventories at 30 April 20X5	7,220	40,840
Gross profit		27,360
Less: Expenditure		
Rent	3,600	
Reduction in the allowance for irrecoverable receivables	(130)	
Light and heat	4,280	
Stationery	2,430	
Irrecoverable receivables	610	
Depreciation on plant	6,000	16,790
Profit for the period		10,570

T. King: Statement of financial position as at 30 April 20X5			
ASSETS	£	£	£
Non-current assets	Cost	Acc. Depn	WDV
Plant and machinery	87,000	33,000	54,000
Current assets			
Inventories			7,220
Trade receivables		15,200	
Less: Allowance for irrecoverable receivables		760	14,440
Prepayments			600
Cash			1,170
			23,430
Total assets			77,430
OWNER'S CAPITAL AND LIABILITIES			
Owner's capital			
Opening balance			59,640
Add: Net profit			10,570
			70,210
Less: Drawings			7,600
Closing balance			62,610
Current liabilities			
Bank overdraft			1,540
Trade payables			12,700
Accruals			580
Total current liabilities			14,820
Total capital and liabilities			77,430

Finally, it should be observed that although the extended trial balance is common in practice (it is particularly used at the start of a trainee accountant's contract to refresh double-entry knowledge), the time allocated to answering examination questions is unlikely to allow for full presentation of the extended trial balance, and this is rarely a requirement.

Another approach to adjusting the trial balance is to reopen the ledger accounts and post the omitted transaction/adjustment and then to amend the trial balance, as is shown in Worked Example 17.3 in the previous chapter. The exercises at the end of this chapter use both approaches and the approach is shown in Worked Example 18.2. This example uses all the information from Worked Example 18.1 hence the question and workings are not re-prepared. In an examination setting, if you are not asked to prepare an extended trial balance then this approach will save you time. However, all workings and journals should also be prepared.

Learning Activity 18.1

Write out the journal entries in full for the accrual and inventory adjustment in Worked Example 18.1.

Some software packages keep the adjustments in the background, in a black box; however, some still allow the user to see the extended trial balance. An example is VT Final Accounts. You can get free access to this software package for a short period of time.

Learning Activity 18.2

Use Google images to see examples of extended trial balances. A variety of examples are available from different sources showing the layout and typical postings.

You could also go to the VT final accounts website to see how the accounting adjustments are catered for in an accounting software package.

REAL WORLD EXAMPLE 18.1

VT Final Accounts

VT Final Accounts runs in Microsoft Excel and produces professionally formatted statutory, sole trader and partnership accounts. A trial balance and up to 250 journals can be entered and a nominal report printed. A trial balance can also be imported from VT Transaction +, VT Cash Book and most other accounting packages.

Source: http://www.vtsoftware.co.uk/final_accounts/index.htm, September 2013.

WORKED EXAMPLE 18.2

T. King has an accounting year ending on 30 April.

The trial balance and additional information are as provided in Worked Example 18.1.

Using this information and the workings from Worked Example 18.1, you are required to prepare an amended trial balance at 30 April 20X5 after all workings have been posted. There is no need to re-prepare the financial statements.

The adjusted trial balance is prepared for the year ended 30 April 20X5 by amending the question as follows:

	Debit	Credit
	£	£
Capital		59,640
Drawings	7,600	
Bank overdraft		1,540
Cash	1,170	
Plant and machinery	87,000	
Provision for depreciation on plant (Cr 6,000)		33,000 ~~27,000~~
Sales revenue		68,200
Purchases	42,160	
Trade receivables	15,200	
Trade payables		12,700
Allowance for irrecoverable receivables (Dr 130)		760 ~~890~~
Irrecoverable receivables	610	
Rent (Cr 600)	3,600 ~~4,200~~	
Light and heat (Dr 580)	4,280 ~~3,700~~	
Stationery	2,430	
Inventories	5,900	
New ledger accounts		
Depreciation (Dr 6,000)	6,000	
Decrease in allowance for irrecoverable receivables (Cr 130)		130
Accrual – gas (Cr 580)		580
Prepayment – rent (Dr 600)	600	
Closing inventory – SOFP (Dr 7,220)	7,220	
Closing inventory – COGS (Cr 7,220)		7,220
	183,770	183,770

The financial statements can now be extracted from this adjusted trial balance.

Summary

The process of preparing final financial statements from a trial balance involves a number of adjustments relating to accounting for inventories, provisions for depreciation, allowances for irrecoverable receivables, and accruals and prepayments. In addition, it will be necessary to make further adjustments in respect of any inventories of tools, stationery, fuel, and so on. These are treated as a debit balance on the relevant expense account, and shown on the statement of financial position as a current asset. The remaining difference between the two sides of the expense account is transferred to the statement of profit or loss account, and represents the value of goods consumed during the year.

When trainee accountants start their training contract it is common practice to prepare final financial statements using an extended trial balance. This comprises the usual trial balance money columns but with additional money columns to the right. The first pair of these comprises adjustment columns that are used to make the adjustments referred to above. The second pair represents the entries in the statement of profit or loss; and the third pair represents the amounts shown in the statement of financial position. The amounts that are entered in the statement of profit or loss and statement of financial position columns are ascertained by cross-casting the figures relating to each ledger account shown in the original trial balance and the adjustment columns.

Key terms and concepts

adjustments 310

extended trial balance 310

An asterisk after the question number indicates that there is a suggested answer in Appendix 2.

Exercises

connect

BASIC

18.1 The trial balance for Jock at 31 December 20X4 is as follows:

	Debit £	Credit £
Sales revenue		10,000
Trade receivables	5,000	
Allowance for irrecoverable receivables		250
Purchases	2,000	
Trade payables		1,000
Provision for discounts		100
Rent	200	
Rates	300	
Inventories	100	
Motor car	10,000	
Provision for depreciation		2,000
Bank	5,000	
Capital account		9,250
	22,600	22,600

Additional information

1 Closing inventory value is £500.

2 The rates in the trial balance cover the 15 months to 31 March 20X5.

3 The motor car is depreciated using 20 per cent straight-line method.

4 A credit customer with a balance on his account of £1,000 is bankrupt.

5 Remove the provision for discounts and provide for a 10 per cent allowance for irrecoverable receivables.

Required

a Prepare the statement of profit or loss for Jock for the year ended 31 December 20X4.

b Prepare the statement of financial position at the same date.

(*Note*: An adjusted trial balance is not required. Show all the adjustments to the ledger accounts.)

BASIC

18.2 B. Good drew up the following trial balance as at 31 March 20X5.

	Debit £	Credit £
Sundry expenses	1,090	
Rent received		200
Office expenses	560	
Insurance	525	
Wages and expenses	4,580	
Telephone	1,250	
Purchases and sales revenue	125,560	189,560
Motor expenses	569	
Rent	2,500	
Rates	1,250	
Carriage outwards	546	
Carriage inwards	200	
Returns outwards		302
Return inwards	560	
Building	230,000	
Motor vehicle	12,500	
Fixtures	5,365	
Trade receivables and payables	28,560	48,560
Cash	12	
Bank		32,250
Drawings	5,562	
Capital		178,907
Opening inventories	28,590	
	449,779	449,779

Closing information included the following:

1 Inventories at the year end were valued at £35,650.

2 An accrual for wages of £400 has still to be posted.

3 The last rent payment (on 15 February) for £1,000 covered the period 1 February to 31 May 20X5.

4 A rates prepayment has been calculated at £250.

5 An accrual for sundry expenses of £110 has still to be posted.

6 Rent income owing at the year end amounted to £100.

Required

Prepare the statement of profit or loss for the year ended 31 March 20X5 and the statement of financial position as at 31 March 20X5.

(*Note*: An adjusted trial balance is not required. Show all the adjustments to the ledger accounts.)

18.3 The balances extracted from the books of Cara Van at 31 December 20X4 are given below:

BASIC

	£
Drawings	7,180
Heating and lighting	1,234
Stationery and postage	268
Carriage outwards	1,446
Insurance	1,818
Wages and salaries	18,910
Inventories at 1 January 20X4	42,120
Purchases	74,700
Sales revenue	131,040
Rent and rates	2,990
General expenses	1,460
Discount received	426
Plant and machinery	9,060
Cash at bank	3,222
Cash in hand	65
Trade receivables	1,920
Trade payables	630
Sales returns	1,310
Purchases returns	747

Required

a Prepare the trial balance.

b What is the missing account?

Additional information

At 31 December 20X4:

1 Inventories are valued at £33,990.

2 Rent amounting to £310 is still owing.

3 Insurance paid in advance is £220.

Required

c Prepare the statement of profit or loss for the year ended 31 December 20X4 and a statement of financial position at that date, after adjusting for the other information that has come to light.

(*Note*: An adjusted trial balance is not required; show the adjustments to the ledger accounts.)

BASIC

18.4 The following trial balance has been prepared from the books and records of Sulphur Products as at 30 September 20X4. We are also told that the figures have to be amended to take into account further adjustments (see below).

Sulphur Products
Trial balance at 30 September 20X4

	Debit	Credit
	£	£
Capital		99,000
Drawings	9,000	
Vehicles	60,000	
Trade payables		47,000
Trade receivables	37,000	
Inventories (1 October 20X3)	12,000	
Rent	15,400	
Telephone	1,800	
Postage	300	
Electricity	2,100	
Bank	22,000	
Returns inwards	4,000	
Returns outwards		2,500
Allowance for irrecoverable receivables		900
Purchases	213,000	
Sales revenue		370,000
Plant and equipment	147,000	
Discounts received		6,000
Bank charges	1,800	
	525,400	525,400

Additional information

1 A trade customer has become bankrupt and £2,000 of their balance owing has yet to be written off.

2 The allowance for irrecoverable receivables is to be 3 per cent of trade receivables.

3 There are unpaid bills for electricity £200 and telephone £300.

4 Rent is payable at £3,300 per quarter, and has been paid until the end of November 20X4.

5 The value of inventories at 30 September 20X3 is £16,500.

6 Depreciation is to be provided on Plant and Equipment (25 per cent reducing balance method).

Required

Prepare a statement of profit or loss for Sulphur Products for the period ending 30 September 20X4 and a statement of financial position at that date.

(*Note*: An adjusted trial balance is not required. Show all the adjustments to the ledger accounts).

INTERMEDIATE

18.5* The following is the trial balance of C. Jones as at 31 December 20X4:

	Debit £	Credit £
Owner's capital		45,214
Drawings	9,502	
Purchases	389,072	
Sales revenue		527,350
Wages and salaries	33,440	
Rent and rates	9,860	
Light and heat	4,142	
Irrecoverable receivables	1,884	
Allowance for irrecoverable receivables		3,702
Trade receivables	72,300	
Trade payables		34,308
Cash at bank	2,816	
Cash in hand	334	
Inventories	82,124	
Motor car – cost	7,200	
– depreciation		2,100
	612,674	612,674

Additional information

1 Inventories at 31 December 20X4 are valued at £99,356.

2 The rent of the premises is £6,400 per annum, payable half-yearly in advance on 31 March and 30 September.

3 Rates for the year ending 31 March 20X5 amounting to £1,488 were paid on 10 April 20X4.

4 Wages and salaries to be accrued amount to £3,012.

5 Depreciation on the car is to be provided using the straight-line method at a rate of 20 per cent per annum.

6 It has been agreed that further receivables amounting to £1,420 are to be written off against specific customers, and the closing allowance is to be adjusted to 5 per cent of the revised trade receivables figure.

Required

Prepare the statement of profit or loss for the year ended 31 December 20X4, and a statement of financial position at that date. This should be done using an extended trial balance.

INTERMEDIATE

18.6* The following is the trial balance of J. Clark at 31 March 20X5:

	Debit £	Credit £
Capital		60,000
Drawings	5,600	
Purchases/sales revenue	34,260	58,640
Returns inwards/outwards	3,260	2,140
Carriage inwards	730	
Carriage outwards	420	
Discount allowed/received	1,480	1,970
Plant and machinery at cost	11,350	
Provision for depreciation on plant		4,150
Motor vehicles	13,290	
Provision for depreciation on vehicles		2,790
Goodwill	5,000	
Quoted investments	6,470	
Freehold premises at cost	32,000	
Mortgage on premises		10,000
Interest paid/received	1,000	460
Inventories	4,670	
Bank and cash	2,850	
Salaries	7,180	
Rent and rates	4,300	
Allowance for irrecoverable receivables		530
Trade receivables/payables	8,070	4,340
Light and heat	2,640	
Stationery	450	
	145,020	145,020

Additional information

1 Goods on sale or return have been treated as sales. These cost £300 and were invoiced to the customer for £400.

2 The allowance for irrecoverable receivables is to be adjusted to 10 per cent of trade receivables.

3 At 31 March 20X5 there is electricity accrued of £130 and rates prepaid amounting to £210.

4 Inventories at 31 March 20X5 were valued at £3,690.

5 During the year the proprietor has taken goods costing £350 from the business for his own use.

6 Depreciation on plant is 25 per cent on the reducing balance method and on vehicles 20 per cent by the same method.

7 Unrecorded in the ledger is the sale on credit on 1 July 20X4 for £458 of a motor vehicle bought on 1 January 20X3 for £1,000.

8 There are irrecoverable receivables of £370 that have not been entered in the ledger.

9 There was an inventory of stationery at 31 March 20X5, which cost £230.

Required

Prepare a statement of profit or loss for the year and a statement of financial position at the end of the year.

INTERMEDIATE

18.7 The following trial balance has been extracted from the ledger of Andrea Howell, a sole trader, as at 31 May 20X5, the end of her most recent financial year.

	Debit £	Credit £
Property, at cost	90,000	
Equipment, at cost	57,500	
Provision for depreciation (as at 1 June 20X4)		
– property		12,500
– equipment		32,500
Inventories as at 1 June 20X4	27,400	
Purchases and sales revenue	259,600	405,000
Discounts allowed and received	3,370	4,420
Wages and salaries	52,360	
Irrecoverable receivables	1,720	
Loan interest	1,560	
Carriage out	5,310	
Other operating expenses	38,800	
Trade receivables and payables	46,200	33,600
Allowance for irrecoverable receivables		280
Cash on hand	151	
Bank overdraft		14,500
Drawings	28,930	
13% loan		12,000
Capital, as at 1 June 20X4		98,101
	612,901	612,901

The following additional information as at 31 May 20X5 is available:

1 Inventories as at the close of business were valued at £25,900.

2 Depreciation for the year ended 31 May 20X5 has yet to be provided as follows:

Property: 1 per cent using the straight-line method.
Equipment: 15 per cent using the straight-line method.

3 Wages and salaries are accrued by £140.

4 'Other operating expenses' include certain expenses prepaid by £500. Other expenses included under this heading are accrued by £200.

5 The allowance for irrecoverable receivables is to be adjusted so that it is 0.5 per cent of trade receivables as at 31 May 20X5.

6 'Purchases' include goods valued at £1,040 that were withdrawn by Mrs Howell for her own personal use.

Required

Prepare Mrs Howell's statement of profit or loss for the year ended 31 May 20X5 and her statement of financial position as at 31 May 20X5.

(AAT, adapted)

INTERMEDIATE

18.8 S. Trader carries on a merchandising business. The following balances have been extracted from his books on 30 September 20X5:

	£
Capital – S. Trader, at 1 Oct 20X4	24,239
Office furniture and equipment	1,440
Cash drawings – S. Trader	4,888
Inventories on hand – 1 Oct 20X4	14,972
Purchases	167,760
Sales revenue	203,845
Rent	1,350
Light and heat	475
Insurance	304
Salaries	6,352
Stationery and printing	737
Telephone and postage	517
General expenses	2,044
Travellers' commission and expenses	9,925
Discounts allowed	517
Discounts received	955
Irrecoverable receivables written off	331
Trade receivables	19,100
Trade payables	8,162
Balance at bank to S. Trader's credit	6,603
Petty cash in hand	29
Allowance for irrecoverable receivables	143

The following further information is to be taken into account:

1 Inventories on hand on 30 September 20X5 were valued at £12,972.

2 Provision is to be made for the following liabilities and accrued expenses as at 30 September 20X5: rent £450; lighting and heating £136; travellers' commission and expenses £806; accountancy charges £252.

3 Allowance for irrecoverable receivables is to be raised to 3 per cent of the closing trade receivable balance.

4 Office furniture and equipment is to be depreciated by 10 per cent on book value.

5 Mr Trader had removed inventory costing £112 for his own use during the year.

Required

a Prepare a statement of profit or loss for the year ended 30 September 20X5 grouping the various expenses under suitable headings; and

b a statement of financial position as at that date.

(ACCA, adapted)

INTERMEDIATE

18.9 F. Harrison is in business as a trader. A trial balance taken out as at 31 January 20X5 was as follows:

	Debit £	Credit £
Purchases	42,400	
Sales revenue		50,240
Returns inwards and outwards	136	348
Salaries and wages	4,100	
Rent, rates and insurance	860	
Sundry expenses	750	
Irrecoverable receivables	134	
Allowance for irrecoverable receivables at 1 February 20X4		280
Inventories on hand at 1 February 20X4	13,630	
Fixtures and fittings:		
At 1 February 20X4	1,400	
Additions on 30 September 20X4	240	
Motor vehicles:		
At 1 February 20X4	920	
Sale of vehicle (book value at 1 February 20X4: £80)		120
Sundry trade receivables and payables	4,610	3,852
Cash at bank and in hand	3,820	
F. Harrison: Capital a/c		20,760
F. Harrison: Drawings a/c	2,600	
	75,600	75,600

The following information is to be taken into account:

1 Included in sales are goods on sale or return that cost £240 and which have been charged out with profit added at 20 per cent of sale price.

2 Outstanding amounts not entered in the books were: rent £36, sundry expenses £90.

3 Prepayments were: rates £60, insurance £10.

4 Inventories on hand on 31 January 20X5 were valued at £15,450.

5 Allowance for irrecoverable receivables is to be changed to £340.

6 Depreciation is to be provided for as follows: fixtures and fittings 10 per cent per annum, motor vehicles 25 per cent per annum.

Required

Prepare a statement of profit or loss for the year ended 31 January 20X5, and draw up a statement of financial position as on that date.

(ACCA, adapted)

INTERMEDIATE

18.10 The trial balance extracted from the books of Mary, a sole trader, as at 31 December 20X5 was as follows:

	Debit £	Credit £
Capital		112,190
Furniture and equipment (cost £21,000)	16,400	
Motor vans (cost £17,000)	11,200	
Purchases	362,910	
Sales revenue		456,220
Rent and rates	8,000	
Salaries	39,690	
Irrecoverable receivables	2,810	
General expenses	10,620	
Bank balance	3,080	
Allowance for irrecoverable receivables		2,690
Inventory at 1 January 20X5	87,260	
Trade receivables	42,890	
Trade payables		31,640
Drawings	17,880	
	602,740	602,740

Additional information

1 Inventory on hand on 31 December 20X5 is £94,280.

2 Rates paid in advance at 31 December 20X5 are £600.

3 General expenses unpaid at 31 December 20X5 are £1,660.

4 Allowance for irrecoverable receivables is to be adjusted to £2,410.

5 A motor van purchased on 1 January of this year at a cost of £8,000 was traded in for £3,500 on 31 December 20X5 and a new van purchased at a cost of £10,000 on the same day. The amount due on the new van was payable on 1 January 20X6. No entries had been made in the books in respect of this transaction when the trial balance at 31 December 20X5 was extracted.

6 Depreciation is to be charged on furniture and equipment at the rate of 5 per cent per annum on cost and at the rate of 25 per cent per annum (reducing balance method) on motor vehicles.

Required

Prepare Mary's statement of profit or loss for the year ended 31 December 20X5 and statement of financial position as at 31 December 20X5.

PART FOUR
Internal control and check

19 The bank reconciliation statement 329
20 Control accounts 347
21 Errors and suspense accounts 367
22 Single entry and incomplete records 383

Chapter 19

The bank reconciliation statement

Learning Objectives:

After reading this chapter you should be able to do the following:

1. Explain the purpose and nature of bank reconciliations.
2. Identify and correct errors and omissions in a cash book.
3. Identify outstanding/unpresented items that are not yet in the bank statement.
4. Prepare a bank reconciliation statement.
5. List the advantages of preparing a bank reconciliation statement.

19.1 The purpose and preparation of bank reconciliations

The purpose of preparing a **bank reconciliation statement** is to ascertain whether or not the balance shown in the cash book at the end of a given accounting period is correct by comparing it with that shown on the bank statement supplied by the bank. In practice, these two figures are rarely the same because of errors, omissions and the timing of bank deposits and cheque payments.

The bank reconciliation is not part of the double-entry system. It must be prepared at least yearly before the final financial statements are compiled. Because most businesses usually have a large number of cheque transactions, they often prepare a bank reconciliation statement either monthly or at least quarterly. The bank reconciliation should always be prepared by someone who is not involved in either writing cheques or dealing with lodgements (not the cashier). There should be segregation of duties. The bank reconciliation is not only the first step to take when preparing an entity's financial statements, it also has a very important control function within a company's accounting systems as it helps to verify the validity and accuracy of transactions and serves as an important deterrent to fraud. An example of fraud where this control was not being exercised is given in Real World Example 19.1. In this example the employee kept the cash records and prepared the daily cash reconciliation, therefore was able to exclude items from the records and hence the reconciliation. This highlights the importance of having segregation of duties when cash is involved. A recommendation is that two people are present when the post is opened, one to open the post and to list the items received, the other to record the funds received in the relevant ledger; both should be present at the same time.

REAL WORLD EXAMPLE 19.1

HM Treasury publishes case notes on recent UK frauds

Transactions involving receipts of cash or cheques are high risk. Of the cases of staff fraud reported to the Treasury each year, a significant proportion involves misappropriation of cash. In this sample case, a member of staff committed a number of frauds over a period of five years, resulting in a loss of over £10,000.

The organisation's business included the *receipt of cheques* through the post and cash and cheques over the counter. It was the responsibility of the member of staff to receive, record and *prepare the receipts for banking*. She had been in the job several years and her line managers, who trusted her implicitly, had given her *sole responsibility for these duties*. They were no longer carrying out checks or monitoring the process.

She would arrive early each morning, usually before her colleagues, *and open the post on her own*. Money handed in over the counters was also passed to her for banking. However, she *did not record or account for the cheques or money* prior to banking. She would, however, complete a daily cash balance record as part of the *banking reconciliation procedures*, but by this time she had already removed some of the cash and a number of cheques. There were *no independent cross-checks* between the documentation which came with the receipts and the amounts sent for banking. To make matters worse *written procedures were out of date* and had fallen into disuse.

The fraud came to light during the officer's *infrequent absences on leave*. A minor query by a member of the public regarding a previous payment led to an unexplained difference between the amount quoted in the documentation accompanying the payment and the amount recorded by the officer and banked. Internal audit were brought in to carry out an initial investigation. They identified major discrepancies between records of receipts kept by counter staff, documentation accompanying payments from members of the public and the amounts being banked. The police were called in and under questioning the officer admitted the offences. She had opened a bank account with the initials of the organisation and had been paying in cash and cheques over a five-year period. The case was taken to court and on conviction she was given a custodial sentence and had to repay the amounts stolen.

Source: HM Treasury, 'Fraud Case Notes', pp. 1–45, http://www.xact.org.uk/information/downloads/Fraud/Fraud_case_notes.pdf, accessed September 2013.

The adjustment and reconciliation items to look out for when preparing a bank reconciliation are summarized in Figure 19.1.

Figure 19.1

Unrecorded items

- Omitted items
- Payments and sometimes receipts that are on the bank statement but which have not been entered in the cash book
- **Unrecorded cheques** include dishonoured cheques, bank charges and interest, standing orders for hire purchase instalments, insurance premiums and loan interest
- **Unrecorded lodgements** include interest and dividends received by credit transfer

Unpresented items

- Also called outstanding items
- Timing differences
- These are receipts and payments in the cash book that at the date of the reconciliation have not yet been entered by the bank on the bank statement
- **Unpresented lodgements** are debit entries in the cash book but are not on the bank statement (not yet cleared)
- **Unpresented cheques** are credit entries in the cash book but are not on the bank statement (either the supplier has not yet put the cheque in the bank or the cheque has not yet cleared)

Other adjustments

- Dishonoured cheques
- Out-of-date cheques
- Errors. For example, a transposition error (a cheque for £189 has been entered into the cash book as £198), an incorrect entry to the cash book or an incorrect entry by the bank

Procedures when preparing a bank reconciliation

The reconciliation procedure

The reconciliation procedure can be split into four areas as identified in Figure 19.2.

Worked Example 19.1 shows the procedure involved in preparing a bank reconciliation statement.

Figure 19.2

Step 1: • Tick off the items that appear in both the cash book and the bank statement.

Step 2: • Identify all the items that have not been ticked

Step 3: • Adjust the bank ledger account in our books for items in the bank statement of which we have no record (unrecorded transactions).

Step 4: • Reconcile the adjusted balance in the cash book to the balance on the bank statement in a bank reconciliation statement – differences are those of timing (outstanding transactions).

Step 5: • Adjust for any errors (typically the cash book only).

The reconciliation procedure

WORKED EXAMPLE 19.1

The following is the cash book of J. Alton for the month of June 20X4

Cash book

20X4	Details	£		20X4	Details	£	
1 June	Balance b/d	1,000		2 June	D. Cat	240	√
11 June	A. Hand	370	√	13 June	E. Dog	490	√
16 June	B. Leg	510	√	22 June	F. Bird	750	
24 June	C. Arm	620		30 June	Balance c/d	1,200	
30 June	Cash	180					
		2,680				2,680	

The following is the statement of J. Alton received from his bank:

Bank statement

Date	Details	Debit £		Credit £		Balance £
20X4						
1 June	Balance					1,000
5 June	D. Cat	240	√			760
15 June	A. Hand			370	√	1,130

18 June	E. Dog	490	√			640
20 June	Dividend received			160		800
21 June	B. Leg			510	√	1,310
30 June	Bank charges	75				1,235

In practice, bank statements do not usually show the names of the people from whom cheques were received and paid. It is therefore necessary to identify the payments by means of the cheque number. However, the use of names simplifies the example for ease of understanding. The procedure is essentially the same.

The first step is to tick all those items which appear in both the cash book and on the bank statement during the month of June. A note is then made of the items which are unticked:

1 *Outstanding lodgements*: Cheques and cash paid into the bank and entered in the cash book but not credited on the bank statement by 30 June 20X4 = C. Arm £620 + Cash £180 = £800.

2 *Outstanding cheques*: Cheques drawn and entered in the cash book not presented for payment by 30 June 20X4 = F. Bird £750.

3 *Unrecorded lodgements*: Amounts received by credit transfer shown on the bank statement not entered in the cash book = Dividends £160.

4 *Unrecorded cheques*: Standing orders and other payments shown on the bank statement not entered in the cash book = Bank charges £75.

Clearly, items 1 and 2 above will eventually appear on the bank statement in a later month. Items 3 and 4 must be entered in the cash book. However, the purpose of the bank reconciliation statement is to ascertain whether the difference between the balance in the cash book at 30 June 20X4 of £1,200 and that shown on the bank statement at the same date of £1,235 is explained by the above list of unticked items. Alternatively, are there other errors or omissions that need to be investigated?

The bank reconciliation statement will appear as follows:

J. Alton: Bank reconciliation statement as at 30 June 20X4

		£	£
Balance per cash book			1,200
Add:	Dividends received not entered in cash book	160	
	Cheques not yet presented	750	910
			2,110
Less:	Bank charges not entered in cash book	75	
	Amounts not yet credited	800	875
Balance per bank statement			1,235

It can thus be seen that since the above statement reconciles the difference between the balances in the cash book and on the bank statement, there are unlikely to be any further errors or omissions.

Notes

1 The dividends received are added to the cash book balance because it is lower than the bank statement balance as a result of this omission. In addition, it will increase by this amount when the dividends are entered in the cash book.

2 The bank charges are deducted from the cash book balance because the bank statement balance has been reduced by this amount but the cash book balance has not. In addition, the cash book balance will decrease by this amount when the bank charges are entered in the cash book.

3 The cheques not yet presented are added to the cash book balance because it has been reduced by this amount whereas the bank statement balance has not.

4 The amounts not yet credited are deducted from the cash book balance because it has been increased by this amount whereas the bank statement balance has not.

Sometimes in examination questions the student is not given the cash book balance. In this case the bank reconciliation statement is prepared in reverse order as follows:

	£	£
Balance per bank statement		1,235
Add: Amounts not yet credited	800	
Payments on bank statement not in the cash book	75	875
		2,110
Less: Cheques not yet presented	750	
Receipts on bank statement not in the cash book	160	910
= Balance per cash book		1,200

An alternative method of dealing with bank reconciliation is to amend the cash book for any errors and omissions, and only include in the bank reconciliation statement those items that constitute timing differences. Pro forma cash book (ledger account) entries are now prepared for reference when doing questions (see Figures 19.3 and 19.4), as is the bank reconciliation.

Figure 19.3

Bank 'T'/ledger account adjustments

Cash book

Bal b/d	XX	Bounced cheques	XX
Unrecorded lodgements	XX	Unrecorded cheques	XX
Errors	X	Errors	X
		Bal c/d	XX
	XXX		XXX
Bal b/d	XX		

A pro forma example of the entries required to adjust the cash book (ledger account) when performing a bank reconciliation

Figure 19.4

Bank statement adjustments	
Balance per statement	XX
Add: outstanding lodgements	XX
	XX
Less: outstanding cheques	XX
Balance per adjusted cash book	XX

A pro forma example of a bank statement reconciliation

This approach is illustrated in Worked Example 19.2, along with some other items frequently found in examination questions.

WORKED EXAMPLE 19.2

The following is a summary from the cash book of Home Shopping Ltd for March 20X4:

Cash book			
	£		£
Opening balance b/d	5,610	Payments	41,890
Receipts	37,480	Closing balance c/d	1,200
	43,090		43,090

When checking the cash book against the bank statement the following discrepancies were found:

1 Bank charges of £80 shown in the bank statement have not been entered in the cash book.

2 The bank has debited a cheque for £370 in error to the company's account.

3 Cheques totalling £960 have not yet been presented to the bank for payment.

4 Dividends received of £420 have been credited on the bank statement but not recorded in the cash book.

5 There are cheques received of £4,840 that are entered in the cash book but not yet credited to the company's account by the bank.

6 A cheque for £170 has been returned by the bank marked 'refer to drawer' but no entry relating to this has been made in the books.

7 The opening balance in the cash book should have been £6,510 and not £5,610.

8 The bank statement shows that there is an overdraft at 31 March 20X5 of £1,980.

Required

a Make the entries necessary to correct the cash book.

b Prepare a bank reconciliation statement as at 31 March 20X5.

Cash book			
	£		£
Balance b/d	1,200	Bank charges	80
Dividends	420	Refer to drawer	170
Error in balance	900	Balance c/d	2,270
	2,520		2,520
Balance b/d	2,270		

Home Shopping Ltd
Bank reconciliation statement as at 31 March 20X5

	£	£
Balance per cash book		2,270
Add: Cheques not yet presented		960
		3,230
Less: Amounts not yet credited	4,840	
Cheque debited in error	370	5,210
Balance per bank statement (overdrawn)		(1,980)

Note

The cheque debited in error is shown in the bank reconciliation statement rather than the cash book because it will presumably be corrected on the bank statement in due course and thus will not affect the cash book.

Sometimes in examination questions the cash book contains a credit (i.e. overdrawn) balance. In this case, the bank reconciliation statement is prepared by reversing the additions and subtractions that are made when there is a favourable cash book balance. The bank reconciliation statement will thus appear as follows:

Balance per cash book (credit/overdrawn)
Add: Amounts not yet credited
Less: Cheques not yet presented
= Balance per bank statement

Alternatively, if the cash book balance is not given in the question and the bank statement contains an overdrawn balance, the bank reconciliation statement would be prepared as follows:

Balance per bank statement (debit/overdrawn)
Add: Cheques not yet presented
Less: Amounts not yet credited
= Balance per cash book

Learning Activity 19.1

Collect all the receipts received for purchases made using your debit card within the past two weeks and record them in a list. Then log onto your internet banking site and download your most recent bank statement. Prepare a reconciliation between the items recorded on your bank statement with that shown on your transaction list. The transactions should affect your bank balance either on the date of the receipt or on the following day. Alternatively if you have a cheque book, prepare a reconciliation of the transactions shown on your bank statement with that shown on your record of cheques received and drawn. A longer delay is expected as it takes a couple of days for a cheque to be processed. Note the number of items that are automatically taken from your bank account – these are unrecorded items.

Summary

After extracting a trial balance but before preparing final financial statements at the end of each accounting year, the first thing that needs to be done is to check the accuracy of the cash book (or *bank account* in the ledger). This takes the form of a bank reconciliation, which involves reconciling the balance in the cash book at the end of the year with that shown on the statement received from the bank. These will probably be different for two main reasons. First, there may be errors or omissions where amounts shown on the bank statement have not been entered properly in the cash book. These should be corrected in the cash book. Second, there are likely to be timing differences. These consist of cheques paid into the bank and cheques drawn entered in the cash book, but not shown on the bank statement at the end of the year. These timing differences are entered on the bank reconciliation statement as explanations for the difference between the balance in the cash book and that on the bank statement. If the timing differences provide a reconciliation of the two balances, the cash book balance is deemed to be correct. Otherwise, the reasons for any remaining difference will need to be investigated.

Key terms and concepts

bank reconciliation statement	330	unrecorded cheques	331
unpresented cheques	331	unrecorded lodgements	331
unpresented lodgements	331		

An asterisk after the question number indicates that there is a suggested answer in Appendix 2.

Review questions

connect

19.1 Explain the purpose of a bank reconciliation statement.

19.2 Describe the procedures involved in the collection of the data needed to prepare a bank reconciliation statement.

Exercises

connect

INTERMEDIATE

19.3 The following is the cash book of T. Trading for the month of September 20X4:

20X4		£	20X4		£
1 Sept	Balance b/d	2,000	2 Sept	Cheque 101	480
11 Sept	Lodgement	740	13 Sept	Cheque 102	980
16 Sept	Lodgement	1,020	22 Sept	Cheque 103	1,500
24 Sept	Lodgement	1,240	30 Sept	Balance c/d	2,400
30 Sept	Lodgement	360			
		5,360			5,360

The following is the bank statement received for T. Trading for the month of September 20X4:

Date	Details	Debit	Credit	Balance
20X4				
1 Sept	Balance			2,000
5 Sept	101	480		1,520
15 Sept	Lodgement		740	2,260
18 Sept	102	980		1,280
20 Sept	Credit transfer		320	1,600
21 Sept	Lodgement		1,020	2,620
30 Sept	Bank charges	150		2,470

Required

Prepare the bank reconciliation as at 30 September 20X4.

INTERMEDIATE

19.4 The following is a summary from the cash book of Hozy Co. Ltd for October 20X4:

Cash book

	£		£
Opening balance b/d	1,407	Payments	15,520
Receipts	15,073	Closing balance c/d	960
	16,480		16,480

On investigation you discover that:

1 Bank charges of £35 shown on the bank statement have not been entered in the cash book.

2 A cheque drawn for £47 has been entered in error as a receipt.

3 A cheque for £18 has been returned by the bank marked 'refer to drawer', but it has not been written back in the cash book.

4 An error of transposition has occurred in that the opening balance in the cash book should have been carried down as £1,470.

5 Three cheques paid to suppliers for £214, £370 and £30 have not yet been presented to the bank.

6 The last page of the paying-in book shows a deposit of £1,542 that has not yet been credited to the account by the bank.

7 The bank has debited a cheque for £72 in error to the company's account.

8 The bank statement shows an overdrawn balance of £124.

Required

a Show what adjustments you would make in the cash book.

b Prepare a bank reconciliation statement as at 31 October 20X4.

(ACCA, adapted)

19.5* The following is a summary of the cash book of Grow Ltd for March 20X5: INTERMEDIATE

Cash book

	£		£
Opening balance b/d	4,120	Payments	46,560
Receipts	45,320	Closing balance c/d	2,880
	49,440		49,440

On investigation you discover that at 31 March 20X5:

1 The last page of the paying-in book shows a deposit of £1,904 that has not yet been credited by the bank.

2 Two cheques paid to suppliers for £642 and £1,200 have not yet been presented to the bank.

3 Dividends received of £189 are shown on the bank statement but not entered in the cash book.

4 Bank charges of £105 shown on the bank statement have not been entered in the cash book.

5 A cheque for £54 has been returned by the bank marked 'refer to drawer', but it has not been written back in the cash book.

6 A cheque drawn for £141 has been entered in error as a receipt in the cash book.

7 The bank has debited a cheque for £216 in error to the company's account.

Required

a Show the adjustments that should be made in the cash book.

b Prepare a bank reconciliation statement at 31 March 20X5.

19.6* On 15 May 20X5 Mrs Lake received her monthly bank statement for the month ended 30 April 20X5. The bank statement contained the following details: INTERMEDIATE

Date	Particulars	Payments	Receipts	Balance
		£	£	£
1 Apr	Balance			1,053.29
2 Apr	236127	210.70		842.59
3 Apr	Bank Giro Credit		192.35	1,034.94
6 Apr	236126	15.21		1,019.73
6 Apr	Charges	12.80		1,006.93
9 Apr	236129	43.82		963.11
10 Apr	427519	19.47		943.64
12 Apr	236128	111.70		831.94
17 Apr	Standing Order	32.52		799.42
20 Apr	Sundry Credit		249.50	1,048.92
23 Apr	236130	77.87		971.05
23 Apr	236132	59.09		911.96
25 Apr	Bank Giro Credit		21.47	933.43
27 Apr	Sundry Credit		304.20	1,237.63
30 Apr	236133	71.18		1,166.45

For the corresponding period, Mrs Lake's own records contained the following bank account:

Date	Details	£	Date	Details	Cheque No	£
1 Apr	Balance	827.38	5 Apr	Purchases	128	111.70
2 Apr	Sales revenue	192.35	10 Apr	Electricity	129	43.82
18 Apr	Sales revenue	249.50	16 Apr	Purchases	130	87.77
24 Apr	Sales revenue	304.20	18 Apr	Rent	131	30.00
30 Apr	Sales revenue	192.80	20 Apr	Purchases	132	59.09
			25 Apr	Purchases	133	71.18
			30 Apr	Wages	134	52.27
			30 Apr	Balance		1,310.40
		1,766.23				1,766.23

Required

a Prepare a statement reconciling the balance at 30 April as given by the bank statement to the balance at 30 April as stated in the bank account.

b Explain briefly which items in your bank reconciliation statement would require further investigation.

(ACCA, adapted)

INTERMEDIATE

19.7 A young and inexperienced bookkeeper is having great difficulty in producing a bank reconciliation statement at 31 December. He gives you his attempt to produce a summarized cash book, and also the bank statement received for the month of December. These are shown below. You may assume that the bank statement is correct. You may also assume that the trial balance at 1 January did indeed show a bank overdraft of £7,000.12.

Cash book summary – draft

	£	£	£	
1 Jan			35,000.34	Payments Jan–Nov
Opening overdraft		7,000.12		
Jan–Nov receipts	39,500.54			
Add: Discounts	500.02			
		40,000.56	12,000.34	Balance 30 Nov
		47,000.68	47,000.68	
1 Dec		12,000.34		Payments Dec
				Cheque No.
Dec receipts	178.19		37.14	7654
	121.27		192.79	7655
	14.92		5,000.00	7656
	16.88		123.45	7657
		329.26	678.90	7658
			1.47	7659
Dec receipts	3,100.00		19.84	7660
	171.23		10.66	7661
	1,198.17	4,469.40	10,734.75	Balance c/d
		16,799.00	16,799.00	
31 Dec balance		10,734.75		

Bank statement – 31 December					
	Withdrawals	Deposits			Balance
	£	£			£
			1 Dec	O/D	800.00
7650	300.00	178.19			
7653	191.91	121.27			
7654	37.14	14.92			
7651	1,111.11	16.88			
7656	5,000.00	3,100.00			
7655	129.79	171.23			
7658	678.90	1,198.17			
Standing order	50.00	117.98			
7659	1.47				
7661	10.66				
Bank charges	80.00		31 Dec	O/D	3,472.34

Required

a A corrected cash book summary and a reconciliation of the balance on this revised summary with the bank statement balance as at 31 December, as far as you are able.

b A brief note as to the likely cause of any remaining difference.

(ACCA)

INTERMEDIATE

19.8 The statement of financial position and statement of profit or loss of Faults Ltd show the following two items:

Bank balance – overdrawn	£3,620
Statement of profit or loss – profit for year	£23,175

However, the balance as shown on the bank statement does not agree with the balance as shown in the cash book. Your investigation of this matter reveals the following differences, and additional information:

1 Cheque payments entered in the cash book but not presented to the bank until after the year end – £3,138.

2 Bankings entered in the cash book but not credited by the bank until after the year end – £425.

3 Cheques for £35 and £140 received from customers were returned by the bank as dishonoured, but no entries concerning these events have been made in the cash book.

4 Items shown on bank statements but not entered in the cash book:

- Bank charges, £425.
- Standing order – hire purchase repayments on purchase of motor car, 12 @ £36.
- Standing order – being quarterly rent of warehouse, £125, due on each quarter day.
- Dividend received on investment, £90.

5 The cheques were returned by the bank for the following reasons: the £35 cheque requires an additional signature and should be honoured in due course; the £140 cheque was unpaid due to the bankruptcy of the drawer and should be treated as an irrecoverable receivable.

6 The hire purchase repayments of £36 represent £30 capital and £6 interest.

7 A cheque for £45 received from a customer in settlement of his account had been entered in the cash book as £450 on the payments side, analysed to the purchases ledger column and later posted.

Required

a Prepare a statement reconciling the cash book balance with the bank statement.

b A statement showing the effect of the alterations on the profit for the period.

(ACCA, adapted)

INTERMEDIATE

19.9 The bank statement for G. Graduate for the period ended 30 June 20X5 was received. On investigation it emerged that the balance per the statement was different to the balance per the cash book. The cash book showed a debit balance of £5,944. On examination the following differences were found:

1 Cheques issued amounting to £9,350 were still outstanding and did not go through the bank until July 20X5.

2 A customer, who received a cash discount of 5 per cent on his account of £500, paid the company by cheque on 15 June 20X5. The bookkeeper, in error, entered the gross amount in the cash book.

3 A deposit of £984 paid into the bank on 29 June 20X5 had not yet appeared on the bank statement.

4 Bank charges of £140 were omitted from the cash book.

5 In March the company had entered into an agreement to pay for its electricity bill by direct debit on the 28th of each month. The amount relating to June was £52. No entries appeared for this in the cash book.

6 A cheque for £82 had been lodged on 20 June. On 22 June this appeared on the debit side with the cheque being returned to the company as out of date. A new cheque has been requested from the customer.

7 Two customers paid amounts directly into the bank account by standing order on 28 June. The amounts were £998 and £1,314. No entries had been made in the cash book.

8 £768 paid into the bank had been entered twice in the cash book.

9 A standing order to a charity for £130 had not been entered in the cash book.

10 On 15 June the manager had given the bookkeeper a cheque for £500 to lodge into his personal account. By mistake the bookkeeper lodged it to the business account and recorded it in the cash book.

After correcting the cash book and adjusting the balance on the bank statement, both balances reconciled.

Required

a Show the necessary adjustments in the cash book of G. Graduate, highlighting the corrected balance at 30 June 20X5.

b Prepare a bank reconciliation at that date showing the balance per the bank statement.

INTERMEDIATE

19.10 Catherine Big has a cash balance of £52,900 on 1 June 20X5. She opens a current account on that date, with Belfast Bank, depositing £50,000. Her transactions during the next three days included the following:

1 June

- Cash sales £4,500.
- Received a cheque for £25,200 from Sean Dargan, a customer.
- Paid £2,400 as rent by cheque number 0001.

- Paid £48 as wages in cash.
- Paid the petty cashier £168 as the week's imprest. The petty cashier has a cash float of £500 at the beginning of each week and has produced vouchers to the cashier to evidence the payment out of petty cash of £168 in the last week of May.
- Deposited all amounts into bank, leaving a cash float with the cashier of £4,000.

2 June

- Paid £76 for stationery by cheque number 0002.
- Cash sales £3,680.
- £9,600 is paid as business rates by a standing order.
- Paid £290 for electricity by cheque number 0003.
- Paid £72 as wages in cash.
- Received a cheque for £36,800 from Tony Kirk, a customer.
- Deposited all amounts into bank, retaining a float of £4,000.

3 June

- Sean Dargan's cheque for £25,200 is returned to Catherine Big marked 'refer to drawer'. Catherine telephoned Sean, who apologised that he was temporarily short of funds and requested Catherine to re-present the cheque to the bank on 4 June.
- The bank approves a loan to the business of £20,000. Catherine is informed that this is lodged to the current account.
- Paid £56,000 for a car by cheque number 0004.
- Wrote cheque number 0005 to draw £1,200 in cash for office use.
- Catherine drew £2,000 cash for her personal use.

Required

a Write up the cash account and the bank account.

Catherine Big receives the following bank statement on 4 June:

Statement of Catherine Big BELFAST BANK plc, 50 Main Street, Belfast, BT1 3HO				
Date	**Details**	**Debits**	**Credits**	**Balance**
20X5		**£**	**£**	**£**
2 Jun	Deposit		50,000	50,000
2 Jun	Deposit		28,384	78,384
3 Jun	Standing order	9,600	–	68,784
3 Jun	Cheque 0001	400	–	68,384
3 Jun	Loan		20,000	88,384
3 Jun	Cheque 0003	290	–	88,094
3 Jun	Cheque dishonour	25,200	–	62,894
3 Jun	Cheque 0005	1,200	–	61,694
3 Jun	Bank charges	20	–	61,674

Required

b Prepare the bank reconciliation as at 3 June 20X5.

INTERMEDIATE

19.11 The following is an extract of the cash book for J. Robin:

		£			£
July	Balance	702.00	3 July	L. Sheep	68.00
3	R. Cow	43.00	5	Carriage	15.00
5	Q. Stallion	87.00	9	R. Pig	77.00
4	Cash sales	48.00	10	Advertising	25.00
8	R. Cow	89.50	12	Cash purchases	25.50
12	Cash sales	12.00	12	Insurance	39.00
23	J. Dog	95.00	18	L. Sheep	3.50
23	S. Cat	158.35	30	S. Horse	85.00
31	T. Farmer	19.99	31	Stationery	15.50

The bank statement of J. Robin in the account with the Bank of ABC is as follows:

		Dr £	Cr £	Balance £
July				
1	Balance c/f			702.00
3	Interest received		15.00	717.00
3	Bank charges	5.50		711.50
4	Cash sales		48.00	759.50
5	Cheque 100	86.00		673.50
6	Cheque 101	15.00		658.50
7	Deposit		43.00	701.50
8	Deposit		87.00	788.50
9	Deposit		98.50	887.00
10	S/O: F. Hen		112.00	999.00
11	Bounced cheque	87.00		912.00
12	Deposit		12.00	924.00
15	S/O: F. Wren		108.00	1032.00
17	Cheque 104	25.50		1006.50
18	D/D: Guinness	125.58		880.92
18	Cheque 105	93.00		787.92
27	Deposit		253.35	1041.27
27	D/D: Rent	125.00		916.27
31	Cheque 103	25.00		891.27

Required

a Complete the cash book and prepare the bank reconciliation as at 31 July 20X4.

INTERMEDIATE

19.12 David Greene, the bookkeeper for Botanic, a wholesale distributor of garden equipment, prepares accounts without the aid of a computerized accounting system. He carries out a bank reconciliation on a monthly basis. The details of the cash book for December 20X4 are set out below:

Botanic cash book							
Date	**No**	**Receipts Details**	**£**	**Date**	**No**	**Payments Details**	**£**
20X4				**20X4**			
1 Dec		Balance b/d	1,501.80	1 Dec	100	P. Potter	55.00
2 Dec	001	Lodgement	1,500.00	1 Dec	101	T. Taylor	222.33
16 Dec	002	Lodgement	1,456.32	6 Dec	102	S. Summer	329.00
21 Dec	003	Lodgement	560.00	6 Dec	103	W. White	1,200.00
30 Dec	004	Lodgement	171.00	8 Dec	104	M. Moore	10.00
				8 Dec	105	R. Rover	52.00
				10 Dec	106	Y. Young	18.50
				10 Dec	107	E. Edwards	32.00
				15 Dec	108	H. Howard	21.50
				15 Dec	109	G. George	180.00
				15 Dec	110	K. Kelly	700.56
				23 Dec	111	F. French	211.00
				23 Dec	112	V. Vance	150.00
				23 Dec	113	D. Downes	89.00
				31 Dec		Balance c/d	1,918.23
			5,189.12				5,189.12

David received Botanic's monthly bank statement for December 20X4 on 6 January 20X5. Details of the bank statement are set out below:

Date	**Details**	**Dr**	**Cr**	**Balance**
20X4		£	£	£
3 Dec	Balance b/fwd			2,905.11
4 Dec	Cheque no. 101	222.33		2,682.78
5 Dec	Bank Giro Credit (Customer A)		298.34	2,981.12
6 Dec	Lodgement 001		1,500.00	
6 Dec	Cheque no. 099	1,189.19		3,291.93
10 Dec	Cheque no. 100	55.00		3,236.93
11 Dec	N.E. Electricity S.O.	100.00		3,136.93
12 Dec	Transfer to savings a/c	1,500.00		
12 Dec	Cheque no. 097	312.12		1,324.81
13 Dec	Cheque no. 105	25.00		1,299.81
14 Dec	Interest	104.23		1,195.58
17 Dec	Cheque no. 102	329.00		866.58
18 Dec	Lodgement 002		1,456.32	2,322.90
19 Dec	Cheque no. 107	32.00		
19 Dec	D.C. 00300 (Customer B)	109.00		
19 Dec	Fee for dishonoured cheque	5.00		2,176.90
20 Dec	Cheque no. 103	1,200.00		
20 Dec	AB Insurance D.D.	550.00		426.90

21 Dec	Cheque no. 110	700.56		– 273.66
24 Dec	T.Y. Ltd.		140.00	– 133.66
25 Dec	Lodgement 003		560.00	426.34
26 Dec	G.T. Properties S.O.	300.00		126.34
31 Dec	Cheque no. 098	352.00		– 225.66

D.C.: Dishonoured Cheque
D.D.: Direct Debit
S.O.: Standing Order

Additional information

1 All of the cheque payments in December 20X4 were made to suppliers.

2 The cheques paid to suppliers during November 20X4 and not presented to the bank by 30 November 20X4 were:

097	£312.12
098	£352.00
099	£1,189.19

3 David Greene has made a transposition error when entering the opening balance for December 20X4 into the cash book. It should have read £1,051.80 debit instead of £1,501.80 debit.

4 The credit appearing in the bank statement in respect of T.Y. Ltd. is a dividend.

5 The standing order for G.T. Properties has been debited to Botanic's bank account in error by the bank. David Greene has written to the bank highlighting the error and has asked for the funds to be credited back to Botanic's account as soon as possible. This was the only error made by the bank in December's bank statement.

6 Customer A and Customer B are both credit customers.

7 N.E. Electricity has an account in the creditors' ledger. However, since payments made to AB Insurance vary on a monthly basis, Botanic has decided not to open an account for them in the creditors' ledger.

Required

a Show the adjustments that should be made to Botanic's cash book for December 20X4.

b Prepare a bank reconciliation statement at 31 December 20X4.

c Identify the entries required in Botanic's ledgers as a result of the adjustments in a above.

Chapter 20

Control accounts

Learning Objectives:

After reading this chapter you should be able to do the following:

1. Describe the division of the general ledger into several different ledgers.
2. Explain the nature of control accounts, including the sources of the entries.
3. Prepare sales ledger control and purchases ledger control accounts.
4. Explain the purposes of control accounts.
5. Identify and correct errors and omissions relating to the different personal ledgers and control accounts.

20.1 The nature and preparation of control accounts

The **general ledger** is typically split into three different ledgers as outlined in Figure 20.1.

Figure 20.1

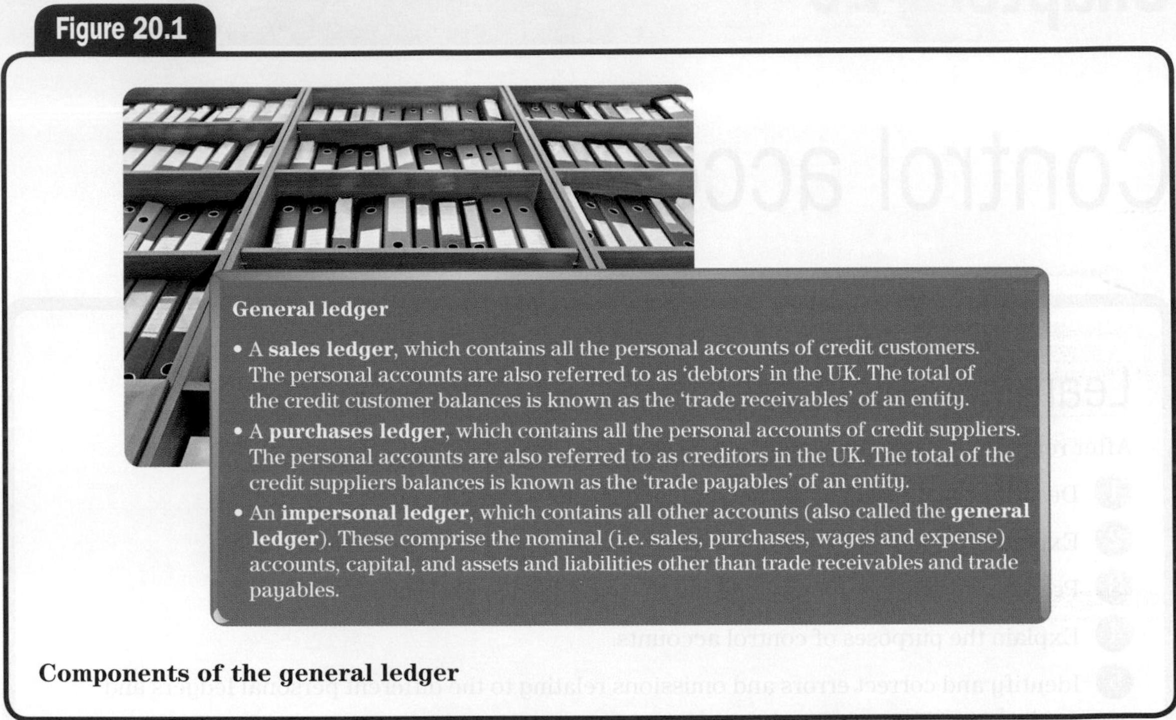

General ledger
• A **sales ledger**, which contains all the personal accounts of credit customers. The personal accounts are also referred to as 'debtors' in the UK. The total of the credit customer balances is known as the 'trade receivables' of an entity.
• A **purchases ledger**, which contains all the personal accounts of credit suppliers. The personal accounts are also referred to as creditors in the UK. The total of the credit suppliers balances is known as the 'trade payables' of an entity.
• An **impersonal ledger**, which contains all other accounts (also called the **general ledger**). These comprise the nominal (i.e. sales, purchases, wages and expense) accounts, capital, and assets and liabilities other than trade receivables and trade payables.

Components of the general ledger

The main reasons for dividing the general ledger into three ledgers in a manual accounting system are:

1 Where there are a large number of transactions (in a manual bookkeeping system), a single ledger becomes physically too heavy to handle.

2 It allows more than one person to work on the ledgers at the same time.

3 It provides a means of **internal control** for checking the accuracy of the ledgers, facilitates the location of errors, and can deter fraud and the misappropriation of cash. This is achieved through the use of control accounts that are described below.

The above also serves to highlight that the advantages of dividing the general ledger, and having control accounts (where the accounting system is computerized) are largely confined to security matters such as restricting access to minimize the possibility of fraud.

Learning Activity 20.1

Before reading further prepare a list of ledgers that you consider will impact on the control account for purchases and separately for sales. Review your list after reading the rest of this section and note the differences.

In a manual accounting system with the above three ledgers, it is usual for the impersonal ledger to contain a **control account** for each of the other ledgers. These will comprise a **sales ledger control account** and a **purchases ledger control account** (sometimes also referred to as **total accounts**). These control accounts contain, *in total*, the entries that are made in the personal ledgers, and are normally written up monthly from the totals of the relevant books of prime entry. For example, in the case of credit sales, the individual invoices shown in the sales day book are entered in each of the credit customer's *personal accounts* in the sales ledger, and the total sales for the month as per the sales day book is debited to the sales ledger control account in the impersonal ledger and credited to the *sales account*.

Where an impersonal ledger contains sales ledger and purchase ledger control accounts, these constitute part of the double entry and therefore enter into the trial balance that would be prepared for the impersonal ledger alone. In these circumstances the balances on the sales and purchases ledgers are outside the double-entry system and are thus not entered in the trial balance. The entries to a typical sales ledger control account are set out in Figure 20.2 (this can be used for reference).

Figure 20.2

Pro forma sales ledger control account

	£		£
Balances b/d	XX	Cash/cheques received	XXX
Credit sales	XXX	Cash discount allowed	XX
Returned cheques	XX	Sales returns	XX
Interest charged	XX	Irrecoverable receivables written off	XX
		Set-off/contra entries	XX
		Balance c/d	XX
	XXX		XXX
Balance b/d	XX		

A pro forma of the typical entries in a sales ledger control account

The entries to a typical purchases ledger control account are set out in Figure 20.3 (this can be used for reference).

Figure 20.3

Purchases ledger control account

	£		£
Cash/cheques paid	XXX	Balance b/d	XX
Cash discount received	XX	Credit purchases	XXX
Purchases returns	XX	Interest charged	XX
Set-off/contra entries	XX		
Balance c/d	XX		
	XXX		XXX
		Balance b/d	XX

A pro forma of the typical entries required to prepare a purchase ledger control account

A simple illustration of the preparation of control accounts is shown in Worked Example 20.1.

WORKED EXAMPLE 20.1

The books of Copper Tree Ltd include three ledgers comprising an impersonal ledger, sales ledger and purchases ledger. The impersonal ledger contains sales ledger and purchases ledger control accounts as part of the double entry.

The following information relates to the accounting year ended 30 June 20X4:

	£
Sales ledger control account balance on 1 July 20X3 (debit)	5,740
Purchases ledger control account balance on 1 July 20X3 (credit)	6,830
Sales revenue	42,910
Purchases	38,620
Cheques received from credit customers	21,760
Cheques paid to credit suppliers	19,340
Returns outwards	8,670
Returns inwards	7,840
Carriage outwards	1,920
Carriage inwards	2,130
Discount received	4,560
Discount allowed	3,980
Bills of exchange payable	5,130
Bills of exchange receivable	9,720
Irrecoverable receivables	1,640
Allowance for irrecoverable receivables	2,380
Amounts due from customers as shown by the sales ledger, transferred to purchases ledger	950
Cash received in respect of a debit balance on a purchases ledger account	810

Required

Prepare the sales ledger and purchases ledger control accounts.

Sales ledger control account

	£		£
Balances b/d	5,740	Bank	21,760
Sales revenue	42,910	Returns inwards	7,840
		Discount allowed	3,980
		Bills receivable	9,720
		Irrecoverable receivables	1,640
		Transfer to the purchase ledger (contra entry)	950
		Balance c/d	2,760
	48,650		48,650
Balance b/d	2,760		

Purchase ledger control account			
	£		£
Bank	19,340	Balance b/d	6,830
Returns outwards	8,670	Purchases	38,620
Discount received	4,560	Cash	810
Bills payable	5,130		
Transfer from the sales ledger (contra entry)	950		
Balance c/d	7,610		
	46,260		46,260
		Balance b/d	7,610

Notes

1 The carriage inwards, carriage outwards and allowance for irrecoverable receivables are not entered in the control accounts since they do not appear in the individual *credit customers'* or *credit suppliers' accounts* in the personal ledgers.

2 The transfer of £950 between the sales ledger and the purchase ledger control accounts (called a **contra entry**) is intended to reflect the total of the transfers between the sales and purchases ledgers during the year. These usually occur where the business buys from and sells goods to the same firm. Thus, instead of exchanging cheques, the amount due as shown in the sales ledger is set against the amount owed as shown in the purchases ledger (or vice versa depending on which is the smaller).

3 The cash received of £810 in respect of a debit balance on a *purchase ledger account* is credited to the *credit supplier's account* and the purchases ledger control account. A debit balance in the purchases ledger usually arises because a supplier has been overpaid as a result of either duplicating a payment or paying for goods that are the subject of a credit note. The cash received is a refund to correct the previous overpayment.

4 Bills of exchange were explained briefly at the end of Chapter 8, 'Basic Documentation and Books of Account'. The most relevant characteristics are that bills of exchange are a method of payment where the business, which owes the money, signs a document undertaking to make payment after the expiry of a specified period (usually 30, 60 or 90 days). This document is referred to as a **bill of exchange receivable** in the case of a trade receivable and a **bill of exchange payable** in the case of a trade payable. The essential point is that in the *credit customers'* and *credit suppliers' personal accounts*, the debt is treated as paid on the date the bill of exchange is signed (and not when the money is actually received or paid, which is at a later date). The same therefore applies in the control accounts.

5 The balances carried down on the control accounts at the end of the period are the difference between the two sides of the accounts.

6 Some examination questions contain amounts described as a *credit* balance on the sales ledger control account and/or a *debit* balance on the purchases ledger control account (at the beginning and/or end of the period). Although individual *credit customers'* and *credit suppliers' personal accounts* can have credit or debit balances, respectively (for the reasons outlined in note 3 above), it is unclear how the control accounts can have such balances. Each control account can only throw up one balance, which is the difference between the two sides of the

account. However, if these perverse balances are encountered in an examination question, the following procedure should be adopted: a credit balance on the sales ledger control account should be entered as a credit balance brought down (and debit balance carried down), and the closing debit balance calculated as the difference between the two sides of the control account in the normal way. Similarly, a debit balance on the purchases ledger control account should be entered as a debit balance brought down (and credit balance carried down), and the closing credit balance calculated as the difference between the two sides of the control account in the normal way.

7 The entries for any irrecoverable receivables recovered are the reverse of those for irrecoverable receivables. Allowances given and allowances received should be treated in the same way as returns inwards and outwards, respectively. Any interest charged on overdue (credit customers') accounts should be debited to the sales ledger control account and credited to an interest receivable account.

20.2 The purpose of control accounts

The main purpose of a control account is to provide a check on the accuracy of the ledger to which it relates. Since the entries in the control account are the same (in total) as those in the ledger to which it relates, the balance on the control account should equal the total of a list of balances of the individual personal accounts contained in the ledger. If the balance on the control account is the same as the list of balances, this proves that the ledger is arithmetically accurate and that all the items in the books of prime entry have been entered in the ledger on the correct side.

The main function of control accounts is therefore to facilitate the location of errors highlighted in the trial balance by pinpointing the personal ledger in which these errors are likely to be found. Furthermore, the existence of control accounts is likely to deter fraud and the misappropriation of funds since it is usually prepared by the accountant as a check on the clerk who is responsible for the personal ledger.

The importance of having controls over purchasing is highlighted in Real World Example 20.1. When one person is in charge of invoicing and cheque payments then the risk of fraud is high.

REAL WORLD EXAMPLE 20.1

Bride stole £200,000 from bosses to pay for lavish wedding

A bride, who stole £200,000 from her employer to pay for a magician, fireworks and a free bar at her wedding, has been jailed for 20 months. Kirsty Lane, 30, swindled the money from her bosses to fund an extravagant reception for her and her husband Graham Lane in January last year. The court heard that Lane, who worked for Pure Audio Visual, had made 122 payments to her personal bank account between December 2008 and January 2011.

She was found to have created false invoices to channel the money from the company. The theft had been discovered by Peter Sutton, the managing director of the firm, who was forced to make two members of staff redundant as a result of the financial damage inflicted by the fraud. Lane, of

Adlington, Lancashire, admitted 10 counts of fraud and asked for 112 other offences to be taken into consideration. Speaking after the hearing, Mr Sutton said that, due to added tax and VAT payments, Lane had cost the company a total of around £300,000.

Source: Adapted from The Telegraph, 20 June 2012, http://www.telegraph.co.uk/news/uknews/crime/9344668/Bride-stole-200000-from-bosses-to-pay-for-lavish-wedding.html, accessed July 2014.

Finally, control accounts facilitate the preparation of (monthly or quarterly) final financial statements since the total values of trade receivables and trade payables are immediately available. The use of control accounts in the location of errors is illustrated in Worked Example 20.2.

WORKED EXAMPLE 20.2

The books of C. Hand Ltd include three ledgers comprising an impersonal ledger, a sales ledger and a purchases ledger. The impersonal ledger contains sales ledger and purchases ledger control accounts as part of the double entry.

The following information relates to the accounting year ended 30 April 20X5:

	£
Sales ledger control account balance on 1 May 20X4 (debit)	8,460
Cheques received from credit customers	27,690
Sales revenue	47,320
Returns outwards	12,860
Returns inwards	7,170
Carriage inwards	3,940
Bills receivable	8,650
Bills payable	4,560
Discount received	5,710
Discount allowed	2,830
Allowance for irrecoverable receivables	1,420
Irrecoverable receivables	970
Proceeds of bills receivable	6,150
Amounts due from customers as shown by sales ledger transferred to purchases ledger	830
Total of balances in the sales ledger on 30 April 20X5	9,460

a You are required to prepare the sales ledger control account for the year ended 30 April 20X5.

b After the preparation of the control account the following errors were identified:

i The total of the sales returns day book has been overcast by £360.

ii A cheque received for £225 has been entered on the wrong side of a *credit customer's personal account*.

iii The total of the discount allowed column in the cash book is shown as £2,830 when it should be £3,820.

iv A sales invoice for £2,000 has been entered in the sales day book as £200 in error.

Solution

Prepare a statement showing the amended balances on the sales ledger and the sales ledger control account. Compute the amount of any remaining undetected error.

a

Sales ledger control account			
	£		£
Balances b/d	8,460	Bank	27,690
Sales revenue	47,320	Returns inwards	7,170
		Bills receivable	8,650
		Discount allowed	2,830
		Irrecoverable receivables	970
		Transfer to the purchase ledger	830
		Balance c/d	7,640
	55,780		55,780
Balance b/d	7,640		

b

Sales ledger		
		£
Original balances		9,460
Add: Sales day book error (£2,000 – £200)		1,800
		11,260
Less: Cheque received posted to wrong side of a credit customers' account (£225 × 2)		450
Amended balance		10,810

Sales ledger control account		
		£
Original balance		7,640
Add: Sales returns day book overcast	360	
Sales day book error (£2,000 – £200)	1,800	2,160
		9,800
Less: Discount allowed undercast		990
Amended balance		8,810
Undetected error = £10,810 – £8,810 = £2,000		

Notes

1 The returns outwards, carriage inwards, bills payable, discount received and allowance for irrecoverable receivables are not entered in the sales ledger control account. The proceeds of bills of exchange receivable should also not be entered in the sales ledger control account. As explained above, the entry in the control account in respect of bills receivable of £8,650 is made when the bills were signed as accepted by the credit customer and not when the proceeds are received. This is dealt with in a separate account, shown below.

Bills receivable			
	£		£
Sales ledger control a/c	8,650	Bank	6,150
		Balance c/d	2,500
	8,650		8,650
Balance b/d	2,500		

2 The difference of £2,000 between the amended balances on the sales ledger and the sales ledger control account indicates that there are still one or more errors in the sales ledger and/or the sales ledger control account.

3 Instead of computing the amended balance on the sales ledger control account in vertical/statement form above, some examination questions require this to be done in the sales ledger control account. This method can take two forms. One way is to prepare a control account containing the correct amounts for all the items. The other method is to prepare a control account with the original (uncorrected) amounts and, after computing the closing balance, show the entries necessary to correct the errors. Notice that this is essentially the same procedure as that shown in Worked Example 19.2 relating to bank reconciliations. The first method is usually expected where an examination question describes the errors before stating the requirement to prepare a control account. The second method is usually expected where an examination question states the requirement to prepare a control account before describing the errors, such as in Worked Example 20.2 above, but unlike the example above, does not explicitly require a statement showing the amended balance on the control account. In this case the items shown in the answer to Worked Example 20.2 that have been added to the 'original' sales ledger control account balance would be simply debited to the control account, and those that have been deducted would be credited to the control account. In practice, errors are not normally identified until after the control accounts have been prepared and thus these would usually be corrected as separate entries in the control accounts.

20.3 Alternative systems

Sometimes, in practice, control accounts are not part of the double entry in the impersonal ledger. Instead, they are prepared on a loose sheet of paper and are thus purely memoranda. The entries still consist of totals from the relevant day books and other books of prime entry. However, in this case the impersonal and personal ledgers must be taken together to produce a trial balance. The values of trade receivables and trade payables in such a trial balance are therefore a list of the balances in the personal ledgers.

Summary

It is common for medium and large enterprises to divide their general ledger into at least three ledgers including: a general ledger (otherwise known as the impersonal ledger as it does not contain any customer/supplier names), a sales ledger and a purchases ledger. The general ledger usually contains a control account for each of the other two personal ledgers. These constitute a part of the double entry and are thus included in the trial balance that would be prepared for the general ledger alone. Thus, sales and purchases ledgers are maintained separately on a single entry memorandum basis and are not included in the trial balance.

The purchases and sales ledger control accounts are written up from the totals of the relevant books of prime entry. The main purpose of a control account is to provide a check on the accuracy of the ledger to which it relates, and facilitate the location of errors. The balance on a control account should equal the total of a list of balances in the ledger to which it relates. If this is not the case the reasons for the difference will need to be investigated.

Key terms and concepts

bill (of exchange) payable	351	internal control	348
bill (of exchange) receivable	351	purchases ledger	348
contra entry	351	purchases ledger control account	349
control account	348	sales ledger	348
general ledger	348	sales ledger control account	348
impersonal ledger	348	total accounts	349

An asterisk after the question number indicates that there is a suggested answer in Appendix 2.

Review question

connect

20.1 Explain the main purposes of control accounts.

Exercises

connect

BASIC

20.2 The following information has been extracted from the books of a trader at 1 July 20X4:

	£
Amount owing by credit customers	40,000
Amount owing by credit suppliers	31,200

The transactions during the year ended 30 June 20X5 were as follows:	
Returns inwards	15,750
Returns outwards	8,660
Discount received	3,187
Discount allowed	5,443
Sales revenue	386,829
Purchases	222,954
Irrecoverable receivables written off	3,400
Cheques received from credit customers	230,040
Cheques paid to credit suppliers	108,999

Required

Write up the sales ledger control account and the purchases ledger control account for the year ended 30 June 20X5.

20.3 The books of original entry for James Plc showed the following for the month ended 31 March 20X5: BASIC

Cash book:	**£**
Discounts allowed	7,300
Cash and cheques received from credit customers	294,100
Discounts received	3,150
Cash and cheques paid to credit suppliers	249,200
Journal:	**£**
Irrecoverable receivables written off	1,500
Purchases day book	253,200
Sales day book	316,250
Returns inward	5,100
Returns outward	4,710
Contra	1,000

Previous trade receivable/trade payable balances were £53,450/£42,150.

Required

Prepare the sales ledger and the purchase ledger control accounts.

20.4 A list of balances on the individual customer accounts in the sales ledger did not agree with the balance on the sales ledger control account. INTERMEDIATE

Sales ledger	£205,640
Sales ledger control account	£225,000

You are told that:

1 A sales invoice of £12,900 included in the sales day book had not been posted to the personal account in the sales ledger.

2 Discounts allowed to customers of £1,260 had been credited to the individual accounts in the sales ledger but no other entry was made for them in the books.

3 The returns inwards journal was wrongly totalled: it was overcast by £3,000.

4 A sales invoice for £9,400 had been entirely omitted from the books.

5 A debit balance of £7,400 on the personal account of a customer had been included in the list of balances as £4,700.

6 The balance on a customer account in the sales ledger of £5,500 had been omitted from the list of balances.

Required

a Write up the control account to correct it for those errors that affect it.

b Revise the list of customer balances for errors.

20.5 Formica purchases inventory on credit from a large number of suppliers. The company maintains a purchases ledger control account as an integral part of its double-entry system and in addition maintains supplier accounts on a memorandum basis in a purchases ledger. At the end of October 20X4 the balance of £25,450 on the purchases ledger control account failed to agree with the total of the balances from the purchases ledger. The total of the list of credit suppliers' balances is £27,620. The following errors have been subsequently discovered:

1 Goods costing £350 purchased on credit from Yellow had been entered into the purchases day book at £600.

2 An amount of £1,500 paid to Hunt had been correctly entered into the cash book but had been entered into Jack's account at £1,550.

3 The return of goods purchased on credit costing £800 had been completely omitted from the books.

4 The purchases day book has been undercast by £2,220.

Required

a Adjust the purchase ledger control account to show the amendments to the original balance.

b Adjust the list of balances in the purchases ledger to agree with the control account.

INTERMEDIATE

20.6 The following particulars relating to the year ended 31 March 20X5 have been extracted from the books of a trader:

	£
Sales ledger control account balance on 1 April 20X4 (debit)	7,182
Sales revenue	69,104
Cash received from credit customers	59,129
Discounts allowed	1,846
Discounts received	1,461
Returns inwards	983
Returns outwards	627
Bills receivable accepted by credit customers	3,243
Irrecoverable receivables written off	593
Cash paid in respect of a credit balance on a sales ledger account	66
Amounts due from customers as shown by sales ledger transferred to purchases ledger	303
Interest charged on credit customers overdue account	10
Credit balance on sales ledger control account on 31 March 20X5	42

Prepare the sales ledger control account for the year ended 31 March 20X5, using relevant figures selected from the data shown above.

(ACCA)

20.7* The books of Trader Ltd include three ledgers comprising an impersonal ledger, sales ledger and purchases ledger. The impersonal ledger contains sales ledger and purchases ledger control accounts as part of the double entry.

INTERMEDIATE

The following information relates to the month of January 20X5:

	£	
Sales ledger control account balance on 1 January 20X5	4,200	debit
Sales ledger control account balance on 1 January 20X5	300	credit
Purchases ledger control account balance on 1 January 20X5	250	debit
Purchases ledger control account balance on 1 January 20X5	6,150	credit
Credit sales for the month	23,000	
Credit purchases for the month	21,500	
Returns inward	750	
Returns outward	450	
Carriage inwards	25	
Carriage outwards	15	
Cheques received from credit customers	16,250	
Cheques paid to credit suppliers	19,800	
Discount allowed	525	
Discount received	325	
Irrecoverable debts	670	
Allowance for irrecoverable receivables	400	
Cheques received from credit customers, dishonoured	1,850	
Bills of exchange payable, accepted by us	4,500	
Bills of exchange receivable, accepted by credit customers	5,300	
Irrecoverable receivables recovered	230	
Cash received from bills receivable	4,850	
Credit customers balances set against accounts in the purchases ledger	930	
Cash paid on bills payable	3,700	
Interest charged on credit customers overdue accounts	120	
Allowances received	280	
Allowances given	340	
Sales ledger control account balance on 31 January 20X5	240	credit
Purchases ledger control account balance on 31 January 20X5	420	debit

Required

Prepare the sales ledger and purchases ledger control accounts for January 20X5.

20.8* The following particulars relating to the year ended 31 March 20X5 have been extracted from the books of Ball and Chain Ltd. All sales have been recorded in personal accounts in the sales ledger, and the sales ledger control account is part of the double entry in the impersonel ledger.

INTERMEDIATE

	£
Sales ledger control account balance on 1 April 20X4 (debit)	14,364
Sales revenue	138,208
Cheques received from credit customers including irrecoverable receivables recovered of £84	118,258
Discounts allowed	3,692
Discounts received	2,922
Returns inwards	1,966
Returns outwards	1,254
Bills receivable	6,486
Irrecoverable receivables written off	1,186
Allowance for irrecoverable receivables	1,800
Cash paid in respect of a credit balance on a sales ledger account	132
Amounts due from customers as shown by the sales ledger transferred to the purchases ledger	606
Interest charged on credit customers overdue accounts	20
Total of balances in the sales ledger on 31 March 20X5 (debit)	20,914

Required

a Prepare the sales ledger control account for the year ended 31 March 20X5 using relevant figures selected from the data shown above.

b Subsequently, the following errors have been discovered:

i The total of the sales day book has been undercast by £1,000.

ii An entry of £125 in the returns inward book has been entered on the wrong side of the credit customer's personal account.

iii Discount allowed of £50 had been entered correctly in a credit customer's personal account but no other entries have been made in the books.

iv A cheque for £3,400 from a credit customer has been entered correctly in the cash book but has been posted to the credit customer's personal account as £4,300.

Required

Prepare a statement showing the amended balances on the sales ledger and the sales ledger control account.

20.9* The books of K. Wills include three ledgers comprising the impersonal ledger, sales ledger and purchases ledger. The impersonal ledger contains sales ledger and purchases ledger control accounts as part of the double entry.

The following information relates to the accounting year ended 30 June 20X5:

	£
Sales ledger control account balance on 1 July 20X4 (debit)	17,220
Purchases ledger control account balance on 1 July 20X4 (credit)	20,490
Cheques received from credit customers	45,280
Cheques paid to credit suppliers	38,020
Sales revenue	98,730
Purchases	85,860

Returns outwards	16,010
Returns inwards	18,520
Bills of exchange payable	21,390
Bills of exchange receivable	29,160
Discount received	7,680
Discount allowed	6,940
Irrecoverable receivables	4,920
Cash received in respect of a debit balance on a credit supplier's ledger account	2,430
Amount due from credit customers as shown by sales ledger, transferred to purchases ledger	2,850
Total balances in purchases ledger on 30 June 20X5 (credit)	20,700

Required

a You are required to prepare the sales ledger and purchases ledger control accounts.

b After the preparation of the above control accounts the following errors were discovered:

i The total of the purchases day book has been overcast by £500.

ii Returns outwards of £180 have been entered on the wrong side of the personal account concerned.

iii Discount received of £120 has been entered correctly in the appropriate personal account but is shown in the cash book as £210.

iv A cheque paid for £340 has been entered correctly in the cash book but has been posted to the credit supplier's personal account as £3,400.

Required

Prepare a statement showing the amended balances on the purchases ledger and the purchases ledger control account. Compute the amount of any remaining undetected error.

20.10 The following figures relating to the year ended 31 March 20X5 have been extracted from the books of a manufacturer: INTERMEDIATE

	£
Total of sales ledger balances as per list	8,300
Total of bought ledger balances as per list	1,270
Balance on sales ledger control account	8,160
Balance on bought ledger control account	1,302

The balances on the control accounts, as shown above, have been included in the trial balance and in this trial balance the total of the credit balances exceeded the total of the debit balances by £58.

Subsequently, the following errors have been discovered:

1 Goods returned by a customer to the value of £10 have been entered on the wrong side of his personal account.

2 The total of the sales day book for the month of March has been undercast by £80.

3 The total of the purchases for the month of March had been correctly shown as £653 in the bought day book and control account, but incorrectly posted to the purchases account as £635.

4 An allowance of £10 made by a supplier because of a slight defect in the goods supplied had been correctly entered in the personal account concerned, but no other entries had been made in the books.

5 A credit balance of £22 on a supplier's personal account had been overlooked and therefore did not appear in the list of bought ledger balances.

An undetected error still remained in the books after the discovery of the above-mentioned errors.

Required

a Prepare a statement showing the amended totals of the balances on the sales and bought ledgers and the amended balances on each of the control accounts assuming that the errors discovered have been corrected.

b Calculate the amount of undetected error and state where in the books you consider such an error is to be found.

(ACCA)

INTERMEDIATE

20.11 Fox & Co. maintain control accounts, in respect of both the sales ledger and purchases ledger, within their nominal ledger. On 31 December 20X4 the net total of the balances extracted from the sales ledger amounted to £9,870, which did not agree with the balance shown on the sales ledger control account. An examination of the books disclosed the following errors and omissions, which when rectified resulted in the corrected net total of the sales ledger balances agreeing with the amended balance of the control account.

1 £240 standing to the credit of Rice's account in the purchase ledger had been transferred to his account in the sales ledger, but no entries had been made in the control accounts in respect of this transfer.

2 Debit balances of £42 in the sales ledger had been extracted as credit balances when the balances were listed at 31 December 20X4.

3 £8,675, a month's total in the sales day book, had been posted to the control account as £8,765 although posted correctly to the sales account.

4 A balance of £428 owing by Stone had been written off to irrecoverable receivables as irrecoverable, but no entry had been made in the control account.

5 Entries on the debit side of Hay's account in the sales ledger had been undercast by £100.

6 The following sales ledger balances had been omitted from the list of balances at 31 December 20X4 – debits £536, credits £37.

7 The sale of goods to Croft amounting to £60 had been dealt with correctly and debited to his account. Croft had returned such goods as not being up to standard and the only treatment accorded thereto was the crossing out of the original entry in Croft's account.

8 £22 allowed to Field as discount had been correctly recorded and posted. Subsequently, this discount had been disallowed and a like amount had been entered in the discounts received column in the cash book and posted to Field's account in the purchases ledger and included in the total of discounts received.

Required

a Give the journal entries, where necessary, to rectify these errors and omissions, and, if no journal entry is necessary, state how they should be rectified.

b Prepare the sales ledger control account showing the balance before and after rectification has been made, and reconcile the balance carried forward on this account with the total of balances extracted from the sales ledger.

(ACCA)

INTERMEDIATE

20.12 Prepare the sales ledger control account and the individual credit customer's accounts for the month of November 20X4 from the details provided below.

(*Note*: see questions 11.8 and 12.8 – you should already have prepared many of the ledger account entries.)

Balances in sales ledger		£
1 November 20X4	Boycey	200
	Del Boy	100
	Rachel	100
	Rodney	150
		550

Cash book (receipts side)		Discount allowed £	Amount received from credit customers £
8 Nov	Boycey	20	180
11 Nov	Rodney	15	135
14 Nov	Del Boy	10	90
		45	405

Credit sales		£
8 Nov	Boycey	320
11 Nov	Rodney	250
14 Nov	Del Boy	80
		650

Sales returns		£
16 Nov	Boycey	70

It was decided that Rachel would not pay her debt as she is away in America pursuing her singing career and cannot be contacted.

INTERMEDIATE

20.13 The following particulars relating to the year ended 31 March 20X5 have been extracted from the books of Heel and Toe, footwear wholesalers. All sales have been recorded in personal accounts in the sales ledger, and the sales ledger control account is part of the double-entry system in the general ledger.

	£
Sales ledger control account balance at 1 April 20X4 (debit)	28,728
Credit sales	276,416
Cheques received from credit customers including irrecoverable receivables recovered of £168	249,188
Discounts allowed	7,384
Discounts received	5,844
Returns inwards	3,932
Returns outwards	2,508
Irrecoverable receivables written off	2,372
Allowance for irrecoverable receivables	3,600
Cash paid in respect of a credit balance on a sales ledger account	264
Amounts due from credit customers as shown by sales ledger transferred to purchases ledger	1,212
Interest charged on credit customer overdue account	40
Total of balances in sales ledger on 31 March 20X5 (debit)	41,828

Required

a Prepare the sales ledger control account for the year ended 31 March 20X5 using relevant figures selected from the data shown above.

b Subsequently, the following errors have been discovered:

- The total of the sales day book has been undercast by £2,000.
- An entry of £250 in the returns inward book has been entered on the wrong side of the credit customer's personal account.
- Discount allowed of £100 had been entered correctly in a credit customer's personal account but no entries have been made in the books.
- A cheque for £6,800 from a credit customer has been entered correctly in the cash book but has been posted to the credit customer's personal account as £8,600.

Prepare a statement showing the amended balances on the sales ledger and the sales ledger control account.

c Discuss the purposes of control accounts.

INTERMEDIATE

20.14 (*Note*: See questions 11.9 and 12.9 – you should already have prepared many of the ledger account entries.)

The balance of the purchases ledger control account in the general ledger of A. Brook and Co. at 1 September is £1,984.50, the details being as follows:

J. Smith & Co	£378.71	
A. Brown	£459.33	
C. Jones	£235.38	
M. Mann	£684.17	
Payne & Co	£245.18	
		£2,002.77
Less: debit – J. Cann & Co		£18.27
		£1,984.50

The following are the transactions relating to the purchases ledger accounts in September:

		£	£
Sep 4	Paid J. Smith & Co		150.00
	J Cann & Co. – Goods purchased from Brook		48.38
	A. Gray – Goods		30.55
	Paid A. Brown	268.08	
	Discount	8.25	276.33
Sep 11	Paid C. Jones	169.93	
	Discount	5.25	175.18
	C. Jones – Goods		39.33
	A. Brown – Goods		75.48
Sep 18	Goods returned to A. Brown		9.80
	Paid M. Mann		300.00
	M. Mann contra for goods purchased by him		89.80
	Paid Payne & Co	164.14	
	Discount	5.08	169.22
	Payne & Co – Goods		83.33
25 Sep	A. Read – Goods		120.15
30 Sep	Allowance by Gray for soiled goods		3.50
	Trade discount allowed by A. Read (Not previously deducted from the invoice)		24.03

Required

a Open accounts in the purchases ledger with balances at 1 September and post therein the above transactions. Bring down balances, list and total them.

b Open and write up a control account and bring down balance to agree.

Chapter 21

Errors and suspense accounts

Learning Objectives:

After reading this chapter you should be able to do the following:

1. Describe the types of error that do and do not cause a trial balance to disagree.
2. Explain how errors should be corrected in ledger accounts.
3. Explain the purposes of a suspense account.
4. Show journal and ledger entries for the correction of both errors that do and do not cause a trial balance to disagree, including those relating to suspense accounts.
5. Prepare a revised statement of profit or loss and statement of financial position after the correction of errors.

—21.1 Introduction

As explained in Chapter 10, 'The Balancing of Accounts and the Trial Balance', one of the main purposes of the trial balance is to check the accuracy of the ledger. If a trial balance agrees this indicates the following:

1 There are no arithmetic errors in the ledger accounts.

2 Every transaction recorded in the ledger has been entered once on each side.

However, there can still be errors in the ledger that do not cause a trial balance to disagree. These are explained below.

—21.2 Types of error that do not cause a trial balance to disagree

There are six different types of error that can occur and that do not cause a trial balance to disagree.

Learning Activity 21.1

Before reading further prepare a list of the types of transaction that may occur that will not cause the trial balance to go out of balance. Compare your answer to the examples provided in Figure 21.1.

Figure 21.1

An **error of commission** occurs when a transaction has been entered on both sides of the ledger correctly and in the correct *class/type* of account, but one of the entries is in the wrong account. For example, stationery has been entered in the purchases account in error, or cheques are posted to the wrong personal account.

An **error of principle** occurs when a transaction has been entered on both sides of the ledger correctly but one of the entries is in the wrong *class/type* of account. For example, an expense has been debited to an asset account in error (or vice versa), or income credited to a liability account in error (or vice versa).

An **error of omission** occurs when a transaction has not been recorded anywhere in the books of account. A typical example is bank charges omitted from the cash book.

An **error of original/prime entry** occurs when an incorrect amount has been entered in a book of prime entry. That is, the amount entered in the book of prime entry is different from that shown on the original document. This will mean that the wrong amount has been entered on both sides of the ledger. For example, a sales invoice for ₭980 entered in the sales day book as ₭890 will result in both the sales and sales ledger (control) accounts containing a figure of ₭890 instead of ₭980.

A **compensating error** is two separate errors that are totally unrelated to each other except that they are both of the same amount. Neither of these two errors is of the four types above but rather would individually cause a trial balance to disagree.

A **double posting error** refers to where the correct amount has been entered in a day book (of prime entry) but the wrong amount is shown on both sides of the ledger or when the correct amount of a transaction has been entered on the wrong side of both of the accounts to which it has been posted. A slightly different example is rent received recorded as rent paid.

Errors that do not cause the trial balance to disagree

Illustrations of these errors and their correction are shown in Worked Example 21.1.

WORKED EXAMPLE 21.1

State the title of each of the following errors and show the journal entries needed for their correction.

1. Plant that was acquired at a cost of £5,000 has been credited in the cash book but debited to the purchases account in error.
2. The purchase of consumable tools for £80 has been debited to the repairs account in error.
3. Bank charges of £27 shown on the bank statement have not been entered in the cash book.
4. A purchase invoice received from A. Creditor for £1,000 has been entered in the purchases day book as £100.
5. Wages paid of £40 have not been posted to the wages account, and the debit side of the purchases account has been overcast by £40.
6. Rent received of £400 has been entered in both the cash book and the ledger as rent paid.

The journal

			Debit	**Credit**
			£	**£**
1	*Plant and machinery*	Dr	5,000	
	Purchases account	Cr		5,000
	Being correction of an error of principle			
2	*Consumable tools*	Dr	80	
	Repairs account	Cr		80
	Being correction of an error of omission			
3	*Bank charges*	Dr	27	
	Cash book	Cr		27
	Being correction of an error of omission			
4	*Purchases account*	Dr	900	
	A. Creditor/purchase ledger control account	Cr		900
	Being correction of an error of prime entry (no correction of purchases day book is necessary)			
5	*Wages account*	Dr	40	
	Purchases account	Cr		40
	Being correction of a compensating error – wages not posted and purchases account overcast			
6	*Cash book*	Dr	800	
	Rent payable account	Cr		400
	Rent receivable account	Cr		400
	Being correction of rent receivable of £400 entered as rent payable			

Inventory error example

Sometimes, in examination questions, goods on sale or return are recorded as sales. This is an error and must be reversed by means of the following entries:

Debit:	*Sales account*	£'XXX	
Credit:	*Trade receivables*		£'XXX

Debit:	*Inventories account*	£'XXX	
Credit:	*Profit or loss account*		£'XXX

Note that the entries in the *inventory account* and the *profit or loss account* take the form of increasing the amount of closing inventory.

21.3 Types of error that cause a trial balance to disagree

As explained above, one of the purposes of a trial balance is to ascertain whether the total of the debit balances in the ledger is the same as the total of the credit balances. The reason why this may not be the case is because of the existence of one or more errors. The types of error that may cause this are outlined in Figure 21.2.

Figure 21.2

Arithmetic errors

The incorrect addition of the amounts on one side of an account, and/or in the calculation of a balance. Adding in accounting is sometimes referred to as to **casting** the account. So **overcast** means the balance was over-stated, and **undercast** means the balance was under-stated.

Posting errors (Three forms)

- Where a transaction has been entered on one side of the ledger but not on the other side
- Where a transaction has been entered twice on the same side
- Where the correct amount of a transaction has been entered on one side of the ledger account but the wrong amount has been entered on the other side. The most common errors of the latter type are of two forms:
  - Where a zero is omitted from the end of an amount (for example, a transaction for £33,000 entered on one side of the ledger as £3,300), and
  - **Transposed figures**, where the correct amount of a transaction has been entered on one side of the ledger but two or more of the figures have been reversed when the entry was made on the other side (for example, an amount of £323 entered on one side as £332). A difference of a number divisible by 9 on the trial balance may indicate that there is a transposition error.

Extraction error

Where the correct balance is shown in the ledger account but the wrong amount is entered on the trial balance, or the correct amount is put on the wrong side of the trial balance.

Errors that cause the trial balance to disagree

Arithmetic and posting errors have to be corrected by a one-sided ledger entry. The correction may be done by changing the figure to the correct amount. However, it is argued that the correction should take the form of double entry so that some record exists of the correction of the error. Furthermore, in practice it is frequently impractical to correct errors by simply changing a figure to the correct amount, since this usually also necessitates numerous other changes to subsequent totals and balances (e.g. an error in the *bank account* which occurred several months previously). Where an error is corrected by means of another entry, it is essential that the details of the correction indicate where the original error is located. For these reasons, it is recommended that *suspense accounts* be created to capture the net error balances and double entry to this account be used to fix the original errors. An illustration of the types of error described above and their correction is given in Worked Example 21.2.

WORKED EXAMPLE 21.2

The following examples are shown in the same order as the types of error described in Figure 21.2:

Error	Correction
1 The debit side of the *cash account* has been overcast by £1,000 and this is reflected in the balance brought down	1 Credit the *cash account* with £1,000
2a Cash purchases of £200 have been credited in the *cash account* but not entered in the *purchases account*	2a Debit the *purchases account* with £200
2b Rent paid of £50 has been credited in the *cash account* but also credited in error to the *rent account*	2b Debit the *rent account* with £100 (i.e. £50 × 2)
2c Bank charges of £23 shown in the *bank account* have been debited to the *bank charges account* as £32	2c Credit the *bank charges account* with £9
3 The *sales revenue account* shows a balance of £2,000, which has been entered on the trial balance as £200	3 Delete the wrong figure on the trial balance and insert the correct amount

These types of error are typically corrected with the use of a suspense account.

21.4 Suspense accounts

Suspense accounts are used for two purposes:

1 *Recording undefined transactions*: That is, where money is received or paid but there is no record of what it relates to, the amount would be entered in the cash book and posted to a suspense account. When the nature of the transaction is known, the amount is transferred from the suspense account to the appropriate account.

2 *To record in the ledger any difference on a trial balance and thus make it agree*: If a trial balance fails to agree by a relatively small amount and the error(s) cannot be found quickly, the difference is inserted in the trial balance (to make it agree) and in a suspense account. The entry in the *suspense account* must be on the same side of the ledger as the entry in the trial balance. At a later date when the error(s) are located they are corrected by double entry – by means of an entry in the suspense account and the other in the account containing the error. This correction through the suspense account is necessary because the original entry in the suspense account (which made the trial balance agree) in effect corrected all the errors in total. Thus, the correction must effectively be moved from the suspense account to the account that contains the error.

An illustration of the use of suspense accounts is given in Worked Example 21.3.

WORKED EXAMPLE 21.3

A trial balance failed to agree because the debit side exceeds the credit side by £2,509. A suspense account has been opened into which the difference is entered. Subsequently, the following errors were identified:

1 The debit side of the cash book has been overcast by £1,000.

2 Goods bought by cheque for £200 have been credited in the cash book but not entered in the *purchases account.*

3 Rent paid of £50 has been credited in the cash book but also credited in error to the *rent account.*

4 Car repairs of £23 shown in the cash book have been debited to the *motor expenses account* as £32 in error.

5 The sales account contains a balance of £2,000 but this has been entered in the trial balance as £200.

You are required to prepare the journal entries needed to correct the above errors and show the entries in the suspense account.

The journal

			Debit	**Credit**
			£	**£**
1	*Suspense account*	Dr	1,000	
	Cash book	Cr		1,000
	Being correction of arithmetic error			
2	*Purchases account*	Dr	200	
	Suspense account	Cr		200
	Being correction of posting error			
3	*Rent account*	Dr	100	
	Suspense account	Cr		100
	Being correction of posting error (£50 × 2)			
4	*Suspense account*	Dr	9	
	Motor expenses	Cr		9
	Being correction of transposed figures			
5	*Suspense account*	Dr	1,800	
	Trial balance (no ledger entry)	Cr		1,800
	Being correction of extraction error			

Suspense account			
Cash book	1,000	Difference on trial balance	2,509
Motor expenses	9	Purchases	200
Extraction error on sales	1,800	Rent	100
	2,809		2,809

Notes

1 It should be noted that only errors of the type that cause a trial balance to disagree are corrected by means of an entry in the *suspense account*. This is because errors that cause a trial balance to disagree give rise to the original entry in the suspense account.

2 The correction of errors via a *suspense account* always involves a double entry to the individual ledger account, with one exception. This relates to the correction of extraction errors, such as item 5 above, where the only ledger entry is in the *suspense account*. A useful way of working out whether the entry in the *suspense account* is a debit or credit is to imagine what entry is needed to correct the trial balance; the entry in the *suspense account* will be on the opposite side of the ledger.

3 Sometimes in examination questions, and in practice, the errors that have been identified are not the only errors. In this case there will still be a balance on the *suspense account* after the known errors have been corrected. This shows the amount of the remaining errors.

4 Occasionally in examination questions and in practice the final financial statements are prepared before the errors in the *suspense account* have been found and corrected. In this instance the *suspense account* will be shown on the statement of financial position. In practice, it will disappear when the errors in the *suspense account* are corrected along with the necessary changes to the items in the final financial statements that are incorrect. However, instead of correcting the final financial statements, some examination questions require students to prepare a statement amending the original/draft (i.e. wrong) figure of profit. In this case it will be necessary also to show the effect of correcting each error on the original profit, as an addition to or subtraction from this figure, thus arriving at a revised amount of profit.

WORKED EXAMPLE 21.4

When Jane, a senior accountant from Balance Accountancy Services, extracted the trial balance from the general ledger of Smith Applepie Limited she noticed that the trial balance did not agree. The debit side was £504 more than the credit balance. Jane is an experienced accountant and she knows from experience that the bookkeeper in Smith Applepie Limited is well trained and normally has everything posted correctly.

What will her first steps be to finding out the source of this error?

As an experienced accountant, Jane's first reaction will be to check her own totals. Then it is likely that she will divide the difference by nine. £504/9 = 56. If the difference is divisible by 9 then it is possible that the error is due to a transposition error. The next step will be to check the trial balance figures to the ledger balances with a focus on ensuring that the balances have been transposed correctly. If this does not uncover the problem, the bank reconciliation, the sales and purchases control accounts and the balances on the corresponding day books will all be checked. If all this is clear then it is likely that the problem lies in the other accounts. This process helps to narrow down the areas that require very labour-intensive review. It is likely that Jane will also get the bookkeeper to help to locate the error.

Errors in bookkeeping are typically corrected internally and, unless material or unethical, are rarely brought to the attention of stakeholders. In some instances, entities make errors that are deemed to be so material that the financial statements require restatement (i.e. to be re-prepared) and reissued to the market. In some instances the regulators will demand restatement in light of their review of the financial statements. The next real world example explains the economic consequence on a company's share price of an error of principle wherein expenses were incorrectly posted to asset accounts.

REAL WORLD EXAMPLE 21.1

Accounting errors may force Harvest Natural to restate results

Reuters reported on 19 March 2013 that Harvest Natural's stock fell 46 percent to a four-year low of $2.97 in early trading, making it the biggest percentage loser on the New York Stock Exchange.

Harvest Natural also estimated a loss of about $9.6 million, or 26 cents per share, for 2012, in contrast to analysts' expectation of a profit of 87 cents per share (Thomson Reuters I/B/E/S).

The company, which now has a market value of about $120 million, had reported profits on a per-share basis for the last nine quarters.

Harvest Natural said in a regulatory filing that there were errors related to incorrect capitalization of some lease maintenance costs and internal selling, general and administrative costs.

Source: Adapted from Reuters website, http://uk.reuters.com/article/2013/03/19/us-harvestnatural-restatment-idUKBRE92I0LU20130319, accessed September 2013.

Summary

If the total of the debit ledger account balances in a trial balance does not equal the total of the credit ledger account balances, this means that certain types of error must have occurred. The types of error that cause a trial balance to disagree comprise arithmetic error, posting error and extraction error. These need to be corrected by a one-sided entry in the general ledger or trial balance. There are six types of error that do not cause a trial balance to disagree. These consist of errors of principle, errors of commission, errors of omission, errors of original/prime entry, compensating errors and double posting errors. Errors that do not cause a trial balance to disagree are always corrected by means of a two-sided ledger (and journal) entry.

Suspense accounts are used for two purposes. One is to record transactions, the nature of which is unknown. The other is to record in the ledger any difference on a trial balance, and thus make it agree. When the error(s) that gave rise to the difference are located, they are corrected by means of one entry in the *suspense account* and a corresponding entry in the account containing the error. Only errors that cause a trial balance to disagree are corrected by means of an entry in the suspense account.

Errors giving rise to the creation of a *suspense account* should be located and corrected before final financial statements are prepared. However, if errors are discovered after the preparation of the final financial statements, the effect of their correction on the statement of profit or loss and statement of financial position should be taken into consideration. This may involve preparing revised final financial statements.

Key terms and concepts

arithmetic error	370	error of principle	368
cast (add)	370	extraction error	370
compensating error	368	overcast	370
double posting error	368	posting errors	370
error of commission	368	suspense accounts	371
error of omission	368	transposed figures	370
error of original/prime entry	368	undercast	370

An asterisk after the question number indicates that there is a suggested answer in Appendix 2.

Review questions

connect

21.1 Describe the types of errors that:

a cause a trial balance to disagree;

b do not cause a trial balance to disagree.

21.2 Describe the two main uses of a suspense account.

Exercises

connect

BASIC

21.3 Write journals to correct the following errors. These errors are not *suspense account* errors.

1 £150 sales invoice posted to the credit customer, *D. Brown's account* – should have been posted to the credit customer, *D. Black's account.*

2 £50 stationery paid for in cash was debited to the *cash account* and credited to the *stationery account.*

3 £100 paid for equipment by cheque was debited to *purchases.*

BASIC

21.4 Write journals to correct the following errors. These errors are not *suspense account* errors.

1 A payment of £4,000 for rent was incorrectly posted to the *insurance account.*

2 The cost of purchasing a delivery van, £12,400, is incorrectly debited to the *motor expenses account.*

3 The day's cash sales takings, £13,400, were not paid into the bank or entered into the *cash book.*

4 A payment of £400 for insurance has been entered in the cash book correctly but posted to the *insurance account* as £40. This is balanced by a transposition error in posting another payment into the *motor expenses account* where £480 was posted as £840.

BASIC

21.5 Write journals to correct the following errors (*suspense account* errors):

1 The debit side of the cash book is undercast by £3,000.

2 A payment of £475 for an electricity bill is correctly entered in the cash book but debited to the *telephone account* as £457.

3 A payment of £4,750 for an electricity bill is again correctly entered in the cash book but is not debited to the *telephone account* at all.

4 In preparing the trial balance the debit balance of £1,940 on the electricity bill is omitted.

5 A credit balance of £280 on the *heat and light account* was not brought forward into the current year.

BASIC

21.6* A trial balance failed to agree. On investigation the following errors were found:

a Wages of £250 have been credited in the *cash account* but no other entry has been made.

b The credit side of the *sales revenue account* has been undercast by £100 and this is reflected in the balance brought down.

c Purchases of £198 shown in the *purchases account* have been entered in the *credit suppliers' account* as £189.

d The *drawings account* contains a balance of £300, but this has been entered on the trial balance as £3,000.

e Bank interest received of £86 has been credited in the *bank account* and the *interest received account.*

Required

Describe the entries needed to correct the above errors.

INTERMEDIATE

21.7 Arthur started a new business on 1 January 20X5. You are supplied with the following nominal ledger accounts, which have been closed off and a trial balance extracted. These are Arthur's only transactions in this period.

Cash account						***Sales revenue account***					
Date	**Details**	**£**	**Date**	**Details**	**£**	**Date**	**Details**	**£**	**Date**	**Details**	**£**
6 Jan	Sales	100	9 Jan	H&L	80				6 Jan	Cash	100
8 Jan	Sales	89							8 Jan	Cash	98
									10 Jan	Bank	129
			10 Jan	Bal c/d	119	10 Jan	PL a/c	327			
		189			189			327			327
11 Jan	Bal b/d	119									

Capital introduced account						Bank account					
Date	Details	£	Date	Details	£	Date	Details	£	Date	Details	£
			1 Jan	Bank	1,000	1 Jan	Cap int.	1,000	2 Jan	H&L	50
						10 Jan	Sales	192	3 Jan	Van	500
10 Jan	Cap a/c	100							10 Jan	Bal c/d	742
		100			100			1,192			1,192
						11 Jan	Bal b/d	742			

Heat and light account (H&L)						Motor vehicle account					
Date	Details	£	Date	Details	£	Date	Details	£	Date	Details	£
2 Jan	Bank	50				3 Jan	Bank	500			
9 Jan	Cash	80	10 Jan	PL a/c	130				10 Jan	PL a/c	500
		130			130			500			500

Trial balance for Arthur as at 10 January 20X5:

	Debit	Credit
	£	£
Cash	119	
Sales		372
Capital introduced		100
Bank account	742	
Heat and light	130	
Motor vehicles	500	
	1,491	572

The trial balance should balance.

There are seven errors (six are double-entry errors, the other is a description error).

Required

a Describe the entries required to correct the errors.

b Redraft the amended ledger accounts and trial balance as on 10 January 20X5.

21.8 Chocolate is a confectionery shop owned by Thomas McKee. Thomas operates a manual bookkeeping system and employs a cashier and a bookkeeper. When writing up the books of account for the year ended 31 December 20X4, the following errors were discovered: INTERMEDIATE

1 The sale of cakes for £128 was not recorded in the cash book or ledger.

2 Payment of £1,600 as rent was recorded as £16,000 in the cash book and ledger.

3 £500 received from a supplier for returned goods was recorded in the cash book only.

4 A payment of £16,000 for a vehicle was recorded in the cash book as a 'purchase'.

5 A payment (£750) to a supplier 'Stephen McCann' was recorded in his account but not in the cash book.

6 £70 paid for stationery was posted to the *telephone account* in the ledger.

7 £425 paid for advertising has not been posted in the ledger.

Required

In respect of each of the errors you are to identify:

a which member of staff is responsible for the error;

b whether the balancing of the trial balance would have been affected;

c the journal required to correct the error (with description).

INTERMEDIATE

21.9 The draft trial balance of Regent Ltd as at 31 May 20X5 agreed. The business proceeded with the preparation of the draft final financial statements and these showed a profit of £305,660.

However, a subsequent audit revealed the following errors:

1 Bank charges of £56 had been omitted from the cash book.

2 The purchases journal had been overcast by £400.

3 The sales journal had been undercast by £100.

4 An invoice for £127 received from Alpha Ltd had been entered into the purchases journal as £217. (This is quite independent of the error made in the purchases journal referred to above.)

5 It is now considered prudent to write off the balance of £88 on *P. Shadey's account* as irrecoverable.

6 An invoice from Caring Garages Ltd for £550 in respect of servicing Regent Ltd's motor vehicles had been posted to the debit of *motor vehicles account*.

7 Depreciation of 10 per cent per annum has been provided for on motor vehicles inclusive of the £550 invoice referred to in point 6 above.

Regent Ltd maintains control accounts for credit sales and credit purchases in its general ledger. Individual accounts for credit customers and credit suppliers are maintained on a memorandum basis only.

Required

a Prepare journal entries to show how the above errors would be corrected. (*Note*: Dates and narratives not required.)

b What is the profit for the year after correcting the above errors?

(AAT)

INTERMEDIATE

21.10* When preparing a trial balance the bookkeeper found it disagreed by £600, the credit side being that much greater than the debit side. The difference was entered in a *suspense account*. The following errors were subsequently found:

1 A cheque for £32 for electricity was entered in the cash book but not posted to the ledger.

2 The debit side of the *wages account* is overcast by £28.

3 There is a debit in the *rent account* of £198 that should be £918.

4 The purchase of a van for £3,000 has been posted to the debit side of the *purchases account* in error.

5 A cheque received from A. Watt for £80 has been credited to *A. Watson's account* in error.

6 The sale of some old loose tools for £100 had been credited to *sales account* in error.

7 An amount of £17 paid for postage stamps has been entered in the *carriage outwards account* in error.

8 Bank charges of £41 shown on the bank statement have not been entered in the books.

9 An amount of £9 for stationery has been entered in the cash book but not posted to the *stationery account*. Cash sales of £43 are entered correctly in the cash book but posted to the *sales account* as £34.

10 A credit sale to J. Bloggs of £120 was entered in the sales day book as £12.

11 A credit balance of £62 shown in the *discount received account* has been entered on the debit side of the trial balance.

Required

Prepare the journal entries necessary to correct the above errors and show the *suspense account*.

21.11 INTERMEDIATE At the end of January 20X5 a trial balance extracted from the ledger of Gerald Ltd did not balance and a *suspense account* was opened for the amount of the difference. Subsequently, the following matters came to light:

1 £234 had been received during January from a credit customer who owed £240. No entry has been made for the £6 outstanding but it is now decided to treat it as a cash discount.

2 Returns to suppliers during January were correctly posted individually to personal accounts but were incorrectly totalled. The total, overstated by £100, was posted to the *returns account*.

3 A bank statement drawn up to 31 January 20X5 showed a credit balance of £120 while the balance of the *bank account* in the trial balance was an overdraft of £87. The difference was found on reconciliation to comprise:

a a direct debit for the annual subscription to a trade association of £70, for which no entry had been made in the books of account;

b an entry in the bank account for payment to a supplier shown as £230 instead of £320;

c unpresented cheques on 31 January totalled £327;

d the remainder of the difference was due to an addition error in the *bank account*.

4 A cheque for £163 was received during January in full settlement of a receivable that was written off in the previous financial year. It was correctly entered in the *bank account* but not posted elsewhere, pending instructions.

5 A credit customer's account with a balance of £180 had been taken out of the loose-leaf ledger when a query was investigated and not replaced at the time the trial balance was extracted.

6 A credit note for £5 sent to a customer in respect of an allowance had been posted to the wrong side of the *customer's personal account*.

Required

Show what correcting entries need to be made in the ledger accounts in respect of these matters. Set out your answer as follows:

Item	Account(s) to be debited £	Account(s) to be credited £

(ACCA, adapted)

21.12 INTERMEDIATE Chi Knitwear Ltd is an old-fashioned firm with a handwritten set of books. A trial balance is extracted at the end of each month, and a statement of profit or loss and statement of financial position are computed. This month, however, the trial balance does not balance, the credits exceeding debits by £1,536.

You are asked to help and after inspection of the ledgers, you discover the following errors:

1 A balance of £87 on a *credit customer's account* has been omitted from the schedule of outstanding balances, the total of which was entered as trade receivables in the trial balance.

2 A small piece of machinery purchased for £1,200 had been written off to repairs.

3 The receipts side of the cash book had been undercast by £720.

4 The total of one page of the sales day book had been carried forward as £8,154, whereas the correct amount was £8,514.

5 A credit note for £179 received from a supplier had been posted to the wrong side of his account.

6 An electricity bill in the sum of £152, not yet accrued for, is discovered in a filing tray.

7 Mr Smith, whose past debts to the company had been the subject of an allowance, at last paid £731 to clear his account. His *personal account* has been credited but the cheque has not yet passed through the cash book.

Required

a Write up the *suspense account* to clear the difference.

b State the effect on the accounts of correcting each error.

(ACCA)

ADVANCED

21.13 The draft final financial statements of RST Ltd for the year ended 30 April 20X5 showed a net profit for the year of £78,263.

During the subsequent audit, the following errors and omissions were discovered. At the draft stage a *suspense account* had been opened to record the net difference.

1 Trade receivables were shown as £55,210. However:

a irrecoverable receivables of £610 had not been written off;

b the existing allowance for irrecoverable receivables, £1,300, should have been adjusted to 2 per cent of trade receivables;

c an allowance of 2 per cent for discounts on trade receivables should have been raised.

2 Rates of £491, which had been prepaid at 30 April 20X4, had not been brought down on the rates account as an opening balance.

3 A vehicle held as a non-current asset, which had originally cost £8,100 and for which £5,280 had been provided as depreciation, had been sold for £1,350. The proceeds had been correctly debited to *bank* but had been credited to *sales*. No transfers had been made to a *disposals account*.

4 Credit purchases of £1,762 had been correctly debited to the *purchases account* but had been credited to the *supplier's account* as £1,672.

5 A piece of equipment costing £9,800 and acquired on 1 May 20X4 for use in the business had been debited to the *purchases account*. (The company depreciates equipment at 20 per cent per annum on cost.)

6 Items valued at £2,171 had been completely omitted from the closing inventory figure.

7 At 30 April 20X5 an accrual of £543 for electricity charges and an insurance prepayment of £162 had been omitted.

8 The credit side of the *wages account* had been under-added by £100 before the balance on the account had been determined.

Required

Using relevant information from that given above:

a Prepare a statement correcting the draft net profit.

b Post and balance the *suspense account*. (*Note*: The opening balance of this account has not been given and must be derived.)

(ACCA)

ADVANCED

21.14* Miscup showed a difference on their trial balance of £14,650. This was posted to a *suspense account* so that the financial statements for the year ended 31 March 20X5 could be prepared. The following statement of financial position was produced:

Statement of financial position for Miscup as at 31st March 20X5			
ASSETS	£	£	£
Non-current assets	*Cost*	*Deprec*	*NBV*
Tangible assets			
Freehold premises	60,000	–	60,000
Motor vehicles	25,000	11,935	13,065
Fixtures and fittings	1,500	750	750
	86,500	12,685	73,815
Current assets			
Inventories			75,410
Trade and other receivables			37,140
Cash			75
			112,625
Suspense account			14,650
Total assets			201,090
OWNERS' EQUITY AND LIABILITIES			
Equity and reserves			
Equity share capital			125,000
Reserves			33,500
			158,500
Current liabilities			
Trade and other payables			41,360
Bank overdraft			1,230
Total liabilities			42,590
Total equity and liabilities			201,090

On checking the books to eliminate the *suspense account* you find the following errors:

1. The debit side of the cash book is undercast by £10,000.
2. A credit item of £5,000 in the cash book on account of a new building has not been posted to the nominal ledger.
3. The purchases day book has been summarized for posting to the nominal ledger but an item of purchases of £100 has been entered in the summary as £1,000 and a further transport charge of £450 has been entered as £45.
4. An item of rent received, £45, was posted twice to the nominal ledger from the cash book.
5. The debit side of the sales ledger control account was undercast by £100.
6. On reconciling the bank statement with the cash book, it was discovered that bank charges of £3,250 had not been entered in the cash book.
7. Depreciation of motor vehicles was undercharged by £500.
8. Inventories were undervalued by £1,250.
9. Suppliers' invoices totalling £2,110 for goods included in inventory had been omitted from the books.

Required

a Show the journal entries necessary to eliminate the balance on the *suspense account*.

b Show the statement of financial position of Miscup as at 31 March 20X5, after correcting all the above errors.

(ACCA)

INTERMEDIATE

21.15 Jacobs Ltd has recently completed its draft financial statements for the year ended 30 December 20X4, which showed a draft profit for the year of £300,000. During the audit a number of mistakes and omissions were uncovered. These are listed below.

1 A cheque from a credit customer amounting to £7,100 had been received on 27 December 20X4 but had not been banked or included in the financial statements.

2 Depreciation on a non-current asset had been incorrectly calculated. The asset's cost was £125,000, it was being depreciated on a straight-line basis over four years. £16,250 was charged in the financial statements.

3 Although included in inventory an invoice for goods sold by Jacobs amounting to £17,500, dated 26 December 20X4, had not been included in the financial statements.

4 Two items of inventory, currently valued at a total cost of £35,000, are now considered obsolete. The director estimates that they will only realize about £10,000 between them.

5 The company accountant forgot to include a charge for interest on the 10 per cent long-term loan of £240,000 for the final six months of the year.

6 Rates of £1,500 for the year to 1 April 20X4 were paid for in April 20X3. No entries have been made in the financial statements in relation to this item other than correctly recording the original payment.

7 An item of capital worth £3,000 had been incorrectly entered into the prepayments account instead of non-current assets. The asset has a useful life of three years and a residual value of £600. The accounting policy states that the reducing balance method is most appropriate for this type of asset.

8 One of the credit customers contacted Jacobs Ltd to inform them that the cashier had not given him the correct agreed trade discount of 20 per cent. The invoices affected were noted by the accountant as follows:

30 November 20X4	£3,500
2 December 20X4	£1,500
15 December 20X4	£2,000

Required

a For each of the items (1) to (8) above, state and describe the effect on the profit for the year and calculate the total effect on Jacobs' draft profit figure.

b For each of the items (1) to (8) above, describe the changes, if any, which will have to be made on the statement of financial position of Jacobs Ltd.

Chapter 22

Single entry and incomplete records

Learning Objectives:

After reading this chapter you should be able to do the following:

1. List the three main forms of incomplete records.
2. Determine the profit/(loss) for the year from a reconstruction of the statement of changes in owner's equity accounts between the start and end of the year.
3. Explain how an accountant would approach preparing the financial statements for an entity that has single entry recordkeeping.
4. Reconstruct the ledger accounts to determine the missing entries in an entity that has single entry record keeping.
5. Prepare final financial statements from incomplete records and single entry.

22.1 Introduction

Incomplete records is a general term given to a situation where the transactions of an organization have not been recorded in double-entry form (or using a computer system), and thus there is not a full set of records of the enterprise's transactions. This is quite common in practice in the case of sole traders. It is often too expensive for small businesses to maintain a complete system of double-entry bookkeeping. In addition, many sole traders often claim to have little practical use for any records other than to know how much money they have, and the amounts of trade receivables and trade payables. Many sole traders are usually able to remember, without records, what non-current assets they own, and any non-current liabilities they owe. In the case of small businesses the accountant is therefore usually engaged not to write up the books, but to ascertain the profit of the business for tax purposes. Often, but not always, a statement of financial position is also prepared.

In practice, there are three different forms of incomplete records:

1 *Incomplete records of revenue income and expenditure*: That is, there are no basic documents or records of revenue income and expenditure or the records are inadequate. This situation usually arises where the books and documents have been accidentally destroyed (e.g. in a fire) or the owner failed to keep proper records. In these circumstances it is not possible to construct a statement of profit or loss. However, it may still be possible to ascertain the profit for the period provided there is information available relating to the assets and liabilities of the business at the start and end of the relevant period.

2 *Single entry*: The term **single entry** is used to describe a situation where the business transactions have only been entered in a book of prime entry, usually a cashbook, and not in the ledger. However, one would also expect to be able to obtain documents or information relating to the value of non-current assets, inventories, trade receivables, trade payables, accruals, prepayments and any non-current liabilities. Given that this is available, it would be possible to prepare a statement of profit or loss and statement of financial position.

3 *Incomplete single entry*: This term may be used to describe a variation on point 2 where there are no books of account (or these are incomplete) but the receipts and payments can be ascertained from the bank statements and/or supporting documents. In this case it would be necessary to produce a cashbook summary from the information given on the bank statements, paying-in book and cheque book stubs. The final financial statements will then be prepared from the cashbook summary together with the supporting documents and information referred to in point 2.

The procedure for preparing final financial statements from these three different forms of incomplete records is described below.

22.2 Incomplete records of revenue income and expenditure

As explained in the introduction to this chapter, in these circumstances it is not possible to construct a statement of profit or loss. However, it may still be possible to ascertain the profit for the relevant period provided that the information to prepare a statement of financial position at the start and end of the period is available.

This involves the application of the comparative static approach to profit measurement described in Chapter 7, 'The Accounting Equation and its Components'. The profit (or loss) is found by calculating the difference between the net asset value of the business at the start and end of the period as shown by the two statements of financial position. The logic behind this computation is that an increase in net assets can only come from two sources, either additional capital introduced by the owner or profits generated from the sale of goods and/or other assets. This is illustrated below.

Statement of financial position as at 1 January 20X5	
ASSETS	£
Total assets	25,000
EQUITY AND LIABILITIES	
Capital	20,000
Liabilities	5,000
Total equity and liabilities	25,000

Statement of financial position as at 31 December 20X5	
ASSETS	£
Total assets	38,000
EQUITY AND LIABILITIES	
Capital	30,000
Liabilities	8,000
Total equity and liabilities	38,000

Ignoring the possibility of additional capital introduced during the year, this business has a profit for the year of £30,000 − £20,000 = £10,000. This is computed by ascertaining the increase in either the net assets or the capital. Both must give the same answer. Any decrease in net assets or capital will mean there has been a loss for the year.

However, part of the increase in net assets and capital may be due to additional capital being introduced during the year of, say, £3,000. In this case the profit for the year is that part of the increase in net assets and capital, which is not the result of additional capital introduced during the year, thus:

	£
Net/assets/capital at end of year	30,000
Less: Net assets/capital at start of year	20,000
Increase in capital	10,000
Less: Capital introduced	3,000
Profit for the year	7,000

In addition, the owner of the business may have made drawings during the year of, say, £4,000. These will reduce the capital and net assets at the end of the year. In this case the profit for the year is the increase in net assets/capital less the capital introduced, plus the drawings for the year – that is, £10,000 – £3,000 + £4,000 = £11,000.

In summary, profits (or losses) are reflected in an increase (or decrease) in the net asset value of a business over a given period. The net asset value corresponds to the capital. The profit or loss can thus be ascertained by computing the change in capital over the year and adjusting this for any capital introduced and/or drawings during the year. This is presented in the form of a statement, as shown below. Notice that this statement is simply a reordering of the entries normally shown in the capital account of a sole trader, as presented in the statement of financial position.

Statement of changes in owner equity for the year ended 31 December 20X5	
	£
Capital at end of current year	30,000
Less: Capital at end of previous year	20,000
Increase in capital	10,000

Add: Drawings during the year including any goods taken by the proprietor for his or her own use	4,000
	14,000
Less: Capital introduced during the year either in the form of cash or any other asset	3,000
Profit for the year	11,000

Before this statement can be prepared, it is necessary to calculate the capital at the end of the current year and at the end of the previous year. This is done by preparing a statement of financial position at each of these dates. These are referred to as **statements of affairs**. This is illustrated in Worked Example 22.1.

WORKED EXAMPLE 22.1

A. Ferry has been in business for the last 10 years as an electrical retailer, and has asked you to compute her profit for the year ended 31 December 20X4.

She has no business bank account and kept no records of her income and expenditure apart from the purchase and sale of non-current assets, inventory, trade receivables and trade payables, and a running cash balance. She has been able to give you the following information relating to her affairs:

1 At 31 December 20X4 the business owns freehold land and buildings used as a shop and workshop. This cost £10,000 on 1 July 20W8.

2 During the year ended 31 December 20X4 the business owned the following vehicles:

Date of purchase	Cost	Date of sale	Proceeds
31 Mar 20X1	£1,000	31 Oct 20X4	£625
1 May 20X2	£1,200	unsold at 31 Dec 20X4	
1 July 20X4	£2,000	unsold at 31 Dec 20X4	

You estimate that the above vehicles have a useful working life of five years and no residual value. In previous years these have been depreciated using the straight-line method.

3 During the year ended 31 December 20X4 the owner has put £5,280 in cash into the business and has taken out £15,900 as drawings.

4 Amounts outstanding at:

	31 Dec 20X3	31 Dec 20X4
	£	£
Trade receivables	865	645
Trade payables	390	480
Accruals	35	20
Prepayments	40	25

Included in trade receivables at 31 December 20X4 are doubtful receivables of £85.

5 Inventories have been valued at £565 on 31 December 20X3, and £760 on 31 December 20X4. The latter amount includes a television that cost £60 and was worthless at that date due to it having been accidentally damaged beyond repair.

6 The cash balances at 31 December 20X3 and 20X4 were £285 and £165, respectively.

Required

Calculate the profit for the year ended 31 December 20X4, showing clearly your workings.

Workings

20X3	**£**	**£**	**20X4**	**£**	**£**
Motor vehicles owned at 31 December 20X3			*Motor vehicles* owned at 31 December 20X4		
Purchased 31/3/X1		1,000	Purchased 1/5/X2		1,200
Purchased 1/5/X2		1,200	Purchased 1/7/X4		2,000
Total cost		2,200	Total cost		3,200
Depreciation using the straight-line method			Depreciation using the straight-line method		
20% × £1,000 × 2 years 9 months	(550)		20% × £1,200 × 2 years 8 months	(640)	
20% × £1,200 × 1 year 8 months	(400)		20% × £2,000 × 6 months	(200)	
		(950)			(840)
Written-down value at 31 December 20X3		1,250	Written down value at 31 December 20X4		2,360

A. Ferry	
Statement of financial position as at 1 January 20X4	
ASSETS	£
Non-current assets	
Freehold land and buildings	10,000
Motor vehicles	1,250
	11,250
Current assets	
Inventories	565
Trade receivables	865
Prepayments	40
Cash	285
	1,755
Total assets	13,005
EQUITY AND LIABILITIES	
Capital	12,580
Liabilities	
Trade payables	390
Accruals	35
	425
Total equity and liabilities	13,005

Statement of financial position as at 31 December 20X4			
ASSETS	Cost (£)	Deprec (£)	NBV (£)
Non-current assets			
Freehold land and buildings	10,000	–	10,000
Motor vehicles	3,200	840	2,360
	13,200	840	12,360
Current assets			
Inventories (£760 – £60)			700
Trade receivables		645	
Allowance for irrecoverable receivables		85	560
Prepayments			25
Cash			165
			1,450
Total assets			13,810
EQUITY AND LIABILITIES			
Capital			13,310
Liabilities			
Trade payables			480
Accruals			20
			500
Total equity and liabilities			13,810

Statement of changes in owner equity for the year ended 31 December 20X4	
	£
Capital at 31 December 20X4	13,310
Less: Capital at 31 December 20X3	12,580
	730
Add: Drawings	15,900
	16,630
Less: Capital introduced	5,280
Net profit for the year	11,350

Notes

1 There is no need to compute the profit or loss on disposals of non-current assets since this will automatically be reflected in the increase in net assets/capital. However, it is necessary to compute the written-down value (or possibly market value) of non-current assets at the end of each year as shown in the workings in order to prepare the statements of financial position.

2 The inventory at 31 December 20X4 excludes the cost of the television that was damaged beyond repair of £60.

3 Doubtful receivables have been provided for by reducing the amount of trade receivables at 31 December 20X4.

4 The amounts for capital in the statement of affairs are the difference between the two sides of these statements of financial position.

5 It is usual to treat the statement of financial position at the end of the previous year as workings not requiring any formal presentation. However, the statement of financial position at the end of the current year should contain the usual headings and subtotals and be in a form presentable to the owner and other interested parties such as HM Revenue and Customs.

22.3 Single entry

As explained in the introduction, **single entry** refers to the situation where a business has some record of its receipts and payments, non-current assets, inventories, trade receivables, trade payables, accruals, prepayments and non-current liabilities. However, these records are not in double-entry form and usually consist of just a cashbook.

One possibility is for the accountant to complete the records by posting the receipts and payments to the appropriate accounts in the ledger either in full or summarized form. The final financial statements are then prepared from the trial balance in the normal way. This is common in practice. However, in very small businesses this may be too expensive and/or impractical. In this case the final financial statements are prepared directly from the cashbook or a summary thereof, and the appropriate adjustments made for trade receivables, trade payables, provisions, accruals, prepayments, and so on. Examination questions on this topic also usually take the same form. An illustration of this treatment of single-entry records is given in Worked Example 22.2. Because of the importance and length of the workings, the procedure for answering the question is presented as a series of steps. These are well worth memorizing as a model for answering such questions.

WORKED EXAMPLE 22.2

The following is the statement of financial position of L. Cook at 1 January 20X4:

Statement of financial position as at 1 January 20X4	
ASSETS	**£**
Non-current assets	
Freehold land and buildings	12,500
Motor vehicles (cost £5,000)	2,900
	15,400
Current assets	
Inventories	1,650
Trade receivables	3,270
Prepayments (rates)	60
Bank	1,500
	6,480
Total assets	21,880

EQUITY AND LIABILITIES	
Capital	19,240
Liabilities	
Trade payables	2,610
Accruals (electricity)	30
	2,640
Total equity and liabilities	21,880

The only book kept by Cook is a cashbook, a summary of which for the year ended 31 December 20X4 has been prepared as follows:

Cashbook			
	£		£
Balance b/d	1,500	Rates	140
Cash takings banked	4,460	Salaries	2,820
Cheques from credit customers	15,930	Electricity	185
Additional capital	500	Bank charges	10
		Motor expenses	655
		Payments to credit suppliers	16,680
		Stationery	230
		Sundry expenses	40
		Balance c/d	1,630
	22,390		22,390

From the supporting documents it has been ascertained that:

1 The following amounts have been paid from cash takings before they were banked:

Drawings	£22,000
Purchases	£560
Petrol	£85
Repairs to buildings	£490

2 Cook has taken goods out of the business for his own use that cost £265.

3 Motor vehicles have been depreciated in past years at 20 per cent per annum by the reducing balance method.

4 Inventory at 31 December 20X4 was valued at £1,960.

5 The trade receivables and trade payables outstanding at the end of the year are £2,920 and £2,860, respectively.

6 At 31 December 20X4 there are rates prepaid of £70 and electricity accrued of £45.

7 You expect to charge Cook £100 for your services.

Required

Prepare a statement of profit or loss for the year ended 31 December 20X4 and a statement of financial position at that date. Show all your workings clearly.

Workings/procedure

1 If necessary, prepare a statement of financial position as at the end of the previous year to ascertain the capital at that date.

2 If necessary, prepare a summarized cashbook from the bank statements, and so on, to ascertain the balance at the end of the year and the total amounts received and spent on each type of income and expenditure, and assets.

3 **a** Compute the net credit purchases by preparing a purchase ledger control account as follows:

Purchase ledger control account

20X4	Details	£	20X4	Details	£
31 Dec	Bank	16,680	1 Jan	Balance b/d	2,610
31 Dec	Balance c/d	2,860	31 Dec	Net purchases	16,930
		19,540			19,540

The net purchases figure is the difference between the two sides.

b Compute the cash and cheque purchases and then the total purchases:

Total purchases = £560 + £16,930 = £17,490

4 **a** Compute the net credit sales by preparing a sales ledger control account as follows:

Sales ledger control account

20X4	Details	£	20X4	Details	£
1 Jan	Balance b/d	3,270	31 Dec	Bank	15,930
31 Dec	Net sales	15,580	31 Dec	Balance c/d	2,920
		18,850			18,850

The net sales figure is the difference between the two sides.

b Compute the cash and cheque sales and then the total sales:

Cash sales = £4,460 + £22,000 + £560 + £85 + £490 = £27,595

Total sales = £27,595 + £15,580 = £43,175

Note that sometimes the computations in (a) and (b) have to be combined. This is necessary when the cash and/or cheque sales are not given separately from the cheques received from credit customers. In this case the total cash and cheques received in respect of sales are credited to the control account. The same principle would also have to be used in the case of purchases when cash and/or cheque purchases are not given separately from cheques paid to credit suppliers.

5 Compute the charges to the statement of profit or loss for those expenses with accruals or prepayments by preparing the relevant ledger accounts. Alternatively, in examinations this may be shown as workings in the statement of profit or loss.

Light and heat					
20X4	Details	£	20X4	Details	£
31 Dec	Bank	185	1 Jan	Accrual b/d	30
31 Dec	Accrual c/d	45	31 Dec	Profit or loss a/c	200
		230			230

Rates					
20X4	Details	£	20X4	Details	£
1 Jan	Prepayment b/d	60	31 Dec	Profit or loss a/c	130
31 Dec	Bank	140	31 Dec	Prepayment c/d	70
		200			200

6 Compute the charges and/or credits to the statement of profit or loss in respect of any allowance for irrecoverable receivables, depreciation, sales of non-current assets, and so on. Alternatively, if these are relatively simple, in examinations, they may be shown as workings in the statement of profit or loss.

Motor vehicles

Depreciation expense = 20% × £2,900 = £580

Aggregate depreciation = (£5,000 − £2,900) + £580 = £2,680

7 Prepare the final financial statements, remembering to add together any cheque and cash expenditure of the same type (e.g. motor expenses in this example), and include any non-current assets acquired, drawings (e.g. goods taken by the proprietor), capital introduced, and so on.

L. Cook		
Statement of profit or loss for the year ended 31 December 20X4		
	£	**£**
Sales revenue		43,175
Less: cost of sales		
Inventories at 1 Jan 20X4	1,650	
Add: Purchases (£17,490 − £265)	17,225	
	18,875	
Less: Inventories at 31 Dec 20X4	1,960	16,915
Gross profit		26,260
Less: expenditure		
Rates (£60 + £140 − £70)	130	
Salaries	2,820	
Light and heat (£185 + £45 − £30)	200	
Bank charges	10	
Motor expenses (£655 + £85)	740	
Stationery	230	

Sundry expenses	40	
Repairs to buildings	490	
Depreciation on vehicles (20% × £2,900)	580	
Accountancy fees	100	5,340
Profit for the year		20,920

L. Cook

Statement of financial position as at 31st December 20X4

	£ Cost	£ Prov depn	£ WDV
ASSETS			
Non-current assets			
Freehold land and buildings	12,500	–	12,500
Motor vehicles	5,000	2,680	2,320
	17,500	2,680	14,820
Current assets			
Inventories			1,960
Trade receivables			2,920
Prepayments			70
Bank			1,630
			6,580
Total assets			21,400
EQUITY AND LIABILITIES			
Equity capital (owners)			
Balance at 1 Jan 20X4			19,240
Add: Capital introduced			500
Net profit			20,920
			40,660
Less: Drawings (£22,000 + £265)			22,265
Balance at 31 Dec 20X4			18,395
Current liabilities			
Trade payables			2,860
Accruals (£45 + £100)			145
Total liabilities			3,005
Total equity and liabilities			21,400

Notes

1 The goods taken by the proprietor for his own use of £265 have been added to drawings and deducted from purchases (rather than added to sales) because the question gives their cost.

2 In the workings for the sales ledger control account, the term 'net sales' is used to emphasize that this is after deducting returns, the amount of which is unknown and cannot be ascertained.

However, if the returns were known, these would be entered in the sales ledger control account and the statement of profit or loss in the normal manner. More importantly, if the value of any irrecoverable receivables, discount allowed, and so on, were known, these would have to be entered in the sales ledger control account and statement of profit or loss in the normal way. The same principles apply to the purchases ledger control account where there are returns, discount received, and so on.

3 In some single entry questions there are petty cash balances at the start and end of the accounting year. Where the balance in cash at the end of the year is greater than at the start, the increase must be added to the cash takings that were banked in order to ascertain the cash sales (in Workings 4(b) above). The reason is simply because the increase in the cash float must have come from cash sales. Put another way, the cash takings banked are after deducting/excluding the increase in the cash balance. To ascertain the cash sales therefore necessitates adding back any increase in the cash float, or deducting any decrease from the cash takings that were banked. Where there are cash balances/floats at the start and end of the year, an alternative to the one-line computation of cash sales shown in Workings 4(b) above is to prepare a petty cash account. The cash sales will be the difference between the two sides of the account after entering the opening and closing cash balances, the amounts paid from the cash takings, and the takings that were banked. This may have the added advantage of reminding students to include the various items of petty cash expenditure in the final financial statements.

4 Many businesses accept credit cards such as Visa or MasterCard in payment for goods that they sell to the public. This gives rise to special problems where there are incomplete records in the form of single entry. Most credit card companies charge a commission of up to 5 per cent of the value of goods sold. Thus, if a business sells goods with a selling price of, say, £200 the amount it receives will be £190 (i.e. 95 per cent of £200). The normal ledger entries for this sale will be to credit the sales account with £200 and debit a credit card trade receivable account with the amount it expects to receive of £190. The difference of £10 commission should be debited to a commission account that will be transferred to the statement of profit or loss at the end of the year.

Where there is only single entry, the accounting records in respect of **credit card sales** will consist of a debit in the cashbook of the amounts received from the credit card company during the year. It is therefore necessary to compute the value of sales before deducting the commission. This is done in two stages. The first stage is to calculate the total credit card sales for the year after deducting commission by means of a credit card receivables account in which the amount received is adjusted to take into account the opening and closing amounts owing. The second stage is to gross up the total credit card sales after deducting commission to ascertain the total credit card sales before deducting commission. Using the example above, this would be $100/95 \times £190 = £200$. The £200 is then included in sales in the trading account, and the difference of £200 − £190 = £10 commission is shown as a separate item of expense in the statement of profit or loss.

Learning Activity 22.1

Construct a list of your personal assets and liabilities from one year ago (for example, car, phone, etc.). Construct a list of your personal assets and liabilities today. How has your tangible net worth changed?

22.4 Record keeping for tax purposes

There are likely to be improvements in small business record-keeping as HM Revenue and Customs have recently implemented a policy of fining tax payers up to £3,000 for poor record-keeping as highlighted in Real World Example 22.1.

REAL WORLD EXAMPLE 22.1

HMRC could fine small businesses up to £3,000 for bad record keeping

Fears of a fresh attack on small businesses have emerged over the imminent deadline for an HMRC inquiry on business records checks that could see small businesses investigated and fines issued for bad record keeping. The proposals indicate HMRC wants to target small businesses keeping inaccurate trading records dating back the past six years, with penalties of up to £3,000. The proposals would affect 50,000 businesses a year – with the aim of bringing in up to £600m in fines for the government.

Essentially, it will amount to HMRC demanding small businesses keep their records in order on an ongoing basis rather than once a year.

Source: Adapted from 'HMRC could fine small businesses up to £3,000 a year for bad record keeping', The Guardian Money Blog 16 February 2011, http://www.theguardian.com/money/blog/2011/feb/16/hmrc-small-businesses-record-keeping accessed August 2014

The proposals have since been implemented but HMRC provides guidelines and advice on its website and if a business is found to have inadequate records, it will be given the chance to bring them up to standard before the fine is imposed. (http://www.hmrc.gov.uk/dealingwith/bus-record-checks.htm)

Summary

There are three different forms of incomplete records. The first is incomplete records of revenue income and expenditure. This refers to where there are no documents or records of revenue income and expenditure. It is therefore not possible to prepare a statement of profit or loss. However, the profit may be ascertained by calculating the difference between the capital/net asset value of the business at the start and end of the year by preparing a statement of financial position at each of these dates. The profit is found by adjusting the change in capital over the year for any capital introduced and/or drawings.

The second form of incomplete records is known as 'single entry'. This refers to where the business transactions have been entered in a cashbook but not posted to a ledger. The third form of incomplete record is incomplete single entry. This refers to where there are no books of account but a cashbook summary can be prepared from the bank statements and/or supporting documents.

In the case of incomplete single entry and single entry, it is therefore possible to prepare a statement of profit or loss and statement of financial position. This can be done by posting the amounts shown in the summarized cashbook to the ledger, extracting a trial balance and preparing final financial statements in the normal way. Alternatively, students are normally required in examinations to prepare final financial statements from the summarized cashbook by means of workings. These usually take the form of purchases ledger and sales ledger control accounts, in order to ascertain the purchases and sales, respectively, together with those expense accounts that have accruals and/or prepayments at the start and end of the year.

Key terms and concepts

credit card sales	394	single entry	384
incomplete records	384	statement of affairs	386

An asterisk after the question number indicates that there is a suggested answer in Appendix 2.

Review question

connect

22.1 Describe the different forms of incomplete records with which you are familiar.

Exercises

connect

BASIC

22.2 Capital at the end of 20X4 is £2,000.

Capital at the end of 20X5 is £3,000.

There were no drawings; and no capital had been introduced.

Required

Calculate the profit for the year ended 20X5 from the above information.

BASIC

22.3 Capital at the end of 20X4 is £2,000.

Capital at the end of 20X5 is £3,000.

Drawings were £700.

Required

Calculate the profit for the year ended 20X5 from the above information.

BASIC

22.4 Happy did not keep proper books of account. At 31 August 20X3 his balances were:

	£
Lorry (at valuation)	3,000
Tools	4,000
Inventories	16,740
Trade receivables	11,890
Bank	2,209
Cash	115
Trade payables	9,052

Details of transactions in year to 31 August 20X4:

Tools purchased	2,000
Drawings	7,560
Legacy	2,800

At 31 August 20X4 the assets and liabilities were:

Depreciation on tools £600, lorry now valued at £2,500, trade receivables £15,821, prepaid expenses £72, inventories £21,491, trade payables £6,002, payables for expenses £236, cash £84, bank overdraft £165.

Required

Draw up a statement showing the profit or loss made by Happy for the year ended 31 August 20X4.

INTERMEDIATE

22.5* The following is the statement of financial position of Round Music as at 30 June 20X4:

Statement of financial position for Round Music as at 30 June 20X4	
ASSETS	£
Non-current assets	
Plant	31,000
	31,000
Current assets	
Inventories	9,720
Trade receivables	6,810
Prepayments	150
Bank	820
	17,500
Total assets	48,500
EQUITY AND LIABILITIES	
Equity capital (owners)	42,770
Current liabilities	
Trade payables	5,640
Accruals (electricity)	90
Total liabilities	5,730
Total equity and liabilities	48,500

During the year ended 30 June 20X5 there was a fire that destroyed the books of account and supporting documents. However, from questioning the proprietor you have been able to obtain the following information:

1 The plant at 30 June 20X4 cost £50,000 and has been depreciated at 10 per cent per annum by the straight-line method on a strict time basis. Additional plant was purchased on 1 April 20X5 at a cost of £20,000. Plant costing £10,000 on 1 January 20X2 was sold on 1 October 20X4 for £4,450.

2 Inventories at 30 June 20X5 were valued at £8,630. This includes goods costing £1,120 that are worthless because of fire damage.

3 Trade receivables and trade payables at 30 June 20X5 were £6,120 and £3,480, respectively. Trade receivables include doubtful receivables of £310.

4 Accruals and prepayments at 30 June 20X5 were £130 and £80, respectively.

5 There was a bank overdraft at 30 June 20X5 of £1,430.

6 During the year the business had borrowed £7,000 from Lickey Bank, which was repayable on 1 January 20X8.

7 During the year the owner introduced additional capital of £5,000 and made drawings of £18,500 by cheque. The proprietor also took goods costing £750 from the business for his own use.

You are required to compute the profit for the year ended 30 June 20X5 and prepare a statement of financial position at that date. Show separately the cost of non-current assets and the aggregate depreciation in the statement of financial position.

22.6 Jane Grimes, retail fruit and vegetable merchant, does not keep a full set of accounting records. However, the following information has been produced from the business's records:

1 Summary of the bank account for the year ended 31 August 20X5:

Bank account			
	£		£
1 Sep 20X4 balance brought forward	1,970	Payments to credit suppliers	72,000
Receipts from credit customers	96,000	Purchase of motor van (E471 KBR)	13,000
Sale of private yacht	20,000	Rent and rates	2,600
Sale of motor van (A123 BWA)	2,100	Wages	15,100
		Motor vehicle expenses	3,350
		Postage and stationery	1,360
		Drawings	9,200
		Repairs and renewals	650
		Insurances	800
		31 Aug 20X5 balance carried forward	2,010
	120,070		120,070

2 Assets and liabilities, other than balance at bank:

As at	1 Sept 20X4	31 Aug 20X5
	£	£
Trade payables	4,700	2,590
Trade receivables	7,320	9,500
Rent and rates accruals	200	260

Motor vans:		
A123 BWA – At cost	10,000	–
Provision for depreciation	8,000	–
E471 KBR – At cost	–	13,000
Provision for depreciation	–	To be determined
Inventory in trade	4,900	5,900
Insurances prepaid	160	200

3 All receipts are banked and all payments are made from the business bank account.

4 A trade debt of £300 owing by Peter Blunt and included in the trade receivables at 31 August 20X5 (see point 2 above) is to be written off as an irrecoverable receivable.

5 It is Jane Grimes' policy to provide depreciation at the rate of 20 per cent on the cost of motor vans held at the end of each financial year; no depreciation is provided in the year of sale or disposal of a motor van.

6 Discounts received during the year ended 31 August 20X5 from credit suppliers amounted to £1,000.

Required

a Prepare Jane Grimes' statement of profit or loss for the year ended 31 August 20X5.

b Prepare Jane Grimes' statement of financial position as at 31 August 20X5.

(AAT)

INTERMEDIATE

22.7* The following is the statement of financial position of A. Fox at 31 July 20X4.

Statement of financial position for A. Fox as at 31 July 20X4			
	£	**£**	**£**
ASSETS	**Cost**	**Prov depn**	**WDV**
Non-current assets			
Freehold land and buildings	35,000	–	35,000
Fixtures and fittings	10,000	4,200	5,800
	45,000	4,200	40,800
Current assets			
Inventories			3,300
Trade receivables			6,540
Prepayments (telephone)			120
Bank			3,000
			12,960
Total assets			53,760
EQUITY AND LIABILITIES			
Equity capital (owners)			48,480
Current liabilities			
Trade payables			5,220
Accruals (electricity)			60
Total liabilities			5,280
Total equity and liabilities			53,760

The only book kept by A. Fox is a cashbook in which all transactions passed through the bank account are recorded. A summary of the cashbook for the year ended 31 July 20X5 has been prepared as follows:

Cashbook

	£		£
Balance b/d	3,000	Wages	5,640
Cash takings banked	18,920	Telephone	280
Cheques from credit customers	31,860	Electricity	370
Additional capital	1,000	Motor expenses	1,810
		Payments to credit suppliers	33,360
		Printing	560
		Purchases	4,500
		Balance c/d	8,260
	54,780		54,780

From the supporting documents it has been ascertained that:

1 The following amounts have been paid from the cash takings before they were banked:

	£
Drawings	4,000
Purchases	1,120
Car repairs	980
Window cleaning	170

2 Inventory at 31 July 20X5 was valued at £3,920.

3 At 31 July 20X5 there are telephone charges prepaid of £140 and electricity accrued of £290.

4 The trade receivables and trade payables outstanding at the end of the year are £5,840 and £5,720, respectively.

5 Fox has taken goods out of the business for his own use that cost £530.

6 Fixtures and fittings have been depreciated in past years at 20 per cent per annum by the reducing balance method.

Required

Prepare a statement of profit or loss for the year ended 31 July 20X5 and a statement of financial position at that date.

ADVANCED

22.8 Jock is a clothing retailer. At 31 December 20X4 he asks you to prepare his final financial statements from very incomplete records. You were able to extract the following information from the limited records that were available.

	31/12/X3	31/12/X4
	£	£
Fixtures and fittings (valued)	9,900	19,648
Motor vehicle	1,000	1,500
Building	25,000	24,500

Inventories	39,050	34,255
Trade receivables	2,500	4,500
Trade payables	7,435	9,995
Cash in hand	925	2,350
Cash at bank	9,500	16,850
Rent accrual	500	–
Cash received in settlement of fire claim for goods (cost £1,050) lost by fire	–	1,050

Accruals and prepayments

In addition to the above Jock extracted the following invoices, which need to be adjusted for.

Rates		
Invoice date	**Period covering**	**Amount paid**
		£
30/03/X3	01/04/X3–31/03/X4	£800
20/03/X4	01/04/X4–31/03/X5	£880

Electricity

Electricity bills are paid for in arrears. The quarters are end of February, May, August and November. The bill paid on 15 March 20X4 was £315. It is expected that the February 20X5 bill will be 20 per cent higher than last year's bill.

Jock records cash received and paid, except for his own drawings.

Jock's cash transactions for the year are as follows:

Payments by cash	**£**
Wages	25,560
General expenses	1,350
Goods for resale	10,352
Receipts by cash	**£**
Cash received from credit customers	185,650
Sale of motor car	750
Paid into bank	**£**
Cheques and cash	123,704

Jock always paid credit suppliers in sufficient time to avail of a cash discount of 5 per cent. A summary of the cheque payments are as follows:

Payments by cheque	**£**
Fixtures and fittings	15,654
Rent and rates	5,625
Trade suppliers (credit)	86,500
Heat and light	3,215
Personal expenditure	3,560
New car	1,800

Jock did not keep a record of his own personal cash takings.

Required

a Prepare an opening statement of financial position for Jock as at 1 January 20X4.

b Prepare the sales, purchases, bank, cash, accruals, prepayments (with corresponding expense accounts) and non-current asset adjustment accounts.

c Draft a statement of profit or loss for the year ended 31 December 20X4 and a statement of financial position at that date.

(*Note*: All workings must be provided.)

ADVANCED

22.9 Miss Fitt owns a retail shop. The statement of profit or loss and statement of financial position are prepared annually by you from records consisting of a bank statement and a file of unpaid suppliers and outstanding trade receivables.

The following balances were shown on her statement of financial position at 1 January 20X4:

	£
Shop trade payables	24,500
Shop fittings (cost £25,000) at written-down value	20,000
Inventory in hand	47,500
Trade receivables	5,000
Cash at bank	11,000
Cash float in till	1,000

The following is a summary of her bank statement for the year ended 31 December 20X4:

	£
Takings banked	698,300
Payments to credit suppliers	629,000
Rent of premises to 31 December 20X4	40,000
A. Smith – shop fitters	8,500
Advertising in local newspaper	5,000
Sundry expenses	3,800

You obtain the following additional information:

1 Takings are banked daily and all suppliers are paid by cheque, but Miss Fitt keeps £1,500 per week for herself, and pays her assistant £1,100 per week out of the takings.

2 The work done by A. Smith was for new shelving and repairs to existing fittings. The cost of new shelves was estimated at £5,000.

3 The cash float in the till was considered insufficient and raised to £1,500.

4 Miss Fitt took £7,500 worth of goods for her own use without payment.

5 Your charges will be £2,500 for preparing the financial statements.

6 The outstanding accounts file shows £23,000 due to credit suppliers, £1,000 due in respect of sundry expenses, and £8,500 outstanding trade receivables.

7 Depreciation on shop fittings is provided at 10 per cent on cost, a full year's charge being made in year of purchase.

8 Inventory in hand at 31 December 20X4 was £71,000.

You are required to prepare Miss Fitt's statement of profit or loss for the year ended 31 December 20X4, and her statement of financial position as at that date.

(ACCA, adapted)

ADVANCED

22.10 A year ago, you prepared financial statements for A. Wilson, a retailer. His closing position was then:

Statement of financial position for A. Wilson as at 31 March 20X4			
	£	**£**	**£**
	Cost	**Prov depn**	**WDV**
ASSETS			
Non-current assets			
Delivery van (cost £4,800 in May 20X2)	4,800	1,920	2,880
Current assets			
Inventories			6,410
Trade receivables		1,196	
Less: allowance for irrecoverable receivables		72	1,124
Owing from Askard Ltd			196
			7,730
Total assets			10,610
EQUITY AND LIABILITIES			
Equity capital (owners)			7,726
Current liabilities			
Bank overdraft			70
Trade payables			2,094
Accruals (accountant's fee)			120
Provision for legal claim			600
Total liabilities			2,884
Total equity and liabilities			10,610

Mr Wilson does not keep full records (despite your advice) and once again you have to use what information is available to prepare his financial statements to 31 March 20X5. The most reliable evidence is a summary of the bank statements for the year. It shows:

	£	£
Balance at 1 Apr 20X4 (overdraft)		(70)
Cash and cheques from credit customers		33,100
Cheques from Askard Ltd.		7,840
		40,870
Less: cheques drawn for:		
Wilson's personal expenses	7,400	
Van – tax, insurance, repairs	440	
Rent, rates and general expenses	2,940	
Cash register	400	
Accountant's fee	120	
Trade payables	28,284	
Legal claim settled	460	40,044
Balance at 31 Mar 20X5		826

For some of the sales Askard credit cards are accepted. Askard Ltd charges 2 per cent commission. At the end of the year the amount outstanding from Askard Ltd was £294.

Some other sales are on credit terms. Wilson keeps copies of the sales invoices in a box until they are settled. Those still in the 'unpaid' box at 31 March 20X5 totalled £1,652, which included one for £136 outstanding for four months – otherwise they were all less than two months old. Wilson thinks he allowed cash discounts of about £150 during the year. The debt of £72 outstanding at the beginning of the year for which an allowance was made was never paid.

The amount of cash and cheques received from credit customers and from cash sales were all paid into the bank except that some cash payments were made first. These were estimated as:

	£
Part-time assistance	840
Petrol for van	800
Miscellaneous expenses	200
Wilson's drawings	2,000

Invoices from suppliers of goods outstanding at the year end totalled £2,420. Closing inventory was estimated at £7,090 (cost price) and your fee has been agreed at £200. It has been agreed with the Inspector of Taxes that £440 of the van expenses should be treated as Wilson's private expenses.

Required

Prepare the statement of profit or loss for Wilson's business for the year to 31 March 20X5 and a statement of financial position at that date.

(ACCA)

ADVANCED

22.11 David Denton set up in business as a plumber a year ago, and he has asked you to act as his accountant. His instructions to you are in the form of the following letter.

Dear Henry

I was pleased when you agreed to act as my accountant and look forward to your first visit to check my records. The proposed fee of £2,500 p.a. is acceptable. I regret that the paperwork for the work done during the year is incomplete. I started my business on 1 January last, and put £65,000 into a business bank account on that date. I brought my van into the firm at that time, and reckon that it was worth £36,000 then. I think it will last another three years after the end of the first year of my business use.

I have drawn £900 per week from the business bank account during the year. In my trade it is difficult to take a holiday, but my wife managed to get away for a while. The travel agent's bill for £2,800 was paid out of the business account. I bought the lease of the yard and office for £65,000. The lease has 10 years to run, and the rent is only £3,000 a year payable in advance on the anniversary of the date of purchase, which was 1 April. I borrowed £40,000 on that day from Aunt Jane to help pay for the lease. I have agreed to pay her 10 per cent interest per annum, but have been too busy to do anything about this yet.

I was lucky enough to meet Miss Prism shortly before I set up on my own, and she has worked for me as an office organizer right from the start. She is paid a salary of £30,000 per annum. All the bills for the year have been carefully preserved in a tool box, and we analysed them last week. The materials I have bought cost me £96,000, but I reckon there was £5,800's worth left in the yard on 31 December. I have not paid for them all yet; I think we owed £7,140 to the suppliers on 31 December. I was surprised to see that I had spent £48,000 on plumbing equipment, but it should last me five years or so. Electricity bills received up to 30 September came to £11,220; motor expenses were £9,120, and general expenses £13,490 for the year. The insurance premium for the year to 31 March next was £8,000. All these have been paid by cheque but Miss Prism has lost the rates demand.

I expect the Local Authority will send a reminder soon since I have not yet paid. I seem to remember that the rates came to £1,800 for the year to 31 March next.

Miss Prism sent out bills to my customers for work done, but some of them are very slow to pay. Altogether the charges made were £298,630, but only £256,130 had been received by 31 December.

Miss Prism thinks that 10 per cent of the remaining bills are not likely to be paid. Other customers for jobs too small to bill have paid £34,180 in cash for work done, but I only managed to bank £26,000 of this money. I used £4,000 of the difference to pay the family's grocery bills, and Miss Prism used the rest for general expenses, except for £1,230 which was left over in a drawer in the office on 31 December.

Yours sincerely,

David.

Required

Draw up a statement of profit or loss for the year ended 31 December, and a statement of financial position as at that date.

(ACCA, adapted)

22.12 Bugs Bunny, a wholesale dealer in ready-made menswear, achieves a gross profit ratio of 50 per cent. The statement of financial position of the business as at 30 June 20X4 was as follows: ADVANCED

Bugs Bunny
Statement of financial position as at 30 June 20X4

	£ Cost	£ Prov depn	£ WDV
ASSETS			
Non-current assets			
Motor vehicles	60,000	24,000	36,000
Fixtures and fittings	43,000	12,900	30,100
	103,000	36,900	66,100
Current assets			
Inventories			79,300
Trade receivables less allowance for irrecoverable receivables			76,475
Cash and bank			17,125
			172,900
Total assets			239,000
EQUITY AND LIABILITIES			
Equity capital			
Opening balance			114,750
Profit for the year			38,900
			153,650
Drawings			29,150
Closing balance			124,500
Current liabilities			
Trade payables			94,472
Accruals – salary			9,200
Accruals – other expenses			10,828
Total current liabilities			114,500
Total equity and liabilities			239,000

Since this date the accounting function has been neglected. However, on the basis of records in his personal diary, Bugs Bunny confirms the following:

1 As at 30 June 20X5, £138,000 is due from credit customers and £108,000 is owed to credit suppliers.

2 During the year ended 30 June 20X5, the payments set out below have been made:

	£
Paid for purchases	252,000
Staff salaries	80,130
Rent for shop premises	10,000
Entertainment	2,250
Office equipment	15,200
Motor vehicles	17,500
Other expenses	33,020
Personal expenses	13,250

3 A vehicle acquired for £15,000 on 1 April 20X1 was sold for £3,830 in the year to 30 June 20X5. Motor vehicles and equipment are depreciated at 20 per cent and 10 per cent per annum on cost, respectively. The depreciation policy is to charge a full year's depreciation in the year of acquisition and none in the year of disposal.

4 An allowance for irrecoverable receivables is maintained at 5 per cent of trade receivables outstanding at the year end. A receivable amounting to £22,000 is deemed to be irrecoverable and was written off in the year.

5 Accruals as at 30 June 20X5 consisted of salaries £10,200, rent £3,000 and other expenses amounting to £13,000.

6 Cash in hand and at bank on 30 June 20X5 is £400.

7 Inventories in trade on 30 June 20X5 (valued at cost) is £99,405.

8 With Bugs Bunny's permission, his teenage sons have been regularly helping themselves to readymade garments from the shop.

9 All sales and purchases are on credit.

Required

Prepare the statement of profit or loss for Bugs Bunny for the year ended 30 June 20X5 and the statement of financial position as at that date.

(*Note*: All workings must be shown.)

ADVANCED

22.13 T. Murray has prepared the following bank ledger account for the year ended 31 March 20X5:

Bank account

	£			£
Balance at 1 April 20X4	782	Repairs		256
Commission	4,930	Renewals		507
Rent income	567	Heat and light		350
Sundry income	58	Telephone		125
Capital introduced	652	Salary and wages		3,328
Bank interest	120	Extension to premises		800
Sale of land	3,600	General expenses		89
Sales	3,250	Stationery		25
		Rent		3,300
		Purchases		2,800
		Rates		200
		Furniture		250
		Motor vehicle		1,250
		Motor expenses		354
		Balance c/d – Cash	100	
		– Bank	225	325
	13,959			13,959

T. Murray has also supplied you with the following information.

a Commissions received included £85, which had been in arrears at 31 March 20X4, and £55, which had been paid for the year commencing 1 April 20X5. In addition, three customers still owed commission for the year to 31 March 20X5. One was commission for a type A product (£15), the other two were commission for the sale of type B products (£45).

b The land that was sold was valued in the company's books at £1,500.

c Depreciation is to be charged as follows.

Buildings	5 per cent per annum straight line basis
Motor vehicle	Sum of digits method over five years
Fixtures and fittings	25 per cent reducing balance method
Furniture	20 per cent reducing balance method

A full year's depreciation is charged in the year of purchase but none is charged in the year of sale.

d Accrued expenses:

	31/03/X4	31/03/X5
	£	£
Stationery	15	656
Wages	560	545

The electricity bill for the period to 30 April 20X5 (£450) was paid for on 23 May 20X5.

The rent paid in advance was to cover three full financial years including 20X4.

The interest received in the year is for the period from 1 April 20X4 to 31 December 20X4.

e General expenses includes an amount of £35 for a telephone bill that was posted here in error.

f The closing inventory has been valued at £990.

g Repairs include £200, which was paid for a brand new pool table.

h The following balances are from T. Murray's books at 31 March 20X4:

	£
Land at cost	8,000
Buildings at cost	6,400
Buildings provision for depreciation	800
Fixtures and fittings at cost	1,250
Fixtures provision for depreciation	250
Furniture at cost	580
Furniture provision for depreciation	180
Commission in arrears (including £15 from a bankrupt client)	100
Commission in advance	30
Inventories	250

Required

a Prepare the opening statement of financial position for T. Murray as at 31 March 20X4.

b Prepare the statement of profit or loss for T. Murray for the year ended 31 March 20X5.

c Prepare the statement of financial position for T. Murray as at 31 March 20X5.

Further questions on incomplete records arise in Chapter 25, 'The Final Financial Statements of Partnerships' and in online Chapter 32, 'The Final Financial Statements of Clubs'.

PART FIVE
Preparing final financial statements for manufacturing entities

23	Inventory valuation	411
24	Financial statements for manufacturing entities	429

Chapter 23

Inventory valuation

Learning Objectives:

After reading this chapter you should be able to do the following:

1. Describe the methods for valuing work-in-progress (WIP) and explain the relationship between these methods and the treatment of WIP in manufacturing accounts.
2. Discuss the method of valuation of finished goods inventory including its impact on gross profit.
3. Describe the perpetual inventory system.
4. Describe the main methods of identifying the cost of fungible inventories and demonstrate their application in the valuation of inventories and the cost of sales.
5. Discuss the circumstances in which each of the main methods of identifying the cost of fungible inventories may be justifiable, and describe their impact on gross profit.

—23.1 Introduction

Accounting for inventories is a perfect example of the matching concept. Goods purchased or manufactured in one period that are not sold, are carried into the next period to be matched against the sales revenue when it occurs. The accounting for inventory is examined in Chapter 14, though this chapter only considers inventory that has been purchased for resale. In practice different entities have different types of inventory. For example, the inventory in service-type organizations (such as accountancy firms or law firms) is typically partly completed service roles, such as half an audit. This type of inventory is called **work-in-progress**. Chapter 24 examines accounting within manufacturing entities, which have four different types of inventory as identified in Figure 23.1.

Figure 23.1

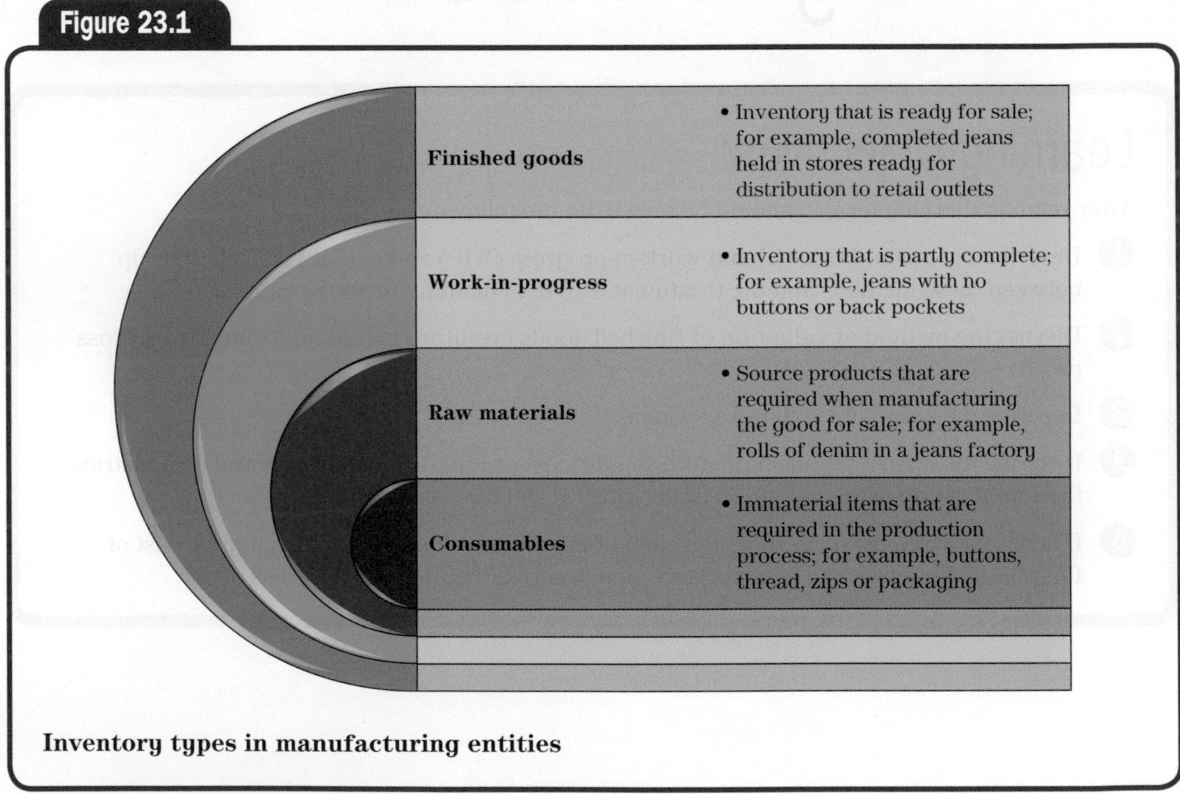

Finished goods
• Inventory that is ready for sale; for example, completed jeans held in stores ready for distribution to retail outlets
Work-in-progress
• Inventory that is partly complete; for example, jeans with no buttons or back pockets
Raw materials
• Source products that are required when manufacturing the good for sale; for example, rolls of denim in a jeans factory
Consumables
• Immaterial items that are required in the production process; for example, buttons, thread, zips or packaging

Inventory types in manufacturing entities

A retail entity is likely to have only two types of inventory:

1 *Goods for sale* – clothes, shoes, and so on.

2 *Consumables* – immaterial items such as coat hangers, price stickers, plastic bags, and so on.

— 23.2 Monitoring inventory

There are several different methods used to monitor inventory within an entity, and two are considered briefly in this chapter – the perpetual and periodic inventory control systems. These are explained briefly in Figure 23.2.

—23.3 The valuation of goods for sale and raw materials

Though the accounting for inventories is relatively straightforward, the valuation of inventory has been manipulated in the past to window-dress financial statements. **Window-dressing** is a term used to describe

Figure 23.2

Periodic inventory control system	• The number of items in inventory are physically checked periodically (monthly, quarterly, yearly) and orders for more items are made in light of expected demand relative to the number of items in stores • The review period is usually fixed and hence high levels of inventory are typically held • In many instances the business closes for the counts, or it is performed overnight
Perpetual inventory control systems	• Constant monitoring of inventory levels and frequent reorders • Computerized control system usually with point of sale technology which records inventory receipts and issues from stores • Physical counts take place continuously, are organized and focus on rotated areas (for example, in a large supermarket, baby products may be covered in one day, vegetables the next, cereals the next, etc.)

Inventory control systems

the selection of valuation techniques and presentation ploys to portray the performance and financial position of an entity in a more favourable light than perhaps it should be. Inventorics are material in many entities, and changes in valuation directly impact on profitability; therefore, the accounting and valuation of inventories is afforded its own standard, *International Accounting Standard 2 – Inventories* (IASB, 2013). The remainder of this chapter focuses on the valuation of inventories.

IAS 2 recommends that inventories be valued at the lower of purchase cost and **net realizable value** (NRV), where purchase cost includes:

1 invoice price, net of trade discount and value added tax (VAT is recoverable);

2 import duties (if sourced in a foreign country) and other taxes that are not recoverable;

3 transport costs (delivery costs);

4 handling costs;

5 other costs that are directly attributable to obtaining the inventory.

Raw materials should be valued in the same manner.

Sometimes goods in inventory may have to be sold at a price that is below their cost. If there are goods in inventory at the end of a given accounting year that are expected to result in a loss, those goods should be valued and entered in the financial statements at their expected NRV and not their cost. NRV is the estimated proceeds from the sale of items of inventory less all costs to be incurred in marketing, selling and distributing that are directly related to the items in question. The comparison of cost and NRV needs to be made in respect of each item of inventory separately (see Worked Example 23.1).

WORKED EXAMPLE 23.1

Martin is a clothes retailer. At the year-end his inventory was valued at its cost price of £21,560. Included in this inventory is a line of clothing that is no longer in fashion. The inventory cost £5,600. Martin is sure that this inventory can be sold at 80 per cent of its cost price. It will cost £200 to market the line.

Required

Calculate the value of inventory that should appear in the financial statements of Martin.

Workings

The £5,600 needs to be written down to its NRV, which is its sale value less any costs of sale.

£5,600 × 80% = £4,480 less £200 = £4,280.

This amounts to a total reduction of £1,320 (£5,600 – £4,280).

Therefore, the inventory will appear in the financial statements of Martin valued at £20,240 (£21,560 – £1,320).

Accounting policy for valuing inventory

Most entities provide details of how they value their inventories. An example can be found in the financial statements of Wm Morrison Supermarkets PLC as follows:

REAL WORLD EXAMPLE 23.1

Wm Morrison Supermarkets plc

Stocks

Stocks are measured at the lower of cost and net realisable value. Provision is made for obsolete and slow moving items. Cost is calculated on a weighted average basis and comprises purchase price, import duties and other non-recoverable taxes less rebates. Stocks represent goods for resale. Net realisable value is the estimated selling price in the ordinary course of business, less the estimated costs necessary to make the sale.

Source: Extract from the accounting policies note, Annual Report and Financial Statements 2013, p. 66.

Learning Activity 23.1

Using Wm Morrison Supermarket plc's financial statements (to be found on their website) for guidance, draft a pro forma note showing a breakdown of an inventory note for a company that manufactures furniture.

23.4 The valuation of **finished goods** and work-in-progress

IAS 2 provides guidance on how to value inventories – 'the cost of inventories shall comprise all costs of purchase, costs of conversion and other costs incurred in bringing inventories to their present location and condition'. The costs of purchase are covered in the previous section. The **costs of conversion** comprise:

1 costs directly attributable to the units of production; for example, direct labour, direct materials and subcontract work;

2 allocated production overheads (fixed and variable):

a ***Fixed production overheads*** – indirect costs of production that remain relatively constant regardless of the production quantity. Examples include depreciation of the factory building, maintenance of the factory building, factory rent and rates, factory management costs and factory administration costs.

b ***Variable production overheads*** – indirect costs of production that vary with production volume. Examples include indirect labour and indirect materials.

The specific costs that impact on the valuation of internally produced inventory are discussed in more detail in the next chapter that focuses on manufacturing entities.

Fungible inventory: **cost flow assumptions**

In the case of both manufacturing and non-manufacturing businesses, the determination of the cost/purchase price of goods in inventory often presents a major problem. It is frequently not possible to identify the particular batch(es) of goods that were purchased, which are in inventory at the end of the year. These are referred to as **fungible inventories**, which means substantially indistinguishable goods. In these circumstances it is necessary to make an *assumption* about the cost of goods in inventory. There are a number of possible assumptions, but the most reasonable assumption will depend on the type of good involved, the procedure for handling the receipt and sale of inventories, prices, and so on. The most appropriate assumption is one that provides a fair approximation to the expenditure actually incurred.

To provide a systematic method of valuing this type of inventory, most large businesses operate what is called a **perpetual inventory system**, which is a continuous record of the quantity and value of inventory. It includes a stores ledger containing an account for each type of good that is purchased. The **stores ledger** accounts are used to record the quantities and prices of goods purchased, the quantities and cost of goods sold (or issued to production in the case of direct materials in manufacturing entities), and the balance and cost of goods in inventories after each receipt and sale. This system requires an assumption or decision on how to attribute value to the goods that leave the stores (cost of goods sold/produced) and the inventory that remains. This is required as all the inventory in stores may have been purchased at different times and at different costs.

There are a number of possible assumptions or what are referred to as bases/methods of identifying/pricing the cost of inventories. The bases make assumptions about the flow of items in inventory. These flow assumptions are not selected as a result of the actual way in which inventory is used but to reflect a particular view of the economic effects of inventory usage in financial statements. They are outlined in Figure 23.3.

Figure 23.3

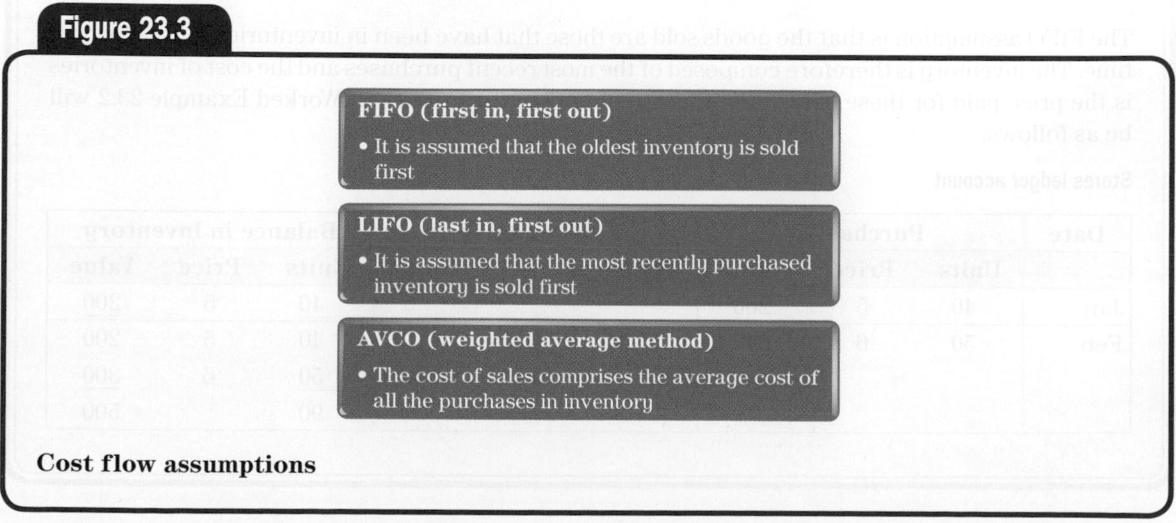

FIFO (first in, first out)
• It is assumed that the oldest inventory is sold first
LIFO (last in, first out)
• It is assumed that the most recently purchased inventory is sold first
AVCO (weighted average method)
• The cost of sales comprises the average cost of all the purchases in inventory

Cost flow assumptions

Each of these methods is described using Worked Example 23.2.

WORKED EXAMPLE 23.2

P. Easton commenced business on 1 January 20X5 as a dealer in scrap iron. The following purchases and sales were made during the first six months of 20X5:

Jan Purchased 40 tonnes at £5 per tonne

Feb Purchased 50 tonnes at £6 per tonne

Mar Sold 30 tonnes at £10 per tonne

Apr Purchased 70 tonnes at £7 per tonne

May Sold 80 tonnes at £15 per tonne

Required

a Prepare a perpetual inventory record of the quantities and values of goods purchased, sold and inventory.

b Prepare a statement of profit or loss showing the gross profit for the six months to 30 June 20X5 given that the above are the only purchases and sales.

State any assumptions that you make.

Learning Activity 23.2

Attempt part (b) of Worked Example 23.2 before proceeding further.

WORKED EXAMPLE 23.2 CONTINUED

1 First in, first out (FIFO)

The FIFO assumption is that the goods sold are those that have been in inventories for the longest time. The inventory is therefore composed of the most recent purchases and the cost of inventories is the price paid for these. Given the FIFO assumption, the answer to Worked Example 23.2 will be as follows.

Stores ledger account

Date	Purchases			Cost of sales			Balance in inventory		
	Units	Price	Value	Units	Price	Value	Units	Price	Value
Jan	40	5	200				40	5	200
Feb	50	6	300				40	5	200
							50	6	300
							90		500

Mar				30	5	150	10	5	50
							50	6	300
							60		350
Apr	70	7	490				10	5	50
							50	6	300
							70	7	490
							130		840
May				10	5	50			
				50	6	300			
				20	7	140	50	7	350
				80		490			
Totals	160		990	110		640	50		350

The FIFO method is based on the premise that the physical movement of goods over time will have this sequence of events, particularly where the goods are perishable. The use of the FIFO method is favoured by IAS 2 and by HM Revenue and Customs.

P. Easton		
Statement of profits or losses for the six months ended 30 June 20X5		
	£	**£**
Sales revenue: 30 tonnes @ £10	300	
80 tonnes @ £15	1,200	1,500
Less: Cost of sales –		
Purchases	990	
Less: Inventories at 30 June 20X5	350	640
Gross profit		860

2 Last in, first out (LIFO)

The LIFO assumption is that the goods sold are those that have been in inventory for the shortest time. The inventory is therefore composed of those goods that have been held for the longest time, and the cost of inventory is the price paid for these. Given the LIFO assumption, the answer to Worked Example 23.2 will be as follows:

Stores ledger account

Date	Purchases			Cost of sales			Balance in inventory		
	Units	Price	Value	Units	Price	Value	Units	Price	Value
Jan	40	5	200				40	5	200
Feb	50	6	300				50	6	300
							40	5	200
							90		500
Mar				30	6	180	20	6	120
							40	5	200
							60		320

Apr	70	7	490				70	7	490
							20	6	120
							40	5	200
							130		810
May				70	7	490			
				10	6	60	10	6	60
				80		550	40	5	200
							50		260
Totals	160		990	110		730	50		260

P. Easton		
Statement of profits or losses for the six months ended 30 June 20X5		
	£	£
Sales revenue		1,500
Less: Cost of sales –		
Purchases	990	
Less: Inventories at 30 June 20X5	260	730
Gross profit		770

The LIFO method may be in accordance with the physical movement of goods in some circumstances. For example, purchases of coal, iron ore, sand and gravel are likely to be piled one on top of the other, and thus goods taken from the top of the heap will probably consist of the most recent purchases. In most other instances it is an unrealistic assumption. However, even where this is the case, the LIFO method may be justified in times of rising prices on the grounds that the cost of sales will reflect the most recent prices. This is said to give a more realistic figure of profit since the most recent price is an approximation of the current cost of the goods sold (i.e. their replacement cost). Thus, one argument for the LIFO method is that where historical cost accounting is used it gives a 'true and fair view' of the profit in times of changing prices.

The LIFO method is not allowed under IAS 2 or by HM Revenue and Customs. The arguments put forward against its use are that LIFO 'results in inventories being stated in the statement of financial position at amounts that bear little relationship to recent cost levels, and it is a poor substitute for a proper system of accounting for changing prices'.

3 Weighted average method (AVCO)

The weighted average method is based on the assumption that the goods sold and the inventory comprise a mixture of each batch of purchases. The cost of sales and inventory is therefore taken to be a weighted average of the cost of purchases. Given the weighted average assumption, the answer to Worked Example 23.2 will be as follows (notice that a new weighted average is computed after each purchase):

Stores ledger account

Date	Purchases			Cost of sales			Balance in inventory		
	Units	Price	Value	Units	Price	Value	Units	Price	Value
Jan	40	5	200				40	5.000	200
Feb	50	6	300				90	5.556[1]	500
Mar				30	5.556	167	60	5.556	333
Apr	70	7	490				130	6.331[2]	823
May				80	6.331	506	50	6.331	317
Totals	160		990	110		673	50		317

Workings for weighted average cost:

1 February = £500 ÷ 90 units = £5.556

2 April = £823 ÷ 130 units = £6.331

All calculations to three decimal places.

P. Easton		
Statement of profits or losses for the six months ended 30 June 20X5		
	£	£
Sales revenue		1,500
Less: Cost of sales –		
Purchases	990	
Less: Inventories at 30 June 20X5	317	673
Gross profit		827

Where purchases are mixed together, the weighted average method can be justified on the grounds that it is in accordance with the physical events. This often occurs when goods are stored in a single container that is rarely completely emptied, such as in the case of nuts and bolts, liquids and granular substances, and so on. Another justification is that when prices are fluctuating it gives a more representative normal price and thus more comparable cost of sales figures.

The weighted average method is approved by IAS 2 and is acceptable to HM Revenue and Customs.

23.5 FIFO and LIFO compared

Clearly, each of the methods of calculating the cost of inventory results in different values for inventory and profit. In times of constantly rising prices, FIFO will give a higher figure of profits and value of inventory than LIFO because it matches older, lower costs against revenues. A business should choose whichever method is appropriate to its particular circumstances and apply this consistently in order that meaningful comparisons can be made. FIFO is by far the most common method used in practice in the UK because it is favoured by the UK accounting standard *SSAP 9 – Stocks and Long Term Contracts* (ASC, 1988), by IAS 2 and by HM Revenue and Customs. The valuation of inventories is a controversial issue in accounting, and is one of the areas most open to deliberate manipulation as can be seen in the following real world example.

REAL WORLD EXAMPLE 23.2

Sims Metal Management under investigation

Metal recycler Sims Metal Management Limited's share price fell by five per cent yesterday as an internal investigation into 'control failures and potential fraudulent conduct' began.

The Australian metal recycling company, which also operates in the US and UK, closed trading on Monday (21 January), with shares selling for $AUS 50 cents less than they had earlier in the day, after the metal recycler announced that there would be 'recognition of goodwill impairment in the first half results'. The suspected fraudulent activity centres on an overvaluation of the company's Long Marston and Newport waste electronic and electrical equipment (WEEE) recycling business in the UK.

In a statement, Sims Metal Management Limited said that the inventory of the UK business at Long Marston and Newport had been overstated by 'circa $60 million' (£39.7m) and relates to 'both changes in the assessment of the net realizable value of certain stock and physical adjustments'.

According to the company, 'preliminary findings' indicate that the situation arose due to 'control failures and potential fraudulent conduct by local and regional plant management responsible for technology and downstream processing systems in the UK'.

Source: Reece, A. (2013) 'Sims Metal Management under Investigation', Resource Media Limited, 22 January, http://www.resource.uk.com/article/News/Sims_Metal_Management_under_investigation-2654, accessed September 2013.

Summary

Work-in-progress and finished goods inventories are usually valued at their factory cost. Direct materials inventories and goods purchased for resale are normally valued at cost. However, IAS 2 dictates that if the NRV of any of these inventories is lower than their cost, they must be included in the final financial statements at their NRV. Furthermore, it is frequently not possible to identify the cost of goods in inventories. This is referred to as 'fungible inventories', which means that the goods are substantially indistinguishable from each other. In these circumstances it is necessary to make an assumption about the cost of goods in inventory and thus the cost of goods sold or issued to production in the case of direct materials in manufacturing entities. The most common assumptions are first in, first out (FIFO), last in, first out (LIFO), and a weighted average cost (AVCO). In times of changing prices, each will give a different value of inventories, cost of sales and thus profit.

Key terms and concepts

consumables	412	first in, first out (FIFO)	415
cost flow assumptions	415	fixed production overheads	415
costs of conversion	414	fungible inventories	415
finished goods	414	last in, first out (LIFO)	415

net realizable value (NRV)	413	weighted average method (AVCO)	415
perpetual inventory system	415	window-dressing	412
stores ledger	415	work-in-progress	412
variable production overheads	415		

An asterisk after the question number indicates that there is a suggested answer in Appendix 2.

Review questions

connect

23.1 Work-in-progress and finished goods inventories should be valued at the cost of purchase and conversion. Explain.

23.2 Explain how the matching principle is applied to the valuation of inventories.

23.3 Explain the circumstances in which inventories might be shown in the financial statements at a value different from their historical cost.

23.4 Explain fully the basis on which finished goods and work-in-progress inventories should be valued in final financial statements.

23.5 a What is a perpetual inventory system?

b Describe three methods of calculating the cost of fungible inventories.

c Explain the circumstances in which each of these methods may be justifiable.

23.6* 'In selecting a method of calculating the cost of inventory, management should ensure that the method chosen bears a reasonable relationship to actual costs. Methods such as . . . LIFO do not usually bear such a relationship' (ASC, 1988). Discuss.

Exercises

connect

INTERMEDIATE

23.7 On 1 April 20X4 Modern Dwellings Ltd commenced business as builders and contractors. It spent £14,000 on the purchase of six acres of land with the intention of dividing the land into plots and building 72 houses thereon.

During the year ended 31 March 20X5 roads and drains were constructed for the project at a total cost of £8,320. Building was commenced, and on 31 March 20X5 30 houses had been completed and eight were in the course of construction.

During the year the outlay on houses was as follows:

	£
Materials, etc.	36,000
Labour and subcontracting	45,000

The value of the work-in-progress on the uncompleted houses at 31 March 20X5 amounted to £8,500, being calculated on the actual cost of materials, labour and subcontracting to date.

During the year, 24 houses had been sold, realizing £80,000.

Required

Prepare a statement of profit or loss for the year ended 31 March 20X5. It can be assumed that the plots on which the 72 houses are to be built are all of equal size and value.

(ACCA, adapted)

INTERMEDIATE

23.8 After stocktaking for the year ended 31 May 20X4 had taken place, the closing inventory of Cobden Ltd was aggregated to a figure of £87,612.

During the course of the audit that followed, the undernoted facts were discovered:

1 Some goods stored outside had been included at their normal cost price of £570. They had, however, deteriorated and would require an estimated £120 to be spent to restore them to their original condition, after which they could be sold for £800.

2 Some goods had been damaged and were now unsaleable. They could, however, be sold for £110 as spares after repairs estimated at £40 had been carried out. They had originally cost £200.

3 One inventory sheet had been overcast by £126 and another undercast by £72.

4 Cobden Ltd had received goods costing £2,010 during the last week of May 20X4 but because the invoices did not arrive until June 20X4, they have not been included in inventories.

5 An inventory sheet total of £1,234 had been transferred to the summary sheet as £1,243.

6 Invoices totalling £638 arrived during the last week of May 20X4 (and were included in purchases and in trade payables) but, because of transport delays, the goods did not arrive until late June 20X4 and were not included in closing inventory.

7 Portable generators on hire from another company at a charge of £347 were included, at this figure, in inventories.

8 Free samples sent to Cobden Ltd by various suppliers had been included in inventories at the catalogue price of £63.

9 Goods costing £418 sent to customers on a sale or return basis had been included in inventories by Cobden Ltd at their selling price, £602.

10 Goods sent on a sale or return basis to Cobden Ltd had been included in inventories at the amount payable (£267) if retained. No decision to retain had been made.

Required

Using such of the above information as is relevant, prepare a schedule amending the inventory figure as at 31 May 20X4. State your reason for each amendment or for not making an amendment.

(ACCA, adapted)

INTERMEDIATE

23.9* Universal Shoes Ltd is a Northern Ireland company that sells a range of casual, dress and work footwear through the internet. The accountant has asked you to calculate the value of the company's closing inventory at 31 December 20X4 for inclusion in the financial statements. The following additional information is available:

a Pairs of shoes counted in the warehouse at the year-end stocktake were as follows:

Casual	10,000 pairs
Work	5,000 pairs
Dress	2,000 pairs

b 2,000 pairs of casual footwear were received into stores on 3 January 20X5. The goods were ordered on 23 December 20X4 and invoiced on 24 December, but were still in transit from the US supplier when the stocktake was being performed. The invoice for these goods is included in the purchase ledger and the trade payable has been recognized at 31 December 20X4.

c Due to an increase in the price of toughened leather, the supplier of work shoes had to increase the cost of each pair from 1 November 20X4. Since this date, Universal Shoes has received 3,000 pairs into its stores.

d Due to a sharp change in fashion over the months of November and December 20X4, dress shoes in inventory have become worthless. They cannot be sold in Northern Ireland. However, the sales manager has secured a contract with a shoe retailer in Sweden. This retailer has agreed to purchase all of the dress shoes at a reduced price.

e Selling price and cost per pair of shoes in 20X4.

	Casual shoes	Work shoes	Dress shoes
	£	£	£
Selling prices in 20X4	30	55	75
Selling prices in 20X5	30	55	40
Purchase cost:			
01/01/X4–01/11/X4	5	10	45
01/11/X4–Present	5	15	45
Carriage inwards per pair	1	2	2
Marketing costs per pair:			
In 20X4	3	5	10
Expected in 20X5	3	5	10

f It is company policy to use the FIFO method of recording the flow of inventory cost.

Required

a Prepare a schedule showing the calculation of the value of inventories to be included in the year end (31 December 20X4) financial statements, in accordance with IAS 2 – *Inventories*.

b Write a brief memorandum to the chief accountant explaining the reasons (under IAS 2) for valuing the inventories on the bases you applied in (a).

23.10 Anna started a picture framing business on 1 July 20X5. The following transactions occurred in the six months ended 31 December 20X5: INTERMEDIATE

Purchases		*Sales*	
20/07/X5	150 units at £20 each	18/09/X5	305 units at £45 each
25/08/X5	225 units at £30 each	02/10/X5	50 units at £45 each
15/11/X5	410 units at £40 each	20/12/X5	100 units at £75 each

Additional information

1 On 1 July 20X5 Anna started the business by putting £10,000 into the bank account.

2 Two months' credit is taken from suppliers.

3 One month's credit is given to customers.

4 Expenses of £1,400 are paid each month as incurred.

Required

a Calculate the value of closing inventory using the first in, first out (FIFO) method and the average cost (AVCO) method.

b Prepare extracts from the statement of profit or loss for the six months to 31 December 20X5 and the statement of financial position at that date, to show the presentation of the above information, for each cost flow assumption used to value inventories.

INTERMEDIATE

23.11 John Ltd starts selling mobile phones in 20X4. Details of purchases in the year are as follows:

Date completed	Number purchased	Unit cost of mobile phone
		£
01/06/X4	100	150
05/08/X4	150	160
21/10/X4	75	176
25/12/X4	100	180
	425	

Details of sales in the year are as follows:

Date of sale	Number sold	Unit sale price
		£
05/06/X4	50	200
10/08/X4	115	220
23/12/X4	50	210
30/12/X4	150	240
	365	

Required

a Calculate the cost of sales for the year ended 31 December 20X4 and detail the value of the closing inventory using the FIFO and weighted average inventory valuation cost flow methods (inventory movement sheets are required).

b Prepare the statement of profit or loss for the year ended 31 December 20X4 based on both valuation methods.

INTERMEDIATE

23.12 Brian Ltd starts selling footballs in 20X4. Although each ball looks the same, the unit cost of manufacture (which is done in batches) has fluctuated during the period. Details of the costs are as follows:

Date completed	Number completed	Unit costs
		£
02/07/X4	200	75
01/08/X4	300	80
24/12/X4	150	88
15/03/X5	200	90
	850	

Details of sales are as follows:

Date of sale	Number sold	Unit sale price
		£
05/07/X4	100	100
10/08/X4	230	110
30/12/X4	100	105
16/03/X5	300	120
	730	

The closing inventory was counted on 30 June and found to be 70 units.

Required

a Calculate the cost of sales for the year ended 30 June 20X5 and detail the value of the closing inventory using the FIFO, LIFO and weighted average inventory valuation cost flow methods (inventory movement sheets are required).

b Prepare extracts from the statement of profit or loss for the year ended 30 June 20X5 based on the three valuation methods – explain why a different profit is reported under each method.

c What inventory valuation method is not permitted under IAS 2?

d Explain in which circumstances (if any) it would be appropriate to use the following cost flow assumptions:

i first in first out (LIFO) assumption;

ii last in, first out (LIFO) assumption;

iii specific identification assumption;

iv weighted average cost assumption.

23.13 Your company sells, for £275 each unit, a product that it purchases from several different manufacturers, all charging different prices. The manufacturers deliver at the beginning of each week throughout each month. The following details relate to the month of February. INTERMEDIATE

		Quantity	Cost each	Sales (units)
Opening inventories		10	£145	
Deliveries:	Week 1	20	£150	15
	Week 2	34	£165	33
	Week 3	50	£145	35
	Week 4	30	£175	39

From the above data you are required to:

a Prepare inventory records detailing quantities and values using the following pricing techniques:

i last in, first out (LIFO);

ii first in, first out (FIFO);

iii weighted average cost (calculated monthly to the nearest £).

b Prepare statements of profit or loss using each of the inventory cost flow pricing methods in (a) above and show the gross profit for each method.

c Compare the results of your calculations and state the advantages and disadvantages of FIFO and LIFO pricing methods in times of inflation.

(JMB, adapted)

INTERMEDIATE

23.14* A businessman started trading with a capital in cash of £6,000, which he placed in the business bank account at the outset.

His transactions, none of which were on credit, were as follows (in date sequence) for the first accounting period. All takings were banked immediately and all suppliers were paid by cheque. He traded in only one line of merchandise.

Purchases		***Sales***	
Quantity	**Price per unit**	**Quantity**	**Price per unit**
No.	**£**	**No.**	**£**
1,200	1.00		
1,000	1.05	800	1.70
600	1.10	600	1.90
900	1.20	1,100	2.00
800	1.25	1,300	2.00
700	1.30	400	2.05

In addition, he incurred expenses amounting to £1,740, of which he still owed £570 at the end of the period.

Required

Prepare separately using the FIFO (first in, first out), the LIFO (last in, first out) and (AVCO) weighted average cost (calculated for the period to the nearest penny) methods of inventory valuation:

a a statement of cost of sales for the period;

b a statement of financial position at the end of the period.

Note: Workings are an integral part of the answer and must be shown.

(ACCA, adapted)

ADVANCED

23.15 S. Bullock, a farmer, makes up his financial statements to 31 March each year. The trial balance extracted from his books as at 31 March 20X5 was as follows:

	Debit	Credit
	£	£
Purchases – livestock, seeds, fertilizers, fodder, etc.	19,016	
Wages and National Insurance	2,883	
Rent, rates, telephone and insurance	1,018	
Farrier and veterinary charges	34	
Carriage	1,011	
Motor and tractor running expenses	490	
Repairs – Farm buildings	673	
– Implements	427	
Contracting for ploughing, spraying and combine work	308	
General expenses	527	
Bank charges	191	
Professional charges	44	
Sales revenue		29,162
Motor vehicles and tractors – as at 1 April 20X4	1,383	
– Additions	605	
Implements – as at 1 April 20X4	2,518	
– Additions	514	
Valuation as at 1 April 20X4:		
Livestock, seeds, fertilizers, fodder, etc.	14,232	
Tillages and growing crops	952	
Loan from wife		1,922
Minister Bank		4,072
S. Bullock – capital at 1 April 20X4		6,440
Current account at 1 April 20X4		6,510
Drawings during the year	1,280	
	48,106	48,106

On 31 March 20X5:	£	£
Trade receivables and prepayments were:		
Livestock sales	1,365	
Motor licence	68	
Liabilities were: seeds and fertilizers		180
Rent, rates and telephone		50
Motor and tractor running expenses		40
Professional charges		127
Contracting		179
General expenses		54

Included in the above-mentioned figure of £50 is £15 for rent and this is payable for the March 20X5 quarter. In arriving at this figure the landlord has allowed a deduction of £235 for materials purchased for repairs to the farm buildings, which were carried out by S. Bullock, and is included in the 'Repairs to farm buildings' shown in the trial balance. In executing these repairs it was estimated that £125 labour costs were incurred and these were included in 'Wages and National Insurance'. This cost was to be borne by S. Bullock.

The valuation as at 31 March 20X5 was:

	£
Livestock, seeds, fertilizers, fodder, etc.	12,336
Tillages and growing crops	898

Depreciation, calculated on the book value as at 31 March 20X5, is to be written off as follows:

- Motor vehicles and tractors 25 per cent per annum
- Implements 12 per cent annum

Required

a Prepare the statement of profit or loss for the year ended 31 March 20X5.

b Prepare the statement of financial position as at that date.

(ACCA, adapted)

References

Accounting Standards Committee (1988) *Statement of Standard Accounting Practice 9 – Stocks and Long-term Contracts* (ICAEW).

International Accounting Standards Board (2013) *International Accounting Standard 2 – Inventories* (IASB).

Chapter 24

Financial statements for manufacturing entities

Learning Objectives:

After reading this chapter you should be able to do the following:

1. Describe the main differences between the final financial statements of a commercial enterprise and those of a manufacturing business.
2. Explain the classification of costs into direct and indirect costs.
3. Describe the different categories of inventories found in a manufacturing business and show how these are treated in the ledger and final financial statements.
4. Explain the purpose of a manufacturing account and the various subtotals normally found in this account.
5. Prepare a manufacturing account, a statement of profit or loss and a statement of financial position for a manufacturing business.
6. Explain the nature of manufacturing profits and show the entries in final financial statements.

24.1 Introduction

The main differences between the financial statements of commercial and manufacturing businesses stem from the former buying goods for resale without further processing, whereas the latter buy raw materials and components that are processed into **finished goods** to be sold. This makes it necessary for a manufacturing business to calculate the total factory cost of goods produced. The amount is computed in what is termed 'a manufacturing account' and the result shown in place of 'purchases' in the statement of profit or loss of a non-manufacturing business. Furthermore, the inventories in the statement of profit or loss are the inventories of finished goods unsold at the start and end of the accounting year. Apart from these differences the statement of profit or loss of a manufacturing business is the same as that of a commercial business, in that they both contain selling and distribution costs/overheads, administrative expenses/overheads and financial charges (such as interest). However, unlike a sole trader, the costs are analysed into these categories and subtotals for each are determined. The statement of financial position is also the same, except a manufacturing business will also include a number of different categories of inventory, which will be described later. The manufacturing account does not form part of the published financial statements. It is for internal management use, therefore does not fall within the presentation requirements of *International Accounting Standard (IAS) 1 – Presentation of Financial Statements* (IASB, 2013).

REAL WORLD EXAMPLE 24.1

Bespoke accounting packages for manufacturing accounts

Manufacturing accounts provide vital information for manufacturing entities and bespoke accounting packages are widely available with relevant charts of accounts (a tailored journal) and the ability to deal with the allocation of direct costs and factory overhead costs to work-in-progress and finished goods. Examples include DBA manufacturing software and JD Edwards EnterpriseOne Manufacturing.

Source: Author.

24.2 The classification of costs

One of the major differences between the financial statements of a commercial and a manufacturing business concerns the classification of costs. In a manufacturing business, costs are usually classified as either direct costs or indirect costs/overheads. **Direct costs** are those that can be traced, attributed to or identified with a particular product. These main types are explained in Figure 24.1.

Indirect costs/overheads are those costs that cannot be traced, attributed to or identified with a particular product, and comprise **factory/production/manufacturing overheads**, **selling and distribution overheads**, and **administrative overheads**. Examples are provided in Figure 24.2.

24.3 Categories of inventory

A manufacturing business also differs from a commercial business in that it has a number of different categories of inventories. These were mentioned in the previous chapter and are now revisited in the context of manufacturing entities. They are outlined in Figure 24.3.

Figure 24.1

Direct material

- Any goods that form a part of the final product
- Includes raw materials and components that are used to create the finished product
- For example, iron ore is a raw material in the manufacture of engines for motor vehicles or the car manufacturer may purchase steel, which is the finished product of another industry. Many companies find it cheaper to buy rather than manufacture parts of their finished product. For example, car manufacturers buy components such as tyres and lighting equipment from outside suppliers.

Direct labour

- Comprises the wages of those employees who physically work on the products or operate the machines that are used to produce the finished products
- For example, wages paid to machine operators
- Wages paid to foremen, supervisors, cleaners, maintenance staff, and so on, are not direct wages.

Other direct expenses

- Any other expenses that are directly attributable to a specific product. The most common direct expenses are royalties paid for the right to produce the finished product, the cost of any special drawings and subcontracted work.

Direct manufacturing costs

Figure 24.2

Factory overheads

- Indirect wages – supervisors' wages, cleaners' wages, foremen's wages, maintenance staff wages
- Power, factory heat and light
- Depreciation of plant and machinery
- Depreciation of the factory building
- Repairs to plant and machinery
- Factory running costs such as factory rent (if rented), factory rates, factory insurance, factory stationery, and so on
- Consumable tools
- Other

Indirect factory overhead costs

Figure 24.3

Direct materials

- This category is composed of raw materials and components that have been purchased but not put into production at the end of the accounting year.

Work-in-progress (WIP)

- This refers to goods that are partially complete (part way through the production process) at the end of the accounting period.

Finished goods

- This category consists of goods that are fully complete and are available for sale but which are unsold at the end of the accounting year. These goods have exited the production process.

Manufacturing inventory types

24.4 Purposes and preparation of a manufacturing account

As has already been mentioned, the main purpose of a **manufacturing account** is to calculate the **factory cost of completed production**. This replaces purchases in the statement of profit or loss. Therefore, it is prepared after the trial balance has been extracted but before the statement of profit or loss is completed. In calculating the cost of the products that have been completed during the accounting year, it is usual to show the following in the manufacturing account (in the order shown below):

1 *The direct material cost* of goods that have been put into production during the year. To calculate this, it will be necessary to adjust the cost of purchases of **direct materials** for the opening and closing inventories thus:

Direct materials in inventories at start of year
Add: Purchases of direct materials during year
Less: Direct materials in inventories at end of year
= Cost of direct materials put into production during year

It is also common to add any carriage inwards to the cost of purchases.

2 *The* **direct labour** *costs*

3 *The* **direct expenses**

4 *The* **prime cost** *of production*

This is the sum of the direct materials, direct labour and direct expenses.

5 *The factory overheads*

6 *The* **total factory costs**

This is the sum of the prime costs and the factory overheads.

7 *The factory cost of completed production.*

The total factory costs relate to both those products that have been completed during the year and those which are only partially completed at the end of the year. To arrive at the factory cost of completed production, it is therefore necessary to make an adjustment for the opening and closing WIP thus:

WIP at start of year
Add: Total factory costs
Less: WIP at end of year
= Factory cost of completed production

The pro forma shown in Figure 24.4 should serve as a useful guide for the preparation of the manufacturing account.

Figure 24.4

Pro forma manufacturing account for 'X' for the year ended 31/12/X5		
	£	£
Production cost for the period		
Opening inventory of raw materials	XX	
Direct materials	XX	
Raw material returns	(XX)	
Carriage inwards	X	
	XX	
Closing inventory of raw materials	(XX)	
Cost of raw materials consumed		XX
Direct labour		XX
Direct expenses		XX
Prime cost		XX
Factory overhead expenses		
Indirect wages	XX	
Factory rent	XX	
Factory rates	XX	
Factory cleaners' wages	XX	
Total factory overheads		XXX
Total factory costs		XXX
Opening work-in-progress		XX
		XXX
Closing work-in-progress		(XX)
Factory cost of completed production c/d (to statement of profit or loss)		XXX

A pro forma of the layout of a manufacturing account

The factory cost of completed production is transferred to the statement of profit or loss in place of 'purchases' in a non-manufacturing business. The cost of sales is computed by adjusting the factory cost of completed production for the opening and closing inventories of finished goods:

Inventories of finished goods at start of year
Add: Factory costs of completed production
Less: Inventories of finished goods at end of year
= Cost of goods sold

The expenses in the statement of profit or loss in a manufacturing entity are normally categorized into distribution expenses, administration expense and finance costs.

Examples of distribution expenses are:

1 salesmen's salaries;

2 credit control staff salaries;

3 commission;

4 advertising;

5 marketing;

6 depreciation on salesmen's motor vehicles;

7 depreciation on delivery trucks;

8 carriage outwards;

9 irrecoverable receivables;

10 increases/(decreases) in the allowance for irrecoverable receivables.

Sometimes irrecoverable receivables and the movement in the allowance for irrecoverable receivables are regarded as being administrative expenses. It depends whether the credit control department is regarded as being either selling or administration. In this book we are treating the credit control department as a selling department.

Therefore, this should be assumed unless a question states that the administration department has control over the granting of credit and the collection of receivables.

Examples of administrative costs are:

1 salaries of accounting staff;

2 office overheads, heat and light, insurance, rent, rates, and so on;

3 cleaners' wages;

4 depreciation on office fixtures and fitting;

5 depreciation of the office manager's motor vehicle;

6 depreciation of the general manager's motor vehicle;

7 stationery.

The last category is finance costs.

Examples of finance costs are:

1 loan interest;

2 bank charges;

3 discounts allowed.

The pro forma shown in Figure 24.5 should serve as a useful guide for the preparation of the statement of profit or loss for a manufacturing entity.

Figure 24.5

Pro forma statement of profit or loss for 'X' for the year ended 31/12/X5	
	£
Revenue	XXX
Cost of sales	(XX)
Gross profit	XX
Other income	X
Distribution expenses	(X)
Administrative expenses	(X)
Other expenses	(X)
Finance costs	(X)
Profit before income tax	X
Income tax expense	(X)
Profit for the period	X

A pro forma of the layout of a statement of a statement of profit or loss for a manufacturing entity

Note that all the adjustments in respect of direct materials inventories, WIP and finished goods are applications of the matching principle. An illustration of the preparation of a manufacturing account is shown in Worked Example 24.1.

WORKED EXAMPLE 24.1

The following information relating to the year ended 30 April 20X5 has been extracted from the books of A. Bush, a motor vehicle component manufacturer:

	£		£
Sales revenue	298,000	Sales staff salaries	41,700
Inventories of direct materials at 1 May 20X4	7,900	Accounting staff salaries	38,200
Inventories of direct materials at 30 Apr 20X5	6,200	Royalties paid for products produced under licence	17,500
Work in progress at 1 May 20X4	8,400	Cost of power for machinery	9,200
Work in progress at 30 Apr 20X5	9,600	Repairs to plant	6,700
Inventories of finished goods at 1 May 20X4	5,400	Irrecoverable receivables	5,100
Inventories of finished goods at 30 Apr 20X5	6,800	Interest on bank loan	7,400
Purchase of direct materials	68,400	Depreciation on plant	18,600
Direct wages	52,600	Depreciation on delivery vehicles	13,200
Production supervisors' salaries	34,800	Depreciation on accounting office equipment	11,500

Required

Prepare a manufacturing account and a statement of profit or loss for the year ended 30 April 20X5, showing clearly the total direct/prime costs, manufacturing/factory costs, cost of completed production and cost of sales.

Solution

Manufacturing account for A. Bush for the year ended 30/4/X5		
	£	**£**
Production cost for the period		
Opening inventory of raw materials	7,900	
Direct materials	68,400	
	76,300	
Closing inventory of raw materials	(6,200)	
Cost of raw materials consumed		70,100
Direct labour		52,600
Direct expenses		17,500
Prime cost		140,200
Factory overhead expenses		
Supervisors' salaries	34,800	
Power	9,200	
Repairs to plant	6,700	
Depreciation on plant	18,600	
Total factory overheads		69,300
Total factory costs		209,500
Opening work-in-progress		8,400
		217,900
Closing work-in-progress		(9,600)
Factory cost of completed production c/d (to statement of profit or loss)		208,300

Note: Any proceeds from the sale of scrap direct materials are normally credited to the manufacturing account, thus reducing the cost of completed production.

Statement of profit or loss for A. Bush for the year ended 30/4/X5		
	Note	**£**
Sales revenue		298,000
Cost of goods produced	1	206,900
Gross profit		91,100
Distribution expenses	2	60,000
Administrative expenses	3	49,700
Finance costs	4	7,400
(Loss) for the period		(26,000)

Notes

1 Cost of sales

	£
Opening inventory of finished goods	5,400
Factory cost of completed production (b/d from manufacturing account)	208,300
	213,700
Closing inventory of finished goods	(6,800)
	206,900

2 Distribution expenses

	£
Sales staff salaries	41,700
Depreciation on delivery vehicles	13,200
Irrecoverable receivables	5,100
	60,000

3 Administration expenses

	£
Accounting staff salaries	38,200
Depreciation on office equipment	11,500
	49,700

4 Finance costs

	£
Interest on loan	7,400
	7,400

24.5 Manufacturing profits

In some businesses, manufactured goods are transferred from the factory to the warehouse at market prices or an approximation thereof in the form of cost plus a given percentage for profit. This is intended to represent the price that the warehouse would have to pay if it bought the goods from an external supplier, or the price that the factory would receive if it sold the goods to an external customer. This is commonly referred to as the **transfer price**. The purpose of having internal transfer prices is to make the managers in the factory and warehouse more aware of the impact of market forces, to increase motivation and to facilitate the evaluation of their performance.

The accounting entries are relatively straightforward. The figure for completed production carried down from the manufacturing account to the statement of profit or loss will simply be at some transfer price or valuation other than cost. This gives rise to a **manufacturing profit** (or loss), which will be the difference between the two sides of the manufacturing account. The double entry for this profit (or loss) is to credit (or debit) the profit or loss account. While this accounting treatment of the manufacturing profit (or loss) may be adopted in the final financial statements prepared for internal management purposes, it would not be acceptable for external reporting because it contravenes IAS 2, which requires that finished goods inventories are valued at the lower of factory cost (discussed later) and net realizable value (NRV) (discussed in the previous chapter). The finished goods inventories will have been valued at the transfer price, which means that the manufacturing profit includes unrealized profit contained in any increase in finished goods inventories over the year. Any such unrealized profit should be transferred to a provision for unrealized (manufacturing) profit account by crediting this account and debiting the profit or loss account. Where there is a decrease in finished goods inventories over the year, the entries are the opposite. After these entries have been made, there should be a balance on the provision for unrealized profit account equal to the manufacturing profit contained in the finished goods inventory at the end of the year. This is deducted from the value of finished goods inventories (at transfer price) in the statement of financial position, thus reducing it to factory cost.

WORKED EXAMPLE 24.2

Using the information from Worked Example 24.1, assume that the manufacturing division of A. Bush has a transfer price, for the goods that have left the production process, of £220,000.

Required

Prepare a summarized manufacturing account and a summarized statement of profit or loss for the year ended 30 April 20X5 showing the split in profits between the manufacturing division and the trading division.

Manufacturing account for A. Bush for the year ended 30/4/X5	
	£
Transfer price	220,000
Factory cost of completed production	208,300
Gross profit on manufacturing	11,700

Statement of profit or loss for A. Bush for the year ended 30/4/X5	
	£
Sales revenue	298,000
Cost of goods produced	206,900
Gross profit	91,100
Distribution expenses	60,000
Administrative expenses	49,700
Finance costs	7,400
(Loss) for the period	(26,000)

There is no change in the reported statement of profit or loss.

Notes

1 Cost of sales (internal use)

Opening inventory of finished goods	5,400
Factory cost of completed production (b/d from manufacturing account)	220,000
	225,400
Closing inventory of finished goods	(6,800)
	218,600

2 Gross profit (internal use)

Manufacturing	11,700
Trading (298,000 – 218,600)	79,400
Total gross profit (manufacturing and trading)	91,100

24.6 The valuation of finished goods and work-in-progress

The work-in-progress (WIP) shown in the manufacturing account is usually valued at production/factory cost; that is, prime costs plus factory overheads. This is why the adjustment for the opening and closing WIP is made after the total factory costs have been computed. Similarly, the finished goods inventory shown in the statement of profit or loss is normally valued at factory cost after the costs of conversion. The **costs of conversion** comprise costs that are specifically attributable to units of production, that is, direct labour, direct expenses and subcontracted work and production overheads. This does not include selling and distribution overheads, administrative overheads or finance costs. This is consistent with the valuation of the completed production, which is also included in the statement of profit or loss at factory cost. Thus, neither the WIP nor finished goods inventory includes other overheads such as selling and distribution costs, administrative expenses and interest. Sometimes WIP is valued at prime cost: that is, excluding factory overheads. In this case the adjustment for WIP must be made before the factory overheads in the manufacturing account. The allocation of costs to inventory is an area that can be controversial as it moves costs from one period into the next period; the result – overstated profits in the earlier period. This is appropriate if the costs are direct or indirect production costs and there is an expectation of selling the inventory for a profit. However, in other instances it is fraudulent, as highlighted in Real World Example 24.2.

REAL WORLD EXAMPLE 24.2

Accounting Fraud Prompts $580 Million Write-Down at CAT

Caterpillar purchased ERA Mining Ltd, a Chinese company that made mine safety equipment, for $734 million; however, accounting irregularities of $580 million were uncovered in 2012. One of the problems was inventory valuation. The company had been capitalising yearly running costs as inventory costs. The impact of this was to reduce reported costs in the statement of profit or loss. This resulted in overstated profits being reported as the costs are carried forward in closing inventory to the next period. In addition, the overstated inventory would cause the company's statement of financial position to seem stronger than what it truly was.

'...Caterpillar said it noticed discrepancies in inventories after taking its own physical inventory following the acquisition. Upon further investigation, it found several years' worth of faulty costs allocations that overstated profits and improper revenue recognition practices that boosted sales.

"The actions carried out by these individuals are offensive and completely unacceptable. This conduct does not represent, in any way, shape, or form, the way Caterpillar does business or how we expect our employees to work, which is spelled out in Caterpillar's Worldwide Code of Conduct," said Caterpillar Chairman and CEO Doug Oberhelman in a statement. "Once our investigation confirmed that misconduct had taken place at Siwei, we moved quickly and decisively to hold the responsible leaders directly accountable for the wrongdoing," Oberhelman said. "Accountability is a critical way that we measure leaders at Caterpillar, and it is my expectation that leaders set an example and are accountable for their actions and results."'

Source: Byrt, F. (2013) 'Accounting Fraud Prompts $580 Million Write-Down at CAT', accountingweb website, http://www.accountingweb.com/article/accounting-fraud-prompts-580-million-write-down-cat/220829, accessed September 2013.

Learning Activity 24.1

Visit the website of a known manufacturing company and review its financial statements. For example, Bombardier – a Canadian-based company which manufactures aeroplanes, trains, etc. This Canadian company has a subsidiary in Belfast (called Shorts) (http://www.bombardier.com/en/corporate/investor-relations/financial-results).

Examine the format of its published financial statements. These will typically follow the format for company financial statements (see Chapters 1 or 29 for a proforma) as the details provided in manufacturing accounts would be deemed to be too sensitive to be made available for competitors to see. However, you will see non-standard items separately identified, such as research and development.

Summary

Manufacturing businesses usually classify all their costs as either direct or indirect/overheads. Direct costs comprise direct materials, direct labour and direct expenses. Overheads are classified as either factory overheads, selling and distribution costs or administrative expenses. Manufacturing businesses also normally have a number of different types of inventory that comprise inventories of direct materials, WIP and finished goods.

The main difference between preparing the financial statements of manufacturing businesses and preparing the financial statements of commercial undertakings is that the former includes preparing a manufacturing account. This is used to ascertain the cost of completed production that is entered in the statement of profit or loss in place of the purchases of a non-manufacturing business. The computation of the cost of completed production necessitates certain adjustments in respect of inventories of direct materials and WIP that are similar to those relating to the calculation of the cost of sales.

Key terms and concepts

administrative overheads	430	finished goods	430
costs of conversion	439	indirect costs/overheads	430
direct costs	430	manufacturing account	432
direct expenses	432	manufacturing profit	438
direct labour	432	prime cost	432
direct materials	432	selling and distribution overheads	430
factory cost of completed production	432	total factory costs	432
factory/production/manufacturing overheads	430	transfer price	437

An asterisk after the question number indicates that there is a suggested answer in Appendix 2.

Review questions

connect

24.1 a Explain the difference between direct costs and overheads.

b Describe the different types of direct cost and overhead found in a manufacturing business.

24.2 Describe the different categories of inventory normally held by a manufacturing business.

24.3 a Explain the main purpose of a manufacturing account.

b Describe the structure and main groups of costs found in a manufacturing account.

24.4 a Explain the difference between the total factory cost of production and the factory cost of completed production.

b What is the justification for adjusting the total factory cost for work-in-progress rather than, say, the total prime/direct cost?

Exercises

connect

24.5

BASIC

	£
Inventories, 1 January 20X5	
Raw materials	7,500
Finished goods	14,300
Work-in-progress	10,070

Wages and salaries	
Factory direct	98,500
Factory indirect	17,500
Purchases – raw materials	90,600
Power and fuel	28,260
Sales revenue	385,400
Insurance	6,640
Returns inwards (finished goods)	6,000
Inventories, 31 December 20X5	
Raw materials	9,200
Finished goods	8,600
Work-in-progress	8,700

Additional information

1 The manufacturing entity's machinery cost £102,000.

2 Provision for depreciation at the start of the period is £47,000. The company has a policy of providing for depreciation at the rate of 20 per cent per year calculated using the reducing balance method.

3 At the year end £740 is outstanding for fuel and power.

4 In addition, the manager informs you that insurance of £240 is prepaid at the year end. The factory proportion of this is 75 per cent, whereas the administration is to be allocated 25 per cent of the expense.

Required

Prepare the manufacturing account and the statement of profit or loss for the year ended 31 December 20X5.

INTERMEDIATE

24.6* The trial balance extracted at 30 April 20X5 from the books of Upton Upholstery, a furniture manufacturer, is given below.

	Debit	Credit
	£	£
Factory machinery at cost	28,000	
Factory machinery depreciation 1/5/X4		5,000
Office equipment	2,000	
Office equipment depreciation 1/5/X4		800
Trade receivables and payables	15,000	16,000
Cash and bank	2,300	
Bank loan		11,000
Inventories 1/5/X4 – Raw materials	4,000	
– Incomplete production	16,400	
– Finished goods	9,000	
Carriage inwards	1,200	
Carriage outwards	700	
Purchases – raw materials	84,000	
Light and heat	3,000	

Rent and rates	6,600	
Direct factory wages	19,900	
Office wages	5,200	
Sales commission to selling agents	1,400	
Sales of finished goods		140,000
Capital account		35,000
Drawings	9,100	
	207,800	207,800

Notes

1 At 30 April 20X5 accrued direct factory wages amounted to £600 and office wages £100; rent paid included £600 paid on 20 January 20X5 for the period 1 January to 30 June 20X5.

2 Records showed that, at the year end, inventory values were as follows; raw materials £5,400; incomplete production £17,000; finished goods £8,000.

3 Depreciation should be allowed for factory machinery on the straight line method over seven years, and office equipment on the reducing balance method at 25 per cent per annum.

4 An allowance of £1,000 should be made for irrecoverable receivables.

5 Light and heat should be apportioned between the factory and office in the ratio 4 : 1, respectively; rent and rates in the ratio 3 : 1, respectively.

Required

Prepare a manufacturing account and a statement of profit or loss for the year ended 30 April 20X5 and a statement of financial position at that date.

24.7* From the following information prepare a manufacturing account and a statement of profit or loss for the year ended 31 December 20X4. Show clearly the prime cost, factory cost of completed production, cost of sales, gross profit, selling and distribution overheads, administrative overhead, and net profit.

INTERMEDIATE

	£
Inventory of raw materials at 1 January 20X4	2,453
Work-in-progress valued at factory cost at 1 January 20X4	1,617
Inventory of finished goods at 1 January 20X4	3,968
Purchases of raw materials	47,693
Purchases of finished goods	367
Raw materials returned to suppliers	4,921
Carriage outwards	487
Carriage inwards	683
Direct wages	23,649
Administrative salaries	10,889
Supervisors' wages	5,617
Royalties payable	7,500
Electricity used in factory	2,334
Light and heat for administrative offices	998
Sales staff salaries and commission	8,600

Irrecoverable receivables	726
Discount received	2,310
Discount allowed	1,515
Depreciation – plant	13,400
– delivery vehicles	3,700
– office fixtures and furniture	1,900
Rent and rates (factory 3/4 office 1/4)	4,800
Delivery expenses	593
Postage and telephone	714
Printing and stationery	363
Proceeds from the sale of scrap metal	199
Interest payable on loan	3,000
Bank charges	100
Insurance on plant	1,750
Advertising	625
Repairs to plant	917
Sales revenue	145,433
Purchases of raw materials includes £2,093, and direct wages £549, for materials and work done in constructing an extension to the factory.	
Inventory of raw materials at 31 December 20X4	3,987
Work-in-progress valued at factory cost at 31 December 20X4	2,700
Inventory of finished goods at 31 December 20X4	5,666

INTERMEDIATE

24.8 W. Wagner, a manufacturer, provided the following information for the year ended 31 August 20X5:

	£
Inventories at 1 September 20X4	
– Raw materials	25,000
– Work-in-progress	15,900
– Finished goods	26,600
Raw materials purchased	176,600
Factory general expenses	14,800
Direct wages	86,900
Repairs to plant and machinery	9,900
Factory lighting and heating	20,010
Carriage inwards	1,910
Carriage outwards	2,500
Sales revenue	320,000
Raw materials returned	7,800
Factory maintenance wages	19,000
Administrative expenses	30,000
Selling and distribution expenses	15,100
Plant and machinery at cost	178,000
Freehold land and buildings at cost	160,000
Provision for depreciation on plant and machinery (1/9/X4)	80,000

Additional information

1 Amounts owing at 31 August 20X5:

	£
Direct wages	4,800
Factory heating and lighting	1,500

2 Depreciation on plant and machinery is to be provided at 10 per cent per annum on cost. There were no sales or purchases of plant and machinery during the year.

3 All manufactured goods are transferred to the warehouse at factory cost plus 10 per cent.

4 Inventories at 31 August 20X5:

	£
Raw materials	30,000
Work-in-progress	17,800
Finished goods	35,090

The raw materials are valued at cost, the work-in-progress at factory cost, while the inventory of finished goods is valued at the factory transfer price.

Required

a A manufacturing account for the year ended 31 August 20X5.

b A statement of profit or loss for the year ended 31 August 20X5.

(AEB, adapted)

24.9 Veronica is the owner of a manufacturing business. The following trial balance was extracted from her books as at 31 December 20X4: ADVANCED

	Dr	Cr
	£	£
Cash in hand	200	
Bank		7,220
Purchase ledger balances		7,160
Sales ledger balances	12,200	
Allowance for irrecoverable receivables		2,000
Administration expenses	5,620	
Electricity and power	12,000	
Sales expenses	2,880	
Repairs to building	2,000	
Rates and insurance	3,200	
Factory wages	27,280	
Administration wages	10,800	
Sales department wages	6,000	
Sales revenue		132,000
Raw material purchases	37,000	
Purchases of tools and utensils	1,600	

Opening inventories		
– *Raw materials*	6,600	
– *Work-in-progress*	5,000	
– *Finished goods*	12,000	
– *Loose tools and utensils*	2,400	
Motor vehicles (selling and distribution)	8,000	
Provision for depreciation on motor vehicles		5,600
Plant and machinery	29,000	
Provision for depreciation on plant and machinery		14,000
Land	30,000	
Capital account		45,800
	213,780	213,780

The following information was also made available:

1 Expenses are to be allocated as follows:

	Factory	Administration
Electricity and power	90%	10%
Repairs	80%	20%
Rates and insurance	70%	30%

2 Closing inventories included: raw materials £5,600; loose tools and utensils £3,200; finished goods £7,800; and work-in-progress £5,000.

3 Irrecoverable receivables amounting to £1,000 are to be written off and the allowance for irrecoverable receivables reduced to £1,200.

4 The following amounts have yet to be provided for in the trial balance: electricity and power £1,600 and new machinery £1,000.

5 The following amounts have been prepaid as at the year end: rates £600 and vehicle licences on sales representatives' cars £80.

6 A vehicle costing £3,000 and written down to £1,000 was sold for £1,200. None of these entries have been recorded in the trial balance as the bookkeeper did not know how to adjust for the sale.

7 Annual depreciation on plant and machinery and on motor vehicles is to be provided using the reducing balance method. The rates used for each class of asset are 15 per cent (plant and machinery) and 20 per cent (motor vehicles).

8 An invoice for £200 for repairs to the building had been incorrectly posted to the administration expenses account.

9 A building costing £100,000 was purchased using a long-term loan on 1 January 20X4. Interest payable on the loan is 10 per cent per year. No entries for this transaction have been included in the trial balance. It has been decided to depreciate buildings at 5 per cent on cost.

Required

Prepare the following:

a The manufacturing account and the statement of profit or loss for the year ended 31 December 20X4.

b The statement of financial position as at 31 December 20X4.

(*Note*: All workings must be shown including adjustments to ledger accounts.)

ADVANCED

24.10 Zacotex Ltd, a manufacturer, produced the following financial information for the year ended 31 March 20X5.

	£
Raw material purchases	250,000
Direct labour	100,000
Direct expenses	80,900
Indirect factory labour	16,000
Factory maintenance costs	9,700
Machine repairs	11,500
Sales of finished goods during the year	788,100
Inventories at 1 April 20X4	
– *Raw materials*	65,000
– *Finished goods*	48,000
– *Work-in-progress*	52,500
Other factory overhead	14,500
Factory heating and lighting	19,000
Factory rates	11,500
Administration expenses	22,000
Selling and distribution expenses	36,800

Additional information

1 The inventories held at 31 March 20X5 were:

Raw materials	£51,400
Finished goods	£53,800
Work-in-progress	£41,000

Note: Raw materials are valued at cost; finished goods at factory cost; work-in-progress at factory cost. Of the raw materials held in inventories at 31 March 20X5, £15,000 had suffered flood damage and it was estimated that they could only be sold for £2,500. The remaining raw material inventory could only be sold on the open market at cost less 10 per cent.

2 One-quarter of the administration expenses are to be allocated to the factory.

3 The raw materials purchases figure for the year includes a charge for carriage inwards. On 31 March 20X5 a credit note for £1,550 was received in respect of a carriage inwards overcharge. No adjustment had been made for this amount.

4 Expenses in arrears at 31 March 20X5 were:

	£
Direct labour	6,600
Machine repairs	1,700
Selling and distribution expenses	4,900

5 Plant and machinery at 1 April 20X4:

	£
At cost	250,000
Aggregate depreciation	75,000

During the year an obsolete machine (cost £30,000, depreciation to date £8,000) was sold as scrap for £5,000. On 1 October 20X4 new machinery was purchased for £70,000 with an installation charge of £8,000.

The company depreciates its plant and machinery at 10 per cent per annum on cost on all items in company ownership at the end of the accounting year.

6 An analysis of the sales of finished goods revealed the following:

	£
Goods sold for cash	105,000
Goods sold on credit	623,100
Goods sold on sale or return: returned	25,000
Goods sold on sale or return: retained and invoice confirmed	35,000
	788,100

7 On 1 April 20X4 the company arranged a long-term loan of £250,000 at a fixed rate of interest of 11 per cent per annum. No provision had been made for the payment of the interest.

Required

Prepare for the year ended 31 March 20X5

a A manufacturing account showing prime cost and factory cost of goods produced.

b A statement of profit or loss.

(AEB, adapted)

ADVANCED

24.11 Ashley Ltd is a manufacturing firm. The bookkeeper supplies you with the following financial information for the year ended 31 March 20X5.

	£
Factory buildings	100,000
Provision for depreciation on buildings	15,000
Plant and equipment	500,000
Provision for depreciation on plant	150,000
Motor vehicles (administration)	25,000
Provision for depreciation on motor vehicles	9,000
Trade receivables	156,000
Bank	8,000
Cash	700
Trade payables	56,000
Other selling and distribution expenses	33,600
Other administration expenses	24,000
Raw material purchases	500,000

Factory rates	23,000
Direct labour	200,000
Factory heat and light	38,000
Direct expenses	161,800
Other factory overheads	29,000
Indirect factory labour	32,000
Inventories at 1 April 20X4	
– *Raw materials*	130,000
– *Finished goods*	96,000
– *Work-in-progress*	105,000
Factory maintenance costs	176,000
Machine repairs	23,000
Sales of finished goods in the year	1,903,400
Sales representatives' salaries	30,000
Commission to sales representatives	10,000
Irrecoverable receivables	4,000
Bookkeeper's salary	15,000
Postage	1,000

Other information

1 On 1 April 20X4 the company arranged a long-term loan of £500,000 at a fixed rate of interest of 10 per cent per annum. The loan was used to buy a building worth £300,000, plant worth £150,000 (including an installation charge of £16,000) and three sales representatives' vehicles for £50,000. No provision had been made for the payment of the interest.

2 During the year an obsolete machine costing £60,000, but written down to £44,000, was sold as scrap for £10,000.

3 The company depreciates its assets as follows:

Buildings	5 per cent per annum
Plant and equipment	20 per cent reducing balance
Motor vehicles (administration)	25 per cent reducing balance
Motor vehicles (sales representatives) over four years using the sum of digits method. A full year's depreciation is provided for all assets in ownership at the end of the year.	

4 The inventories held at the end of the year were:

	£
Raw materials per inventory sheet	102,800
Finished goods	107,600
Work in progress	82,000

Of the raw materials held in inventories at the year end, £30,000 had suffered fire damage. It was estimated that they could be sold for £5,000.

5 The raw material purchases figure included in the list above includes £100,000 for carriage inwards. A credit note for £3,000, correcting an overcharge on an original invoice for carriage, was received on 31 March 20X5. The figures had not been adjusted for this.

6 Accruals and prepayments at the year end were:

	£
Direct labour accrued	13,200
Machine repairs accrued	3,400
Factory maintenance prepaid	2,000

Required

Prepare the following:

a The manufacturing account and the statement of profit or loss for the year ended 31 March 20X5.

b The statement of financial position as at 31 March 20X5.

(*Note*: All workings must be shown including the adjustments to ledger accounts.)

ADVANCED

24.12 (*Note*: This question should be attempted after the chapter on incomplete records has been studied.)

ABC manufacturing entity (sole trader) has provided you with the following information at the year ended 31 July 20X4:

	£
Inventories:	
– Raw materials	25,000
– Work-in-progress	6,700
– Finished goods	100,000
Trade payables	47,500
Trade receivables	68,000
Bank	3,500
Administration expenses prepaid	300
Non-current assets (cost £60,000)	59,400

During the year ended 31 July 20X5 the following transactions took place:

	£
Sales invoiced	254,000
Cash received from customers	245,700
Discounts allowed	5,900
Irrecoverable receivables written off	900
Purchases invoiced	92,000
Purchase returns	1,500
Payments to suppliers	93,500
Discounts received	1,800
Factory wages paid	42,600
Manufacturing expenses paid	51,500
Administration expenses paid	15,800
Selling and distribution expenses paid	18,100
Payments to purchase plant and machinery	28,000

ABC informed you that the balances at 31 July 20X5 were as follows:

	£
Inventories:	
– *Raw materials*	24,000
– *Work-in-progress*	5,900
– *Finished goods*	102,000
Trade payables	?
Trade receivables	?
Bank	?
Administration expenses accrued	1,000
Non-current assets (cost £88,000)	59,000

Additional information

1 Depreciation on non-current assets should be apportioned between manufacturing (60 per cent), administration (25 per cent) and selling and distribution (15 per cent).

2 Discounts allowed and irrecoverable receivables are regarded as selling expenses.

3 Discounts received should be regarded as administration expenses.

Required

a Compute the balances on the trade receivables account, the trade payables account and the bank account at 31 July 20X5 *(the ledger accounts should be provided)*.

b Prepare the manufacturing account and the statement of profit or loss for the company for the year ended 31 July 20X5.

Reference

International Accounting Standards Board (2013) *International Accounting Standard 1 – Presentation of Financial Statements* (IASB).

PART SIX
Partnerships

25 The final financial statements of partnerships 455

26 Changes in partnerships 485

27 Partnership dissolution and conversion to a limited company 521

Chapter 25

The final financial statements of partnerships

Learning Objectives:

After reading this chapter you should be able to do the following:

1. Describe the main characteristics of partnerships.
2. Explain how profits may be shared between partners, including the nature and purpose of partners' salaries, interest on capital and interest on drawings.
3. Explain the difference between partners' capital, current and drawings accounts.
4. Show the journal and ledger entries relating to those items normally found in partners' capital, current and drawings accounts.
5. Prepare partnership final financial statements, including an appropriation account.
6. Show the entries in the ledger and final financial statements relating to partners' commission and a guaranteed share of profit.
7. Explain the difference between a partnership and a limited liability partnership.

Learning Activity 25.1

Before starting this chapter, return to Chapter 1, 'Entities and Financial Reporting Statements' and read sections 1.7 and 1.8 on Sole Traders and Partnerships and list the differences in the two types of entity and the differences in the format of their financial statements.

25.1 The law and characteristics of partnerships

For a number of commercial reasons, it may be mutually advantageous for two or more people to form a partnership. The Partnership Act 1890 defines a **partnership** as *'the relation which subsists between persons carrying on business in common with a view of profit'*. It cannot have fewer than two partners and, at one time, the Act set a limit of 20 partners. However, with the introduction of the Companies Act 1967, this maximum has been relaxed in the case of a number of professional firms, such as accountants and solicitors.

Since partnerships are not able to limit their liability to creditors and other members of the public, there is no need for any special legislation to protect these groups. Thus, partners are largely free to make whatever agreements between themselves that they wish to cover their mutual relationships. The powers and rights of the partners between themselves are governed by any written agreement they may make. This is referred to as the **articles** or **deed of partnership**. It is important for partners to reach an agreement on matters such as those listed in Figure 25.1.

Figure 25.1

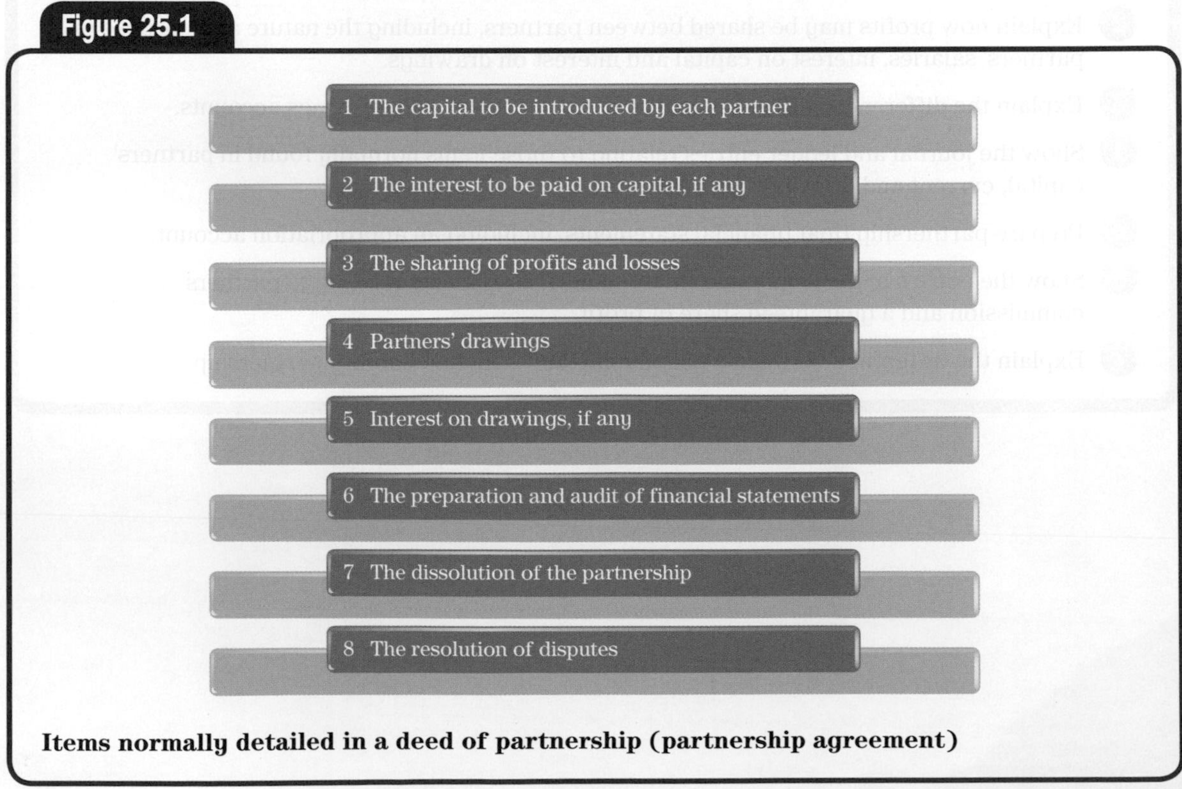

1 The capital to be introduced by each partner
2 The interest to be paid on capital, if any
3 The sharing of profits and losses
4 Partners' drawings
5 Interest on drawings, if any
6 The preparation and audit of financial statements
7 The dissolution of the partnership
8 The resolution of disputes

Items normally detailed in a deed of partnership (partnership agreement)

In the absence of any partnership agreement, or if the agreement is silent on any of the items listed, then the partnership is subject to the provisions of the Partnership Act 1890, which includes the following:

1 Each partner has **unlimited liability**. That is, if the debts of the partnership cannot be paid because the business has insufficient assets to do so, the creditors have recourse to the private property of the individual partners. The partners are said to be jointly and severally liable for the debts of the firm and therefore a creditor may sue the partnership or any individual partner.

2 Voting powers: in the ordinary day-to-day running of a partnership, individual partners often make routine business decisions without consulting the other partners. At the other extreme, certain fundamental decisions, such as to change the type of business in which the partnership is engaged, or the admission of a new partner, require the consent of all the partners. Other major decisions are supposed to be determined by a majority vote. Each partner has one vote. However, a partnership deed may specify some other distribution of voting power.

3 Every partner is entitled to take part in the management of the business. However, some partnership agreements provide for certain partners to be sleeping or limited partners. Neither of these normally takes part in the management of the business.

4 Every partner is entitled to have access to the books and papers of the partnership. This includes sleeping and limited partners.

5 Each partner is an agent of the partnership and can thus sign contracts on behalf of the partnership, which will then be legally bound to honour them.

6 A new partner can only be admitted to the partnership if all the existing partners give their consent. However, a partnership deed may specify otherwise.

7 A partnership will be dissolved by:

   a any partner giving notice to the other partner(s) of his or her intention to leave the partnership;

   b the death, insanity or bankruptcy of a partner.

25.2 The sharing of profits between the partners

Learning Activity 25.2

Consider the following situation. A and B enter into partnership; A is to work full time in the business while B will only spend a few hours each week on partnership business; B is to put into the business £100,000 as capital whereas A is to contribute capital of only £10,000. You are asked by A and B to suggest how the profits might be shared so as to recompense A for working more hours than B in the business, and to compensate B for having put into the business (and therefore put at risk) substantially more capital than A.

The way this is normally achieved is to give each partner a prior share of the profits as: (1) a **partnership salary** related to the amount of time each devotes to the business; and (2) **interest on the capital** each invests. The remaining profit, which is often referred to as the **residual profit/loss**, can then be divided between the partners according to whatever they agree is fair. This might be equal, since both have already been compensated for the unequal time and capital they contribute.

Another aspect of sharing partnership profits concerns **interest on drawings**. This is intended to compensate the partner who has annual drawings that are less than those of the other partner. Each partner is charged interest on drawings for the period from the date of the drawings to the end of the accounting year in which the drawings took place.

It is important to appreciate that partners' 'salaries', 'interest on capital' and 'interest on drawings' are not actual payments of money; they are only part of a profit-sharing formula. If any such payments are made to a partner, these should be treated as drawings. Indeed, as a general rule *all* payments to partners must be treated as drawings. It should also be observed that salaries, interest on capital and interest on drawings will still arise even if the business makes a loss. In these circumstances they effectively become part of a loss-sharing formula.

If there is no agreement between the partners concerning how profits and losses should be shared, section 24 of the Partnership Act 1890 would be applied as follows:

1 Profits and losses are to be shared equally between the partners.

2 No partner will receive a salary or interest on capital, or be charged interest on drawings.

3 Any loans made by a partner to the business (as distinct from capital introduced) will be entitled to interest at the rate of 5 per cent per annum.

25.3 Capital and current accounts

In the financial statements of sole traders, there is a **capital account** and usually a drawings account. The typical entries in these accounts are outlined in Figure 25.2.

Figure 25.2

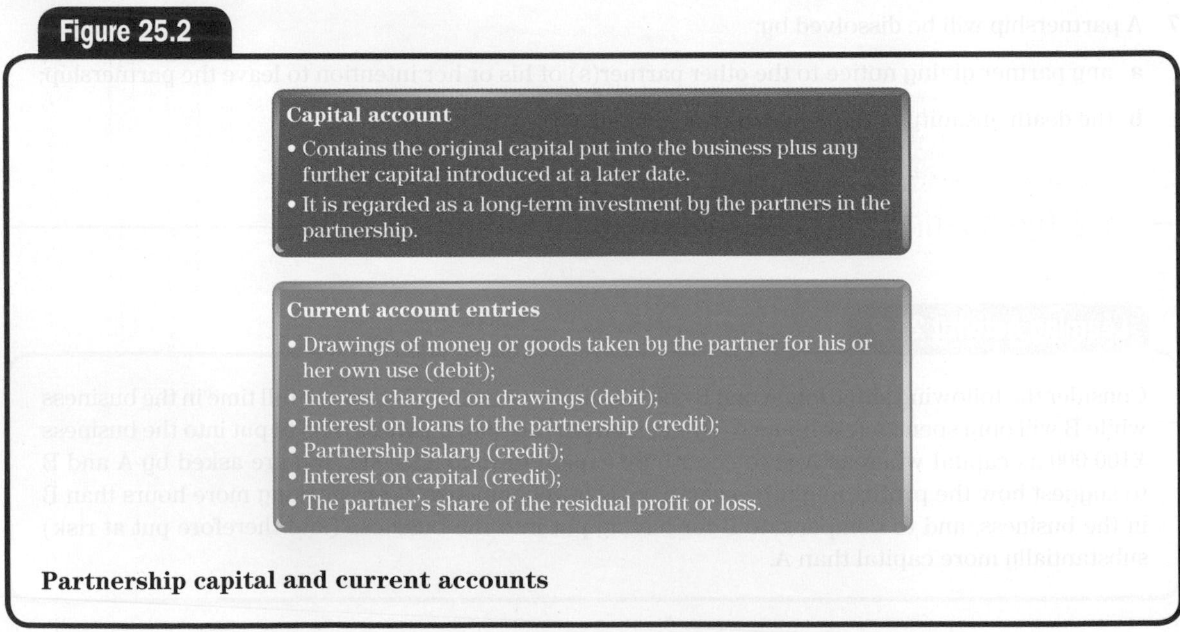

Capital account
• Contains the original capital put into the business plus any further capital introduced at a later date.
• It is regarded as a long-term investment by the partners in the partnership.
Current account entries
• Drawings of money or goods taken by the partner for his or her own use (debit);
• Interest charged on drawings (debit);
• Interest on loans to the partnership (credit);
• Partnership salary (credit);
• Interest on capital (credit);
• The partner's share of the residual profit or loss.

Partnership capital and current accounts

There may also be a separate **drawings account** for each partner in which all goods or money taken by the partners during the year are entered instead of putting them in the partners' **current accounts**. However, at the end of the year these are transferred to the partners' current accounts. Note also that current accounts are sometimes labelled 'drawings accounts'.

The partners' capital accounts are shown on the statement of financial position in the same place as the capital account of a sole trader. Underneath these are entered the balances on the partners' current accounts at the end of the year. If a current account has a debit balance, it may be entered after the net current assets but it is more common to deduct (in parentheses) this from the other partners' current accounts.

25.4 The appropriation account

In partnership final financial statements, the statement of profit or loss contains exactly the same entries as that of a sole trader.

After the statement of profit or loss has been prepared, the profit (or loss) for the year is carried down to an **appropriation account** in which is shown the sharing of the profit (or loss) between the partners. The basis for sharing may include partners' salaries, interest on capital and interest on drawings. It will also always contain the division of the remaining amount (the residual profit or loss) in some agreed proportion. The appropriation account is part of the double entry in the ledger and as a general rule it is worth remembering that the double entry for each item in the appropriation account is on the opposite side of the relevant *partner's current account*. The typical contents of an appropriation account (ledger style) are shown in Figure 25.3. This can be used as a reference to check your double entry.

Figure 25.3

Appropriation account			
Salaries		*Profit*	XXX
– Salary A (to current account)	XX		
– Salary B (to current account)	XXX	*Interest on drawings*	
Interest on capital X%		– A (to current account)	X
– A (to current account)	X	– B (to current account)	X
– B (to current account)	X	– C (to current account)	X
– C (to current account)	X		
Balance (to current account)			
– A 40%	XXX		
– B 40%	XXX		
– C 20%	XX		
	XXX		XXX

A pro forma layout of a typical partnership appropriation account (ledger style)

The corresponding pro forma entries to the current account are shown in Figure 25.4.

Figure 25.4

Current account							
	A	B	C		A	B	C
Drawings	XX	XX	XX	Balance b/d	XX	XX	XX
Interest on drawings	X	X	X	Salary	XX	XXX	–
				Interest on capital	X	X	X
Balance c/d	XX	XX	XX	Profit	XXX	XXX	XX
	XXX	XXX	XXX		XXX	XXX	XXX
				Balance b/d	XX	XX	XX

A pro forma example of the layout of a typical partnership current account

The contents of the appropriation account are illustrated in Worked Example 25.1.

WORKED EXAMPLE 25.1

Bonnie and Clyde are in partnership sharing profits in the ratio 2 : 1. From the following, you are required to prepare the appropriation account for the year ended 31 December 20X4 and show the relevant items in the statement of financial position at that date.

	Bonnie	Clyde
	£	£
Capital at 31 Dec 20X3	100,000	80,000
Current account balances at 31 Dec 20X3	16,340	28,290
Drawings – 1 Apr 20X4	4,000	8,000
31 Aug 20X4	6,000	9,000
30 Sep 20X4	8,000	–
Salaries	20,000 p.a.	25,000 p.a.
Interest on capital	10% p.a.	10% p.a.
Interest on drawings	5% p.a.	5% p.a.

Clyde introduced additional capital of £10,000 on 1 January 20X4 and Bonnie lent the business £20,000 on 30 June 20X4. The profit for the year ended 31 December 20X4 was £78,700.

Before dividing the profit between the partners, the *partners' capital accounts* need to be adjusted. These ledger accounts are often prepared in columnar form as follows:

Capital account

		Bonnie	Clyde			Bonnie	Clyde
		£	£			£	£
20X4				20X4			
				1 Jan	Balance b/d	100,000	80,000
31 Dec	Balance c/d	100,000	90,000	1 Jan	Bank		10,000
		100,000	90,000			100,000	90,000
				20X5			
				1 Jan	Balance b/d	100,000	90,000

The loan from Bonnie is not entered in his *capital account* but rather in a separate *loan account*, which constitutes a non-current liability.

Next, it may be useful to prepare a schedule which shows the division of the profits as follows:

	Bonnie	Clyde	Total
	£	£	£
Profit for 20X4			78,700
Loan interest ($\frac{6}{12}$ × 5% × £20,000)	500	–	(500)
Partners' salaries	20,000	25,000	(45,000)

Interest on capital:			
10% × £100,000	10,000	–	(10,000)
10% × £90,000	–	9,000	(9,000)
	30,500	34,000	14,200
Interest on drawings (see note 3)	(350)	(450)	800
	30,150	33,550	15,000
Share of residual profit (2 : 1)	10,000	5,000	(15,000)
Totals	40,150	38,550	–

Notes

1 The interest on partners' loans is computed using the rate of 5 per cent per annum specified in the Partnership Act 1890, unless you are told that some other rate has been agreed by the partners.

2 The interest on capital is computed using the balances on the partners' capital accounts and not the current accounts, unless you are told the contrary. Note also that in this example the balance on the capital account at the end of the year can be used because the additional capital was introduced at the start of the year. Where additional capital is introduced at some other date, it will be necessary to compute the interest on a strict time basis.

3 The interest on drawings is calculated on a monthly basis as follows:

Bonnie $\frac{9}{12} \times 5\% \times £4{,}000 = 150$

$\frac{4}{12} \times 5\% \times £6{,}000 = 100$

$\frac{3}{12} \times 5\% \times £8{,}000 = 100$

350

Clyde $\frac{9}{12} \times 5\% \times £8{,}000 = 300$

$\frac{4}{12} \times 5\% \times £9{,}000 = 150$

450

4 The sum of the total of each column in the profit appropriation schedule should always equal the profit for the year (i.e. £40,150 + £38,550 = £78,700; £30,150 + £33,550 + £15,000 = £78,700, etc.)

The above appropriation schedule can be used to make the necessary entries in the appropriation account and the *partners' current accounts* in the ledger. The preparation of a schedule is very efficient because the total of each of the columns, showing each partner's total share of the annual net profit, can be entered in the appropriation account and *partners' current accounts* as single amounts thus:

		Debit	Credit
Debit:	*Appropriation account*	£78,700	
Credit:	*Current accounts: – Bonnie*		£40,150
	– Clyde		£38,550

However, for a fuller presentation and to emphasize the double entry, the separate elements are all shown below:

Bonnie and Clyde appropriation account for the year ended 31 December 20X4

	£	£		£	£
Loan interest – Bonnie			Net profit for year b/d		78,700
($\frac{0}{12}$ × 5% × £20,000)		500	Interest on drawings:		
Salaries – Bonnie	20,000		– Bonnie	350	
– Clyde	25,000	45,000	– Clyde	450	800
Interest on capital:					
– Bonnie (10% × £100,000)	10,000				
– Clyde (10% × £90,000)	9,000	19,000			
Shares of residual profit:					
– Bonnie (2/3)	10,000				
– Clyde (1/3)	5,000	15,000			
		79,500			79,500

The double entry for the items in the appropriation account is in the *partners' current accounts*, which are usually prepared in columnar form as follows:

Current accounts

	Bonnie	Clyde		Bonnie	Clyde
	£	£		£	£
Drawings	18,000	17,000	Balance b/d	16,340	28,290
Interest on drawings	350	450	Loan interest	500	–
Balance c/d	38,490	49,840	Salaries	20,000	25,000
			Interest on capital	10,000	9,000
			Shares of profit	10,000	5,000
	56,840	67,290		56,840	67,290
			Balance b/d	38,490	49,840

The relevant balances will then be included in the statement of financial position as follows:

Bonnie and Clyde statement of financial position as at 31 December 20X4

	£	£
EQUITY AND LIABILITIES		
Owners' equity		
Capital		
– Bonnie		100,000
– Clyde		90,000
		190,000
Current accounts		
– Bonnie	38,490	
– Clyde	49,840	88,330
		278,330

Non-current liabilities	
Loan – Bonnie	20,000
Total non-current liabilities	20,000
Total equity and liabilities	298,330

Alternatively, these can be shown on the statement of financial position in columnar form, as follows:

	Bonnie	**Clyde**	**Total**
EQUITY AND LIABILITIES	£	£	£
Owners' equity			
Capital	100,000	90,000	190,000
Current accounts	38,490	49,840	88,330
Total owners' equity	138,490	139,840	278,330
Non-current liabilities			
Loan – Bonnie			20,000
Total non-current liabilities			20,000
Total equity and liabilities			298,330

In practice and when answering examination questions it is not usual to show final financial statements in account form. Thus, the appropriation account is not normally prepared in account form. Instead this can either be presented as a schedule, as shown above, or in a vertical format as illustrated below. Whichever presentation is adopted, it is advisable to show each of the entries in the *partners' current accounts* relating to salaries, interest on capital, and so on as above, rather than the totals of each of the partner's columns in the schedule. Moreover, the vertical format shown below is generally preferable to a schedule because the use of an analysis column for each partner serves little purpose when the entries in the *partners' current accounts* are done individually. This format has thus been used in the solutions to the exercises in the student OLC.

Bonnie and Clyde appropriation account for the year ended 31 December 20X4

	£	£	£
Profit for the year			78,700
Add: Interest on drawings:			
– Bonnie		350	
– Clyde		450	800
			79,500
Less: Loan interest – Bonnie		500	
Salaries:			
– Bonnie	20,000		
– Clyde	25,000	45,000	
Interest on capital:			
– Bonnie	10,000		
– Clyde	9,000	19,000	64,500
Residual profit			15,000

Shares of residual profit:	
– Bonnie	10,000
– Clyde	5,000
	15,000

Notes

1 Interest on partners' loans is commonly entered in the appropriation account, particularly in examination questions that do not require the preparation of a statement of profit or loss. However, this is not strictly an appropriation of profit but rather an expense that should be entered in the *statement of profit or loss* as a charge/deduction in arriving at the profit (or loss) for the year.

2 Where money which is described as 'salaries' has actually been paid to the partners this must be treated as drawings and not included in the statement of profit or loss as wages and salaries. However, this may be interpreted as indicating that the partners wish to give themselves a prior share of profits in the form of a salary. In this case the amounts paid must still be treated as drawings but an equivalent amount is also entered in the appropriation account as salaries, as described above.

3 Additional capital introduced during the year may include assets other than cash. This would usually be entitled to interest on capital from the date the assets were introduced until the end of the year in question (and subsequent years).

4 Interest is usually only charged on cash and cheque drawings and not on goods taken by the partners for their own use.

5 Losses would be shared in the same ratio as profit. If, in the case of Worked Example 25.1, the profit for the year had been only £55,000, the schedule of division of profits would be as follows:

	Bonnie	**Clyde**	**Total**
	£	**£**	**£**
Profit for year			55,000
Loan interest	500	–	(500)
Salaries	20,000	25,000	(45,000)
Interest on capital	10,000	9,000	(19,000)
	30,500	34,000	(9,500)
Interest on drawings	(350)	(450)	800
	30,150	33,550	(8,700)
Shares of residual loss (2 : 1)	(5,800)	(2,900)	8,700
	24,350	30,650	–

Note that loan interest, salaries, interest on capital and interest on drawings are included even if there is a net loss for the year (i.e. before the appropriation). Salaries, and so on, simply increase the amount of the residual loss.

25.5 Partners' commission

Some partnership businesses are departmentalized, with each of the selling departments being managed by a different partner. In such circumstances it is common for partners' salaries to take the form of an agreed **partners' commission** expressed as a percentage of the profit of their department. This necessitates the preparation of a trading account for each department, which normally takes the form of a columnar trading account, containing columns on both the debit and credit sides for each department. Computing the profits of each partner's department is done in the same way as departmental accounts, a short description of which is given in Appendix A (p. 467) to this chapter. Having ascertained the profit of each department, the partner's commission can be calculated and then accounted for in exactly the same way as partners' salaries.

25.6 A guaranteed share of profit

Some partnership agreements include a clause which states that if a particular partner's share of profit in any year is below some agreed figure, then all or certain other partners will make it up to the agreed amount from their shares of profit. The agreed amount is referred to as a **guaranteed share of profit**; the amount by which the actual share of profit falls short of the guaranteed amount is usually shared (i.e. made up) by the other partners in their profit-sharing ratio. Such a guarantee is fairly common in professional firms as an enticement to an employee to become a partner while at the same time being guaranteed an amount equal to the employee's existing remuneration. The guaranteed amount may include or exclude the partner's interest on capital and/or salary, but in the absence of information to the contrary it is usually taken to be the residual profit share that is guaranteed. Worked Example 25.2 shows how to account for a guaranteed share of profit.

WORKED EXAMPLE 25.2

If, in the amended Worked Example 25.1, when profits are only £55,000, Bonnie was guaranteed a share of residual profit of at least £2,000, the profit-sharing schedule would appear as follows:

	Bonnie	Clyde	Total
	£	£	£
Profit for year	–	–	55,000
Salaries, interest on loan, capital, and drawings	30,150	33,550	(63,700)
Share of residual loss	2,000	(10,700)	8,700
	32,150	22,850	–

25.7 Limited liability partnerships

Limited liability partnerships (LLP) were introduced in the UK under the Limited Liability Partnership Act 2000 and the Limited Liability Partnerships Act (Northern Ireland) 2002. They have some characteristics that are similar to companies – the partners are seen as being legally independent from the partnership, which has its own legal identity. Just like a company, the responsibility of the partners for the debts of the LLP is limited to the amounts invested by the partners – hence their liability is limited. However, the partners are taxed in a similar manner to partners in a normal partnership. Many accountancy and law partnerships have became LLPs in response to negligence claims being made against partnerships (see Real World Example 25.1).

REAL WORLD EXAMPLE 25.1

Deloitte opts for limited liability

'Deloitte & Touche yesterday became the last of the Big Four accounting firms to say it would adopt limited liability status in an attempt to protect partners from Enron-style negligence claims.

The UK arm, which absorbed Andersen's former partners and much of its business after the firm's collapse last year, announced its intention to convert in early summer.

Partners, who share the firm's liabilities as well as its profits, are concerned that a successful negligence claim could leave them destitute.

Limited liability ringfences the liability only around those partners involved in a failed audit, leaving others in the partnership unaffected. As a condition, however, the firm must open up its books like a public company.'

Source: Adapted from *The Telegraph*, 25 March, 2003; www.telegraph.co.uk/finance/2847063/Deloitte-opts-for-limited-liability.html (Accessed September 2014)

Learning Activity 25.3

Visit the Deloitte LLP website and view their financial statements for the most recent year (http://www.deloitte.com/view/en_GB/uk/about/annual-reports/). Note how the format of LLP financial statements is consistent with that of a company, not a partnership. *Also, in the UK the heading Balance Sheet is still used by many companies instead of Statement of Financial Position.*

Summary

A partnership exists when between 2 and 20 persons (or more in the case of professional firms) carry on business with a view of profit. One of the main characteristics of partnerships is that the partners have unlimited liability. They are thus jointly and severally liable for the partnership debts. Each partner is also an agent of the partnership, entitled to take part in the management, and has equal voting rights.

However, the articles or deed of partnership may contain any form of agreement relating to the rights of partners between themselves. This is particularly important with regard to the sharing of profits and losses. Where partners contribute unequal amounts of capital and/or time, it is common to find a profit-sharing formula that includes giving each partner a prior share of profits as interest on capital and/or a salary. Similarly, where partners have unequal amounts of drawings, they may decide to charge each other interest on drawings as a part of the profit-sharing formula.

The statements of profit or loss of partnerships are the same as those of sole traders. However, the net profit (or loss) is carried down into an appropriation account in which is shown the shares of profit appropriated to each partner. The statement of financial position of partnerships is the same as that of a sole trader, except that instead of having a single *capital account* there is a *capital* and *current account* for each partner.

Sometimes partners' salaries take the form of a commission that is expressed as a percentage of the gross (or net) profit of a department or branch that is managed by each partner. Some partnership agreements also contain a clause guaranteeing a particular partner a minimum amount as his or her share of the annual profit. In this case, the amount by which the actual share of the annual profit falls short of the minimum is made up from the other partners' share(s) of profit (in their profit-sharing ratio).

Key terms and concepts

appropriation account	459	interest on the capital	457
articles/deed of partnership	456	limited liability partnership (LLP)	465
capital account	458	partners' commission	465
current account	458	partnership	456
drawings account	458	partnership salary	457
guaranteed share of profit	465	residual profit/loss	457
interest on drawings	457	unlimited liability	457

Appendix A: Departmental accounts

Where it is decided to produce separate profit or loss results for each trading department within a business, in addition to identifying the sales for each unit and tracking costs that are specifically identifiable to the departments, it is necessary to apportion (i.e. divide up on the basis of ratios) the untraceable overhead costs. No matter how carefully the apportionment ratios are selected, they will depend on the exercise of judgement, and to that extent are arbitrary. The basis should be chosen to attempt to reflect the extra cost likely to be caused by the particular department or, failing that, the benefits the department receives. An illustration of the preparation of departmental financial statements is given in Worked Example 25.3.

WORKED EXAMPLE 25.3

Status Stores run three sales departments: clothing, footwear and stationery. For accounting purposes departmental financial statements are to be prepared, apportioning building costs (rent, etc.) on the basis of floor space occupied and office administration in proportion to gross profit.

The following information has been extracted from the store's accounting records for the year ended 31 December 20X5:

	Clothing	Footwear	Stationery
	£	£	£
Sales revenue	47,000	27,000	26,000
Purchases	23,000	16,000	10,500
Wages	2,500	2,100	1,800
Inventories at 1 Jan 20X5	6,000	1,000	500
Inventories at 31 Dec 20X5	4,000	2,000	1,000
Floor space (in sq. m)	3,000	2,000	1,000
Rent, rates, lighting, heating and building maintenance (all departments)		£13,800	
Administration and office salaries, etc.		£20,000	

Status Stores

Departmental statement of profit or loss for the year ended 31 December 20X5

	Clothing		Footwear		Stationery	
	£	£	£	£	£	£
Sales revenue		47,000		27,000		26,000
Less: Cost of sales:						
Opening inventory	6,000		1,000		500	
Add: Purchases	23,000		16,000		10,500	
	29,000		17,000		11,000	
Less: Closing inventory	4,000	25,000	2,000	15,000	1,000	10,000
Gross profit		22,000		12,000		16,000
Less: Wages	2,500		2,100		1,800	
Building costs (3:2:1)	6,900		4,600		2,300	
Administration (22:12:16)	8,800	18,200	4,800	11,500	6,400	10,500
		3,800		500		5,500

It is not usual to have separate statements of financial position for each department.

An asterisk after the question number indicates that there is a suggested answer in Appendix 2.

Review questions

connect

25.1 **a** Define a partnership.

b What are the legal limits on the number of partners?

c Outline the principal matters normally found in the articles or deed of partnership.

25.2* Describe the main characteristics of a partnership.

25.3 If there is no partnership agreement the provisions of the Partnership Act 1890 apply. List the main provisions of this Act with regard to the rights of partners between themselves, including the sharing of profits or losses.

25.4 Explain each of the following in the context of partnership profit sharing:

a partners' salaries;

b interest on capital;

c interest on drawings;

d residual profit.

25.5 Lane and Hill have decided to form a partnership. Lane is to contribute £150,000 as capital and Hill £20,000. Hill is to work full time in the business and Lane one day a week. Because Hill has no other income, she anticipates making drawings of £1,000 per month from the partnership. Lane expects to make drawings of about £1,000 per quarter.

You have been asked to advise the partners on how to share profits in such a way as to compensate each of them for their unequal contributions of capital, labour and withdrawals.

25.6 Explain the difference between each of the following ledger accounts in the books of a partnership:

a capital account;

b current account;

c drawings account.

Exercises

connect

25.7* Clayton and Hammond are in partnership sharing profits and losses equally. The partnership agreement provides for annual salaries of Clayton: £17,000 and Hammond: £13,000. It also provides for interest on capital of 8 per cent per annum and interest on drawings of 4 per cent per annum. BASIC

The following additional information relates to the accounting year ending 30 June 20X5:

	Clayton	Hammond
	£	£
Capital at 1 July 20X4	90,000	60,000
Current account at 1 July 20X4	16,850	9,470
Drawings – 1 October 20X4	3,000	2,000
– 1 March 20X5	5,000	1,000
Capital introduced – 1 November 20X4	10,000	–
Loan by Hammond – 1 April 20X5	–	20,000

The profit for the year shown in the statement of profit or loss for the year ended 30 June 20X5 was £67,500.

Required

Prepare the appropriation account, capital account and current account. Show all the accounts in account format.

25.8 Mary and Seamus are in partnership sharing profits and losses equally. The partnership agreement provides for annual salaries of £34,000 for Mary and £22,000 for Seamus. It also provides for interest on capital of 8 per cent per annum and interest on drawings of 5 per cent per annum. BASIC

You are given the following additional information relating to the accounting year ending 30 June 20X5.

	Mary	Seamus
	£	£
Capital at 1 July 20X4	180,000	60,000
Current account at 1 July 20X4	33,850	20,470
Drawings – 1 October 20X4	6,000	5,000
– 1 March 20X5	12,000	4,000
Capital introduced – 1 November 20X4	30,000	–
Loan by Seamus (5%) – 1 April 20X5		50,000

The profit for the year shown in the statement of profit or loss for the year ended 30 June 20X5 was £150,000.

Required

a Prepare the following accounts:

i Appropriation account

ii Capital accounts

iii Current accounts

b Describe the main characteristics of a partnership.

BASIC

25.9 Anna and Thomas are in partnership sharing profits and losses equally. The partnership agreement provides for an annual salary to Anna of £57,000. It also provides for interest on capital of 10 per cent per annum and interest on drawings of 12 per cent per annum.

The following additional information relates to the accounting year ending 30 June 20X5:

	Anna	Thomas
	£	£
Opening capital balance	150,000	50,000
Opening current account balance	5,000	12,000
Drawings – 1 July 20X4	10,000	10,000
Drawings – 1 October 20X4	10,000	15,000
Drawings – 1 December 20X4	12,000	10,000
Drawings – 1 March 20X5	5,000	8,000
Capital introduced – 1 December 20X4	50,000	
Loan by Anna – 1 December 20X5 (15%)	100,000	

The profit for the year shown in the statement of profit or loss for the year ended 30 June 20X5 was £180,000.

Required

Prepare the following accounts:

a Appropriation account

b Capital accounts

c Current accounts

BASIC

25.10 Light and Dark are in partnership sharing profits and losses in the ratio 7 : 3, respectively. The following information has been taken from the partnership records for the financial year ended 31 May 20X5:

Partners' capital accounts, balances as at 1 June 20X4:

Light	£200,000
Dark	£140,000

Partners' current accounts, balances as at 1 June 20X4:

Light	£15,000 Credit
Dark	£13,000 Credit

During the year ended 31 May 20X5 the partners made the following drawings from the partnership bank account:

Light	£10,000 on 31 August 20X4 £10,000 on 30 November 20X4 £10,000 on 28 February 20X5 £10,000 on 31 May 20X5
Dark	£7,000 on 31 August 20X4 £7,000 on 30 November 20X4 £7,000 on 28 February 20X5 £7,000 on 31 May 20X5

Interest is to be charged on drawings at the rate of 12 per cent per annum. Interest is allowed on *capital accounts* and credit balances on *current accounts* at the rate of 12 per cent per annum. Dark is to be allowed a salary of £15,000 per annum.

The net profit of the partnership for the year ended 31 May 20X5 is £102,940.

Required

a A computation of the amount of interest chargeable on each partner's drawings for the year ended 31 May 20X5.

b The partnership appropriation account for the year ended 31 May 20X5.

c A computation of the balance on each partner's *current account* as at 31 May 20X5.

(AAT)

INTERMEDIATE

25.11 The partnership of Sewell, Grange and Jones has just completed its first year in business. The partnership agreement stipulates that profits should be apportioned in the ratio of Sewell 3, Grange 2 and Jones 1 after allowing interest on capital at 12 per cent per annum and crediting Sewell with a salary of £15,000.

The following information relates to their first financial year that ended on 31 October 20X5.

1 The partners introduced the following amounts as capital on 1 November 20X4:

	£
Sewell	50,000
Grange	40,000
Jones	20,000

2 Cash drawings during the year were:

	£
Sewell	3,900
Grange	4,500
Jones	2,400

3 The draft statement of profit or loss for the year showed a profit for the year of £61,720.

4 Included in the *motor expenses account* for the year was a bill for £300 that related to Grange's private motoring expenses.

5 No entries had been made in the financial statements to record the following:

a As a result of a cash flow problem during April, Grange invested a further £10,000 as capital with effect from 1 May 20X5, and on the same date Jones brought into the business additional items of equipment at an agreed valuation of £6,000. In addition, in order to settle a debt, Jones had privately undertaken some work for Foster, a creditor of the partnership. Foster accepted the work as full settlement of the £12,000 the partnership owed her for materials.

b Sewell had accepted a holiday provided by Miller, a credit customer of the partnership. The holiday, which was valued at £1,000, was accepted in full settlement of a debt of £2,500 that Miller owed to the partnership and that he was unable to pay.

c Each partner had taken goods for his own use during the year at cost as follows:

	£
Sewell	1,400
Grange	2,100
Jones	2,100

Note: It is the policy of the firm to depreciate equipment at the rate of 10 per cent per annum based on the cost of equipment held at the end of each financial year.

Required

a The appropriation account for the year ended 31 October 20X5 showing clearly the corrected profit from the first year's trading.

b The *capital* and *current accounts* of Sewell, Grange and Jones for the year ended 31 October 20X5.

(AEB)

INTERMEDIATE

25.12* The following is the trial balance of Peace and Quiet, grocers, as at 31 December 20X4.

	Debit £	Credit £
Capital: Peace		10,000
Capital: Quiet		5,000
Current account: Peace		1,280
Current account: Quiet		3,640
Purchases/sales revenue	45,620	69,830
Trade receivables/trade payables	1,210	4,360
Leasehold shop at cost	18,000	

Equipment at cost	8,500	
Depreciation on equipment		1,200
Shop assistants' salaries	5,320	
Light and heat	1,850	
Stationery	320	
Bank interest and charges	45	
Inventory	6,630	
Bank	3,815	
Drawings – Peace 1 May 20X4	2,200	
– Quiet 1 September 20X4	1,800	
	95,310	95,310

Additional information

1 The inventory at 31 December 20X4 was valued at £5,970.

2 There is electricity accrued at the end of the year of £60.

3 Stationery unused at 31 December 20X4 was valued at £50.

4 The equipment is depreciated at 10 per cent per annum on the reducing balance method.

5 There is a partnership deed that says that each partner is to be credited with interest on capital at 10 per cent per annum; salaries of £6,200 per annum for Peace and £4,800 per annum for Quiet; and charged interest on drawings of 8 per cent per annum. The remainder of the profit is to be divided equally between the partners.

6 Included in the capital of Peace is capital introduced of £1,000 on 1 April 20X4 and a loan to the partnership of £2,000 on 1 October 20X4.

Required

Prepare the statement of profit or loss and appropriation account for the year and a statement of financial position at 31 December 20X4.

25.13 Peter and Paul, whose year end is 30 June, are in business as food wholesalers. Their partnership deed states that:

INTERMEDIATE

a profits and losses are to be shared equally;

b salaries are: Peter £20,000 per annum; Paul £18,000 per annum;

c interest on capital of 10 per cent is allowed;

d interest on drawings of 5 per cent is charged;

e interest on loans from partners is given at the rate shown in the Partnership Act 1890.

The trial balance as at 30 June 20X5 is as follows:

	Debit	Credit
	£	£
Capital – Peter		100,000
– Paul		80,000
Current accounts – Peter	804	
– Paul		21,080
Loan at 1 July 20X4 – Peter		12,000
Freehold premises at cost	115,000	

Plant and machinery at cost	77,000	
Provision for depreciation on plant		22,800
Motor vehicles at cost	36,500	
Provision for depreciation on vehicles		12,480
Loose tools at 1 July 20X4	1,253	
Inventories	6,734	
Trade receivables and payables	4,478	3,954
Bank	7,697	
Electricity accrued at 1 July 20X4		58
Paid for electricity	3,428	
Purchases and sales revenue	19,868	56,332
Warehouse wages	23,500	
Rates	5,169	
Postage and telephone	4,257	
Printing and stationery	2,134	
Allowance for irrecoverable receivables		216
Selling expenses	1,098	
	308,920	308,920

You also ascertain the following:

1 Inventory at 30 June 20X5 is £8,264.

2 Depreciation by the straight line method is 10 per cent per annum on plant and machinery and 20 per cent per annum on motor vehicles. The latter are used by the administrative staff. The revaluation method of depreciation is used for loose tools. These have a value at 30 June 20X5 of £927.

3 Included in wages are drawings of £6,000 by Peter on 1 March 20X5 and £8,000 by Paul on 1 October 20X4.

4 The allowance for irrecoverable receivables at 30 June 20X5 is to be £180.

5 Trade receivables include irrecoverable receivables of £240.

6 Sales revenue includes goods that are on sale or return at a price of £200. The cost price of these is £160.

7 Electricity accrued at 30 June 20X5 amounts to £82.

8 Rates prepaid at 30 June 20X5 are £34.

Required

Prepare a statement of profit or loss and appropriation account for the year ended 30 June 20X5 and a statement of financial position at that date. Present your answer in vertical form.

ADVANCED

25.14* Simon, Wilson and Dillon are in partnership. The following trial balance has been prepared on 31 December 20X4:

	Debit	Credit
	£	£
Capital accounts – Simon		35,000
– Wilson		25,000
– Dillon		10,000
Current accounts – Simon		5,600
– Wilson		4,800
– Dillon	1,800	
Freehold land and buildings	65,000	
Inventories	34,900	
Bank	10,100	
Delivery vehicles at cost	30,000	
Provision for depreciation on vehicles		18,000
Goodwill at cost	11,000	
8% mortgage on premises		40,000
Salesmen's salaries	19,480	
Sales ledger control account	28,000	
Purchases ledger control account		25,000
Unquoted investments	6,720	
Loose tools at valuation	1,200	
Sales revenue		130,000
Investment income		800
Returns	400	600
Purchases	64,000	
Rates	12,100	
Motor expenses	2,800	
Allowance for irrecoverable receivables		400
Mortgage interest paid	1,600	
Printing and stationery	1,100	
Extension to premises	5,000	
	295,200	295,200

Additional information

1 The inventory at 31 December 20X4 was valued at £31,000.

2 There is investment income accrued at 31 December 20X4 of £320.

3 The inventory of stationery at 31 December 20X4 was £170.

4 At the same date there were motor expenses accrued of £240 and rates paid in advance of £160.

5 The allowance for irrecoverable receivables at 31 December 20X4 is to be adjusted to 2 per cent of trade receivables.

6 Mortgage interest accrued should be provided for at the end of the year.

7 Depreciation on vehicles, on a strict time basis, is 10 per cent per annum using the straight-line method.

8 The loose tools in inventory at 31 December 20X4 were valued at £960.

9 The following errors have been found:

a unrecorded in the ledger is the sale of a delivery vehicle on credit on 1 November 20X4 for £1,900 – this vehicle cost £2,400 when it was purchased on 1 April 20X2;

b irrecoverable receivables for this year of £2,000 have not been written off;

c bank charges of £130 have been omitted from the books.

Simon and Dillon are to be allocated salaries of £15,000 and £10,000 per annum, respectively. All partners will be entitled to interest on capital of 10 per cent per annum. The remaining profit or loss is shared between Simon, Wilson and Dillon in the ratio of 2 : 2 : 1, respectively.

Required

Prepare in vertical form a statement of profit or loss and appropriation account for the year ended 31 December 20X4 and a statement of financial position at that date.

ADVANCED

25.15 A, B, C and D were partners in a garage business comprising (1) petrol sales, (2) repairs and servicing and (3) second-hand car dealing. A was responsible for petrol sales, B for repairs and servicing and C for second-hand car deals, while D acted purely in an advisory capacity.

The partnership agreement provided the following:

i Interest on fixed capital is to be provided at a rate of 10 per cent per annum.

ii Each working partner is to receive commission of 10 per cent of the gross profit of that partner's own department.

iii Profits are shared as follows: A: $\frac{2}{10}$, B: $\frac{3}{10}$, C: $\frac{3}{10}$, D: $\frac{2}{10}$

iv Financial statements are to be made up annually to 30 September.

A trial balance extracted from the books at 30 September 20X5 showed the following balances:

		Debit	Credit
		£	£
A	Capital account		3,500
	Current account		1,350
	Drawings account	6,000	
B	Capital account		7,500
	Current account		7,500
	Drawings account	13,250	
C	Capital account		6,500
	Current account		5,500
	Drawings account	10,500	
D	Capital account		12,500
	Current account		2,150
	Drawings account	3,500	
Freehold premises at cost		25,000	
Goodwill at cost		10,000	
Servicing tools and equipment at cost		9,000	
Servicing tools and equipment – accumulated depreciation to 1 October 20X4			1,350
Bank balance			10,105

Inventories at 1 October 20X4 – petrol	950	
– spares	525	
– second-hand cars	6,350	
Trade receivables and payables	4,350	2,350
Cash in hand	125	
Sales – petrol		68,650
– servicing and repairs		86,750
– cars		156,000
Purchases – petrol	58,500	
– spares	51,650	
– second-hand cars	118,530	
Wages – forecourt attendants	5,750	
– mechanics	31,350	
– car sales staff	8,550	
– office personnel	1,850	
Rates	2,500	
Office expenses	1,800	
Heating and lighting	550	
Advertising	775	
Bank interest	350	
	371,705	371,705

Additional information

1 Inventories at 30 September 20X5:

	£
Petrol	1,050
Spares	475
Second-hand cars	9,680

2 Depreciation on tools and equipment is to be provided at 5 per cent per annum by the straight-line method.

3 Your fee for preparation of the financial statements will be £175.

4 The service department did work valued at £11,300 on the second-hand cars.

5 The service department used old cars valued at £550 for spare parts in services and repairs.

Required

a Prepare a statement of profit or loss for the year ended 30 September 20X5.

b Prepare a statement of financial position at 30 September 20X5.

c Prepare the partners' current accounts in columnar form for the year.

(ACCA)

INTERMEDIATE

25.16 a When accounting for the relationship of partners *inter se*, the partnership agreement provides the rules which, in the first instance, are to be applied.

What information would you expect to find in a partnership agreement to provide such rules, and what should you do if the agreement fails to deal with any aspect of the partnership relationship that affects the financial statements?

b A, B and C are in partnership, agreeing to share profits in the ratio 4 : 2 : 1. They have also agreed to allow interest on capital at 8 per cent per annum; a salary to C of £5,000 per annum; and to charge interest on drawings made in advance of the year end at a rate of 10 per cent per annum.

A has guaranteed B a minimum annual income of £6,500, gross of interest on drawings. The statement of financial position as at 30 June 20X4 disclosed the following:

EQUITY AND LIABILITIES			
Owners' equity		£	£
Capital	A	50,000	
	B	30,000	
	C	10,000	90,000
Current accounts	A	2,630	
	B	521	
	C	(418)	2,733
			92,733
Non-current liabilities			
Loan account	A		15,000
Total equity and liabilities			107,733

Drawings during the year were: A £6,400; B £3,100; C £2,000.

Profit for the year to 30 June 20X5 was £24,750.

You are required to prepare the *current accounts* for the partners as at 30 June 20X5.

(ACCA, adapted)

ADVANCED

25.17 Brick, Stone and Breeze carry on a manufacturing business in partnership, sharing profits and losses: Brick one-half, Stone one-third and Breeze one-sixth. It is agreed that the minimum annual share of profit to be credited to Breeze is to be £2,200, and any deficiency between this figure and her true share of the profits is to be borne by the other two partners in the ratio that they share profits. No interest is to be allowed or charged on partners' capital or current accounts.

The trial balance of the firm as on 30 June 20X5 was as follows:

	Debit	Credit
	£	£
Inventory on 1 July 20X4	7,400	
Purchases	39,100	
Manufacturing wages	8,600	
Salaries	5,670	
Rates, telephone and insurance	1,744	
Incidental trade expenses	710	
Repairs and renewals	1,250	
Cash discounts allowed and received	280	500

Office expenses	3,586	
Carriage inwards	660	
Carriage outwards	850	
Professional charges	500	
Sales revenue		69,770
Allowance for irrecoverable receivables as at 1 July 20X4		400
Provision for depreciation as at 1 July 20X4:		
Machinery and plant		2,500
Motor vehicles		1,300
Capital accounts:		
Brick		9,000
Stone		5,000
Breeze		4,000
Current accounts as at 1 July 20X4:		
Brick		1,900
Stone	500	
Breeze		400
Freehold buildings, at cost	9,800	
Machinery and plant, at cost	8,200	
Motor vehicles, at cost	2,500	
Bank balance	750	
Sales ledger balances	7,000	
Bought ledger balances		4,330
	99,100	99,100

Additional information

1 An amount of £3,000, for goods sent out on sale or return, has been included in sales. These goods were charged out to customers at cost plus 25 per cent and they were still in the customers' hands on 30 June 20X5, unsold.

2 Included in the item, repairs and renewals is an amount of £820 for an extension to the factory.

3 Telephone and insurance paid in advance amounted to £424 and £42 was owing in respect of a trade expense.

4 A receivable of £80 has turned out to be irrecoverable and is to be written off.

5 The allowance for irrecoverable receivables is to be increased to £520.

6 Provision for depreciation on machinery and plant and on motor vehicles is to be made at the rate of 10 per cent and 20 per cent per annum, respectively, on the cost.

7 The value of the inventory on hand on 30 June 20X5 was £7,238.

8 Each month Brick has drawn £55, Stone £45 and Breeze £20, and the amounts have been included in salaries.

Required

a Prepare the statement of profit or loss for the year ended 30 June 20X5.

b Write up the *partners' current accounts*, in columnar form, for the year.

c Draw up the statement of financial position as on 30 June 20X5.

(ACCA)

ADVANCED

25.18 A. Cherry owned a farmhouse and land, the latter being used by him and his sons, Tom and Leo, in carrying on a fruit and poultry business in partnership. The partnership agreement stipulated that the father should take one-sixth of the profits, such to be not less than £1,200 per annum, the sons sharing the remainder equally.

The following are extracts from the trial balance of the business as on 31 December 20X5:

	Debit	Credit
	£	£
Purchases – poultry	2,160	
– feeding stuffs	30,720	
– sprays and fertilizers	14,510	
– spraying machine	4,600	
Wages	29,080	
General expenses (not apportionable)	8,420	
Sales – fruit		60,220
– poultry		5,580
– eggs		58,430
– motor mower (cost £900 written down to £500)		460
Capital accounts – A. Cherry		64,500
– Tom		33,400
– Leo	8,400	
Drawings – A. Cherry	9,300	
Equipment at 1 January 20X5 at cost	34,200	
Equipment at 1 January provision for depreciation		15,100

Inventories on hand were as follows:

	31 Dec 20X4	31 Dec 20X5
	£	£
Sprays and fertilizers	3,100	2,890
Poultry	3,200	1,540
Feeding stuffs	3,630	4,120

Additional information

1. Drawings by Tom and Leo have been £150 and £140 per week, respectively. The amounts have been included in the *wages account*. Of the wages, one-quarter is to be charged to the fruit department and three-quarters to the poultry department.
2. The father and son Tom live in the farmhouse and are to be charged jointly per annum £300 for fruit, and £680 for eggs and poultry, such charges being shared equally. Leo is to be charged £380 for fruit and £620 for eggs and poultry.
3. Independent of the partnership, Leo kept some pigs on the farm and in respect of this private venture he is to be charged £1,400 for feeding stuffs and £400 for wages.

4 A. Cherry is to be credited with £3,600 for rent of the land (to be charged as to two-thirds to the fruit and one-third to the poultry departments), and Tom is to be credited with £840 by way of salary for packing eggs and dressing poultry.

5 Eggs sold in December 20X5 and paid for in January 20X6 amounted to £2,430 and this sum was not included in the trial balance.

6 An account to 31 December 20X5 for £240 was received from a veterinary surgeon after the trial balance had been prepared. This account included a sum of £140 in respect of professional work as regards Leo's pigs, which he himself paid.

7 Annual provision was to be made for depreciation on equipment at 10 per cent on cost at the end of the year.

Required

a A trading account (showing separately the trading profit on the fruit and poultry departments) and appropriation accounts for the year ended 31 December 20X5.

b The *partners' capital accounts* in columnar form showing the balances as on 31 December 20X5.

(ACCA)

ADVANCED

25.19 Field, Green and Lane are in partnership making up financial statements annually to 31 March. Owing to staff difficulties proper records were not maintained for the year ended 31 March 20X5, and the partners request your assistance in preparing the financial statements for that year.

The statement of financial position on 1 April 20X4 was as follows:

ASSETS	£	£	£
Non-current assets	**Cost**	**Acc depn**	**WDV**
Fixed plant	15,000	6,000	9,000
Motor vehicles	4,000	1,000	3,000
Fixtures and fittings	500	250	250
	19,500	7,250	12,250
Current assets			
Inventories			19,450
Trade receivables			10,820
Prepayments			250
Cash			75
			30,595
Total assets			42,845
OWNERS' EQUITY AND LIABILITIES			
Owners' equity			
Capital accounts			
– Field		10,000	
– Green		10,000	
– Lane		2,500	22,500
Current accounts			
– Field		5,000	

– Green	2,000	
– Lane	500	7,500
		30,000
Current liabilities		
Bank overdraft		6,370
Trade payables		1,125
Accruals		5,350
Total current liabilities		12,845
Total capital and liabilities		42,845

The accruals in the statement of financial position comprised: audit fee £600, heat and light £400 and advertising £125. The prepayment of £250 was in respect of rates.

A summary of the bank statement provides the following information for the year to 31 March 20X5.

	£
Takings banked	141,105
Purchases	111,805
Wages	6,875
Rates and water	6,850
Heat and light	1,720
Delivery and travelling	3,380
Repairs and renewals	1,475
Advertising	375
Printing and stationery	915
Sundry office expenses	215
Bank charges	1,100
Audit fee	600

The following items were paid from the takings before they were banked:

- Wages: cleaner £5 per week; van driver's mate £10 per week
- Casual labour for the year: £555
- Paraffin for shop heating: £445
- Advertising: £75
- Sundry office expenses: £515
- Purchases for resale: £12,635
- Hire of delivery vehicle: £20 per week
- Partners' drawings per week: Field £40, Green £30, Lane £30.

Additional information

1 The partners are allowed interest of 5 per cent per annum on their *capital accounts*.

2 Profits or losses are shared in the ratio Field 5, Green 3, Lane 2, with the proviso that Lane is guaranteed by Field an income of £3,000 per annum, excluding his interest on capital.

3 Certain goods had been appropriated by the partners during the year. The selling price of these goods was £460, allocated as follows: Field £235; Green £110; Lane £115.

4 Depreciation on non-current assets is to be provided at the following rates: fixed plant 5 per cent; motor vehicles 25 per cent; and fixtures and fittings 10 per cent; using the straight-line method.

5 Accrued charges for heat and light at 31 March 20X5 were £450.

6 Rates of £750 were prepaid at 31 March 20X5.

7 Your charges for the 20X4/X5 audit were estimated at £650.

8 At 31 March 20X5, inventories were £22,345, trade receivables £11,415, trade payables £5,920 and cash in till £100.

Required

a Prepare the partnership's statement of profit or loss, and appropriation account for the year ended 31 March 20X5.

b Prepare the statement of financial position as at 31 March 20X5. (Movements in the *partners' current accounts* should be shown on the face of the statement of financial position.)

(ACCA)

Chapter 26

Changes in partnerships

Learning Objectives:

After reading this chapter you should be able to do the following:

1. List the different circumstances that may lead to a change in partnerships.
2. Discuss the nature, valuation and accounting treatment of goodwill. Compute the value of goodwill.
3. Show the journal and ledger entries for the admission of a new partner and/or an outgoing partner, including those relating to goodwill and the effects of revaluing assets.
4. Show the journal and ledger entries relating to a change in partners' profit-sharing ratio, including the appropriation of profits in the year of the change.
5. Prepare the appropriation account and statement of financial position of a partnership where there is a change in partners or there is a change in their profit-sharing ratio.

26.1 Introduction

When a partner leaves a partnership owing to, for example, retirement or death, or whenever a new partner is admitted, it has the effect of bringing the old partnership to an end and transferring the business to a new partnership. The retiring partner(s) will want to take out their share of the business assets and any new partner(s) may be expected to introduce capital. Furthermore, a new profit-sharing agreement must be reached. The situation would be relatively simple, in accounting terms, if three conditions could be met:

1 The change occurs at the start or end of an accounting year.

2 The separate assets and liabilities of the business are all included in the financial statements at values that the partners agree to be current.

3 No account is taken of 'goodwill'.

The difficulties that arise when these conditions do not apply (which is nearly always) are discussed later in this chapter. The new partnership that is formed takes on the appearance of being a continuous business as it frequently takes over the assets and liabilities of the old partnership and normally retains the name of the old partnership (with perhaps a minor amendment to reflect the change of partners). For these reasons the partnership usually continues to use the same set of books of account with various adjustments to the *capital* and *current accounts* to reflect the change of partners. These are described below.

26.2 Retirement of a partner

This is considered initially using the simplifying assumptions 1, 2 and 3 set out in the introduction. The first step in dealing with the retirement of a partner is to ensure that the financial statements are complete at the date of retirement, including crediting the *partner's current account* with the partner's share of profit and debiting the *current account* with the partner's drawings to this date. The retiring partner's share of the partnership assets is then represented by the sum of the balances on his or her *current* and *capital accounts*. As soon as the individual ceases to be a partner, that person no longer has capital invested in the partnership and must thus be treated as a loan creditor. The balances on the former *partner's current* and *capital accounts* are, therefore, transferred to a *loan account* in the individual's name. This loan is eliminated either by one payment, or alternatively there may be a clause in the partnership agreement to make repayment by instalments over time. Since the person is no longer a partner, any interest payable on this loan is an expense of the partnership to be charged in the statement of profit or loss and not an appropriation of profits as in the case of interest on loans made by partners.

The accounting entries relating to the retirement of a partner are illustrated in Worked Example 26.1.

WORKED EXAMPLE 26.1

Britten, Edwards and Howe are partners sharing profits equally after interest on partners' loans of 5 per cent per annum. Edwards retires on 1 January 20X5 and is to be repaid one year later. Interest on money due to her is to be at 8 per cent per annum.

The statement of financial position at 31 December 20X4 is summarized as below, before the appropriation of profit:

EQUITY AND LIABILITIES		
Owners' equity	£	£
Capital accounts		
– Britten	10,000	
– Edwards	6,000	
– Howe	5,000	21,000
Current accounts		
– Britten	1,000	
– Edwards	1,500	
– Howe	1,100	3,600
Statement of profit or loss – profit for year		1,000
		25,600
Non-current liabilities		
Partners' loan from Edwards		2,000
Total equity and liabilities		27,600

First, the appropriation of profits should be carried out as follows:

	B	E	H	Total
	£	£	£	£
Profit for year				1,000
Interest on loan (5% × £2,000)		100		(100)
				900
Shares of residual profit	300	300	300	(900)
	300	400	300	–

The journal and ledger entries in respect of Edwards' interest on loan and share of profit will be as follows:

			£	£
Debit:	*Appropriation account*	Dr	400	
Credit:	*Current account – Edwards*	Cr		400

This produces a balance on *Edwards' current account* of £1,500 + £400 = £1,900. The balances on the retiring partner's *capital, current* and *loan accounts* are then transferred to a *new loan account* as shown by the following journal entries:

			£	£
Debit:	*Capital account – Edwards*	Dr	6,000	
Debit:	*Current account – Edwards*	Dr	1,900	
Debit:	*Partners' loan account – Edwards*	Dr	2,000	
Credit:	*Loan account – Edwards*	Cr		9,900
			9,900	9,900

After crediting the other *partners' current accounts* with their shares of profit the statement of financial position on 1 January 20X5 after Edwards' retirement will be as follows:

EQUITY AND LIABILITIES		
Owners' equity	£	£
Capital accounts		
– Britten	10,000	
– Howe	5,000	15,000
Current accounts		
– Britten	1,300	
– Howe	1,400	2,700
		17,700
Non-current liabilities		
Loan – Edwards		9,900
Total equity and liabilities		27,600

26.3 Admission of a new partner

When a new partner is admitted to a partnership, the value of the assets he or she introduces into the business will be debited to the appropriate asset accounts (e.g. *bank*) and credited to the new *partner's capital account*. If the new partner is admitted in the circumstances set out in the introduction to this chapter as three conditions or simplifying assumptions, then these are the only entries that are necessary to account for the admission of a new partner. However, such circumstances are rarely the case. In particular, the change of partners may not occur at the start or end of an accounting year, but more likely at some time during the accounting year. We will thus now examine the accounting requirements when this condition does not apply, but the other two are still met.

When a new partner is admitted (or an existing partner leaves) part way through an accounting year it is usual, at least in examination questions, to retain the same accounting year. This means that it will be necessary to ascertain the partners' shares of profit for the period from the start of the accounting year to the date of the change, separately from that for the period from the date of the change until the end of the accounting year.

One possibility is to start by preparing two statements of profit or loss, one for each of these two periods. However, it is more common, at least in examination questions, to assume that the profit has arisen evenly over the accounting year, and thus simply prepare a statement for profit or loss for the year and divide the profit (or loss) between the two periods on a time basis. Two appropriation accounts are then prepared: one for the period from the start of the accounting year to the date of the change; and the other from the date of the change until the end of the accounting year. The reason for this is that the partners' shares of profit will be different for each period, as may be their salaries, rates of interest on capital and interest on drawings. Note that the salaries, interest on capital and interest on drawings for each of the two periods will have to be computed separately, and on a strict time basis.

The two appropriation accounts are usually prepared in columnar form since this is quicker and easier. Moreover, it means that each partner's salary, interest on capital, interest on drawings and share of residual profit for each of the two periods can be added together to give the total of each for the year. Obviously, this only applies to those partners who were partners before and after the change. An illustration of the preparation of an appropriation account where a new partner is admitted part way through an accounting year is given in Worked Example 26.2. Notice that there is no impact on the statement of profit or loss, and the only effects on the statement of financial position relate to the capital introduced by the new partner and the appropriation of profit to the partners' current accounts.

WORKED EXAMPLE 26.2

Brick and Stone are in partnership sharing profits and losses Brick $\frac{3}{5}$ and Stone $\frac{2}{5}$ after giving each partner 6 per cent per annum interest on capital and annual salaries of £28,000 to Brick and £22,000 to Stone.

On 1 July 20X4 Wall was admitted as a partner. From this date profits or losses will be shared equally after giving each partner 10 per cent per annum interest on capital and annual salaries of £34,000 to Brick, £26,000 to Stone and £24,000 to Wall.

The financial statements are made up to 31 December of each year. The profit for the year ended 31 December 20X4 was £150,000 and this is believed to have arisen evenly over the year. The following is the statement of financial position at 31 December 20X4 before the appropriation of the profit between the partners:

ASSETS	£'000	£'000
Non-current assets		675
Current assets		180
Total assets		855
EQUITY AND LIABILITIES		
Owners' equity		
Capital accounts:		
– Brick	300	
– Stone	200	
– Wall	100	600
Current accounts:		
– Brick	27	
– Stone	23	50
Profit for the year		150
Total owners' equity		800
Current liabilities		55
Total equity and liabilities		855

The above balances on the *capital accounts* of Brick and Stone have not changed since 31 December 20X3. The balance on *Wall's capital account* is the capital she introduced on 1 July 20X4.

You are required to prepare:

a An appropriation account for the year ended 31 December 20X4;

b A statement of financial position as at 31 December 20X4 showing all the entries in the partners' current accounts after giving effect to the change in partners.

Workings

a

	Brick	Stone	Wall
	£'000	£'000	£'000
From 1 Jan to 30 June 20X4:			
Salaries			
$\frac{6}{12} \times$ £28,000	14		
$\frac{6}{12} \times$ £22,000		11	
Interest on capital			
$\frac{6}{12} \times$ 6% × £300,000	9		
$\frac{6}{12} \times$ 6% × £200,000		6	
From 1 July to 31 Dec 20X4:			
Salaries			
$\frac{6}{12} \times$ £34,000	17		
$\frac{6}{12} \times$ £26,000		13	
$\frac{6}{12} \times$ £24,000			12
Interest on capital			
$\frac{6}{12} \times$ 10% × £300,000	15		
$\frac{6}{12} \times$ 10% × £200,000		10	
$\frac{6}{12} \times$ 10% × £100,000			5

Brick, Stone and Wall

Appropriation account for the year ended 31 December 20X4

	Total		1 Jan to 30 June		1 July to 31 Dec	
	£'000	£'000	£'000	£'000	£'000	£'000
Profit for the year		150		75		75
Less: salaries						
– Brick	31		14		17	
– Stone	24		11		13	
– Wall	12		–		12	
	67		25		42	

Less: interest on capital			
– Brick	24	9	15
– Stone	16	6	10
– Wall	5	–	5
	45	15	30
	112	40	72
Residual profit	38	35	3
Shares of residual profit:			
– Brick	22	21	1
– Stone	15	14	1
– Wall	1	–	1
	38	35	3

b

Brick, Stone and Wall				
Statement of financial position as at 31 December 20X4				
ASSETS	**£'000**	**£'000**	**£'000**	**£'000**
Non-current assets				675
Current assets				180
Total assets				855
EQUITY AND LIABILITIES				
Owners' equity	*Brick*	*Stone*	*Wall*	*Total*
Capital accounts	300	200	100	600
Current accounts:				
Balance at 1 Jan 20X4	27	23	–	
Add: – salaries	31	24	12	
– interest on capital	24	16	5	
– shares of residual profit	22	15	1	
Balance at 31 Dec 20X4	104	78	18	200
Total equity	404	278	118	800
Current liabilities				55
Total equity and liabilities				855

Notes

1 In some examination questions the profit does not accrue evenly over the accounting year. These questions usually specify the amounts of profit before and after the change in partners. With this exception the same principles as above would be applied to the preparation of the appropriation account. It is unlikely, but students may be required to compute the amounts of profit before and after the change, in which case the necessary information would have to be

supplied in the question. This will probably involve apportioning some expenses between the two periods on a time basis.

2 When a partner leaves part-way through an accounting year, the above principles and procedure would also have to be applied to the appropriation of profits. However, where the outgoing partner leaves the amount due to him or her in the partnership as an interest-bearing loan, it will be necessary to prepare the appropriation account for the period up to the change in partners before that for the period after the change. This is because the outgoing partner's share of profit, salary, and so on, will need to be credited to his or her *current account* and then transferred to a *loan account* at the date of the change in partners. The balance on this account will then be used to ascertain the interest on the loan that needs to be deducted in arriving at the net profit of the period after the change in partners.

Learning Activity 26.1

Imagine you are in business with reported assets of £100,000. You decide to admit me to your business as a partner. I will bring in capital of £100,000 in cash, and we will share profits and losses equally. The assets of your old business have a market value of £150,000, but we have agreed that they will remain in the books at their historical cost of £100,000 on the grounds of prudence. The day after my admission I give you notice to dissolve our partnership, and the assets of your old business are sold for £150,000. The profit of £150,000 – £100,000 = £50,000 must be shared equally, and thus our capital is now £100,000 + £25,000 = £125,000 each. This is repaid in cash and I therefore walk away with a gain of £25,000 after only having been a partner for two days.

Describe your feelings about the way in which the profit on realization of the assets has been shared, and whether in retrospect you would have done anything differently. The answer is given in Learning Activity 26.2.

26.4 The revaluation of assets on changes in partners

The values of assets and liabilities shown in the ledger and the statement of financial position (i.e. the book values) are not normally the current market values. Therefore, when a new partner is admitted to a business or an existing partner dies or retires, it is usually necessary to revalue all the assets and liabilities. The reason for this revaluation is that since assets are normally shown in the financial statements at their historical cost, there will be **unrealized holding gains and losses** that have not been recorded in the books (e.g. arising from an increase in the market value of property since the date of purchase). These must be taken into account by means of a **revaluation**, and each old partner's capital account credited with their share of the unrealized gains (or debited with their share of any unrealized losses).

Thus, when an existing partner dies or retires, the revaluation ensures that the former partner receives his or her share of any unrealized holding gains. Similarly, when a new partner is admitted, the revaluation is necessary to ensure that the old partners receive recognition of their shares of the unrealized holding gains. If this was not done the new partner would be entitled to a share of these gains when they were eventually realized, despite the fact that they arose prior to the partner's admission to the partnership.

Learning Activity 26.2

Answer

You should not have agreed to the assets remaining in the books at their historical cost. The whole of the difference between their market value and historical cost belongs to you. The principle of prudence does not apply because the assets of your old business were sold to the new partnership, and thus the gain was realized. You should have brought the revaluation of the assets into the books before admitting me as a partner. That way, the whole of the gain would have been credited to your capital account.

An illustration of the ledger entries relating to the revaluation of assets on changes in partners is given in Worked Example 26.3.

WORKED EXAMPLE 26.3

Bill and Harry are in partnership sharing profits equally. On 1 July 20X5 Harry retired and Jane was admitted as a partner. She is to contribute cash of £9,000 as capital. Future profits are to be shared, Bill three-fifths and Jane two-fifths.

The statement of financial position at 30 June 20X5 was as follows:

ASSETS	£	£	£
Non-current assets	**Cost**	**Acc Depn**	**WDV**
Plant	13,500	3,300	10,200
Fixtures and fittings	10,500	2,700	7,800
	24,000	6,000	18,000
Current assets			
Inventories			13,800
Trade receivables			9,450
Cash			3,900
			27,150
Total assets			45,150
OWNERS' EQUITY AND LIABILITIES			
Owners' equity			
Capital accounts			
– Bill		17,000	
– Harry		17,500	34,500
Current accounts			
– Bill		4,800	
– Harry		2,100	6,900

Total owners' equity	41,400
Current liabilities	
Trade payables	3,750
Total current liabilities	3,750
Total capital and liabilities	45,150

It was decided that inventory is to be valued at £12,000 and fixtures are to be valued at £10,350. Of the trade receivables, £1,350 are considered to be doubtful receivables.

The ledger entries relating to the above revaluation and change of partners are required.

It is necessary first to set up a revaluation account in the ledger and enter the increases and decreases in value of all the assets. The resulting profit or loss on revaluation must then be shared between the old partners in their old profit-sharing ratio and entered in their *capital accounts*. The cash introduced by the new partner is simply credited to her *capital account*. This is shown below.

Fixtures

Balance b/d	10,500	Provision for depreciation	2,700
Revaluation a/c	2,550	Balance c/d	10,350
	13,050		13,050
Balance b/d	10,350		

Inventory

Balance b/d	13,800	Revaluation a/c	1,800
		Balance c/d	12,000
	13,800		13,800
Balance b/d	12,000		

Allowance for irrecoverable receivables

Balance b/d	13,800	Revaluation a/c	1,350

Revaluation a/c

Write down of inventory	1,800	Write up of fixtures		2,550
Allowance for irrecoverable receivables	1,350	Loss on revaluation –		
		Capital Bill	300	
		Capital Harry	300	600
Balance b/d	3,150			3,150

Capital

	Bill	Harry	Jane		Bill	Harry	Jane
Revaluation a/c	300	300	–	Balance b/d	17,000	17,500	–
Balance c/d	16,700	17,200	9,000	Bank	–	–	9,000
	17,000	17,500	9,000		17,000	17,500	9,000
				Balance b/d	16,700	17,200	9,000

Finally, the transfers in respect of Harry's capital and current accounts must be made, which would involve the following journal entry:

		Debit	Credit
Debit:	*Capital account – Harry*	17,200	
Debit:	*Current account – Harry*	2,100	
Credit:	*Loan account – Harry*		19,300
		19,300	19,300

So far, consideration has only been given to situations where any deceased or retiring *partners' capital accounts* have credit balances and the remaining partners are required to make payments to them. If there is a debit balance on a *capital account*, a retiring partner will be due to pay this to the partnership. However, if the retiring partner is unable to make this payment, there will be a deficiency to be shared among the remaining partners. The partnership agreement may specify how this sharing is to take place. In the absence of such an agreement, then the precedence of a court ruling in the case of ***Garner v. Murray*** will apply under English law. Under this rule, the deficiency is shared in proportion to the partners' credit balances on their *capital accounts* at the last statement of financial position date before the retirement. Subsequent revaluations are not taken into account in calculating these proportions, nor are profit-sharing ratios.

26.5 The nature of goodwill

The precise nature of goodwill is difficult to define in a theoretically sound manner. However, it is generally recognized that goodwill exists, since a value is normally attached to it when a business is purchased. Goodwill usually arises in the financial statements where another business has been purchased at some time in the past. Its value frequently takes the form of the excess of the purchase price of the other business over the market value of its net assets. The existence of this excess shows that the purchaser of a business is prepared to pay for something in addition to the net assets. Goodwill is the label given to that something. *IFRS 3 – Business Combinations* (IASB, 2013b), states that (in a business combination) **goodwill** represents an

> "*asset representing future economic benefits arising from assets acquired in a business combination that are not individually identified and separately recognised.*"

Goodwill is therefore by definition incapable of realization separately from the business as a whole. **Separable/identifiable net assets** are the assets and liabilities of an entity that are capable of being disposed of or settled separately, without necessarily disposing of the business as a whole. **Fair value** is

> "*the price that would be received to sell an asset or paid to transfer a liability in an orderly transaction between market participants at the measurement date.*"
>
> (*IFRS 3, 2013*)

Where the value of a business as a whole exceeds the total value of its separable net assets this is described as **positive goodwill**. Where the value of a business as a whole is less than the total value of its separable net assets, this is referred to as a **gain on bargain purchase.** This may arise when there is a forced liquidation or distressed sale. When this occurs the gain on purchase is recognized in profit or loss on the acquisition date.

Most ongoing businesses are normally worth more as a going concern than is shown by the value of their net tangible assets; otherwise, it would probably be better to shut the business down and sell the separate assets. From this standpoint, goodwill may be said to represent the present value of the future profits accruing from an existing business. Thus, goodwill arises from a number of attributes that an ongoing business possesses, such as the following:

1 The prestige and reputation attaching to the name of a business or its products and thus the likelihood that present customers will continue to buy from the business in future (e.g. Rolls-Royce, Microsoft).

2 Existing contracts for the supply of goods in the future (e.g. construction, aerospace, defence equipment).

3 The location of the business premises (e.g. a newsagent next to a railway station) and other forms of captive customers (e.g. a milk distributor's clientele).

4 The possession of patents, trademarks, brand names and special technical knowledge arising from previous expenditure on advertising and research and development. However, some of these may be accounted for as separate assets.

5 The existence of known sources of supply of goods and services, including the availability of trade credit.

6 The existing staff, including particular management skills. The costs of recruiting and training present employees give rise to an asset that is not recorded in the statement of financial position but nevertheless represents a valuable resource to the business. Furthermore, these costs would have to be incurred if a business were started from scratch.

7 Other set-up factors. An existing business has the advantage of having collected together the various items of equipment and other assets necessary for its operations. Obtaining and bringing together these assets usually involves delay and expense, and avoiding this is an advantage of an ongoing business.

26.6 The recognition of goodwill in partnership financial statements

IFRS 3 recommends that positive ***purchased*** **goodwill** should be capitalized as an intangible asset on the statement of financial position at cost. Then goodwill should be reviewed for impairment on a regular basis. When it is clear that there is impairment, the capitalized value should be written down to its current fair value. **Internally generated**, that is **non-purchased goodwill**, is not allowed to be recognized as an asset. The main reason for this is that the valuation of non-acquired goodwill is regarded as highly subjective and thus is unlikely to provide a faithful representation of the underlying asset. An example of this is evident from Real World Example 26.1. In the last few years there have been a number of very high profile goodwill write-offs – HP wrote off $18 billion following a decade of poor takeovers including Autonomy (a UK company) in 2012, Palm in 2010 and Compaq back in 2002 and Tata Steel wrote off $1.6 billion following a review of the value of Corus, a British steelmaker (P. F., 2013).

REAL WORLD EXAMPLE 26.1

Impairment of goodwill

'The most highly publicized write-downs of goodwill have been in the banking sector. Wachovia (a US bank) alone reported a goodwill impairment charge of nearly $19 billion in the third quarter of 2008. The phenomenon was not limited to U.S. banks. The Royal Bank of Scotland Group wrote off £15.5 billion of goodwill in 2008 related to series of mergers, including £7.7 billion for ABN AMRO, £4.4 billion for Citizens and Charter One, and £2.7 billion for NatWest.'

Source: Gore, R. and Zimmerman, D. (2010) 'Is Goodwill an Asset?', *The CPA Journal*, 80 (6), 46–48.

In the case of a partnership, goodwill is likely to occur when a new partner is admitted or an existing partner retires or dies. The law states that in each instance the old partnership is dissolved, and thus effectively taken over by the new partnership. The financial statements of the new partnership may therefore include goodwill acquired from the purchase of the old partnership. This is examined in detail later in the chapter.

The accounting for goodwill has changed dramatically over the past three decades but the current established thinking is that acquired goodwill is an asset that has a cost. Its value is impacted on by changes in the economic climate, changes in business trends, changes in human capital (personnel), changes in intellectual capital, and so on. The value may increase or decrease. Therefore, the best way to determine whether there has been a change in the economic value (its ability to generate future income) of goodwill is to review it periodically for impairment (goodwill is never revalued upwards). In simple terms, an **impairment review** is essentially a revaluation to ensure that the value of goodwill has not fallen below its book/carrying value. Some indicators that might spark a full impairment review include a decline in sales, or the introduction into the market of a new competitor. These events may be taken as indicators that the future earnings to be expected from goodwill have declined and its value is not as it once was. Determining the new value is subjective and is beyond the scope of this text. Any exercises in this text that deal with capitalized goodwill will provide the impairment amount. At this level, an awareness of how to account for the impairment is sufficient.

Figure 26.1

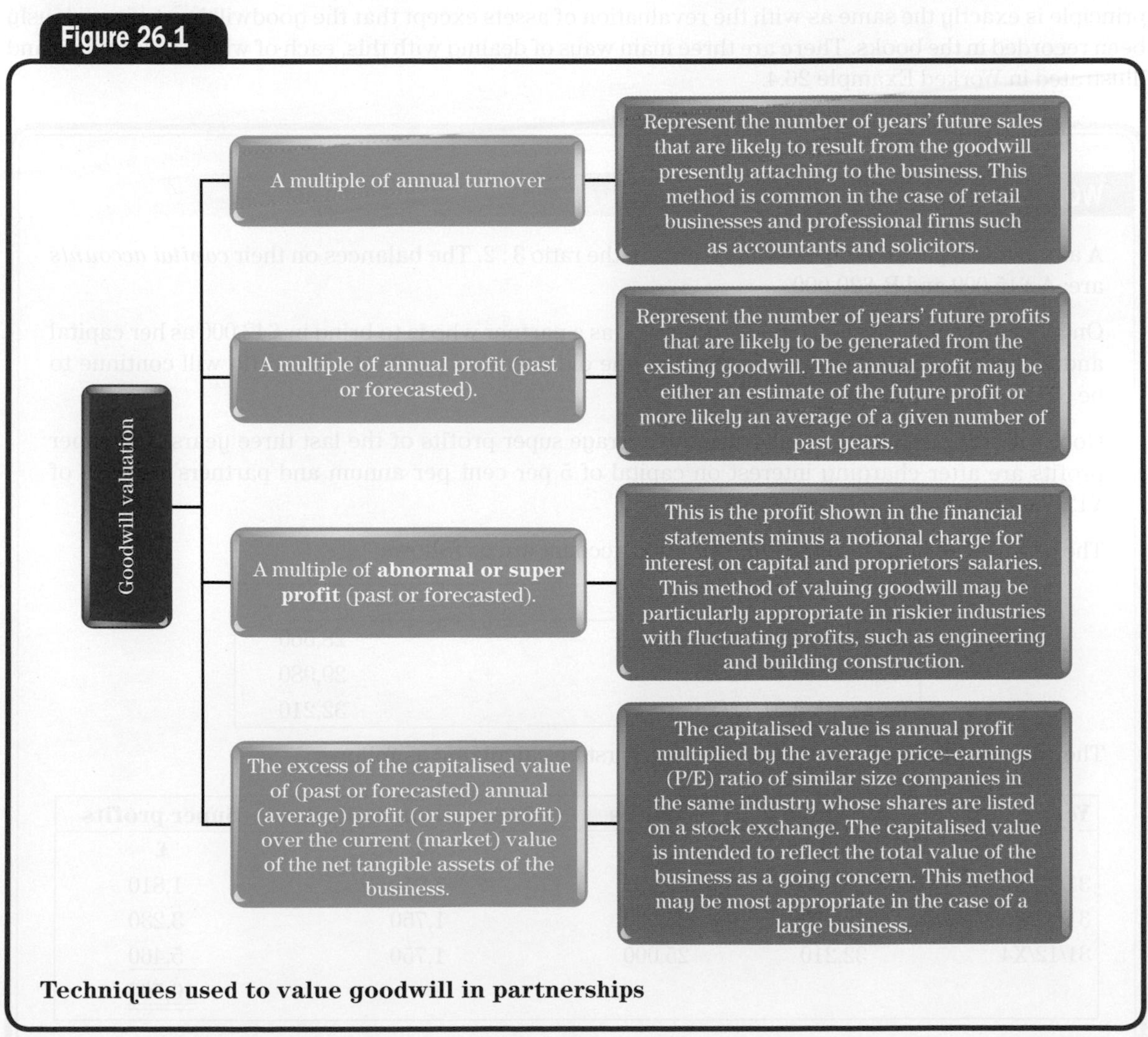

Goodwill valuation
A multiple of annual turnover
Represent the number of years' future sales that are likely to result from the goodwill presently attaching to the business. This method is common in the case of retail businesses and professional firms such as accountants and solicitors.
A multiple of annual profit (past or forecasted).
Represent the number of years' future profits that are likely to be generated from the existing goodwill. The annual profit may be either an estimate of the future profit or more likely an average of a given number of past years.
A multiple of abnormal or super profit (past or forecasted).
This is the profit shown in the financial statements minus a notional charge for interest on capital and proprietors' salaries. This method of valuing goodwill may be particularly appropriate in riskier industries with fluctuating profits, such as engineering and building construction.
The excess of the capitalised value of (past or forecasted) annual (average) profit (or super profit) over the current (market) value of the net tangible assets of the business.
The capitalised value is annual profit multiplied by the average price–earnings (P/E) ratio of similar size companies in the same industry whose shares are listed on a stock exchange. The capitalised value is intended to reflect the total value of the business as a going concern. This method may be most appropriate in the case of a large business.

Techniques used to value goodwill in partnerships

26.7 The valuation of goodwill

As explained previously, the cost of acquired goodwill is deemed to be the excess of the purchase price of a business over the market/fair value of its net assets. In the case of company financial statements, the value of goodwill is usually computed in precisely this manner. However, in the case of sole traders and partnerships, the purchase price of a business is frequently arrived at by valuing the net tangible assets (often at market prices) and, as a separate item, goodwill. This is particularly common where a new partner is admitted or an existing partner leaves.

There are several methods of valuing goodwill. These reflect the customs/conventions of businesses generally and certain trades and professions in particular. It should be emphasized that in practice the amount arrived at using one of these methods is frequently regarded as a starting point in negotiating a final value for goodwill. The most common methods are outlined in Figure 26.1.

26.8 The admission of a new partner and the treatment of goodwill

When a new partner is admitted to a partnership, an adjustment to the old partners' capital accounts is necessary to recognize the value of goodwill that they have created and therefore belongs to them. The principle is exactly the same as with the revaluation of assets except that the goodwill has not previously been recorded in the books. There are three main ways of dealing with this, each of which is described and illustrated in Worked Example 26.4.

WORKED EXAMPLE 26.4

A and B are in partnership sharing profits in the ratio 3 : 2. The balances on their *capital accounts* are: A £15,000 and B £20,000.

On 31 December 20X4 they decide to admit C as a partner who is to bring in £42,000 as her capital and will receive half of all future profits. The old partners' profit-sharing ratio will continue to be 3 : 2.

Goodwill is to be calculated at twice the average super profits of the last three years. The super profits are after charging interest on capital of 5 per cent per annum and partners' salaries of £12,500 per annum each.

The profits transferred to the appropriation account are as follows:

	£
Year ended 31/12/X2	28,560
Year ended 31/12/X3	29,980
Year ended 31/12/X4	32,210

The value to be ascribed to goodwill would first be calculated as follows:

Year ended	Net profits	Salaries	Interest on capital	Super profits
	£	£	£	£
31/12/X2	28,560	25,000	1,750	1,810
31/12/X3	29,980	25,000	1,750	3,230
31/12/X4	32,210	25,000	1,750	5,460
				10,500

$$\text{Goodwill} = 2 \times \frac{£10,500}{3} = £7,000$$

Note that the new profit-sharing ratio will be A3 : B2 : C5. This can be explained thus: since C is to receive one-half of all future profits, A's share will be 3 divided by 3 + 2 multiplied by the remaining one-half, i.e. $\frac{3}{5} \times \frac{1}{2} = \frac{3}{10}$. Similarly, B's share will be $\frac{2}{5} \times \frac{1}{2} = \frac{2}{10}$. Thus, the new profit-sharing ratio is A $\frac{3}{10}$, B $\frac{2}{10}$ and C $\frac{5}{10}$, or A3 : B2 : C5.

The different methods of treating goodwill on the admission of a new partner can now be shown as follows.

Method 1

The value of goodwill is debited to a *goodwill account* and credited to the *old partners' capital accounts* in their old profit-sharing ratio. This method recognizes the existence of the previously unrecorded asset of goodwill by bringing it into the books. The goodwill is shared between the old partners in their old profit-sharing ratio because it is an asset created by the old partnership which thus belongs to the old partners.

Goodwill

20X4		£	20X4		£
31 Dec	Capital A	4,200			
31 Dec	Capital B	2,800	31 Dec	Balance c/d	7,000
		7,000			7,000
20X5					
1 Jan	Balance b/d	7,000			

Capital

		A	B	C			A	B	C
20X4		£	£	£	20X4		£	£	£
					31 Dec	Balance b/d	15,000	20,000	–
					31 Dec	Bank	–	–	42,000
31 Dec	Balance c/d	19,200	22,800	42,000	31 Dec	Goodwill	4,200	2,800	–
		19,200	22,800	42,000			19,200	22,800	42,000
					20X5				
					1 Jan	Balance b/d	19,200	22,800	42,000

Method 2

In partnerships it is common practice to write the goodwill off against the *partners' capital accounts*. In Method 1 above, the goodwill would be impaired. Method 2 is the alternative treatment. The value of goodwill is first debited to a *goodwill account* and credited to the *old partners' capital accounts* in their old profit-sharing ratio (as in Method 1). Then the goodwill is written off by crediting the *goodwill account* and debiting all the partners in the new partnership in their new profit-sharing ratio. The debit to the *partners' capital accounts* is in their new profit-sharing ratio because the writing off of goodwill effectively amounts to recognizing a (paper) loss that would otherwise have been charged to future years' statements of profit or loss (as the impairment of goodwill) and thus shared between the new partners in their new profit-sharing ratio.

Goodwill

20X4		£	20X4		£
31 Dec	Capital A	4,200	31 Dec	Capital A	2,100
31 Dec	Capital B	2,800	31 Dec	Capital B	1,400
			31 Dec	Capital C	3,500
		7,000			7,000

Capital

		A	B	C			A	B	C
20X4		£	£	£	20X4		£	£	£
31 Dec	Goodwill	2,100	1,400	3,500	31 Dec	Balance b/d	15,000	20,000	–
					31 Dec	Bank	–	–	42,000
31 Dec	Balance c/d	17,100	21,400	38,500	31 Dec	Goodwill	4,200	2,800	–
		19,200	22,800	42,000			19,200	22,800	42,000
					20X5				
					1 Jan	Balance b/d	17,100	21,400	38,500

The entries in the *goodwill account* are a waste of time and paper, and thus Method 2 normally involves only the two sets of entries for goodwill on each side of the *partners' capital accounts*. Note that this method should be used when you are told that no account for goodwill is to be kept/maintained in the books or that goodwill is not to be recorded in the books.

It should also be observed that this method has the effect of charging the new partner with what is referred to as a premium of £3,500, in that her capital introduced has been reduced by £3,500. This premium represents the purchase by the new partner of her share of goodwill, that is $\frac{1}{2}$ of £7,000 = £3,500. She will get this back when the goodwill is eventually realized (if the business is sold) or she leaves.

Method 3

This method is essentially a further shortcutting of Method 2. The net effects of the entries for goodwill in the *partners' capital accounts* in Method 2 are: C is debited with £3,500; A is credited with £4,200 − £2,100 = £2,100; and B is credited with £2,800 − £1,400 = £1,400. Method 3 consists of simply entering in the *partners' capital accounts* these net effects, which are referred to as a **premium contra**. The amount of the premium is debited to the *new partners' capital account* and credited to the *old partners' capital accounts* in their old profit-sharing ratio A $\frac{3}{5}$ × £3,500 = £2,100 and B $\frac{2}{5}$ × £3,500 = £1,400

Capital

		A	B	C			A	B	C
20X4		£	£	£	20X4		£	£	£
31 Dec	Premium	–	–	3,500	31 Dec	Balance b/d	15,000	20,000	–
					31 Dec	Bank	–	–	42,000
31 Dec	Balance c/d	17,100	21,400	38,500	31 Dec	Premium	2,100	1,400	–
		17,200	21,400	42,000			17,100	21,400	42,000
					20X5				
					1 Jan	Balance b/d	17,100	21,400	38,500

This method should normally only be used where you are told that the new partner is to pay a premium representing the purchase of his or her share of goodwill. The premium is usually given but can be calculated from the goodwill. In this example the premium can be calculated as $\frac{1}{2}$ of £7,000 = £3,500. The ledger entries would be as shown immediately above. It must be emphasized that this method only gives a correct answer where the old partners share profits (and losses) in the new partnership in the same ratio as the old partnership. If this is not the case, Method 2 must be used instead.

Sometimes it is not possible to compute the premium from the figure of goodwill because the partners have not agreed a method of valuation for goodwill. Instead, you may be told something along the lines that the new partner receives an interest in the new partnership equity/assets, which is less than the amount he or she is to invest/pay into the firm.

WORKED EXAMPLE 26.5

Using the data in Worked Example 26.4 this can be illustrated as follows. C is to be admitted as a partner with a one-half interest in both capital and profits in exchange for £42,000. C's interest in the capital/assets is computed as follows:

	£
Capital/assets/equity of old partnership (£15,000 + £20,000)	35,000
Investment by C	42,000
Capital/assets/equity of new partnership	77,000
C's share of equity of new partnership	
(½ × £77,000)	38,500

The premium which C is being charged is therefore £42,000 − £38,500 = £3,500. The ledger entries will be similar to those in Method 3. However, these can be shortened to the following:

Journal

		Debit	*Credit*
		£	£
Debit:	Bank	42,000	
Credit:	Capital – C		38,500
Credit:	Capital – A		2,100
Credit:	Capital – B		1,400
		42,000	42,000

Remember that this method only gives the correct answer where the old partners continue to share profits in the same ratio. If this is not the case Method 2 must be used, which will require a notional figure for goodwill to be computed by multiplying the premium by the inverse of the new partner profit-sharing ratio (i.e. £3,500 × $\frac{2}{1}$ = £7,000).

Finally, it should be mentioned that it is possible for the new partner to receive an interest greater than the amount he or she is to invest. This results in a **negative premium**, sometimes referred to as a 'bonus' or **negative goodwill**.

26.9 An outgoing partner and the treatment of goodwill

When a partner leaves, the balances on his or her *capital* and *current accounts* are repaid. However, it is necessary first to make an adjustment to the *partners' capital accounts* in recognition of the value of goodwill that has been created, some of which belongs to the outgoing partner. There are three main ways of dealing with this, which correspond to Methods 1 to 3 (Worked Example 26.4), respectively, of treating goodwill on the admission of a new partner.

1 The value of goodwill is debited to a *goodwill account* and credited to the *old partners' capital accounts* in their old profit-sharing ratio.
2 The value of goodwill is credited to the *old partners' capital accounts* in their old profit-sharing ratio and debited to the remaining *partners' capital accounts* in their new profit-sharing ratio. This effectively results in the remaining partners purchasing the outgoing partners' share of goodwill. No goodwill account is maintained in the books.
3 The outgoing partner's share of goodwill is credited to his or her *capital account* and debited to the remaining *partners' capital accounts* in their new profit-sharing ratio. Again, no goodwill account is maintained in the books. This method only gives a correct answer where the remaining partners share profits in the new partnership in the same ratio as the old partnership. If this is not the case, Method 2 must be used instead.

Sometimes it is not possible to compute the outgoing partner's share of goodwill from the figure of goodwill, because the partners have not agreed a method of valuation for goodwill. Instead, you may be told something along the lines that the outgoing partner is to receive more than the balance of his or her capital account. This excess is the outgoing partner's share of goodwill. If necessary, a notional figure for goodwill can be computed by multiplying this excess by the inverse of the outgoing partner's profit-sharing ratio.

26.10 Incoming and outgoing partners and goodwill

We have thus far dealt with the revaluation of assets on changes in partners and the treatment of goodwill where there is either an incoming or outgoing partner. The final step is to combine all of these and examine the situation where there is both an incoming and outgoing partner. This is a fairly simple step since the treatment of goodwill involves exactly the same principles whether there is an incoming or outgoing partner. An illustration is given in Worked Example 26.6.

WORKED EXAMPLE 26.6

Beech and Oak are in partnership, sharing profits and losses in the ratio 3 : 5, respectively. The statement of financial position drawn up on 31 December 20X4 showed the following position:

ASSETS	£	£
Non-current assets		*NBV*
Premises		16,000
Fixtures		6,000
		22,000

Current assets		
Inventories		4,000
Trade receivables		3,000
Cash		5,000
		12,000
Total assets		34,000
OWNERS' EQUITY AND LIABILITIES		
Owners' equity		
Capital accounts		
– Beech	11,000	
– Oak	14,000	25,000
Current liabilities		
Trade payables		9,000
Total current liabilities		9,000
Total capital and liabilities		34,000

Beech retired as from 1 January 20X5 and at the same date Maple was admitted to the partnership. For the purpose of these changes, the premises were revalued at £19,500, fixtures at £4,500, inventories at £5,800 and goodwill was agreed at £10,000. An allowance for irrecoverable receivables of £200 is also to be created. The new valuations are to be included in the business books but no account for goodwill is to be maintained. In the new partnership, profits or losses will be divided in the proportions 3 : 2 between Oak and Maple, respectively. Maple will introduce cash of £15,000 and Beech is to receive payment for his capital in cash, but no other cash is to change hands between partners in implementing the change.

Required

Show the above changes in the revaluation account and the partners' capital accounts.

Revaluation account

		£		£
Fixtures		1,500	Premises	3,500
Allowance for irrecoverable receivables		200	Inventory	1,800
Profit on revaluation				
– Beech (£3,600 × 3/8)	1,350			
– Oak (£3,600 × 5/8)	2,250	3,600		
		5,300		5,300

Capital accounts

	Beech	Oak	Maple		Beech	Oak	Maple
Goodwill contra	–	6,000	4,000	Balance b/d	11,000	14,000	–
Cash	16,100		–	Profit on revaluation	1,350	2,250	–
Balance c/d	–	16,500	11,000	Goodwill contra	3,750	6,250	–
				Cash	–	–	15,000
	16,100	22,500	15,000		16,100	22,500	15,000
				Balance c/d	–	16,500	11,000

Notes

1 The double entry for the items in the *revaluation account* will be in the respective *asset accounts* and the *allowance for irrecoverable receivables account.*

2 The goodwill is credited to the *old partners' capital accounts* in their old profit-sharing ratio (Beech $\frac{3}{8}$ × £10,000 = £3,750; Oak $\frac{5}{8}$ × £10,000 = £6,250) and debited to the *new partners' capital accounts* in their new profit-sharing ratio (Oak $\frac{3}{5}$ × £10,000 = £6,000; Maple $\frac{2}{5}$ × £10,000 = £4,000).

3 The cash paid to Beech of £16,100 is the balance on his *capital account* after the revaluation of assets and adjustments for goodwill.

26.11 Changes in partners' profit-sharing ratio

Sometimes partners decide to change the proportions in which they share profits or losses. This may occur when the partners agree that one partner is to spend more (or less) time on partnership business, or alternatively one partner's skills have become more (or less) valuable to the partnership.

If a change in the profit-sharing ratio occurs at some time during the accounting year, it will be necessary to divide the profit before appropriations into the periods before and after the change. This is usually done on a time basis. The interest on capital and on drawings, salaries and shares of residual profit are then computed for each period separately. It should be noted that this procedure is the same as when a new partner is admitted and/or a partner leaves during the accounting year.

When there is a change in the profit-sharing ratio, it is also necessary to revalue the assets, including goodwill. As in the case of changes in partners, the profit or loss on revaluation is computed in a *revaluation account* and transferred to the *partners' capital accounts*. An adjustment must also be made in respect of goodwill, using the principles already described. A simple illustration is given in Worked Example 26.7 and a more complicated version is shown in Worked Example 26.8.

WORKED EXAMPLE 26.7

X and Y are in partnership sharing profits and losses equally. They have decided that as from 1 October 20X4 the profit-sharing ratio is to become X three-fifths and Y two-fifths.

The financial statements are made up to 31 December each year. The profit for the year ended 31 December 20X4 was £60,000. The statement of financial position at 31 December 20X4 prior to sharing profits is as follows:

	£
Net assets	210,000
Capital X	80,000
Capital Y	70,000
Profit for the year	60,000
	210,000

It was decided that the impact of the change in profit-sharing ratio on each partner's share of the assets would be effected at 31 December 20X4 when the net assets were valued at £250,000. The goodwill was valued at £25,000. No *goodwill account* is to be maintained in the books.

You are required to show the entries in the *partners' capital accounts* and a statement of financial position at 31 December 20X4.

Distribution of profit 20X4

	£	£	£
	Total	1 Jan–30 Sep	1 Oct–31 Dec
Profit for the year apportioned			
on a time basis	60,000	45,000	15,000
Share of profit – X	31,500	22,500	9,000
– Y	28,500	22,500	6,000
	60,000	45,000	15,000

Revaluation account

Profit on revaluation:			Net assets	40,000
– Capital X	20,000		(£250,000 – £210,000)	
– Capital Y	20,000	40,000		
		40,000		40,000

Capital accounts

	X	Y		X	Y
Goodwill contra	15,000	10,000	Balance b/d	80,000	70,000
			Share of profit	31,500	28,500
			Profit on revaluation	20,000	20,000
Balance c/d	129,000	121,000	Goodwill contra	12,500	12,500
	144,000	131,000		144,000	131,000
			Balance b/d	129,000	121,000

X and Y statement of financial position as at 31 December 20X4

	£
TOTAL ASSETS	250,000
EQUITY AND LIABILITIES	
Owners' equity	
– Capital X	129,000
– Capital Y	121,000
Total equity and liabilities	250,000

WORKED EXAMPLE 26.8

Hill and Dale are in partnership sharing profits and losses: Hill three-fifths and Dale two-fifths after giving each partner 8 per cent per annum interest on capital and annual salaries of £28,000 to Hill and £18,000 to Dale.

They have decided that as from 1 July 20X4 the profits or losses will be shared equally after giving each partner 10 per cent per annum interest on capital and annual salaries of £32,000 to Hill and £30,000 to Dale.

The financial statements are made up to 31 December of each year. The profit for the year ended 31 December 20X4 was £150,000 and this is believed to have accrued evenly over the year. The following is the statement of financial position at 31 December 20X4 before the appropriation of the profit between the partners and any other entries relating to the change in the partners' profit-sharing ratio:

ASSETS	£'000	£'000
Non-current assets		
Freehold land and buildings at cost		600
Current assets		
Inventories		105
Trade receivables		45
Bank		25
		175
Total assets		775
EQUITY AND LIABILITIES		
Owners' equity		
Capital accounts:		
– Hill	300	
– Dale	250	550
Current accounts:		
– Hill	26	
– Dale	14	40
Profit for the year		150
Total owners' equity		740
Current liabilities		
Trade payables		35
Total current liabilities		35
Total equity and liabilities		775

The forementioned balances on the *partners' capital accounts* and the *land and buildings account* are as at 31 December 20X3.

On 1 July 20X4 the freehold land and buildings were revalued at £650,000. The partners have also agreed that the book values of the other assets and liabilities at 1 July 20X4 were their current net realizable values. The goodwill at 1 July 20X4 was valued at £100,000 but no *goodwill account* is to be maintained in the books.

Required

Prepare:

a the *partners' capital accounts* as at 1 July 20X4 showing the effects of the change in the partners' profit-sharing ratio on their claims on the partnership assets;

b an appropriation account for the year ended 31 December 20X4;

c a statement of financial position as at 31 December 20X4 showing all the entries in the *partners' current accounts* after giving effect to the change in the partners' profit-sharing ratio.

Workings

a

Capital accounts

	Hill	Dale		Hill	Dale
	£'000	**£'000**		**£'000**	**£'000**
Goodwill	50	50	Balance b/d	300	250
Balance c/d	340	260	Profit on revaluation		
			(£650k – £600k)	30	20
			Goodwill	60	40
	390	310		390	310
			Balance b/d	340	260

b

	Hill £'000	Dale £'000
From 1 Jan to 30 June 20X4:		
Salaries		
$\frac{6}{12} \times$ £28,000	14	
$\frac{6}{12} \times$ £18,000		9
Interest on capital		
$\frac{6}{12} \times$ 8% × £300,000	12	
$\frac{6}{12} \times$ 8% × £250,000		10
From 1 July to 31 Dec 20X4:		
Salaries		
$\frac{6}{12} \times$ £32,000	16	
$\frac{6}{12} \times$ £30,000		15
Interest on capital		
$\frac{6}{12} \times$ 10% × £340,000	17	
$\frac{6}{12} \times$ 10% × £260,000		13

Hill and Dale
Appropriation account for the year ended 31 December 20X4

		Total		1 Jan to 30 June		1 July to 31 Dec
	£'000	£'000	£'000	£'000	£'000	£'000
Profit for the year		150		75		75
Less: salaries						
– Hill	30		14		16	
– Dale	24		9		15	
	54		23		31	
Less: interest on capital						
– Hill	29		12		17	
– Dale	23		10		13	
	52		22		30	
		106		45		61
Residual profit		44		30		14
Shares of residual profit:						
– Hill		25	$\frac{3}{5}$	18	$\frac{1}{2}$	7
– Dale		19	$\frac{2}{5}$	12	$\frac{1}{2}$	7
		44		30		14

c

Current accounts

	Hill	Dale		Hill	Dale
	£'000	£'000		£'000	£'000
			Balance b/d	26	14
			Salaries	30	24
			Interest on capital	29	23
Balance c/d	110	80	Share of residual profit	25	19
	110	80		110	80
			Balance b/d	110	80

Hill and Dale
Statement of financial position as at 31 December 20X4

ASSETS	£'000	£'000	£'000
Non-current assets			
Freehold land and buildings			650
Current assets			
Inventories			105
Trade receivables			45
Bank			25
			175
Total assets			825

EQUITY AND LIABILITIES	Hill	Dale	Total
Owners' equity			
Capital accounts	340	260	600
Current accounts:	110	80	190
Total owners' equity	450	340	790
Current liabilities			
Trade payables			35
Total current liabilities			35
Total equity and liabilities			825

Notes

1 The requirement in part 'a' of the example, to prepare the *partners' capital accounts*, is not always explicitly required by examination questions. However, it is always necessary in these circumstances and, where there is interest on capital, will need to be done first.

2 Then the *appropriation accounts* for the periods prior to and after the change in the partners' profit-sharing ratio are prepared. These could be done as two separate accounts but it is quicker and easier to show them in columnar form, as in the above answer. Each partner's salary, interest on capital and share of residual profit for the year shown in the total column of the *appropriation account* is found by simply adding together the respective amounts for each of the periods prior to and after the change in the profit-sharing ratio.

Summary

When a new partner is admitted to a partnership, an existing partner leaves or there is a change in the profit-sharing ratio, it is usually necessary to revalue all the assets and liabilities. This ensures that the existing/old partners receive their share of the unrealized holding gains (and losses) that arose prior to the change.

When assets are revalued, it is also usually necessary to make certain adjustments to the *partners' capital accounts* in respect of goodwill. According to IFRS 3 goodwill represents an:

> *asset representing future economic benefits arising from assets acquired in a business combination that are not individually identified and separately recognised.*

It is valued as 'the residual cost of the business combination after recognising the acquiree's identifiable assets, liabilities and contingent liabilities'. In the case of partnerships, goodwill is normally valued as a given multiple of the annual sales or profits. When there is a change of partners, goodwill is brought into the books by debiting a *goodwill account* and crediting the *capital accounts* of the existing/old partners in their old profit-sharing ratio. The goodwill must either be capitalized at cost and impaired, or alternatively, written off against the new *partners' capital accounts* in their profit-sharing ratio (assuming it is just an accounting adjustment). This latter treatment can be short-cut by means of adjusting entries on both sides of the *partners' capital accounts*.

Subsequent to the revaluation of assets and goodwill adjustments, when a new partner is admitted, the capital introduced is credited to his or her *capital account*. When a partner leaves, the balance on this *partner's capital*, *current* and any *loan account* is transferred to a new *loan account*, which is repaid in due course.

Key terms and concepts

abnormal profit	497	non-purchased goodwill	496
fair value	495	positive goodwill	495
gain on bargain purchase	495	premium contra	500
Garner *v.* Murray	495	purchased goodwill	496
goodwill	495	revaluation	492
impairment review	497	separable/identifiable net assets	495
internally generated goodwill	496	super profit	497
negative goodwill	502	unrealized holding gains and losses	492
negative premium	502		

An asterisk after the question number indicates that there is a suggested answer in Appendix 2.

Review questions

connect

26.1* a Explain the nature of goodwill.

b Describe the business attributes that are thought to give rise to goodwill.

26.2 a What is the difference between positive and negative goodwill?

b What is the difference between purchased goodwill and non-purchased goodwill?

26.3 a Explain the circumstances in which goodwill might appear in the books of a partnership.

b Describe how it would be treated in the statement of financial position.

26.4 A member of the board of Shoprite Enterprises plc has suggested two accounting policies for consideration by the financial director in preparing the latest set of financial statements. These have been summarized as follows:

1 The incorporation of goodwill in the financial statements as a permanent non-current asset in recognition of the favourable trading situations of several of the business's outlets and also to reflect the quality of management experience in the business.

2 No depreciation to be provided in future on the buildings owned by the company, because their market value is constantly appreciating and, in addition, this will result in an increase in the profit of the company.

Required

a Briefly explain your understanding of each of the following:

i goodwill;

ii depreciation.

b Discuss the acceptability of each of the above suggested accounting policies, highlighting any conflict with accounting concepts and standards.

(AEB)

25.5 Describe three different methods of valuing goodwill where the purchase price is unknown.

Exercises

connect

BASIC

26.6 Al and Bert are in partnership sharing profits equally. At 30 June they have balances on their *capital accounts* of £12,000 (Al) and £15,000 (Bert). On that day they agree to bring in their friend Hall as a third partner. All three partners are to share profits equally from now on. Hall is to introduce £20,000 as capital into the business. Goodwill on 30 June is agreed at £18,000.

Required

a Show the *partners' capital accounts* for 30 June and 1 July on the assumption that the goodwill, previously unrecorded, is to be included in the financial statements.

b Show the additional entries necessary to eliminate goodwill again from the financial statements.

c Explain briefly what goodwill is. Why are adjustments necessary when a new partner joins a partnership?

(ACCA)

INTERMEDIATE

26.7* Brown and Jones are in partnership sharing profits and losses equally. The statement of financial position drawn up on 31 March 20X4 showed the following position:

ASSETS	
Non-current assets	£
Premises	80,000
Fixtures	60,000
	140,000
Current assets	
Inventories	40,000
Trade receivables	30,000
Cash	85,000
	155,000
Total assets	295,000
EQUITY AND LIABILITIES	
Equity capital	
– Brown	110,000
– Jones	87,000
Total equity	197,000

Current liabilities	
Sundry payables	98,000
Total current liabilities	98,000
Total equity and liabilities	295,000

Brown retired as from 1 April 20X4 and at the same date Smith was admitted to the partnership. For the purpose of these changes, the premises were revalued at £115,000, fixtures at £68,000, inventory at £36,000 and goodwill was agreed at £90,000. An allowance for irrecoverable receivables of £3,000 is also to be created. The new valuations are to be included in the business accounts, but no account for goodwill is to be maintained. In the new partnership, profits and losses will be divided in the proportion 3 : 2 between Jones and Smith, respectively. Smith will introduce cash of £100,000 and Brown is to receive payment for his capital in cash but no other cash is to change hands between partners in implementing the change.

Required

Show the above changes in the *revaluation account* and *partners' capital accounts*.

ADVANCED

26.8* Blackburn, Percy and Nelson are in partnership, sharing profits equally. On 1 January 20X4 Nelson retired and Logan was admitted as a partner. Nelson has agreed to leave the amounts owing to her in the business as a loan until 31 December 20X4. Logan is to contribute £6,000 as capital. Future profits are to be shared; Blackburn one-half and Percy and Logan one-quarter each.

A *goodwill account* is to be opened and kept in the books. The goodwill should be valued at the difference between the capitalized value of the estimated super profits for the forthcoming year and the net asset value of the partnership at 31 December 20X3 after revaluing the assets. The capitalized value of the expected super profits is to be computed using the price–earnings ratio, which for this type of business is estimated as 8. The super profits are after deducting notional partners' salaries but not interest on capital. The profit for 20X4 is estimated as £48,750 and it is thought that the partners could each earn £15,000 a year if they were employed elsewhere.

The statement of financial position at 31 December 20X3 was as follows:

ASSETS	Cost	Prov for depn	WDV
Non-current assets	£	£	£
Plant	9,000	2,200	6,800
Vehicles	7,000	1,800	5,200
	16,000	4,000	12,000
Current assets			
Inventories			9,200
Trade receivables			6,300
Prepaid expenses			2,600
			18,100
Total assets			30,100
EQUITY AND LIABILITIES			
Equity capital			
Capital			
– Blackburn		10,000	
– Percy		8,000	
– Nelson		5,000	23,000

Current accounts		
– Blackburn	1,300	
– Percy	1,900	
– Nelson	1,400	4,600
Total equity capital		27,600
Current liabilities		
Trade payables		2,500
Total current liabilities		2,500
Total equity and liabilities		30,100

It was decided that inventory is to be valued at £8,000 and vehicles at £6,700. Of the trade receivables £900 are considered doubtful receivables.

Required

Show the ledger entries relating to the above revaluation and change of partners.

26.9 Gupta, Richards and Jones are in partnership sharing profits and losses in the ratio 5 : 4 : 3. On 1 January 20X5 Richards retired from the partnership and it was agreed that Singh should join the partnership, paying a sum of £30,000. From this date, profits are to be shared equally between the three partners and, in view of this, Jones agrees to pay a further £10,000 into the partnership as capital. ADVANCED

The statement of financial position at 31 December 20X4 showed:

ASSETS	£	£
Non-current assets		
Property		60,000
Fixtures		30,000
		90,000
Current assets		
Inventories		30,000
Trade receivables		15,000
Bank		5,000
		50,000
Total assets		140,000
EQUITY AND LIABILITIES		
Owners' equity		
Capital accounts		
– Gupta	60,000	
– Richards	40,000	
– Jones	25,000	125,000
Current accounts		
– Gupta	1,000	
– Richards	2,500	
– Jones	1,500	5,000
Total equity		130,000
Current liabilities		
Trade payables		10,000
Total current liabilities		10,000
Total equity and liabilities		140,000

It was agreed that in preparing a revised opening statement of financial position of the partnership on 1 January 20X5, the following adjustments should be made:

1 Property is to be revalued at £70,000 and fixtures are to be revalued at £32,000.

2 Inventory is considered to be shown at a fair value in the financial statements. An allowance for irrecoverable receivables of £1,200 is required.

3 Professional fees of £600 relating to the change in partnership structure are to be regarded as an expense of the year to 31 December 20X4, but were not included in the statement of profit or loss of that year. They are expected to be paid in March 20X5.

4 Goodwill of the partnership as at 31 December 20X4 is estimated at £30,000. No account for goodwill is to be entered in the books, but appropriate adjustments are to be made in the *partners' capital accounts*.

5 On retirement, Richards is to be paid a sum of £40,000. The balance owing to her will be recorded in a loan account carrying interest of 12 per cent, to be repaid in full after two years.

6 All balances on *current accounts* are to be transferred to *capital accounts*. All balances on capital accounts in excess of £20,000 after this transfer are to be transferred to loan accounts carrying interest at 12 per cent.

Required

a Compute the balances on the loan accounts of Richards and the new partners on 1 January 20X5, following completion of these arrangements.

b Prepare an opening statement of financial position for the partnership on 1 January 20X5, following completion of these arrangements.

c Explain briefly *three* factors to be taken into account when establishing profit-sharing arrangements between partners.

(JMB, adapted)

ADVANCED

26.10 Street, Rhode and Close carried on business in partnership sharing profits and losses, in the ratio 5 : 4 : 3. Their draft statement of financial position as on 31 March 20X5 was as follows:

ASSETS	Cost	Prov for depn	WDV
Non-current assets	£	£	£
Leasehold premises	8,000	800	7,200
Plant and machinery	9,200	2,700	6,500
	17,200	3,500	13,700
Current assets			
Inventories			5,400
Trade receivables		4,200	
Allowance for irrecoverable receivables		(750)	3,450
Bank			8,000
			16,850
Total assets			30,550
EQUITY AND LIABILITIES			
Equity capital			
Capital			
– Street		8,500	

– Rhode	6,000	
– Close	4,500	19,000
Current accounts		
– Street	850	
– Rhode	1,300	
– Close	1,150	3,300
Total equity		22,300
Non-current liabilities		
Loan: Street		4,000
Total non-current liabilities		4,000
Current liabilities		
Trade payables		4,250
Total current liabilities		4,250
Total equity and liabilities		30,550

Street retired from the partnership on 31 March 20X5 and Rhode and Close decided to carry on the business and to admit Lane as a partner who is to bring in capital of £10,000. Future profits are to be shared equally among Rhode, Close and Lane.

By agreement, the following adjustments were to be incorporated in the books of account as at 31 March 20X5:

1 Plant and machinery to be increased to £6,900 in accordance with a valuer's certificate.

2 Inventory to be reduced to £4,860, since some items included therein were regarded as unsaleable.

3 The allowance for irrecoverable receivables to be increased to £830.

4 Provision to be made for the valuer's charges, £140.

The partnership deed provided that on the retirement of a partner, the value of goodwill was to be taken to be an amount equal to the average annual profit of the three years ending on the date of retirement. The profits of such three years were:

Year ended 31 Mar 20X3	£7,800
Year ended 31 Mar 20X4	£9,400
Year ended 31 Mar 20X5	£11,600

The partners agreed that, in respect of the valuing of goodwill, the profits should be regarded as not being affected by the revaluation. It was decided that an account for goodwill should not be opened in the books, but that the transactions between the partners should be made through their *capital accounts*.

£3,000 was repaid to Street on 1 April 20X5 and she agreed to leave £12,000 as a loan to the new partnership. Rhode, Close and Lane promised to repay the balance remaining due to Street within six months.

Required

You are required to prepare:

a the *revaluation account*;

b the *partners' capital accounts* (in columnar form);

c *Street's account* showing the balance due to her;

d the statement of financial position of Rhode, Close and Lane as on 1 April 20X5.

(ACCA, adapted)

INTERMEDIATE

26.11 Matthew, Mark and Luke were in partnership sharing profits and losses in the ratio 5 : 3 : 2, financial statements being made up annually to 30 June. Fixed capital accounts were to bear interest at the rate of 5 per cent per annum, but no interest was to be allowed or received on *current accounts* or *drawings*. Any balance on *current accounts* was to be paid at each year end.

Luke left the partnership on 30 September 20X4, but agreed to leave his money in the business until a new partner was admitted, provided interest at 5 per cent was paid on all amounts due to him.

John was admitted to the partnership on 1 January 20X5, providing capital of £2,000. It was agreed that the new profit-sharing ratio be Matthew 5, Mark 4, John 1, but Mark was to guarantee John an income of £3,000 per annum in addition to his interest on capital.

At 1 July 20X4 each partner had a fixed capital of £4,000.

Drawings during the year 20X4/20X5 were as follows:

Matthew	£750
Mark	£600
Luke	£220 (to 30 September 20X4)
John	£80

The profit for the year to 30 June 20X5 was £20,000, which may be assumed to have accrued evenly over that period.

You are required to show:

a the *appropriation account*;

b the *partners' current accounts* for the year ended 30 June 20X5.

(ACCA)

INTERMEDIATE

26.12 Hawthorn and Privet have carried on business in partnership for a number of years, sharing profits in the ratio of 4 : 3 after charging interest on capital at 4 per cent per annum. Holly was admitted into the partnership on 1 October 20X4, and the terms of the partnership from then were agreed as follows:

1 Partners' annual salaries to be: Hawthorn £1,800, Privet £1,200, Holly £1,100.

2 Interest on capital to be charged at 4 per cent per annum.

3 Profits to be shared: Hawthorn four-ninths, Privet three-ninths, Holly two-ninths.

On 1 October 20X4 Holly paid £7,000 into the partnership bank and of this amount £2,100 was in respect of the share of goodwill acquired by her. Since the partnership has never created, and does not intend to create, a *goodwill account*, the full amount of £7,000 was credited for the time being to *Holly's capital account* at 1 October 20X4.

The trial balance of the partnership at 30 June 20X5 was as follows:

	Debit	***Credit***
	£	**£**
Cash at bank	3,500	
Inventories at 1 July 20X4	11,320	
Purchases	102,630	

Sales revenue		123,300
Wages and salaries	6,200	
Rates, telephone, lighting and heating	2,100	
Printing, stationery and postage	530	
General expenses	1,600	
Irrecoverable receivables written off	294	
Capital accounts: – Hawthorn		22,000
– Privet		11,000
– Holly		7,000
Current accounts: – Hawthorn	2,200	
– Privet	1,100	
– Holly	740	
Trade receivables and trade payables	27,480	13,744
Freehold premises	12,000	
Furniture, fixtures and fittings at 1 July 20X4	5,800	
Irrecoverable receivables reserve		450
	177,494	177,494

After taking into account the following information and the adjustment required for goodwill, prepare a statement of profit or loss for the year ended 30 June 20X5 and a statement of financial position as on that date. On 30 June 20X5:

1 Inventory was £15,000.

2 Rates (£110) and wages and salaries (£300) were outstanding.

3 Telephone rental paid in advance was £9.

4 Allowance for irrecoverable receivables is to be adjusted to 2.5 per cent of trade receivables.

5 Depreciation is to be provided on furniture, fixtures and fittings at 10 per cent.

Apportionments required are to be made on a time basis.

(ACCA)

26.13 A, B and C are in partnership sharing profits and losses in the ratio of 50 : 25 : 25 per cent. Each partner receives a salary of £40,000 and interest on opening capital balance of 15 per cent per year. The draft statement of financial position at the year end 31 March 20X5 is as follows: INTERMEDIATE

Draft statement of financial position for ABC as at 31 March 20X5			
ASSETS	Cost	Prov for depn	WDV
Non-current assets	£'000	£'000	£'000
Fixtures	500	300	200
Motor vehicles	240	120	120
	740	420	320
Current assets			
Inventories			280
Trade receivables		200	
Allowance for irrecoverable receivables		(40)	160
Bank			240
			680
Total assets			1,000

EQUITY AND CAPITAL		
Equity capital		
Capital accounts:		
– A	80	
– B	160	
– C	80	320
Current accounts:		
– A	40	
– B	(20)	
– C	60	80
		400
Profit for the year (not yet apportioned)		320
Total equity		720
Non-current liabilities		
Long-term loan		80
Total non-current liabilities		80
Current liabilities		
Trade payables		200
Total current liabilities		200
Total equity and liabilities		1,000

The partners agreed to admit D on 31 March 20X5. D agreed to introduce £200,000 of capital. The partners have agreed to share the profits as follows A (40 per cent), B (30 per cent), C (20 per cent) and D (10 per cent). Goodwill on that date is valued at £600,000 and is not to be brought into the books. It is agreed that inventories are worth £360,000 and trade receivables £140,000. All other entries are of similar value to the book value amounts shown in the above statement of financial position.

You are required to prepare the:

a appropriation account for the year ended 31 March 20X5;

b revaluation account;

c partners' capital and current accounts;

d revised final statement of financial position at 31 March 20X5, after the introduction of D as partner.

26.14 X, Y and Z are in partnership sharing profits and losses in the ratio 4 : 2 : 2. Z died on 30 June 20X5. The partnership statement of financial position as at that date was:

Statement of financial position for X, Y and X partners on 30 June 20X5		
ASSETS	£'000	£'000
Non-current assets		280
Current assets		800
Total assets		1,080
EQUITY AND LIABILITIES		
Owners' equity		

Partner capital accounts		
– X	200	
– Y	240	
– Z	160	600
Partner current accounts		
– X	60	
– Y	100	
– Z	40	200
Total owners' equity		800
Current liabilities		280
Total equity and liabilities		1,080

Additional information

It was agreed between X, Y and Z's representatives that on 30 June 20X5 (for the purposes of settling the affairs of Z) goodwill be valued at £120,000 and the freehold land (the only non-current asset) at £360,000. The balance owing to Z will remain on loan to the partnership for five years at a rate of 10 per cent interest per annum. X and Y agree that goodwill should not be reflected as an asset in the financial statements; however, the new value of freehold land should. They also agree that in the future they will share profits and losses equally.

Required

a Prepare the *capital* and *current accounts* for the three partners, the *revaluation account* and the opening statement of financial position for the new X and Y partnership.

b Explain goodwill and outline why it is important to be able to value it in the context of partnership financial statements.

References

Gore, R. and Zimmerman, D. (2010) 'Is Goodwill an Asset?', *The CPA Journal*, 80 (6), 46–48.

International Accounting Standards Board (2013) *International Financial Reporting Standard 3 – Business Combinations* (IASB).

P. F. (2013) 'Goodwill Hunting', *The Economist*, 14 May, http://www.economist.com/blogs/schumpeter/2013/05/tata-steel, accessed September 2013.

Chapter 27

Partnership dissolution and conversion to a limited company

Learning Objectives:

After reading this chapter you should be able to do the following:

1. **List the circumstances that result in a partnership dissolution.**
2. **Critically evaluate the conversion decision.**
3. **Show the journal and ledger entries for the dissolution of a partnership.**
4. **Show the journal and ledger entries relating to the conversion of a partnership to a limited company.**
5. **Prepare the opening statement of financial position for the new limited company on the date of formation.**

—27.1 Introduction

The previous chapter dealt with changes to a partnership that continued in operation into the future. This chapter focuses on the accounting for a complete cessation of the partnership. This usually happens in two circumstances: when the partnership is dissolved and when the partnership converts to a limited company. Accounting for limited companies is covered in detail in Part 7 of this book. This chapter will only deal with the basic format of company financial statements. The two types of permanent cessation are now considered.

—27.2 Dissolution of partnerships

As explained in the previous chapter, when a partner leaves and/or a new partner is admitted, the law states that the old partnership is dissolved and a new partnership is created. However, the phrase '**dissolution** of partnerships' refers to the circumstances where all the partners wish to leave, and thus the activities of the partnership are wound up without a new partnership being created. Partnerships are usually dissolved because either it is unprofitable to carry on trading or the partners no longer wish to be associated with each other for personal reasons.

Accounting for the dissolution of partnerships can be quite complicated when the assets are disposed of over a prolonged period; known as the piecemeal realization of assets, and/or one or more of the partners is insolvent, which may involve the application of the *Garner* v. *Murray* rule described in Chapter 26 in the section, 'The revaluation of assets on changes in partners'. However, these circumstances are not covered in this book. The basic model of accounting for the dissolution of partnerships is relatively simple, at least after having grasped the contents of Chapter 26.

The chronological sequence of events on the dissolution of partnerships is as follows:

1 Prepare a set of final financial statements from the end of the previous accounting year to the date of dissolution, including the usual entries in the *partners' current accounts*. These will be no different from the usual final financial statements apart from relating to a period of less than one year.

2 The assets will be disposed of usually by sale (some may be taken over by the partners) and the money collected from trade receivables.

3 The liabilities are repaid in the order – trade payables, loans and then any partners' loans.

4 The balances on the *partners' capital* (and *current*) *accounts* are paid to them.

A simplifying assumption is usually made that all the above events occur on the date of dissolution or within a short period thereafter.

The simplest and also a perfectly acceptable way of accounting for a dissolution is to transfer *all* the balances on the *asset* (except for bank/cash), *liability* and *provision accounts* to a *realization account*. Then, all the money received from the sale of assets (including that collected from trade receivables) and paid to trade payables and loan creditors is entered in this account. If any assets (or liabilities) are taken over by the partners, the value placed on these will be entered in the *realization account* with a double entry to the relevant *partners' capital accounts*.

However, since liabilities such as trade payables and loans are technically not realized, some accountants do not enter these in the realization account. Instead, the amounts paid are entered in the relevant liability accounts, and any difference between the book values and amounts paid, such as discount received, are transferred to the *realization account*.

This highlights an important feature of the *realization account* concerning its purpose, and brings us to the next stage in the accounting procedure. The *realization account* performs a similar function to the *revaluation account* except that instead of being used to determine the profit or loss on revaluation, it is used to ascertain the profit or loss on dissolution. This is then transferred to the *partners' capital accounts* in their profit-sharing ratio.

Finally, the balances on the *partners' current accounts* are transferred to their *capital accounts*, and the resulting balances on the *capital accounts* are paid to the partners. This will eliminate the balance on the *bank* and *cash accounts*, leaving all the ledger accounts now closed. One last complication arises if the resulting balance on any of the *partners' capital accounts*, before repaying the partners, is a debit balance. In this text it is assumed that the partner is solvent and thus will pay to the partnership any debit balance on his or her *capital account*. This should then provide enough money with which to repay the other partners the credit balances on their *capital accounts*.

An illustration of accounting for the dissolution of partnerships is given in Worked Example 27.1.

WORKED EXAMPLE 27.1

Tom and Jerry, whose accounting year end is 31 December, have been in partnership for several years sharing profits equally. They have decided to dissolve the partnership as on 14 February 20X5. You have already prepared a statement of profit or loss for the period 1 January 20X5 to 14 February 20X5 and a statement of financial position as at the latter date as follows:

	Cost	Dep'n	NBV
ASSETS	£	£	£
Non-current assets			
Motor vehicles	20,000	6,600	13,400
Current assets			
Inventories			6,700
Trade receivables		5,900	
Allowance for irrecoverable receivables		(600)	5,300
Prepaid expenses			500
			12,500
Total assets			25,900
EQUITY AND LIABILITIES			
Equity capital			
Capital – Tom		8,000	
– Jerry		4,200	12,200
Current accounts – Tom		4,800	
– Jerry		(1,900)	2,900
Total equity capital			15,100
Current liabilities			
Bank overdraft			1,600
Trade payables			3,200
Bank loan			2,000
Loan – Tom			4,000
Total current liabilities			10,800
Total equity and liabilities			25,900

One of the motor vehicles was taken over by Jerry at an agreed valuation of £5,700. The remainder were sold for £6,200. The inventory realized £7,100 and £4,900 was received from trade receivables. A refund of the full amount of prepaid expenses was also received.

There were selling expenses in respect of advertising the vehicles and inventory for sale of £800. Trade payables were paid £2,900 in full settlement. The bank loan was repaid, including an interest penalty for early settlement of £400.

The partnership also sold its business name and a list of its customers to a competitor for £1,000.

You are required to show all the ledger entries necessary to close the partnership books.

Motor vehicles			
Balance b/d	20,000	Realization a/c	20,000

Provision for depreciation			
Realization a/c	6,600	Balance b/d	6,600

Inventory			
Balance b/d	6,700	Realization a/c	6,700

Trade receivables			
Balance b/d	5,900	Realization	5,900

Allowance for irrecoverable receivables			
Realization a/c	600	Balance b/d	600

Prepaid expenses			
Balance b/d	500	Realization a/c	500

Trade payables			
Bank	2,900	Balance b/d	3,200
Realization a/c	300		
	3,200		3,200

Bank loan			
Bank	2,400	Balance b/d	2,000
		Realization a/c (Int. penalty)	400
	2,400		2,400

Loan – Tom			
Bank	4,000	Balance b/d	4,000

Realization account			
Vehicles	20,000	Provision for depreciation	6,600
Inventories	6,700	Allowance for irrecoverable receivables	600
Trade receivables	5,900	Bank – vehicles	6,200
Prepaid expenses	500	Bank – inventories	7,100
Loan interest	400	Bank – trade receivables	4,900
Bank – expenses	800	Bank – prepayments	500
		Bank – goodwill	1,000
		Trade payables	300
		Capital – Jerry:	5,700
		Loss on realization:	
		– Capital Tom 700	
		– Capital Jerry 700	1,400
	34,300		34,300

Current accounts					
	Tom	**Jerry**	**Tom**	**Jerry**	
Balance b/d	–	1,900	Balance b/d	4,800	–
Capital	4,800	–	Capital	–	1,900
	4,800	1,900		4,800	1,900

Capital accounts					
	Tom	**Jerry**		**Tom**	**Jerry**
Current account	–	1,900	Balance b/d	8,000	4,200
Realization – vehicle	–	5,700	Current a/c	4,800	–
Loss on realization	700	700	Bank	–	4,100
Bank	12,100	–			
	12,800	8,300		12,800	8,300

Bank			
Realization – vehicles	6,200	Balance b/d	1,600
Inventories	7,100	Trade payables	2,900
Trade receivables	4,900	Bank loan	2,400
Prepayments	500	Realization – expenses	800
Goodwill	1,000	Loan – Tom	4,000
Capital – Jerry	4,100	Capital Tom	12,100
	23,800		23,800

27.3 Conversion to a limited company

Sometimes the partners in a partnership decide to convert their partnership into a limited company.

Learning Activity 27.1

Before reading further prepare a list of possible reasons for a partnership forming a limited company. Highlight any disadvantages of becoming a limited company also.

Reasons may include: limiting their personal liability to the creditors of the partnership, or it may be for tax reasons.

REAL WORLD EXAMPLE 27.1

'Why would a partnership wish to convert to a limited liability company?'

'The main reason for a partnership firm becoming incorporated is to enable the partners not to be personally liable for the debts of the business. A partnership has no separate legal identity and each partner has joint and several liability for the debts of the firm. However, a shareholder in a limited company is not responsible for the debts of the company in the event of its insolvency. A shareholder's liability is limited to any amount still unpaid on the issue of the shares. If the shares were issued fully paid (as they normally are), then the shareholder has no liability.

Further, as a company the business should find it easier to attract new capital, as investors become shareholders and not partners. In the long run, companies can be floated on a stock exchange. However, before incorporating the business as a company, the partners will have to carefully consider the tax implications.'

Source: extract from an article by Tom Clendon (1999) 'Conversion of a Partnership to a Limited Company', 1 October, ACCA website, http://www.accaglobal.com/archive/sa_oldarticles/30891#top, accessed September 2013.

A practical example of the benefits of limited liability are provided in the next real world example.

REAL WORLD EXAMPLE 27.2

The BDO Binder Hamlyn Case

The High Court in this case ordered the partners of BDO Binder Hamlyn (BDO) to pay £65 million to ADT (an electronic security group) in damages and £105 million in court costs. This was a famous case as it was the highest-ever award against a firm of auditors. At this time (1996) BDO was not an LLP, and the insurance company did not cover the full claim, meaning that the partners had to make good on the outstanding debt from their personal assets.

The history of the case is as follows: BDO audited the financial statements of Britannia Security Systems (Britannia). When ADT were undertaking their due diligence audit before acquiring

Britannia, they reviewed ADT's financial statements and a representative of ADT met the BDO audit partner who had signed the audit report 11 weeks earlier. The audit partner provided assurances to the ADT representative over the truth and fairness of the audited financial statements. The court concluded that these assurances meant that the BDO partner had accepted responsibility for the audited financial statements and had known about the influence the financial statements had on the decision by ADT to acquire Britannia. After acquisition, ADT discovered that Britannia was worth about £65 million less than the £105 million paid for the company and that the financial statements had contributed to the overvaluation.

Had BDO been an LLP, ADT would not have had recourse for the balance due to them from the partners' (shareholders') personal assets.

Source: http://www.thelawyer.com/reasons-to-be-careful/92609.article, accessed September 2013.

Learning Activity 27.2

Dissolving a partnership does not only impact on accounting ledgers and accounting systems, many other stakeholders are also affected. List at least five steps that you would need to take when dissolving a partnership that are not accounting related. When you have finished, go to http://www.wikihow.com/Dissolve-a-Partnership to see a suggested 10-step process to partnership dissolution. This makes suggestions about the process and the stakeholders involved.

The result of a conversion to a limited company is that the partnership ceases to exist and all the partnership accounts have to be closed and a new company is established with new ledger accounts. The steps to take to convert a partnership to a company are as follows:

1 Open a *realization account* and transfer all assets and liabilities to this (the exception is cash/bank). In addition, some questions may state that items have to be paid, or credit accounts settled before the **conversion** takes place.

2 Transfer the *partners' current accounts* to the *capital accounts*.

3 Open a '*company personal account*' and debit the consideration being given for the partnership to this account. Credit the *realization account* with the other side of this entry.

4 Close off the *realization account*, transferring the profit, or loss, on realization to the partners in their profit-sharing ratio.

5 Credit the '*company personal account*' with the share capital, debentures and cash (this account will now also balance and can be closed) and debit the *partnership capital accounts* with the shares, cash or debentures in the portions stipulated in the question.

6 The balance on the *partners' capital accounts* will be the amount owing to them from the partnership, or the amount they owe to the partnership.

7 Finally, write cheques to settle any balances remaining as owing to the partners (credit *bank*, debit *partners' capital accounts*), or get the partners to introduce cash when they owe the partnership funds (debit *bank*, credit *partners' capital accounts*). At this point the *cash account* should be closed with no balance and the *capital accounts* will be closed with no balances. Indeed, all accounts will now be closed.

The transactions also have to be recorded in the books of the new company. This is normally done through a ***purchase of consideration account***. The assets are usually taken over at fair value and these values are the ones that should be used as the opening balances in the new company. The steps to take when setting up the accounts in the new company are as follows:

1 Determine the value of goodwill (excess of the purchase consideration over the fair value of the assets and liabilities). This is commonly taken to be the balance on the *purchase consideration account.*

2 Open a *purchase of consideration account*. Debit it with the purchase consideration and credit the source of the purchase consideration; for example, *share capital, bank, loan* or *debentures account.*

3 Credit the *purchase consideration account* with the asset values and debit the new *asset accounts.*

4 Debit the *purchase consideration account* with the liabilities value and credit the new *liabilities accounts.*

5 Post the balance (goodwill) to a *goodwill account.*

If the goodwill is negative, then it is important to review the fair values of the assets being recorded; it is likely that they are overstated.

WORKED EXAMPLE 27.2

Anna and Mary, who share profits 3 : 2, decide to become a limited company on 31/03/X5. The statement of financial position at this date is as follows:

Statement of financial position for Anna and Mary as at 31 March 20X5			
	Cost	***Prov for dep'n***	***WDV***
ASSETS	**£**	**£**	**£**
Non-current assets			
Motor vehicles	10,000	8,000	2,000
Equipment	6,000	2,000	4,000
	16,000	10,000	6,000
Current assets			
Inventories			3,200
Trade receivables			4,400
Cash			800
			8,400
Total assets			14,400
EQUITY AND LIABILITIES			
Owners' equity	*Anna*	*Mary*	
Capital account	6,000	3,000	9,000
Current account	960	(160)	800
	6,960	2,840	9,800
Current liabilities			
Trade payables			4,600
Total equity and liabilities			14,400

The company is to be called McKees Ltd.

The purchase consideration is £12,500 to be settled by issuing 10,000 equity shares of £1 each, allotted at £1.20 per share, and £500 cash.

Assume the transfer is at book values.

Required

a Close the accounts of the partnership.

b Prepare the opening statement of financial position of the new company.

Motor vehicles			
Balance b/d	10,000	Realization a/c	10,000

Provision for depreciation – motor vehicles			
Realization a/c	8,000	Balance b/d	8,000

Equipment			
Balance b/d	6,000	Realization account	6,000

Provision for depreciation – equipment			
Realization a/c	2,000	Balance b/d	2,000

Inventories			
Balance b/d	3,200	Realization account	3,200

Trade receivables			
Balance b/d	4,400	Realization account	4,400

Trade payables			
Realization a/c	4,600	Balance b/d	4,600

Personal account				
Realization account (Purchase consideration)	12,500	Cash		500
		Shares allocated:		
		– Anna ($\frac{3}{5}$)	7,200	
		– Mary ($\frac{3}{5}$)	4,800	12,000
	12,500			12,500

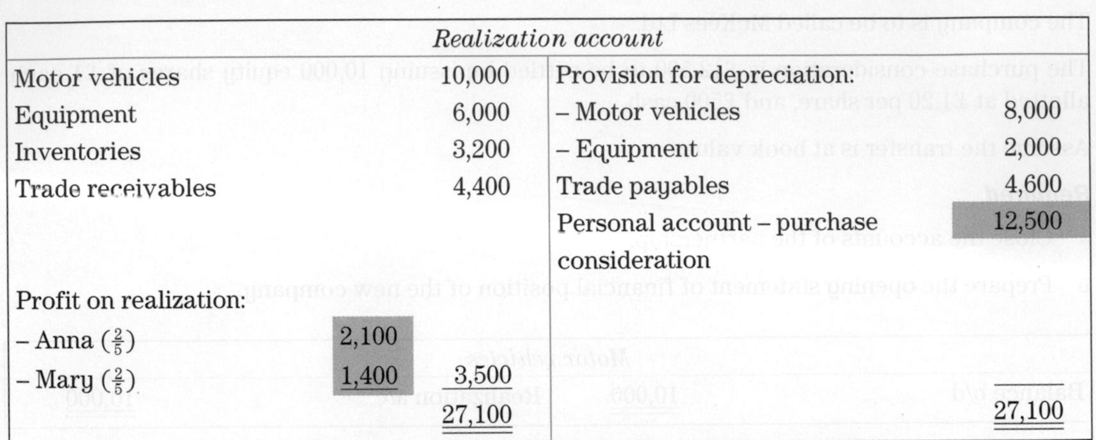

Realization account

Motor vehicles		10,000	Provision for depreciation:	
Equipment		6,000	– Motor vehicles	8,000
Inventories		3,200	– Equipment	2,000
Trade receivables		4,400	Trade payables	4,600
			Personal account – purchase consideration	12,500
Profit on realization:				
– Anna ($\frac{2}{5}$)	2,100			
– Mary ($\frac{2}{5}$)	1,400	3,500		
		27,100		27,100

Current accounts

	Anna	Mary		Anna	Mary
Balance b/d	–	160	Balance b/d	960	–
Capital account	960	–	Capital account	–	160
	960	160		960	160

Capital accounts

	Anna	Mary		Anna	Mary
Current account	–	160	Balance b/d	6,000	3,000
Equity shares	7,200	4,800	Current account	960	–
			Profit on realization	2,100	1,400
Bank	1,860	–	Bank	–	560
	9,060	4,960		9,060	4,960

Bank account

Balance b/d	800	Anna	1,860
Personal account	500		
Mary	560		
	1,860		1,860

Note

1 Mary has to introduce £560 to the partnership, whereas Anna will receive a cheque from the partnership for £1,860.

WORKED EXAMPLE 27.3

Required

Using the information from Worked Example 27.2 prepare the opening statement of financial position of the new company.

Note: the purchase of business account should be completed, but it is unnecessary to open all the ledger accounts.

Purchase of business account			
Trade payables account	4,600	Motor vehicles account	2,000
Purchase consideration:		Equipment account	4,000
– Bank overdraft account	500	Inventories account	3,200
– Equity share capital account	12,000	Trade receivables account	4,400
		Goodwill account	3,500
	17,100		17,100

Statement of financial position for McKees Ltd as at 31/03/X5		
ASSETS	£	£
Non-current assets		
Tangible assets		
Motor vehicles	2,000	
Equipment	4,000	
	6,000	
Intangible assets		
Goodwill	3,500	
Total non-current assets	9,500	
Current assets		
Inventories		3,200
Trade receivables		4,400
		7,600
Total assets		17,100
EQUITY AND LIABILITIES		
Equity and reserves		
Share capital		12,000
Current liabilities		
Bank overdraft		500
Trade payables		4,600
Total current liabilities		5,100
Total equity and liabilities		17,100

The next real world example is taken from the Companies House website and deals with common queries in respect of LLPs.

REAL WORLD EXAMPLE 27.3

Limited Liability Partnerships (LLPs) FAQs

What is an LLP?

It is an alternative corporate business vehicle that gives the benefits of limited liability but allows its members the flexibility of organising their internal structure as a traditional partnership. The LLP is a separate legal entity and, while the LLP itself will be liable for the full extent of its assets, the liability of the members will be limited.

What sort of organisation can become an LLP?

Any new or existing firm of two or more persons can incorporate as an LLP.

Can I convert from being a limited company to an LLP?

The LLP legislation does not allow for a 'conversion process' – in the way that a limited company can convert to PLC status under the Companies Act, for example. The process will involve a closely controlled company change of name and an LLP incorporation. Establishing contact prior to submitting the necessary forms will help ensure that this process is completed as smoothly as possible.

What are the LLP disclosure requirements?

They are similar to those of a company. LLPs are required to provide financial information equivalent to that of companies, including the filing of annual accounts. Among other things, they are also required to:

- File an annual return
- Notify any changes to the LLP's membership
- Notify any changes to their members' names & residential addresses
- Notify any change to their Registered Office Address

How much does it cost to register an LLP?

Registration electronically of a limited liability partnership on its incorporation under the 2000 Act is £14.

Registration on paper of a limited liability partnership on its incorporation under the 2000 Act is £40.

Source: Companies House, http://www.companieshouse.gov.uk/infoAndGuide/faq/llpFAQ.shtml, accessed September 2013.
© Crown copyright 2014

Learning Activity 27.3

Download the article by P. Spicer and A. Fahy on 'The Benefits of Incorporating your Audit Practice' (2011) and summarize the benefits in ten points. See the references for the full source.

Summary

When a partnership's activities cease there is a dissolution of the partnership. All the assets are realized and the liabilities paid. Any profit or loss on realization is ascertained via a *realization account* and transferred to the *partners' capital accounts*. The balances on the *partners' capital* and *current accounts* are then repaid.

Key terms and concepts

conversion	527	purchase of consideration account	528
dissolution	522		

An asterisk after the question number indicates that there is a suggested answer in Appendix 2.

Review questions

connect

27.1* What are the main reasons for dissolving a partnership?

27.2 What happens to the assets and liabilities of a partnership on dissolution?

Exercises

connect

27.3* Martin and Stephen share profits in the ratio 2 : 1. They decide to terminate their partnership on 31 December 20X4. Their statement of financial position is as follows: INTERMEDIATE

Statement of financial position for Martin and Stephen as at 31 December 20X4			
	Cost	*Dep'n*	*NBV*
ASSETS	£	£	£
Non-current assets	6,000	2,400	3,600
Current assets			
Inventory			4,150
Trade receivables			3,850
Cash			250
			8,250
Total assets			11,850
EQUITY AND LIABILITIES			
Equity capital	*Martin*	*Stephen*	
Capital	5,000	3,000	8,000
Current	150	(100)	50
Total equity	5,150	2,900	8,050

Non-current liabilities	
Loan account: Martin	1,000
Total non-current liabilities	1,000
Current liabilities	
Trade payables	2,800
Total current liabilities	2,800
Total equity and liabilities	11,850

The dissolution progressed as follows:

1 £350 of trade receivables could not be recovered.

2 Trade payables gave 10 per cent discount when settled.

3 Non-current assets realized £2,950.

4 Realization costs of £50 were paid.

5 Inventory realized 20 per cent more than anticipated.

6 Partners' claims were met and the books closed.

Required

Prepare the ledger accounts showing the final distributions to be paid to each partner.

ADVANCED

27.4 Alpha, Beta and Gamma were in partnership for many years sharing profits and losses in the ratio 5 : 3 : 2 and making up their financial statements to 31 December each year. Alpha died on 31 December 20X4, and the partnership was dissolved as from that date.

The partnership statement of financial position at 31 December 20X4 was as follows:

Alpha, Beta and Gamma
Statement of financial position as at 31 December 20X4

ASSETS	*Cost*	*Aggregate depreciation*	*Net book value*
Non-current assets	£	£	£
Freehold land and buildings	350,000	50,000	300,000
Plant and machinery	220,000	104,100	115,900
Motor vehicles	98,500	39,900	58,600
	668,500	194,000	474,500
Current assets			
Inventories			110,600
Trade and sundry receivables			89,400
Cash at bank			12,600
			212,600
Total assets			687,100
EQUITY AND LIABILITIES			
Owners' equity			
Capital accounts:			
– Alpha			233,600
– Beta			188,900
– Gamma			106,200
			528,700

Non-current assets	
Loan – Delta (carrying interest at 10 per cent)	40,000
Current liabilities	
Trade and sundry payables	118,400
Total equity and liabilities	687,100

In the period January to March 20X5 the following transactions took place and were dealt with in the partnership records:

1 Non-current assets	£
Freehold land and buildings – sold for:	380,000
Plant and machinery – sold for:	88,000
Motor vehicles: Beta and Gamma took over the cars they had been using at the following agreed values:	
– Beta	9,000
– Gamma	14,000
The remaining vehicles were sold for:	38,000
2 Current assets	
Inventory – taken over by Gamma at agreed value:	120,000
Trade and sundry receivables:	
Cash received	68,400
Remainder taken over by Gamma at agreed value	20,000
3 Current liabilities	
The trade and sundry payables were all settled for a total of:	115,000
4 Non-current liabilities	
Delta's loan was repaid on 31 March 20X5 with interest accrued since 31 December 20X4	
5 Expenses of dissolution £2,400 were paid	
6 *Capital accounts*	
The final amounts due to or from the estate of Alpha, Beta and Gamma were paid/received on 31 March 20X5	

Required

Prepare the following accounts as at 31 March 20X5 showing the dissolution of the partnership:

a realization account;

b partners' capital accounts;

c cash book (cash account).

Ignore taxation and assume that all partners have substantial resources outside the partnership.

(ACCA)

ADVANCED

27.5 Peter, Paul and Mary have been in partnership for several years sharing profits and losses in the ratio 1 : 2 : 3. Their last statement of financial position is as follows:

Peter, Paul and Mary Statement of financial position as at 30 June 20X5			
ASSETS	£	£	£
Non-current assets	40,000	12,000	28,000
Current assets			
Inventories			10,000
Trade receivables			42,000
			52,000
Total assets			80,000
EQUITY AND LIABILITIES			
Owners' equity			
Capital accounts			
– Peter			4,000
– Paul			8,000
– Mary			8,000
Total equity			20,000
Current liabilities			
Bank			26,000
Trade payables			34,000
Total current liabilities			60,000
Total equity and liabilities			80,000

The partnership had become very dependent on one customer, Jefferson, and in order to keep his custom the partners had recently increased his credit limit until he owed them £36,000. Jefferson has just been declared bankrupt and the partnership is unlikely to get any money from him. Reluctantly, the partners have agreed to dissolve the partnership on the following terms:

1 The inventory is to be sold for £8,000.

2 The non-current assets will be sold for £16,000 except for certain items with a book value of £10,000, which will be taken over by Mary at an agreed valuation of £14,000.

3 The trade receivables, except for Jefferson, are expected to pay their accounts in full.

4 The costs of dissolution will be £1,600 and discounts received from trade credit suppliers are expected to be £1,000.

5 Peter is unable to meet his liability to the partnership out of his personal funds.

Required

Prepare the:

a realization account

b partners' capital accounts recording the dissolution of the partnership.

ADVANCED

27.6 Maraid, Wendy and Diane have been in partnership for a number of years sharing profits $\frac{2}{5}$, $\frac{2}{5}$ and $\frac{1}{5}$, respectively. They decide to form a limited company on 1 January 20X5, called McKee Ltd, to carry on the business. The statement of financial position of the partnership on 31 December 20X4 is as follows:

Statement of financial position for Maraid, Wendy and Diane as at 31 December 20X4			
	Cost	*Dep'n*	*NBV*
ASSETS	£	£	£
Non-current assets			
Land	190,000	–	190,000
Plant and equipment	40,000	23,650	16,350
Fixtures and fittings	18,000	8,000	10,000
	248,000	31,650	216,350
Current assets			
Inventories			38,000
Trade receivables		186,490	
Allowance for irrecoverable receivables		(12,000)	174,490
Bank			20,500
Cash			510
			233,500
Total assets			449,850
EQUITY AND LIABILITIES			
Owners' equity			
Capital accounts:			
– Maraid			84,950
– Wendy			45,000
– Diane			30,000
Total equity			159,950
Non-current liabilities			
10% Loan			120,000
Current liabilities			
Trade payables			169,900
Total equity and liabilities			449,850

Additional information

The updated statement of financial position information at 31 December 20X4 is as follows:

1 The land is valued at £210,000 on 31 December 20X4.

2 A machine that was purchased for £10,000 on 1 January 20X2 is now considered to be worthless. Machines are depreciated using the sum of digits method over a period of four years. On 1 January 20X5 the partners considered that this machine would have a residual value of £2,000. (The figures in the statement of financial position above have been adjusted for 20X4's depreciation charge.)

3 The financial statements for the period ended 31 December had omitted the accountancy fee for that period of £3,000.

4 During a review of the inventory on 31 December 20X4, items valued in the books at £9,000 were considered to be worth £1,000.

5 The partners received information that one of their customers, Seamus, is declared bankrupt. On investigation, it is estimated that Seamus will only be able to pay 20p for each £1 he owes. Seamus owes the partnership £50,000.

6 A full year's interest is still outstanding and has not yet been accrued in the above draft figures.

Required

Provide the relevant entries required for amending the statement of financial position to take account of the new up-to-date information and prepare the new updated statement of financial position.

(*Note*: All workings must be shown.)

ADVANCED

27.7 Use the amended information from Exercise 27.6 as a starting point.

Dissolution information

1 On 1 January 20X5 the partners decide to form a company and issue £140,000 worth of shares in the company to the partners. They raise an additional loan (£60,000) and raise £70,000 in cash from the bank by way of an overdraft to enable the newly created company to purchase the partnership. The full £270,000 is to be used to purchase the assets and liabilities of the partnership, with the exception of the loan and the interest owing on the loan.

2 The shares and loan are to be divided between the partners as follows: Maraid (50 per cent), Wendy (25 per cent) and Diane (25 per cent).

3 The expenses associated with the conversion to a limited company are £3,500. These are payable by the partnership.

4 The partnership loan and interest owing must be repaid in full before the conversion takes place.

Required

a Provide the relevant entries required for dissolution of the partnership (each partner will withdraw, or introduce cash to close their *capital account*). Prepare all the necessary ledger accounts, showing all workings.

b Prepare the purchase of business account and the statement of financial position of McKee Ltd as on 1 January 20X5 (the opening accounts in the new business are not required).

Reference

Spicer, P. and Fahy, A. (2011) 'The Benefits of Incorporating your Audit Practice', *Accountancy Ireland*, 43 (1), 34–36.

PART SEVEN Companies

28 The nature of limited companies and their capital 541

29 The final financial statements of limited companies 557

30 Statement of cash flows 609

31 The appraisal of company financial statements using ratio analysis 647

Chapter 28

The nature of limited companies and their capital

Learning Objectives:

After reading this chapter you should be able to do the following:

1. Describe the main characteristics of limited companies with particular reference to how these differ from partnerships.
2. Describe the different classes of companies limited by shares.
3. Outline the legal powers and duties of limited companies with reference to their Memorandum and Articles of Association.
4. Explain the nature and types of shares and loan capital issued by limited companies.
5. Outline the procedure relating to the issue of shares and debentures.
6. Explain the nature of a share premium, debenture discount, preliminary expenses, interim and final dividends.
7. Discuss the contents and purpose of the auditors' report.
8. Describe the contents of a company's statutory books.
9. Describe the purpose and proceedings of a company's annual general meeting.

28.1 Introduction

As discussed in Chapter 1, there are several different legal forms of organization. These can be grouped into two categories, known as **bodies sole** and **bodies corporate**. Bodies sole, or **unincorporated bodies**, consist of sole traders and partnerships. All other forms of organization are bodies corporate. A key feature of bodies corporate, or **incorporated bodies**, is that they are recognized by law as being a legal entity separate from their members.

A body corporate is one that is created either by Royal Charter, such as the Institute of Chartered Accountants in England and Wales or by Act of Parliament. The Act of Parliament may either relate to the creation of a specific organization, such as the British Broadcasting Corporation, or alternatively permit the creation of a particular form of legal entity by any group of individuals. The most common forms of legal entity that can be created under such Acts of Parliament include building societies, life assurance and friendly societies, and companies.

A **company** is defined as a legal entity that is formed by registration under the Companies Act 2006. There are four types of company: companies whose liability is limited by shares, companies with unlimited liability, companies whose liability is limited by guarantee and companies limited by shares and guarantee. Companies limited by guarantee include organizations such as some professional bodies where the liability of its members is limited to the amount of their annual subscription. The remainder of this chapter deals with companies whose liability is limited by shares. These are commonly known as 'limited companies'.

28.2 The characteristics of companies limited by shares

1. A company is a legal entity that is separate from its shareholders (owners). This means that companies enter into contracts as legal entities in their own right. Thus, creditors and others cannot sue the shareholders of the company but must take legal proceedings against the company. This is referred to as not being able to lift the **veil of incorporation**.
2. A company has perpetual existence in that the death of one of its shareholders does not result in its dissolution. This may be contrasted with a partnership, where the death of a partner constitutes a dissolution.
3. The liability of a company's shareholders is limited to the nominal value of their shares. **Limited liability** means that if a company's assets are insufficient to pay its debts, the shareholders cannot be called upon to contribute more than the nominal value of their shares towards paying those debts.
4. The shareholders of a company do not have the right to take part in its management as such. They appoint directors to manage the company. However, a shareholder may also be a director (or other employee).
5. Each voting share carries one vote at general meetings of the company's shareholders (e.g. in the appointment of directors). There may be different classes of shares, each class having different rights and, possibly, some being non-voting.
6. A limited company must have at least two shareholders but there is no maximum number.

28.3 The classes of companies limited by shares

There are two classes of companies limited by shares, namely public and private. Under the Companies Act a **public limited company** must be registered as such. The principal reason for forming a public limited company is to gain access to greater amounts of capital from investment institutions and members of the public. The shares of many, but not all, public companies in the UK are quoted on the London Stock Exchange.

All other limited companies are **private companies**. These are not allowed to offer their shares for sale to the general public and thus do not have a stock exchange quotation. One of the main reasons for forming a private rather than a public company is that it enables its owners to keep control of the business, for example, within a family.

The name of a public company must end with the words 'public limited company' or the abbreviation 'plc'. The name of a private company must end with the word 'limited' or the abbreviation 'Ltd'. A business that does not have either of these descriptions after its name is not a limited company even if its name contains the word 'company' (the only exception being certain companies that have private company status, such as charities, who are permitted under licence to omit the word limited from their name).

28.4 The legal powers and duties of limited companies

A company is formed by sending certain documents and the appropriate fee to the Registrar of Companies. The most relevant of these documents are the Memorandum and Articles of Association. These define a company's powers and duties. The key contents of the **Memorandum of Association** are contained in Figure 28.1.

Figure 28.1

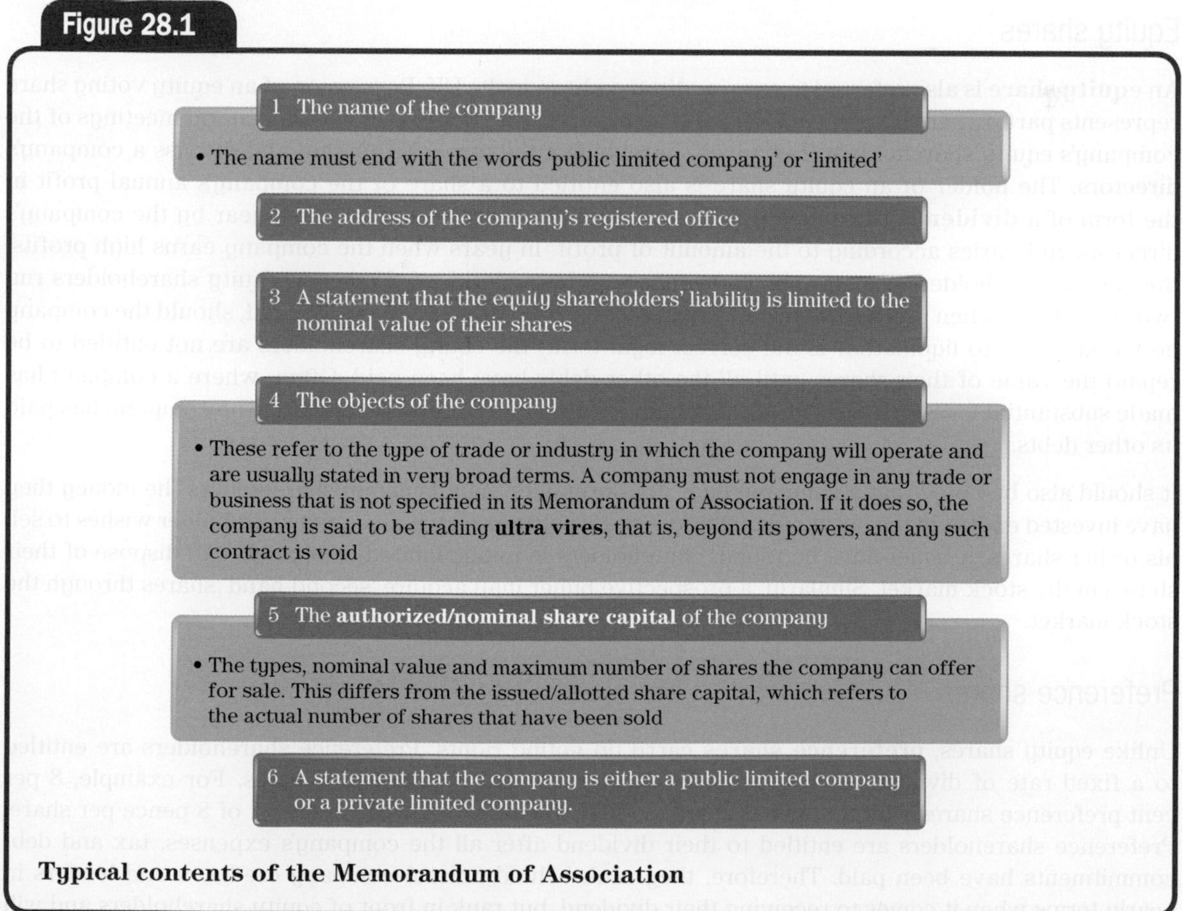

1 The name of the company
• The name must end with the words 'public limited company' or 'limited'
2 The address of the company's registered office
3 A statement that the equity shareholders' liability is limited to the nominal value of their shares
4 The objects of the company
• These refer to the type of trade or industry in which the company will operate and are usually stated in very broad terms. A company must not engage in any trade or business that is not specified in its Memorandum of Association. If it does so, the company is said to be trading ultra vires, that is, beyond its powers, and any such contract is void
5 The authorized/nominal share capital of the company
• The types, nominal value and maximum number of shares the company can offer for sale. This differs from the issued/allotted share capital, which refers to the actual number of shares that have been sold
6 A statement that the company is either a public limited company or a private limited company.

Typical contents of the Memorandum of Association

Any of the above can be subsequently changed by a **special resolution** passed at a general meeting of the company's shareholders. Such a resolution requires at least 75 per cent of the votes cast.

The **Articles of Association** can best be described as a rule book that sets out the rights of a company's shareholders between themselves. It contains regulations relating to the issue of shares, conduct of meetings, borrowing powers, the appointment of directors, and so on. When a company is registered, it is issued with what might be described as a birth certificate by the Register of Companies. This is called a **Certificate of Incorporation**. However, before a public limited company can commence trading, it must satisfy the Registrar that certain regulations relating to its capital structure have been complied with. When this is done the Registrar issues a **Trading Certificate**, on receipt of which the company can commence trading.

The costs of forming a company, including the above documents, are referred to as **preliminary, promotion or formation expenses**.

28.5 The nature and types of share and loan capital

Companies are financed predominantly by the issue (sale) of shares, loan stock and **debentures**, and by retaining part of each year's profit. In the UK all shares, loan stock and debentures have a fixed **nominal, par or face value**. This is often £1 or 25 pence in the case of shares and £100 for debentures and loan stock. There are several different types of share and loan capital, each of which is described below.

Equity shares

An **equity share** is also referred to as an **ordinary share** in the UK. Possession of an equity voting share represents part ownership of a company and it entitles the holder to one vote in general meetings of the company's equity shareholders. This gives shareholders the power to appoint and dismiss a company's directors. The holder of an equity share is also entitled to a share of the company's annual profit in the form of a **dividend**. The amount of the dividend per share is decided each year by the company's directors and varies according to the amount of profit. In years when the company earns high profits, the equity shareholders are more likely to receive a large dividend. However, equity shareholders run two risks. First, when profits are low they may receive little or no dividend. Second, should the company go bankrupt ('into liquidation' is the correct legal term) the equity shareholders are not entitled to be repaid the value of their shares until *all* the other debts have been paid. Often, where a company has made substantial losses, there is little or nothing left for equity shareholders after the company has paid its other debts.

It should also be noted that a company does not normally repay its equity shareholders the money they have invested except in the event of liquidation (or by court order). If an equity shareholder wishes to sell his or her shares, a buyer must be found. Shareholders in public limited companies can dispose of their shares in the stock market. Similarly, a prospective buyer may acquire 'second-hand' shares through the stock market.

Preference shares

Unlike equity shares, **preference shares** carry no voting rights. Preference shareholders are entitled to a fixed rate of dividend each year based on the nominal value of the shares. For example, 8 per cent preference shares with a nominal value of £1 each carry an annual dividend of 8 pence per share. Preference shareholders are entitled to their dividend after all the company's expenses, tax and debt commitments have been paid. Therefore, they rank behind normal company creditors and lenders in yearly terms when it comes to receiving their dividend, but rank in front of equity shareholders and will receive their dividend before equity shareholders can get any distribution (dividend).

In the event of a company going into liquidation, the preference shareholders are normally entitled to be repaid the nominal value of their shares before the equity shareholders. However, if no money is left after paying the other debts they would receive nothing.

As in the case of equity shares, companies do not normally repay preference shareholders the money they have invested except in the event of liquidation. Should a preference shareholder wish to dispose of shares, he or she must find a buyer or sell them in the stock market, if the company has a quotation for the preference shares.

There are two advantages of preference shares from the point of view of a company. One is that, since the rate of dividend is fixed, the company knows in advance what its future annual commitment is in respect of preference dividends. The second advantage is that preference shares are a permanent source of long-term capital, which does not have to be repaid. However, since the introduction of the corporation tax system in 1965, it has become unpopular to issue preference shares, because the dividend is not an allowable charge against income for tax purposes, while interest on debt is allowable. This makes debt a relatively more attractive source of fixed return finance for most companies. Small companies may be able to take advantage of the tax rules applicable to them to offset this difference.

There are a number of different types of preference share with rights that vary from those described above as detailed in Figure 28.2.

Figure 28.2

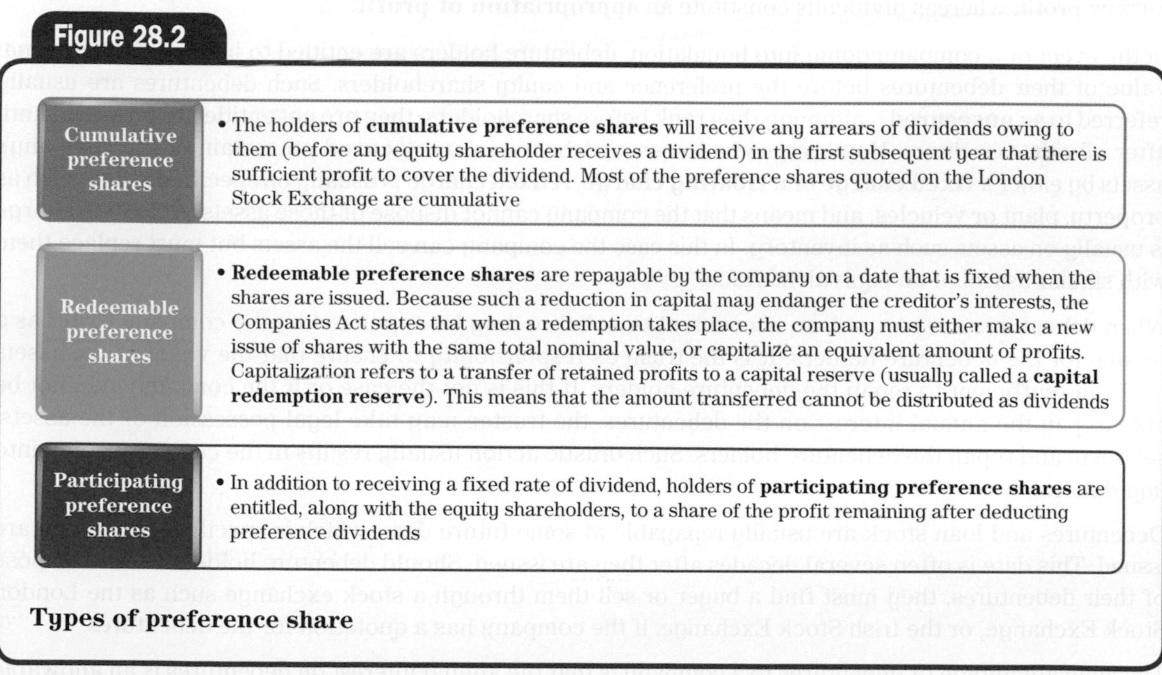

Cumulative preference shares
• The holders of **cumulative preference shares** will receive any arrears of dividends owing to them (before any equity shareholder receives a dividend) in the first subsequent year that there is sufficient profit to cover the dividend. Most of the preference shares quoted on the London Stock Exchange are cumulative
Redeemable preference shares
• **Redeemable preference shares** are repayable by the company on a date that is fixed when the shares are issued. Because such a reduction in capital may endanger the creditor's interests, the Companies Act states that when a redemption takes place, the company must either make a new issue of shares with the same total nominal value, or capitalize an equivalent amount of profits. Capitalization refers to a transfer of retained profits to a capital reserve (usually called a **capital redemption reserve**). This means that the amount transferred cannot be distributed as dividends
Participating preference shares
• In addition to receiving a fixed rate of dividend, holders of **participating preference shares** are entitled, along with the equity shareholders, to a share of the profit remaining after deducting preference dividends

Types of preference share

Accounting for and disclosing preference shares and preference share dividends in the financial statements

Classifying preference shares is quite difficult under IFRS. They can be considered to be debt or equity. The terms of each preference share issue need to be considered to determine the economic substance of the issue, with a view to classifying the shares as either a form of finance (debt), or new owners (equity). Preference shares are not strictly equity as they do not represent a share in the ownership of a company. Yet, in some instances, they have the same rights as owners. For example, they might be classed as equity: when they have voting rights attached that are the same as the voting rights of equity shareholders; when they are non-cumulative and directors can waive the yearly dividend; when they are non-redeemable; and when they are participating. In these circumstances preference shares are more like equity shares than debt.

In the UK most preference shares are cumulative and are non-participating. Some are redeemable. In these instances, though preference shares are called share capital, it is argued that their economic substance is closer to debt. Like debt, they have no voting rights and the company has to pay a finance charge yearly (the dividend). Therefore, unless otherwise stated, it is assumed, in this book, that preference shares are a form of non-current liability and their dividend is a finance charge, albeit a non-taxable deduction.

Debentures/loan stock

These are often referred to in the press as **corporate bonds**. Debentures and loan stock are not shares and have no voting rights. They represent a loan to the company and carry a fixed rate of interest per annum based on the nominal value. For example, 10 per cent debentures with a nominal value of £100 each carry an annual interest of £10 per debenture. A company may make several issues of debentures or loan stock at different times, each of which can have a different rate of interest. Debenture holders are entitled to their interest before the preference and equity shareholders receive their dividends, and the interest must be paid even if there is a loss. The interest on debentures is thus referred to as a charge against profit, whereas dividends constitute an **appropriation of profit**.

In the event of a company going into liquidation, debenture holders are entitled to be repaid the nominal value of their debentures before the preference and equity shareholders. Such debentures are usually referred to as **unsecured** – although they rank before shareholders, they are not entitled to be repaid until after all other creditors. However, some issues of debentures are **secured** on certain of the company's assets by either a **fixed charge** or a **floating charge**. A fixed charge is usually on specified assets such as property, plant or vehicles, and means that the company cannot dispose of those assets. A floating charge is usually on assets such as inventory. In this case the company can sell the assets but must replace them with similar assets of an equivalent value.

When debentures are secured, an accountant or solicitor may be appointed by the company to act as a trustee for the debenture holders. It is the trustee's responsibility to ensure that the value of the assets is always sufficient to repay the debenture holders. If this is not the case or if the company may not be able to pay the annual interest on the debentures, the trustee may take legal possession of the assets, sell them and repay the debenture holders. Such drastic action usually results in the company going into liquidation.

Debentures and loan stock are usually repayable at some future date, which is specified when they are issued. This date is often several decades after they are issued. Should debenture holders wish to dispose of their debentures, they must find a buyer or sell them through a stock exchange such as the London Stock Exchange, or the Irish Stock Exchange, if the company has a quotation for the debentures.

The main advantage of debentures to a company is that the annual interest on debentures is an allowable charge against income for tax purposes.

A variation on debentures that has proved popular is **convertible loan stock/debentures**. These are debentures with a fixed annual rate of interest that also carry the right, at the holder's option, to convert them into a specified number of equity shares within a given time period, which is fixed when they are issued. The attraction of convertible loan stock is that the holder hopes to make a capital gain on conversion at some time in the future by virtue of the conversion rate being such that the equity shares can be acquired at an effective cost that is lower than the market price at the date of conversion. Suppose, for example, a company issues £100 convertible loan stock at a price of £108, the rate of conversion being

90 equity shares for every £100 loan stock. At the date of the issue, the equity shares are quoted on the stock exchange at a price of £1 each. If at some future date the market price of the shares rises to, say, £1.50, it is beneficial to convert, since the shares would effectively cost £1.20 each (i.e. £108 ÷ 90 shares) compared with a market price of £1.50. These could then be sold for 90 @ £1.50 = £135 to give a capital gain of £135 − £108 = £27. Where the effective cost is more than the current market price, it would not be beneficial to convert and so the debentures should be retained.

A summary of the characteristics of shares and loan stock is given in Figure 28.3. A more detailed summary of the different types of preference shares and loan stock is shown in Figure 28.4.

Figure 28.3

Equity shares	Preference shares	Loan stock/debentures
1 Owners of the company who are normally entitled to vote at a general meeting of the company's shareholders (e.g. to elect directors)	1 No voting rights	1 No voting rights
2 Receive a dividend the rate of which is decided annually by the company's directors. It varies each year depending on the profit and is an appropriation of profit	2 Receive a fixed rate of dividend each year which constitutes an appropriation of profit. Have priority over equity dividends	2 Receive a fixed rate of interest that constitutes a charge against income in computing the profit. Have priority over preference dividends
3 Last to be repaid the value of their shares in the event of the company going into liquidation. Also entitled to any surpluses/profits on liquidation	3 Repaid before the equity shareholders in the event of liquidation	3 Repaid before the equity and preference shareholders in the event of liquidation
4 Non-repayable except on the liquidation of the company	4 All but one particular type are non-repayable except on liquidation	4 Normally repayable after a fixed period of time
5 Rights specified in Articles of Association	5 Rights specified in Articles of Association	5 Rights specified in the terms of issue
6 Dividends non-deductible for tax purposes	6 Dividends non-deductible for tax purposes	6 Interest deductible for tax purposes

Summary of the characteristics of shares and loan stock

The Bank of Ireland's Annual Report provides a good example of the use of three of the different types of finance as shown in Real World Example 28.1. The bank has preference shares and equity shares in issue and also has redeemable (dated) and irredeemable (undated) debt. Subordinated means that they rank behind other sources of finance when it comes to repayment by the company, hence the equity and preference shares would be repaid before the loan capital is.

Figure 28.4

Types of preference shares

1 **Non-cumulative** – do not receive arrears of dividends.

2 **Cumulative** – if the dividend on these shares is not paid in any year, the holders are entitled to it in the next year that there are sufficient profits – before any other shareholder receives a dividend. The dividend becomes a liability of the company.

3 **Redeemable** – the only type of preference share that is repaid by the company after the expiration of a period specified when they were issued.

4 **Participating** – in addition to receiving a fixed annual rate of dividend, the holders are also entitled to a further dividend, which is related to profit levels and is similar in nature to a dividend on equity shares.

Issuing preference shares

Advantages: (a) non-repayable (except point 3 above); (b) the annual cost/dividend is known, thus facilitating planning; (c) in extreme circumstances the annual dividend can be waived.

Disadvantages: the dividends are not deductible for tax purposes.

Types of loan stock/debentures

1 **Unsecured/naked** – in the event of the company going into liquidation these are repaid before the equity and preference shareholders, but after other creditors.

2 **With a fixed charge** – secured on assets that the company cannot dispose of without the trustee for the debenture holders' permission. In the event of the security being in jeopardy or the company not paying the annual interest, the trustee can take legal possession of the asset(s), sell them and repay the debenture holders.

3 **With a floating charge** – the same as debentures with a fixed charge, except that the asset(s) on which the debentures are secured can be sold by the company, but must be replaced with asset(s) of an equivalent value.

4 **Convertible loan stock** – carry the right, at the holder's option, to convert them into equity shares within a given time period fixed when they are issued. The rate of conversion is usually such that the holder obtains equity shares at a price that is lower than the market price of the shares at the date of conversion.

Issuing loan stock/debentures

Advantages: (a) the annual cost/interest is known; (b) the interest is deductible for tax purposes.

Disadvantages: (a) they have to be repaid after the expiration of the period specified when they were issued; (b) the interest must be paid before the equity and preference shareholders receive any dividend. This can be a burden when the proceeds of the issue have been used to finance expansion that may not result in revenue during the early years or where there is a reduction in the annual profit or high interest rates.

Summary of the types of preference shares and loan stock

REAL WORLD EXAMPLE 28.1

Bank of Ireland

Capital management

Capital resources

The following table sets out the Group's capital resources.

	31 December 2013	Restated 31 December 2012
Group capital resources	**€m**	€m
Nominal amount outstanding of 2009 Preference Stock	1,300	1,837
Other equity (including equity reserves)	6,575	6,820
Stockholders' equity	7,875	8,657
Non-controlling interests – equity	(6)	(2)
Total equity	**7,869**	**8,655**
Undated subordinated loan capital	162	165
Dated subordinated loan capital	1,513	1,542
Total capital resources	**9,544**	**10,362**

Source: Bank of Ireland: Annual Report for the year ended 31 December 2013, available at http://www.bankofireland.com/fs/doc/wysiwyg/bank-of-ireland-annual-report-for-the-year-ended-31-december-2013.pdf, accessed May 2014.

28.6 The issue of shares and debentures

Shares can be, and usually are, issued (sold) by the company at a price in excess of their nominal value. The amount by which the issue price exceeds the nominal value is referred to as a **share premium**. In the case of a public limited company whose shares are listed on a stock exchange, the price at which the shares are quoted is usually different from both the nominal value and the issue price. The market price may be either above or below the issue price and the nominal value.

Debentures can be issued by the company at a price that is either greater or less than their nominal value. The latter is referred to as a **debenture discount**.

When shares and debentures are issued, the price may be payable by instalments. These consist of amounts payable: (a) on application; (b) on allotment/allocation of the shares by the company; and (c) any number of further instalments, referred to as **calls**.

Public limited companies offer shares, loan stock and debentures for sale to members of the public by means of a document known as a **prospectus**. This usually takes the form of a booklet sent by the company to anyone who expresses an interest in the issue. It may also consist of a full-page advertisement in a national newspaper, such as the *Financial Times*. The typical contents are outlined in Figure 28.5.

Figure 28.5

Prospectus contents

- The total number of shares the company wishes to issue and the minimum subscription (i.e. the smallest number for which the applicant can apply)
- The price of each share, stating the amounts payable on application, allotment and any calls
- Details of the rights attaching to all classes of shares
- A report by the company's auditors on the profits and dividends of the last five years, and the assets and liabilities at the end of the previous accounting year

Prospectus contents

28.7 Interim and final dividends

Most large companies pay both interim and final dividends on their equity and preference shares. An **interim dividend** is paid halfway through the accounting year, when the profit for the first six months is known. The amount is decided by the directors. The **final dividend** is additional to the interim dividend and, although it relates to the same accounting year, is paid just after the end of the year. This is because the final dividend has to be approved by the equity shareholders at the annual general meeting (AGM), and this is always held after the end of the accounting year when the profit for the year is known.

Interest on loan stock and debentures is also often paid in two instalments, one halfway through the accounting year and the other at the end of the year. However, the amount relating to the latter half of the year may be outstanding at the end of the accounting year.

28.8 The books of account and published financial statements

Companies are required by law to keep proper books of account, and to prepare a set of published financial statements each year (i.e. a statement of comprehensive income, a statement of financial position, a statement of cash flows and the related notes), which conform with the books of account. The 'books of account' need not necessarily actually be in the form of books, but there must be some set of records of the business transactions (e.g. a computerized system). A copy of the published financial statements must be sent to each equity shareholder and the Registrar of Companies, and are available for inspection by the general public at Companies House. Most public limited companies also publish a copy of their full final financial statements on their website.

Learning Activity 28.1

You have already been able to view the final financial statements of a large public limited company, Ryanair plc or Diageo plc. Using search engines, locate and view the full financial statements of five other large UK companies.

To fully appreciate the extent of standardization in company annual reports, prepare a table of the main contents as is found at the start of Ryanair plc's annual report (e.g. it includes directors' report, remuneration report, etc.). Put the contents in rows in the table. Turn to the contents of each of the other companies' annual reports and match them to the table you created from Ryanair plc's annual reports (you could create columns for each company and tick if the same report is included).

Then view the statement of comprehensive income and statement of financial position; note the similarity in presentation.

Compare the presentation of accounting information in the financial statements of these companies to that recommended by IAS 1. This is given as a pro forma presentation for companies in Chapter 1 (simple version) and again in more detail in Chapter 29.

28.9 The auditors' report

Most limited companies are required by law to have their books and annual final financial statements audited by an independent qualified accountant. The financial statements covered by the audit consist of the statement of comprehensive income, the statement of financial position, the statement of cash flows (covered in Chapter 30) and the notes to the financial statements. The auditor also has to ensure that the information reported within the annual report is consistent with the financial statements. Audit reporting is covered in Chapter 6, 'Auditing, Corporate Governance and Ethics'. It is important to appreciate that the auditor does not guarantee that fraud or errors have not taken place.

Learning Activity 28.2

Revisit the audit report to the members of Wm Morrison Supermarkets plc (this is reproduced in Chapter 6). Read the audit report again, highlighting the wording of the opinion, and the scope limitation, which specifically details the fact that an audit is not a guarantee that fraud and errors have not taken place.

28.10 Statutory books

Companies are obliged by law to maintain certain records relating to their capital and directors. These are known as **statutory books**. The required statutory books are outlined in Figure 28.6.

Companies are also required by law to submit an annual return to the Registrar of Companies each year, showing changes in the entries in the statutory books during that year. This information is available for inspection by the general public at Companies House. The statutory books (except the Minutes of Directors' Meetings) are also required by law to be available for inspection by members of the public at the company's registered office.

28.11 The annual general meeting

The law demands that companies hold an **annual general meeting** (AGM). This is a meeting of the equity shareholders at which they are entitled to vote on a number of matters. These include the following:

1 To receive and adopt the report of the directors and the published financial statements for the year. This provides shareholders with an opportunity to question the directors on the contents of the financial

Figure 28.6

Statutory books

- Register of Members, containing the name and address.
- Register of interests in shares if the company is a PLC.
- Register of Debenture Holders, containing the name, address and number of debentures/loan stock held by each debenture holder.
- Register of Directors and Company Secretary, stating the name, address and occupation of each.
- Register of Mortgages and Other Charges secured on the company's assets, showing the name and address of the lender and the amount of each loan.
- Minute Book of General Meetings of the company's equity shareholders, containing details of the proceedings and resolutions.
- Minute Book of Directors' Meetings, containing details of the resolutions.
- Memorandum and Articles of Association.

Statutory books

Note: A register of directors' interests is no longer required.

statements. The financial statements are usually adopted, but if shareholders think that the financial statements are inaccurate or misleading, they may vote not to accept the financial statements. If the shareholders vote not to adopt the financial statements, this does not mean that another set has to be prepared.

2 To declare and adopt a proposed final dividend for the year on the equity shares. The amount of the final dividend is proposed by the directors. The shareholders cannot propose some other figure. Thus, if the shareholders vote not to adopt the proposed dividend, they will receive no final dividend for that year.

3 To elect directors. This is a source of the shareholders' power, in that if they are dissatisfied with the financial statements, the dividend or the company's performance, they may vote not to re-elect the existing directors. Shareholders also have the right to nominate other people as directors.

4 To appoint auditors and fix their remuneration. The directors normally suggest a specific firm of auditors, and the power to fix their remuneration is often delegated to the directors by the shareholders at the AGM. Large companies usually appoint a reputable national or international firm of accountants to act as auditors.

REAL WORLD EXAMPLE 28.2

Shareholders becoming more active?

The Walker Report (2009) suggests that owners (shareholders) should protect their own interests by taking a more active role in ensuring that the company is governed appropriately. Shareholders *have* become more active and have used their power to exercise control over director decision-making. For example, in June 2010 at Tesco's Annual General Meeting 47 per cent of shareholders failed to back the remuneration report (Bowers and Finch, 2010). At a British Airways Annual General Meeting (in 2010) one disgruntled shareholder got a round of applause when he reportedly told the board '*you do seem to be feathering your own nests at the expense of the shareholders you are supposed to serve*' (*Guardian*, 2010).

Source: Author.

Summary

A limited company is a separate legal entity that has perpetual existence, and is managed by directors appointed by the members. The liability of its shareholders is limited to the nominal value of their shares. There are two classes of companies limited by shares, known as private limited companies (Ltd) and public limited companies (plc). A company's powers and the rights of the shareholders are contained in its Memorandum and Articles of Association.

Limited companies are financed predominantly by the issue of equity and preference shares, debentures and loan stock. These have a fixed face or nominal value but may be issued at a premium. Equity shares usually carry voting rights that give their holders the power to elect directors. They are also entitled to a share of the annual profits as a dividend that can vary each year. Equity shares are the last to be repaid in the event of the company going into liquidation. Preference shares are also entitled to an annual dividend but this is at a rate fixed at the time of issue. They may be cumulative, redeemable or participating. Preference shares are repaid before the equity shares in the event of liquidation. Most shares are non-repayable except on liquidation. All dividends are an appropriation of profits, and may include both an interim and final dividend. Debentures and loan stock represent a loan to the company. These carry a fixed rate of interest that is a charge against income. Debentures and loan stock are repaid before the shares in the event of liquidation, and may be secured by either a fixed or a floating charge on company assets.

Companies are required by law to keep proper records of their transactions and to prepare annual financial statements. In most cases these must be audited by independent qualified accountants who prepare a report expressing an opinion on whether the financial statements give a true and fair view of the profit and financial state of affairs. A copy of the published financial statements and auditors' report must be sent to all the equity shareholders. Companies are also required by law to maintain statutory books, and to hold an AGM. At the AGM the equity shareholders vote on whether to adopt: the published financial statements; the dividend proposed by the directors; and the election of directors and auditors.

Key terms and concepts

annual general meeting (AGM)	551	authorized/nominal share capital	543
appropriation of profit	546	bodies corporate	542
Articles of Association	544	bodies sole	542

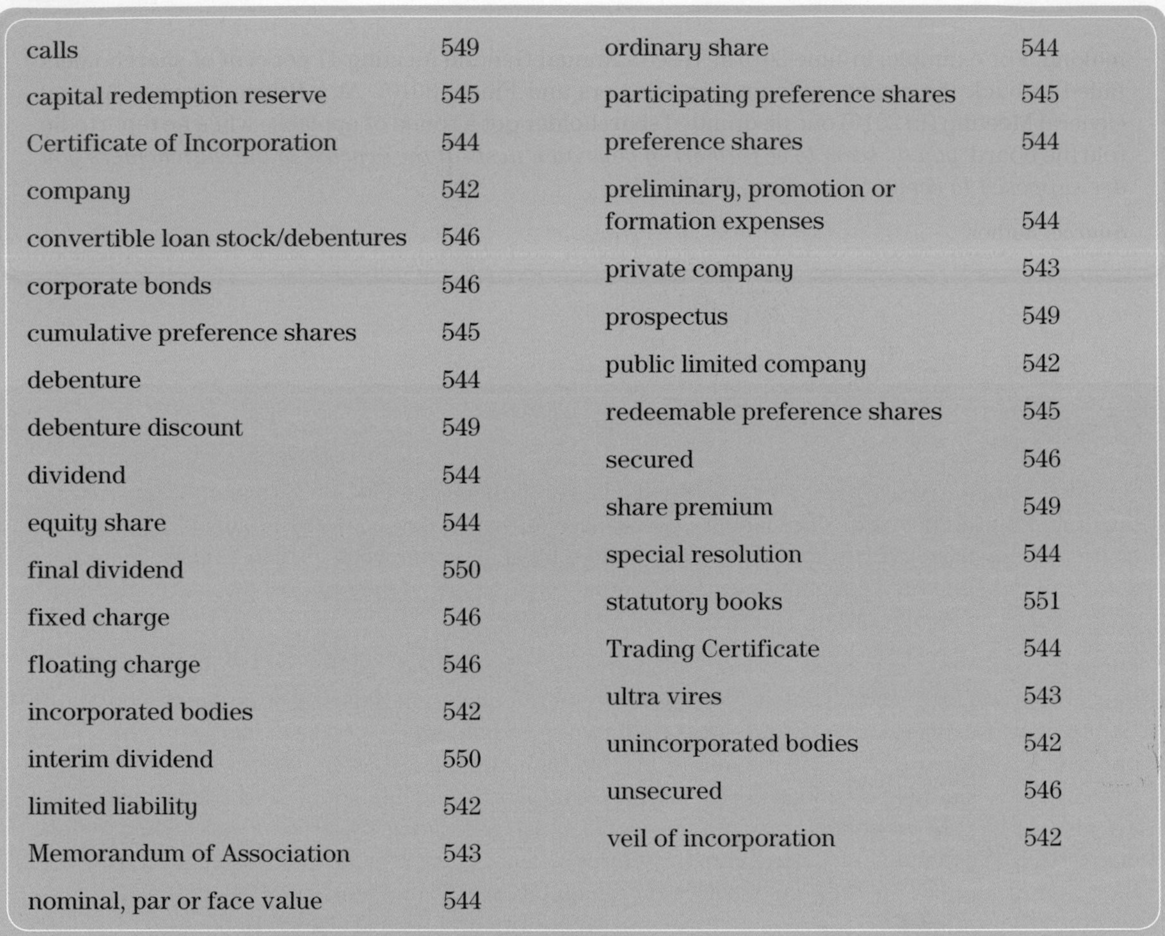

calls 549
capital redemption reserve 545
Certificate of Incorporation 544
company 542
convertible loan stock/debentures 546
corporate bonds 546
cumulative preference shares 545
debenture 544
debenture discount 549
dividend 544
equity share 544
final dividend 550
fixed charge 546
floating charge 546
incorporated bodies 542
interim dividend 550
limited liability 542
Memorandum of Association 543
nominal, par or face value 544
ordinary share 544
participating preference shares 545
preference shares 544
preliminary, promotion or formation expenses 544
private company 543
prospectus 549
public limited company 542
redeemable preference shares 545
secured 546
share premium 549
special resolution 544
statutory books 551
Trading Certificate 544
ultra vires 543
unincorporated bodies 542
unsecured 546
veil of incorporation 542

An asterisk after the question number indicates that there is a suggested answer in Appendix 2.

Review questions

connect

28.1* Describe the characteristics of companies limited by shares.

28.2 How does a public limited company differ from a private limited company?

28.3 Describe the contents of the Memorandum and Articles of Association. What are the purposes of these documents?

28.4 What are preliminary expenses?

28.5 Explain how each of the following arises:

a a share premium;

b a debenture discount.

28.6 Outline the main contents of a prospectus.

28.7 What is the difference between an interim dividend and a final dividend?

28.8 What is the auditors' report? How useful do you think this is in its present form and with its current legal standing in the UK?

28.9 Describe the contents of the statutory books of companies. What is the purpose of each of these books?

28.10 What is the annual general meeting of a company? Describe the proceedings at such a meeting.

28.11 Explain the main difference between a limited company and a sole trader.

28.12* Explain the main similarities and differences between equity shares, preference shares and debentures/loan stock.

28.13 Describe the different kinds of preference share.

Exercises

connect

28.14* Design a table highlighting the attributes of a preference share that might cause it to be regarded as being equity, and the attributes that are more likely to cause it to be regarded as debt. INTERMEDIATE

28.15 Rank the following stakeholders in terms of who would have priority when a company is settling claims of the stakeholders against it. Note, a rank of 1 means this stakeholder should be paid first. INTERMEDIATE

- debenture holders;
- loan stock holders;
- preference shareholders;
- trade supplier;
- equity shareholder;
- bank.

28.16 What is the difference between a fixed charge and a floating charge? INTERMEDIATE

28.17 Describe the main kinds of debenture loan stock. INTERMEDIATE

References

Bowers, S. and Finch, J. (2010) 'Shareholders Fight Back over Executive Pay and Bonuses', *Guardian*, 11 July, http://www.theguardian.com/business/2010/jul/11/shareholders-rebellion-expected-exec-pay, accessed September 2013.

Guardian (2010) 'BA Boss Willie Walsh Heckled at AGM over Strike Claims', *Guardian*, 13 July, http://www.theguardian.com/business/2010/jul/13ba-boss-willie-walsh-heckled-agm-strike-claims, accessed August 2014.

Walker Report (2009) *A Review of Corporate Governance in UK Banks and other Financial Industry Entities*, The Walker Review Secretariat, London, 16 July.

Chapter 29

The final financial statements of limited companies

Learning Objectives:

After reading this chapter you should be able to do the following:

1. Describe the main differences between the final financial statements of sole traders and companies, with particular reference to those arising from the latter being a separate legal entity.
2. Explain the nature and types of reserves.
3. Show the journal and ledger entries relating to the treatment of share issues, preliminary expenses, debenture interest, company income tax, dividends and transfers to reserves.
4. Demonstrate a basic understanding of the legal format of published company final financial statements and the main provisions of International Accounting Standard (IAS) 1 and International Financial Reporting Standards (IFRS) 5.
5. Prepare a simple set of final financial statements in a form suitable for publication and which complies with IAS (and with the Companies Act 2006).
6. Explain the nature and accounting treatment of discontinued operations, material items, prior period adjustments, events after the reporting period and contingencies.

—29.1 Introduction

The Companies Act 2006 requires companies to send their equity shareholders a copy of the annual final financial statements. These are contained in the annual report and referred to as **published accounts**. They include a statement of comprehensive income, a statement of financial position and related notes. Larger entities also have to provide a statement of cash flows. There are detailed legal requirements relating to the content and format of company final financial statements. The first two sections of this chapter deal with the preparation of company final financial statements prior to putting them in a form suitable for publication. The remaining sections describe some of the legal requirements relating to their presentation in published form.

—29.2 Published financial statements

The final financial statements of companies that are published and sent to equity shareholders in the annual report must be presented in a form that complies with the Companies Act 2006. The Companies Acts laid down specific guidance on formats: financial statements must comprise a profit or loss account (statement of comprehensive income) and a balance sheet (statement of financial position). The statement of financial position must portray a true and fair view of the state of the affairs of the entity at the end of the year and the statement of comprehensive income must portray a true and fair view of the profit or loss of the entity for the year.

In terms of format, financial statements now have to be prepared either in accordance with IFRSs, or in accordance with any guidance/provision laid down by the Secretary of State (s396 of the 2006 Companies Act). The latter currently allows presentation under two statutory instruments: the Small Companies and Groups (Accounts and Directors Report) Regulations 2008; and the Large and Medium Sized Companies and Groups (Accounts and Report) Regulations 2008. This book is focusing on IFRS; therefore, the formats presented in *IAS 1 – Presentation of Financial Statements* are utilized. The pro forma formats provided in IAS 1 include certain items with which the student will be unfamiliar and go beyond what is required at introductory level. The formats do not include disclosures for group entities as this is considered in Chapter 34, 'An Introduction to Consolidated Financial Statements', available online at www.mcgrawhill/textbooks/thomas. With the exception of deferred tax, the remainder should be understandable at this level. Deferred tax is not usually examined at this level. The financial statement formats are reproduced in full for reference purposes in Figures 29.1 and 29.2.

—29.3 Determining the profit or loss for the period

IAS 1 allows two options for presenting the profit or loss for an entity for a period of time (usually one year). The first option is to combine all income, whether recognized or not, into a statement called the 'statement of comprehensive income'. This has two parts: the first part deals with realized profits or losses and is called the statement of profit or loss for the period. This ranges from 'revenue' to 'profit for the year'. The second part of this statement is called 'statement of other comprehensive income'. The statement of comprehensive income is as shown in Figure 29.1.

The second option is to present this information in two statements, the 'statement of profit or loss' and the 'statement of other comprehensive income net of tax'. The IASB have stated a preference for a single statement approach and it is likely that published financial statements will use this format. Therefore, in this textbook the single statement approach is utilized.

Figure 29.1

Company name	
Statement of comprehensive income for the year ended 31 March 20X4	
	£
Revenue	XXX
Cost of sales	(XXX)
Gross profit	XXX
Other income	XX
Distribution costs	(XXX)
Administration expenses	(XXX)
Other expenses	(XXX)
Finance costs	(XXX)
Profit before tax	XX
Income tax expense	(XX)
Profit for the year	XX
Other comprehensive income	
Gains on property revaluation	XX
Other comprehensive income	XX
Total comprehensive income for the year	XXX

A pro forma of the layout of a statement of comprehensive income for a company

The contents of the statement of profit or loss for companies are the same as for sole traders and partnerships, with some exceptions. In arriving at the profit for the year, certain items not found in the financial statements of sole traders and partnerships are deducted.

- *Expenses*: These consist of directors' emoluments/remuneration (e.g. fees, salaries, pensions, compensation for loss of office), auditors' fees and expenses, interest on debentures, preliminary/formation/promotion expenses and taxation. Preliminary/formation/promotion expenses refers to the costs incurred in forming a company, such as registration fees, and preparation of the Memorandum and Articles of Association. Preliminary expenses must not be retained in the financial statements as an asset.
- *Income tax expense (tax on income)*: Since a company is a separate legal entity, it is liable for taxation on its annual profit, which takes the form of income tax. This is called **corporation tax** in the UK, but is disclosed as income tax (an international label for the taxation of companies). The income tax is deducted from the profit before tax to give profit for the year. Companies typically have to estimate the expected tax for the period and to pay this to the tax authorities within the year.

  The double entry for the income tax *payment* on the annual profit is:

Debit:	*Income tax expense account*	£'XXX	
Credit:	*Bank account*		£'XXX

Where this payment is insufficient to cover the tax charge for the period the double entry to record the outstanding income tax *charge* on the annual profit is:

Debit:	*Income tax expense account*	£'XXX	
Credit:	*Income tax liability account*		£'XXX

Where this payment is found to exceed the tax charge for the period the double entry to record the *prepaid* income tax on the annual profit is:

Debit:	*Income tax prepayment account*	£'XXX	
Credit:	*Income tax expense account*		£'XXX

- *Preference share dividends*: As mentioned previously, the economic substance of preference share capital is usually regarded as being a form of debt. Therefore, the dividends payable on preference share capital are included as a finance cost and treated as an expense of the company for accounting purposes. However, it is noted that dividends on preference shares are not an allowable expense for taxation purposes, therefore have to be added back in a tax computation to determine the taxable profit. Preference dividends comprise any interim dividend paid plus the final dividend proposed. The interim dividend paid will have been debited to the preference share dividends account in the ledger and thus shown in the trial balance. The final dividend may be outstanding at the end of the accounting year, in which case it is necessary to create an accrual in the preference dividends account and to show the amount owing on the statement of financial position as a current liability. The total of the interim and final dividends is then transferred from the preference share dividend account to the profit or loss account by debiting the profit or loss account with the yearly charge, with a corresponding credit in the preference share dividends account.

The key point at this stage is that the separate items that make up the cost of sales, distribution costs, administrative expenses, finance costs and other income should not be shown on the face of the statement of profit or loss. It is therefore necessary to first ascertain the total of each of these as workings. Note that distribution costs include selling expenses. Guidance on this was provided in Chapter 24, 'Financial Statements for Manufacturing Entities'.

Some of the items that are to be classified as either distribution costs or administrative expenses may be obvious from their descriptions (e.g. salespersons' commission, administrative salaries). Others are either less obvious or based on generally accepted conventions. In particular, distribution costs are usually taken to include advertising, carriage outwards, motor expenses of delivery vehicles (including depreciation, profit/losses on disposal), and any costs associated with a warehouse such as wages, repairs to and depreciation of forklift trucks and similar 'plant and machinery'. Administrative expenses include auditors' fees and expenses, irrecoverable receivables, changes in the allowance for irrecoverable receivables, discount received, directors' remuneration, office salaries, rent and rates, light and heat, telephone and postage, and so on. Finance costs include discount allowed and interest. Frequently, examination questions also require some items (such as those in the previous sentence) to be apportioned between distribution costs and administrative expenses. This is a relatively simple arithmetic exercise in which the amounts are divided between distribution costs and administrative expenses using the basis of apportionment (i.e. percentages for each) given in the question.

—29.4 The statement of financial position

IAS 1 – Presentation of Financial Statements (IASB, 2013a) does not specify a set format for the statement of financial position though separate guidance does offer a couple of options. The one adopted in this text is where the financial position of the entity is presented in the form of the accounting equation: *assets = capital + liabilities*. Assets and liabilities are analysed into current and non-current (see Figure 29.2).

Figure 29.2

Company name	
Statement of financial position as at 31 March 20X4	
ASSETS	£'000
Non-current assets	
Property, plant and equipment	XXX
Goodwill	XX
Other intangible assets	XX
Available-for-sale investments	XX
	XXX
Current assets	
Inventories	XX
Trade receivables	XX
Other current assets	XX
Cash and cash equivalents	XX
	XXX
Total assets	XXX
EQUITY AND LIABILITIES	
Equity attributable to owners	
Share capital	XXX
Retained earnings	XX
Other components of equity	XX
Total equity	XXX
Non-current liabilities	
Long-term borrowing	XX
Deferred tax	X
Long-term provisions	XX
Total non-current liabilities	XX
Current liabilities	
Trade and other payables	XX
Short-term borrowing	XX
Current portion of long-term borrowing	XX
Current tax payable	XX
Short-term provision	XX
Total current liabilities	XXX
Total liabilities	XXX
Total equity and liabilities	XXX

A pro forma of the layout of the financial statement for a company

The content of the statement of financial position of companies is the same as that of sole traders and partnerships, with the following exceptions:

1 The 'trade receivables' includes prepayments, and the 'trade and other payables' includes trade payables and accruals.

2 Property, plant and equipment includes the cost accounts for all tangible non-current assets and their provisions for depreciation.

3 The current liabilities of companies also usually include current tax payable (which is the income tax due on the annual profit – a portion of this is normally paid within the period with a balance still owing at the period end; this will be paid in the next period), current portions of long-term borrowing (debt capital that is repayable within one year), short-term provisions, accrued debenture interest and the outstanding final dividends on preference shares (the latter two will be included with the other finance charges outstanding at the year end – in *trade and other payables*).

4 The non-current liabilities of companies also often include the nominal value of loan stock, debentures and long-term provisions.

5 The financing of a company is categorized as being either equity capital or liabilities. Under the heading 'equity attributable to the owners of the parent', the equity share capital (typically not preference share capital), retained earnings and other components of equity are disclosed.

Where this format is followed exactly in answering examination questions, it will be necessary to prepare workings that clearly show how the amounts of, in particular, property, plant and equipment and trade and other payables (both current and long term) have been computed. This is discussed later in this chapter.

Equity attributable to the owners of the parent

Details about equity share capital should be provided, either on the face of the statement of financial position, the statement of changes in equity or in a note to the financial statements (IAS 1). Two items are usually disclosed as detailed in Figure 29.3.

Figure 29.3

Share capital disclosures

- **Allotted share capital:** This refers to the total nominal value of the number of shares that have actually been issued at the date of the statement of financial position. It is sometimes referred to as the issued share capital.
- **Called-up share capital:** This refers to that part of the allotted share capital that the company has required the equity shareholders to pay. It will consist of the amounts payable on application and allotment plus any calls that have been made by the company up to the date of the statement of financial position.
- A reconciliation of the number of shares outstanding at the start of the year and at the end of the year.
- Details of the rights, preferences and restrictions attaching to each class of share including restrictions on the distribution of dividends and the repayment of capital (restrictive covenants).
- IAS 1 also requires disclosure of the details of any shares held in the entity by the entity itself, or any of its subsidiaries or associates, and details of shares reserved for issue under options and contracts for the sale of shares, including terms and amounts.

Disclosures required for share capital

The figure for share capital that enters into the total of the statement of financial position under 'equity attributable to the owners of the parent' is the called-up equity share capital. This is frequently the same as the allotted share capital. However, if these are different, the allotted capital must be shown as a memorandum figure (i.e. not entering into the total of the statement of financial position). An example of the typical disclosures is as follows.

REAL WORLD EXAMPLE 29.1

Tesco Plc

	2013 *Ordinary shares of 5p each*		*2012* *Ordinary shares of 5p each*	
	Number	*£m*	*Number*	*£m*
Allotted, called up and fully paid:				
At beginning of year	8,031,812,445	402	8,046,468,092	402
Share options exercised	18,632,251	1	23,490,825	1
Share bonus awards issues	3,610,234	–	32,656,313	2
Shares issued for cancellation	–	–	(70,802,785)	(3)
At end of year	8,054,054,930	403	8,031,812,445	402

During the financial year, 19 million (2012: 23 million) ordinary shares of 5p each were issued in relation to share options for an aggregate consideration of £57m (2012: £69m).

During the financial year, 4 million (2012: 33 million) shares of 5p each were issued in relation to share bonus awards for an aggregate consideration of £0.2m (2012: £1.6m).

Between 24 February 2013 and 12 April 2013 options over 1,288,429 ordinary shares were exercised under the terms of the Savings-related Share Option Scheme (1981) and the Irish Savings-related Share Options Scheme (2000). Between 24 February 2013 and 12 April 2013 options over 2,741,490 ordinary shares have been exercised under the terms of the Executive Share Option Schemes (1994 and 1996) and the Discretionary Share Option Plan (2004).

As at 23 February 2013, the Directors were authorised to purchase up to a maximum in aggregate of 804.0 million (2012: 803.6 million) ordinary shares.

The holders of ordinary shares are entitled to receive dividends as declared from time to time and are entitled to one vote per share at general meetings of the Company.

Source: Tesco PLC Annual Report and Financial Statements 2013, p. 120, http://www.tescoplc.com/index.asp?pageid=540#/, accessed September 2013.

29.5 Accounting for share issues (limited companies)

In a limited company the accounting for share issues is typically straightforward. Shares are issued at a price, typically in excess of their nominal value and cash is received. The double entry to record this is:

Debit:	*Bank account (total amount received)*	£'XXX	
Credit:	*Share capital account (nominal value)*		£'XXX
Credit:	*Share premium account (excess value)*		£'XXX

An example showing the ledger entries is provided in Worked Example 29.1.

WORKED EXAMPLE 29.1

Roger Ltd has ordinary equity shares with a nominal value of £1 each. On 30 June 20X4 100,000 shares were issued to a new shareholder at £2.50 each. Roger currently has 50,000 shares in issue. These had been issued at par.

Required

Illustrate how this transaction would be recorded in the ledger accounts of Roger Ltd for the year ended 31 December 20X4.

The company will receive £250,000 in cash by bank transfer or by cheque. The shares are issued at a premium of £1.50 per share, making a total premium of £150,000. The double entry to record the transaction is as follows:

Debit:	*Bank account (total amount received)*	£250,000	
Credit:	*Share capital account (nominal value)*		£100,000
Credit:	*Share premium account (excess value)*		£150,000

And the ledger entries are:

Bank account			
Share capital a/c	100,000		
Share premium a/c	150,000	Balance c/d	250,000
	250,000		250,000
Balance b/d	250,000		

Share capital account			
		Balance b/d	50,000
Balance c/d	150,000	Bank a/c	100,000
	150,000		150,000
		Balance b/d	150,000

Share premium account			
Balance c/d	150,000	Bank a/c	150,000
	150,000		150,000
		Balance b/d	150,000

29.6 Accounting for share issues (public limited companies)

Share issues in plcs often involve very large sums of money and, given that a series of actions needs to be taken, are complex matters. A number of methods may be used to issue shares to the public, but the accounting procedures are similar and these can be presented most appropriately by considering an **offer for sale**. First, an offer is made to the public to apply for shares in the form of a prospectus. At this time the price to be paid for the share is set. This price may be the same as, or above, the par/nominal value of the share. Under the Companies Act shares may not be issued at below their par value.

On **application** it is usual for applicants to be required to send money representing part, but not all, of the price of the shares for which they apply (known as 'application money'). Once the closing date for applications is reached, the number of shares applied for must be compared with the number on offer. If applications are lower than the number on offer, the issue is undersubscribed and the company will be required either to cancel the offer and refund the application money or to call upon the underwriters to take up the remaining shares. If the issue is oversubscribed, then a basis for allotting shares must be established. Some applications may be rejected and the application money must be refunded; some may receive a reduced allocation and their excess application money used as further payment towards the price of the shares.

Having established the basis for allocation, shares can then be issued to those who are to get them – this is known as **allotment**. The balance of the price is, typically, payable in instalments, perhaps some on allotment (known as 'allotment money') and some **calls** at a later date (known as 'call money'). There may be more than one instalment, so there would be a first call, second call, etc. Anyone failing to pay a call is liable to *forfeit* their partly paid shares and, once forfeited, these may be *reissued* to others on terms agreed for this purpose. These are referred to as **forfeited shares** and **reissued shares**, respectively.

Learning Activity 29.1

Search the Web for notification in the financial press of an issue of shares to the public. Details of the issue terms are usually advertised. Read the terms of the issue carefully with particular reference to the amounts payable on application, allotment and any calls. Note also the relevant dates, dividend entitlement, etc.

The major stages of an issue of shares and the associated cash/bank (i.e. cash book effects) are summarized in Figure 29.4.

Figure 29.4

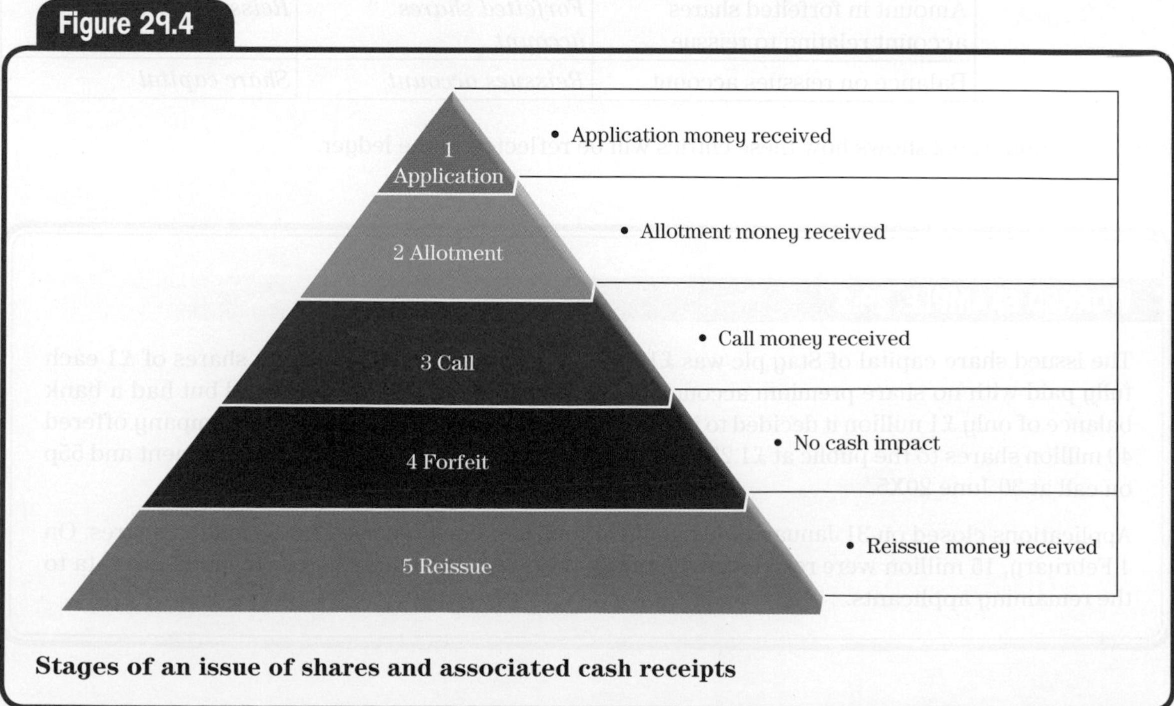

Stages of an issue of shares and associated cash receipts

The double entry to record all of these stages is as follows:

Stage	Transaction	Debit	Credit
1 Application	Money received	*Cash*	*Application and allotment account*
2 Allotment	Refund some application money	*Application and allotment account*	*Cash*
	Allotment money received	*Cash*	*Application and allotment account*
	Issue of shares partly paid	*Cash*	*Share capital*
		Application and allotment account	
	Share premium (if any)	*Application and allotment account*	*Share premium*
3 Call	Call made	*Call account*	*Share capital*
	Call money received	*Cash*	*Call account*
4 Forfeit	Called-up value of forfeited shares excluding share premium	*Share capital*	*Forfeited shares account*
	Premium included in amount called up (if any)	*Share premium*	*Forfeited shares account*
	Amount in the call account relating to arrears on forfeited shares	*Forfeited shares account*	*Call account*
5 Reissue	Nominal value of shares reissued called up	*Reissues account*	*Share capital*
	Money received	*Cash*	*Reissues account*
	Amount in forfeited shares account relating to reissue	*Forfeited shares account*	*Reissues account*
	Balance on reissues account	*Reissues account*	*Share capital*

Worked Example 29.2 shows how these entries will be reflected in the ledger.

WORKED EXAMPLE 29.2

The issued share capital of Stag plc was £100 million, being 100 million equity shares of £1 each fully paid with no share premium account. Since the company wished to expand but had a bank balance of only £1 million it decided to issue more shares. On 2 January 20X5 the company offered 40 million shares to the public at £1.25 each, payable 40p on application, 30p on allotment and 55p on call at 30 June 20X5.

Applications closed on 31 January when applications had been received for 65 million shares. On 4 February, 15 million were rejected and moneys returned, and allotments were made pro rata to the remaining applicants.

Note that since 50 million share applications were not rejected, allotments were on the basis of four shares 50p paid (i.e. 50 million @ 40p ÷ 40 million) for every five shares applied for; a balance of only 30p − (50p − 40p) = 20p per share will be payable on allotment.

The amounts due on allotment were received in full by 28 February.

By 4 July call money for 32 million shares had been received. The remaining shares (8 million) were forfeited. On 18 July 4 million forfeited shares were reissued at 75p each.

Required

a Show the ledger accounts to record the application and allotment of the share capital in the books of Stag plc.

b Show the ledger accounts to record the call and forfeiture of Stag plc's shares.

c Show the ledger accounts to record the reissue of the forfeited shares.

Workings

Application and allotment

Application money = 65 million @ 0.40 = £26 million

Refunded = 15 million @ £0.40 = £6 million

Allotment money = 40 million @ £0.20 = £8 million

Share premium per share = £1.25 − £1 = £0.25

Total share premium = 40 million @ £0.25 = £10 million

Nominal value of application and allotment = 40 million @ (£0.40 + £0.30 − £0.25) = £18 million.

Call

Nominal value of call = 40 million @ £0.55 = £22 million

Call money received = 32 million @ £0.55 = £17.6 million.

Forfeiture

Called-up value of forfeited shares excluding the share premium = 8 million @ £1 = £8 million

Premium included in the amount called up relating to forfeited shares = 8 million @ £0.25 = £2 million

Amount in call account relating to arrears on forfeited shares = 8 million @ £0.55 = £4.4 million.

Reissue

Reissue money received = 4 million @ £0.75 = £3 million

Nominal value of shares reissued called up = 4 million @ £1 = £4 million

Amount in forfeited shares account relating to reissue = 4 million @ (£0.40 + £0.30) = £2.8 million.

a The entries to record the application and allotment will appear in the ledger as shown below (all amounts in £ millions):

Bank					
2 Jan	Balance b/d	1	4 Feb	Appl'n and allotment	6
31 Jan	Appl'n and allotment	26		Balance c/d	29
28 Feb	Appl'n and allotment	8			
		35			35
	Balance b/d	29			

Application and allotment					
4 Feb	Bank	6	31 Jan	Bank	26
4 Feb	Share capital	18	28 Feb	Bank	8
4 Feb	Share premium	10			
		34			34

Share capital					
			2 Jan	Balance b/d	100
			4 Feb	Appl'n and allotment	18
					118

Share premium					
			4 Feb	Appl'n and allotment	10

b The call and forfeiture can then be entered in the ledger as follows:

Bank					
	Balance b/d	29.0			
4 July	Call	17.6			
		46.6			

Call					
30 June	Share capital	22.0	4 July	Bank	17.6
			4 July	Forfeited shares	4.4
		22.0			22.0

Share capital					
4 July	Forfeited shares	8.0		Balance b/d	118.0
	Balance c/d	132.0	30 June	Call	22.0
		140.0			140.0
				Balance b/d	132.0

Share premium					
4 July	Forfeited shares	2.0		Balance b/d	10.0
	Balance c/d	8.0			
		10.0			10.0
				Balance b/d	8.0

Forfeited shares					
4 July	Call	4.4	4 July	Share capital	8.0
	Balance c/d	5.6		Share premium	2.0
		10.0			10.0
				Balance b/d	5.6

c **Finally, the amounts can be entered for the reissue of 4 million shares, thus:**

Bank					
	Balance b/d	46.6			
18 July	Reissues	3.0			
		49.6			

Share capital					
				Balance b/d	132.0
			18 July	Reissues	4.0
					136.0

Share premium					
				Balance b/d	8.0
			18 July	Reissues	1.8
					9.8

Forfeited shares					
18 July	Reissues	2.8		Balance b/d	5.6
	Balance c/d	2.8			
		5.6			5.6
				Balance b/d	2.8

Reissues					
18 July	Share capital	4.0	18 July	Bank	3.0
18 July	Share premium	1.8	18 July	Forfeited shares	2.8
		5.8			5.8
				Balance b/d	2.8

Note

1 The balances can be interpreted thus: the share capital represents the original shares of £100 million plus 36 million shares issued at £1 par value. The forfeited shares account balance of £2.8 million is the remaining 4 million shares not reissued at the 70p application and allotment amounts. The share premium comprises £9 million, being the premium at 25p on the 36 million shares issued, plus the additional premium of £800,000 on the reissue; in the case of the 4 million reissued shares, 75p rather than just the call money of 55p was raised, giving 4 million × 20p = £800,000.

Further detail on the accounting for bonus issues, rights issues, purchase and redemption of shares is provided in the online Chapter 33, 'Changes in Share Capital'.

29.7 Other items in the statement of financial position

Reserves are difficult to define because they take a variety of forms. However, they usually represent some sort of gain or profit, and constitute part of a company's capital. Reserves may be of two types, either distributable or non-distributable. These are also frequently referred to as revenue and capital reserves, respectively. **Revenue/distributable reserves** are those that can be distributed to equity shareholders as dividends. These include any **retained earnings** and other revenue reserves/general reserves that are made up from transfers from retained earnings. These reserves consist of retained profits of the current and previous accounting years.

Capital/non-distributable reserves cannot be distributed as dividends. These may take a number of forms. The most common is the balance on a **share premium** account. This arises from shares having been issued at a price in excess of their nominal value. The excess is credited to a *share premium account*. Another non-distributable reserve is a **revaluation reserve**. This arises if a non-current asset (usually land and buildings) is revalued and shown in the statement of financial position at an amount that exceeds its historical cost. The excess is credited to a revaluation reserve account. A third form of non-distributable reserve is a **capital redemption reserve (CRR)**. This is formed by transfers from retained earnings. This is a statutory reserve, being identified in the Companies Act. It arises when shares are redeemed or purchased back from shareholders. Attention is given to the CRR and share repurchase in Chapter 33, 'Changes in Share Capital', available online at www.mcgraw-hill.uk/textbooks/thomas.

The total amount of reserves is added to the called-up share capital and shown on the statement of financial position as the '**Total equity attributable to owners**'. IAS 1 requires that the company discloses a description of the nature and purpose of each reserve within equity. This information is commonly provided for in a note.

29.8 Statement of changes in equity

Changes in equity reserves and gains and losses in equity that do not form part of the statement of profit or loss (but form part of the other statement of comprehensive income) impact on an additional statement, the **statement of changes in equity**. This statement focuses on reconciling the opening and closing equity position. It provides details on the movements in share capital, reserves, including the share premium account, any revaluation reserve, and the statement of profit or loss (i.e. retained earnings). Movements on these reserves will arise from the issue of shares at a premium, a surplus on the revaluation of non-current assets and the retained earnings for the year, respectively. A pro forma is provided in IAS 1, as shown in Figure 29.5.

Figure 29.5

Statement of changes in equity for the year ended 31 March 20X5					
	Share capital	***Other components of equity***	***Revaluation reserve***	***Retained earnings***	***Total***
	£'000	***£'000***	***£'000***	***£'000***	***£'000***
Balance at 1 April 20X4	XXX	XX	XX	XXX	XXX
Changes in accounting policy	–	–	–	(X)	(X)
Restated balance	XXX	XX	XX	XXX	XX
Changes in equity for 20X5					
Issue of share capital	XXX	–	–	–	XXX
Dividends	–	–		(XX)	(XX)
Total comprehensive income for the period	–	–	XX	XXX	XXX
Balance at 31 March 20X5	XXX	XX	XX	XXX	XXX

A pro forma of the layout of a statement of changes in equity

Items that do not form part of comprehensive income, but are changes in equity

Equity share dividends

These are *not* entered in the statement of comprehensive income. They are not an expense. They should be deducted from retained earnings in the statement of changes, and/or disclosed in a note to the financial statements. Equity dividends comprise an interim dividend paid plus a proposed final dividend. The interim dividend paid will have been debited to the equity share dividends account and thus shown in the trial balance. The proposed final dividend will always be outstanding at the end of the accounting year. However, it is *not* a liability at the statement of financial position date. It does not become a liability until it is agreed by the equity shareholders at the Annual General Meeting (AGM), at which point the financial statements are approved by the equity holders. Therefore, it is *not* an accrual. The amount proposed, however, is disclosed in a note to the financial statements. What is debited to **general reserves** will be the total amount of equity dividend paid in the year, which usually comprises *last year's proposed dividend and the interim dividend paid for this year.*

Transfers to other distributable reserves

The profit for the year is added to the *'retained earnings reserve account'*. Note that it is not transferred to the *capital account*, as in the case of sole traders. However, sometimes companies transfer a part of their retained earnings to a reserve account (though this is not as common now). The reason for this is to indicate to equity shareholders that the directors do not intend to distribute it as dividends but rather have earmarked it for some other use, such as expansion of the business by purchasing additional non-current assets. The entry for a transfer to a reserve is to:

Debit:	*Retained earnings account*	£'XXX	
Credit:	*Reserve account*		£'XXX

An illustration of the preparation of the final financial statements of limited companies is given in Worked Example 29.3.

WORKED EXAMPLE 29.3

The following is the trial balance of XYZ Ltd at 31 March 20X5:

	£	£
Equity shares of £1 each, fully paid		100,000
5% preference shares of £1 each, fully paid		20,000
8% debentures		30,000
Share premium		9,500
Revaluation reserve		10,000
General reserve		2,000
Retained profit from previous years		976
Motor vehicles at revaluation	210,000	
Depreciation on vehicles		19,000
Inventories	14,167	
Trade receivables/trade payables	11,000	8,012
Allowance for irrecoverable receivables		324
Bank balance	9,731	
Purchases/sales revenue	186,000	271,700
Wages and salaries	16,362	
General expenses	3,912	
Directors' remuneration	15,500	
Preliminary expenses	1,640	
Debenture interest	1,200	
Equity dividend paid (interim)	2,000	
	471,512	471,512

Additional information:

1 Inventory at 31 March 20X5 is valued at £23,487.

2 Depreciation of motor vehicles is to be provided at the rate of 10 per cent per annum on the fixed instalment method (straight-line method).

3 The allowance for irrecoverable receivables is to be made equal to 5 per cent of the trade receivables at 31 March 20X5.

4 Debenture interest of £1,200 and preference share dividends of £1,000 are outstanding at 31 March 20X5.

5 Provision is to be made for taxation on the year's profit amounting to £9,700.

6 There is a proposed final equity dividend of 5p per share.

7 The directors have decided to increase the general reserve by a further £3,000.

You are required to prepare in publishable form the statement of comprehensive income for the year ended 31 March 20X4, the statement of financial position at that date and the statement of changes in equity.

Workings

These could be done arithmetically but are shown below in the form of ledger accounts to help students understand the double entry.

Allowance for irrecoverable receivables			
Balance c/d	550	Balance b/d	324
(5% x £11,000)		Profit or loss a/c	226
	550		550
		Balance b/d	550

Provision for depreciation			
Balance c/d	40,000	Balance b/d	19,000
		Profit or loss a/c	21,000
	40,000		40,000
		Balance b/d	40,000

Debenture interest			
Bank	1,200	Profit or loss a/c	2,400
Accrual c/d	1,200		
	2,400		2,400
		Accrual b/d	1,200

Preference dividend			
Balance c/d	1,000	Profit or loss a/c	1,000
	1,000		1,000
		Balance b/d	1,000

Equity dividends			
Bank	2,000	Retained earnings	2,000
	2,000		2,000

In a note to the financial statements the amount of final dividend proposed (100,000 × 5p = £5,000) would be disclosed.

Income tax			
Closing payable c/d	9,700	Profit or loss a/c	9,700
		Opening payable c/d	9,700

General reserve			
Balance c/d	5,000	Balance b/d	2,000
		Retained earnings account	3,000
	5,000		5,000
		Balance b/d	5,000

XYZ Ltd

Statement of profit or loss for the year ended 31 March 20X5

	£
Revenue	271,700
Cost of sales	(176,680)
Gross profit	95,020
Distribution costs	(21,226)
Administration expenses	(35,774)
Other expenses	(1,640)
Finance costs	(3,400)
Profit before tax	32,980
Income tax expense	(9,700)
Profit for the year	23,280

XYZ Ltd

Statement of financial position as at 31 March 20X5

ASSETS	£
Non-current assets	
Property, plant and equipment	170,000
	170,000
Current assets	
Inventories	23,487
Trade receivables	10,450
Bank	9,731
	43,668
Total assets	213,668

EQUITY AND LIABILITIES	
Equity	
Share capital	100,000
Share premium	9,500
Retained earnings	19,256
General reserve	5,000
Revaluation reserve	10,000
Total equity	143,756
Non-current liabilities	
Preference shares	20,000
Debentures	30,000
Total non-current liabilities	50,000
Current liabilities	
Trade and other payables	10,212
Current tax payable	9,700
Total current liabilities	19,912
Total liabilities	69,912
Total equity and liabilities	213,668

Statement of changes in equity for the year ended 31 March 20X5

	Share capital	*Share premium*	*Revaluation reserve*	*General reserve*	*General earnings*	*Total*
	£	£	£	£	£	£
Balance at 1 April 20X4	100,000	9,500	10,000	2,000	976	122,476
Changes in equity for 20X5						
Equity dividends paid	–	–	–	–	(2,000)	(2,000)
Total comprehensive income for the period	–	–	–	–	23,280	23,280
Transfer to general reserve	–	–	–	3,000	(3,000)	–
Balance at 31 March 20X5	100,000	9,500	10,000	5,000	19,256	143,756

Notes

1 The cost of sales is calculated as follows:

	£
Inventories at 1 Apr 20X4	14,167
Add: Purchases	186,000
	200,167
Less: Inventories at 31 Mar 20X5	23,487
Cost of sales	176,680

2 Expenditure is allocated as follows:

	Distribution costs £	Administration expenses £	Other expenses £	Finance costs £
Wages and salaries		16,362		
General expenses		3,912		
Provision for depreciation	21,000			
Allowance for irrecoverable receivables	226			
Directors' remuneration		15,500		
Preliminary expenses			1,640	
Debenture interest				2,400
Preference dividend				1,000
Total	21,226	35,774	1,640	3,400

3 Property, plant and equipment (£170,000) comprises motor vehicles at valuation £210,000 less the amended provision for depreciation £40,000.

4 Trade receivables £10,450 is net of the amended year-end allowance for irrecoverable receivables (£11,000 – £550).

5 The amount of the proposed final dividend on equity shares is computed by multiplying the dividend per share by the number of shares that have been issued/allotted as shown in the trial balance; that is, 5p × (£100,000 ÷ £1) = £5,000. Sometimes the dividend per share is expressed as a percentage. In this case the percentage is applied to the nominal value of the issued/allotted equity share capital (e.g. 5% × £100,000 = £5,000). Where additional equity shares have been issued during the year, these are usually entitled to the full amount of any dividends that are declared after they have been allotted, such as the proposed final dividend for the year. In answering examination questions students should make this assumption unless told otherwise.

Note: The dividend on the new shares is *not* computed on a time basis because it is not a fixed annual rate.

6 It is important to ensure that the amounts entered in the statement of profit or loss in respect of debenture interest and preference share dividends are the amounts paid plus any that are outstanding at the end of the year. Sometimes in examination questions students are not told how much is outstanding or even that anything is outstanding. In these circumstances the total amount to be entered in the statement of profit or loss is ascertained using the information given in the question relating to the rates of debenture interest and preference dividends as follows:

8 per cent debentures £30,000

∴ Annual interest = 8% × £30,000 = £2,400.

5% preference shares £20,000

∴ Annual dividend = 5% × £20,000 = £1,000.

The amounts to be entered as current liabilities in the statement of financial position can then be found by subtracting the amounts paid as shown in the trial balance as follows:

Debenture interest outstanding = £2,400 – £1,200 = £1,200

Preference dividends outstanding = £1,000 – £0 = £1,000

Where debentures or preference shares have been issued during the year, the amount of interest/dividends that is entered in the statement of profit or loss needs to be calculated on a strict time basis.

7 It is generally accepted practice to prepare the final financial statements of companies in vertical form. However, the statement of profit or loss must also be prepared in the ledger by transferring all the balances on the income and expense accounts to this account in the normal manner. The retained earnings of the current year (after deducting any transfers to reserves) is added to the retained earnings reserve and the resulting figure is carried forward to the next year in the statement of financial position. This movement is shown in the statement of changes in equity. It should also be remembered that journal entries are supposed to be made for all the above entries in the ledger.

8 As explained earlier in this chapter, the law allows revenue reserves such as the general reserve and the balance in retained earnings at the end of the previous year to be distributed to shareholders as dividends. This can clearly be seen from the statement of changes in equity, wherein dividends are paid out of the available reserves, which is the current year addition and the balance brought forward.

9 As explained earlier in this chapter, preliminary expenses must not be retained in the financial statements as an asset. When they are incurred they should be posted to a *preliminary expenses account*, the double entry being:

Debit:	*Preliminary expenses account*	£'XXX	
Credit:	*Bank account*		£'XXX

There are two possible ways of dealing with these when the company first comes into operation. One is to charge them to the statement of profit or loss, as in the above worked example:

Debit:	*Profit or loss account (expense)*	£'XXX	
Credit:	*Preliminary expenses account*		£'XXX

However, this reduces the profit, which many companies wish to avoid if possible. The alternative, and preferred treatment, is to charge preliminary expenses against the balance on the *share premium account*, the double entry being:

Debit:	*Share premium account*	£'XXX	
Credit:	*Preliminary expenses account*		£'XXX

The amount entered on the statement of financial position in respect of the *share premium account* will then be the difference between the balance shown in the trial balance and the preliminary expenses; that is, the balance on the *share premium account* after entering the preliminary expenses.

10 Details on share capital will be presented in a note to the financial statements (this information can be provided on the face of the statement of financial position and in the statement of changes in equity).

Share capital	**20X5**
Allotted and fully paid	£
100,000 equity shares of £1 each	100
20,000 5% preference shares of £1 each	20
	120

29.9 Notes to the financial statements

The Companies Act 2006 and IASs also require several 'notes' to be attached to the published statement of comprehensive income and statement of financial position. Those most commonly examined at the introductory level comprise the following:

1 Changes in property, plant and equipment (and accumulated depreciation).

2 A note on allotted and fully paid share capital.

A note on the composition of property, plant and equipment and the related accumulated depreciation is necessary to provide detail on the single figure that is reported in the statement of financial position. In addition, this note must include the cost of acquisitions and disposals, any revaluation, diminution in value, the depreciation charges for the year and the accumulated depreciation on disposals. An illustration is given later in the book.

An illustration of the preparation of published financial statements including the above notes is given in Worked Example 29.4.

WORKED EXAMPLE 29.4

The following is the trial balance of Oasis Ltd as at 30 September 20X5:

	£'000	£'000
Called-up share capital		1,000
Share premium		500
Retained earnings 1 October 20X4		700
10% debentures (repayable 20X8)		600
Land and buildings at cost	2,500	
Buildings – accumulated depreciation		90
Motor vehicles – at cost	1,400	
– accumulated depreciation		470
Inventories	880	
Trade receivables/payables	420	360
Purchases/sales revenue	3,650	6,540
Warehouse wages	310	
Administrative salaries	190	
Sales staff salaries	70	
Irrecoverable receivables	20	
Directors' remuneration	280	
Advertising expenditure	60	
Motor expenses	230	
Light and heat	180	
Telephone and postage	80	
Bank overdraft		19
Discount allowed	9	
	10,279	10,279

Additional information:

1 The called-up share capital consists of 1 million equity shares of £1 each, fully paid.

2 Inventory at 30 September 20X5 was £740,000.

3 The auditors' fees and expenses for the year are expected to be £71,000.

4 The estimated tax charge on the company's profits for the year is £250,000.

5 The directors have proposed a final dividend on the equity shares in issue at 30 September 20X5 of 10p per share.

6 Depreciation is provided on a straight-line basis at 2 per cent per annum for buildings and 20 per cent per annum on vehicles. A full year's charge is made in the year of acquisition and none in the year of disposal.

7 The following items are to be apportioned between distribution costs and administrative expenses as below:

	Distribution	Administrative
Directors' remuneration	25%	75%
Light and heat, telephone and postage, buildings depreciation	40%	60%
Motor expenses, vehicle depreciation	50%	50%

8 The following items were unrecorded in the ledger on 30 September 20X5:

a The issue of 500,000 equity shares at £1.50 each fully paid on 31 August 20X5.

b The acquisition on credit of a motor vehicle costing £100,000 on 31 August 20X5.

c The sale on credit of a motor vehicle for £40,000 on 31 August 20X5. This cost £50,000 when purchased on 1 February 20X3.

9 The land included in the above trial balance cost £1m. The directors have decided to revalue this on 30 September 20X5 at £1.3m.

Required

Prepare the company's statement of comprehensive income for the year and a statement of financial position as at 30 September 20X5. This should be in a form suitable for publication and should include a statement of other comprehensive income for the period (net of tax), a statement of changes in equity and notes relating to changes in non-current assets and details of equity share capital.

Workings

1 Cost of sales

	£'000
Inventories at 1 Oct 20X4	880
Add: Purchases	3,650
	4,530
Less: Inventories at 30 Sep 20X5	740
Cost of sales	3,790

2 Depreciation

	£'000
a Buildings at cost (£2,500 – £1,000)	1,500
Depreciation expense (2% × £1,500)	30
Accumulated depreciation at 30 Sep 20X4 (£90 + £30)	120
b Motor vehicles at 1 Oct 20X5 at cost	1,400
Acquisition	100
	1,500
Disposal	(50)
Motor vehicles at 30 Sep 20X5 at cost	1,450
Disposal –	
Accumulated depreciation (2 × 20% × £50)	20
Book value (£50 – £20)	30
Profit on sale (£40 – £30)	10
Depreciation expense (20% × £1,450)	290
Accumulated depreciation at 30 Sep 20X5 (£470 – £20 + £290)	740

3 Distribution costs and administrative expenses

	Distribution	Administrative
	£'000	£'000
Warehouse wages	310	–
Administrative salaries	–	190
Sales staff salaries	70	–
Irrecoverable receivables	20	–
Directors' remuneration	70	210
Advertising	60	–
Motor expenses	115	115
Vehicle depreciation	145	145
Profit on sale vehicle	(5)	(5)
Light and heat	72	108
Telephone and postage	32	48
Buildings depreciation	12	18
Discount allowed	9	–
Auditors' fees and expenses	–	71
	910	900

4 Trade and other payables

	£'000
Trade payables	360
Auditor's fees and other expenses	71
Car dealer	100
Debenture interest (600 × 10%)	60
	591

Oasis Ltd	
Statement of profit or loss for the year ended 30 September 20X4	
	£'000
Sales revenue	6,540
Cost of sales	(3,790)
Gross profit	2,750
Distribution costs	(910)
Administrative expenses	(900)
Finance costs (10% × £600)	(60)
Profit before taxation	880
Income tax expense	(250)
Profit for the year	630

Oasis Ltd	
Statement of other comprehensive income for the year ended 30 September 20X4	
	£'000
Other comprehensive income for the year, after tax:	
Gain on property revaluation	300
Other comprehensive income for the year, net of tax	300

Oasis Ltd	
Statement of financial position as at 30 September 20X4	
ASSETS	£'000
Non-current assets	
Property, plant and equipment (Note 1)	3,390
Current assets	
Inventory	740
Trade receivables	420
Other current assets	40
Cash and cash equivalents (£750 – £19)	731
	1,931
Total assets	5,321
EQUITY AND LIABILITIES	
Equity	
Share capital	1,500
Share premium account	750
Revaluation reserve	300
Retained earnings	1,330
Total equity	3,880
Non-current liabilities	
Debenture loans	600
Total non-current liabilities	600

Current liabilities	
Trade and other payables	591
Current tax payable	250
Total current liabilities	841
Total assets less current liabilities	1,441
Total equity and reserves	5,321

Statement of changes in equity for Oasis Ltd for the year ended 30 September 20X5

	Share capital	Share premium	Revaluation reserve	Retained earnings	Total
	£'000	*£'000*	*£'000*	*£'000*	*£'000*
Balance at 1 October 20X4	1,000	500	–	700	2,200
Changes in equity for 20X5					
Total comprehensive income for the period	–	–	300	630	930
Issue of share capital	500	250	–	–	750
Balance at 30 September 20X5	1,500	750	300	1,330	3,880

Notes to the financial statements

1 Property, plant and equipment

	Land	Buildings	Vehicles	Total
Cost or valuation	*£'000*	*£'000*	*£'000*	*£'000*
At 1 Oct 20X4	1,000	1,500	1,400	3,900
Additions	–	–	100	100
Disposals	–	–	(50)	(50)
Revaluation	300	–	–	300
At 30 Sep 20X5	1,300	1,500	1,450	4,250
Accumulated depreciation				
At 1 Oct 20X4	–	90	470	560
Charge for year	–	30	290	320
Disposals	–	–	(20)	(20)
At 30 Sep 20X5	–	120	740	860
Net book value				
At 30 Sep 20X5	1,300	1,380	710	3,390
At 1 Oct 20X4	1,000	1,410	930	3,340

2 Dividends

The company proposed a final dividend of 10p per share (£100,000).

3 Share capital

	20X5
Allotted and fully paid	
1,000,000 equity shares of £1 each	1,000

Note

The alternative disclosure for total comprehensive income is to show one statement as follows:

Oasis Ltd	
Statement of comprehensive income for the year ended 30 September 20X5	
	£'000
Sales revenue	6,540
Cost of sales	(3,790)
Gross profit	2,750
Distribution costs	(910)
Administrative expenses	(900)
Finance costs (10% × £600)	(60)
Profit before taxation	880
Income tax expense	(250)
Profit for the year	630
Other comprehensive income	
Gains on property revaluation	300
Total comprehensive income for the year	960

29.10 Reporting financial performance

The Companies Act and various IFRSs require that certain items be shown separately in published financial statements or as notes to the financial statements. The most significant of these, which have not been discussed thus far, are explained below in brief. However, it is first necessary to appreciate why these items are required to be shown separately.

As explained in Chapter 3, one of the main objectives of published financial statements is to provide information that is useful in the evaluation of the performance of the reporting entity. One of the principal means of evaluating performance involves making comparisons over time, with other companies and/or forecasts. It may also involve making predictions of future profits, cash flows, and so on. Comparisons and predictions of profits are likely to be misleading where the profit includes gains and losses of a non-recurring nature such as relating to operations that have been discontinued. In order to facilitate comparisons and predictions, it is therefore desirable that the following items be disclosed separately in published company financial statements.

29.11 Non-current assets held for sale and discontinued operations

IFRS 5 – Non-current Assets Held for Sale and Discontinued Operations (IASB, 2013d) provides guidance on how to define and account for items, operations, and so on that are no longer being utilized for operational activities and are being either sold or abandoned. IFRS 5 defines a **discontinued operation** as:

❝*A component of an entity that either has been disposed of, or is classified as held for sale, and*

a *represents a separate major line of business or geographical area of operations;*

- **b** *is part of a single coordinated plan to dispose of a separate major line of business or geographical area of operations; or*
- **c** *is a subsidiary acquired exclusively with a view to resale.* ”

A non-current asset (or disposal group) should be classed as **held for sale** if

“*Its carrying amount will be recovered principally through a sale transaction rather than through continuing use' (IFRS 5). The following conditions have to be met before an asset/ disposal group can be classed as held for sale.*

- **a** *The asset, or disposal group must be available for immediate sale in its present condition and its sale must be highly probable.*
- **b** *Management should be actively trying to sell the asset, or disposal group.*
- **c** *The sale should be expected to be completed within one year, though may extend beyond this if events occur that are beyond the company's control.*
- **d** *It is unlikely that there will be any significant changes to the plan to sell the asset, or disposal group.* ”

Operations not satisfying all these conditions are classified as continuing.

When a non-current asset/disposal group is classed as discontinued or held for sale, then all the assets and liabilities are measured at the lower of carrying amount and fair value less costs to sell. These assets are not depreciated and are disclosed separately on the face of the statement of financial position. In addition, the results (income and expenditure) of the discontinued operation are shown separately from the results from continuing operations on the face of the statement of comprehensive income (net of tax). Though detail on the results of the discontinued activity can be provided on the face of the statement of comprehensive income, they are normally shown in one line, with detail being provided in a note to the financial statements. This note should include an analysis of revenue, expenses, pre-tax profit/loss, the related income tax expense and the gain/loss on the measurement of the discontinued/held for sale asset to fair value less costs to sell (and the related tax expense). The disclosure on the face of the statement of comprehensive income might be as shown in Figure 29.6.

29.12 Material/exceptional items

IAS 1 recommends that an entity should 'present additional line items, headings and subtotals in the statement of comprehensive income, when such presentation is relevant to an understanding of the entity's financial performance'. Therefore material items and items that are not material in size but are material in nature, should be disclosed separately (with the related tax impact) if non-disclosure would mislead the users of the financial statements. Examples of items that might be considered to impact on the users' ability to see trends in the performance of the company can include: profits or losses on the sale or termination of an operation; costs of a fundamental reorganization or restructuring having a material effect on the nature and focus of the reporting entity's operations; profits or losses on the disposal of non-current assets (all types); discontinued activities; one-off redundancy costs; abnormal losses caused by a natural disaster such as a fire, flood, earthquake – where not insured; irrecoverable receivables; inventory, property, plant or equipment write-downs and subsequent reversal of such write-downs; a legal claim against the company and any other provisions. These items are usually material and if included within, say, administration expenses, would lead users to misinterpret the performance of the company and its management team in the year.

Figure 29.6

Company name	
Statement of comprehensive income for the year ended 31 March 20X4	
	£
Revenue	XXX
Cost of sales	(XXX)
Gross profit	XXX
Other income	XX
Distribution costs	(XXX)
Administration expenses	(XXX)
Other expenses	(XXX)
Finance costs	(XXX)
Profit before tax	XX
Income tax expense	(XX)
Profit for the year from continuing activities	XX
Loss for the year from discontinuing activities	(X)
Profit for the year	XX
Other comprehensive income	
Gains on property revaluation	XX
Other comprehensive income	XX
Total comprehensive income for the year	XXX

A pro forma of the layout of a statement of comprehensive income for a company that has both continuing and discontinuing activities in the reporting period

Learning Activity 29.2

You should find it useful at this point to review the financial statements of three or four large plc companies to examine similarities between their presentation of information when there are acquisitions, discontinued activities and **exceptional items**. In addition, students may wish to attempt Exercise 29.24 or use the solution as an example of how to answer examination questions on this topic.

29.13 Prior period adjustments

IAS 8 – Accounting Policies, Changes in Accounting Estimates and Errors (IASB, 2013b) provides guidance on the most common events to cause a **prior period adjustment**, as summarized in Figure 29.7.

Figure 29.7

The correction of material prior period errors (omissions and misstatements)

Changes to accounting policies caused by the introduction of a new standard or the revision of a standard that does not contain specific transitional arrangements (these are normally arrangements that allow the change in accounting policy to be made prospectively)

Common causes of prior period adjustments

Changes in accounting estimates, such as the useful economic life of a non-current asset, do not require a prior period adjustment. The change is applied prospectively.

Errors found in current period financial statements should be corrected before the statements are signed off (finalized). Errors in respect of prior years should be corrected by restating the opening balances to what they really should be and by amending the comparatives. Indeed, under IAS 1, two years of adjusted comparatives for the statement of financial position only should be provided. When a prior period adjustment has taken place, a note to the financial statements should disclose the nature of the prior period error, the impact that the correction had to each line of the financial statements that it affected (including the tax implications) and the impact of the correction at the beginning of the earliest period presented – the opening retained earnings of the earliest statement of financial position disclosed.

Examples of prior period adjustments are rare but include a change in the method of inventory valuation, and an item previously recorded as a non-current asset that should have been treated as an expense (or vice versa). The most common prior period adjustment arises from the issue of an IFRS that would necessitate a company to change one of its accounting policies.

29.14 Events after the reporting period

These are defined in *IAS 10 – Events after the Reporting Period* (IASB, 2013c) as

> “*those events, both favourable and unfavourable, which occur between the statement of financial position date and the date on which the financial statements are authorised for issue.*”

The statement of financial position date is of course the end of an accounting year. The date on which the financial statements are authorized for issue is the date that they are approved by the board of directors, which is usually before they are approved by the equity shareholders. They are usually authorized for issue a month or two after the end of the accounting year, since it takes this amount of time to prepare the financial statements.

Events after the reporting period are classified as falling into one of two categories as follows:

1 **Adjusting events after the reporting period** are defined as events *'that provide additional evidence of conditions that existed at the end of the reporting period'*.

  Examples of adjusting events include any evidence of a permanent diminution in value of non-current assets, investments, inventories and work-in-progress, the insolvency of a credit customer, changes in the rates of taxation, amounts received or receivable in respect of an insurance claim outstanding at the reporting date, and errors or frauds which show that the financial statements were incorrect.

IAS 10 requires that a material adjusting event should be included in the financial statements. For example, inventories would be reduced to their net realizable value, an allowance created for an insolvent credit customer, errors corrected, and so on.

2 **Non-adjusting events after the reporting period** are defined as *'events that are indicative of conditions that arose after the reporting period'*. In other words, the conditions did not exist during the reporting period. Examples include mergers and acquisitions, reconstructions, issues of shares and debentures, purchases and sales of non-current assets and investments, losses on non-current assets and inventories resulting from a fire or flood, government action (e.g. nationalization), strikes and other labour disputes. Another common example is equity dividends. The final dividend for the year is agreed at a company's annual general meeting (AGM) – this takes place after the year end. Hence, the dividend amount is not confirmed until after the reporting period and therefore should not be accrued. The only time a dividend can be accrued is if it is agreed at a shareholder's meeting that takes place before the period end; however, this is rare. It is normal to agree the total dividend for the period at the AGM which always takes place post period end.

IAS 10 requires that details of material non-adjusting events be disclosed as a note to the financial statements. It is not appropriate to include non-adjusting events in the financial statements since they do not relate to conditions that existed during the reporting period. However, it is appropriate to disclose non-adjusting events as a note to ensure that financial statements are not misleading where there is some subsequent material event that affects a company's financial position. These details should refer to the nature of the event and provide an estimate of the financial effect, or a statement that such an estimate cannot be made.

29.15 Provisions and contingencies

These are the subject of *IAS 37 – Provisions, Contingent Liabilities and Contingent Assets* (IASB, 2013e). This defines a **provision** as *'a liability of uncertain timing or amount'*. A **liability** is *'a present obligation of a reporting entity arising from past events the settlement of which is expected to result in an outflow from the entity of economic benefits'*. A provision should be recognized in the financial statements when it meets the definition of a liability and a reliable estimate can be made of the amount of the obligation. The relevant double entry would be as follows:

Debit:	*Profit or loss account (the relevant expense)*	£'XXX	
Credit:	*The provision account (liability)*		£'XXX

The notes to the financial statements should disclose for each class of provision: (1) the carrying amount at the start and end of the period; (2) increases and decreases in the provision; (3) amounts charged against the provision; (4) a brief description of the nature of the obligation, and the expected timing of any resulting transfers of economic benefits; and (5) an indication of the uncertainties about the amount or timing of those transfers of economic benefits.

A **contingency** is a condition that exists at the end of the reporting period, where the outcome will be confirmed only on the occurrence, or non-occurrence, of one or more uncertain future events. A **contingent liability** can be possible or probable.

It can be

> “a possible *obligation that arises from past events and whose existence will be confirmed only by the occurrence or non-occurrence of one or more uncertain future events not wholly within the control of the entity*
>
> *[or]*
>
> a probable *obligation that arises from past events but is not recognised because: (i) it is not probable that an outflow of resources embodying economic benefits will be required to settle the obligation; or (ii) the amount of the obligation cannot be measured with sufficient reliability.*”

Contingent liabilities should not be recognized in the financial statements. They should be disclosed in a note to the financial statements, except when remote, wherein they should not form part of the financial statements.

A **contingent asset** is

> *a possible asset that arises from past events and whose existence will be confirmed only by the occurrence or non-occurrence of one or more uncertain future events not wholly within the control of the entity.*

Contingent assets should not be recognized in the financial statements. They should be disclosed in a note to the financial statements, except when remote, wherein they should not form part of the financial statements. The note should disclose a brief description of the nature of the contingent asset at the reporting date and, where practicable, an estimate of its financial effect. If the asset becomes certain, then it is not contingent, it is an asset which should be recognized.

Contingent liabilities and contingent assets should be reviewed regularly to determine if they are certain liabilities and assets, whereupon they are recognized.

Examples of contingent losses include possible liabilities arising from bills of exchange received that have been discounted, corporation tax disputes, failure by another party to pay a debt that the reporting entity has guaranteed, and a substantial legal claim against the company. The latter is the most common example and refers to where a legal action has been brought against the company but the court has not yet pronounced judgment regarding the company's innocence or guilt. This is often simply referred to as a pending legal action. It is regarded as a contingency because, whether or not a loss or liability will arise depends on the 'outcome' of the court case (i.e. an 'uncertain future event').

It should also be noted that although contingencies are conditions that exist at the end of the reporting period, their accounting treatment depends on information available up to the date on which the financial statements are approved by the board of directors.

A useful exercise at this point is to consider the similarities and differences between liabilities, provisions and contingent liabilities.

- A liability is a debt owed to a known party of a known certain amount.
- A provision is a known or highly probable future liability or loss, the amount and/or timing of which is uncertain (and thus has to be estimated).
- A contingent liability is uncertain with regard to its existence, timing and amount, and is thus only a possible liability.

Learning Activity 29.3

Examine Wm Morrison Supermarket plc's financial statements for items discussed in this chapter. List the purpose of any provisions made by them. Note any contingencies and related disclosures.

29.16 Accounting for debt

Accounting for debt can be quite complicated depending on the nature of the debt. At introductory level, it is assumed that debt is a liability which is known with certainty. As such the amortized cost of the debt, for example a bank loan, should be capitalized at the outset and the relevant interest and charges should be released using the effective annual interest rate (which may differ from the actual interest payments that have been contracted to be paid) over the period of the loan agreement. The accounting for debt is best explained using an example (Worked Example 29.5).

WORKED EXAMPLE 29.5

Magnetic Ltd requires £500,000 to finance a new investment and enters into a loan agreement with the bank, All First Bank. Magnetic Ltd has been a long-standing customer of the bank, and they inform the bank that they need the repayments to be over a five-year period and to be higher in the later stages of the loan agreement due to current liquidity issues. The bank agrees to provide the £500,000 on the following terms. An arrangement fee of £25,000 is payable, though this can be added to the capital portion of the loan; hence does not have to be paid for up-front. The bank requires Magnetic Ltd to pay interest on the loan of 1 per cent at the end of years 1 and 2, 7 per cent at the end of year 3, 14 per cent at the end of year 4 and 20 per cent at the end of year 5, with all of the capital (£500,000) being repaid on the first day of year 6. The effective annual interest rate is 6.731 per cent.

Required

a Determine the interest charge for each of the five years.

b Show the accounting entries (in journal form) for each of the five years.

c Prepare the ledger account for the financial liability (the loan) showing the movement and balance at the end of each period.

a Calculation of the interest charge in each of the five years.

Year	Opening balance	Interest charge (6.731%)	Repayment	Closing balance
1	£525,000	£35,340	(£5,000)	£555,340
2	£555,340	£37,380	(£5,000)	£587,720
3	£587,720	£39,560	(£35,000)	£592,280
4	£592,280	£39,870	(£70,000)	£562,150
5	£562,150	£37,850	(£100,000)	£500,000
6	£500,000	–	(£500,000)	–

There is rounding (to the nearest £10) in this table in the interest calculation.

b Initial recognition in year 1

Debit:	*Bank account*	£525,000	
Credit:	*Loan account*		£525,000

Journal to post the entries for the financial liability in year 1

Debit:	*Interest expense account*	£35,340	
Credit:	*Loan account*		£30,340
Credit:	*Bank account*		£5,000

Journal to post the entries for the financial liability in year 2

Debit:	*Interest expense account*	£37,380	
Credit:	*Loan account*		£32,380
Credit:	*Bank account*		£5,000

Journal to post the entries for the financial liability in year 3

Debit:	*Interest expense account*	£39,560	
Credit:	*Loan account*		£4,560
Credit:	*Bank account*		£35,000

Journal to post the entries for the financial liability in year 4

Debit:	*Interest expense account*	£39,870	
Credit:	*Loan account*	£30,130	
Credit:	*Bank account*		£70,000

Journal to post the entries for the financial liability in year 5

Debit:	*Interest expense account*	£37,850	
Credit:	*Loan account*	£62,150	
Credit:	*Bank account*		£100,000

Journal to post the entries for the financial liability in year 6

Debit:	*Loan account*	£500,000	
Credit:	*Bank account*		£500,000

c

Loan account

Year 1	*Details*	£	*Year 1*	*Details*	£
31 Dec	Bank account	5,000	1 Jan	Bank account	525,000
			31 Dec	P or L Interest	35,340
31 Dec	Balance c/d	555,340			
		560,340			560,340
			Year 2		
			1 Jan	Balance b/d	555,340
31 Dec	Bank account	5,000	31 Dec	P or L Interest	37,380
31 Dec	Balance c/d	587,720			
		592,720			592,720
			Year 3		
			1 Jan	Balance b/d	587,720
31 Dec	Bank account	35,000	31 Dec	P or L Interest	39,560
31 Dec	Balance c/d	592,280			
		627,280			627,280

			Year 4		
			1 Jan	Balance b/d	592,280
31 Dec	Bank account	70,000	31 Dec	P or L Interest	39,870
31 Dec	Balance c/d	562,150			
		632,150			632,150
			Year 5		
			1 Jan	Balance b/d	562,150
31 Dec	Bank account	100,000	31 Dec	P or L Interest	37,850
31 Dec	Balance c/d	500,000			
		600,000			600,000
			Year 6		
1 Jan	Bank account	500,000	1 Jan	Balance b/d	500,000
31 Dec	Balance c/d	–			
		500,000			500,000

Notes

1 The effective annual interest rate was calculated by the author using the internal rate of return, though can also be determined using a financial calculator. You will be given the effective annual interest rate in questions at introductory level.

2 The difference between the effective yearly interest charge and the amount that Magnetic Ltd pays to the bank either increases the financial liability owing, or reduces it, depending on whether the payment is less than or more than the interest charge.

Learning Activity 29.4

Visit the website of a large listed/quoted public limited company and find their latest annual report and financial statements. Examine the contents of the statement of comprehensive income (or equivalent named), statement of financial position and notes to the financial statements, paying particular attention to the items discussed in this chapter.

Summary

The statements of profit or loss of companies contain the same items as those of sole traders but in addition include others such as directors' remuneration, auditors' fees, interest on debentures/loan stock and company income tax. Many large companies will also have to provide a statement showing other comprehensive income in the period. Other comprehensive income includes unrealized gains on, for example, the revaluation of property, actuarial gains on pension funds and foreign exchange translation differences. At this level only revaluations are examined. The other comprehensive income can be disclosed as a stand-alone statement or it can form part of the main statement (called the 'statement of comprehensive income'). When the latter approach is adopted (i.e. a single statement), the whole statement is called the statement of comprehensive income for the period.

The statements of financial position of companies are similar to those of sole traders, except that the capital account is replaced by the called-up share capital and various reserves. These may be of two sorts, either revenue or capital reserves. Revenue reserves such as the retained earnings and general reserves can be distributed as dividends. Capital reserves such as the share premium, revaluation reserve and capital redemption reserve cannot be distributed as dividends. Loan stock and debentures are normally shown on the statement of financial position as non-current liabilities at their nominal value.

The final financial statements that are published and sent to equity shareholders must be presented in a form that complies with the Companies Act 2006 (i.e. contain a statement of profit or loss and a statement of financial position that show a true and fair view of the company's performance for the reporting period and its financial position at the reporting date), IAS 1 and other IFRSs. One of the main purposes of many accounting standards, particularly IAS 1, IAS 8, IAS 10 and IFRS 5, is to facilitate comparisons and predictions of performance by showing separately in the statement of comprehensive income any items of a non-recurring nature, showing items that belong to the period and adjusting comparatives when non-adjustment would diminish comparability. IFRS 5 requires an analysis of turnover, expenses, profit and tax on discontinued operations to be separately identifiable. In addition, all assets and liabilities of the asset/disposal group that are not classed as disposed, or as being held for sale, are separately disclosed and measured at the lower of realizable value and fair value less the costs of sale. Similarly, IAS 1 also states that some material items should be shown separately in published statements of comprehensive income. Comparisons and predictions may also be distorted where there are material adjustments applicable to prior periods arising from changes in accounting policies or the correction of fundamental errors. These are referred to as 'prior period adjustments'; and IAS 8 requires that the comparative figures for the preceding year be restated. Indeed, two years' adjusted comparatives of the statement of financial position should be disclosed.

In addition to showing certain items separately in final financial statements, the Companies Act 2006 and various accounting standards require notes to form part of the financial statements. These provide a more detailed breakdown, and in some cases, additional information about conditions prevailing at the reporting date, or events that have occurred since. Two examples are contingencies and events after the reporting date, respectively. IAS 10 states that material adjusting events after the reporting period should be provided for in financial statements and material non-adjusting events after the reporting date be disclosed as a note. Similarly, IAS 37 requires that probable material contingent liabilities be recognized in financial statements as provisions and probable material contingent gains be recognized as assets. Possible but not probable material contingent assets and liabilities should be disclosed in a note to the financial statements.

Key terms and concepts

adjusting events after the reporting period 586
allotment 565
allotted share capital 562
application 565
called-up share capital 562
calls 565
capital/non-distributable reserves 570
capital redemption reserve (CRR) 570
contingency 587
contingent asset 588
contingent liability 587

corporation tax	559	prior period adjustment	585
discontinued operation	583	provision	587
events after the reporting period	586	published accounts	558
exceptional items	585	reissued shares	565
forfeited shares	565	reserves	570
general reserve	571	retained earnings	570
held for sale	584	revaluation reserve	570
liability	587	revenue/distributable reserves	570
non-adjusting events after the reporting period	587	share premium	570
		statement of changes in equity	570
offer for sale	564	total equity attributable to owners	570

An asterisk after the question number indicates that there is a suggested answer in Appendix 2

Review questions

connect

29.1 Explain the difference between the allotted share capital and called-up share capital of companies.

29.2 Explain the difference between revenue/distributable reserves and capital/non-distributable reserves, giving three examples of the latter.

29.3 Explain the difference between a reserve and a provision.

29.4 Briefly explain the reason(s) for the separate disclosure of components of financial performance such as discontinued operations and exceptional items in published company financial statements.

29.5 a Explain the nature of acquisitions and discontinued operations.

b Briefly describe the treatment of each of these items in published company financial statements.

29.6 a Explain with examples the nature of exceptional items.

b Briefly describe the treatment of each of these items in published company financial statements.

29.7 a Explain with examples the nature of prior period adjustments.

b Briefly describe the treatment of prior period adjustments in published company financial statements.

29.8 a Explain with examples the nature of events after the reporting period.

b Describe the treatment of events after the reporting period in published company financial statements.

29.9 a Explain with examples the nature of contingent assets and contingent liabilities.

b Describe the treatment of contingent assets and liabilities in published company financial statements.

29.10 Explain with an example the difference between current liabilities, provisions and contingent liabilities.

29.11 Set out below is the capital section of a company's statement of financial position.

	31 Mar 20X5	31 Mar 20X4
	£'000	*£'000*
Equity share capital	140,000	140,000
Preference share capital	–	30,000
Share premium	20,000	20,000
Capital redemption reserve	30,000	–
Revaluation reserve	9,700	7,200
General reserve	27,000	20,000
Retained earnings	84,900	70,300
	311,600	287,500

You are required to explain the five different reserves that are shown on this company's statement of financial position, including in your answer the possible reasons for their existence.

(JMB)

Exercises

connect

BASIC

29.12 a The following items usually appear in the final financial statements of a limited company:

i interim dividend;

ii general reserve;

iii share premium account.

Required

An explanation of the meaning of each of the above terms.

b The following information has been obtained from the books of Drayfuss Ltd:

Retained earnings – 1 Apr 20X4	£355,000
General reserve	£105,000
Issued capital	80,000 8% £1 preference shares (fully paid)
	250,000 50p equity shares (fully paid)
Profit for the year to 31 Mar 20X5	£95,000

The preference share interim dividend of 4 per cent had been paid and the final dividend of 4 per cent had been proposed by the directors. No equity share interim dividend had been declared, but the directors proposed a final dividend of 15p per share. The directors agreed to transfer £150,000 to general reserve.

Required

Prepare the statement of changes in equity for the year ended 31 March 20X5. Ignore taxation.

(AEB, adapted)

INTERMEDIATE

29.13 The following information is available for Aston Products Plc as at 30 April 20X4.

	£'000
Allotted and called-up share capital	
Equity shares of 50p each	2,000
6% preference shares of £1 each	1,000
	3,000
Retained profits	950

There were no other reserves in the statement of financial position at 30 April 20X4.

You are given the following additional information relating to the year ended 30 April 20X5.

1 The company issued one million equity shares at a price of 75 pence each on 1 January 20X5.

2 The management have decided to revalue the land and buildings that cost £400,000 at a value of £600,000.

3 The profit before tax for the year ended 30 April 20X5 was £475,000.

4 The income tax charge on the profit for the year ended 30 April 20X5 was estimated to be £325,000.

5 There are no interim dividends during the year ended 30 April 20X5 but the directors have proposed a final dividend on the preference shares, and a dividend of 10 pence each on the equity shares.

6 The directors have agreed to transfer £350,000 to a general reserve at 30 April 20X5.

You are required to prepare in vertical form the statement of comprehensive income for the year ended 30 April 20X5, a statement of financial position extract at that date showing the composition of the equity and a statement of changes in equity.

INTERMEDIATE

29.14 Cold Heart plc, which has a turnover of £100 million and pre-tax profit of £10 million, has its financial statements drawn up on 30 June each year and at 30 June 20X5 the company's accountant is considering the items specified below.

1 The directors have decided that the change in trading prospects evident during the year means that the goodwill shown at 30 June 20X4 at £200,000 has no value at 30 June 20X5.

2 Research and development expenditure of £7 million has been incurred in the year, and has been written off due to the project being abandoned.

3 Unrealized revaluation surplus of £10 million that arose on the revaluation of the company's buildings during the year.

4 An allowance for irrecoverable receivables of £15 million on the collapse of the company's main customer during the year.

5 A loss of £1 million arising from the closure of the company's retailing activities.

You are required to classify each of the above items into one of the following categories, explaining the reasons for the classification:

a material item that requires separate disclosure on the face of the financial statements;

b transfer direct to reserves;

c discontinued operations.

(JMB, adapted)

INTERMEDIATE

29.15 *IAS 10 – Events after the Reporting Period* defines the treatment to be given to events arising after the statement of financial position date but before the financial statements are approved by the Board of Directors.

Required

a Define the terms 'adjusting events after the reporting period' and 'non-adjustment events after the reporting period' as they are used in IAS 10.

b Consider each of the following four events after the reporting period. If you think the event is an adjusting one, show exactly how items in the financial statements should be changed to allow for the event. If you think the event is non-adjusting, write a suitable disclosure note, including such details as you think fit. You may assume that all the amounts are material but that none is large enough to jeopardize the going concern status of the company.

i The company makes an issue of 100,000 shares that raises £180,000 shortly after the statement of financial position date.

ii A legal action brought against the company for breach of contract is decided, shortly after the reporting period, and as a result the company will have to pay costs and damages totalling £50,000. No provision has currently been made for this event. The breach of contract concerned occurred within the reporting period.

iii Inventory included in the financial statements at cost £28,000 was subsequently sold for £18,000.

iv A factory in use during the reporting period and valued at £250,000 was completely destroyed by fire. Only half of the value was covered by insurance. The insurance company has agreed to pay £125,000 under the company's policy.

(ACCA, adapted)

INTERMEDIATE

29.16 Your managing director is having a polite disagreement with the auditors on the subject of accounting for contingencies. Since the finance director is absent on sick leave, he has come to you for advice.

It appears that your firm is involved in four unrelated legal cases: P, Q, R and S. In case P the firm is suing for £10,000, in case Q the firm is suing for £20,000, in case R the firm is being sued for £30,000 and in case S the firm is being sued for £40,000. The firm has been advised by its expert and expensive lawyers that the chances of the firm winning each case are as follows:

Case	Percentage likelihood of winning
P	8
Q	92
R	8
S	92

Required

Write a memorandum to the managing director that:

1 explains why IAS 37 is relevant to these situations;

2 states the required accounting treatment for each of the four cases in the published financial statements;

3 gives journal entries for any necessary adjustments in the double-entry records;

INTERMEDIATE

4 suggests the contents of any Notes to the Financial Statements that are required by the IFRS;

5 briefly discusses whether IAS 37 leads to a satisfactory representation of the position.

(ACCA, adapted)

29.17 The trial balance of Norr Ltd at 31 December 20X4 appeared as follows:

	Debit	Credit
	£	£
Equity shares of £1 fully paid		50,000
Purchases	220,000	
Retained profit		30,000
Freehold property – cost	80,000	
Fixtures – cost	15,000	
Fixtures – accumulated depreciation		9,000
Rates	3,000	
Motor vehicles – cost	28,000	
Motor vehicles – accumulated depreciation		14,000
Insurance	2,000	
Inventories	40,000	
Trade receivables	30,000	
Trade payables		24,000
Sales revenue		310,000
Bank	12,100	
12% debentures		40,000
Debenture interest	2,400	
Wages and salaries	34,000	
Heat and light	4,100	
Professional fees	3,900	
General expenses	1,200	
Motor expenses	2,000	
Allowance for irrecoverable receivables		1,000
Irrecoverable receivables	300	
	478,000	478,000

Additional information

1 During the year a motor vehicle purchased on 31 March 20X1 for £8,000 was sold for £3,000. The sale proceeds were debited to the bank account and credited to the sales account, and no other entries have been made in the financial statements relating to this transaction.

2 Depreciation has not yet been provided for the year. The following rates are applied on the straight-line basis, with the assumption of no residual value:

Fixtures and fittings	10 per cent
Motor vehicles	20 per cent

The company's policy is to provide a full year's depreciation in the year of acquisition and no depreciation in the year of disposal.

3 Inventory at 31 December 20X4 amounted to £45,000.

4 Rates paid in advance amount to £400. Insurance includes £200 paid in advance. An electricity bill covering the quarter to 31 December 20X4 and amounting to £320 was not received until February 20X5. It is estimated that the audit fee for 20X4 will be £1,500. An accrual also needs to be made in relation to debenture interest.

5 A general allowance for irrecoverable receivables of 4 per cent of trade receivables is to be carried forward.

6 The directors propose a dividend of £10,000.

Required

a Prepare a statement of profit or loss and statement of financial position on the basis of the above information.

b Explain the meaning of the terms 'provision' and 'reserve', giving one example of each from the statement of financial position you have prepared.

(JMB, adapted)

ADVANCED

29.18 The Cirrus Co. Plc has the following balances on its books at 31 December 20X4.

	Debit	Credit
	£	£
50p equity shares		20,000
£1 (6%) preference shares		14,000
Purchases	240,000	
Sales revenue		310,000
Inventories at 1 January 20X4	20,000	
Directors' fees	6,000	
Retained earnings at 1 January 20X4		35,700
10% debentures		20,000
Debenture interest paid	1,000	
Discounts allowed	500	
Administrative expenses	18,400	
Sales staff salaries	18,500	
Selling and distribution expenses	4,000	
Heating and lighting	2,500	
Rent and rates	1,700	
Trade receivables	14,000	
Allowance for irrecoverable receivables at 1 January 20X4		300
Trade payables		9,700
Land and buildings at cost	65,000	
Vans at cost less depreciation	19,800	
Cash in hand	400	
Bank balance		2,100
	411,800	411,800

The following information is also given:

1 The inventory at 31 December 20X4 has been valued at £32,000. Further investigation reveals that this includes some items originally purchased for £3,000, which have been in inventory for a long time. They need modification, probably costing about £600, after which it is hoped they will be saleable for between £3,200 and £3,500. Other items, included in the total at their cost price of £5,000, have been sent to an agent and are still at his premises awaiting sale. It cost £200 for transport and insurance to get them to the agent's premises and this amount is included in the selling and distribution expenses.

2 The balance on the vans account (£19,800) is made up as follows:

	£
Vans at cost (as at 1 Jan 20X4)	30,000
Less: Provision for depreciation to 1 Jan 20X4	13,800
	16,200
Additions during 20X4 at cost	3,600
	19,800

Depreciation is provided at 25 per cent per annum on the diminishing balance method. The addition during the year was invoiced as follows:

	£
Recommended retail price	3,000
Signwriting on van	450
Undersealing	62
Petrol	16
Number plates	12
Licence (to 31 Dec 20X4)	60
	3,600

3 The directors, having sought the advice of an independent valuer, wish to revalue the land and buildings at £80,000.

4 The directors wish to make an allowance for irrecoverable receivables of 2.5 per cent of the balance of trade receivables at 31 December 20X4.

5 Rates prepaid at 31 December 20X4 amount to £400, and sales staff salaries owing at that date were £443.

6 The directors have proposed an equity dividend of 5p per share and the 6 per cent preference dividend.

7 Ignore value added tax (VAT).

Required

a Explain carefully the reason for the adjustments you have made in respect of points 1, 2 and 3 above.

b Prepare a statement of profit or loss for the year ended 31 December 20X4, a statement of financial position as at that date and the statement of changes in equity for the year.

c Briefly distinguish between your treatment of debenture interest and proposed dividends.

(ACCA, adapted)

INTERMEDIATE

29.19* The following is the trial balance of D. Cooper Ltd as at 30 September 20X4:

	Debit	Credit
	£	£
Allotted and called-up share capital:		
100,000 equity shares of £1 each		100,000
50,000 7% preference shares of 50p each		25,000
Leasehold premises at valuation	140,000	
Goodwill	20,000	
Plant and machinery (cost £80,000)	66,900	
Loose tools (cost £13,000)	9,100	
Inventory	9,400	
Trade receivables/trade payables	11,200	8,300
Bank overdraft		7,800
Purchases/sales revenue	49,700	135,250
Directors' salaries	22,000	
Rates	4,650	
Light and heat	3,830	
Plant hire	6,600	
Interest on debentures	1,200	
Preliminary expenses	1,270	
10% debentures		24,000
Allowance for irrecoverable receivables		910
Share premium		35,000
Retained earnings		2,580
Revenue reserve		10,200
Interim dividend on equity shares paid	3,250	
Audit fees	1,750	
Revaluation reserve		9,860
Irrecoverable receivables	700	
Listed investments	8,000	
Investment income		650
	359,550	359,550

Additional information

1 Inventory at 30 September 20X4 is valued at £13,480.

2 Rates include a payment of £2,300 for the six months from 1 July 20X4.

3 Depreciation on plant is 15 per cent per annum of cost and the loose tools were valued at £7,800 on 30 September 20X4. Goodwill did not suffer any diminution in value. The company does not depreciate its premises.

4 The allowance for irrecoverable receivables is to be adjusted to 10 per cent of the trade receivables at the end of the year.

5 The preference share dividends are outstanding at the end of the year and the last half year's interest on the debentures has not been paid.

6 The corporation tax on this year's profit is £6,370.

7 The directors propose to declare a final dividend on the equity shares of 13 pence per share and transfer £2,500 to revenue reserves.

You are required to prepare in publishable form a statement of profit or loss and a statement of changes in equity for the year ended 30 September 20X4, and a statement of financial position at that date.

29.20* The following is the trial balance of L. Johnson Ltd as at 31 December 20X5:

ADVANCED

	Debit	Credit
Issued and called-up capital:	£	£
80,000 equity shares		80,000
50,000 5% preference shares		50,000
Freehold buildings (at valuation)	137,000	
Motor vehicle (cost £35,000)	29,400	
Plant and machinery (cost £40,000)	32,950	
Development costs (cost £10,000)	6,600	
Interim dividend on preference shares	1,250	
Allowance for irrecoverable receivables		860
Wages and salaries	5,948	
Irrecoverable receivables	656	
Discount allowed/received	492	396
Goodwill	10,000	
Listed investments	4,873	
Purchases/sales revenue	78,493	130,846
Capital redemption reserve		9,000
Revaluation reserve		13,500
Formation expenses	250	
Directors' emoluments	13,000	
Returns inwards/outwards	1,629	1,834
Rates	596	
Dividends received		310
Retained earnings		3,126
Light and heat	1,028	
Audit fee	764	
Revenue reserve		8,400
Share premium		5,600
10% debentures		30,000
Inventories	9,436	
Trade receivables/trade payables	11,600	8,450
Bank overdraft		3,643
	345,965	345,965

Additional information

1 Corporation tax of £2,544 will be payable on the profit of 20X5.

2 Rates include £200 for the half year ended on 31 March 20X6.

3 Electricity for the quarter to 31 January 20X6 of £330 is not included in the trial balance.

4 The allowance for irrecoverable receivables is to be adjusted to 5 per cent of the trade receivables at the end of the year.

5 Annual depreciation on the reducing balance method is 25 per cent of vehicles, 20 per cent of plant and 10 per cent of development costs. The value of goodwill did not fall below the value recorded in the trial balance. The company does not depreciate buildings.

6 Formation expenses are to be written off against the share premium account.

7 Inventory at 31 December 20X5 was £12,456.

8 It is proposed to pay a final dividend on the equity shares of 6.25 pence per share.

9 The directors have decided to transfer £4,000 to the revenue reserve this year.

10 The debenture interest for the year and the final dividend on the preference shares are outstanding at the end of the year.

Required

Prepare in publishable form a statement of profit or loss and a statement of changes in equity for the year ended 31 December 20X5, and a statement of financial position at that date.

ADVANCED

29.21* The following is the trial balance of Oakwood Ltd as at 30 June 20X4:

	Debit	Credit
Allotted and called-up capital:	£	£
125,000 equity shares		125,000
60,000 5% preference shares		60,000
Freehold buildings at cost	165,000	
Development costs (cost £12,000)	5,400	
Goodwill	8,000	
Delivery vehicles (cost £28,000)	18,700	
Plant and machinery (cost £34,000)	31,900	
Listed investments	3,250	
10% debentures		20,000
Share premium		9,000
Revenue reserve		6,100
Interim dividend on equity shares	2,000	
Interim dividend on preference shares	1,500	
Allowance for irrecoverable receivables		730
Administrative salaries	6,370	
Irrecoverable receivables	740	
Discount allowed/received	290	440
Purchases/sales revenue	81,230	120,640
Audit fee	390	
Preliminary expenses	200	

Directors' remuneration	14,100	
Returns inwards/outwards	230	640
Carriage inwards	310	
Rates	600	
Interest received		410
Retained earnings		7,700
Light and heat	940	
Postage and telephone	870	
Inventories	8,760	
Trade receivables/trade payables	10,400	7,890
Bank overdraft		2,630
	361,180	361,180

Additional information

1 Corporation tax of £1,080 will be payable on the profit of this year.

2 Rates include a prepayment of £150.

3 Gas used in May and June 20X4 of £270 is not included in the trial balance.

4 Inventory at 30 June 20X4 was £11,680.

5 The allowance for irrecoverable receivables is to be adjusted to 5 per cent of trade receivables at 30 June 20X4.

6 Annual depreciation on the reducing balance method is 20 per cent of plant, 10 per cent of vehicles and 25 per cent of development costs. The value of goodwill did not fall below the value recorded in the trial balance. The company does not depreciate buildings.

7 Sales revenue includes goods on sale or return at 30 June 20X4 that cost £500 and were invoiced to credit customers at a price of £1,000.

8 Included in plant and machinery are consumable tools purchased during the year at a cost of £300.

9 The preliminary expenses are to be written off against the share premium account balance.

10 It is proposed to pay a final dividend on the equity shares of 3.2 pence per share.

11 The directors have decided to transfer £3,000 to the revenue reserve.

Required

Prepare in publishable form a statement of profit or loss and a statement of changes in equity for the year ended 30 June 20X4, and a statement of financial position at that date.

29.22 The trial balance of Harmonica Ltd at 31 December 20X4 is given below. ADVANCED

	Debit	Credit
	£'000	*£'000*
Purchases and sales revenue	18,000	28,600
Inventory at 1 January 20X4	4,500	
Warehouse wages	850	
Salespersons' salaries and commission	1,850	

Administrative salaries	3,070	
General administrative expenses	580	
General distribution expenses	490	
Directors' remuneration	870	
Debenture interest paid	100	
Dividends – interim dividend paid	40	
Non-current assets		
– cost	18,000	
– aggregate depreciation, 1 January 20X4		3,900
Trade receivables and payables	6,900	3,800
Allowance for irrecoverable receivables at 1/1/X4		200
Balance at bank		2,080
10% debentures (repayable 20X7)		1,000
Called-up share capital (£1 equity shares)		4,000
Share premium account		1,300
Retained earnings, 1 January 20X4		8,720
Suspense account (see note 3 below)		1,650
	55,250	55,250

Additional information

1 Closing inventory amounted to £5m.

2 A review of the trade receivables total of £6.9m showed that it was necessary to write off receivables totalling £0.4m, and that the allowance for irrecoverable receivables should be adjusted to 2 per cent of the remaining trade receivables.

3 Two transactions have been entered in the company's cash record and transferred to the suspense account shown in the trial balance. They are:

a The receipt of £1.5m from the issue of 500,000 £1 equity shares at a premium of £2 per share.

b The sale of some surplus plant. The plant had cost £1m and had a written-down value of £100,000. The sale proceeds of £150,000 have been credited to the suspense account but no other entries have been made.

4 Depreciation should be charged at 10 per cent per annum on cost at the end of the year and allocated 70 per cent to distribution costs and 30 per cent to administration.

5 The directors propose a final dividend of 4 pence per share on the shares in issue at the end of the year.

6 Accruals and prepayments still to be accounted for are:

	Prepayments	Accruals
	£'000	*£'000*
General administrative expenses	70	140
General distribution expenses	40	90
	110	230

7 Directors' remuneration is to be analysed between distribution costs and administrative expenses as follows:

	£'000
– distribution	300
– administration	570
	870

8 Ignore taxation.

Required

Prepare the company's statement of profit or loss and statement of changes in equity for the year ended 31 December 20X4, and statement of financial position as at 31 December 20X4 in a form suitable for publication. Notes to the financial statements are not required.

(ACCA adapted)

29.23 The following balances existed in the accounting records of Koppa Ltd at 31 December 20X4: ADVANCED

	£'000
Development costs capitalized, 1 January 20X4	180
Freehold land as revalued 31 December 20X4	2,200
Buildings – cost	900
– aggregate depreciation at 1 January 20X4	100
Office equipment – cost	260
– aggregate depreciation at 1 January 20X4	60
Motor vehicles – cost	200
– aggregate depreciation at 1 January 20X4	90
Trade receivables	1,360
Cash at bank	90
Trade payables	820
12% debentures (issued 20W7 and redeemable 20X9)	1,000
Called up share capital – equity shares of 50p each	1,000
Share premium account	500
Revaluation reserve	200
Retained earnings 1 January 20X4	1,272
Sales revenue	8,650
Purchases	5,010
Research and development expenditure for the year	162
Inventories 1 January 20X4	990
Distribution costs	460
Administrative expenses	1,560
Debenture interest	120
Interim dividend paid	200

In preparing the company's statement of comprehensive income and statement of financial position at 31 December 20X4 the following further information is relevant:

1 Inventory at 31 December 20X4 was £880,000.

2 Depreciation is to be provided for as follows:

Land	Nil
Buildings	2 per cent per annum on cost
Office equipment	20 per cent per annum, reducing balance basis
Motor vehicles	25 per cent per annum on cost

Depreciation on buildings and office equipment is all charged to administrative expenses. Depreciation on motor vehicles is to be split equally between distribution costs and administrative expenses.

3 The £180,000 total for development costs as at 1 January 20X4 relates to two projects:

	£'000
Project 836: completed project (balance being amortized over the period expected to benefit from it. Amount to be amortized in 20X4: £20,000)	82
Project 910: in progress	98
	180

4 The research and development expenditure for the year is made up of:

	£'000
Research expenditure	103
Development costs on Project 910 that continues to satisfy the requirements in IAS 38 for capitalization	59
	162

5 The freehold land had originally cost £2,000,000 and was revalued on 31 December 20X4.

6 Prepayments and accruals at 31 December 20X4 were:

	Prepayments	Accruals
	£'000	£'000
Administrative expenses	40	11
Sundry distribution costs	–	4

7 The share premium account balance arose as a result of the issue during 20X4 of 1,000,000 50p equity shares at £1 each. All shares qualify for the proposed final dividend to be provided for (see note below).

8 A final dividend of 20p per share is proposed.

Required

Prepare the company's statement of profit or loss, a statement of changes in equity for the year ended 31 December 20X4, and statement of financial position as at that date, in a form suitable for publication as far as the information provided permits. No notes are required. Ignore taxation.

(ACCA, adapted)

ADVANCED

29.24 Topaz Ltd makes up its financial statements regularly to 31 December each year. The company has operated for some years with four divisions; A, B, C and D, but on 30 June 20X4 Division B was sold for £8m, realizing a profit of £2.5m. During 20X4 there was a fundamental reorganization of Division C, the costs of which were £1.8m.

The trial balance of the company at 31 December 20X4 included the following balances:

	Division B		**Divisions A, C and D combined**	
	Debit	*Credit*	*Debit*	*Credit*
	£m	*£m*	*£m*	*£m*
Sales revenue		13		68
Costs of sales	8		41	
Distribution costs (including a bad debt of £1.9m – Division D)	1		6	
Administrative expenses	2		4	
Profit on sale of Division B		2.5		
Reorganization costs, Division C			1.8	
Interest on £10m (10% debenture stock) issued in 20W8			1	
Taxation			4.8	
Interim dividend paid			2	
Revaluation reserve				10

A final dividend of £4m is proposed.

The balance on the revaluation reserve relates to the company's freehold property and arose as follows:

	£m
Balance at 1 January 20X4	6
Revaluation during 20X4	4
Balance at 31 December 20X4 per trial balance	10

Required

a Prepare the statement of profit or loss of Topaz Ltd for the year ended 31 December 20X4, complying as far as possible with the provisions of the Companies Act 2006 and *IAS 1 – Presentation of Financial Statements.*

b Explain why the disclosures in the statement of comprehensive income required by IFRS 5 and IAS 1 improve the quality of information available to users of the financial statements.

(ACCA, adapted)

INTERMEDIATE

29.25 Marmite Ltd obtains a £750,000 loan which is repayable over the next five years. The bank has agreed to accept the following repayments. The repayments are varied to match to periods when Marmite Ltd expect to have surplus future cash flows which can be used to reduce their debt. The repayment schedule is as follows. Marmite Ltd is aware that interest is usually paid up front and has proposed the following split in the agreed repayments for the preparation of the financial statements.

	Interest	Capital	Total repayment
End of Year 1	£20,000	£10,000	£30,000
End of Year 2	£60,000	£40,000	£100,000
End of Year 3	£60,000	£90,000	£150,000
End of Year 4	£50,000	£250,000	£300,000
End of Year 5	£40,000	£360,000	£400,000

You are informed that the effective interest rate is 7.05 per cent.

Required

a Advise Marmite Ltd as to whether the above suggested charge for interest and capital is appropriate under International Financial Reporting Standards.

b Calculate the interest charge that is applicable in each of the five years (under IFRS).

c Prepare journals to post the transactions to the financial liability account (the loan account) for the five-year period.

d Prepare the ledger account for the loan for the five-year period.

References

International Accounting Standards Board (2013a) *International Accounting Standard 1 – Presentation of Financial Statements* (IASB).

International Accounting Standards Board (2013b) *International Accounting Standard 8 – Accounting Policies, Changes in Accounting Estimates and Errors* (IASB).

International Accounting Standards Board (2013c) *International Accounting Standard 10 – Events after the Reporting Period* (IASB).

International Accounting Standards Board (2013d) *International Financial Reporting Standard 5 – Non-current Assets Held for Sale and Discontinued Operations* (IASB).

International Accounting Standards Board (2013e) *International Accounting Standard 37 – Provisions, Contingent Liabilities and Contingent Assets* (IASB).

Chapter 30

Statement of cash flows

Learning Objectives:

After reading this chapter you should be able to do the following:

1. Explain the nature and purpose of a statement of cash flows.
2. Explain the advantages and limitations of a statement of cash flows.
3. Explain the relationship between a statement of cash flows and the statement of comprehensive income (statement of profit or loss) and the statement of financial position.
4. Prepare a simple statement of cash flows for sole traders and limited companies.
5. Prepare a classified statement of cash flows using the indirect method for sole traders and limited companies in accordance with International Accounting Standard (IAS) 7 (including notes).
6. Explain the nature of the groups of items and subtotals found in a typical classified statement of cash flows conforming to IAS 7.
7. Outline the main differences between the direct and indirect methods of preparing a statement of cash flows.

30.1 The nature and purpose of statements that analyse the cash flows of a business

In simple terms, the purpose of a **statement of cash flows** is to show the reasons for the change in the cash and bank balance over an accounting period. Another common way of expressing this is to show the manner in which cash has been generated and used (or where it has gone).

30.2 Relationship between the statement of cash flows, the statement of profit or loss and the statement of financial position

Statements of cash flows are intended to complement the statement of profit or loss (statement of comprehensive income) and statement of financial position. The main difference between a statement of cash flows and a statement of profit or loss lies in the observation that profit is not the same as the increase in cash over a given accounting period, but rather is one source of funds. The cash flow statement provides information on the cash that is obtained from operating activities, which are the core objects of an entity and which typically make up most of the entity's ongoing profits/returns. The statement of cash flows also shows the impact on cash of movements in assets, liabilities and capital over the accounting period (financing and investing activities). Therefore, it provides a link between the statement of financial position at the beginning of the period, the statement of profit or loss for the period, and the statement of financial position at the end of the period.

Learning Activity 30.1

List the sources and application of funds that you would expect from a company within the airline industry.

Obtain the financial statements of an airline company such as Ryanair, British Airways or easyJet and review the sources and applications of their cash flows as presented in the statement of cash flows. Note any differences.

30.3 Statements of cash flows – IAS 7

IAS 7 – Statement of Cash Flows (IASB, 2013) defines **cash flows** as *'inflows and outflows of cash and cash equivalents'*. **Cash** is defined as *'cash on hand and demand deposits'*. **Demand deposits** are repayable on demand if they can be withdrawn at any time without notice and without penalty, or if they are at maturity, or have a period of notice of not more than 24 hours or one working day has been agreed. **Cash equivalents** are *'short-term, highly liquid investments that are readily convertible to known amounts of cash and which are subject to an insignificant risk of changes in value'*.

IAS 7 requires the items that are normally contained in a statement of cash flows to be classified, grouped under three headings, the total of which are reconciled to the opening and closing cash position. A simple summarized format portraying the key cash flow information requirements is shown in Figure 30.1.

The detail making up each of the key classifications of cash (operating, investing and financing) are provided on the face of the statement of cash flows. These are now discussed in turn.

1 Cash flows from operating activities

Operating activities are the principal revenue-producing activities of the entity and other activities that are not investing or financial activities. **Cash flows from operating activities** are primarily made up of the net increase (or decrease) in cash that results from a company's normal trading activities.

Figure 30.1

B. Good	
Statement of cash flows for the year ended 31 March 20X5	
	£
Net cash from operating activities	XXX
Net cash from investing activities	XX
Net cash from financing activities	XX
Net cash increase in cash and cash equivalents	XXX
Cash and cash equivalents at 1/04/X4	X
Cash and cash equivalents at 31/03/X5	XXX

A summary of the key headings included in a statement of cash flows under IAS 7

Therefore, they generally result from the transactions and other events that enter into the determination of profit or loss.

'Cash flow from operating activities' is sometimes crudely referred to as 'cash profit', or more accurately 'operating profit computed on a cash basis'. Under IAS 7 the derivation of the 'cash flow from operating activities' is shown first in the statement of cash flows. It can be derived using two methods: the direct method or the indirect method. Both methods give the same figure for cash flows from operating activities.

The direct method

The **direct method** involves converting all the individual items in the statement of profit or loss from an accruals basis to a cash basis. It therefore shows the cash received from customers, cash paid to suppliers, and cash paid in wages and for operating expenses. This is all new information not shown elsewhere in the published financial statements. A pro forma (adapted from an example provided in the appendix to IAS 7) for calculating cash flows from operating activities using the direct method might look like the one shown in Figure 30.2.

The cash generated from operations is before payments to service finance (interest), tax and income from investments.

- *Taxation cash flows*. Tax on operating activities is included in this part of the statement of cash flows and is taken away from 'cash generated from operations' to give 'net cash from operating activities'. The tax cash flows refer to cash received and paid to taxation authorities in respect of a reporting entity's operating activities. If any portion of the tax expense were attributable to, for example, investing activities, then that tax cash flow would be included under that classification. It usually only relates to the income tax (corporation tax) paid on a company's annual profit. It does not include value added tax (VAT) or property taxes. In this introductory textbook, all taxation entries are assumed to arise from operating activities only, so will always be disclosed under the 'cash flows from operating activities' classification.
- *Interest and dividend cash flows*. There is some flexibility within IAS 7 in respect of interest paid, interest received, dividends paid and dividends received. The standard either allows these to be disclosed within 'net cash flows from operating activities' wherein they would be separately disclosed after the 'cash generated from operations' in the same manner as taxation in Figure 30.2. The argument for this treatment stems from the fact that interest and investment income form part of the determination of profit or loss and, therefore, should be disclosed here. Alternatively, interest and dividends paid in the period can be classified as a financing cash flow as these represent the cost of obtaining and

Figure 30.2

Cash flows from operating activities	£	£
Cash received from customers	XXX	
Cash paid to suppliers	(XXX)	
Cash paid to employees	(XX)	
Cash paid for other operating activities	(XX)	
Cash generated from operations	XXX	
Taxation paid	(XX)	
Net cash from operating activities		XXX

A pro forma for calculating cash flows from operating activities using the direct method

retaining finance such as loans and equity, while interest and dividends received in the period can be classified as cash inflows from investing activities as they are the returns from investment activities, not operating activities. In this textbook, for consistency purposes, the latter approach is adopted and all pro formas are portrayed in this manner.

The indirect method

The **indirect method** involves adjusting the profit or loss before tax for:

1 the effects of transactions of a non-cash nature, such as profits and losses on the disposal of non-current assets and movements in allowances (irrecoverable receivables);

2 deferrals or accruals of past or future operating cash receipts or payments (changes in working capital);

This is an area that typically causes confusion in students. Therefore some simplified explanations are provided. An increase in trade payables is a source of funds because the money that would otherwise have been used to pay these credit suppliers is available for other purposes (less has been paid out – therefore there is more in the bank). A decrease in trade receivables is also a source of funds as the credit customers have paid their accounts earlier, hence there will be more in the bank (assuming sales have remained constant or grown). Similarly, a decrease in inventory is a source of funds because the proceeds of the sale of inventory will mean that there is more money in the bank. Conversely, an increase in inventory is an application of funds since money will have been used to pay for it. Similarly, an increase in trade receivables is an application of funds, because allowing customers additional credit is like giving them a loan. A decrease in trade payables is also an application of funds, since money will have been paid out to them.

Items included in points 1 and 2 are purely accounting adjustments that arise from the preparation of the statement of profit or loss using an accruals/matching basis. They do not represent movements of cash funds. It is therefore necessary to adjust the figure of profit shown in the statement of profit or loss in respect of these items to arrive at the cash funds generated from operations that are entered in the statement of cash flows as shown in Figure 30.3.

3 In addition, items included in the statement of profit or loss that are regarded as being income from investing activities (dividends received) or payments to service finance (interest paid) are typically removed from the profit and disclosed separately as sources and applications of funds. Taxation is also removed for the same reason. Therefore, investment income is taken off the profit figure, and the interest and taxation expense are added back. This is illustrated in Worked Example 30.3 (page 621).

Hence the indirect method calculates the cash flows from operating activities by reconciling the reported profit before taxation in the statement of profit or loss with the cash movements in the assets and liabilities in the statement of financial position that are held for the purposes of generating profits through normal operating activities. A pro forma (adapted from an example provided in the appendix to IAS 7) is provided in Figure 30.3.

Figure 30.3

Cash flows from operating activities	£	£
Profit before taxation	XXX	
Adjustments for:		
Depreciation	XX	
Increase/(Decrease) in the allowance for irrecoverable receivables	XX/(XX)	
Investment income	(XX)	
Interest expense	XX	
(Profit)/Loss on sale of non-current asset	(XX)/XX	
Operating profit before working capital changes	XXX	
Increase in trade and other receivables	(XX)	
Decrease in inventories	XX	
Increase in trade and other payables	(XX)	
Cash generated from operations	XXX	
Income taxes paid	(XX)	
Net cash from operating activities		XXX

A pro forma for calculating cash flows from operating activities using the indirect method

IAS 7 permits use of either the direct or indirect method, though recommends use of the direct method. However, most UK and Irish companies use the indirect method. The reasons are probably because it can be prepared from the opening and closing statements of financial position and historically the indirect approach was promoted under UK GAAP. Therefore all the examples and exercises in this book are based on the indirect method.

The amount of cash flows arising from operating activities is a key indicator of the extent to which the operations of an entity have generated sufficient cash flows to repay loans, maintain the operating capability of the entity, pay dividends and make new investments without recourse to external sources of finance.

2 Cash flows from investing activities

According to IAS 7 (IASB, 2013) **investing activities** are '*the acquisition and disposal of non-current assets and other investments not included in cash equivalents*'. This refers to cash flows arising from the acquisition and disposal of non-current assets and the ownership of investments and payments to the providers of non-current finance and non-equity shareholders. In respect of investment in capital items, the entries in the statement of cash flows should distinguish between tangible non-current assets and intangible non-current assets. In each case the receipts from disposals must be shown separately from payments in respect of acquisitions.

In terms of investments in financial assets, cash flows comprise the purchase and sale of financial assets (which are not classed as cash equivalents) and interest and dividends received on these assets.

Examples of cash flows from investing activities that are included in IAS 7 are as follows:

- cash payments to acquire property, plant and equipment;
- cash payments to acquire intangible assets;
- cash payments to acquire other non-current assets;
- cash receipts from the sale of property, plant and equipment;
- cash receipts from the sale of intangible assets;
- cash receipts from the sale of other non-current assets;
- cash payments to acquire the equity or debt instruments of other entities (including joint ventures);
- cash receipts from the sale of equity or debt instruments in other entities (including joint ventures);
- cash advances or loans made to other parties (not banks);
- cash receipts from the repayment of advances and loans from other parties (not banks);
- interest received on investments;
- dividends received from investments.

The latter two examples are not included in the pro forma presented in the appendix of IAS 7 since two disclosure options are permissible, as previously discussed. The separate disclosure of cash flows arising from investing activities is important, because the cash flows represent the extent to which expenditures have been made for resources intended to generate future income and cash flows.

3 Cash flows from financing activities

According to IAS 7, **financing activities** are '*activities that result in changes in the size and composition of the contributed equity and borrowings of the entity*'. This encapsulates cash received and paid to external providers of finance in respect of the principal amounts of finance and the payments required to service these principal amounts (interest and dividends). The most common external providers of finance are equity shareholders, preference shareholders, loan stock holders and debenture holders.

Examples of **cash flows from financing activities** that are included in IAS 7 are as follows (IASB, 2013):

- cash proceeds from issuing shares;
- cash payments to owners to acquire, or redeem shares;
- cash proceeds from issuing debentures, loans, notes, bonds, mortgages and other short or long-term borrowing;
- cash repayments of amounts borrowed;
- cash payments by a lessee for the reduction of the outstanding liability relating to a finance lease;
- dividends paid on 'financing equity';
- interest paid on 'financing debt'.

The latter two examples are not included in the pro forma presented in IAS 7 since two disclosure options are permissible, as previously discussed.

The separate disclosure of cash flows from financial activities is important because it is useful in predicting claims on future cash flows by providers of capital to the entity.

30.4 Presentation: statement of cash flows

Now that each main part of the statement has been discussed, a complete pro forma is provided in Figure 30.4 for reference. This pro forma is adapted from an example provided in the appendix to IAS 7 (IASB, 2013).

Figure 30.4

Statement of cash flows (indirect method)		
Cash flows from operating activities	£	£
Profit before taxation	XXX	
Adjustments for:		
Depreciation	XX	
Loss on sale of non-current assets	XX	
Profit on sale of non-current assets	(X)	
Investment income	(XX)	
Finance charges	XX	
Operating profit before working capital changes	XXX	
Decrease in trade and other receivables	XX	
Increase in inventories	(XX)	
Decrease in trade and other payables	XX	
Cash generated from operations	XXX	
Income tax paid	(XX)	
Net cash from operating activities		XXX
Cash flows from investing activities		
Purchase of property, plant and equipment (note 1)	(XXX)	
Proceeds from sale of equipment	XX	
Interest received	XX	
Dividends received	XX	
Net cash used in investing activities		(XX)
Cash flows from financing activities		
Proceeds from the issue of share capital	XXX	
Proceeds from long-term borrowings	XX	
Payment of finance lease liabilities	(XX)	
Interest paid	(XX)	
Dividends paid	(XX)	
Net cash from financial activities		XX
Net increase in cash and cash equivalents		XXX
Cash and cash equivalents at beginning of period (note 2)		XX
Cash and cash equivalents at end of period (note 2)		XXX

A pro forma of the layout of a statement of cash flows (indirect method) under IAS 7 (IASB, 2013)

30.5 IAS 7 – statement of cash flows: sole traders and partnerships

The cash flows that are particular to sole traders will have to be analysed into cash flows from operating activities, cash flows from investing activities and cash flows from financing activities.

Figure 30.5

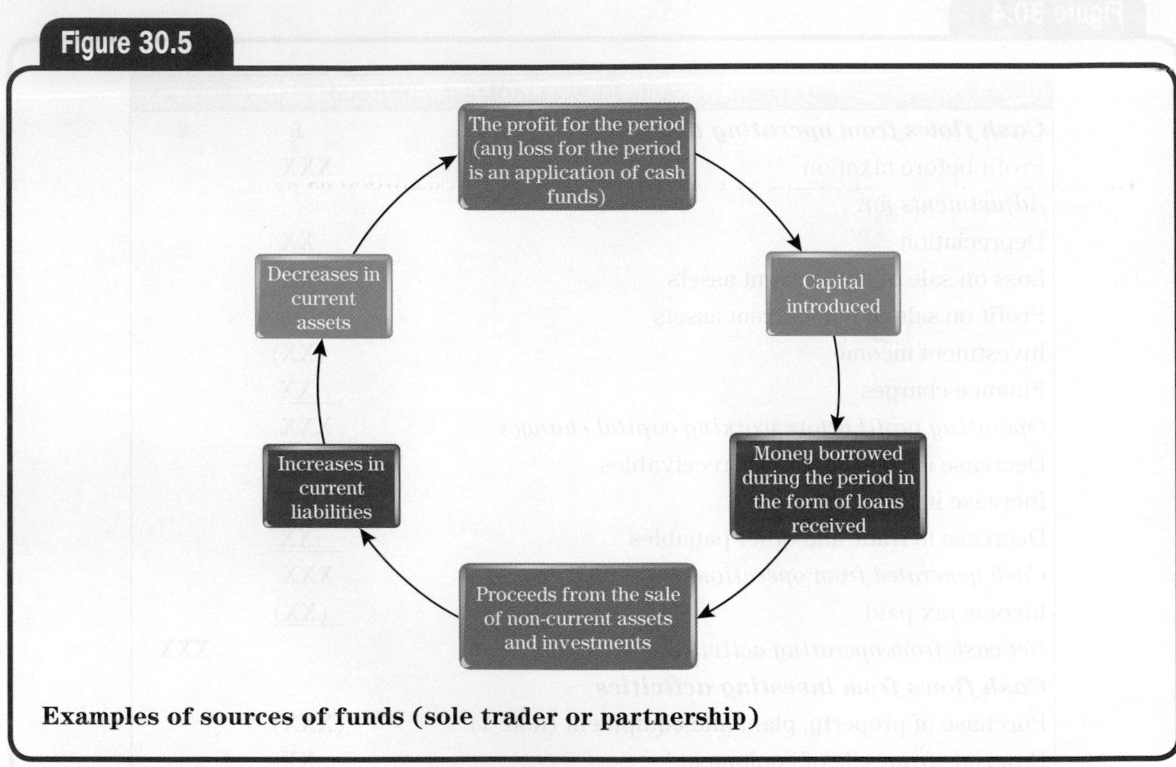

Examples of sources of funds (sole trader or partnership)

Figure 30.6

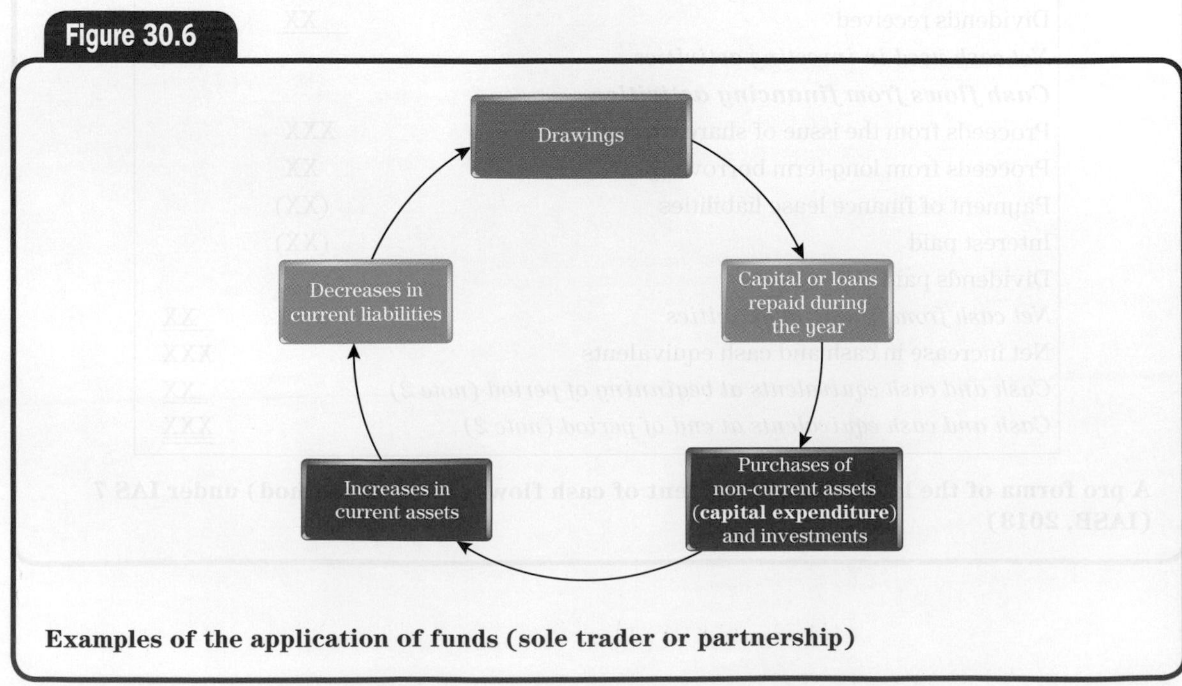

Examples of the application of funds (sole trader or partnership)

The main sources of cash funds in sole traders and partnerships are shown in Figure 30.5.

Applications of cash funds are highlighted in Figure 30.6.

A simple statement of cash flows for a sole trader, or a partnership, might consist of the above list of sources and applications of cash funds. This is illustrated in Worked Example 30.1.

WORKED EXAMPLE 30.1

The following are the statements of financial position of A. Cashwood as at 30 September 20X4 and 30 September 20X5:

	30 Sep 20X4	30 Sep 20X5
	£	£
ASSETS		
Non-current assets (at cost)	85,000	97,000
Current assets		
Inventory	13,600	10,800
Trade receivables	8,400	9,700
Cash and bank	2,500	3,600
	24,500	24,100
Total assets	109,500	121,100
EQUITY AND LIABILITIES		
Equity		
Capital at start of year	77,700	82,200
Add: Capital introduced	2,800	4,300
Profit for the year	21,600	34,200
	102,100	120,700
Less: Drawings	19,900	20,700
Capital at end of year	82,200	100,000
Non-current liabilities		
Bank loan	20,000	15,000
Total non-current liabilities	20,000	15,000
Current liabilities		
Trade payables	7,300	6,100
Total current liabilities	7,300	6,100
Total liabilities	27,300	21,100
Total equity and liabilities	109,500	121,100

Note

1 It is assumed that there is no interest or non-cash item in the statement of profit or loss.

2 Sole trader and partnership financial statements do not contain tax.

Required

Prepare a statement of cash flows for A. Cashwood in accordance with IAS 7 for the year ended 30 September 20X5.

A. Cashwood		
Statement of cash flows for the year ended 30 September 20X5		
Cash flows from operating activities	**£**	**£**
Profit before taxation	34,200	
Adjustments for:		
Decrease in trade payables (£7,300 – £6,100)	(1,200)	
Increase in trade receivables (£9,700 – £8,400)	(1,300)	
Decrease in inventory (£13,600 – £10,800)	2,800	
Net cash flow from operating activities		34,500
Cash flows from investing activities		
Purchase of property, plant and equipment (£97,000 – £85,000)	(12,000)	
Net cash used in investing activities		(12,000)
Cash flows from financing activities		
Repayment of bank loan (£20,000 – £15,000)	(5,000)	
Capital introduced	4,300	
Drawings	(20,700)	
Net cash used in financing activities		(21,400)
Net increase in cash and cash equivalents		1,100
Cash and cash equivalents at beginning of period (note 1)		2,500
Cash and cash equivalents at end of period (note 1)		3,600

1 Cash and cash equivalents

	At 1 Oct 20X4	At 30 Sept 20X5
	£	£
Cash at bank	2,500	3,600
Total cash and cash equivalents	2,500	3,600

30.6 IAS 7 – statement of cash flows: companies

The preparation of a statement of cash flows for companies involves some additional considerations as follows.

Sources of cash funds include:

1 the profit for the year before interest, taxation and income from investing activities, for example dividends received (this is because these items are shown separately as sources or applications of funds);

2 investment income: for example, dividends received;

3 capital introduced. This will comprise the amount received from any issues of shares and debentures during the year;

4 proceeds from the sale of non-current assets and investments;

5 increases in current liabilities;

6 decreases in current assets.

Applications of cash funds include:

1 income tax paid during the period;

2 servicing of finance: for example, interest paid or preference dividends;

3 instead of drawings, the amounts paid during the year in respect of equity share dividends. This will normally comprise the interim dividend plus the final dividend of the previous accounting year;

4 capital repaid will consist of any loans repaid during the year and any shares and debentures redeemed during the year;

5 purchases of non-current assets and investments;

6 increases in current assets;

7 decreases in current liabilities.

The requirements of IAS 7 with regard to the application of the indirect method of deriving the net cash inflow from operating activities are illustrated in Worked Example 30.2 and 30.3. The two questions use the same information; however, in the first the statement of profit or loss is not provided and has to be reconstructed from the movements in reserves. Many examination questions do not contain a statement of profit or loss, this can be quite tricky. In order to ascertain the profit before tax, it is therefore necessary to reconstruct the lower half of the statement of profit or loss. The income tax must either be given as a note in the question or included under current liabilities on the statement of financial position at the end of the current year. Details on both interim dividends paid and proposed dividend and their respective payment dates must be given as further information in the question. Transfers to reserves and the retained profit of the current year are found by calculating the difference between the amounts shown on the statement of financial position at the end of the current year and the end of the previous year for these items (see Worked Example 30.2).

WORKED EXAMPLE 30.2

The following are the statements of financial position of C. Flowers Ltd as at 31 March 20X4 and 31 March 20X5:

	31 Mar 20X4	31 Mar 20X5
ASSETS	£	£
Non-current assets		
Property, plant and equipment	127,000	113,000
Current assets		
Inventory	48,400	56,700
Trade receivables	37,400	34,800
Cash and bank	8,600	17,300
	94,400	108,800
Total assets	221,400	221,800

EQUITY AND LIABILITIES		
Equity		
Equity shares of £1 each	50,000	60,000
Share premium account	18,000	26,000
General reserve	6,400	9,600
Retained earnings	47,900	54,900
Total equity	122,300	150,500
Non-current liabilities		
10% debentures	52,000	20,000
Total non-current liabilities	52,000	20,000
Current liabilities		
Trade payables	31,400	32,800
Current tax payable	15,700	18,500
Total current liabilities	47,100	51,300
Total liabilities	99,100	71,300
Total equity and liabilities	221,400	221,800

Additional information

1 Non-current assets

	31 Mar 20X4	31 Mar 20X5
	£	£
Property, Plant and Equipment (at cost)	173,000	165,000
Aggregate depreciation	(46,000)	(52,000)
	127,000	113,000

2 Non-current assets that cost £8,000 and had a written-down value of £4,200 were disposed of during the year ended 31 March 20X5 at a price of £3,500. There were no other acquisitions or disposals of non-current assets during the year.

3 The total depreciation on non-current assets for the year was £9,800.

4 Trade receivables are made up of the following:

	31 Mar 20X4	31 Mar 20X5
	£	£
Trade receivables	39,100	36,200
Less: Allowance for irrecoverable receivables	(1,700)	(1,400)
	37,400	34,800

5 The current tax payable at 31 March 20X4 of £15,700 was paid in September 20X4.

6 The proposed final equity dividend for the year 31 March 20X5 is £29,600 (31 March 20X4 – £26,200). If approved at the AGM, the proposed final equity dividend will be paid for immediately. The AGM is usually three months after the reporting period end date. In addition, an interim equity dividend is paid each year in October. The interim dividend for 20X5 was £8,600 (20X4 – £5,500).

7 During the year 10,000 equity shares were issued at a price of £1.80 each.

Required

You are required to prepare a statement that reconciles the movement in retained earnings to profit before taxation for the year ended 31 March 20X5.

Solution

Computation of profit before interest and taxation	£	£
Increase in balance in retained earnings (£54,900 – £47,900)		7,000
Transfer to general reserve (£9,600 – £6,400)		3,200
Equity dividends paid –		
Proposed final (20X4)	26,200	
Interim (20X5)	8,600	34,800
Interest paid on debentures (£20,000 × 10%)		2,000
Income tax expense		18,500
Profit before taxation		65,500

Worked Example 30.3 follows on from Worked Example 30.2. However, in this instance the statement of profit or loss is provided, you do not need to reconstruct it. In addition, *investment income is introduced.* The statements of financial position and notes 1 to 7 from Worked Example 30.2 are relevant in this example also.

WORKED EXAMPLE 30.3

You are provided with the following statement of profit or loss for C. Flowers Ltd.

C. Flowers Ltd Statement of profit or loss for the year ended 31/03/X5	
	£
Revenue	1,429,000
Cost of sales	(1,143,200)
Gross profit	285,800
Other income	5,400
Distribution costs	(136,000)
Administration expenses	(89,700)
Finance costs	(2,000)
Profit before tax	63,500
Income tax expense	(18,500)
Profit for the year	45,000

Additional information

Other income represents interest received on investments made (this was not in Worked Example 30.2).

Required

Prepare the statement of cash flows for C. Flowers for the year ended 31/03/X5 using the information provided in this question and the information in Worked Example 30.2.

Solution

C. Flowers Ltd		
Statement of cash flows for the year ended 31 March 20X5		
	£	£
Cash flows from operating activities		
Profit before taxation	63,500	
Adjustments for:		
Depreciation charges	9,800	
Interest received	(5,400)	
Debenture interest paid	2,000	
Loss on sale of tangible non-current assets	700	
Allowance for irrecoverable receivables (decrease)	(300)	
Operating profit before working capital changes	70,300	
Increase in trade payables (£32,800 – £31,400)	1,400	
Decrease in trade receivables (£39,100 – £36,200)	2,900	
Increase in inventory (£56,700 – £48,400)	(8,300)	
Cash generated from operations	66,300	
Income taxes paid	(15,700)	
Net cash flow from operating activities		50,600
Cash flows from investing activities		
Interest received	5,400	
Receipts from sale of tangible non-current assets	3,500	
Net cash from investing activities		8,900
Cash flows from financing activities		
Issue of equity share capital (10,000 × £1.80)	18,000	
Repayment of debenture loan (£52,000 – £20,000)	(32,000)	
Debenture interest paid (£20,000 × 10%)	(2,000)	
Equity dividends paid (£26,200 + £8,600)	(34,800)	
Net cash used in financing activities		(50,800)
Net increase in cash and cash equivalents		8,700
Cash and cash equivalents at beginning of period		8,600
Cash and cash equivalents at end of period		17,300

Notes

1 The proceeds from the issue of shares of £18,000 (given in Additional information above) should correspond with the increase in *equity share capital* (£60,000 – £50,000) and *share premium account* (£26,000 – £18,000) shown in the statement of financial position (i.e. £10,000 + £8,000). The proceeds from an issue of shares are often not given in the Additional

information, and thus have to be calculated in terms of the increase in *share capital* and *share premium accounts*.

2 The details relating to the acquisition and disposal of non-current assets, and depreciation (given in additional information) should also correspond with the changes in non-current assets and aggregate depreciation shown in the statement of financial position as follows:

Non-current assets			
20X4	£	*20X5*	£
1 Apr Balance b/d	173,000	31 Mar Bank	3,500
		31 Mar Provision for depreciation (£8,000 – £4,200)	3,800
		31 Mar Loss on sale	700
		31 Mar Balance c/d	165,000
	173,000		173,000

Provision for depreciation			
20X5	£	20X4	£
31 Mar Non-current assets (£8,000 – £4,200)	3,800	1 Apr Balance b/d	46,000
		20X5	
31 Mar Balance c/d	52,000	31 Mar Depreciation expense	9,800
	55,800		55,800

The reason for understanding how the additional information in respect of issues of shares, non-current assets and depreciation corresponds with changes in the statement of financial position is that sometimes not all the information required is given as additional information (e.g. acquisitions of non-current assets, revaluations of assets). The student will then have to ascertain the missing information by examining the changes in the statement of financial positions. A useful way of doing this is in terms of the ledger accounts.

3 In the preparation of a statement of cash flows, investments held as a non-current asset are treated in the same way as other non-current assets. However, investments held as current assets that are repayable on demand are treated in the same way as cash and bank as per IAS 7 (discussed later). The amount of current asset investments is added to the cash and bank balance and shown on statements of cash flows as 'cash and cash equivalents'.

4 As covered in Chapter 29, dividends do not form part of the statement of profit or loss. They are distributions out of distributable profits (usually retained earnings). They are only taken out of distributable profits when paid, not when proposed. Proposed dividends are disclosed in the financial statements (not accrued). They are typically paid a couple of months after the reporting period end date – when they have been approved by shareholders at the company's AGM. Therefore, the movement in retained earnings between two reporting dates will have been affected by the dividends paid in the year. Dividends paid in the year will comprise the proposed dividend from the previous period (in this instance £26,200) and any interim dividends paid in the year (in this instance £8,600).

5 The income tax expense used to compute the profit before tax is the amount outstanding at the end of the current accounting year (£15,700) because this will have been deducted in arriving

at the retained earnings for the year of £3,600. It is often given as a note in examination questions, failing which the amount can be found as a current liability on the statement of financial position at the end of the *current* year. In contrast, the income tax shown as an application of funds (£18,500) is that outstanding at the end of the previous year since this will have been paid during the current year. It is often given as Additional information in examination questions, failing which, the amount can be found as a current liability on the statement of financial position at the end of the *previous* year.

6 The movement in the retained earnings reserves will also include (in addition to the profit for the year after tax) transfers made to other reserves. Therefore, when working back to find the profit before tax, it is necessary to add any transfer to reserves to the movement in the retained earnings balances as shown in the opening and closing statements of financial position. Details of transfers to other reserves may be found in Additional information; however, they can also be identified from increases in the reserve balances recorded in the opening and closing statements of financial position.

7 Dividends paid in the period might also be determined from the statement of changes in equity if provided in the examination question.

8 The current assets might include prepaid expenses and the current liabilities may include accrued expenses. These could be dealt with separately; however, an acceptable and more expedient treatment is simply to aggregate prepayments with trade receivables, and accruals with trade payables.

9 It is assumed that the interest on the debentures is paid within the year, therefore there is no opening or closing accruals and the statement of profit or loss charge is equal to the cash flow.

Though the statement of cash flows for C. Flowers Ltd (Worked Example 30.3) shows the cash flows for the current year and uses two columns to display subtotals and totals for each main heading, in practice many companies just show the figures in one column, but also show the comparatives (prior year figures). An example of the latter format can be seen in the financial statements of Tesco plc (2013) as shown in the following real world example.

REAL WORLD EXAMPLE 30.1

Tesco plc

Group cash flow statement

Year ended 23 February 2013	notes	52 weeks 2013 £m	52 weeks 2012 £m
Cash flows from operating activities			
Cash generated from operations	29	3,873	5,688
Interest paid		(457)	(531)
Corporation tax paid		(579)	(749)
Net cash from operating activities		2,837	4,408

Cash flows from investing activities			
Acquisition/(disposal) of subsidiaries, net of cash acquired/disposed		(72)	(65)
Proceeds from sale of joint ventures and associates		68	–
Proceeds from sale of property, plant and equipment, investment property and non-current assets classified as held for sale		1,351	1,141
Purchase of property, plant and equipment, investment property and non-current assets classified as held for sale		(2,619)	(3,374)
Purchase of intangible assets		(368)	(334)
Net (increase)/decrease in loans to joint ventures and associates		(43)	122
Investments in joint ventures and associates		(158)	(49)
Net proceeds from sale of/(investments in) short-term and other investments		1,427	(767)
Dividends received from joint ventures and associates		51	40
Interest received		85	103
Net cash used in investing activities		(278)	(3,183)
Cash flows from financing activities			
Proceeds from issue of ordinary share capital	27	57	69
Increase in borrowings		1,820	2,905
Repayment of borrowings		(3,022)	(2,720)
Repayment of obligations under finance leases		(32)	(45)
Purchase of non-controlling interests		(4)	(89)
Dividends paid to equity owners	8	(1,184)	(1,180)
Dividends paid to non-controlling interests		–	(3)
Own shares purchased		–	(303)
Net cash from financing activities		(2,365)	(1,366)
Net (decrease)/increase in cash and cash equivalents		194	(141)
Cash and cash equivalents at beginning of year		2,311	2,428
Effect of foreign exchange rate changes		26	24
Cash and cash equivalents including cash held in disposal group at the end of the year		2,531	2,311
Cash held in disposal group	7	(19)	(6)
Cash and cash equivalents at end of year	18	2,512	2,305

Reconciliation of net cash flow to movement in net debt note

Year ended 23 February 2013	**note**	**52 weeks 2013 £m**	**52 weeks 2012 £m**
Net increase/(decrease) in cash and cash equivalents		194	(141)
Elimination of net (increase)/decrease in Tesco Bank cash and cash equivalents		(475)	126
Investment in Tesco Bank		(45)	(112)
Debt acquired on acquisition		(1)	(98)
Net cash outflow to repay debt and lease financing		1,589	262

Dividend received from Tesco Bank		105	100
(Decrease)/increase in short-term investments		(721)	221
Increase/(decrease) in Retain joint venture loan receivables		36	(122)
Other non-cash movements		(430)	(330)
Elimination of other Tesco non-cash movements		(11)	46
Decrease/(increase) in net debt in the year		241	(48)
Opening net debt	30	(6,838)	(6,790)
Closing net debt	30	(6,597)	(6,838)

NB. The reconciliation of net cash flow to movement in net debt note is not a primary statement and does not form part of the cash flow statement and forms part of the notes to the financial statements.

Source: Tesco PLC Annual Report and Financial Statements 2013, p. 76, http://www.tescoplc.com/index.asp?pageid=540#/, accessed September 2013.

30.7 IAS 7 – statement of cash flows: notes

IAS 7 also requires some notes to the statement of cash flows. Normally, a note provides more information on investing activities, highlighting what was invested and how it was financed. IAS 7 requires that an analysis of the opening and closing balance of cash and cash equivalents, as disclosed in the last two lines of the statement of cash flows, is provided in a note.

An illustration of this latter note is shown in a continuation of Worked Example 30.3 using the information in Worked Example 30.2.

WORKED EXAMPLE 30.3 CONTINUED

Notes to the statement of cash flows (continued)

1 ***Cash and cash equivalents***

	At 1 April 20X4	At 31 Mar 20X5
	£	£
Cash in hand, at bank	8,600	17,300
Total cash and cash equivalents	8,600	17,300

30.8 Purposes and uses of statements of cash flows revisited

The statement of cash flows for C. Flowers Ltd in Worked Example 30.3 can be interpreted as showing the following. The company generated £50,600 from operating activities. There has been no expansion in the company's business activities; indeed, there has been a slight contraction as shown by the net positive **cash flow from investing activities** of which £3,500 comes from the sale of non-current tangible assets. The cash generated from operating activities together with the proceeds from the sale of investments and the proceeds from the issue of additional equity shares have been used to repay part of the debenture loan, the interest on the debenture loan and a dividend of £34,800 to the equity shareholders. In short, this statement of cash flows paints a picture of a company well able to cover its financing charges by cash inflows from operating activities, and which is seeking to reduce its dependence on debt capital by partly replacing it with more permanent equity shares. This scenario is often associated with a process of consolidation likely to result in greater financial stability in times of falling profits that frequently occur during an economic recession.

30.9 Advantages and limitations of statements of cash flows

The advantages of statements of cash flows are often explained in terms of the deficiencies of statements of profit or loss and statements of financial position. This should not be interpreted to mean that statements of cash flows are an alternative to statements of profit or loss. The statement of profit or loss and statement of financial position have a number of limitations; however, they provide different types of information for users. Statements of cash flows provide useful additional information for the following reasons:

1 Most readers and potential readers (e.g. private shareholders) appreciate the meaning and importance of cash and will therefore find statements of cash flows easier to understand and more relevant. In contrast, the nature of profit and capital and the contents of the statement of profit or loss and statement of financial position are more difficult to understand.

2 Statements of cash flows are more objective in that cash received and paid are observable events. In contrast, the statement of profit or loss and statement of financial position are based on the accruals concept and matching principle, which involve subjective allocations, valuations, and so on.

3 Statements of cash flows therefore permit more meaningful comparisons of performance over time, and between actual performance and forecasts.

4 Profit is only a symbol or measure of performance. The ultimate success and survival of an enterprise depends on its ability to generate and use cash in the most efficient manner. The statement of cash flows provides information that facilitates an evaluation of the efficiency with which cash has been generated and used.

5 Future dividends, the repayment of loans and payments to trade payables depend primarily on the availability of cash and not profits. Statements of cash flows provide information that allows users of company published financial statements to make more accurate predictions of future dividends, insolvency, and so on.

Few accountants would quarrel with the assertion that statements of cash flows provide useful additional information. However, most would be opposed to the idea that they should replace the statement of profit or loss for the following reasons:

1 A statement that is easier to understand is not necessarily more relevant or useful.

2 The preparation of statements of cash flows also involves subjective judgements.

3 The use of statements of cash flows in making comparisons and the evaluation of performance can be misleading. The pattern of cash flows over time is often erratic and therefore not indicative of an enterprise's long-term performance.

4 Statements of cash flows focus on the financing activities of an enterprise rather than the economic or trading activities. They therefore do not provide meaningful information on either past or future economic performance.

30.10 The purpose, uses and advantages of classified statements of cash flows

According to IAS 7, the purpose of statements of cash flows is to provide information about the historical changes in cash and cash equivalents of an entity by classifying cash flows during the period from operating, investing and financing activities. The economic decisions that are taken by users require an evaluation of the ability of an entity to generate cash and cash equivalents and to assess the timing and certainty of their generation. In particular, users will wish to assess the liquidity, solvency, investment potential and financial adaptability of the entity. The following objectives may be expanded and expressed in slightly different terms to emphasize the potential uses of statements of cash flows:

1 To enable management, investors, trade payables and others to see how the various activities of the company have been financed (e.g. which activities have net cash outflows and which have net cash inflows).

2 A statement of cash flows, in conjunction with a statement of comprehensive income and statement of financial position, provides information on the financial position and performance as well as liquidity, solvency and financial adaptability of an entity. It also gives an indication of the relationship between profitability and cash-generating ability, and thus of the *quality* of the profit earned. Historical cash flow information could be useful to check the accuracy of past assessments and indicate the relationship between the entity's activities, and its receipts and payments.

3 Historical cash flow information may assist users of financial statements in making judgements on the amount, timing and degree of certainty of future cash flows. The statement of cash flows may therefore be useful to management, investors, trade payables and others in assessing the enterprise's ability to:

  a pay its debts (i.e. loan repayment, trade payables, etc.) as and when they become due;

  b pay loan interest, dividends, and so on;

  c decide whether it will need to raise additional external finance (e.g. issue shares or debentures) in the near future.

4 To explain why an enterprise may have a profit for the year but nevertheless has less cash at the end of that year (or vice versa), and thus, for example, is only able to pay a small dividend.

5 To allow users to see directly the reasons for the difference between the net profit and its associated cash receipts and payments (i.e. the net cash inflow from operating activities).

When answering examination questions, it is often advisable to assume that the function/objective/purpose(s), uses and advantages of statements of cash flows all require similar answers but the amount of detail increases with each, respectively.

Learning Activity 30.2

Examine the most recent financial statements of British Airways plc. Try to construct the statement of cash flows from the information provided in the statement of comprehensive income, the statement of financial position and the related notes where relevant. Some of the entries are beyond the scope of this text; however, you should be able to determine about 80 per cent of the final statement of cash-flow entries. Compare your effort with their published version.

Summary

The purpose of a statement of cash flows is to show the reasons for the change in the cash and bank balance over an accounting year. Another common way of expressing this is that a statement of cash flows shows the manner in which cash has been generated and used. The reasons for the change in cash are shown in this statement as either sources or applications of cash funds. The statement of cash flows is intended to complement the statement of profit or loss and statement of financial position by providing additional information. It is often regarded as an alternative with its own advantages and limitations. However, the statement of cash flows is intended to serve different purposes.

IAS 7 requires that most companies include a classified statement of cash flows in their annual financial statements wherein the cash flows are classified into the three groups: net cash from operating activities, net cash from investing activities and net cash from financing activities. The net cash from operating activities is usually compiled using the indirect method. However, there is another method, referred to as the direct method, which is also permissible under IAS 7. Though the direct method is recommended by IAS 7, the indirect method is used in practice in the UK and Ireland. IAS 7 also requires a note analysing the opening and closing cash and cash equivalent balance as disclosed in the statement of cash flows.

Key terms and concepts

capital expenditure	616	demand deposits	610
cash	610	direct method	611
cash equivalents	610	financing activities	614
cash flows	610	indirect method	612
cash flow from financing activities	614	investing activities	613
cash flow from investing activities	627	operating activities	610
cash flow from operating activities	610	statement of cash flows	610

An asterisk after the question number indicates that there is a suggested answer in Appendix 2.

Review questions

connect

30.1 **a** Explain the purpose(s) of a statement of cash flows.

b Describe the typical sources and applications of cash funds in an entity.

30.2 Describe the advantages and limitations of statements of cash flows.

30.3 Explain how statements of cash flows differ from: (a) statements of profit or loss; and (b) statements of financial position.

30.4 Explain the meaning of each of the following in the context of statements of cash flows:

a cash;

b cash equivalents.

30.5 List and describe the contents of the three headings/groups of items found in a statement of cash flows prepared in accordance with IAS 7.

30.6 Explain the purpose, uses and advantages of classified statements of cash flows prepared in accordance with IAS 7.

30.7 Explain the difference between the direct and indirect methods of ascertaining the 'net cash inflow from operating activities' shown in a statement of cash flows.

30.8 For many years, company financial statements consisted of a statement of financial position and a statement of profit or loss prepared using the accruals basis. Many also have to include a statement of cash flows.

Required

a Explain why a statement of cash flows is considered to add value to the information already available in the statement of financial position and the statement of profit or loss.

b Itemize the different sections that IAS 7 requires to be included in the statement of cash flows and explain the information each one can provide to users.

Exercises

connect

BASIC

30.9 J. White, a sole trader, has produced the following statements of financial position for the years ended 31 March 20X4 and 31 March 20X5.

J. White **Statements of financial position as at 31 March**				
ASSETS		*20X5*		*20X4*
Non-current assets	£	£	£	£
Freehold premises		10,000		10,000
Shop fittings	1,200		1,000	
Depreciation to date	(870)	330	(750)	250
Motor vehicle	800		800	
Depreciation to date	(600)	200	(400)	400
		10,530		10,650
Current assets				
Inventories		15,400		11,000
Trade receivables		540		1,000
Bank		3,000		9,500
Cash in till		30		50
		18,970		21,550
Total assets		29,500		32,200
EQUITY AND LIABILITIES				
Equity				
Capital		15,000		15,000

Current account	5,200		3,000	
Profits	5,800		5,400	
	11,000		8,400	
Drawings	(4,500)	6,500	(3,200)	5,200
Total equity		21,500		20,200
Current liabilities				
Trade payables		8,000		12,000
Total liabilities		8,000		12,000
Total equity and liabilities		29,500		32,200

J. White is unable to understand why, after he has made a profit for the year ended 31 March 20X5 of £5,800, his bank balance has fallen by £6,500.

Required

Prepare a report explaining how this has occurred.

(Adapted from ACCA)

30.10 Prepare a statement of cash flows in accordance with IAS 7 using the information in Question 30.9. There was no investment income or interest paid during the year ended 31 March 20X5. BASIC

30.11 T. Bone is a sole trader and reports the following for the year ended 30 June 20X5: INTERMEDIATE

T. Bone
Statements of financial position as at 30 June

ASSETS	*20X5*	*20X4*
Non-current assets	£	£
Motor vans	10,500	14,500
Depreciation to date	(4,448)	(5,628)
	6,052	8,872
Current assets		
Inventories	16,352	12,558
Trade receivables less allowance for irrecoverable receivables	5,250	6,580
Bank	4,093	2,358
	25,695	21,496
Total assets	31,747	30,368
EQUITY AND LIABILITIES		
Equity		
Capital	10,808	8,799
Profits	28,689	24,009
	39,497	32,808
Drawings	(24,000)	(22,000)
Total equity	15,497	10,808
Non-current liabilities		
10% loan	6,000	7,000
Total non-current liabilities	6,000	7,000

	£	£
Current liabilities		
Trade payables	10,250	12,560
Total current liabilities	10,250	12,560
Total liabilities	16,250	19,560
Total equity and liabilities	31,747	30,368

T. Bone
Statement of profit or loss for the year ended 30 June 20X5 (extract)

	£	£
Gross profit		56,325
Add: discounts received:		1,026
		57,351
Less expenses:		
Wages	18,930	
Motor expenses	6,582	
Loan interest	600	
Irrecoverable receivables	650	
Increase in allowance for irrecoverable receivables	240	
Loss on sale of motor van	570	
Depreciation	1,090	28,662
Profit for the year		28,689

Notes

1 The 20X4 allowance for irrecoverable receivables was £600.

2 The 20X5 allowance for irrecoverable receivables is £840.

3 The motor van was sold for £2,300.

Required

Prepare the statement of cash flows in accordance with IAS 7 for T. Bone for the year ended 30 June 20X5.

INTERMEDIATE **30.12** A. Net is a sole trader and reports the following for the year ended 31 December 20X4:

Statement of profit or loss for the year ended 31 December 20X4 (extract)

	£	£
Gross profit		2,500
Less expenses:		
Wages	300	
Motor expenses	110	
Loss on sale of car	20	
Depreciation	60	490
Profit for the year		2,010

A. Net Statements of financial position as at 31 December		
ASSETS	*20X4*	*20X3*
Non-current assets	£	£
Motor vehicles	1,500	1,750
Depreciation to date	(150)	(270)
	1,350	1,480
Current assets		
Inventories	1,600	1,200
Trade receivables less allowance for irrecoverable receivables	1,200	980
Bank	1,220	500
	4,020	2,680
Total assets	5,370	4,160
EQUITY AND LIABILITIES		
Equity		
Capital	2,060	1,000
Profits	2,010	1,650
	4,070	2,650
Drawings	(950)	(590)
Total equity	3,120	2,060
Non-current liabilities		
Loan	1,800	1,700
Total non-current liabilities	1,800	1,700
Current liabilities		
Trade payables	450	400
Total current liabilities	450	400
Total liabilities	2,250	2,100
Total equity and liabilities	5,370	4,160

Note: The car that was disposed of during the year was sold for £400, which was lodged in A. Net's bank account.

Required

Prepare the statement of cash flows in accordance with IAS 7 for A. Net for the year ended 31 December 20X4.

30.13 The following are the financial statements for A. Tack for the years ended 30 June 20X5 and 20X4: INTERMEDIATE

Statement of profit or loss for the year ended 30 June		
	20X5	*20X4*
	£'000	*£'000*
Sales revenue	2,280	1,230
Less: Cost of goods sold	1,318	422
Gross profit	962	808

	20X5	20X4
Less expenses		
Depreciation	320	310
Office expenses	100	110
Interest paid	27	–
Rent	173	150
Profit for the year	342	238

Statements of financial position as at 30 June

	20X5	20X4
ASSETS	£'000	£'000
Non-current assets (see note)	2,640	2,310
Current assets		
Inventory	450	275
Trade receivables	250	100
Bank	153	23
	853	398
Total assets	3,493	2,708
EQUITY AND LIABILITIES		
Equity		
Capital	2,388	2,050
Capital introduced	300	200
Profits for year	342	238
	3030	2488
Drawings	(252)	(100)
Total equity	2,778	2,388
Non-current liabilities		
9% loan (20Y0)	300	–
Total non-current liabilities	300	–
Current liabilities		
Trade payables	415	320
Total current liabilities	415	320
Total liabilities	715	320
Total equity and liabilities	3,493	2,708

Note: Schedule of non-current assets

	Land and buildings	Plant and machinery	Total
	£'000	£'000	£'000
Cost			
At 1 July 20X4	1,500	1,350	2,850
Additions	400	250	650
At 30 June 20X5	1,900	1,600	3,500

Depreciation			
At 1 July 20X4	–	540	540
Charge for year at 20%	–	320	320
At 30 June 20X5	–	860	860
Net book value at 30 June 20X5	1,900	740	2,640

Required

Prepare a statement of cash flows in accordance with IAS 7 for A. Tack for the year ended 30 June 20X5.

30.14 The following are the financial statements for S. Low for the years ended 30 April 20X4 and 30 April 20X5: INTERMEDIATE

S. Low: Income statements for year ended 30 April

	20X5		*20X4*	
	£'000	*£'000*	*£'000*	*£'000*
Sales revenue		4,850		4,400
Less: cost of sales		2,400		2,310
Gross profit		2,450		2,090
Less: expenses				
Depreciation	162		142	
Interest payable	22		18	
Wages	750		670	
Electricity	520		450	
Rent	286	1,740	286	1,566
Profit for the period		710		524

S. Low: Statements of financial position as at 30 April

	20X5	*20X4*
ASSETS		
Non-current assets	£	£
Property, plant and equipment	1,250	630
Depreciation to date	(432)	(270)
	818	360
Current assets		
Inventories	405	384
Trade receivables less allowance for irrecoverable receivables	698	729
Bank	–	47
	1,103	1,160
Total assets	1,921	1,520
EQUITY AND LIABILITIES		
Equity		
Capital	429	220
Profits	710	524
	1,139	744

Drawings	(391)	(315)
Total equity	748	429
Non-current liabilities		
12% loan	180	150
Total non-current liabilities	180	150
Current liabilities		
Bank overdraft	28	–
Trade payables	965	941
Total current liabilities	993	941
Total liabilities	1,173	1,091
Total equity and liabilities	1,921	1,520

Required

Prepare a statement of cash flows in accordance with IAS 7 for S. Low for the year ended 30 April 20X5.

INTERMEDIATE

30.15* The following are the statements of financial position of A. Brooks as at 30 June 20X4 and 30 June 20X5:

	30 June 20X4	30 June 20X5
ASSETS	£	£
Non-current assets		
Property, plant and equipment (cost)	65,000	72,000
Aggregate depreciation	(13,000)	(14,500)
	52,000	57,500
Current assets		
Inventory	6,700	7,300
Trade receivables	5,400	4,100
Cash and bank	–	900
	12,100	12,300
Total assets	64,100	69,800
EQUITY AND LIABILITIES		
Equity		
Capital at start of year	38,500	43,000
Capital introduced	2,700	20,000
Profit for the year	14,100	–
	55,300	63,000
Loss for the year	–	(1,800)
Drawings	(12,300)	(7,600)
Total equity capital	43,000	53,600
Non-current liabilities		
Bank loan (5 years)	15,000	10,000
Total non-current liabilities	15,000	10,000

Current liabilities		
Trade payables	4,800	6,200
Bank overdraft	1,300	–
Total current liabilities	6,100	6,200
Total liabilities	21,100	16,200
Total equity and liabilities	64,100	69,800

Additional information

1 There were no disposals of non-current assets during the year.

2 During the year ended 30 June 20X5 there was interest received of £900 and bank interest paid of £1,250.

Required

Brooks cannot understand how there can be a loss for the year 20X4/X5 when there has been an increase in the cash and bank balance. You are required to explain this by preparing a statement of cash flows for the year ended 30 June 20X5.

30.16 The statement of financial position of C.F. Ltd for the year ended 31 December 20X4, together with comparative figures for the previous year, is shown below. ADVANCED

	20X4	**20X3**
ASSETS	*£'000*	*£'000*
Non-current assets		
Property, plant and equipment (note 4)	180	124
Current assets		
Inventory	50	42
Trade receivables	40	33
Cash	–	11
	90	86
Total assets	270	210
EQUITY AND LIABILITIES		
Equity		
Equity share capital £1 shares	25	20
Share premium	10	8
Retained earnings	93	81
Total equity	128	109
Non-current liabilities		
15% debentures, repayable 20X8	80	60
Total non-current liabilities	80	60
Current liabilities		
Trade and operating payables	33	24
Current tax payable	19	17
Bank overdraft	10	–
Total current liabilities	62	41
Total liabilities	142	101
Total equity and liabilities	270	210

Additional information

1 There were no sales of non-current assets during 20X4.

2 The company declared a final dividend of £26,000 for 20X4 (20X3 – £28,000). This is paid immediately after the AGM that takes place two months after the year end. The company does not pay any interim dividends.

3 New debentures and shares issued in 20X4 were issued on 1 January.

4 Property, plant and equipment is made up of the following:

	20X4	20X3
	£'000	*£'000*
Equipment	270	180
Provision for depreciation	(90)	(56)
	180	124

Required

a Show your calculation of the operating profit of C.F. plc for the year ended 31 December 20X4.

b Prepare a statement of cash flows for the year, in accordance with *IAS 7 – Statement of Cash Flows.*

c State the headings of any other notes that you would be required to include in practice under IAS 7.

d Comment on the implications of the information given in the question, plus the statements you have prepared, regarding the financial position of the company.

e IAS 7 supports the use of the indirect method of arriving at the net cash inflow from operating activities, which is the method you have used to answer part (b) of this question. What is the direct method of arriving at the net cash inflow from operations? State, with reasons, whether you agree with the IAS 7 acceptance of the indirect method.

(ACCA, adapted)

ADVANCED

30.17* The directors of J. Kitchens Ltd were pleased when their accountants informed them that the company had made a profit of £24,000 during the year ended 31 December 20X4. However, their pleasure was turned into confusion when the cashier showed them a letter he had received from their banker. This indicated that he had reviewed Kitchens' account and was concerned to note the deterioration in their bank position. During 20X4 a small overdraft of £500 had reached £9,800 and was nearing the limit of their security. The directors would like to see an explanation of this increased overdraft, particularly as they had declared lower dividends than for the previous year. You are given the statements of financial position at 31 December 20X3 and 31 December 20X4:

	20X3	20X4
ASSETS	£	£
Non-current assets		
Property, plant and equipment (note 5)	58,000	59,500
Current assets		
Inventory	14,900	22,500
Trade receivables	11,300	16,400
	26,200	38,900
Total assets	84,200	98,400

EQUITY AND LIABILITIES		
Equity		
Share capital	20,000	20,000
Reserves	44,000	51,000
Total equity	64,000	71,000
Current liabilities		
Trade payables	19,700	17,600
Overdraft	500	9,800
Total current liabilities	20,200	27,400
Total equity and liabilities	84,200	98,400

Notes

1 Dividends

	20X3	20X4
	£	£
Interim paid	3,000	8,000
Final proposed	9,000	–

2 During the year, plant costing £10,000 with a net book value of £6,000 was sold for £6,400.

3 The amount included for trade receivables at 31 December 20X4 is after making an allowance for irrecoverable receivables of £600 (20X3: £400).

4 During the year ended 31 December 20X4 £750 was paid in bank interest.

5 Property, plant and equipment is made up of the following:

	20X3		20X4	
	£	£	£	£
Property, plant and equipment				
Leasehold premises – cost	30,000		30,000	
Provision for depreciation	(6,000)	24,000	(9,000)	21,000
Plant – cost	41,000		48,000	
Provision for depreciation	(7,000)	34,000	(9,500)	38,500
		58,000		59,500

Required

You are required to prepare a statement of cash flows in accordance with IAS 7 for the year 20X4 showing why the overdraft has increased.

30.18* The following are the statements of financial positions of L. Tyler Ltd as at 31 May 20X4 and 31 May 20X5: ADVANCED

	20X4	20X5
ASSETS		
Non-current assets	£	£
Property, plant and equipment (note 5)	115,000	94,000
Current assets		
Inventory	21,600	19,400

Trade receivables (note 6)	11,300	13,500
Investments	3,900	17,100
Cash and bank	4,600	12,800
	41,400	62,800
Total assets	156,400	156,800
EQUITY AND LIABILITIES		
Equity		
Equity shares of 50p each	60,000	70,000
Share premium account	25,000	34,000
Revenue reserve	4,200	6,900
Retained earnings	23,000	27,000
Total equity	112,200	137,900
Non-current liabilities		
8% loan stock	30,000	5,000
Total non-current liabilities	30,000	5,000
Current liabilities		
Trade payables	8,400	6,700
Current tax payable	5,800	7,200
Total current liabilities	14,200	13,900
Total liabilities	44,200	18,900
Total equity and liabilities	156,400	156,800

Notes

1 Non-current assets that cost £12,000 and had a book value of £7,500 were sold during the year ended 31 May 20X5 for £8,100. There were no other purchases or sales of non-current assets during that year.

2 The amounts of current tax shown in the statement of financial position as outstanding at 31 May 20X4 were paid during the year ended 31 May 20X5.

3 A dividend of £19,600 was proposed by the directors and later approved by the shareholders for the year ended 20X4 (20X5 – £21,800). In addition, an interim dividend of £6,400 was paid on 1 January 20X5.

4 The company received interest of £1,800 and paid loan stock interest of £1,600 in the year to 31 May 20X5.

5 Property, plant and equipment is made up of the following:

	20X4	20X5
	£	£
Equipment and fixtures at cost	143,000	131,000
Aggregate depreciation	(28,000)	(37,000)
	115,000	94,000

6 Trade receivables is made up of the following:

	20X4	20X5
	£	£
Trade receivables	11,800	14,200
Allowance for irrecoverable receivables	(500)	(700)
	11,300	13,500

Required

Prepare a statement of cash flows in accordance with IAS 7 for the year ended 31 May 20X5.

ADVANCED

30.19 The statement of financial position of Euston Ltd as at 31 December 20X4, with corresponding amounts, showed the following:

	20X4	20X3
ASSETS	*£'000*	*£'000*
Non-current assets		
Property, plant and equipment	4,200	4,000
Current assets		
Inventory	470	400
Trade receivables	800	600
Prepayments	60	50
Bank	20	150
	1,350	1,200
Total assets	5,550	5,200
EQUITY AND LIABILITIES		
Equity		
Share capital	2,500	2,500
Retained earnings	1,650	1,530
Total equity	4,150	4,030
Non-current liabilities		
12% debentures	1,000	800
Total non-current liabilities	1,000	800
Current liabilities		
Trade payables	230	200
Current tax payable	100	80
Accruals	70	90
Total current liabilities	400	370
Total liabilities	1,400	1,170
Total equity and reserves	5,550	5,200

Notes relevant to 20X4

1 Property, plant and equipment includes the following:

	20X4		20X3	
Property, plant and equipment	*£'000*	*£'000*	*£'000*	*£'000*
Freehold property at cost		2,000		2,000
Plant and machinery:				
– Cost	3,500		3,000	
– Provision for depreciation	(1,300)	2,200	(1,000)	2,000
Total		4,200		4,000

2 An item of plant costing £100,000 with a written-down value of £60,000 was sold at a profit of £15,000 during the year. This profit has been included in the statement of profit or loss for the year.

3 The company declared a final dividend at the end of 20X4 of £50,000 (20X3 – £30,000). This was approved by the shareholders one month after the reporting period end and paid two weeks after that. No interim dividend was paid during the year.

4 Tax on company profits is paid nine months after the end of the reporting period.

5 During the year ended 31 December 20X4 there was no interest received but there was debenture interest paid of £108,000. None of the debenture interest was accrued at the end of either 20X3 or 20X4.

Required

Prepare a statement of cash flows in accordance with IAS 7 for the year 31 December 20X4.

(JMB, adapted)

ADVANCED

30.20 The following are the statements of financial positions of Waterloo plc for the last two financial years ended on 30 September.

	20X4	20X3	Notes
ASSETS	*£'000*	*£'000*	
Non-current assets			
Property, plant and equipment	1,320	1,090	1
Goodwill	200	200	2
	1,520	1,290	
Current assets			
Inventories	420	300	
Trade receivables	220	120	
Balance at bank	–	20	
	640	440	
Total assets	2,160	1,730	
EQUITY AND LIABILITIES			
Equity			
Equity shares, of 50p each, fully paid	750	500	4
Share premium account	100	350	4
Revaluation reserve	300	–	
Retained earnings	340	280	
Total equity	1,490	1,130	
Non-current liabilities			
9% debentures	360	400	
Total non-current liabilities	360	400	
Current liabilities			
Bank overdraft	120	–	
Trade payables	190	200	
Total current liabilities	310	200	
Total liabilities	670	600	
Total equity and liabilities	2,160	1,730	

Explanatory notes to the statement of financial positions are as follows:

1 The movement during the year to 30 September 20X4 in property, plant and equipment was as follows:

	Buildings	Plant and machinery	Total
Cost	*£'000*	*£'000*	*£'000*
At 1 October 20X3	820	600	1,420
Surplus on revaluation	300	–	300
Additions	–	100	100
Disposals	–	(50)*	(50)
	1,120	650	1,770
Provision for depreciation			
At 1 October 20X3	100	230	330
Depreciation on disposal	–	(40)*	(40)
Depreciation for year	50	110	160
At 30 September 20X4	150	300	450
Closing net book value	970	350	1,320
Opening net book value	720	370	1,090

* *The plant and machinery disposed of during the year was sold for £5,000.*

2 Goodwill arising from the purchase of a business on 1 November 20X2 was valued at £200,000. Goodwill has not diminished in value over the year.

3 Dividend details for the company are as follows:

	20X4	20X3
Interim paid in year	£25,000	£15,000
Final proposed at year end	£60,000	£45,000

4 There was a bonus issue during the year to 30 September 20X4 of one new equity share for every two held.

Required

Prepare a statement of cash flows for the year ended 30 September 20X4, in accordance with IAS 7. There was no investment income for the year ended 30 September 20X4 but there was debenture interest paid of £35,000 during the year.

(AEB, adapted)

ADVANCED

30.21 The summarized statements of financial position as at 31 March 20X4 and 31 March 20X5 of Higher Ltd are as follows:

	20X5	20X4	Additional information
ASSETS	*£'000*	*£'000*	
Non-current assets	175	150	1
Current assets	90	80	2
Total assets	265	230	
EQUITY AND LIABILITIES			
Equity			
Equity shares of £1 each	90	80	3
Share premium account	25	20	3
Capital redemption reserve	15	–	
Retained earnings	35	20	
Total equity	165	120	
Non-current liabilities			
Debentures	30	30	
8% redeemable preference shares of 50p each	–	30	3
Total non-current liabilities	30	60	
Current liabilities	70	50	
Total liabilities	100	110	
Total equity and liabilities	265	230	

Additional information

1 Non-current assets

	Cost	Depn	Net book value
	£'000	*£'000*	*£'000*
Balance at 31 March 20X4	200	50	150
Additions	60	–	60
Disposals	(40)	(25)	(15)
Depreciation for the year to 31 March 20X5	–	20	(20)
	220	45	175

Non-current assets disposed of during the year were sold for £22,000.

2 Current assets at 31 March for each of the two years comprise the following:

	20X5	20X4
	£'000	*£'000*
Inventories	35	27
Trade receivables	22	28
Bank	24	22
Cash	9	3
	90	80

3 The preference shares were redeemed during the year ended 31 March 20X5. This redemption was funded by a new issue of equity shares at a premium.

4 During the year the company made a transfer of £15,000 from retained earnings to the capital redemption reserve.

Required

Prepare a statement of cash flows for Higher Ltd for the year ended 31 March 20X5, in accordance with IAS 7. Assume that there was no investment income, interest paid or dividends paid during the year ended 31 March 20X5.

(AEB, adapted)

Reference

International Accounting Standards Board (2013) *International Accounting Standard 7 – Statement of Cash Flows* (IASB).

Chapter 31

The appraisal of company financial statements using ratio analysis

Learning Objectives:

After reading this chapter you should be able to do the following:

1. Explain the purposes of ratio analysis.
2. Compute various measures of a company's performance, explain what each is intended to measure and evaluate the results.
3. Compute various measures of liquidity and solvency, explain what each is intended to measure, and evaluate the results.
4. Compute various ratios used in the appraisal of working capital, explain what each is intended to measure and evaluate the results.
5. Compute various measures of return on investment and risk, explain what each is intended to measure and evaluate the results.
6. Explain the nature of capital gearing, compute the gearing ratio and describe the effect of gearing on the profit available for distribution as dividends and the earnings per share.
7. Discuss the limitations of ratio analysis.

31.1 Introduction

Ratio analysis involves relating two numbers from an entity's financial statements to each other to form an easily understood measure (typically a percentage) which facilitates comparison to the same measure from previous years and across entities of different sizes. Most stakeholders with business knowledge will use ratio analysis to evaluate the performance of an entity, both in terms of their previous performance and relative to competitors in the market.

The purpose of ratio analysis

The main function of published company final financial statements is to provide information that will enable users of financial statements to evaluate the financial performance and financial position of a company. However, the absolute amount of profit, or assets and liabilities, shown in the financial statements is not usually a particularly meaningful criterion for evaluating the performance or financial position of businesses. For example, if Company A has a profit of £200,000 and Company B has a profit of £1 million, one cannot conclude that B has better performance than A. Company B may have used net assets of £10 million to generate this profit whereas Company A may have only used net assets of £0.5 million.

Net assets = Total assets less Current liabilities

Therefore, 'net assets' is the same as equity and long-term sources of debt that are used to finance the company. 'Net assets' is also known as **capital employed**. Thus, A is said to be more profitable than B because the profit is 40 per cent of the value of its net assets (£200,000/£500,000) compared with only 10 per cent in the case of B (£1,000,000/£10,000,000). Similarly, if Company B had a profit of £900,000 last year, one cannot conclude that it is more profitable this year. The value of the net assets last year may only have been £8 million, which gives a return of 11.25 per cent (£900,000/£8,000,000) compared with 10 per cent this year.

Indeed, the terms '**profitability**' and '**return**' are taken as referring to the relationship between the profit and the value of the net assets/equity capital used to generate that profit. Thus, in order to evaluate a company's performance and financial position over time, or in relation to other companies, it is necessary to compute various accounting ratios and percentages. These are primarily intended for the use of external groups of users such as shareholders, loan creditors and credit suppliers, whose only source of accounting information is that contained in published financial statements.

It is important to appreciate at the outset that accounting ratios and percentages have a number of limitations.

- One of these stems from the aggregate nature of information in published financial statements. Companies are not required to disclose all the items that enter into the computation of profit or values of assets and liabilities in the statement of financial position. As a result, the information needed to compute some ratios may not be available. This necessitates the use of surrogate data in the calculation of some ratios.
- Furthermore, comparisons of ratios over time and between companies can be misleading when economic conditions change and/or where the companies concerned are operating in substantially different industries. Ratios must therefore always be interpreted in the light of the prevailing economic climate and the particular circumstances of the company or companies concerned. The limitations of ratio analysis are discussed in the context of each ratio and are summarized at the end of the chapter.

A large number of ratios can be calculated from the information contained in published financial statements. These ratios may be grouped under four main headings, each heading reflecting what the ratios are intended to measure: (1) measures of company performance; (2) measures of solvency and **liquidity**; (3) measures of the control of **working capital** (management efficiency); and (4) measures of return on investment and risk. The most common ratios in each of these four classes are described on the following pages and illustrated using the information in Worked Example 31.1.

WORKED EXAMPLE 31.1

The following is an extract from the published financial statements of A. Harry plc, for the year ending 31 January 20X4:

Statement of profit or loss		
	20X4	*20X3*
	£'000	*£'000*
Revenue	5,280	4,900
Cost of sales	(3,090)	3,000
Gross profit	2,190	1,900
Distribution costs	(560)	(500)
Administrative expenses	(230)	(450)
Finance costs	(400)	(600)
Profit before taxation	1,000	350
Income tax expense	(250)	(100)
Profit after taxation	750	250

Statement of financial position		
	20X4	*20X3*
ASSETS	*£'000*	£'000
Non-current assets at cost	9,470	8,000
Aggregate depreciation	(2,860)	(2,400)
	6,610	5,600
Current assets		
Inventories	550	400
Trade receivables	1,070	900
Bank and cash	1,130	2,000
	2,750	3,300
Total assets	9,360	8,900
EQUITY AND LIABILITIES		
Equity		
Called-up share capital: 2,000,000 equity shares of £1 each	2,000	2,000
Retained earnings	2,380	1,630
Total equity	4,380	3,630
Non-current liabilities		
10% loan stock of £100 each	4,000	5,000
Total non-current liabilities	4,000	5,000

Current liabilities		
Trade payables	730	220
Current tax payable	250	50
Total current liabilities	980	270
Total liabilities	4,980	5,270
Total equity and liabilities	9,360	8,900

Additional information

1 The equity shares and loan stock are currently quoted on the London Stock Exchange at £4 and £90, respectively. The figures for 20X3 were £2.40 and £85.

2 A final dividend for the year of £400,000 is proposed (no interim dividend was paid in the year). The dividend for the year 20X3 was £250,000.

31.2 Measures of a company's performance

The main function of financial statements is to provide information that will enable users to evaluate the financial performance and financial position of a company. Performance may relate to a number of things, such as productivity, energy conservation and pollution control. From the equity shareholders' point of view, financial performance is usually equated with the profit available for distribution as dividends or the **earnings per share** (discussed later). However, the term 'financial performance' is normally associated with an entity view of business enterprises. This section therefore examines various measures of a company's performance from the point of view of its being an economic entity separate from the shareholders, and irrespective of the way in which its assets are financed (i.e. the proportion of debt to equity capital).

Return on capital employed (ROCE)

Various accounting ratios are used to measure different aspects of financial performance. Many of these are derived from a single ratio known as the 'return on capital employed'. The **return on capital employed** is a measure of profitability that is used to indicate how efficiently and effectively a company has utilized its assets during a given accounting period. It is a common means of evaluating a company's profitability over time, and comparing the profitability of different companies. As a rough guide, the typical target ROCE of many large companies is about 15 per cent. This is ascertained as follows:

$$\frac{\text{Profit before tax, interest on non-current loans and preference dividends}}{\text{Net capital employed}} \times 100$$

Net capital employed refers to the shareholders' interests + non-current liabilities. Using the data in Worked Example 31.1 for 20X4 this is calculated thus:

$$\frac{£1{,}000{,}000 + £400{,}000}{£4{,}380{,}000 + £4{,}000{,}000} \times 100 = 16.7 \text{ per cent (20X3} - 11.0 \text{ per cent)}$$

The logic behind this ratio is perhaps more obvious when it is calculated as the **return on assets** as follows:

$$\frac{\text{Profit before tax, interest on non-current loans and preference dividends}}{\text{Total assets less current liabilities}} \times 100$$

$$\frac{£1{,}000{,}000 + £400{,}000}{£9{,}360{,}000 - £980{,}000} \times 100 = 16.7 \text{ per cent (20X3 – 11 per cent)}$$

Tailored Interpretation: In this example, A. Harry plc can be regarded as being more efficient in 20X4 relative to 20X3 as the company is generating 5.7p more profit before financing from each £1 invested.

Some authors advocate expressing the return on capital employed in terms of the **gross capital employed**. This refers to the shareholders' interests + non-current + current liabilities. A somewhat easier way of calculating this is non-current assets + current assets. Clearly, the return on gross capital employed/total assets will be different from the return on net capital employed/total assets less current liabilities. The latter is more common in practice.

Whatever method is used, there is a problem concerning the point at which the capital employed should be measured. In the above computation this was taken as being the end of the accounting year, for simplicity. However, this is not really justifiable because the capital employed includes the retained profit for the year and any additional capital raised during the year. The retained profit for the year was not available to generate the profit throughout this year, and it is unlikely that any capital raised during the year provided a significant contribution to the profit for the year. Given the time lags between capital expenditure and assets becoming productive, it may be more appropriate to use the capital employed at the start of the accounting year. Alternatively, if the additional capital is known to have generated profit during the year, the average capital employed for the year would be used. The same considerations apply to the **return on equity** discussed later.

The use of historical cost data in the calculation of this ratio can give a distorted view of the profitability for two reasons. First, during times of rising prices the denominator in the formula comprises a mixture of assets acquired at various times when the prevailing levels of prices were different. In times of rising prices, the denominator is also understated because assets are not shown in the statement of financial position at their current value. Second, the numerator tends to be overstated, since the historical cost profit is calculated by matching current selling prices with historical costs. Thus, the effect of historical cost accounting in both the denominator and the numerator is to inflate the return on capital and encourage the retention of old assets.

The profit margin and asset-turnover ratios

The ROCE can be broken down into two further ratios, as follows:

$$\boxed{\text{ROCE} = \text{Profit margin} \times \text{Asset-turnover ratio}}$$

The **profit margin** is computed thus:

$$\boxed{\frac{\text{Profit before tax, interest on non-current loans and preference dividends}}{\text{Revenue}} \times 100}$$

Using the data in Worked Example 31.1 for 20X4 this will give:

$$\frac{£1{,}000{,}000 + £400{,}000}{£5{,}280{,}000} \times 100 = 26.5 \text{ per cent (20X3 – 19.4 per cent)}$$

Tailored Interpretation: The company's profitability has increased over the two years. In 20X4 A. Harry plc is generating 26.5p profit to cover finance costs from every £1 sale made, an increase of 7.1p in each £1 of revenue generated. This suggests cost efficiencies and a stronger margin on sales.

The profit margin is often described as a measure of profitability that shows what percentage of sales revenue is profit. Different products have different profit margins. Jewellery and greengrocery, for example, usually have a higher profit margin than electrical goods and clothing. In addition, different sized businesses have different profit margins. Small shops, for example, usually have a higher profit margin than supermarkets. Inter-firm comparisons of profit margins should therefore only be made between companies in the same industry and of a comparable size.

The Companies Act 2006 requires the disclosure of an analysis of profit and revenue for each class of business. It is therefore possible to calculate the profit margin for each class of business. These could be used in inter-firm comparisons of performance. However, this can be misleading because the profit margin constitutes an average for all the products comprising one particular class of business, and few firms sell exactly the same combination of products (i.e. product mix). Time-series analysis of profit margins is likely to be more meaningful. Variations in the profit margin over time can be due to a number of factors relating to changes in the product mix, selling prices, unit costs and overhead costs.

The second of the ratios making up the ROCE is referred to as the asset-turnover ratio. It is calculated as follows:

$$\frac{\text{Revenue}}{\text{Total assets less Current liabilities}}$$

Using the data in Worked Example 31.1 for 20X4 this will give:

$$\frac{£5,280,000}{£9,360,000 - £980,000} = 0.63 \text{ times (20X3} - 0.57 \text{ times)}$$

Tailored Interpretation: This shows the amount of sales revenue that has been generated per £ of capital employed. In this instance, £0.63 of revenue has been generated in this year from every £1 invested in the company by equity shareholders and other providers of long-term financing (long-term liabilities). This has increased by 6p from £0.57 in 20X3, suggesting improvements in performance.

The **asset-turnover ratio** is a measure of the level of activity and productivity. Different industries have different asset turnover ratios, primarily because of differences in technology. Labour-intensive industries usually have a high asset turnover ratio, whereas capital-intensive industries tend to have a lower asset-turnover ratio. Inter-firm comparisons of asset-turnover ratios should therefore only be made between companies in the same industry. Time-series analysis of asset-turnover ratios is likely to be more meaningful. Changes in the asset-turnover ratio over time can be due to a number of factors, such as producing at under capacity, labour inefficiency or overstocking.

There is an important relationship between the asset-turnover ratio and the profit margin. In order to achieve a satisfactory return on capital employed, a company with a low asset-turnover ratio (e.g. capital-intensive) will need a high profit margin on its products. Conversely, a company with a high asset-turnover ratio (e.g. labour-intensive) will only require a low profit margin on its products in order to achieve a satisfactory return on capital employed. The former case of a capital-intensive company can be illustrated arithmetically using the asset-turnover ratio, profit margin and ROCE for Worked Example 31.1 for 20X4, as follows:

$$0.63 \times 26.5 \text{ per cent} = 16.7 \text{ per cent}$$

The profit margin ratio may be broken down into a number of other ratios in order to pinpoint more precisely the reasons for changes in performance over time. These are as follows:

Profit margin:

$$\frac{\text{Cost of sales}}{\text{Revenue}} \times 100$$

$$\frac{\text{Gross profit}}{\text{Revenue}} \times 100$$

$$\frac{\text{Distribution costs}}{\text{Revenue}} \times 100$$

$$\frac{\text{Administration expenses}}{\text{Revenue}} \times 100$$

The most important of these is probably the **gross profit ratio**. Using data from Worked Example 31.1 for 20X4, a gross profit percentage of 41.5 per cent results.

$$\frac{£2{,}190{,}000}{£5{,}280{,}000} \times 100 = 41.5 \text{ per cent (20X3 – 38.8 per cent)}$$

This provides information on the percentage of each pound of revenue that contributes towards covering the entity's fixed overhead costs and to profit. It includes the variable costs associated with each sale, such as the purchase cost of the products in non-manufacturing entities, or the manufacturing cost of the products that are for sale in manufacturing entities. It is affected by the selling price of the products, the purchase price of the products and inventory management (inventory losses).

Tailored Interpretation: A. Harry plc's performance has improved. In 20X4 41.5p in each £1 of revenue is available to cover the fixed costs and finance costs of the business. This is up from 38.8p in each £1 in 20X3. This means that either the sales mix has changed to include items with lower direct costs of production (higher profit margins), cheaper/better quality supplies have been obtained (discounts perhaps) or production is more efficient.

The asset-turnover ratio can also be analysed further into a number of other ratios to pinpoint more precisely reasons for changes in performance over time. These are as follows:

Asset-turnover ratio:

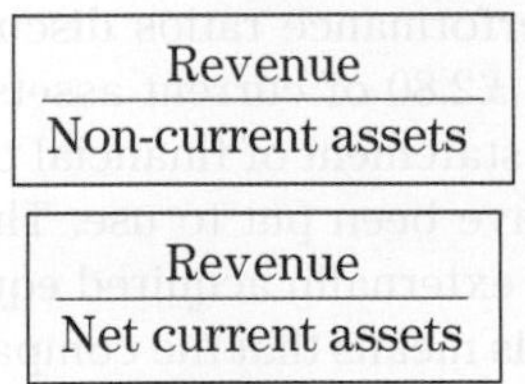

$$\frac{\text{Revenue}}{\text{Non-current assets}}$$

$$\frac{\text{Revenue}}{\text{Net current assets}}$$

The last ratio can be further subdivided into a number of other ratios relating to each constituent of net current assets. These are discussed in a later section on the appraisal of working capital.

31.3 Measures of solvency and liquidity

The main function of published financial statements is to provide information that will enable users to evaluate the performance and financial position of a company. The phrase 'financial position' is normally taken as including whether or not a company will be able to pay its debts as and when they become due. A business that is unable to do so is said to be **insolvent**, and will usually be forced into compulsory liquidation by its creditors. Sometimes profitable businesses face financial crisis, frequently because of overtrading. This broadly means that a company has invested too much in non-current assets and inventory but too little in liquid assets and is thus short of cash.

Solvency does not mean that at any time a business must have enough money to pay its liabilities. These will fall due at various dates in the future. **Solvency** therefore refers to whether or not liabilities are covered by assets that will be realized as the liabilities fall due. Thus, if the value of current assets is less than the amount of current liabilities, a business may be insolvent.

However, even if current assets are equal to or greater than current liabilities, this is no guarantee of solvency, since some current assets are less liquid than others. Liquidity refers to the ease with which an asset can be turned into cash without loss. Cash in hand and money in a bank current account are the most liquid types of asset, followed by listed investments, trade receivables and inventory. Current assets are usually presented in published financial statements in what is referred to as a reverse order of liquidity.

Two fairly crude but common ratios used to measure liquidity are explained below.

The working capital/current ratio

The **working capital/current ratio** is calculated thus:

$$\frac{\text{Current assets}}{\text{Current liabilities}}$$

Using the data in Worked Example 31.1 for 20X4 this gives:

$$\frac{\pounds 2{,}750{,}000}{\pounds 980{,}000} = 2.8 \text{ (20X3 – 12.2)}$$

This is a measure of the extent to which current liabilities are covered by current assets. As a generalization, the current ratio should be between 1.5 and 2, although this depends on the type of industry and the prevailing economic climate. A ratio of lower than 1.5 may indicate a poor liquidity position and thus future insolvency. At the other extreme a business can have too much working capital, which normally means that its assets are not being used as profitably as they otherwise might (investment in non-current assets typically generates a higher return than investment in current assets).

Tailored Interpretation: The current ratio in 20X3 was very high (£12.20 of current assets for every £1 of current liabilities) suggesting inefficient use of liquid funds. Further evidence of this can be seen directly from the statement of financial position, wherein a cash and bank balance of £2,000,000 is evident. These funds are not being used productively (funds in a bank account typically earn a very low return). This may in part help to explain why the performance ratios discussed earlier in this chapter were lower for 20X3. The ratio has fallen in 20X2 to £2.80 of current assets to £1 of current liabilities. This is also considered to be high. An analysis of the statement of financial position provides some indication of how the excessive funds recorded in 20X3 have been put to use. There have been increases in non-current assets, yet no corresponding increase in externally acquired equity or long-term debt. Indeed long-term debt has actually fallen by £1,000,000. This means that the company has used its surplus cash to purchase non-current assets and to pay off some of the expensive debt. This will improve reported performance and also explains why the interest cost has fallen in 20X4.

The working capital ratio has a serious limitation as a measure of liquidity, which is that some current assets are less liquid than others. In particular, inventories and work-in-progress are not easily realized without loss in the short term. A better criterion for measuring a company's ability to pay its debts as and when they become due is the **liquidity ratio**. In this ratio, inventories and work-in-progress are excluded from current assets.

The liquidity/quick ratio or acid test

This is calculated thus:

$$\frac{\text{Current assets} - \text{Inventories}}{\text{Current liabilities}}$$

Using the data in Worked Example 31.1 for 20X4 this gives:

$$\frac{\pounds 2{,}750{,}000 - \pounds 550{,}000}{\pounds 980{,}000} = 2.24 \text{ (20X3 – 10.74)}$$

Tailored Interpretation: The results show that A. Harry plc is not at risk from over-investment in inventory. The discussion for the current ratio applies here also.

Bank overdrafts are frequently excluded from the current liabilities in the calculation of this ratio because, although an overdraft is usually legally repayable at short notice, in practice it is often effectively a non-current liability.

The liquidity ratio indicates whether a company is likely to be able to pay its credit suppliers, current taxation, other current liabilities and dividends proposed (but not accrued) from its cash at bank, the proceeds of sale of listed investments and the amounts collected from trade receivables, that is, without having to raise additional capital or sell non-current assets. As a generalization, the liquidity ratio should therefore be at least 1 (expressed as 1:1). However, this criterion cannot be applied to all types of business. Large retailing companies, for example, often have a liquidity ratio of less than 1. They buy goods on credit, sell them for cash and turn over their inventory rapidly. Thus, inventory is a relatively liquid asset. It is therefore only necessary for the working capital ratio to be at least 1.

A poor liquidity position usually arises from continual losses, though it can also be the result of overtrading. At the other extreme a business can have too much liquidity. Where this is not temporary, the excess should be invested in non-current assets (assuming that there are profitable investment opportunities).

The prediction of insolvency

The working capital and liquidity ratios are, at best, crude conventional measures of liquidity. Most users of published financial statements are interested in liquidity as an indicator of whether a company will be able to pay its debts, or alternatively whether it is likely to go into liquidation in the near future. There is empirical research that demonstrates that the working capital and liquidity ratios are not particularly good predictors of insolvency. However, certain other ratios have been found to be useful in predicting corporate failure. The two most often cited studies of bankruptcy are by Altman (1968) in the USA and Taffler (1982) in the UK. They each identify a set of five accounting ratios that provide successful predictions of company failure. These are as follows:

Altman	***Taffler***
$\frac{\text{Profit before interest and tax}}{\text{Total assets}}$	$\frac{\text{Profit before interest and tax}}{\text{Opening total assets}}$
$\frac{\text{Working capital}}{\text{Total assets}}$	$\frac{\text{Working capital}}{\text{Net worth}}$
$\frac{\text{Revenue}}{\text{Total assets}}$	$\frac{\text{Revenue}}{\text{Average inventory}}$
$\frac{\text{Revenue earnings}}{\text{Total assets}}$	$\frac{\text{Quick assets}}{\text{Total assets}}$
$\frac{\text{Market value of equity}}{\text{Book value of total debt}}$	$\frac{\text{Total liabilities}}{\text{Net capital employed}}$

Both of these studies make use of a statistical technique known as 'multiple discriminant analysis'. This involves taking several ratios together in a multiple regression model. The set of five ratios in Altman's model enabled him correctly to classify as bankrupt or non-bankrupt 95 per cent of the cases in a sample of failed and non-failed US companies. He further claims that these ratios can be used to predict bankruptcy up to two years prior to actual failure. Similarly, Taffler correctly classified all but one company in a sample of UK companies, and asserts that his model exhibits predictive ability for about three years prior to bankruptcy. Several other studies have revisited this area (Ohlson, 1980; Dambolena and Khoury, 1980; Ding, 2007), making revisions to the methodology used and the ratios being focused on.

However, there are doubts about the validity of the results of studies such as these for a number of reasons. First, the research is not based on a theory that explains why particular ratios should provide successful predictions of insolvency. Second, these studies make use of historical cost data, the deficiencies of which have already been explained. Finally, there are several problems involved in the use of statistical techniques, such as discriminant analysis, which make the results questionable.

31.4 The appraisal of working capital

The phrase 'working capital' has two slightly different meanings. In computational terms it relates to the amount of the **net current assets**.

$$\text{Net current assets} = \text{Current assets} - \text{Current liabilities}$$

However, it is also used in a general sense to refer to the current assets and current liabilities. In this section the phrase 'working capital' is intended to be interpreted in the latter sense.

One way of looking at the appraisal of working capital is in terms of the interrelationship between a company's performance and liquidity position. As regards performance, the analysis of working capital is an extension of the asset turnover ratio (or more precisely the ratio of revenue to net current assets), which shows how effective a company's management has been in utilizing the various constituents of working capital. This in turn affects a company's liquidity position.

If there has been a significant change in the working capital and/or liquidity ratios, one would want to try to pinpoint the cause(s). In crude terms, the appraisal of working capital reveals whether too much or too little is invested in, for example, trade receivables and inventory relative to a company's level of activity (i.e. revenue). In theory, there is an optimal level of working capital. However, in practice all that users of published financial statements can do is to identify changes in the relative level of current assets such as trade receivables and inventory. These are taken as prima facie indicators of the effectiveness of credit control and inventory control, respectively.

A number of ratios can be calculated relating to those items that make up the working capital. Each of these must be considered in the light of the particular circumstances of the company, the type of industry and the prevailing economic climate. The most common ratios used in the appraisal of working capital are given below.

The trade receivables ratio – average period of credit taken by credit customers

This is calculated thus:

$$\frac{\text{Trade receivables}}{\text{Revenue}} \times \text{Number of days in a year}$$

Using the data in Worked Example 31.1 for 20X4 this gives:

$$\frac{£1{,}070{,}000}{£5{,}280{,}000} \times 365 = 74 \text{ days (20X3} - \text{67 days)}$$

Tailored Interpretation: It takes A. Harry plc's customers on average 74 days to pay for their goods. This is high and in addition the increase from 20X3 would suggest that the company is not as efficient at collecting its receivables in 20X4 as it was in 20X3. This may indicate that the balance includes balances that are not recoverable or that the debt collection department needs to be investigated.

Instead of using the trade receivables at the end of the accounting year in the numerator some authors compute the average trade receivables as follows:

$$\frac{\text{Trade receivables at the end of the previous year} + \text{Trade receivables at the end of the current year}}{2}$$

The argument for using this method of computation is that it gives a more representative figure for the 'normal' level of trade receivables. However, the important point is that the ratio should be computed on a consistent basis, otherwise comparisons will be misleading.

As the title suggests, this ratio shows the average number of days' credit taken by trade receivables. The most common terms of credit in the UK are that an invoice is due for payment by the end of the calendar month following the calendar month in which the goods are delivered/invoiced. The minimum average period of credit is thus approximately 45 days (i.e. one and a half months). However, many credit customers take a longer period than this if they can, since it is obviously beneficial for them to do so. Another method of expressing this ratio is referred to as the trade receivables' turnover ratio. It is calculated by inverting the fraction (and excluding the number of days in a year).

$$\frac{\text{Revenue}}{\text{Trade receivables}}$$

Using the data in Worked Example 31.1 for 20X4 this gives:

$$\frac{£5,280,000}{£1,070,000} = 4.9 \text{ times (5.4 times)}$$

Tailored Interpretation: This means that trade receivables turn over slower in 20X4 at 4.9 times in the year compared to 5.4 times in 20X3.

When the **trade receivables ratio** is calculated from the information in published financial statements, it may be nothing like any of these figures. This occurs if a company has both cash and credit sales. Since trade receivables arise because of credit sales, the denominator in the ratio should obviously comprise only the credit sales. However, these are not disclosed separately in published financial statements. Consequently, the aggregate of cash and credit sales has to be used in the computation, which results in a lower trade receivables collection period than if the denominator comprises only the credit sales. This is therefore clearly not the 'real' average period of credit, and a change in the proportion of cash to credit sales can distort the ratio over time.

The trade receivables collection period can also be abnormally high or low because a business's sales are seasonal, such as where these are heavily concentrated either in the summer (e.g. ice cream, soft drinks) or winter, or at Easter or Christmas. This can result in an exceptionally high or low trade receivables' figure depending on when the accounting year ends, and thus a correspondingly high or low trade receivables' ratio.

The average period of credit taken by credit customers varies between industries and according to the economic situation. Retailers, for example, usually grant little or no credit, whereas wholesalers and manufacturers often allow a considerable period of credit. Comparisons should therefore really only be made between businesses in the same industry and for a particular company over time. Where the period of credit is high compared with other firms (or with the average for the industry), and/or increasing over time, this is normally taken as indicating inadequate credit control procedures.

The trade payables ratio – average period of credit received from credit suppliers

The basic principle used in the calculation of the ratio for trade receivables can also be applied to trade payables in order to ascertain the average period of credit taken by the reporting entity. This is calculated as follows:

$$\frac{\text{Trade payables}}{\text{Purchases}} \times \text{Number of days in a year}$$

As in the case of trade receivables, the figure of trade payables used in the computation of the **trade payables ratio** may be an average of those at the end of the previous year and the end of the current year.

Another method of expressing this ratio is referred to as the 'trade payables turnover ratio'. It is calculated by inverting the fraction (and excluding the number of days in a year).

$$\frac{\text{Purchases}}{\text{Trade payables}}$$

The amount of purchases is not normally disclosed in published financial statements. However, if the company is a non-manufacturing business, these can be calculated by adjusting the cost of sales figure (given in the statement of profit or loss) by the change in inventory (given in the statement of financial position) over the year as follows:

Cost of sales
Add : inventory at end of current year
Less : inventory at end of previous year
= Purchases

Where the company is a manufacturing business, or the inventory at the end of the previous year is not given as a comparative figure instead of purchases, a surrogate has to be used, such as the cost of sales.

Using the data in Worked Example 31.1 for 20X4 this will give:

$$\frac{\pounds730{,}000}{\pounds3{,}090{,}000} \times 365 = 86 \text{ days (20X3 – 26 days)}$$

Tailored Interpretation: A. Harry plc is taking far longer to pay its suppliers in 20X4 (86 days) than it did in 20X3 (26 days). This is very long; however, given the other information in the question it is concluded that this is an agreed long credit period. This is inferred as the gross margin ratio has improved, suggesting that supplies have not increased in price. This is what normally happens when suppliers are not paid what they are due within the agreed timeframe and also A. Harry plc has plenty of money in the bank so can easily pay.

It is beneficial to delay paying credit suppliers for as long as possible. However, this may adversely affect the company's credit rating, and credit suppliers may refuse to supply further goods on credit. In addition, where the period of credit is high compared with other firms (or with the average for the industry) and/or increasing over time, this may be an indication of financial weakness.

The inventory turnover ratio

This is calculated thus:

$$\frac{\text{Cost of sales}}{\text{Inventory (finished goods)}}$$

Using the data in Worked Example 31.1 for 20X4 this will give:

$$\frac{\pounds3{,}090{,}000}{\pounds550{,}000} = 5.6 \text{ (20X3 – 7.5 times)}$$

Tailored Interpretation: Inventory turnover is slowing down. In general, this is a sign of inefficiency. The reduction may be as a result of reductions in demand (sales) not being predicted by the production manager, hence production remaining at a higher level than is necessary. Alternatively, it may suggest that some of the inventory on hand at the period end is obsolete.

The **inventory turnover ratio** shows the number of times that a business 'turns over'/sells its average/normal level of inventory during the accounting year. In very simple terms, a greengrocer who goes to market once a week and sells all those goods during that week would have an inventory turnover ratio of 52 (because there are 52 weeks in a year). Inventory turnover ratios vary between industries. Food retailers, for example, have a relatively high inventory turnover ratio, whereas jewellery retailers normally have a much lower ratio. Comparisons should therefore really only be made between firms in the same industry and for a particular company over time. Where the inventory turnover ratio is low compared with other firms (or with the average for the industry), and/or decreasing over time, this is normally taken as indicating a lack of adequate inventory control.

As in the calculation of the average period of credit for trade receivables and trade payables, there is an argument for using an average of the inventory at the end of the previous year and the current year as the denominator in this ratio. Once again, the important point is that a consistent basis of computation should be used to ensure meaningful comparisons. Another method of expressing this ratio is referred to as the 'number of days' sales from inventory'. It is calculated by inverting the fraction and multiplying the answer by 365.

31.5 Measures of return on investment and risk

This group of ratios is primarily intended for the use of equity shareholders, although a company's management will probably monitor these ratios as a guide to how investors view the company. There are several investment ratios, some of which are published in the *Financial Times*. These include the following.

The dividend yield

This is calculated as:

$$\frac{\text{Annual equity dividend}}{\text{Current market value of equity shares}}$$

For Worked Example 31.1 for 20X4 this will give:

$$\frac{£400{,}000 \div £2{,}000{,}000}{£4} \text{ or } \frac{£400{,}000}{2{,}000{,}000 \times £4} \times 100 = 5 \text{ per cent (20X3 – 5.2 per cent)}$$

Tailored Interpretation: Though the dividend increased from 12.5p per share in 20X3 (£250,000/2,000,000) to 20p per share in 20X4 (£400,000/2,000,000), the increase in share price from £2.50 to £4.00 has resulted in a reduction in the dividend yield from 5.2 per cent in 20X3 to 5 per cent in 20X4. The increase in share price suggests that investors are more confident about the future of the company in 20X4 than they were in 20X3.

The same principle can be used to calculate the **dividend yield** on preference shares and the interest yield on debentures and loan stock.

The dividend yield is said to measure the equity shareholder's annual cash return on investment, and may be compared with what could be obtained by investing in some other company. However, such comparisons can be misleading, for two main reasons. First, companies have different risk characteristics. A comparison of the dividend yields of, for example, a steel company and a large retailer such as Tesco plc would be misleading because the former is a riskier investment than the latter. Second, companies have different dividend policies, in that some distribute a greater proportion of their annual profit than others. Put slightly differently, the annual dividend is only part of an investor's total return, in that the investor will also expect to make a capital gain in the form of an increase in the market price of shares. This partly results from companies retaining a proportion of their annual profits.

The dividend yield is often between 2 and 5 per cent, but varies between companies for the reasons outlined above. Some investors regard the dividend yield as important because they are primarily interested in maximizing their annual cash income (e.g. retired people). However, for other investors the dividend yield may only be of limited importance because they are more interested in capital gains (for tax reasons) resulting from an increase in the share price. They are therefore often attracted to companies with a low dividend yield but high retained profits.

Dividend cover

This is calculated as:

$$\frac{\text{Profit for the year}}{\text{Annual equity dividend}}$$

For Worked Example 31.1 for 20X4 this will give:

$$\frac{£750{,}000}{£400{,}000} = 1.875 \ (20X3 - 1)$$

Tailored Interpretation: The dividend cover ratio has strengthened. In 20X3 all of the company's profits were distributed as a dividend, hence the dividend cover ratio of 1. This suggests that the dividend policy is risky as a reduction in profit means that the company will not be able to pay out the same dividend without affecting built up historical reserves. However, the situation improved and in 20X4 distributable profits covered the dividend 1.875 times.

The profit for the year is used in the calculation of this ratio because it represents the profit available for distribution as dividends to equity shareholders.

The **dividend cover** indicates how likely it is that the company will be able to maintain future dividends on equity shares at their current level if profits were to fall in future years. It is thus a measure of risk. The amount by which the dividend cover exceeds unity represents what might be called 'the margin of safety'. Thus, a company with a high dividend cover would be more likely to be able to maintain the current level of equity dividends than a company with a low dividend cover.

Earnings per share (EPS)

This is calculated as:

$$\frac{\text{Profit for the year}}{\text{Number of equity shares in issue}}$$

For Worked Example 31.1 for 20X4 this will give:

$$\frac{£750{,}000}{2{,}000{,}000} = £0.375 \ (20X3 - £0.125)$$

Tailored Interpretation: This ratio reflects the earlier performance ratios. Earnings per share have increased from 12.5p in 20X3 to 37.5p in 20X4. Investors will be happier with the reported ratio in 20X4.

The profit for the year is used in the calculation of this ratio because it represents the profit available for distribution as dividends to equity shareholders. This is referred to as the 'earnings'. There are complex rules for ascertaining the number of equity shares when there are movements in the number of shares during the year but these are beyond the scope of this book.

EPS is not strictly a measure of return on investment. However, it is included in the calculation of another widely used accounting ratio, the price–earnings ratio (discussed next). Furthermore, EPS is generally regarded as an important consideration in investment decisions, as such, and because of the significance investors place on this ratio, it has been given special attention by the IASB and has its own standard, *IAS 33 – Earnings per Share* (IASB, 2013). This standard requires that the EPS be disclosed in the published financial statements of all listed companies.

EPS provides a useful means of evaluating performance (where performance is defined from the shareholders' point of view as relating to the profit available for distribution as dividends). The trend in EPS over time indicates growth or otherwise in the profit attributable to each equity share. Inter-firm comparisons of EPS are not advisable.

The price–earnings (P/E) ratio

The **price–earnings (P/E) ratio** is calculated as:

$$\frac{\text{Current market price of each equity share}}{\text{EPS}}$$

For Worked Example 31.1 for 20X4 this will give:

$$\frac{£4}{£0.375} = 10.67 \text{ (20X3 – 20)}$$

Tailored Interpretation: The P/E ratio has fallen from 20 times in 20X3 to 10.67 times in 20X4. Given the increases in share price that have occurred over the year, it would seem that investors in 20X3 considered that earnings would increase, as at that time shareholders were willing to pay 20 times the yearly earnings for each share in the company. Over the year 20X4 earnings did increase; however, the share price increased also and by the end of the year it can be concluded that investors are not as positive about the future expected increases in earnings as they were at the end of 20X3.

The P/E ratio is often between 10 and 25 but varies considerably between different industries and companies in the same industry. The P/E ratio is a reflection of risk in that it represents the number of years' earnings that investors are prepared to buy at their current level. This is probably better explained in terms of what is essentially a payback period. The P/E ratio shows the number of years it will take to recoup the current price of the shares at the present level of EPS (the share price being recouped in the form of dividends and retained profits). In the context of A. Harry plc, the P/E ratio can be explained as follows. Share price covers earnings 10.67 times. Therefore, it will take 10.67 years to recoup the share price investment in earnings.

Where an investment is risky, investors will want to get their money back relatively quickly, whereas if an investment is comparatively safe, a longer payback period will be acceptable. Thus, companies in risky industries such as mining and construction tend to have a low P/E ratio, whereas companies in relatively safe industries such as food manufacturers, and those which are diversified tend to have a high P/E ratio.

The P/E ratio also varies between companies in the same industry. If investors think that a company's earnings are going to decline, the P/E ratio will tend to be lower than the average for the industry. Conversely, if profits are expected to rise, the P/E ratio will tend to be higher, both of which occur because of decreases and increases in the share price, respectively. The P/E ratio is therefore also a reflection of the expected earnings growth potential of a company. This also means that sometimes industries which one would expect to have a high P/E ratio, since they are relatively safe, in fact have a low P/E ratio because the earnings are expected to decline (and vice versa).

It appears that the P/E ratio is sometimes also used in practice to identify shares that are over or underpriced. A share is said to be overpriced if its P/E ratio is higher than the norm for the industry or other similar companies, and underpriced if the P/E ratio is lower than the norm for the industry or other similar companies. However, as explained above, this is probably an oversimplification, because the intrinsic/real value of a share will depend on the expected future earnings of the particular company.

Another way of looking at the P/E ratio is to invert the formula and express the result as a percentage. This is referred to as the **earnings yield**. For Worked Example 31.1 this will give:

$$\frac{£0.375}{£4} \text{ or } \frac{£750{,}000}{2 \text{ million } @ £4} \times 100 = 9.375 \text{ per cent (20X3 – 5 per cent)}$$

The earnings yield is not really a yield in the same sense as the dividend yield, since not all the earnings are distributed as dividends. However, it is often referred to as a measure of return on investment. As in the case of EPS, the earnings yield is a useful means of evaluating performance (where performance is defined from the shareholders' point of view as relating to the profit available for distribution as dividends). The trend in the earnings yield over time indicates how efficiently and effectively a company has utilized the amount of money the shareholders have invested in the company in terms of the current share price. It can also be used to compare the performance of different companies.

Learning Activity 31.1

Obtain two copies of the *Financial Times*, one for a Monday and one for any other day of the week. Turn to the last two pages but one of the section called 'Companies and Markets' headed 'London Share Service'. Look at the last two columns in the Tuesday to Saturday editions headed 'Yield' and 'P/E', which refer to the dividend yield and price–earnings ratio, respectively. Similarly, look at the column in the Monday edition headed 'Div.cov.', which refers to the dividend cover. Examine the values of these three ratios for some large public limited companies in different industries. What do these ratios tell you about those companies?

The return on equity (ROE)

This is calculated as:

$$\frac{\text{Profit for the year}}{\text{Equity}} \times 100$$

For Worked Example 31.1 for 20X4 this will give:

$$\frac{£750{,}000}{£4{,}380{,}000} \times 100 = 17.1 \text{ per cent (20X3 – 6.9 per cent)}$$

Tailored Interpretation: Earnings generated for each £1 invested in the company in the form of equity generated 17.1p in 20X4, up from 6.9p per £1 invested in 20X3. This is consistent with the earlier performance ratios discussed earlier in this chapter. The company is more efficient and is reporting better performance, hence the returns are greater.

Sometimes this ratio is calculated using the profit before tax (but after preference dividends) to avoid the distortions that can arise when comparing companies with different tax positions. As in the ROCE ratio, it is more appropriate to use the equity shareholders' interests at the start of the accounting year, or an average, rather than at the end of the year. The latter is unjustifiable and has only been used in this example because it is the only figure available for simplicity.

The ROE is essentially the same as the earnings yield. The difference is that, instead of expressing the earnings as a percentage of the market price/value of the equity shares, this is expressed as a percentage of the book value of the equity shares in the form of the equity shareholders' interests. Since the latter is not the 'real' (i.e. market) value of the equity shareholders' investment, this ratio can be said to be inferior to the earnings yield.

However, the ROE, like the earnings yield, is a common measure of return on investment which is used to evaluate profitability (where profitability is defined from the equity shareholders' point of view as relating to the profit available for distribution as dividends). It is said to indicate how efficiently and effectively a company's management has utilized the equity shareholders' interests. The ratio may be used to compare the profitability of different companies and/or to examine trends over time.

The gearing ratio

Gearing, or **leverage** as it is called in the USA, refers to the relationship between the amount of fixed interest capital (i.e. loan stock, debentures, preference shares, etc.) and the amount of equity capital (i.e. equity shares). In discussions of gearing, the fixed interest capital is frequently referred to as the **debt capital**, which is taken to include preference shares. As a broad generalization, where the value of fixed interest capital is less than the value of equity, a company is said to have low gearing. Where the value of debt capital is more than the value of equity, a company is said to have high gearing.

There are two main ways of expressing the **gearing ratio**. The basis most commonly used in the financial press is to express the debt capital as a fraction (or percentage) of the equity capital thus:

$$\text{Debt/equity ratio} = \frac{\text{Debt capital}}{\text{Equity capital}} \ (\times 100)$$

However, in accounting it is more common to compute the gearing ratio by expressing the debt capital as a fraction (or percentage) of the total capital thus:

$$\text{Gearing ratio} = \frac{\text{Debt capital}}{\text{Debt capital} + \text{Equity capital}} \ (\times 100)$$

Try Worked Example 31.2 before proceeding.

WORKED EXAMPLE 31.2

	Company with low gearing	Company with high gearing
	£	£
Equity shares of £1 each	400,000	100,000
10% preference shares of £1 each	30,000	150,000
10% debentures of £100 each	70,000	250,000
	500,000	500,000
Gearing ratio	20% or 1:4	80% or 4:1

The next issue concerns how the debt and equity capital are to be measured/valued. Two methods are discussed here.

1 The first uses the *nominal values* of the equity accounts including share capital, the share premium account, other equity reserves and retained profits. Debt capital refers to the preference shares, loan stock, debentures, bank loans, mortgages and any other non-current borrowing, such as an overdraft for more than one year. Thus:

Returning to the data in Worked Example 31.1 for 20X4, gearing would be calculated as follows:

$$\frac{£4{,}000{,}000}{£4{,}000{,}000 + £4{,}380{,}000} \times 100 = 47.7 \text{ per cent (20X3} - 57.9 \text{ per cent)}$$

Tailored Interpretation: Gearing has fallen from 57.9 per cent in 20X3 to 47.7 per cent in 20X4. This is a positive movement that has been caused by the company retaining more funds from distributable profits and also by paying back £1,000,000 of the long-term debt. The company will have less interest to pay in the future and this reduces the riskiness of the company.

This method of expressing the gearing ratio is considered to be superior to the first because reserves and retained earnings constitute part of the equity shareholders' interests and thus the capital that they provide. The logic behind this is perhaps more obvious when the gearing ratio is calculated in terms of the book value of the assets, thus:

$$\frac{\text{Nominal value of debt capital}}{\text{Total assets} - \text{Current liabilities}} \times 100$$

Using the data in Worked Example 31.1 for 20X4 this would be calculated as follows:

$$\frac{£4{,}000{,}000}{£9{,}360{,}000 - £980{,}000} \times 100 = 47.7 \text{ per cent (20X3} - 57.9 \text{ per cent)}$$

This formula highlights that the gearing ratio shows the proportion of the assets, which are financed by fixed interest capital.

2 *Using the current market prices* of a company's equity shares and debt capital, thus:

$$\frac{\text{Market value of debt capital}}{\text{Market value of debt capital} + \text{Market value of equity shares}} \times 100$$

Using the data in Worked Example 31.1 for 20X4 this would be calculated as follows:

$$\frac{40{,}000@£90 \text{ (or } £4{,}000{,}000 \times £90 \,/\, £100)}{(40{,}000@£90) + (2{,}000{,}000@£4)} \times 100 = 31 \text{ per cent (20X3} - 45.9 \text{ per cent)}$$

This is generally regarded as being a more theoretically sound method of expressing the gearing ratio, because market prices are said to represent the 'real' value of the debt capital and shareholders' interests as distinct from the nominal or book values.

The gearing ratio is a measure of the '**financial risk**' attaching to a company's equity shares that arises because of the prior claim that fixed interest capital has on the annual income and assets (in the event of liquidation). This financial risk is additional to the '**operating risk**' that is associated with the particular industry or industries in which a company is trading.

Companies are said to engage in gearing because it usually produces substantial benefits for the equity shareholders. In crude terms, the money provided by loan creditors is used to generate income in excess of the loan interest. The tax deductibility of interest contributes to this benefit. In technical terms, gearing usually increases the profit available for distribution as dividends to equity shareholders and thus the EPS, although it does have an impact on the riskiness of the earnings. These effects are illustrated numerically in Worked Example 31.3. The data are taken from Worked Example 31.2. These two companies are assumed to be identical in all respects except their gearing. Both have a profit after tax (but before interest) of £50,000 and an EPS of 10 pence in year 1. Although this example is clearly unrealistic, it illustrates vividly the impact of gearing.

Now suppose the profit of both companies doubles in year 2, as shown in Worked Example 31.4. In the case of the company with low gearing, a 100 per cent increase in the profit after tax (but before interest) in year 2 results in a 125 per cent increase (from £40,000 to £90,000) in the profit available for distribution

WORKED EXAMPLE 31.3

	Company with low gearing		Company with high gearing	
Year 1	£	£	£	£
Profit before interest		50,000		50,000
Preference dividends	3,000		15,000	
Interest	7,000	10,000	25,000	40,000
Distributable profit		40,000		10,000
Earnings per share		10p		10p

as dividends to equity shareholders. By contrast, in the case of the highly geared company, a 100 per cent increase in the profit after tax in year 2 results in a 500 per cent increase (from £10,000 to £60,000) in the distributable profit. Similarly, a 100 per cent increase in the profit after tax results in a 125 per cent increase in the EPS of the low-geared company, compared with a 500 per cent increase for the company with high gearing.

WORKED EXAMPLE 31.4

	Company with low gearing		Company with high gearing	
Year 2	£	£	£	£
Profit before interest		100,000		100,000
Preference dividends	3,000		15,000	
Interest	7,000	10,000	25,000	40,000
Distributable profit		90,000		60,000
Earnings per share		22.5p		60p

This can be summarized in the form of a general rule as follows: any increase in profit (before charging interest) will result in a *proportionately greater* increase in the profit available for distribution (and the EPS) of a high-geared company, compared with an equivalent increase for a company with low gearing.

However, gearing is a double-edged sword, in that the same occurs in reverse when there is a decrease in profit, as often happens when there is an economic recession. Imagine that the chronological sequence in Worked Example 31.4 is reversed, giving profit before interest of £100,000 in year 1 and £50,000 in year 2 representing a 50 per cent decrease in the profit after tax (but before interest). This results in a reduction in the distributable profit and EPS of 56 per cent in the case of the low-geared company, compared with 83 per cent for the company with high gearing. This can also be summarized in the form of a general rule as follows: any decrease in the profit (before charging interest) will result in a proportionately greater reduction in the profit available for distribution (and the EPS) of a high-geared company compared with an equivalent decrease for a company with low gearing.

Furthermore, the level of gearing affects a company's break-even point. A company with high gearing will have a larger break-even point than an equivalent company with low gearing. This is because the interest charges of a high-geared company are greater than for an equivalent company with low gearing. In Worked Example 31.3 the break-even point of the high-geared company is £30,000 (i.e. £40,000 – £10,000) higher than that of the low-geared company. This means that a company with high gearing has to earn a greater profit (before interest) before it can declare a dividend compared with an equivalent company that has low gearing. Thus, if the profit after tax of these companies fell to, say, £20,000, the company with low gearing would still be able to declare an equity dividend from the current year's trading profit whereas the high-geared company could not.

To sum up, the equity shareholders in a high-geared company benefit from gearing when profits are relatively large. However, they run two risks. First, when profits are small the dividends will be less than would be the case with low gearing. Second, if the company goes into liquidation, they will not be repaid the value of their shares until after all the fixed interest capital has been repaid. Usually very little or nothing is left for the equity shareholders. Thus, the tendency to assume that gearing is advantageous may be a misconception because, while it frequently results in a proportionately greater increase in the distributable profit, it also makes the equity shares riskier. To use an analogy, one should not bet on an outsider in a horse race merely because the winnings would be greater than betting on the favourite. One must weigh up the possible return in relation to the perceived risk.

Learning Activity 31.2

Assess the liquidity, solvency, profitability, efficiency and investment potential of Ryanair plc. Find the disclosures in respect of their EPS ratio. Try to calculate it using the information provided.

Learning Activity 31.3

Search the Web for a copy of the financial statements of a large public limited company. Try to obtain the financial statements of a company that is known to have had recent financial problems. Using the information contained in this document, compute all the ratios discussed in this chapter for the current and previous year. List any apparent material changes in the value of these ratios, and outline their possible causes.

31.6 The limitations of ratio analysis

Worked Example 31.1 was deliberately kept simple for the purpose of illustration. In particular, it contains no comparative figures for the previous year. Thus, no time-series analysis was possible. In addition, in the calculation of some ratios (e.g. EPS, ROE, ROCE) the amount at the end of the accounting year was used when it would have been more appropriate to take the figure at the beginning of the year or an average for the year. Companies are required by law to include comparative figures for the previous year in their published financial statements. These would therefore usually be available and should be used where appropriate.

Ratio analysis has a number of limitations. Most of these have already been explained in the context of particular ratios but can be summarized as follows:

1. Comparisons between companies and for a particular company over time may be misleading if different accounting policies are used to calculate profits and value assets.
2. Ratios usually have to be calculated using historical cost data since few companies publish a current cost statement of comprehensive income and statement of financial position. These ratios will therefore be distorted because of the effects of inflation and thus comparisons may be misleading.
3. The data needed to compute some ratios are not disclosed in published financial statements and thus surrogates have to be used (e.g. the aggregate cash and credit sales in the calculation of the average period of credit taken by trade receivables). This may also mean that comparisons are misleading.

4 The general yardsticks or performance criteria that may be applied to particular ratios (e.g. a liquidity ratio of at least 1) are not appropriate for all types of industry.

5 Changes in a given ratio over time and differences between companies must be considered in the light of the particular circumstances of the reporting entity, the type of industry and the general economic situation. They may also be due to deliberate policy decisions by management such as a build-up of inventories prior to a sales promotion campaign, to rent or own non-current assets, and so on.

6 A single ratio may not be very informative by itself, but a number of related ratios taken together should give a general picture of the company's performance or financial position (e.g. in the prediction of insolvency).

In practice

To aid the interpretation of performance, most plcs include important ratios in a statement at the front of their annual report called the Business Review. This can either be a narrative overview of the performance of the entity or a table highlighting trends in certain ratios. An example is now provided. Note how CRH have analysed the percentage change in figures; this is known as trend analysis.

REAL WORLD EXAMPLE 31.1

CRH plc

2012 FULL YEAR RESULTS

Year ended 31 December	**2012 € m**	**2011 € m**	**% change**
Sales revenue	**18,659**	**18,081**	**Up 3%**
EBITDA*	**1,640**	**1,656**	**Down 1%**
Operating profit (EBIT)*	**845**	**871**	**Down 3%**
Profit on disposals	230	55	
Finance costs	(289)	(257)	
Associates' results, net of impairment	(112)	42	
Profit before tax	**674**	**711**	**Down 5%**
	€ cent	**€ cent**	
Earnings per share	**76.5**	**82.6**	**Down 7%**
Cash earnings per share	**206.8**	**194.0**	**Up 7%**
Dividend per share	**62.5**	**62.5**	**Maintained**

** EBIT (earnings before interest and tax) and EBITDA (earnings before interest, tax, depreciation, amortisation and impairment charges) exclude profit on disposals and CRH's share of associates' profit after tax.*

Financial Highlights

- Sales up 3% to €18.7 billion; EBITDA of €1.64 billion, ahead of November guidance
- Americas sales up 15% and EBITDA up 12% to €0.85 billion
- European sales down 7% and EBITDA down 12% at €0.79 billion
- Continuing tight management of working capital and capital expenditure

- Net debt down €0.5 billion to under €3 billion; net debt to EBITDA cover of 1.8 times
- One of the strongest balance sheets in the global building materials sector
- Dividend per share maintained at 62.5c

Source: CRH (2012) Extract from the CRH Annual Report 2012, http://www.crh.com/docs/press-releases-2013/crh-2012-full-year-results-report.pdf?sfvrsn = 4, accessed September 2013.

Summary

The main purpose of ratio analysis is to enable users of financial statements to evaluate a company's financial performance and financial position over time, and/or in relation to other companies. Ratios may be grouped under four main headings, each reflecting what the ratios are intended to measure, as outlined in Figure 31.1:

Figure 31.1

Measures of a company's performance
- Return on capital employed
- Profit margin (net and gross)
- Asset-turnover ratio

Measures of solvency and liquidity
- Solvency refers to whether a company is able to pay its debts as they become due (gearing ratio)
- Liquidity refers to the ease with which an asset can be turned into cash without loss. Measures include the current and liquidity ratios

The appraisal of working capital (management efficiency)
- The trade receivables' ratio
- Trade payables' ratio
- Inventory-turnover ratio

Measures of return on investment and risk
- Dividend yield
- Dividend cover
- Earnings per share
- Price–earnings ratio
- Earnings yield
- Return on equity
- Capital-gearing ratio

A single ratio may not be very informative, but a number of related ratios taken together can provide strong indications of a company's performance or financial position, such as in the prediction of insolvency. However, these must be interpreted in the light of the particular circumstances of the company, the type of industry and the current economic climate. General yardsticks are not always appropriate. Furthermore, ratios must be interpreted with caution. The use of historical cost and surrogate data, as well as different accounting policies, can distort comparisons.

Key terms and concepts

asset-turnover ratio	652	liquidity ratio	654
capital employed	648	net current assets	656
debt capital	663	operating risk	664
dividend cover	660	price–earnings (P/E) ratio	661
dividend yield	659	profitability	648
earnings per share	650	profit margin	651
earnings yield	662	return	648
financial risk	664	return on assets	650
gearing	663	return on capital employed	650
gearing ratio	663	return on equity	651
gross capital employed	651	solvency	653
gross profit ratio	653	trade payables ratio	657
insolvent	653	trade receivables ratio	657
inventory turnover ratio	658	working capital	648
leverage	663	working capital/current ratio	654
liquidity	648		

An asterisk after the question number indicates that there is a suggested answer in Appendix 2.

Review questions

connect

31.1 Explain what each of the following is intended to measure:

a return on capital employed;

b profit margin;

c asset-turnover ratio;

d working capital and liquidity ratios;

e average period of credit taken by trade receivables;

f inventory turnover ratio.

31.2 Examine the empirical evidence relating to the predictive ability of accounting ratios with regard to insolvency.

31.3 Explain what each of the following is intended to measure: (a) dividend yield; (b) dividend cover; (c) earnings per share; (d) price–earnings ratio; and (e) return on equity.

31.4 a Explain what is meant by capital gearing/leverage.

b Why might this influence a prospective investor's decision concerning whether or not to buy equity shares in a company?

31.5 Explain the limitations of using accounting ratios in time-series analysis and inter-firm comparisons, giving examples where appropriate.

31.6 How does inflation affect ratio analysis?

31.7 What is the difference between solvency and liquidity?

Exercises

connect

BASIC

31.8 Bastante plc has 40,000 equity shares in issue. They are currently trading at £3.00 each. Bastante plc also has 400 debentures, trading at par.

Required

a Calculate the gearing ratio for Bastante plc using market values.

b Explain the outcome.

INTERMEDIATE

31.9 Dale is in business as a sole trader. You are presented with the following summarized information relating to his business for the year to 31 October 20X4:

Statement of profit or loss for the year to 31 October 20X4		
	£'000	*£'000*
Sales revenue: cash	200	
credit	600	800
Less: Cost of goods sold –		
opening inventory	80	
purchases	530	
	610	
Less: closing inventory	70	540
Gross profit		260
Expenses		(205)
Profit for the year		55

Statement of financial position at 31 October 20X4	
ASSETS	*£'000*
Non-current assets	550
Current assets	
Inventories	70
Trade receivables	120
Cash	5
	195
Total assets	745

EQUITY AND LIABILITIES	
Equity	
Capital at 1 November 20X3	410
Net profit for the year	55
	465
Drawings	(50)
Total equity	415
Non-current liabilities	
Loan	200
Total non-current liabilities	200
Current liabilities	
Trade payables	130
Total current liabilities	130
Total liabilities	330
Total equity and liabilities	745

Required

a Based on the above information, calculate eight recognized accounting ratios.

b List what additional information you would need in order to undertake a detailed ratio analysis of Dale's business for the year to 31 October 20X4.

Note: In answering part (a) of the question, each ratio must be distinct and separate. Marks will *not* be awarded for alternative forms of the same ratio.

(AAT)

31.10* White and Black are sole traders. Both are wholesalers dealing in a similar range of goods. Summaries of the profit calculations and statements of financial position for the same year have been made available to you, as follows:

Statements of profit or loss for the year				
	White		**Black**	
	£'000	*£'000*	*£'000*	*£'000*
Sales revenue		600		800
Cost of goods sold		(450)		(624)
Gross profit		150		176
Administrative expenses	(64)		(63)	
Selling and distribution expenses	(28)		(40)	
Depreciation – equipment and vehicles	(10)		(20)	
Depreciation – buildings	–	(102)	(5)	(128)
Profit for the year		48		48

Statements of financial position as at end of year		
	White	**Black**
ASSETS		
Non-current assets	*£'000*	*£'000*
Buildings	29	47
Equipment and vehicles	62	76
	91	123
Current assets		
Inventory	56	52
Trade receivables	75	67
Bank balance	8	–
	139	119
Total assets	230	242
EQUITY AND LIABILITIES		
Equity		
Capital	192	160
Total equity	192	160
Current liabilities		
Trade payables	38	78
Bank balance	–	4
Total current liabilities	38	82
Total equity and liabilities	230	242

Required

Compare the performance and financial position of the two businesses on the basis of the above figures, supporting your comments where appropriate with ratios and noting what further information you would need before reaching firmer conclusions.

(ACCA)

INTERMEDIATE

31.11 The following are the summarized financial statements of Alpha and Omega, two companies that operate in the same industry:

Summarized statement of financial position		
	Alpha	**Omega**
	£m	*£m*
ASSETS		
Non-current assets	790	1,000
Current assets		
Inventories	1,200	1,800
Trade receivables	720	1,200
Bank	190	–
	2,110	3,000
Total assets	2,900	4,000

EQUITY AND LIABILITIES		
Equity		
Capital	1,160	1,756
Retained earnings	340	404
Total equity	1,500	2,160
Non-current liabilities		
Loan	500	–
Current liabilities		
Trade payables	900	1,040
Bank overdraft	–	800
Total current liabilities	900	1,840
Total liabilities	1,400	1,840
Total equity and liabilities	2,900	4,000

Summarized statements of profit or loss

	Alpha		Omega	
	£m	*£m*	*£m*	*£m*
Revenue		6,000		7,200
Less: Cost of goods sold				
Opening inventory	1,000		1,500	
Add: purchases	4,760		5,916	
	5,760		7,416	
Less: closing inventory	1,200	4,560	1,800	5,616
Gross profit		1,440		1,584
Expenses				
Overhead expenditure		(1,100)		(1,180)
Profit for the year		340		404

Required

a Using ratio analysis, comment on the profitability, efficiency, liquidity and gearing of *both* companies.

b List three limitations of ratio analysis for the purposes of interpreting financial statements.

31.12* The following is an extract from the published financial statements of Blue Light plc for the year ended 31 March 20X4. INTERMEDIATE

Blue Light Plc: Statement of profit or loss

	£'000
Revenue	4,230
Cost of sales	(2,560)
Gross profit	1,670
Distribution costs	(470)
Administrative expenses	(380)
Finance costs	(240)
Profit before taxation	580
Income tax	(270)
Profit for the year	310

Blue Light Plc: Statement of financial position	
ASSETS	*£'000*
Non-current assets	4,870
Current assets	
Inventories	480
Trade receivables	270
Bank and cash	320
	1,070
Total assets	5,940
EQUITY AND LIABILITIES	
500,000 equity shares of £1 each	500
Retained earnings	1,910
Total equity	2,410
Non-current liabilities	
8% debentures of £100 each	3,000
Total non-current liabilities	3,000
Current liabilities	
Trade payables	260
Current tax payable	270
Total current liabilities	530
Total liabilities	3,530
Total equity and liabilities	5,940

Additional information:

The equity shares and debentures are currently quoted on the London Stock Exchange at £5 and £110, respectively.

Required

Calculate the ratios that you would include in a report to a prospective investor relating to measures of performance, liquidity, the appraisal of working capital, and return on investment and risk. Comment briefly on the results and the limitations of your analysis.

INTERMEDIATE

31.13* The following is a summary of some of the accounting ratios of two companies in the same industry and of a comparable size for the year ended 30 June 20X5.

	Fish plc	Chips plc
Dividend yield	4%	7%
Dividend cover	3.6	2.1
Earnings per share	17p	23p
P/E ratio	14	8
Return on equity	22%	27%
Return on capital employed	18%	15%
Profit margin	20%	25%
Asset turnover ratio	0.9	0.6
Gearing ratio	28%	76%

Required

Write a report to a prospective investor on the comparative return on investment, risk and performance of these two companies.

31.14* Key working capital and liquidity ratios for A plc are as follows: INTERMEDIATE

	20X3	20X4
Working capital ratio	1.5	1.7
Liquidity ratio	1.1	0.8
Inventory turnover	6.3	5.9
Trade receivables' ratio	52 days	63 days
Trade payables' ratio	71 days	78 days

Required

Write a report to one of A plc's major shareholders on the change in its liquidity and working capital position over the year ended 30 April 20X4.

31.15 Two retailers show the following financial statements for the year to 31 December 20X4. INTERMEDIATE

Statements of financial position as at 31 December 20X4		
	A. Ltd	**B. Ltd**
ASSETS	*£'000*	*£'000*
Non-current assets		
Premises	5,000	8,000
Fixtures	500	1,000
	5,500	9,000
Current assets		
Inventory	800	900
Trade receivables	50	60
Bank	330	720
	1,180	1,680
Total assets	6,680	10,680
EQUITY AND LIABILITIES		
Equity		
Equity shares of £1	3,000	2,000
Retained earnings	2,030	2,700
Total equity	5,030	4,700
Non-current liabilities		
Long-term loans	800	5,000
Total non-current liabilities	800	5,000
Current liabilities	850	980
Total liabilities	1,650	5,980
Total equity and liabilities	6,680	10,680

Statements of profit or loss for the year ended 31 December 20X4		
	£'000	£'000
Revenue	13,360	16,020
Cost of sales	(8,685)	(10,090)
Gross profit	4,675	5,930
Distribution	(2,300)	(2,870)
Administration	(1,375)	(1,670)
Finance costs	(65)	(400)
Profit for the year	935	990

Additional information

1 **A. Ltd paid a dividend of £300,000 during the year.**

2 **B. Ltd paid a dividend of £400,000 during the year.**

Required

a **Compute for each of the two companies:**

i **one ratio relevant to an assessment of liquidity;**

ii **one ratio relevant to an assessment of gearing;**

iii **three ratios relevant to an assessment of profitability and performance.**

b **Summarize briefly the overall strengths and weaknesses of Company A, using each of the ratios you have computed.**

(JMB)

INTERMEDIATE

31.16 The outline statements of financial position of the Nantred Trading Co. Ltd were as shown below:

Statements of financial position as at 30 September		
ASSETS	*20X3*	*20X4*
Non-current assets	£	£
Premises	40,000	98,000
Plant and equipment	65,000	162,000
	105,000	260,000
Current assets		
Inventory	31,200	95,300
Trade receivables	19,700	30,700
Bank and cash	15,600	26,500
	66,500	152,500
Total assets	171,500	412,500
EQUITY AND LIABILITIES		
Equity		
Equity share capital	100,000	200,000
Retained earnings	36,200	43,600
Total equity	136,200	243,600

Non-current liabilities		
7% debentures	–	100,000
Total non-current liabilities	–	100,000
Current liabilities		
Trade payables	23,900	55,800
Current tax payable	11,400	13,100
Total current liabilities	35,300	68,900
Total liabilities	35,300	168,900
Total equity and liabilities	171,500	412,500

Additional information

The only other information available is that the revenue for the years ended 30 September 20X3 and 20X4 was £202,900 and £490,700, respectively, and that on 30 September 20X2 reserves were £26,100.

Required

a Calculate, for each of the two years, six suitable ratios to highlight the financial stability, liquidity and profitability of the company.

b Comment on the situation revealed by the figures you have calculated in your answer to (a) above.

(ACCA)

31.17 You are given below, in draft form, the financial statements of Algernon Ltd for 20X4 and 20X5. They are not in publishable format. ADVANCED

Statements of financial position

	20X4			20X5		
	Cost	**Depn**	**Net**	**Cost**	**Depn**	**Net**
ASSETS	£	£	£	£	£	£
Plant	10,000	4,000	6,000	11,000	5,000	6,000
Building	50,000	10,000	40,000	90,000	11,000	79,000
	60,000	14,000	46,000	101,000	16,000	85,000
Financial assets			50,000			80,000
Land			43,000			63,000
Inventory			55,000			65,000
Trade receivables			40,000			50,000
Bank			3,000			–
Total assets			237,000			343,000

EQUITY AND LIABILITIES		
Equity shares £1 each	40,000	50,000
Share premium	12,000	14,000
Revaluation reserve	–	20,000
Retained earnings	45,000	45,000
10% debentures	100,000	150,000
Trade payables	40,000	60,000
Bank	–	4,000
	237,000	343,000

Statements of profit or loss		
	20X4	**20X5**
	£	£
Sales revenue	200,000	200,000
Cost of sales	(100,000)	(120,000)
Gross profit	100,000	80,000
Expenses	(60,000)	(60,000)
Profit for the year	40,000	20,000

Required

a Calculate for Algernon Ltd, for 20X4 and 20X5, the following ratios:

- **i** return on capital employed;
- **ii** return on owners' equity (return on shareholders' funds);
- **iii** trade receivables' turnover;
- **iv** trade payables' turnover;
- **v** current ratio;
- **vi** quick assets (acid test) ratio;
- **vii** gross profit percentage;
- **viii** net profit percentage;
- **ix** dividend cover;
- **x** gearing ratio.

b Using the summarized financial statements given, and the ratios you have just prepared, comment on the position, progress and direction of Algernon Ltd.

(ACCA adapted)

INTERMEDIATE

31.18 Delta Ltd is an old-established light engineering company. The key performance data for the company between 20X1 and 20X5 are given below.

	20X1	20X2	20X3	20X4	20X5
Profit before interest/revenue (%)	3.6	0.5	0.6	8.1	9.8
Revenue/non-current assets (times)	4.6	3.4	3.3	3.5	3.7
Revenue/net current assets (times)	2.2	2.5	2.9	3.7	5.1
Cost of sales/inventory (times)	1.9	2.0	2.4	2.7	2.9
Trade receivables/ave. days sales (days)	80.0	77.0	75.0	67.0	64.0
Trade payables/ave. days sales (days)	58.0	57.0	61.0	64.0	71.0
Cost of sales/revenue (%)	71.0	73.7	75.0	71.0	69.5
Selling and distribution/revenue (%)	19.0	18.7	18.5	16.0	15.6
Administrative/revenue (%)	6.4	7.1	5.9	4.9	5.1
Current ratio	4.9	2.8	3.3	2.1	1.8

Required

Examine the above data and write a report to the directors of Delta Ltd analysing the performance of the company between 20X1 and 20X5.

(JMB)

ADVANCED

31.19 Aragon (a bank) has recently received a request for a term loan from one of its customers, Valencia plc, a company listed on the Alternative Investment Market of the London Stock Exchange. Valencia plc's directors have requested a further £6 million (five-year floating rate) term loan at an initial interest rate of 12 per cent per annum, in order to purchase new equipment. The equipment will not materially change the company's current average percentage return on investment. Valencia plc's turnover increased by 9 per cent during the last financial year. Prior to receiving the request, the regional commercial manager of Aragon had conducted a review of Valencia plc's financial position, and had decided to ask Valencia plc's management to reduce the company overdraft by 25 per cent within the next six months.

Summarized financial statements for Valencia plc are as follows:

Statements of financial position		
	20X4	20X3
ASSETS	*£'000*	*£'000*
Non-current assets		
Property, plant and equipment	16,060	14,380
Current assets		
Inventories	31,640	21,860
Trade receivables	24,220	17,340
Investment	8,760	10,060
Cash and cash equivalents	1,700	960
	66,320	50,220
Total assets	82,380	64,600

EQUITY AND LIABILITIES		
Equity		
Share capital	3,800	3,800
Retained earnings	16,900	13,500
Total equity	20,700	17,300
Non-current liabilities		
Long-term borrowings	6,000	–
Debentures	16,000	16,000
Total non-current liabilities	22,000	16,000
Current liabilities		
Overdraft	16,340	13,220
Trade and other payables	20,920	15,280
Current taxation	2,420	2,800
Total current liabilities	39,680	31,300
Total liabilities	61,680	47,300
Total equity and liabilities	82,380	64,600

Extract information from the statement of profit or loss of Valencia plc

	20X4
	£'000
Revenue	99,360
Profit before interest and taxation	10,760
Finance costs	(3,840)
Profit before tax	6,920
Income tax expense	(2,420)
Profit for the period	4,500
Dividend paid in the year	1,100

The company's debentures are currently trading at £96.50 and equity 10p shares at £1.50.

Comparative ratio information for Valencia plc's industry (averages)

	20X4
Share price	£51.20
Dividend yield	2.5%
Dividend payout ratio	50%
Gross asset turnover	1.4 times
Earnings per share	17.8 pence
Gearing	52.4%
Acid test	1 : 1
Interest cover	4 times
Return on revenue (PBIT)	9%
Return on investment	16.5%

Required

a You are a consultant for Aragon. You are required to produce a reasoned case explaining why the bank should request a 25 per cent reduction in the company's overdraft.

b You are a consultant for Valencia plc:

i Prepare a reasoned case to present to Aragon in support of the new term loan.

ii Make recommendations to the board of Valencia plc in respect of how you think the company's financial position might be improved.

Note: Clearly state any assumptions made. All assumptions must relate to all parts of the question.

31.20 The directors of Atono plc were informed at a golf outing by fellow directors that it is more valuable to have debt in a company's capital structure than equity, as debt is cheaper than equity. Atono plc currently has no debt in its capital structure, though is considering borrowing funds, which it will use to buy back the more expensive equity capital. The capital structure of Atono plc is as follows: INTERMEDIATE

	Current	Suggested
	£'000	*£'000*
Assets	10,000	10,000
Equity and reserves	10,000	5,000
Long-term debt	–	5,000
Total equity and liabilities	10,000	10,000
Shares outstanding	500,000	250,000

Additional information:

1 The company's equity shares are currently trading at £20 each, and it is assumed that this value does not change when the suggested capital structure change takes place.

2 The long-term debt attracts an interest rate of 8 per cent.

3 Taxation is 30 per cent.

Required

Calculate the gearing ratio for Atono plc under both scenarios.

31.21 Using the information provided in 31.20, assume the company faces three differing external environment scenarios: boom; steady state; and recession. Each scenario has different income potentials: if there is a boom economy, then earnings before interest and taxation (EBIT) of £1 million are expected; if the economy stays steady, EBIT are expected to remain at £660,000; whereas if the economy goes into recession, EBIT are expected to fall to £450,000. ADVANCED

Required

Calculate the impact of the change in gearing on the *return on equity* and the *earnings per share* for each scenario.

31.22 The following are the summarized financial statements of Ingrid Ltd and Epona Ltd, two firms that operate in identical industries. INTERMEDIATE

Summarized statements of profit or loss		
	Ingrid Ltd	Epona Ltd
	£'000	*£'000*
Sales revenue	6,000	7,200
Cost of goods sold	(4,560)	(5,616)
Gross profit	1,440	1,584
Overhead expenditure (including interest)	(1,140)	(1,260)
Profit for the year	300	324

Summarized statements of financial position		
ASSETS		
Non-current assets	790	1,000
Current assets		
Inventories	1,200	1,800
Trade receivables	720	1,200
Bank	190	–
	2,110	3,000
Total assets	2,900	4,000
EQUITY AND LIABILITIES		
Equity		
Share capital and retained earnings	1,500	2,160
Non-current liabilities		
8% long-term loan	500	–
Current liabilities		
Trade payables	900	1,040
Bank overdraft	–	800
Total current liabilities	900	1,840
Total liabilities	1,400	1,840
Total equity and liabilities	2,900	4,000

Note: The rate of interest on Epona's overdraft is 10 per cent per annum.

Required

a Calculate three ratios for each company showing profitability and three showing liquidity.

b Discuss three reasons why a potential investor would choose Ingrid Ltd.

c Identify three further pieces of information necessary before making the recommendation in (b) above.

References

Altman, E.A. (1968) 'Financial Ratios, Discriminant Analysis and the Prediction of Corporate Bankruptcy', *Journal of Finance* (September), 589–609.

International Accounting Standards Board (2013) *IAS 33 – Earnings Per Share* (IASB).

Dambolena, I.G. and Khoury, S.J. (1980) 'Ratio Stability and Corporate Failure', *Journal of Finance*, 35(4), 1017–26.

Ding, A. (2007) 'Early Discovery of Individual Firm Insolvency', *IMA Journal of Management Mathematics*, 18(3), 269–95.

Ohlson, J.A. (1980) 'Financial Ratios and the Probabilistic Prediction of Bankruptcy', *Journal of Accounting Research*, 18(1), 109–31.

Taffler, R.J. (1982) 'Forecasting Company Failure in the UK using Discriminant Analysis and Financial Ratio Data', *Journal of the Royal Statistical Society*, 145, Part 3.

Appendix 1

Case studies

Case Study 1 684

Case Study 2 689

Case Study 3 690

Case Study 4 691

Case study 1

The following case study shows how to track entries from the book of original entries right through to the preparation of final financial statements for a sole trader. Knowledge is required of Part 2, 'Double-entry Bookkeeping', Part 3 'Preparing Final Financial Statements for Sole Traders' and Chapter 35, 'Value Added Tax, Columnar Books of Prime Entry and the Payroll'.

Trading details and supporting documentation

Mr O'Donnell, a sole trader, has owned and operated an antique furniture store for a number of years. He specializes in the purchase and sale of antique furniture from different countries and deals with a small number of reputable suppliers and reliable customers.

You have been employed by Mr O'Donnell as a qualified accountant to maintain his accounts and prepare his financial statements. Following discussions with Mr O'Donnell, from which he believes he has supplied you with all the necessary details, and after obtaining a copy of all relevant documentation, you have established an opening trial balance at the start of the financial year, 1 October 20X3. Furthermore, you identify all his business transactions for the year ended 30 September 20X4. You also ascertain that VAT of 25 per cent applies to the sale, purchase and return of goods. In all other respects VAT can be ignored. VAT and PAYE returns are submitted on an annual basis and are paid by direct debit every December.

O'Donnell's Opening Trial Balance as at 1 October 20X3

	Debit £	Credit £
Non-current assets		
Delivery vans (2)	26,000	
Accumulated depreciation on delivery vans		11,500
Fittings	12,000	
Accumulated depreciation on fittings		2,000
Current assets		
Inventories	44,000	
Trade receivables (Murphy £7,000; Foley £7,000)	14,000	
Cash at bank		1,750
Petty cash	130	
Current liabilities		
Trade payables (Cronin £11,000; Broderick £4,000)		15,000
VAT		1,000
PAYE		100
Equity		
Capital		67,150
Drawings		
Selling and distribution expenses		
Motor delivery expenses	600	
Administration expenses		
Postage, stationery and telephone		130
Light and heat		100
Rent	2,000	
	98,730	98,730

The transactions that occurred during the year to 30 September 20X4 are listed below:

October:

2 Sold goods on credit to Murphy for £5,000, invoice no. 580.

6 Purchased goods on credit from Cronin for £3,750.

11 Paid £7 for stationery from petty cash.

23 Received and lodged to bank all money outstanding from Foley (no discount allowed).

November:

4 Returned £1,250 worth of goods purchased from Cronin.

11 Sold goods on credit to Foley for £5,000, invoice no. 581.

19 Paid cheques no. 23985, £45, for electricity and no. 23986, £175, for petty cash.

24 Purchased goods on credit from Broderick for £1,250.

December:

1 Murphy returned goods worth £1,000 and credit note 14 was issued to him.

12 Received and lodged cheque for £3,000 from Murphy and allowed him discount of £100.

19 Paid cheque no. 23987 in the amount of £2,000 to Cronin and received £200 discount.

24 Withdrew £2,500 for personal use.

27 Paid VAT and PAYE outstanding from previous year by direct debit.

30 Paid motor insurance, £1,200 by cheque no. 23988 to cover the following six months.

31 Paid from petty cash: £7 postage; £11 motor repairs; £50 advertising.

January:

7 Sold goods on credit to Foley for £400, invoice no. 582, and to Doolan for £4,000, invoice no. 583.

8 Lodged cash sales of £1,250.

9 Purchased goods on credit for £1,500 from Broderick.

22 Foley returned goods worth £1,000 so credit note 15 was issued to him.

23 Sent cheque no. 23989 for £100 to Foley to cover the cost of returning goods.

30 Paid £6,000 by cheque no. 23990, being rent due for 12 months from 1 February 20X4.

February:

1 Received and lodged all money due from Foley after allowing him discount of £400.

7 Sold goods to Doolan for £3,000, invoice no. 584; paid cheque no. 23991 worth £73 for motor expenses.

17 Purchased goods from Cronin on credit, £7,200.

22 Returned goods to Cronin to the value of £3,000.

30 Paid from petty cash: £12 postage; £20 stationery; £20 petrol.

March:

3 Sold goods on credit to Doyle to the value of £5,000, invoice no. 585.

7 Sold goods on credit to O'Haire, £11,000, invoice no. 586.

11 Paid cheque no. 23992 worth £2,700 to Getaway Travel for a family holiday.

12 Withdrew £3,000 from bank for use on holiday.

April:

7 Returned to find that Doyle was in financial difficulties and his accountant has temporarily suspended all payment. However, you decided to take no action yet.

8 Paid cheque no. 23993 to Cronin to the amount of £3,200 and received a discount of £200.

9 Paid motor tax, £133 by cheque no. 23994.

10 Paid cheque no. 23995 to the value of £400 to cover repairs to delivery van.

17 Sold goods on credit to Brennan for £7,000, invoice no. 587.

19 Purchased goods on credit from Cronin, £3,000.

25 Paid Cronin £5,000 (cheque no. 23996) and received a discount of £200.

31 Paid from petty cash: advertising £22; postage £12; petrol £44.

May:

7 Sold goods to Kelly on credit for £4,000, invoice no. 588.

10 Received £400 unexpectedly from Doyle's accountants, lodged money immediately.

17 Kelly returned damaged goods worth £2,000. Credit note 16 was issued to him.

22 Purchased goods from Sabura on credit worth £2,000.

23 Received and lodged cheques from Brennan in full settlement after allowing for a discount of £100.

31 Paid from petty cash: stationery £5; motor expenses £81; postage £12.

June:

2 Sold goods on credit to O'Haire worth £5,000, invoice no. 589.

3 Purchased goods on credit from Broderick to the value of £3,000.

9 Purchased goods from Cronin on credit worth £1,750.

17 Lodged cash sales worth £400.

22 Paid Broderick the full amount due less discount £350 (cheque no. 23997).

29 Withdrew £2,000 for personal use. O'Donnell also received letter from bank dated 28 June stating that his bank account was seriously overdrawn and that if money was not lodged soon to reduce it, serious action would have to be taken.

July:

2 Sold goods on credit to O'Haire for £7,000, invoice no. 590.

3 Paid cheque no. 23998 to the amount of £300 to petty cash.

11 O'Haire returned goods of £1,000. Credit note 17 was issued.

14 O'Haire settled his account in full, less agreed discount of £450. Proceeds lodged.

19 Sold goods on credit to Doolan for £11,000, invoice no. 591.

25 Withdrew £3,000 for personal use.

30 Paid motor insurance of £1,200 by cheque no. 23999 to cover following three months.

August:

3 Purchased goods on credit from Cronin for £9,000.

7 Returned goods worth £2,000 to Cronin. Credit note N274 received.

11 Cash sales of £500 lodged.

20 Paid telephone bill of £432 by cheque no. 24000.

20 Sold goods to O'Haire on credit for £500, invoice no. 592.

21 Sold goods on credit to Doolan worth £4,000, invoice no. 593.

26 Paid Cronin £10,000 on account, cheque no. 24001. Discount received £100.

29 Received and lodged £12,000 from Doolan. Discount allowed £500.

30 Doolan returned goods in the amount of £100. Credit note 18 issued.

September:

1 Purchased goods on credit from Slatery worth £5,000.

3 Sold goods on credit to O'Haire for £3,000, invoice no. 594.

6 Received and lodged balance due from O'Haire, less an agreed discount of £100.

7 Paid electricity bill of £298 by cheque no. 24002.

9 Sold goods to Murphy on credit worth £2,000, invoice no. 595 and to Doolan for £3,000, invoice no. 596.

13 Lodged cash sales worth £490.

16 Sold goods to O'Sullivan on credit for £3,000, invoice no. 597.

19 Received and lodged £2,500 from O'Sullivan. Discount allowed £200.

20 Received and lodged £1,000 from Murphy. Discount allowed £50.

21 Paid Cronin by cheque no. 24003 to the amount of £4,000. Discount received £200.

22 Paid Slatery £2,500 by cheque no. 24004. Discount received £100. Cash sales £2,450 lodged by Credit Transfer.

23 Paid Sergi, a temporary employee, to the amount of £1,300 by cheque no. 24005.

24 Withdrew £7,000 for personal use.

30 Paid from petty cash: stationery £42; postage £35; petrol £88; delivery expenses £94.

31 Received and lodged £3,500 from J. Cunningham to whom you sold a delivery van.

Mr O'Donnell's bank, First Time Bank, have supplied you with the following bank statement:

Account Number: 809234
Customer: O'Donnell's Furniture, New Street, Ballydune, Cork
Statement No 9

Date	Details	Debit	Credit	Balance
20X3/20X4		£	£	*dr = overdrawn*
1 Oct	Balance			1,750 dr
23 Oct	Lodgement		7,000	5,250 cr
22 Nov	Cheque no 23985	45		5,205 cr
25 Nov	Cheque no 23986	175		5,030 cr
12 Dec	Lodgement		3,000	8,030 cr
23 Dec	Cheque no 23987	2,000		6,030 cr
24 Dec	Withdrawal	2,500		3,530 cr
27 Dec	Direct debit 7422986	1,000		2,530 cr
27 Dec	Direct debit 7422987	100		2,430 cr
31 Dec	Cheque no 23988	1,200		1,230 cr
31 Dec	Interest and charges	90		1,140 cr
8 Jan	Lodgement		1,250	2,390 cr
26 Jan	Cheque no 23989	100		2,290 cr
1 Feb	Lodgement		4,000	6,290 cr
6 Feb	Cheque no 23990	6,000		290 cr
12 Mar	Withdrawal	3,000		2,710 dr
20 Mar	Cheque no 23992	2,700		5,410 dr
21 Mar	Cheque no 23991	73		5,483 dr
12 Apr	Cheque no 23994	133		5,616 dr
15 Apr	Cheque no 23995	400		6,016 dr
28 Apr	Cheque no 23996	5,000		11,016 dr
10 May	Lodgement		400	10,616 dr
23 May	Lodgement		6,900	3,716 dr
17 June	Lodgement		400	3,316 dr
17 June	Cheque no 23993	3,200		6,516 dr
28 June	Cheque no 23997	9,400		15,916 dr
29 June	Withdrawal	2,000		17,916 dr
30 June	Interest and charges	1,185		19,101 dr
3 July	Cheque no 23998	300		19,401 dr
14 July	Lodgement		21,550	2,149 cr
25 July	Withdrawal	3,000		851 dr
11 Aug	Lodgement		500	351 dr
25 Aug	Cheque no 24000	432		783 dr
26 Aug	Lodgement		12,000	11,217 cr
30 Aug	Cheque no 24001	10,000		1,217 cr
6 Sep	Lodgement		3,400	4,617 cr
13 Sep	Lodgement		490	5,107 cr
19 Sep	Lodgement		2,500	7,607 cr
20 Sep	Lodgement		1,000	8,607 cr
23 Sep	Cheque no 24004	2,500		6,107 cr
24 Sep	Cheque no 24005	1,300		4,807 cr
24 Sep	Withdrawal	7,000		2,193 dr
30 Sep	Lodgement		3,500	1,307 cr

Required

First, prepare the books of original entry; that is, journals (sales, sales returns, purchases and purchases returns), cheque payments book, cash receipts book and petty cash book. This requires that you make one entry in these books for each transaction listed above.

Next, you must complete the sales and purchases ledgers. To do this you extract the relevant information from the books of original entry, which you have just completed. Include the opening balances for individual credit customers and credit suppliers as shown in the trial balance at 1 October 20X3. You should also extract trade receivables and trade payables schedules. These will be used later to check control account balances.

The next stage is writing up the nominal ledger. Remember to enter the opening balances for the individual relevant ledger accounts shown in the trial balance at 1 October 20X3. You complete this stage by preparing a bank reconciliation statement at 30 September 20X4.

At this point you may extract a preliminary trial balance by extracting balances from the nominal ledger accounts you have just completed. Remember to enter the individual opening balances for the relevant accounts shown in the trial balance at 1 October 20X3.

Note: Case study 2: Preparing final financial statements is a continuation from this point.

(*Sandra Brosnan, adapted*)

Case study 2

Using the preliminary trial balance you extracted in Case study 1, and taking account of the following post trial balance adjustments, you are required to prepare the statement of profit or loss and statement of financial position for Mr O'Donnell for the year ended 30 September 20X4.

Post-trial balance adjustments:

1 Closing inventory is valued at £35,000.

2 On 30 September 20X4 Mr O'Donnell decided to dispose of one of his vans. This had been acquired in 20X1 at a cost of £10,000 and had been depreciated at a rate of 25 per cent per annum on cost. Sale proceeds amounted to £3,500 and this was lodged by Mr O'Donnell into his account in First Time Bank on 30 September. No other entry relating to this transaction has been made in the books.

3 Mr O'Donnell's depreciation policy is as follows: Depreciation is to be charged on delivery vans at 25 per cent on cost and on fittings at 10 per cent using the reducing balance method. Depreciation is not to be charged in the year of disposal.

4 Light and heat worth £120 and telephone worth £215 are outstanding at the year end.

5 You have decided to charge Mr O'Donnell £2,000 for your accounting services.

6 There is PAYE of £256 outstanding in respect of Sergi that must be forwarded to the tax authorities.

7 The rent payment made on 30 January was in respect of the subsequent 12 months. The motor insurance payment made on 30 July related to the subsequent three months.

8 After discussing matters with Mr O'Donnell, you decide that there is little likelihood of any further payments from Doyle and that the remaining balance should be written off as an irrecoverable receivable.

9 In the light of the experience with Doyle, you have advised Mr O'Donnell that it would be prudent to create an allowance for irrecoverable receivables. He has agreed that an allowance equal to 6 per cent of closing trade receivables should be established.

Note: A statement of cash flows may also be requested here.

(*Sandra Brosnan, adapted*)

Case study 3

This case study tests your understanding of the incomplete records topic. In order to fully answer the questions in the case study, it is necessary to draw upon earlier topics including accruals and prepayments, depreciation, allowance for irrecoverable receivables and the purpose of financial statements.

Wendy set up the printing shop business on 2 January 20X4. She is new to running a business, and so has only been able to maintain some basic records, including those of her cash transactions. Wendy has hired you for an agreed fee of £1,000 to prepare her end of year financial statements and to explain some accounting principles that are puzzling her. The agreed fee will be paid after you have completed the accountancy work. She has provided you with the following letter that contains information about her business activities during the year.

Dear Accounting Expert, 31 January 20X5

Thank you very much for agreeing to act as my accountant and also for agreeing to deal with some rather puzzling points which, I have to confess, have been making my brain hurt! I started the printing shop business with just £2,000 in cash, which I deposited in the business bank account on 2 January 20X4. All cash transactions have gone through the business bank account. I was fortunate in obtaining a loan of £28,000, from the Sunnydale Bank, on 2 January. I immediately used the loan to purchase some essential desktop printing equipment for £20,000 in cash. I used the remainder of the loan to purchase a van, to be used for delivering printing orders to clients, for £8,000 in cash. I also purchased on 2 January a stock of paper on good credit terms for £30,000. An experienced businesswoman friend of mine has explained that I need to depreciate both my printing equipment and the van. I do not understand this point at all, as I paid for both of the items in cash – surely that is the only cost that matters, as I have paid for both the assets in full? Anyway, my friend tells me that it is standard practice in my line of business to depreciate the printing equipment evenly over its six-year life, and to depreciate the van at 25 per cent on the reducing balance basis. I am told that the printing equipment has a scrap value of £2,000. I am not clear as to what all of this advice on depreciation means, but I am sure that you will be able to explain it and work it all out for me.

During the year, I paid an assistant a salary of £10,000, but I still owe her £1,000 for the overtime which she kindly agreed to work for me in December 20X4. I have also drawn £25,000 in cash for myself out of the business bank account over the year. I obtained premises to rent at the start of the year, and paid rent of £12,000 in advance in cash on 2 January to cover me up to the end of June 20X5. There have been several van expenses which have arisen during the year and have been paid in cash. Petrol expenses amounted to £1,500. Also, there were van repairs which totalled £500 and additional payments for tax and insurance which came to £1,000. Electricity expenses paid in cash during the year amounted to £1,000. This figure for electricity included the last bill for £300 for three months: it covered the months of November and December 20X4 as well as the month of January 20X5. Business rates of £9,600 were paid in cash in advance on 1 April 20X4, and covered the 12 months up to 31 March 20X5. The council kindly agreed not to charge me rates for the first three months of 20X4.

At the end of the year, I was advised by friends to carry out a comprehensive stock-take for the business. This revealed that I had an inventory of paper worth £40,000. I also found that I had spent £60,000 in cash on purchases of paper during the year, and also owed credit suppliers £50,000 for purchases of paper during the year. I have received cash from sales of printing work of £120,000 during 20X4. I also discovered that I had credit customers who owed me £40,000 for printing work, which I had carried out for them during the year. I also appear to have a problem credit customer. The bank has informed me that a cheque from one credit customer, Shark Enterprises, which owes me £4,000, has 'bounced' many times and so unfortunately I am not likely to obtain any money from that firm now or in the future. The bank manager has also suggested that I should make an allowance of 10 per cent of the remaining trade receivables in order to allow for possible problems with people who do not settle their debts in future.

I am not clear as to how this might be done, but hope that this suggestion makes sense to you when you put all this business information together.

During the year, as you may want to know, I took a modest amount of paper for my own use out of the business. This paper was worth £1,000. Also, I was able to pay the total interest of £3,000 which was due on the loan in cash, and was able to repay £2,000 of the loan to the Sunnydale Bank.

I hope that you can make sense of all the information that I have provided for you above.

I understand that you can prepare some financial statements for me, although I am not really sure if it is necessary to do this. If I can aim just to end up with a cash surplus at the end of the year, then is that not sufficient to show everyone that the business is doing well?

Best wishes

Yours sincerely

Wendy

Required

1 Draw up a statement of profit or loss for Wendy's Printing Shop for the year ended 31 December 20X4 and a statement of financial position as at that date. Include in your workings both the depreciation policies suggested by Wendy's friend and the treatment of irrecoverable and doubtful receivables suggested by her bank manager.

2 Explain to Wendy the purpose and importance of depreciating non-current assets.

3 Explain to Wendy the purpose and importance of making a provision for doubtful debts.

4 Compare the cash position of Wendy's business at the end of the year with the performance shown by the statement of profit or loss. Explain the difference between the two, and how a statement of profit or loss and a statement of financial position can be useful to Wendy.

(Robert Jupe, adapted)

Case study 4

Mr O'Donnell, originally a sole trader, had owned and operated an antique furniture store in Cork for a number of years. He specialized in the purchase and sale of antique furniture from different countries and dealt with a small number of reputable suppliers and reliable customers. However, due to growing demand and growing opportunities Mr O'Donnell decided two years ago to register as a private limited company named Antique Furniture Supplies Ltd to facilitate expansion into a growing international market and secured a number of interested investors to provide the necessary capital. Antique Furniture Supplies Ltd filed all the necessary documentation (Memorandum of Association and Articles of Association) with the Registrar of Companies in accordance with the Companies Act 2006. Antique Furniture Supplies Ltd maintained all its existing customer base and suppliers but has also attracted a number of large customers that have enabled the company to be quite successful.

You have been employed by Antique Furniture Supplies Ltd, as a qualified accountant, to maintain the company's accounts and prepare the necessary financial statements. Following discussions with Antique Furniture Supplies Ltd, and after obtaining a copy of all relevant documentation, you have established an opening trial balance at the start of the financial year, 1 October 20X3. Furthermore, you identify all his business transactions for the year ended 30 September 20X4. You also ascertain that VAT of 25 per cent applies to the sale, purchase and return of goods. In all other respects VAT can be ignored. VAT returns are submitted on an annual basis and are paid by direct debit every December.

Antique Furniture Supplies Ltd Opening trial balance as at 1 October 20X3		
	Debit **£**	**Credit** **£**
Non-current assets		
Delivery vans	42,000	
Accumulated depreciation on delivery vans		11,500
Fittings	16,000	
Accumulated depreciation on fittings		2,000
Premises	200,000	
Accumulated depreciation		40,000
Current assets		
Inventories	54,000	
Trade receivables (Murphy £12,000; Foley £12,000)	24,000	
Cash at bank	35,550	
Petty cash	130	
Current liabilities		
Trade payables (Cronin £11,000; Broderick £4,000)		15,000
VAT		2,400
Income tax		10,000
Equity		
Share capital (200,000 £1 shares)		200,000
Share premium	20,000	
Retained earnings 1 October 20X3		53,150
10 per cent long-term loan		60,000
Selling and distribution expenses		
Motor delivery expenses	600	
Administration expenses		
Postage, stationery and telephone		130
Light and heat		100
Rent	2,000	
	394,280	394,280

The transactions that occurred during the year to 30 September 20X4 are listed below:

October:

2 Sold goods on credit to Murphy for £5,000.

5 Sold goods on credit to Hulgerstein for £20,000.

6 Purchased goods on credit from Cronin for £53,750.

11 Paid £70 for stationery from petty cash.

23 Received and lodged to bank all money outstanding from Foley (no discount allowed).

30 Paid employee wages of £8,000 by direct debit.

November:

4 Returned £10,250 worth of goods purchased from Cronin.

11 Sold goods on credit to Foley for £5,000.

12 Sold goods on credit to Williams for £15,000.

19 Paid cheques no. 23985 for light and heat (£1,450) and no. 23986 for petty cash £600.

24 Purchased goods on credit from Broderick for £21,250.

30 Paid employee wages of £8,000 by direct debit.

December:

1 Murphy returned goods in the amount of £1,000 and credit note 14 was issued to him.

2 Received and lodged £19,000 from Hulgerstein after allowing him a 5 per cent discount.

12 Received and lodged cheque in amount of £13,000 from Murphy and allowed him a discount of £650.

19 Paid cheque no. 23987 in amount of £42,000 to Cronin and received £1,500 discount.

24 Received £13,000 from Williams and allowed him a discount of £750.

27 Paid VAT outstanding from previous year by direct debit.

30 Paid motor insurance, £2,400 by cheque no. 23988 to cover the following six months.

30 Paid employee wages of £8,000 by direct debit.

31 Paid from petty cash: £27 postage; £350 stationery.

January:

7 Sold goods on credit to Foley for £4,000 and to Doolan for £4,000.

8 Lodged cash sales of £24,500.

9 Purchased goods on credit for £31,500 from Broderick.

22 Foley returned goods worth £1,000 so credit note 15 was issued to him.

26 Murphy lodged the amount outstanding on his account.

30 Paid £8,000 by cheque no. 23989, being rent due for 12 months from 1 February 20X4.

30 Paid employee wages of £8,000 by direct debit.

February:

1 Received and lodged all money due from Foley after allowing him discount of £400.

7 Sold goods to Doolan for £3,000; paid cheque no. 23990 worth £5,300 for motor expenses.

10 Sold goods on credit for £20,000 to Williams.

17 Purchased goods from Cronin on credit, £37,500.

22 Returned goods to Cronin to the value of £3,000.

28 Paid from petty cash: £80 postage; £200 stationery.

28 Paid employee wages of £8,000 by direct debit.

March:

3 Sold goods on credit to Doyle to the value of £8,000.

7 Sold goods on credit to O'Haire, £11,000.

8 Paid £36,750 to Broderick for goods previously purchased (cheque no. 23991).

10 Purchased goods on credit for £21,000 from Broderick.

11 Paid cheque no. 23992 to Cronin to the amount of £33,200 and received a discount of £2,000.

16 Paid for light and heat to the amount of £4,350 with cheque no. 23993.

25 Williams lodged £18,000 into bank account.

26 Paid £3,500 for advertising with cheque no. 23994.

30 Paid employee wages of £8,000 by direct debit.

30 Received a letter from Doyle's accountant to state that Doyle is in financial difficulty and probably will not be able to settle his debt.

April:

7 Paid motor tax, £1,000 by cheque no. 23995.

8 Paid cheque no. 23996 to the value of £900 to cover repairs to delivery van.

17 Sold goods on credit to Brennan for £17,000.

19 Purchased goods on credit from Cronin, £13,000.

20 Sold goods worth £25,000 to Hulgerstein on credit.

25 Paid Cronin £15,000 (cheque no. 23997) and received a discount of £800.

28 Sold a further £50,000 worth of goods on credit to Williams.

30 Received a letter from your bank stating that the company has overdrawn beyond its agreed credit limits and that if the overdraft was not reduced serious action will have to be taken.

30 Paid employee wages of £8,000 by direct debit.

30 Paid £12 from petty cash for postage.

May:

7 Sold goods to Kelly on credit for £4,000.

12 Received £1,000 unexpectedly from Doyle's accountants, lodged money immediately.

17 Kelly returned damaged goods in the amount of £2,000.

19 Hulgerstein paid £20,000 on his account and was allowed a discount of £500.

22 Purchased goods from Sabura on credit worth £2,000.

23 Received and lodged cheques from Brennan in full settlement after allowing for a discount of £100.

30 Paid employee wages of £8,000 by direct debit.

31 Paid from petty cash: stationery £50; postage £12.

June:

2 Sold goods on credit to O'Haire worth £25,000.

3 Purchased goods on credit from Broderick to the value of £13,000.

9 Purchased goods from Cronin on credit worth £15,750.

17 Lodged cash sales worth £14,000.

20 Credit sale of £10,000 to Hulgerstein.

22 Paid Broderick £53,650 due, less discount £350 (cheque no. 23998).

29 Paid motor and delivery expenses of £3,500 (cheque no. 23999)

30 Williams settled his account (no discount allowed).

30 Paid employee wages of £8,000 by direct debit.

July:

2 Sold goods on credit to O'Haire for £17,000.

3 Paid cheque no. 24000 to the amount of £300 to petty cash.

13 O'Haire returned goods of £1,000.

14 O'Haire settled account in full, less agreed discount of £450. Proceeds lodged.

19 Sold goods on credit to Doolan for £11,000.

24 Hulgerstein settled his account (discount allowed of £450).

30 Paid employee wages of £8,000 by direct debit.

31 Paid motor insurance of £2,400 by cheque no. 24001 to cover following three months.

August:

3 Purchased goods on credit from Cronin for £19,000.

7 Returned goods worth £6,000 to Cronin.

10 Sold goods on credit to Baralux Ltd to the amount of £50,000.

11 Cash sales of £6,000 lodged.

20 Paid telephone bill of £4,500 by cheque no. 24002.

20 Sold goods to O'Haire on credit for £5,000.

21 Sold goods on credit to Doolan worth £4,000.

26 Paid Cronin £26,000 on account, cheque no. 24003. Discount received £250.

29 Received and lodged £12,000 from Doolan. Discount allowed £500.

30 Doolan returned goods in the amount of £100.

30 Paid employee wages of £8,000 by direct debit.

September:

1 Purchased goods on credit from Slatery worth £20,000.

3 Sold goods on credit to O'Haire for £6,000.

6 Received and lodged balance due from O'Haire, less an agreed discount of £100.

7 Paid light and heat worth £2,528 by cheque no. 24004.

9 Sold goods to Murphy on credit worth £6,000, and to Doolan for £3,000.

13 Lodged cash sales worth £4,900.

14 Baralux Ltd paid £35,000 on its account. Discount allowed £1,000.

16 Sold goods to O'Sullivan on credit for £3,000.

19 Received and lodged £2,500 from O'Sullivan. Discount allowed £200.

20 Received and lodged £4,000 from Murphy. Discount allowed £100.

21 Paid Cronin by cheque no. 24005 to the amount of £9,000.

22 Paid Slatery £2,500 by cheque no. 24006. Discount received £100. Cash sales £2,450 lodged by credit transfer.

23 Purchased goods on credit from Slatery for £26,000.

30 Paid from petty cash: stationery £42; postage £35.

30 Received and lodged £5,500 from J. Cunningham to whom you sold a delivery van.

30 Paid employee wages of £8,000 by direct debit.

Antique Furniture Supplies Ltd's bank, First Time Bank, have supplied you with the following bank statement:

Account Number: 659289

Customer: Antique Furniture Supplies Ltd, Link Road, Ballydune, Cork.

Statement No 11

Date	Details	Debit	Credit	Balance
20X3/20X4		£	£	*dr = overdrawn*
1 Oct	Balance			35,550 cr
23 Oct	Lodgement		12,000	47,550 cr
30 Oct	Direct debit 7422984	8,000		39,550 cr
19 Nov	Cheque no 23985	1,450		38,100 cr
19 Nov	Cheque no 23986	600		37,500 cr
30 Nov	Direct debit 7422985	8,000		29,500 cr
2 Dec	Lodgement		19,000	48,500 cr
12 Dec	Lodgement		13,000	61,500 cr
19 Dec	Cheque no 23987	42,000		19,500 cr
24 Dec	Lodgement		13,000	32,500 cr
27 Dec	Direct debit 7422986	2,400		30,100 cr
30 Dec	Cheque no 23988	2,400		27,700 cr
30 Dec	Direct debit 7422987	8,000		19,700 cr
31 Dec	Interest and charges	1,900		17,800 cr
8 Jan	Lodgement		24,500	42,300 cr
27 Jan	Lodgement		2,350	44,650 cr
30 Jan	Cheque no 23989	8,000		36,650 cr
30 Jan	Direct debit 7422988	8,000		28,650 cr
1 Feb	Lodgement		7,600	36,250 cr
8 Feb	Cheque no 23990	5,300		30,950 cr
28 Feb	Direct debit 7422989	8,000		22,950 cr
15 Mar	Cheque no 23992	33,200		10,250 dr

21 Mar	Cheque no 23991	36,750		47,000 dr
25 Mar	Lodgement		18,000	29,000 dr
28 Mar	Cheque no 23994	3,500		32,500 dr
30 Mar	Direct debit 7422990	8,000		40,500 dr
15 Apr	Cheque no 23995	1,000		41,500 dr
16 Apr	Cheque no 23996	900		42,400 dr
28 Apr	Cheque no 23997	15,000		57,400 dr
30 Apr	Direct debit 7422991	8,000		65,400 dr
12 May	Lodgement		1,000	64,400 dr
20 May	Lodgement		20,000	44,400 dr
23 May	Lodgement		16,900	27,500 dr
30 May	Direct debit 7422992	8,000		35,500 dr
17 June	Lodgement		14,000	21,500 dr
17 June	Cheque no 23993	4,530		26,030 dr
28 June	Cheque no 23998	53,650		79,680 dr
29 June	Cheque no 23999	3,500		83,180 dr
30 June	Lodgement		53,250	29,930 dr
30 June	Interest and charges	1,185		31,115 dr
30 June	Direct debit 7422993	8,000		39,115 dr
3 July	Cheque no 24000	300		39,415 dr
14 July	Lodgement		51,550	12,135 cr
25 July	Lodgement		9,550	21,685 cr
30 July	Direct debit 7422994	8,000		13,685 cr
3 Aug	Cheque no 24001	2,400		11,285 cr
11 Aug	Lodgement		6,000	17,285 cr
25 Aug	Cheque no 24002	4,500		12,785 cr
29 Aug	Lodgement		12,000	24,785 cr
30 Aug	Cheque no 24003	26,000		1,215 dr
30 Aug	Direct debit 7422995	8,000		9,215 dr
6 Sep	Lodgement		10,900	1,685 cr
13 Sep	Lodgement		4,900	6,585 cr
15 Sep	Lodgement		35,000	41,585 cr
20 Sep	Lodgement		2,500	44,085 cr
21 Sep	Lodgement		4,000	48,085 cr
23 Sep	Cheque no 24004	2,528		45,557 cr
24 Sep	Cheque no 24005	9,000		36,557 cr
24 Sep	Lodgement		2,450	39,007 cr
24 Sep	Cheque no 24006	2,500		36,507 cr
30 Sep	Lodgement		5,500	42,007 cr
30 Sep	Direct debit	8,000		34,007 cr

Required

First, prepare the books of original entry (sales, sales returns, purchases and purchases returns journals), cheque payments book, cash receipts book and petty cash book. This requires that you make one entry in these books for each transaction listed above.

Next, you must complete the sales and purchases ledgers. To do this you extract the relevant information from the books of original entry, which you have just completed.

Include the opening balances for individual credit customers and credit suppliers as shown in the trial balance at 1 October 20X3. You should also extract trade receivables and trade payables schedules. These will be used later to check control account balances.

The next stage is writing up the nominal ledger. Remember to enter the opening balances for the individual relevant accounts shown in the trial balance at 1 October 20X3. You complete this stage by preparing a bank reconciliation statement at 30 September 20X4.

At this point you may extract a preliminary trial balance by extracting balances from the nominal ledger accounts you have just completed. Remember to enter the individual opening balances for the relevant accounts shown in the trial balance at 1 October 20X3.

Using the preliminary trial balance you extracted above, and taking account of the following post-trial balance adjustments, you are required to prepare the statement of profit or loss for Antique Furniture Supplies Ltd for the year ended 30 September 20X4 and a statement of financial position at that date. Also, comment on Antique Furniture Supplies Ltd's cash flow position throughout the year and suggest ways to improve its working capital cycle.

Post trial balance adjustments

1. Closing inventory is valued at £35,000.
2. On the 30 September 20X4 Antique Furniture Supplies Ltd decided to dispose of one of its vans. This had been acquired in 20X1 at a cost of £12,000 and had been depreciated at a rate of 20 per cent per annum on cost. Sale proceeds amounted to £5,500 and this was lodged by Mr O'Donnell into his account in First Time Bank on 30 September. No other entry relating to this transaction has been made in the books.
3. Antique Furniture Supplies Ltd's depreciation policy is as follows. Depreciation is to be charged on both delivery vans and premises at 20 per cent on cost and on fittings at 10 per cent using the reducing balance method. Depreciation is not to be charged in the year of disposal.
4. Light and heat worth £175 and telephone worth £265 are outstanding at the year end along with wages of £2,000.
5. You have decided to charge Antique Furniture Supplies Ltd £12,000 for your accounting services.
6. The rent payment made on 30 January was in respect of the subsequent 12 months. The motor insurance payment made on 30 July related to the subsequent three months.
7. After discussing matters with Antique Furniture Supplies Ltd, you decide that there is little likelihood of any further payments from Doyle and that the remaining balance should be written off as an irrecoverable receivable.
8. In the light of the experience with Doyle, you have advised Antique Furniture Supplies Ltd that it would be prudent to create an allowance for irrecoverable receivables. It is agreed that a provision equal to 5 per cent of closing trade receivables should be established.
9. Income tax for this accounting period is £10,000 and has not been paid.
10. Interest on the long-term loan is outstanding at the year end.
11. It is proposed that a final dividend of 5 per cent equity share capital should be paid.

Note: A statement of cash flows may also be requested here.

(Sandra Brosnan, adapted)

Appendix 2

Solutions to Exercises

1 Entities and financial reporting statements 700
2 Financial reporting: institutional framework and standards 702
3 The Conceptual Framework 1: objective of financial statements, stakeholders and other reports 704
4 The Conceptual Framework 2: concepts, principles and policies 707
5 The Conceptual Framework 3: the qualitative characteristics of financial information 709
6 Auditing, corporate governance and ethics 709
7 The accounting equation and its components 710
8 Basic documentation and books of account 711
9 Double entry and the general ledger 712
10 The balancing of accounts and the trial balance 715
11 Day books and the journal 719
12 The cash book 723
13 The petty cash book 730
14 The final financial statements of sole traders (introductory) 731
15 Depreciation and non-current assets 734
16 Irrecoverable receivables and allowance for irrecoverable receivables 738
17 Accruals and prepayments 742
18 The extended trial balance and final financial statements (advanced) 744
19 The bank reconciliation statement 749

20 Control accounts 750
21 Errors and suspense accounts 753
22 Single entry and incomplete records 757
23 Inventory valuation 760
24 Financial statements for manufacturing entities 765
25 The final financial statements of partnerships 769
26 Changes in partnerships 776
27 Partnership dissolution and conversion to a limited company 779
28 The nature of limited companies and their capital 780
29 The final financial statements of limited companies 781
30 Statement of cash flows 791
31 The appraisal of company financial statements using ratio analysis 795

1 Entities and Financial Reporting Statements

1.1 Nature and functions of financial accounting

Financial accounting includes bookkeeping which is the process of designing and operating an information system for collecting, measuring and recording an enterprise's transactions. It also is concerned with financial statements which summarize and communicate the results of these transactions to users to facilitate making financial/economic decisions. The financial statements show the profit earned during a given period (statement of profit or loss) and the financial position at the end of that period (statement of financial position).

The key functions covered by an appropriate accounting system include:

- *The recording and control of business transactions*
  Accounting systems need to keep a record of the cash in and out of the business and the assets and liabilities of the business.
- *Maintaining accuracy in recording*
  Transactions are usually recorded using 'double entry'.
- *To meet the requirements of the law*
  The law, in the form of the Companies Act 2006, states that companies must keep a proper record of their transactions.
- *To present final financial statements to the owners of the business*
- *To present other financial reports and analyses*
  For example, the operating and financial review, the directors' report, the chairman's statement, the remuneration report and the corporate social responsibility report. Summary analysis of the performance and financial standing of the business are usually provided in these other reports.
- *To facilitate the efficient allocation of resources*

1.5 a Describe the recording and control function of financial accounting

Accounting systems need to keep a record of the cash in and out of the business and the assets and liabilities of the business.

This should include capturing details of:

- When cash or cheques are received including from whom and for what.
- When cash or cheques are paid including from whom and for what.

Any liabilities owing by the business for loans, goods, expenses for example and any assets of the business such as buildings, inventory, amounts receivable from customers and money in the bank.

The owners of a business wish to safeguard their assets and to ensure that they are being utilized efficiently to produce wealth. An appropriate accounting system should have controls in place to protect business assets and to determine how the company is performing. The control aspect of an accounting system includes ensuring that the correct amounts are paid to those entitled to them at the appropriate time, to ensure that the business's debts are paid when due, and to ensure that assets are safeguarded against fraud and misappropriation. For example, an appropriate accounting system will have an up-to-date list of all non-current assets (buildings, etc.), including their location and state of condition. These will be inspected periodically to verify that they have not been misappropriated. The latter function is often referred to as internal control.

1.5 b Explain the role of financial accounting with regard to the presentation of final financial statements

The two main financial statements are the statement of financial position and the statement of profit or loss. The statement of financial position provides information on the assets, liabilities and capital of the business. The assets include the amount of cash the business has, assets including tangible assets, inventory and trade receivables. The liabilities of the business include payables and loans and the capital includes amounts invested by the owners in the business. This is arranged to enable the user to determine the reported net worth of the business (though this may be different to the market value of the business).

The statement of profit or loss provides information on the income earned by the business from operating activities and other activities and the expenses incurred in the generation of that income in the period. It shows the overall profit made by the business in the period.

Financial statements are prepared to provide information for stakeholders. They succinctly inform the stakeholders about the company's financial performance in the period and the net worth of the business on a particular date. They are typically standardized for types of organization but vary in the disclosures that they provide across type of organization. For example: In the case of a sole trader, final financial statements are primarily used to determine the owner's tax liability, though they also show the owner his or her 'earnings' for the period and can be used by others (such as the bank) to evaluate the profitability of the business.

Final financial statements perform similar functions in the case of companies, though the primary aim of the final financial statements is to give information to third parties to enable them to evaluate the profitability and financial stability of the company. The third parties include current and prospective equity shareholders, trade unions and employees, customers, creditors and those who have lent the company money, government departments, social pressure groups and the public.

1.6 Knowledge of items in the financial reporting statements

Statement	Classification
a Statement of financial position	Non-current asset
b Statement of profit or loss	Revenue expense
c Statement of profit or loss	Revenue expense
d Statement of financial position	Current liability
e Statement of financial position	Current asset

1.10 Explanation of terms

Internal control – A system of internal checks, and control procedures that are designed to ensure that assets are not misappropriated and liabilities are complete.

Internal check – Procedures, tests and controls in place to ensure that transactions are correct and are being processed correctly.

Stewardship accountability – The accountability of an enterprise's management for the resources entrusted to them.

Accountability – Management's responsibility to provide an account/report on the way in which the resources entrusted to them have been used.

2 Financial Reporting: Institutional Framework and Standards

2.1 Objectives of the IASB

Under the IFRS Foundation Constitution the objectives of the IASB are:

> "*(a) to develop, in the public interest, a single set of high quality, understandable and enforceable global accounting standards that require high quality, transparent and comparable information in financial statements and other financial reporting to help participants in the world's capital markets and other users make economic decisions;*
>
> *(b) to promote the use and rigorous application of those standards;*
>
> *(c) in fulfilling the objectives associated with (a) and (b), to take account of, as appropriate, the special needs of small and medium-sized entities and emerging economies; and*
>
> *(d) to bring about convergence of national accounting standards and International Accounting Standards and International Financial Reporting Standards to high quality solutions.*"

2.9 Describe the sources of the rules and regulations that govern the content and format of company final financial statements in the UK

Company law

International financial reporting standards

Stock exchange guidance

In addition – commonly accepted good practice

2.10 Describe the current institutional framework concerned with the setting and enforcement of accounting standards in the UK

The institutional framework for setting accounting standards and regulating accounts preparation is depicted by the following diagram.

Figure 1

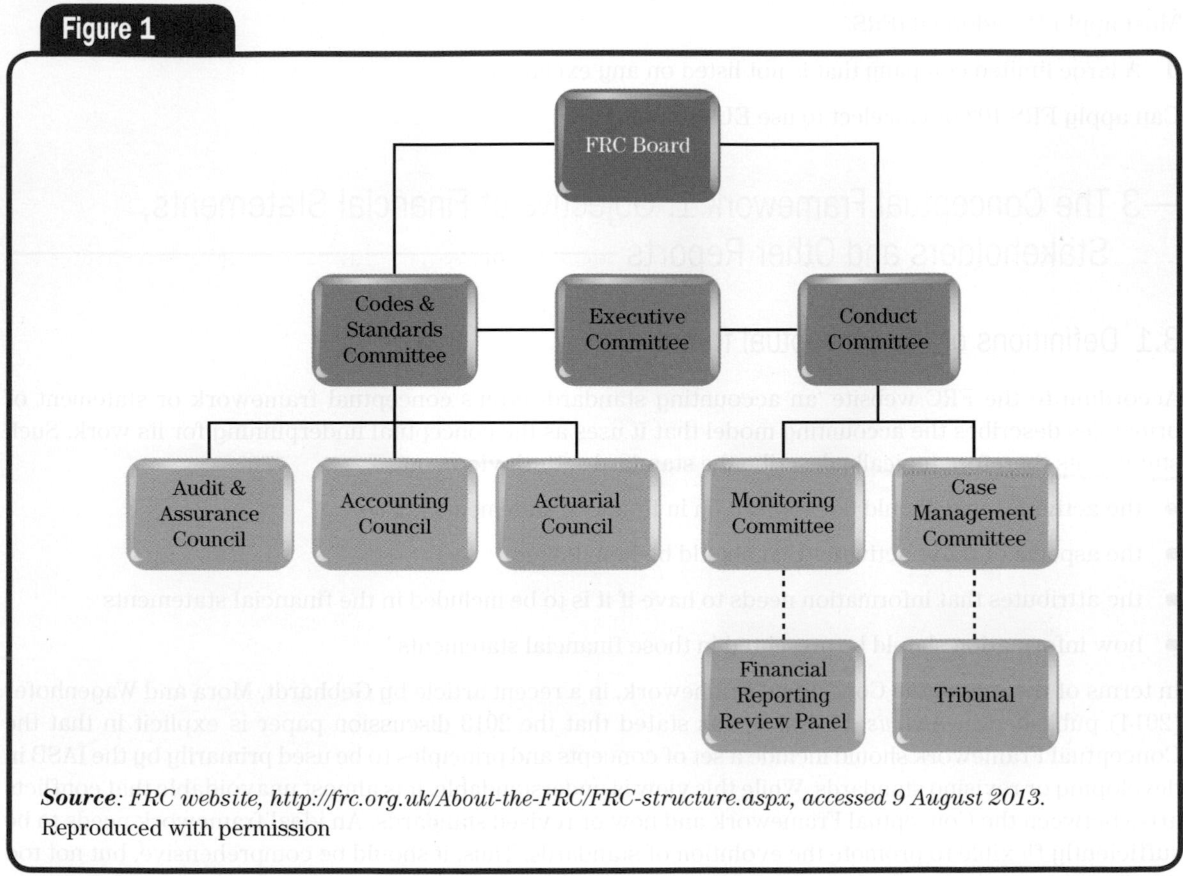

Source: *FRC website, http://frc.org.uk/About-the-FRC/FRC-structure.aspx, accessed 9 August 2013.* Reproduced with permission

> *"The FRC Board is supported by three Committees: the Codes and Standards Committee, the Conduct Committee and the Executive Committee. The Codes and Standards Committee advises the FRC Board on matters relating to codes, standard-setting and policy questions, through its Accounting, Actuarial and Audit & Assurance Councils. The Conduct Committee advises the FRC Board in matters relating to conduct activities to promote high-quality corporate reporting, including monitoring, oversight, investigative and disciplinary functions, through its Monitoring Committee and Case Management Committee. The Executive Committee supports the Board by advising on strategic issues and providing day-to-day oversight of the work of the FRC'."*
>
> (FRC website, 2013)

Financial reporting standards are set by the 'Accounting Council' who report to the 'Codes and Standards Committee' who in turn report to the FRC Board.

2.11 Explain the accounting framework options open to the following types of UK entity from 1 January 2015

a A subsidiary of a company that has prepared consolidated financial statements using EU-adopted IFRS

They can use the reduced disclosure framework under FRS 101 or apply the full EU adopted IFRS.

b A small limited company

They have a choice under FRS 101. They can use the FRSSE, or FRS 102 or EU-adopted FRS. Most likely will apply the FRSSE.

c A public limited company

Must apply EU-adopted IFRS.

d A large limited company that is not listed on any exchange

Can apply FRS 102 or can elect to use EU-adopted IFRS.

3 The Conceptual Framework 1: Objective of Financial Statements, Stakeholders and Other Reports

3.1 Definitions of the conceptual framework

According to the FRC website 'an accounting standard-setter's conceptual framework or statement of principles describes the accounting model that it uses as the conceptual underpinning for its work. Such statements therefore typically describe the standard-setter's views on:

- the activities that should be reported on in financial statements
- the aspects of those activities that should be highlighted
- the attributes that information needs to have if it is to be included in the financial statements
- how information should be presented in those financial statements.'

In terms of the role of the Conceptual Framework, in a recent article by Gebhardt, Mora and Wagenhofer (2014) published in *Abacus*, 50 (1), it was stated that the 2013 discussion paper is explicit in that the Conceptual Framework should include a set of concepts and principles to be used primarily by the IASB in developing or revising standards. While this view is understandable, it is almost unavoidable that conflicts arise between the Conceptual Framework and new or revised standards. An ideal framework needs to be sufficiently flexible to promote the evolution of standards. Thus, it should be comprehensive, but not too detailed in its prescriptions.

3.8

a. Investors are defined in the *Conceptual Framework* as providers of risk capital. They are concerned with evaluating the 'risk in, and return provided by, their investment'. A basic premise in the *Conceptual Framework* is that 'investors require information to help them determine whether they should buy, hold or sell. Shareholders are also interested in information which enables them to assess the ability of the entity to pay dividends'.

1. Employees and their representative groups are interested in information about the stability and profitability of their employers. They are also interested in information which enables them to assess the ability of the entity to provide remuneration, retirement benefits and employment opportunities.

   Employee representatives (trade unions) will be interested in information for the purpose of wage bargaining. Employees are likely to be interested in indications of the position, progress and prospects of the employing enterprise as a whole and about individual establishments and bargaining unit.

2. Lenders are interested in information that enables them to determine whether their loans, and the interest attaching to them, will be paid when due. Lenders encapsulate entities like the bank and

investors in debt capital (bonds). Holders of debt capital that is traded on a recognized stock exchange will have similar information requirements to equity investors as they will also have to decide whether to hold, buy or sell their bonds.

3. Suppliers and other creditors will have similar interests to lenders. When a supplier provides goods in advance of receiving payment, this is like giving a loan. Therefore, they will be interested to determine at the outset whether to trade with the entity or not, and will want to make judgements on the length of credit period to give and the amount of credit to allow. Credit suppliers are likely to be interested in an entity over a shorter period than lenders unless they are dependent upon the continuation of the entity as a major customer'. Therefore, they are most interested in liquidity and changes in liquidity.

4. Customers have an interest in information about the continuance of an entity, especially when they have a long-term involvement with, or are dependent on, the entity. Going concern will be of particular interest.

5. Governments and their agencies are interested in the allocation of resources and, therefore, the activities of entities. They also require information in order to regulate the activities of entities, determine taxation policies and as the basis for national income and similar statistics. The government needs to estimate economic trends, including balance of payments figures (imports versus exports), employment figures and inflation levels. In the UK most of this information is collected through special government returns. However, in some other countries corporate reports perform this function. The government is interested in profits and the resultant tax – statement of profit or loss. Growth is also important and this is typically calculated from the income figures. They are also interested in employment – so the wages note is of interest.

6. Entities affect members of the public in a variety of ways. For example, entities may make a substantial contribution to a local economy in many ways, including the number of people they employ and their patronage of local suppliers. Financial statements may assist the public by providing information about the trends and recent developments in the prosperity of the entity and its range of activities. The public has a right to information about a local entity as most entities use community-owned assets such as roads and car parks. Their employment requirements may bring an influx of people to the area. More people means more places required in schools, longer waits for the doctor, and so on. Some members of the public may be concerned about the employment policies of the reporting entity and therefore want information relating to local employment levels or discrimination in employment, for example. Other members of the public may be interested in any plans that the reporting entity has that affect the environment, including issues relating to conservation and pollution, and congestion. Other matters of a political or moral nature may also be of particular concern to some sections of the community, such as contributions to political organizations, pressure groups or charities, and whether the reporting entity is trading with countries having repressive political regimes.

b. In the main financial statements do meet the needs of their key stakeholders. Now outlined in brief for each stakeholder.

Investors

Investors will typically be most interested in all three of the main statements in an annual return (including the related notes – depending on the sophistication of the investor), though they will pay particular regard to the communications from the chairman and the directors' report as this will provide information on the future plans of the company.

Information needs

Information on financial strength can be obtained from the statement of financial position. This will in part be able to inform them on whether to hold or sell their shares. In addition they will be interested in profitability and its sustainability (statement of profit or loss and comparatives to assess trends).

In terms of dividend payments, financial adaptability is of importance. They will be interested to see if the dividend payout can be maintained. They will want to see the statement of cash flows and the statement of profit or loss. If an entity is profitable, it is more likely to be able to maintain the dividend payout policy. Dividends are also paid in cash (typically) so the quality of cash flows is important to see if the surplus cash made is substantial enough for the dividend (this can be observed from the statement of cash flows – in particular, the cash flows from operating activities in the year (the engine of the entity).

Employees

Employees typically are interested in knowing the company is profitable and not carrying too much debt (secure for the future).

Information on the latter can be obtained from the statement of profit or loss – shows the profit strength of the entity. A wages note shows the payments made to employees in aggregate, including to their pension scheme. A remuneration note/pensions note identifies the type of pension scheme and gives details of its position. The statement of financial position provides guidance on the liabilities and debts that the company is exposed to. It also will provide information on the net standing of the pension scheme (asset, or liability).

Information on the statement of profit or loss and information on dividends is of interest to trade unions as they can see the cut of the profits of the business that goes to employees, directors and owners. They can use this information to determine if wage rates are fair.

Employees will be particularly interested in the wages note, the remuneration report (which deals with the remuneration paid to directors) and the employee note (typically included in the directors' report).

Lenders

Lenders will be interested in information on the present and likely future cash position, since this will determine whether the company will be able to pay the annual interest on loans and repay the money borrowed as and when it becomes due (liquidity and solvency). This can be obtained from the statement of financial position and also the statement of cash flows.

They will be interested in assessing the economic stability and vulnerability of the company in so far as this reflects the risk of possible default in repayment of money borrowed by the company (risk). Information on this can be obtained from the statement of financial position (notes on risk and gearing) and the statement of profit or loss (interest cover ratio).

They will want to know if there are any prior claims on the company's assets in the event of its going into liquidation (security). This information is typically disclosed in a note to the statement of financial position (contingent liabilities).

Other creditors/suppliers

(same as lenders – see above)

Customers

Customers are most interested that the firm is a going concern. Information on this can be obtained from the accounting policies and the audit report as well as an overview of performance and financial position/strength. They will also be interested in the profitability of the firm, in particular the gross profit margin, as this lets them know if the price they are being charged is fair.

Government

The government is interested in profits and the resultant tax. This can be obtained from the statement of profit or loss. Growth is also important and this is typically calculated from the income figures. It is also interested in employment – so the wages note is of interest.

Public

Though interested in profitability and financial strength, the public are most interested in what the company is doing within the community, including the employment it brings to the area and its impact on the environment. To this end most companies now include a Corporate Social Responsibility report which provides information on all these issues typically in narrative form.

Problems and improvements with financial statement might include:

The amount of detail is great. Some annual reports extend to nearly 200 pages. This is too much information for any user. Steps should be taken to reduce the information.

Some information is not of interest to some of the user groups, yet they have to sift through this to get what is important for them as only one report is utilized. Separate reports might be a possibility.

The financial reports contain a lot of narrative information now; though good at explaining things simply, these can be subject to bias and are not appropriately audited. Auditors just have to read this information and to say whether it is inconsistent or not.

Some firms could use graphics more to highlight trends over a longer timeframe (this would be particularly useful for the investor grouping).

4 The Conceptual Framework 2: Concepts, Principles and Policies

4.1 Concept governing drawings

The relevant concept is the 'entity concept'. This concept assumes that the financial statements represent all the transactions of the business entity only, which is not considered to be separate in law (unincorporated entities), however, in accounting it is. Therefore, any expenditure by the owner for his/her own personal needs or wants is not to be included, so must be removed from the financial statements through the drawings account.

4.3 a Definition of the elements

i. Assets

'Resources controlled by an entity as a result of past events and from which future economic benefits are expected to flow to the entity'.

ii. Liabilities

'Present obligations of an entity arising from past events, the settlement of which is expected to result in an outflow from the entity of resources embodying economic benefits'.

iii. Ownership interest

'The residual interest in the assets of the entity after deducting all its liabilities'.

iv. Income

'Increases in economic benefits during the accounting period in the form of inflows or enhancements of assets or decreases of liabilities that result in increases in equity, other than those relating to contributions from equity participants' (owners).

v. Expenditure

'Decreases in economic benefits during the accounting period in the form of outflows or depletions of assets or incurrences of liabilities that result in decreases in equity, other than those relating to distributions to equity participants' (owners).

Conceptual Framework (IASB, 2011)

4.3 b Definition of terms

i. Off-balance sheet finance

Method of getting access to resources (assets) without having the associated commitment to pay for the asset recorded in the statement of financial position.

ii. Substance over form

Information that represents faithfully the transactions and other events it either purports to represent or could reasonably be expected to represent. The economic substance of the transaction is considered over its legal form.

iii. Threshold quality

Materiality is the threshold quality – wherein only material information is relevant and therefore only material information should be included in an entity's financial statements.

4.15 (solution – brief points which should be referred to)

The first point relates to the realization concept and the prudence concept.

Profits should not be anticipated but losses should. Though this used to be one of the fundamental concepts of accounting, it has been downgraded due to the abuse of the prudence concept by preparers, wherein it was used for earnings manipulation (smoothing). In January 2009 IAS 1 *Preparation and Presentation of Financial Information* (IASB, 2009) introduced the statement of comprehensive income, which basically requires that holding gains (such as gains on the value of investments) are shown under 'other comprehensive income'. This can be shown as part of a single 'statement of comprehensive income' which shows the profit or loss for the year (as normal) from realized transactions and impairments and a second part which deals with holding gains made; or, alternatively, the holding gains (unrealized profits) can be shown in a separate statement to the statement of profit or loss – called the 'statement of comprehensive income'.

Therefore, though not treated as realized, holding gains are provided for the user as the information is deemed to be relevant for economic decision-making.

The prudence concept, though downgraded, is still important and impairments in value will always be realized in the statement of profit or loss.

Advertising – IAS 38 'Intangible Assets' – does not allow advertising to be capitalized as development expenditure. Though it is assumed to generate future revenues it is an example of an internally generated intangible asset – which cannot be capitalized.

The main reasoning for disallowing the treatment is uncertainty as to whether the expenditure qualifies as the element 'asset' and uncertainty as to the measurement of the value to include in the financial statements. Advertising creates brands which do not have an active readily available market to determine market value, they are bespoke and no two brands are the same. Cost may not provide an appropriate measurement basis. The potential revenue generation may be questionable. Therefore reliability takes precedence over relevance in this instance.

5 Conceptual Framework 3: The Qualitative Characteristics of Financial Information

5.2 Relevance

According to the *Conceptual Framework* information is relevant if it has 'the ability to influence the economic decisions of users by helping them to evaluate past, present or future events or confirming, or correcting, their past evaluations'. Therefore, according to the *Conceptual Framework* relevant information should have predictive value or confirmatory value. Information has **predictive value** if it helps users to evaluate or assess past, present or future events. To have predictive value, information need not be in the form of an explicit forecast. However, the ability to make predictions from financial statements is enhanced by the manner in which the information on the past is presented. For this reason, comparatives are provided and exceptional, one-off and abnormal items are identified separately in the financial statements from normal activities. In addition, transactions involving newly acquired businesses, or businesses that are being disposed of, are reanalysed and separately disclosed from transactions from continuing operations. Therefore, a diligent user can determine changes in the performance and financial position of the entity that resulted from normal activities that are expected to continue into the future.

Information has **confirmatory value** if it helps users to confirm or correct their past evaluations and assessments. Information may have both predictive and confirmatory value. Though not mentioned in the *Conceptual Framework*, it is commonly considered that relevant information is more relevant when it is provided in a timely manner as it is more likely to influence decision-making (**timeliness**).

6 Auditing, Corporate Governance and Ethics

6.9 The ethical dilemma suggested by your father

The suggestion put forward by your father (assuming no country risk) will more than likely increase the profitability of the company in these hard times. However, the board of directors should consider the ethical consequences. Ethical practices can restrict the extent to which a company can achieve its primary objective. In the global economy in which we operate, there is much to be made by companies who have products that can be made in countries that have no employment laws. Profits and company value will theoretically increase if a company is able to access cheap labour, or even child labour, for next to nothing. In these circumstances, companies justify their actions by arguing that some income to a family is better than none; or by highlighting the fact that, though the salaries paid are low, they are higher than those paid by indigenous companies. Many companies also use some of the profits made for social purposes in the communities that they are located in by, for example, building schools, building churches, building hospitals, or getting running water. These are all deemed to be signs of these companies acting ethically. However, this does not get away from the fact that the local population is being abused for financial gain. Whether the board feels that the financial gain is worth the drop in ethical standards is a matter for debate. Given that this company is a UK company, I would suggest that this action is not consistent with how he should be running a company. In addition, the consequences of this action becoming public might be great. There is likely to be an adverse reaction from trade unions, the public and from the government.

The use of bribery or corruption may be seen as part and parcel of normal trade within certain countries. In a global economy when there is much pressure to perform, unethical approaches (such as bribery) might be considered to be 'fair game' when attempting to achieve the company's primary objectives. However, unethical behaviour cannot be defended on the grounds of it being normal practice in a country, nor can it be defended by the argument 'if I did not do it, someone else would', or 'we would lose the business to a competitor, who does it'. Taking bribes is not considered to be appropriate in the UK and is not appropriate behaviour for UK companies. Were the use of bribery to become public, the company might be subject to public attention and enquiry.

All in all these unethical actions may end up with the company in a worse financial state. However, on a positive note looking globally to obtain cheaper running costs and labour is an option that he should look into; however, child labour and bribery should not form part of any investment package.

7 The Accounting Equation and its Components

7.1 Relevance of the entity concept in accounting

A **reporting entity** is defined in the *Statement of Principles for Financial Reporting* (ASB, 1999) as 'an entity for which there are users who rely on the financial statements as their major source of financial information about the entity'. Accounting for a reporting entity focuses on setting up a means of recording all accounting information in relation to that entity, as distinct from information that does not relate to the entity. The use of the word entity emphasises the properties of being separate and discrete. Boundaries are created to separate out the **accounting entity**. Realizing that these boundaries are necessary, even though they may be artificial, is the key to the entity concept. It becomes possible, for example, to accept that a business may be separate from its sole proprietor.

By defining the boundaries of the organizational unit, the accounting entity concept determines the transactions that will be recorded in the financial statements. For example, when a local plumber buys tools to carry out his work, that action can be regarded as a purchase by the business, while when the same man buys a cinema ticket this would be seen as a personal purchase. In the same way, the salary paid to a company director is treated not as some internal transfer within a company but as a payment to an officer as a separate individual. In general, accounting sets up 'the business', 'the company' and 'the club' as entities that are artificial constructs, separate from their owners and employees as individuals.

7.7

J. Frank **Statement of financial position as at 1 January 20X4**	
ASSETS	**£**
Non-current assets	
Land and buildings	7,500
Fixtures	560
	8,060
Current assets	
Bank	1,740
Total assets	9,800
EQUITY AND LIABILITIES	**£**
Equity	
Owners' capital (to balance)	5,800
Total equity	5,800
Non-current liabilities	
Mortgage	4,000
Total non-current liabilities	4,000
Total equity and liabilities	9,800

J. Frank Statement of financial position as at 31 December 20X4	
ASSETS	£
Non-current assets	
Land and buildings	7,500
Fixtures	560
Delivery van	650
	8,710
Current assets	
Inventory	940
Sundry receivables	470
Bank	1,050
Cash	80
	2,540
Total assets	11,250
EQUITY AND LIABILITIES	£
Equity	
Owners' capital (to balance)	5,450
Total equity	5,450
Non-current liabilities	
Mortgage	5,000
	5,000
Current liabilities	
Sundry payables	800
	800
Total equity and liabilities	11,250

J. Frank Determining income for the year ended 31 December 20X4	
	£
Capital at 31 December	5,450
Less: Capital at 1 January	5,800
Apparent loss	(350)
Add: Drawings	500
Profit for the year	150

8 Basic Documentation and Books of Account

8.9 Books of prime entry that record inventory movement

Sales day book

Purchase day book

Returns inward book

Returns outward book

8.10 Making a cheque safe

The cheque should be crossed and the words 'Account payee only' written between the crossing lines.

9 Double Entry and the General Ledger

9.3 H. George

Cash					
20X4		£	*20X4*		£
1 Oct	Capital	5,000	1 Oct	Rent	200
6 Oct	S. Ring	3,500	2 Oct	Purchases	970
12 Oct	Sales revenue	1,810	4 Oct	Fixtures and fittings	1,250
24 Oct	Sales revenue	1,320	9 Oct	Motor vehicles	2,650
			15 Oct	Wages	150
			18 Oct	Purchases	630
			19 Oct	Drawings	350
			21 Oct	Motor expenses	25
			22 Oct	Printing	65
			25 Oct	Motor expenses	45
			27 Oct	Wages	250
			28 Oct	Stationery	35
			30 Oct	Rates	400
			31 Oct	Drawings	175
			31 Oct	Balance c/d	4,435
		11,630			11,630
1 Nov	Balance b/d	4,435			

Capital					
			1 Oct	Cash	5,000

Loan – S. Ring					
			6 Oct	Cash	3,500

Sales revenue					
			12 Oct	Cash	1,810
			24 Oct	Cash	1,320

Rent and rates					
1 Oct	Cash	200			
30 Oct	Cash	400			

Purchases					
2 Oct	Cash	970			
18 Oct	Cash	630			

Fixtures and fittings					
4 Oct	Cash	1,250			

Motor vehicles					
9 Oct	Cash	2,650			

Wages					
15 Oct	Cash	150			
27 Oct	Cash	250			

Drawings					
19 Oct	Cash	350			
31 Oct	Cash	175			

Motor expenses					
21 Oct	Cash	25			
25 Oct	Cash	45			

Printing and stationery					
22 Oct	Cash	65			
28 Oct	Cash	35			

9.4 L. Johnson

Bank					
20X5		£	*20X5*		£
1 Mar	Capital	10,000	1 Mar	Leasehold premises	5,000
18 Mar	Sales revenue	540	2 Mar	Office equipment	1,400
28 Mar	G. Lion	280	6 Mar	Postage	35
			9 Mar	Purchases	420
			13 Mar	Drawings	250
			20 Mar	Telephone	120
			24 Mar	Light and heat	65
			26 Mar	E. Lamb	230
			30 Mar	Light and heat	85
			31 Mar	Bank charges	45
			31 Mar	Balance c/d	3,170
		10,820			10,820
1 Apr	Balance b/d	3,170			

Capital					
			1 Mar	Bank	10,000

Sales revenue					
			11 Mar	G. Lion	880
			18 Mar	Bank	540

G. Lion					
11 Mar	Sales	880	22 Mar	Sales returns	310
			28 Mar	Bank	280

Sales returns					
22 Mar	G. Lion	310			

Leasehold premises					
1 Mar	Bank	5,000			

Office equipment					
2 Mar	Bank	1,400			

Postage and telephone					
6 Mar	Bank	35			
20 Mar	Bank	120			

Purchases					
4 Mar	E. Lamb	630			
9 Mar	Bank	420			

E. Lamb					
16 Mar	Purchases returns	180	4 Mar	Purchases	630
26 Mar	Bank	230			

Purchases returns					
			16 Mar	E. Lamb	180

Drawings					
13 Mar	Bank	250			

Light and heat					
24 Mar	Bank	65			
30 Mar	Bank	85			

Bank charges					
31 Mar	Bank	45			

10 The Balancing of Accounts and the Trial Balance

10.2 S. Baker

Cash account					
20X5	*Details*	£	*20X5*	*Details*	£
1 Jan	Capital	1,000	1 Jan	Rent	100
1 Jan	Loan – London Bank Ltd	500	2 Jan	Fixtures and fittings	300
31 Jan	Sales revenue	600	8 Jan	Purchases	400
			9 Jan	Carriage inwards	25
			10 Jan	Stationery	50
			15 Jan	Wages	200
			20 Jan	Drawings	150
			31 Jan	Balance c/d	875
		2,100			2,100
1 Feb	Balance b/d	875			

Capital introduced account					
20X5	*Details*	£	*20X5*	*Details*	£
31 Jan	Capital account	1,000	1 Jan	Cash	1,000
		1,000			1,000

Loan – London Bank account					
20X5	*Details*	£	*20X5*	*Details*	£
31 Jan	Balance c/d	500	1 Jan	Cash	500
		500			500
			1 Feb	Balance b/d	500

Sales revenue account					
20X5	*Details*	£	*20X5*	*Details*	£
31 Jan	Statement or P or L a/c	600	31 Jan	Cash	600
		600			600

Rent account					
20X5	*Details*	£	*20X5*	*Details*	£
1 Jan	Cash	100	31 Jan	Statement or P or L a/c	100
		100			100

Fixtures and fittings account					
20X5	*Details*	£	*20X5*	*Details*	£
2 Jan	Cash	300	31 Jan	Balance c/d	300
		300			300
1 Feb	Balance c/d	300			

Purchases account					
20X5	*Details*	£	*20X5*	*Details*	£
8 Jan	Cash	400	31 Jan	Statement or P or L a/c	400
		400			400

Carriage inwards account					
20X5	*Details*	£	*20X5*	*Details*	£
9 Jan	Cash	25	31 Jan	Statement or P or L a/c	25
		25			25

Stationery account					
20X5	*Details*	£	*20X5*	*Details*	£
10 Jan	Cash	50	31 Jan	Statement or P or L a/c	50
		50			50

Wages account					
20X5	*Details*	£	*20X5*	*Details*	£
15 Jan	Cash	200	31 Jan	Statement or P or L a/c	200
		200			200

Drawings account					
20X5	*Details*	£	*20X5*	*Details*	£
20 Jan	Cash	150	31 Jan	Capital a/c	150
		150			150

10.3

S. Baker
Trial balance as at 31 January 20X5

	Debit £	*Credit* £
Cash	875	
Capital		1,000
Loan – London Bank		500
Sales revenue		600
Rent	100	
Fixtures and fittings	300	
Purchases	400	
Carriage inwards	25	
Stationery	50	
Wages	200	
Drawings	150	
	2,100	2,100

10.4 H. George (Q9.3)

Cash a/c

20X4		£	20X4		£
1 Oct	Capital	5,000	1 Oct	Rent	200
6 Oct	S. Ring	3,500	2 Oct	Purchases	970
12 Oct	Sales revenue	1,810	4 Oct	Fixtures & fittings	1,250
24 Oct	Sales revenue	1,320	9 Oct	Motor vehicles	2,650
			15 Oct	Wages	150
			18 Oct	Purchases	630
			19 Oct	Drawings	350
			21 Oct	Motor expenses	25
			22 Oct	Printing	65
			25 Oct	Motor expenses	45
			27 Oct	Wages	250
			28 Oct	Stationery	35
			30 Oct	Rates	400
			31 Oct	Drawings	175
			31 Oct	***Balance c/d***	***4,435***
		11,630			11,630
1 Nov	***Balance b/d***	***4,435***			

Capital introduced a/c

31 Oct	***Capital a/c***	***5,000***	1 Oct	Cash	5,000
		5,000			5,000

Loan – S. Ring a/c

31 Oct	***Balance c/d***	***3,500***	6 Oct	Cash	3,500
		3,500			3,500
			1 Nov	***Balance b/d***	***3,500***

Sales revenue a/c

			12 Oct	Cash	1,810
31 Oct	***P or L a/c***	***3,130***	24 Oct	Cash	1,320
		3,130			3,130

Rent & rates a/c

1 Oct	Cash	200			
30 Oct	Cash	400	***31 Oct***	***P or L a/c***	***600***
		600			600

Purchases a/c

2 Oct	Cash	970			
18 Oct	Cash	630	***31 Oct***	***P or L a/c***	***1,600***
		1,600			1,600

Fixtures & fittings a/c					
4 Oct	Cash	1,250	***31 Oct***	***Balance c/d***	***1,250***
		1,250			1,250
1 Nov	***Balance b/d***	***1,250***			

Motor vehicles a/c					
9 Oct	Cash	2,650	***31 Oct***	***Balance c/d***	***2,650***
		2,650			2,650
1 Nov	***Balance b/d***	***2,650***			

Wages a/c					
15 Oct	Cash	150			
27 Oct	Cash	250	***31 Oct***	***P or L a/c***	***400***
		400			400

Drawings a/c					
19 Oct	Cash	350			
31 Oct	Cash	175	***31 Oct***	***Capital a/c***	***525***
		525			525

Motor expenses a/c					
21 Oct	Cash	25			
25 Oct	Cash	45	***31 Oct***	***P or L a/c***	***70***
		70			70

Printing & stationery a/c					
22 Oct	Cash	65			
28 Oct	Cash	35	***31 Oct***	***P or L a/c***	***100***
		100			100

H. George
Trial balance as at 31 October 20X4

	Debit	*Credit*
	£	£
Cash	4,435	
Capital		5,000
Loan — S. Ring		3,500
Sales revenue		3,130
Rent & rates	600	
Purchases	1,600	
Fixtures & fittings	1,250	
Motor vehicles	2,650	

Wages	400	
Drawings	525	
Motor expenses	70	
Printing & stationery	100	
	11,630	11,630

10.5 (Q9.4)

L. Johnson
Trial balance as at 31 March 20X5

	Debit	Credit
	£	£
Bank	3,170	
Capital		10,000
Sales revenue		1,420
G. Lion	290	
Sales returns	310	
Leasehold premises	5,000	
Office equipment	1,400	
Postage and telephone	155	
Purchases	1,050	
E. Lamb		220
Purchases returns		180
Drawings	250	
Light and heat	150	
Bank charges	45	
	11,820	11,820

11 Day Books and the Journal

11.5

Purchases day book

Date	*Name of supplier*	*Amount*
20X5		£
1 Aug	Desks Ltd	750
3 Aug	Chairs Ltd	350
18 Aug	Cabinets Ltd	720
		1,820

Purchases returns day book

Date	*Name of supplier*	*Amount*
20X5		£
10 Aug	Desks Ltd	225
21 Aug	Chairs Ltd	140
		365

Sales day book

Date	*Name of supplier*	*Amount*
20X5		£
6 Aug	British Cars Ltd	630
13 Aug	London Beds Ltd	680
23 Aug	English Carpets Ltd	1,170
		2,480

Sales returns day book

Date	*Name of supplier*	*Amount*
20X5		£
16 Aug	British Cars Ltd	270
25 Aug	London Beds Ltd	85
		355

The ledger

Purchases					
20X5					
31 Aug	Per PDB	1,820			

Purchases returns					
			20X5		
			31 Aug	Per PRDB	365

Desks Ltd					
10 Aug	Returns	225	1 Aug	Purchases	750
31 Aug	Balance c/d	525			
		750			750
			1 Sep	Balance b/d	525

Chairs Ltd					
21 Aug	Returns	140	3 Aug	Purchases	350
31 Aug	Balance c/d	210			
		350			350
			1 Sep	Balance b/d	210

Cabinets Ltd					
			18 Aug	Purchases	720

Sales revenue					
			31 Aug	Per SDB	2,480

Sales returns					
31 Aug	Per SRDB	355			

British Cars					
6 Aug	Sales revenue	630	16 Aug	Returns	270
			31 Aug	Balance c/d	360
		630			630
1 Sep	Balance b/d	360			

London Beds					
13 Aug	Sales revenue	680	25 Aug	Returns	85
			31 Aug	Balance c/d	595
		680			680
1 Sep	Balance b/d	595			

English Carpets					
23 Aug	Sales revenue	1,170			

11.6

The journal

Date	*Details account*		*Debit*	*Credit*
20X5			£	£
20 Apr	Plant and machinery	Dr	5,300	
	To Black Ltd	Cr		5,300
	Being purchase of machine on credit			
23 Apr	White Ltd	Dr	3,600	
	To Motor vehicles	Cr		3,600
	Being sale of delivery vehicle on credit			
26 Apr	Fixtures and fittings	Dr	480	
	To Grey Ltd	Cr		480
	Being purchase of shop fittings on credit			
28 Apr	Yellow Ltd	Dr	270	
	To Office equipment	Cr		270
	Being sale of typewriter on credit			

The ledger

Plant and machinery					
20X5		£			
20 Apr	Black Ltd.	5,300			

Black Ltd					
			20X5		
			20 Apr	Plant and machinery	5,300

White Ltd					
23 Apr	Motor vehicles	3,600			

Motor vehicles					
			23 Apr	White Ltd	3,600

Fixtures and fittings					
26 Apr	Grey Ltd	480			

Grey Ltd					
			26 Apr	Fixtures and fittings	480

Yellow Ltd					
28 Apr	Office equipment	270			

Office equipment					
			28 Apr	Yellow Ltd	270

11.7

The journal

Date	*Details account*		*Debit*	*Credit*
20X4			£	£
1 Aug	Premises	Dr	55,000	
	Plant and machinery	Dr	23,000	
	Inventory	Dr	14,600	
	Trade receivables	Dr	6,300	
	To Trade payables	Cr		2,900
	To Capital	Cr		96,000
			98,900	98,900
	Being assets and liabilities introduced into business by owner from takeover of L. House			

The ledger

Premises					
20X4		£			
1 Aug	Capital	55,000			

Plant and machinery					
1 Aug	Capital	23,000			

Inventory					
1 Aug	Capital	14,600			

Trade receivables					
1 Aug	Capital	6,300			

Trade payables					
			20X4		
			1 Aug	Capital	2,900

Capital					
			1 Aug	Assets and liabilities	96 ,000

Note: The trade receivables and trade payables would be entered in their individual personal accounts.

12 The Cash Book

12.3 The cash book

Date	*Details*	*Memo. discount allowed*	*Debit amount*	*Date*	*Details*	*Memo. discount received*	*Credit amount*
20X5		£	£	20X5		£	£
1 May	Balance b/d		3,680	7 May	Purchases		510
3 May	Capital		2,000	10 May	Wages		200
4 May	Revenue		840	13 May	Rent		360
15 May	Revenue		490	18 May	Fixtures & fittings		2,450
31 May	Oak Ltd	30	160	20 May	Light & heat		180
31 May	Pine Ltd	25	485	23 May	Printing & stationery		70
31 May	Lime Ltd		575	26 May	Drawings		250
				31 May	Brick Ltd	45	850
				31 May	Stone Ltd	20	220
				31 May	Slate Ltd	40	480
				31 May	Balance c/d		2,660
		55	8,230			105	8,230
1 June	Balance b/d		2,660				

12.4 The ledger

Capital					
			20X5		£
			1 May	Balance b/d	3,680

Capital introduced					
20X5		£	20X5		£
31 May	Capital a/c	2,000	3 May	Bank	2,000
		2,000			2,000

The capital introduced and drawings account are balanced to the capital account; however, for the purpose of preparing the trial balance, for extracting the financial statements, these are all kept separate.

Sales revenue					
			30 Apr	Per SDB	1,910
			4 May	Bank	840
31 May	P or L a/c	3,240	15 May	Bank	490
		3,240			3,240

Oak Ltd					
1 May	Balance b/d	190	31 May	Bank	160
			31 May	Discount allowed	30
		190			190

Pine Ltd					
1 May	Balance b/d	510	31 May	Bank	485
			31 May	Discount allowed	25
		510			510

Lime Ltd					
15 Apr	Sales	630	31 May	Bank	575
			31 May	Balance c/d	55
		630			630
1 June	Balance b/d	55			

Discount allowed					
31 May	Total per Cash Book	55	31 May	P or L a/c	55
		55			55

Purchases					
30 Apr	Per PDB	1,850			
7 May	Bank	510	31 May	P or L a/c	2,360
		2,360			2,360

Brick Ltd					
31 May	Bank	850	1 May	Balance b/d	895
31 May	Discount rec'd	45			
		895			895

Stone Ltd					
31 May	Bank	220	1 May	Balance b/d	240
31 May	Discount rec'd	20			
		240			240

Slate Ltd					
31 May	Bank	480	11 Apr	Purchases	520
31 May	Discount rec'd	40	31 May	Discount disallowed	40
31 May	Balance c/d	40			
		560			560
			1 June	Balance c/d	40

Discount received					
31 May	Slate Ltd – disallowed	40	31 May	Total per Cash Book	105
31 May	P or L a/c	65			
		105			105

Wages					
10 May	Bank	200	31 May	P or L a/c	200
		200			200

Rent					
13 May	Bank	360	31 May	P or L a/c	360
		360			360

Fixtures & fittings					
18 May	Bank	2,450	31 May	Balance c/d	2,450
		2,450			2,450
1 June	Balance b/d	2,450			

Light & heat					
20 May	Bank	180	31 May	P or L a/c	180
		180			180

Printing & stationery					
23 May	Bank	70	31 May	P or L a/c	70
		70			70

Drawings					
26 May	Bank	250	31 May	Capital a/c	250
		250			250

B. Jones Trial balance as at 31 May 20X5		
	Debit	*Credit*
	£	£
Bank	2,660	
Capital		3,680
Capital introduced		2,000
Sales revenue		3,240
Sales returns	580	
Lime Ltd (trade receivable)	55	
Discount allowed	55	
Purchases	2,360	
Purchases returns		195
Slate Ltd (trade payable)		40
Discount received		65
Wages	200	
Rent	360	
Fixtures & fittings	2,450	
Light & heat	180	
Printing & stationery	70	
Drawings	250	
	9,220	9,220

Note

1. The discount relating to Slate Ltd has been entered in the cash book and then reversed as discount disallowed because the latter will probably have occurred at a later date, and to illustrate the entry for discount disallowed. This reversal is often shown as a deduction (in red ink) in the discount received column of the cash book. However, if it was known to have been disallowed on 31 May, as implied in the question, the student would be justified in simply not entering the discount in the cash book in the first place.

12.5 The cash book

Date	*Details*	*Memo discount received*	*Bank*	*Cash*	*Date*	*Details*	*Memo discount received*	*Bank*	*Cash*
20X5		£	£	£	20X5		£	£	£
1 Sep	Balance b/d		1,950	860	4 Sep	Purchases			230
3 Sep	Sales revenue		470		6 Sep	Light and heat		510	
9 Sep	Sales revenue		380		10 Sep	Wages		250	
12 Sep	Sales revenue			290	15 Sep	Travelling expenses			40
22 Sep	Cash		350		16 Sep	Rates		410	
24 Sep	Capital		500		19 Sep	Drawings			150
26 Sep	B. Jones – loan		1,000		20 Sep	Purchases		320	
27 Sep	Purchases returns			170	21 Sep	Postage and telephone			30

					22 Sep	Bank			350
29 Sep	Bank			180	22 Sep	Bank			350
30 Sep	British Cars	10	350		25 Sep	Vehicles		2,500	
30 Sep	London Beds	15	580		28 Sep	Motor expenses			280
30 Sep	English Carpets		1,100		29 Sep	Cash		180	
					30 Sep	Desks Ltd	25	500	
					30 Sep	Chairs Ltd	20	190	
					30 Sep	Cabinets Ltd		500	
					30 Sep	Balance c/d		1,320	420
		25	6,680	1,500			45	6,680	1,500
1 Oct	Balance c/d		1,320	420					

12.6 The ledger

Capital

			20X5		£
			1 Sep	Balance b/d	2,810
30 Sep	Balance c/d	3,310	24 Sep	Bank	500
		3,310			3,310
			1 Oct	Balance b/d	3,310

Loan – B. Jones

30 Sep	Balance c/d	1,000	26 Sep	Bank	1,000
			1 Oct	Bal b/d	1,000

Sales revenue

			31 Aug	Per SDB	2,480
			3 Sep	Bank	470
			9 Sep	Bank	380
30 Sep	P/L a/c	3,620	12 Sep	Cash	290
		3,620			3,620

Sales returns

20X5					
31 Aug	Per SRDB	355	30 Sep	P or L a/c	355

British Cars

1 Sep	Balance b/d	360	30 Sep	Bank	350
			30 Sep	Discount allowed	10
		360			360

London Beds

1 Sep	Balance b/d	595	30 Sep	Bank	580
			30 Sep	Discount allowed	15
		595			595

Discount allowed

30 Sep	Total per Cash Book	25	30 Sep	P or L a/c	25

English Carpets

23 Aug	Sales revenue	1,170	30 Sep	Bank	1,100
			30 Sep	Balance c/d	70
		1,170			1,170
1 Oct	Balance b/d	70			

Purchases

31 Aug	Per PDB	1,820			
4 Sep	Cash	230			
20 Sep	Bank	320	30 Sep	P or L a/c	2,370
		2,370			2,370

Purchases returns

			31 Aug	Per PRDB	365
30 Sep	P or L a/c	535	27 Sep	Cash	170
		535			535

Desks Ltd

30 Sep	Bank	500	1 Sep	Balance b/d	525
30 Sep	Discount received	25			
		525			525

Chairs Ltd

30 Sep	Bank	190	1 Sep	Balance b/d	210
30 Sep	Discount received	20			
		210			210

Discount received

	Profit or loss account	45	30 Sep	Total per Cash Book	45

Cabinets Ltd

30 Sep	Bank	500	18 Aug	Purchases	720
30 Sep	Balance c/d	220			
		720			720
			1 Oct	Balance b/d	220

Light and heat

6 Sep	Bank	510		Profit or loss a/c	510

Wages

10 Sep	Bank	250		Profit or loss a/c	250

		Travelling expenses			
15 Sep	Cash	40		Profit or loss a/c	40

		Rates			
16 Sep	Bank	410		Profit or loss a/c	410

		Drawings			
19 Sep	Cash	150		Profit or loss a/c	150

		Postage and telephone			
21 Sep	Cash	30		Profit or loss a/c	30

		Motor vehicles			
25 Sep	Bank	2,500	30 Sep	Bal c/d	2,500

B. Player
Trial balance as at 30 September 20X5

	Debit	*Credit*
	£	£
Cash	420	
Bank	1,320	
Capital		3,310
Loan – B. Jones		1,000
Sales revenue		3,620
Sales returns	355	
Discount allowed	25	
English Carpets	70	
Purchases	2,370	
Purchases returns		535
Discount received		45
Cabinets Ltd		220
Light and heat	510	
Wages	250	
Travelling expenses	40	
Rates	410	
Drawings	150	
Postage and telephone	30	
Motor vehicles	2,500	
Motor expenses	280	
	8,730	8,730

Note: Discount taken by trade receivables such as English Carp etc, which is not allowed, is usually simply not entered in the discount allowed column of the cash books since the business whose books we are preparing has disallowed the discount.

13 The Petty Cash Book

13.3

Petty cash book

Debit amount	*Date*	*Details*	*Credit amount*	*Purchases*	*Wages*	*Motor expenses*	*Travelling expenses*	*Printing and stationery*	*Postage and telephone*	*Misc.*
£	20X5		£	£	£	£	£	£	£	£
400	1 Feb	Balance b/d								
	1 Feb	Purchases	31	31						
	3 Feb	Wages	28		28					
	6 Feb	Petrol	9			9				
	8 Feb	Bus fares	3				3			
	11 Feb	Pens and pencils	8					8		
	12 Feb	Casual labour	25		25					
	14 Feb	Repairs	17			17				
	16 Feb	Paper	15					15		
	19 Feb	Purchases	22	22						
	20 Feb	Train fares	12				12			
	21 Feb	Repairs to premises	35							35
	22 Feb	Postage	6						6	
	23 Feb	Drawings	20							20
	24 Feb	Taxi fares	7				7			
	25 Feb	Envelopes	4					4		
	26 Feb	Purchases	18	18						
	27 Feb	Wages	30		30					
	28 Feb	Petrol	14			14				
304	28 Feb	Bank	304	71	83	40	22	27	6	55
	28 Feb	Balance c/d	400							
704			704							
400	1 Mar	Balance b/d								

The ledger

Purchases					
20X5		£			
28 Feb	Per PCB	71			

Wages					
28 Feb	Per PCB	83			

Motor expenses					
28 Feb	Per PCB	40			

Travelling expenses				
28 Feb	Per PCB	22		

Printing and stationery				
28 Feb	Per PCB	27		

Postage and telephone				
28 Feb	Per PCB	6		

Repairs to premises				
21 Feb	Cash (PCB)	35		

Drawings				
23 Feb	Cash (PCB)	20		

Bank					
			20X5		£
			28 Feb	Cash (PCB)	304

14 The Final Financial Statements of Sole Traders (Introductory)

14.7 R. Woods

Statement of profit or loss for the year ended 30 September 20X5		
	£	£
Sales revenue		18,922
Less : Cost of sales		
Inventory at 1 Oct 20X4	2,368	
Add : purchases	12,389	
	14,757	
Less : inventory at 30 Sep 20X5	2,946	
		11,811
Gross profit		7,111
Less : Expenditure		
Salaries and wages	3,862	
Rent and rates	504	
Insurance	78	
Motor expenses	664	
Printing and stationery	216	
Light and heat	166	
General expenses	314	5,804
Profit for year		1,307

R. Woods Statement of financial position as at 30 September 20X5		
ASSETS	£	£
Non-current assets		
Premises		5,000
Motor vehicles		1,800
Fixtures and fittings		350
		7,150
Current assets		
Inventory		2,946
Trade receivables		3,896
Bank		482
		7,324
Total assets		14,474
EQUITY AND LIABILITIES		
Equity capital		
Balance at 1 Oct 20X4		12,636
Add : profit for the year		1,307
		13,943
Less : drawings		1,200
Balance at 30 Sep 20X5		12,743
Current liabilities		
Trade payables		1,731
Total liabilities		1,731
Total equity and reserves		14,474

14.9 A. Evans

Statement of profit or loss for the year ended 30 June 20X5			
	£	£	£
Sales revenue			81,640
Less : returns inwards			840
Net sales			80,800
Less : Cost of sales			
Inventory at 1 July 20X4		5,610	
Add : purchases	49,870		
Less : returns outwards	960	48,910	
		54,520	
Less : inventory at 30 June 20X5		4,920	
			49,600
Gross profit			31,200
Add : interest received			620
			31,820

Less : Expenditure		
Carriage outwards	390	
Rent and rates	1,420	
Light and heat	710	
Telephone and postage	540	
Printing and stationery	230	
Bank interest	140	3,430
Profit for the year		28,390

A. Evans
Statement of financial position as at 30 June 20X5

	£	£	£
ASSETS			
Non-current assets			
Leasehold premises			52,500
Motor vehicles			13,650
			66,150
Current assets			
Inventory			4,920
Trade receivables			2,630
Investments			4,980
Cash			460
			12,990
Total assets			79,140
EQUITY AND LIABILITIES			
Equity capital			
Balance at 1 July 20X4			39,980
Add : profit for the year			28,390
			68,370
Less : drawings			14,760
Balance at 30 June 20X5			53,610
Non-current liabilities			
Loan – Solihull Bank			20,000
Total non-current liabilities			20,000
Current liabilities			
Trade payables			1,910
Bank overdraft			3,620
Total current liabilities			5,530
Total liabilities			25,530
Total equity and liabilities			79,140

Note: The student should state that she or he is assuming that the investments are intended to be held for less than one year from the date of the statement of financial position and are thus a current asset. Alternatively, it may be assumed that the investments are to be held for more than one accounting year and are therefore a non-current asset.

15 Depreciation and Non-Current Assets

15.7 Is depreciation the loss in value of a non-current asset?

A common misconception is that depreciation reflects the loss in value of a non-current asset. However, this is not its purpose. Depreciation is a systematic means of allocating the cost of a non-current asset to the revenue which the asset helps to generate. It is a prime example of the application of the matching concept. The allocation should reflect the reduction in the useful economic life of the asset (the reduction in the revenue-generating powers of the asset). Though it may equate, or be close, to the reduction in the market value of the asset this is not its purpose and may not happen in some cases. For example, when a non-current asset is bespoke (like a mine-shaft). In this instance the asset can only be used by that particular company and its market value would be scrap value. The market value would be very different to the net book value (the unallocated portion of the original cost).

15.17 Workings

Cost of machines purchased on 1 October 20X4 should include all transportation and installation expenditure:

$$£3{,}100 + £130 + £590 + £180 = £4{,}000$$

$$\text{Cost per machine} = £4{,}000 \div 2 = £2{,}000$$

Disposal

Aggregate depreciation from the date brought into use (1 April 20X5) until the date of disposal (31 March 20Y3) = 10% × £2,000 × 8 years = £1,600. Book value at 31 March 20Y3 = £2,000 – £1,600 = £400. Proceeds of sale = £800 – £100 = £700. Profit on sale = £700 – £400 = £300.

a The journal

			Debit	Credit
20Y3			£	£
31 Mar	Machinery disposals account	Dr	2,000	
	Machinery account	Cr		2,000
	Being the transfer of the cost of the machine sold to the disposals account			
31 Mar	Depreciation expense	Dr	100	
	Provision for depreciation	Cr		100
	Being depreciation for the current year on the machine sold			
31 Mar	Provision for depreciation	Dr	1,600	
	Machinery disposals account	Cr		1,600
	Being the aggregate depreciation on the disposal			
31 Mar	H. Johnson bank account	Dr	800	
	Machinery disposals account	Cr		800
	Being proceeds of sale of machinery sold			
31 Mar	Machinery disposals	Dr	100	
	Wages	Cr		100
	Being the labour cost of dismantling the machine sold			

31 Mar	Machinery disposals account	Dr	300	
	Profit or loss account	Cr		300
	Being profit on sale of machine			
1 May	Machinery account	Dr	2,800	
	R. Adams bank account	Cr		2,800
	Being purchase of new machine			

Notes

1 It is likely that in practice the entries relating to depreciation and the profit on sale would be done at the end of the accounting year. However, examination questions like this often expect students to do them on the date of disposal.

2 Although not required by the question, students may find it useful to start by constructing the machinery disposals account in rough form as follows:

Machinery disposals			
Machinery – cost	2,000	Provision for depreciation	
Wages – dismantling costs	100	– aggregate depreciation	1,600
P/L – profit on sale	300	H. Johnson – proceeds of sale	800
	2,400		2,400

b Provision for depreciation for year ended 30 September 20Y3:

Machine owned all year: 10% × £2,000 = £200

Machine sold: 10% × £2,000 × 6 months = £100

Machine acquired: depreciation from the date brought in to use (1 July 20Y3) to the end of the accounting year: 10% × £2,800 × 3 months = £70

Total depreciation expense for year: £200 + £100 + £70 = £370

15.19 Workings

Plant

Cost at 31 December 20X3 = £96,920 + £33,080 – £40,000 = £90,000

Depreciation for 20X3 = 10% × £90,000 = £9,000

Disposal:

Aggregate depreciation = 10% × £40,000 × 6 years = £24,000

Book value at disposal = £40,000 – £24,000 = £16,000

Loss on sale = £16,000 – £15,000 = £1,000

Vehicles

Disposal 1:

Aggregate depreciation –

20X1 = 25% × £3,200 = £800

20X2 = 25% × (£3,200 – £800) = £600

20X3 = 25% × (£3,200 – [£800 + £600]) = £450

Total = £800 + £600 + £450 = £1,850

Book value at disposal = £3,200 – £1,850 = £1,350

Loss on sale = £1,350 – £1,300 = £50

Disposal 2:

Aggregate depreciation –

20X2 = 25% × £4,800 = £1,200

20X3 = 25% × (£4,800 – £1,200) = £900

Total = £1,200 + £900 = £2,100

Book value at disposal = £4,800 – £2,100 = £2,700

Profit on sale = £2,960 – £2,700 = £260

Remainder

Cost at 31 December 20X4 = £25,060 + £4,750 – £3,200 – £4,800 = £21,810

Aggregate depreciation at 31 December 20X4 = £14,560 – £1,850 – £2,100 = £10,610

Depreciation for 20X4 = 25% × (£21,810 – £10,610) = £2,800

a The ledger

Plant					
20X4		£	*20X4*		£
1 Jan	Balance b/d	96,920	31 Dec	Bank	15,000
31 Dec	Bank	33,080	31 Dec	Provision for dep'n	24,000
			31 Dec	P or L – loss	1,000
			31 Dec	Balance c/d	90,000
		130,000			130,000
20X5					
1 Jan	Balance b/d	90,000			

Provision for depreciation on plant					
20X4		£	*20X4*		£
31 Dec	Plant	24,000	1 Jan	Balance b/d	50,120
31 Dec	Balance c/d	35,120	31 Dec	P or L	9,000
		59,120			59,120
			20X5		
			1 Jan	Balance b/d	35,120

Vehicles					
20X4		£	*20X4*		£
1 Jan	Balance b/d	25,060	31 Dec	Bank – vehicle	1,300
31 Dec	Bank	4,750	31 Dec	Provision for depn	1,850
			31 Dec	P or L – loss	50
			31 Dec	Bank – vehicle	2,960
31 Dec	P or L – Profit	260	31 Dec	Provision for depn	2,100
			31 Dec	Balance c/d	21,810
		30,070			30,070
20X5					
1 Jan	Balance b/d	21,810			

Provision for depreciation on vehicles					
20X4		£	*20X4*		£
31 Dec	Vehicles	1,850	1 Jan	Balance b/d	14,560
31 Dec	Vehicles	2,100	31 Dec	P or L	2,800
31 Dec	Balance c/d	13,410			
		17,360			17,360
			20X5		
			1 Jan	Balance b/d	13,410

Statement of P or L			
Depn on plant	9,000	Profit on sale vehicle	260
Depn on vehicles	2,800		
Loss on sale plant	1,000		
Loss on sale vehicle	50		

b The journal

				Debit	*Credit*
20X4				£	£
31	Dec	Profit or loss account	Dr	9,000	
		Provision for depn – plant	Cr		9,000
		Being depreciation on plant for 20X4			
31	Dec	Profit and loss account	Dr	2,800	
		Provision for depn vehicles	Cr		2,800
		Being depreciation on vehicles for 20X4			

Alternative method – disposals account

Plant					
20X4		£	*20X4*		£
1 Jan	Balance b/d	96,920	31 Dec	Disposals	40,000
31 Dec	Bank	33,080	31 Dec	Balance c/d	90,000
		130,000			130,000
20X5					
1 Jan	Balance b/d	90,000			

Plant disposals					
20X4		£	*20X4*		£
31 Dec	Plant	40,000	31 Dec	Bank	15,000
			31 Dec	Provision for depn	24,000
			31 Dec	P or L – loss	1,000
		40,000			40,000

Vehicles					
20X4		£	*20X4*		£
1 Jan	Balance b/d	25,060	31 Dec	Disposal 1	3,200
31 Dec	Bank	4,750	31 Dec	Disposal 2	4,800
			31 Dec	Balance c/d	21,810
		29,810			29,810
20X5					
1 Jan	Balance b/d	21,810			

Vehicle disposals					
20X4		£	*20X4*		£
31 Dec	Vehicles 1	3,200	31 Dec	Bank – vehicle	1,300
31 Dec	Vehicles 2	4,800	31 Dec	Provision for depn	1,850
			31 Dec	P or L – loss	50
			31 Dec	Bank – vehicle	2,960
31 Dec	P or L – profit	260	31 Dec	Provision for depn	2,100
		8,260			8,260

16 Irrecoverable receivables and allowance for irrecoverable receivables

16.6 Workings

	£
Trade receivables at 31 July 20X5	15,680
Less : irrecoverable receivables (£410 + £270)	680
Revised trade receivables at 31 July 20X5	15,000
Allowance for irrecoverable receivables = 4% × £15,000 = £600	

The ledger

A. Wall					
20X5		£	20X5		£
31 July	Balance b/d	410	31 July	Irrec. Rec.	410

B. Wood					
31 July	Balance b/d	270	31 July	Irrec. Rec.	270

Irrecoverable receivables					
31 July	A. Wall	410	31 July	P or L a/c	680
31 July	B. Wood	270			
		680			680

Allowance for irrecoverable receivables					
			31 July	P or L a/c	600

Statement of P or L a/c		
Irrec. Rec.	680	
Allowance for irrecoverable receivables	600	

16.7 Workings

	£
Trade receivables at 30 Apr 20X5	19,500
Less : Irrecoverable receivables (£620 + £880)	1,500
Revised trade receivables at 30 Apr 20X5	18,000
Allowance for irrecoverable receivables at 30 Apr 20X5 (3% x £18,000)	540
Less : Allowance for irrecoverable receivables at 30 Apr 20X4	750
Reduction in allowance for irrecoverable receivables.	210

The ledger

A. Winters					
20X5		£	20X5		£
30 Apr	Balance b/d	620	30 Apr	Irrec. Rec.	620

D. Spring					
30 Apr	Balance b/d	880	30 Apr	Irrec. Rec.	880

Irrecoverable Receivables					
30 Apr	A. Winters	620	30 Apr	P or L a/c	1,500
30 Apr	D. Spring	880			
		1,500			1,500

Allowance for Irrecoverable Receivables					
20X5		£	*20X4*		£
30 Apr	P or L a/c	210	30 Apr	Balance b/d	750
30 Apr	Balance c/d	540			
		750			750
			20X5		
			1 May	Balance b/d	540

Statement of profit or loss account			
Irrecoverable receivables	1,500	Allowance for irrecoverable receivables	210

16.13 Workings

Allowance for irrecoverable receivables	£	£	£
Specific allowance (£320 – £70)			250
General allowance			
Trade receivables at 31 Dec 20X5		12,610	
Less : irrecoverable receivables (£210 + [£260 – £110])	360		
Specific allowance	250	610	
Revised trade receivables at 31 Dec 20X5		12,000	
Allowance at 31 Dec 20X5 (5% x £12,000)			600
Total allowable for irrecoverable receivables at 31 Dec 20X5			850
Less : allowance for irrecoverable receivables at 31 Dec 20X4			1,260
Reduction in allowance for irrecoverable receivables			410

Provision for depreciation			
Date of purchase or sale	**Details**	**Depreciation on disposal**	**Depreciation year ended 31 Dec 20X5**
		£	£
	Depreciation on disposal		
1 July 20X3	For year ending 31.12.X3 – 25% × £8,000 × $\frac{6}{12}$	1,000	
	For year ending 31.12.X4 – 25% × (£8,000 – £1,000)	1,750	
31 Mar 20X5	For year ending 31.12.X5 – 25% × (£8,000 – [£1,000 + £1,750]) × $\frac{3}{12}$	328	328
		3,078	

	Book value at 31.3.X5: £8,000 − £3,078 = £4,922	
	Loss on sale: £4,922 − £4,000 = £922	
	Depreciation on acquisition	
31 Mar 20X5	25% × (£4,000 + £1,000) × $\frac{9}{12}$	938
	Depreciation on remainder	
	Cost = £30,000 − £8,000 = £22,000	
	Aggregate depreciation:	
	£12,500 − (£1,000 + £1,750) = £9,750	
	WDV = £22,000 × £9,750 = £12,250	
	Depreciation = 25% × £12,250	3,063
		4,329

a The ledger

A. Bee					
20X5		£	*20X5*		£
1 Jan	Balance b/d	320	30 Apr	Bank	70
			30 Apr	Balance c/d	250
		320			320
1 May	Balance b/d	250			

J. Kay					
1 Jan	Balance b/d	210	15 June	Irrec. rec.	210

C. Dee					
1 Jan	Balance b/d	180	3 Aug	Bank	180

F. Gee					
1 Jan	Balance b/d	260	7 Oct	Bank	110
			7 Oct	Irrec. rec.	150
		260			260

Irrecoverable receivables					
15 June	J. Kay	210	31 Dec	P or L a/c	360
7 Oct	F. Gee	150			
		360			360

Allowance for irrecoverable receivables					
31 Dec	P or L a/c	410	1 Jan	Balance b/d	1,260
31 Dec	Balance c/d	850			
		1,260	20X6		1,260
			1 Jan	Balance b/d	850

Plant and machinery					
1 Jan	Balance b/d	30,000	31 Mar	Part exchange	4,000
31 Mar	Bank	1,000	31 Dec	Provision for depreciation	3,078
31 Mar	Part exchange	4,000	31 Dec	P or L a/c – loss on sale	922
			31 Dec	Balance c/d	27,000
		35,000			35,000
20X6					
1 Jan	Balance b/d	27,000			

Provision for depreciation					
31 Dec	Plant and machinery	3,078	1 Jan	Balance b/d	12,500
31 Dec	Balance c/d	13,751	31 Dec	P or L a/c	4,329
		16,829			16,829
			20X6		
			1 Jan	Balance b/d	13,751

Statement of profit or loss account			
Irrecoverable receivables	360	Allowance for receivables	410
Provision for depreciation	4,329		
Loss on sale of plant	922		

b

A provision is the setting aside of income to meet a known or highly probable future liability or loss, the amount and/or timing of which cannot be ascertained exactly, and thus an estimate has to be made. Allowances for irrecoverable receivables are intended to provide for a future loss. An allowance for irrecoverable receivables provides for the loss that occurs when credit customers fail to pay their debts.

Depreciation is the reduction in the useful economic life of a non-current asset.

17 Accruals and Prepayments

17.2 The ledger

Rent					
20X4		£	*20X4*		£
1 Jan	Prepayment b/d	300	31 Dec	P or L a/c	3,730
29 Jan	Bank	930	31 Dec	Prepayment c/d	320
2 May	Bank	930			
30 July	Bank	930			
5 Nov	Bank	960			
		4,050			4,050
20X5					
1 Jan	Prepayment b/d	320			

Light and heat					
20X4		£	*20X4*		£
6 Mar	Bank	420	1 Jan	Accrual b/d	140
4 June	Bank	360	31 Dec	P or L a/c	1,450
3 Sep	Bank	270			
7 Dec	Bank	390			
31 Dec	Accrual c/d	150			
		1,590			1,590
			20X5		
			1 Jan	Accrual b/d	150

Workings

Rent prepaid at 1 Jan 20X4 = $\frac{1}{3} \times 900 = £300$

Rent prepaid at 31 Dec 20X4 = $\frac{1}{3} \times 960 = £320$

Light and heat accrued at 1 Jan 20X4 = $\frac{1}{3} \times 420 = £140$

Light and heat accrued at 31 Dec 20X4 = $\frac{1}{3} \times 450 = £150$

17.8

The entries in a rent receivable account are on the opposite side to those in a rent payable account. The credit to the profit or loss account is the difference between the two sides of the ledger account after entering all the prepayments (or accruals).

The derivation of the purchases on credit will be unfamiliar to students at this point in their studies. It is discussed in depth in Chapter 20. However, the principle is very similar to expense accounts containing accruals. A total purchase ledger (control) account is used in place of the individual personal accounts of the credit suppliers. The trade payables (total credit suppliers) at the start and end of the year are entered on the same sides as accruals in an expense account, as are the payments. The credit purchases for the year are then the difference between the two sides of the purchase ledger control account.

The ledger

Rents receivable					
20X5		£	*20X4*		£
31 May	P or L a/c	4,004	1 June	Prepayment b/d	463
			20X5		
31 May	Prepayment c/d	517	31 May	Bank	4,058
		4,521			4,521
			1 June	Prepayment b/d	517

Rent and rates payable					
20X4		£	*20X4*		£
1 June	Prepayment b/d	1,246	1 June	Accrual b/d	315
20X5			*20X5*		
31 May	Bank – rent	7,491	31 May	P or L a/c	10,100
31 May	Bank – rates	2,805	31 May	Prepayment c/d	1,509
31 May	Accrual c/d	382			
		11,924			11,924
1 June	Prepayment b/d	1,509	1 June	Accrual b/d	382

Total trade payables					
20X5		£	*20X4*		£
31 May	Bank	75,181	1 June	Balance b/d	5,258
31 May	Discount rec'd	1,043	*20X5*		
31 May	Balance c/d	4,720	31 May	P or L – purchases	75,686
		80,944			80,944
			1 June	Balance b/d	4,720

—18 The Extended Trial Balance and Final Financial Statements (Advanced)—

18.5 Workings

Rent prepaid $= \frac{3}{6} \times \frac{6}{12} \times$ £6,400 = £1,600

Rates prepaid $= \frac{3}{12} \times$ £1,488 = £372

Rent and rates prepaid = £1,600 + £372 = £1,972

Allowance for irrecoverable receivables:

At 31 December 20X4 = 5% × (£72,300 − £1,420) = £3,544

Reduction in allowance = £3,702 − £3,544 = £158

Depreciation on car = 20% × £7,200 = £1,440

C. Jones
Extended trial balance as at 31 December 20X4

	Trial balance		*Adjustments*		*Statement of profit or loss*		*Statement of financial position*	
	Dr	*Cr*	*Dr*	*Cr*	*Dr*	*Cr*	*Dr*	*Cr*
	£	£	£	£	£	£	£	£
Capital		45,214	9,502					35,712
Drawings	9,502			9,502				
Purchases	389,072				389,072			
Sales revenue		527,350				527,350		
Wages and salaries	33,440		3,012	3,012	36,452			3,012
Rent and rates	9,860		1,972	1,972	7,888		1,972	
Light and heat	4,142				4,142			
Irrecoverable receivables	1,884		1,420		3,304			
Allowance for irrecoverable receivables		3,702	158			158		3,544
Trade receivables	72,300			1,420			70,880	
Trade payables		34,308						34,308
Bank	2,816						2,816	
Cash	334						334	
Inventory	82,124		99,356	82,124	82,124	99,356	99,356	
Motor car – cost	7,200						7,200	
Motor car – depreciation		2,100		1,440	1,440			3,540
Profit for the year					102,442			102,442
	612,674	612,674			626,864	626,864	182,558	182,558

C. Jones
Statement of profit or loss for the year ended 31 December 20X4

	£	£
Sales revenue		527,350
Less : cost of sales		
Inventory at 1 Jan 20X4	82,124	
Add : purchases	389,072	
	471,196	
Less : inventory at 31 Dec 20X4	99,356	371,840
Gross profit		155,510
Add : reduction in allowance for irrecoverable receivables		158
		155,668
Less : Expenditure		
Wages and salaries	36,452	
Rent and rates	7,888	
Light and heat	4,142	
Irrecoverable receivables	3,304	
Depreciation	1,440	53,226
Profit for the year		102,442

C. Jones Statement of financial position as at 31 December 20X4		
ASSETS	£	£
Non-current assets		
Motor car at cost		7,200
Less: provision for depreciation		3,540
		3,660
Current assets		
Inventory		99,356
Trade receivables	70,880	
Less: allowance for irrecoverable receivables	3,544	67,336
Prepayments		1,972
Bank		2,816
Cash		334
		171,814
Total assets		175,474
EQUITY AND LIABILITIES		
Equity capital		
Balance at 1 Jan 20X4		45,214
Add: profit for the year		102,442
		147,656
Less: drawings		9,502
Balance at 31 Dec 20X4		138,154
Current liabilities		
Trade payables		34,308
Accruals		3,012
Total liabilities		37,320
Total equity and liabilities		175,474

18.6

J. Clark Statement of profit or loss for the year ended 31 March 20X5			
	£	£	£
Sales revenue (£58,640 – £400)			58,240
Less : Returns inwards			3,260
Net sales revenue			54,980
Less : Cost of sales			
Opening inventory		4,670	
Add : Purchases (£34,260 – £350)	33,910		
Less : Returns outwards	2,140		
	31,770		
Add : Carriage inwards	730	32,500	
		37,170	

Less : Closing inventory (£3,690 + £300)	3,990	33,180
Gross profit		21,800
Add : Discount received		1,970
Investment income		460
		24,230
Less : Expenditure		
Wages	7,180	
Carriage outward	420	
Discount allowed	1,480	
Depreciation on plant (25% x [£11,350 – £4,150])	1,800	
Depreciation on vehicles	1,986	
Loss on sale of vehicle	264	
Interest payable	1,000	
Rent and rates (£4,300 – £210)	4,090	
Allowance for irrecoverable receivables ([10% x (£8,070 – £370 – £400)] – £530)	200	
Irrecoverable receivables	370	
Light and heat (£2,640 + £130)	2,770	
Stationery (£450 – £230)	220	21,780
Profit for the year		2,450

J. Clark
Statement of financial position as at 31 March 20X5

	£	£	£
ASSETS	*Cost*	*Prov depn*	*WDV*
Non-current assets			
Freehold premises	32,000		32,000
Plant and machinery (£4,150 + £1,800)	11,350	5,950	5,400
Motor vehicles (£13,290 – £1,000)	12,290	4,498	7,792
	55,640	10,448	45,192
Goodwill			5,000
			50,192
Current assets			
Stationery inventory		230	
Inventory (£3,690 + £300)		3,990	
Trade receivables (£8,070 – £370 – £400)	7,300		
Less : Allowance for irrecoverable receivables	730	6,570	
Sundry receivables		458	
Prepayments		210	
Quoted investments		6,470	
Bank and cash		2,850	
		20,778	
Total assets		70,970	

EQUITY AND LIABILITIES	
Equity capital	
Balance at 1 April 20X4	60,000
Add : profit for year	2,450
	62,450
Less : Drawings (£5,600 + £350)	5,950
Balance at 31 March 20X5	56,500
Non-current liabilities	
Mortgage on premises	10,000
Total non-current liabilities	10,000
Current liabilities	
Trade payables	4,340
Accruals	130
Total current liabilities	4,470
Total liabilities	14,470
Total equity and liabilities	70,970

Workings: Depreciation on vehicles

	Previous years	*This year*
	£	£
Disposal		
20X2/X3: 20% × £1,000 × $\frac{3}{12}$	50	
20X3/X4: 20% × (£1,000 − £50)	190	
	240	
20X4/X5 (current year charge)		
20% × [£1,000 − (£50 + £190)] × $\frac{3}{12}$	38	38
	278	
Book value at sale = £1,000 − £278 = £722		
Loss on sale = £722 − £458 = £264		
Depreciation on remaining		
20% × [(£13,290 − £1,000) − (£2,790 − £240)]		1,948
		1,986
Aggregate depreciation at 31 March 20X5		
£2,790 + £1,986 − £278 = £4,498		

Note

1 It is assumed that the quoted investments are to be held for less than one accounting year.

19 The Bank Reconciliation Statement

19.5 The ledger

Cash book			
Balance b/d	2,880	Bank charges	105
Dividends	189	Refer to drawer	54
		Error (£141 × 2)	282
		Balance c/d	2,628
	3,069		3,069

Grow Ltd **Bank reconciliation statement at 31 March 20X5**		
	£	£
Balance per cash book		2,628
Add : Cheques not yet presented (£642 + £1,200)		1,842
		4,470
Less : Amounts not yet credited	1,904	
Cheque debited in error by bank	216	2,120
Balance per bank statement		2,350

19.6 Mrs Lake

a Bank reconciliation statement as at 30 April 20X5

	£	£
Balance per bank account		1,310.40
Add : Error cheque no. 236130 (£87.77 – £77.87)	9.90	
Receipts not entered in bank account	21.47	
Cheques not yet presented (£30 + £52.27)	82.27	113.64
		1,424.04
Less : Payments not entered in bank account (£12.80 + £32.52)	45.32	
Amounts not yet credited	192.80	238.12
		1,185.92
Less : Undetected error		19.47
Balance per bank statement		1,166.45

b

The undetected error would require further investigation. The amount is the same as cheque number 427519 on 10 April. This cheque number is different from the sequence of the others, which suggests that it may have been debited to Mrs Lake's account in error.

Note

1 Students should have realized that cheques numbered 236126 and 236127 shown on the bank statement are in the cash book for March and were unpresented at 31 March (Reconciliation at 31 March 20X5: £1,053.29 – £15.21 – £210.70 = £827.38). No entries are required in the bank reconciliation at 30 April 20X5 since these are on the bank statement for April.

20 Control Accounts

20.7 The ledger

Sales ledger control account					
20X5		£	*20X5*		£
1 Jan	Balance b/d	4,200	1 Jan	Balance b/d	300
31 Jan	Sales revenue	23,000	31 Jan	Returns inward	750
31 Jan	Dishonoured cheques	1,850	31 Jan	Bank	16,250
31 Jan	Irrecoverable receivables recovered	230	31 Jan	Discount allowance	525
31 Jan	Interest on overdue accts	120	31 Jan	Irrecoverable receivables	670
			31 Jan	Bills receivable	5,300
			31 Jan	Purchase ledger contra	930
			31 Jan	Allowances	340
31 Jan	Balance c/d	240	31 Jan	Balance c/d	4,575
		29,640			29,640
1 Feb	Balance b/d	4,575	1 Feb	Balance b/d	240

Purchase ledger control account					
20X5		£	*20X5*		£
1 Jan	Balance b/d	250	1 Jan	Balance b/d	6,150
31 Jan	Returns outward	450	31 Jan	Purchases	21,500
31 Jan	Bank	19,800			
31 Jan	Discount rec'd	325			
31 Jan	Bills payable	4,500			
31 Jan	Sales ledger contra	930			
31 Jan	Allowances rec'd	280			
31 Jan	Balance c/d	1,535	31 Jan	Balance c/d	420
		28,070			28,070
1 Feb	Balance b/d	420	1 Feb	Balance b/d	1,535

Notes

1 The following items do not appear in control accounts: carriage inwards, carriage outwards; allowance for irrecoverable receivables; cash received from bills receivable; cash paid on bills payable.

2 The debit balance on the sales ledger control account is calculated by subtracting the total of the credit side from the debit side. The credit balance on the purchases ledger control account is calculated in a similar way.

3 The credit balances on the sales ledger control account are probably the result of credit customers overpaying, possibly in instances where they have been sent a credit note for goods and also paid for them. Similarly, the debit balances on the purchases ledger control account may be due to this business overpaying some of its credit suppliers.

4 Although credit balances on the sales ledger control account and debit balances on the purchase ledger control account are frequently encountered in examinations, in practice each control account can only throw up one balance which would naturally be the difference between the two sides of the control account. This balance should then agree with the difference between the total of the debit and credit balances of the personal accounts in the personal ledger.

5 Sometimes goods are bought from a business to which goods were also sold. In these circumstances the amounts owed may be set off against each other and a cheque paid/received for the difference. The amount set off is referred to as a personal ledger contra and in the above example is £930.

6 It is assumed that the actual money received that relates to debts that were previously written off as bad (£230) is included in cheques received from credit customers. Thus, the item 'irrecoverable receivables recovered' is treated as an instruction to reverse the entry by which they were originally written off.

20.8 a The ledger

Sales ledger control account

Balance b/d	14,364	Bank	118,258
Sales revenue	138,208	Discount allowed	3,692
Irrecoverable receivables recovered	84	Returns inwards	1,966
Cash	132	Bills receivable	6,486
Interest on overdue accounts	20	Irrecoverable receivables	1,186
		Purchase ledger contra	606
		Balance c/d	20,614
	152,808		152,808
Balance b/d	20,614		

b Sales ledger control account

	£
Original balance	20,614
Add : Sales day book undercast	1,000
	21,614
Less : Discount allowed omitted	50
Amended balance	21,564
Sales ledger	
Original balances	20,914
Add : Amount of cheque transposed (£4,300 – £3,400)	900
	21,814
Less : Returns posted incorrectly (£125 × 2)	250
Amended balance	21,564

20.9

a The ledger

Sales ledger control account			
	£		£
Balance b/d	17,220	Bank	45,280
Sales revenue	98,730	Returns inwards	18,520
		Bills receivable	29,160
		Discount allowed	6,940
		Irrecoverable receivables	4,920
		Transfer to purchase ledger	2,850
		Balance c/d	8,280
	115,950		115,950
Balance b/d	8,280		

Purchase ledger control account			
Bank	38,020	Balance b/d	20,490
Returns outwards	16,010	Purchases	85,860
Bills payable	21,390	Cash	2,430
Discount received	7,680		
Transfer to sales ledger	2,850		
Balance c/d	22,830		
	108,780		108,780
		Balance b/d	22,830

b Purchase ledger

	£
Original balances	20,700
Add : cheque posted wrongly (£3,400 – £340)	3,060
	23,760
Less : returns outward error (£180 × 2)	360
Amended balance	23,400
Purchase ledger control account	
Original balance	22,830
Add : discount received (£210 – £120)	90
	22,920
Less : purchases day book overcast	500
Amended balance	22,420
Undetected error = £23,400 – £22,420 = £980	

21 Errors and suspense accounts

21.6

a Debit wages account with £250.

b Credit sales account with £100.

c Credit suppliers personal account with £9 (i.e. £198 – £189).

d Change the amount shown in the trial balance in respect of drawings to £300.

e Debit the bank account with £172 (i.e. £86 × 2).

21.10

The journal

			Debit	*Credit*
			£	£
1	Light and heat	Dr	32	
	Suspense	Cr		32
	Being correction of posting error			
2	Suspense	Dr	28	
	Wages	Cr		28
	Being correction of arithmetic error			
3	Rent	Dr	720	
	Suspense	Cr		720
	Being correction of transposed figures			
4	Motor vehicles	Dr	3,000	
	Purchases	Cr		3,000
	Being correction of error of principle			
5	A. Watson	Dr	80	
	A. Watt	Cr		80
	Being correction of an error of commission			
6	Sales revenue	Dr	100	
	Loose tools	Cr		100
	Being correction of error of principle			
7	Postage and telephone	Dr	17	
	Carriage outwards	Cr		17
	Being correction of error of commission			

8	Bank charges	Dr	41	
	Cash book	Cr		41
	Being correction of error of omission			
9	Stationery	Dr	9	
	Sales revenue	Cr		9
	Being correction of a compensating error			
10	J. Bloggs Sales control	Dr	108	
	Sales revenue	Cr		108
	Being correction of error of prime entry			
11	Suspense	Dr	124	
	Trial balance	Cr		124
	Being correction of extraction error			

The ledger

Suspense			
Difference per trial balance	600	Light and heat	32
Wages	28	Rent	720
Extraction error	124		
	752		752

21.14

a The journal

		Debit	*Credit*
20X5		£	£
31 March Cash book	Dr	10,000	
Suspense account	Cr		10,000
Being correction of undercast on debit side of cash book			
Freehold premises:	Dr	5,000	
Suspense account	Cr		5,000
Being correction of purchase of building in cash book not posted to ledger			
Suspense account	Dr	900	
Purchases	Cr		900
Being correction of purchases of £100 entered in PDB summary as £1,000			
Carriage	Dr	405	
Suspense account	Cr		405
Being correction of transport charge of £450 entered in PDB summary as £45			

Rent receivable	Dr	45	
Suspense account	Cr		45
Being correction of rent received of £45 posted twice to the ledger			
Sales ledger control account	Dr	100	
Suspense account	Cr		100
Being correction of undercast on debit side of sales ledger control account			

Notes

1 Item 3 relates to errors in a PDB summary that is used to post the nominal ledger. It is assumed that the credit supplier's personal ledger is posted from the PDB and not the summary, and thus the individual supplier's personal account and control account are correct.

2 Item 5 assumes that the sales ledger control account is part of the double entry in the ledger and thus the balance is included in the statement of financial position.

3 Items 6 to 9 do not necessitate entries in the suspense account but will require journal entries for their correction.

4 Check that the balance on the suspense account has been eliminated as follows:

Suspense			
Per trial balance	14,650	Cash book	10,000
Purchases	900	Freehold premises	5,000
		Carriage	405
		Rent receivable	45
		Sales ledger control account	100
	15,550		15,550

b Workings

Bank account			
Correction of undercast	10,000	Balance b/d	1,230
		Bank charges	3,250
		Balance c/d	5,520
	10,000		10,000
Balance b/d	5,520		

Freehold premises			
Balance b/d	60,000		
Correction of posting error	5,000		
	65,000		

Sales ledger control account			
Balance b/d	37,140		
Correction of undercast	100		
	37,240		

Provision for depreciation on vehicles			
		Balance b/d	11,935
		I/S a/c	500
			12,435

Inventory			
Balance b/d	75,410		
Undervaluation	1,250		
	76,660		

Purchase ledger control account			
		Balance b/d	41,360
		Purchases	2,110
			43,470

Profit or loss account			
Carriage	405	Balance b/d	33,500
Rent receivable	45	Purchases	900
Bank charges	3,250	Inventory	1,250
Depreciation on vehicles	500		
Purchases	2,110		
Revised profit	29,340		
	35,650		35,650

Miscup
Statement of financial position as at 31 March 20X5

ASSETS	£	£	£
Non-current assets	*Cost*	*Agg/depn*	*WDV*
Freehold premises	65,000	–	65,000
Motor vehicles	25,000	12,435	12,565
Fixtures and fittings	1,500	750	750
	91,500	13,185	78,315
Current assets			
Inventory			76,660
Trade receivables			37,240
Bank			5,520
Cash			75
			119,495
Total assets			197,810

EQUITY AND LIABILITIES	
Equity capital (start of year)	125,000
Add : profit for the year	29,340
Total equity	154,340
Current liabilities	
Trade payables and accrued charges	43,470
Total current liabilities	43,470
Total equity and liabilities	197,810

22 Single Entry and Incomplete Records

22.5 Workings for plant

	£	£
Cost at 30 June 20X4		50,000
Add : additions		20,000
		70,000
Less : disposals		10,000
Cost at 30 June 20X5		60,000
Aggregate depreciation		
Depreciation at 30 June 20X4		
(£50,000 – £31,000)		19,000
Add : depreciation for the year		
on addition (10% × £20,000 × 3 mths)	500	
on disposal (10% × £10,000 × 3 mths)	250	
on rest (10% × [£50,000 – £10,000])	4,000	4,750
		23,750
Less : aggregate depreciation on disposal		
10% × £10,000 × 2 years 9 mths		2,750
Depreciation at 30 June 20X5		21,000

Round Music
Statement of financial position as at 30 June 20X5

ASSETS	£	£	£
Non-current assets			
Plant at cost			60,000
Less : aggregate depreciation			21,000
			39,000
Current assets			
Inventory (£8,630 – £1,120)			7,510
Trade receivables		6,120	
Less : allowance for irrecoverable receivables		310	5,810
Prepayments			80
			13,400
Total assets			52,400

EQUITY AND LIABILITIES	
Equity	
Capital at 30 June 20X5	40,360
Total equity	40,360
Non-current liabilities	
Long-term loan	7,000
Total non-current liabilities	7,000
Current liabilities	
Trade payables	3,480
Accruals	130
Bank overdraft	1,430
Total current liabilities	5,040
Total liabilities	12,040
Total equity and liabilities	52,400

Round Music
Statement of profit or loss for the year ended 30 June 20X5

	£
Capital at 30 June 20X5	40,360
Less : capital at 30 June 20X4	42,770
	(2,410)
Add : drawings (£18,500 + £750)	19,250
	16,840
Less : capital introduced	5,000
Profit for the year	11,840

22.7 Workings

1 Credit purchases = £5,720 + £33,360 – £5,220 = £33,860

2 Total purchases = £33,860 + £1,120 + £4,500 = £39,480

3 Credit sales = £5,840 + £31,860 – £6,540 = £31,160

4 Cash sales = £18,920 + £4,000 + £1,120 + £980 + £170 = £25,190

5 Total sales = £25,190 + £31,160 = £56,350

6 Telephone = £120 + £280 – £140 = £260

7 Light and heat = £370 + £290 – £60 = £600

8 Motor expenses = £1,810 + £980 = £2,790

9 Depreciation on fixtures and fittings = 20% × £5,800 = £1,160

10 Accumulated depreciation on fixtures and fittings = £10,000 – £5,800 + £1,160 = £5,360

A. Fox
Statement of profit or loss for the year ended 31 July 20X5

	£	£
Sales revenue		56,350
Less : cost of sales		
Inventory at 1 Aug 20X4	3,300	
Add : purchases (£39,480 – £530)	38,950	
	42,250	
Less : inventory at 31 July 20X5	3,920	38,330
Gross profit		18,020
Less : expenditure		
Wages	5,640	
Telephone (£120 + £280 – £140)	260	
Light and heat (£370 + £290 – £60)	600	
Motor expenses (£1,810 + £980)	2,790	
Printing	560	
Cleaning	170	
Depreciation (20% × £5,800)	1,160	11,180
Profit for the year		6,840

A. Fox
Statement of financial position as at 31 July 20X5

ASSETS	£	£	£
Non-current assets	*Cost*	*Agg/depn*	*WDV*
Freehold land and buildings	35,000	–	35,000
Fixtures and fittings	10,000	5,360	4,640
	45,000	5,360	39,640
Current assets			
Inventory			3,920
Trade receivables			5,840
Prepayments			140
Bank			8,260
			18,160
Total assets			57,800

EQUITY AND LIABILITIES	
Equity capital	
Balance at 1 Aug 20X4	48,480
Add : capital introduced	1,000
Profit for year	6,840
	56,320
Less : drawings (£4,000 + £530)	4,530
Balance at 31 July 20X5	51,790
Current liabilities	
Trade payables	5,720
Accruals	290
Total current liabilities	6,010
Total equity and liabilities	57,800

23 Inventory Valuation

23.6 Discussion on the relationship between inventory valuation method and actual costs

When a firm elects not to separately identify each individual item of inventory either because this is impossible as the items cannot be separately identified (coal, oil, etc.) or because the cost of this type of system would exceed the benefit, then three common methods are typically used for valuing the inventory that is sold (or released to production). These are the LIFO, FIFO and AVCO methods of inventory valuation. Each of the three methods of calculating the cost of inventory results in different values for inventory and hence profit. In times of constantly rising prices, FIFO will give the highest figure for profits of the three methods (as the cheaper values relating to items that are purchased earlier/first will be released as an expense first) and the highest value of inventory at the period end (as the remaining inventory will be valued at the latest higher priced). In summary under FIFO older, lower costs are matched against revenues than is the current reality; however, the value of inventory in the statement of financial position will be current. The opposite impact on profit and inventory valuation will occur in times of falling prices (uncommon).

When prices are rising, the lowest profit figure will be reported under the LIFO method as the more expensive values relating to the more recently purchased items will be released to the statement of profit or loss first. Under this method inventory will have the lowest valuation of the three methods as the remaining items will be assigned the earliest price values (which are the lowest in times of rising prices). In summary under LIFO the statement of profit or loss reflects the most recent costs; however, the statement of financial position will be out of date as inventory will be valued at old values. The opposite impact on profit and inventory valuation will occur in times of falling prices (uncommon).

Under AVCO average prices are used and the value of the inventory released to the statement of profit or loss will lie between the LIFO and FIFO methods as will the value of year-end inventory.

A business should choose whichever method is appropriate to its particular circumstances and apply this consistently in order that meaningful comparisons can be made. FIFO is by far the most common method used in practice in the UK because it is favoured by the UK accounting standard *SSAP 9 – Stocks and Long Term Contracts* (ASC, 1988), by IAS 2 and by HM Revenue and Customs. The valuation of inventories is a controversial issue in accounting, and is one of the areas most open to deliberate manipulation.

23.9 Universal shoes

(a) Inventories schedule as at 31 December 20X4

	Cost		Net realizable value	Lower of cost and NRV
Casual shoes	£		£	£
10,000 × 6	60,000	10,000 × 30	300,000	
2,000 × 6	12,000	2,000 × 30	60,000	
	72,000		360,000	72,000
Work shoes				
3,000 × 17	51,000	3,000 × 55	165,000	
2,000 × 12	24,000	2,000 × 55	110,000	
	75,000		275,000	75,000
Dress shoes				
2,000 × 47	94,000	2,000 × 30	60,000	60,000
				207,000

(b) Memorandum to chief accountant

TO: Chief accountant

FROM: An Accountant

Subject: Inventory valuation

Date: 15 January 20X5

(the contents of the answer should refer to the following points)

I refer to your recent request regarding the valuation of inventories as at 31 December 20X4. IAS 2 'Inventories' sets out the methods allowed for valuing inventories.

Points that might be included

- Under IAS 2, inventories includes assets that are held for sale in the ordinary course of the business.
- It states that inventory value includes the cost of purchase (purchase price), import duties and transport and handling costs (but excludes trade discounts)

FIFO and the weighted average method are allowable but LIFO is not. So the FIFO policy adopted by Universal Shoes is fine.

- In terms of valuation, inventory should be held at the lower of cost and the net realizable value (NRV). When the sale price expected is below inventory cost then inventory should be written down to this value (less any costs to sell the assets). This value is called the NRV.

When calculating the closing costs for the shoes the following matters arose:

1. Casual shoes – there were goods in transit at the year end. In accordance with cut-off principles, the goods need to be included in inventories as they have been included in purchases and in trade payables.

2. **Work shoes – the cost of these shoes increased on 1 November 20X4. In order to apply the FIFO method for inventory valuation, account is taken of the jackets in inventory from 1 November 20X4, which will be valued at the new cost. Any remaining inventory will be valued at the old cost.**

3. **Dress shoes – the market for these shoes changed from 1 January 20X5. Although this is after the year end, it still has to be taken account of when arriving at the inventory valuation. The effect of the market changing has resulted in a reduction in the NRV of the shoes from £75 to £40, with associated costs of £10 reducing the NRV further to £30 per pair. As the NRV is lower than cost this is the value that is used for the year-end inventory figure.**

I hope this explains the valuation of inventory at the year-end.

Any issues – ask, etc.

23.14 a Cost of sales

FIFO

Quantity	Purchase price £	Value £	Quantity	COS price £	Value £	Quantity	Inventory price £	Value £
1,200	1.00	1,200				1,200	1.00	1,200
1,000	1.05	1,050				1,000	1.05	1,050
						2,200		2,250
			800	1.00	800	400	1.00	400
						1,000	1.05	1,050
						1,400		1,450
600	1.10	660				400	1.00	400
						1,000	1.05	1,050
						600	1.10	660
						2,000		2,110
			400	1.00	400			
			200	1.05	210	800	1.05	840
			600		610	600	1.10	660
						1,400		1,500
900	1.20	1,080				800	1.05	840
						600	1.10	660
						900	1.20	1,080
						2,300		2,580
			800	1.05	840			
			300	1.10	330	300	1.10	330
			1,100		1,170	900	1.20	1,080
						1,200		1,410
800	1.25	1,000				300	1.10	330
						900	1.20	1,080
						800	1.25	1,000
						2,000		2,410

			300	1.10	330			
			900	1.20	1,080			
			100	1.25	125	700	1.25	875
			1,300		1,535	700		875
700	1.30	910				700	1.25	875
						700	1.30	910
						1,400		1,785
			400	1.25	500	300	1.25	375
						700	1.30	910
5,200		5,900	4,200		4,615	1,000		1,285

LIFO

Quantity	Purchase price £	Value £	Quantity	COS price £	Value £	Quantity	Inventory price £	Value £
1,200	1.00	1,200				1,200	1.00	1,200
1,000	1.05	1,050				1,000	1.05	1,050
						2,200		2,250
						1,200	1.00	1,200
			800	1.05	840	200	1.05	210
						1,400		1,410
600	1.10	660				1,200	1.00	1,200
						200	1.05	210
						600	1.10	660
						2,000		2,070
			600	1.10	660	1,200	1.00	1,200
						200	1.05	210
						1,400		1,410
900	1.20	1,080				1,200	1.00	1,200
						200	1.05	210
						900	1.20	1,080
						2,300		2,490
			900	1.20	1,080			
			200	1.05	210	1,200	1.00	1,200
			1,100		1,290	1,200		1,200
800	1.25	1,000				1,200	1.00	1,200
						800	1.25	1,000
						2,000		2,200
			800	1.25	1,000			
			500	1.00	500	700	1.00	700
			1,300		1,500	700		700

700	1.30	910				700	1.00	700
						700	1.30	910
						1,400		1,610
			400	1.30	520	300	1.30	390
						700	1.00	700
5,200		5,900	4,200		4,810	1,000		1,090

Weighted average (AVCO)	
	£
Purchases	5,900
Less : inventory 1,000 @ (£5,900 ÷ £5,200)	1,135
Cost of sales	4,765

23.14 Workings

Sales revenue	*Quantity* Units	*Price* £	*Value* £
	800	1.70	1,360
	600	1.90	1,140
	1,100	2.00	2,200
	1,300	2.00	2,600
	400	2.05	820
	4,200		8,120

Bank			
Capital	6,000	Purchases	5,900
Sales revenue	8,120	Expenses	
		(£1,740 – £570)	1,170
		Balance c/d	7,050
	14,120		14,120
Balance b/d	7,050		

	FIFO	*LIFO*	*AVCO*
Statements of profit or loss	£	£	£
Sales revenue	8,120	8,120	8,120
Less : cost of sales	4,615	4,810	4,765
Gross profit	3,505	3,310	3,355
Less : expenses	1,740	1,740	1,740
Profit for the year	1,765	1,570	1,615

Statements of financial position			
ASSETS			
Inventory	1,285	1,090	1,135
Bank	7,050	7,050	7,050
Total assets	8,335	8,140	8,185
EQUITY AND LIABILITIES			
Equity			
Capital at start of period	6,000	6,000	6,000
Profit for year	1,765	1,570	1,615
Capital at end of period	7,765	7,570	7,615
Current liabilities			
Accrued expenses	570	570	570
Total equity and liabilities	8,335	8,140	8,185

—24 Financial Statements for Manufacturing Entities

24.6

Upton Upholstery Manufacturing Account for the year ended 30 April 20X5		
	£	£
Raw materials:		
Inventory at 1 May 20X4		4,000
Add : purchases	84,000	
carriage inwards	1,200	85,200
		89,200
Less : inventory at 30 Apr 20X5		5,400
Cost of raw materials consumed		83,800
Direct wages (£19,900 + £600)		20,500
Prime cost		104,300
Factory overheads:		
Depreciation: machinery (£28,000 ÷ 7)	4,000	
Light and heat (£3,000 × $\frac{4}{5}$)	2,400	
Rent and rates (£6,600 – [$\frac{1}{3}$ × £600]) × $\frac{3}{4}$	4,800	
Factory costs		11,200
Manufacturing costs		115,500
Add : WIP at 1 May 20X4		16,400
		131,900
Less : WIP at 30 Apr 20X5		17,000
Factory cost of completed production		114,900

Statement of profit or loss for the year ended 30 April 20X5		
	Note	£
Sales revenue		140,000
Cost of sales	1	(115,900)
Gross profit		24,100
Selling and distribution	2	(3,100)
Administration	3	(7,800)
Profit for the year		13,200

Workings for the statement of profit or loss

1. Cost of sales	
Inventory at 1 May 20X4	9,000
Add : factory cost of production	114,900
	123,900
Less : inventory at 30 Apr 20X5	8,000
Cost of sales	115,900
2. Selling and distribution overheads	
Carriage outwards	700
Sales commission	1,400
Allowance for irrecoverable receivables	1,000
	3,100
3. Administrative overheads	
Depreciation: equipment 25% × (£2,000 – £800)	300
Light and heat (£3,000 × $\frac{1}{5}$)	600
Rent and rates (£6,600 – [$\frac{1}{3}$ × £600]) × $\frac{1}{4}$	1,600
Office wages (£5,200 + £100)	5,300
	7,800

Upton Upholstery Statement of financial position as at 30 April 20X5			
	£	£	£
ASSETS	*Cost*	*Aggr. depn*	*WDV*
Non-current assets			
Factory machinery (£5,000 + £4,000)	28,000	9,000	19,000
Office equipment (£800 + £300)	2,000	1,100	900
	30,000	10,100	19,900
Current assets			
Inventories (£5,400 + £17,000 + £8,000)			30,400
Trade receivables		15,000	
Less : allowance for receivables		1,000	14,000
Prepaid rent			200
Cash and bank			2,300
			46,900
Total assets			66,800

EQUITY AND LIABILITIES		
Equity capital		
Capital	1	39,100
Non-current liabilities		
Bank loan		11,000
Current liabilities		
Trade payables		16,000
Accrued costs (£600 + £100)		700
Total current liabilities		16,700
Total liabilities		27,700
Total equity and liabilities		66,800

Workings for the statement of financial position

1. Equity capital	
Balance at 1 May 20X4	35,000
Add : profit for the year	13,200
	48,200
Less : drawings	9,100
Balance at 30 April 20X5	39,100

24.7

Manufacturing account for the year ended 31 December 20X4		
	£	£
Raw materials:		
Inventory at 1 Jan 20X4		2,453
Add : purchases (£47,693 – £2,093)	45,600	
Add: carriage inwards	683	
	46,283	
Less : returns outward	4,921	41,362
		43,815
Less : inventory at 31 Dec 20X4		3,987
Cost of raw materials consumed		39,828
Direct wages (£23,649 – £549)		23,100
Direct expenses:		
Royalties		7,500
Prime cost		70,428
Factory overheads:		
Supervisors' wages	5,617	
Electricity – factory	2,334	
Depreciation on plant	13,400	
Rent and rates – factory	3,600	
Insurance on plant	1,750	
Repairs to plant	917	27,618

Manufacturing costs	98,046
Add : WIP at 1 Jan 20X4	1,617
	99,663
Less : WIP at 31 Dec 20X4	2,700
	96,963
Less : proceeds from the sale of scrap	199
Factory cost of completed production	96,764

Statement of profit or loss for the year ended 31 December 20X4		
	Note	£
Sales revenue		145,433
Cost of sales	2	95,433
Gross profit		50,000
Discount received		2,310
		52,310
Selling and distribution	3	(16,246)
Administrative	4	(16,064)
Financial charges	5	(3,100)
Profit for the year		16,900

Notes

1 The proceeds from the sale of scrap metal could have been deducted from the cost of raw materials.

2 Cost of sales

Inventory of finished goods at 1 Jan 20X4	3,968
Add : factory cost of production	96,764
Purchases of finished goods	367
	101,099
Less : inventory of finished goods at 31 Dec 20X4	5,666
Cost of sales	95,433

3 Selling and distribution overheads

Salaries and commission	8,600
Carriage outwards	487
Irrecoverable receivables	726
Discount allowed	1,515
Depreciation – vehicles	3,700
Delivery expenses	593
Advertising	625
	16,246

4 Administrative overheads	
Salaries	10,889
Light and heat	998
Depreciation – fixtures and furniture	1,900
Rent and rates	1,200
Postage and telephone	714
Printing and stationery	363
	16,064

5 Financial charges	
Loan interest	3,000
Bank charges	100
	3,100

25 The Final Financial Statements of Partnerships

25.2 Main characteristics of a partnership

A partnership is the relationship which exists between individuals carrying on business in common with a view of profit. A partnership must have two or more partners to exist. Partnerships are typically not able to limit their liability to creditors and other members of the public (unless the partnership is an LLP). Therefore, partners are largely free to make whatever agreements between themselves that they wish to cover their mutual relationships. The powers and rights of the partners between themselves are governed by any partnership agreement they may make. Items typically agreed in this agreement include: the capital to be introduced by each partner; the interest to be paid on capital, if any; the sharing of profits and losses; partners' drawings; interest on drawings, if any; the preparation and audit of financial statements; the dissolution of the partnership and how to deal with disputes.

25.7 Workings

Interest on loan:

Hammond – 5% × £20,000 × $\frac{3}{12}$ = £250

Interest on capital:

Clayton – (8% × £90,000) + (8% × £10,000 × $\frac{8}{12}$) = £7,733

Hammond – 8% × £60,000 = £4,800

Interest on drawings:

Clayton –

4% × £3,000 × $\frac{9}{12}$ = £ 90

4% × £5,000 × $\frac{4}{12}$ = £ 67

£ 157

Hammond –

4% × £2,000 × $\frac{9}{12}$ = £ 60

4% × £1,000 × $\frac{4}{12}$ = £ 13

£ 73

Clayton and Hammond
Appropriation account 30 June 20X5

	£	£		£	£
Interest on loan:			Net profit b/d		67,500
Hammond		250	Interest on drawings:		
			Clayton	157	
Salaries:			Hammond	73	230
Clayton	17,000				
Hammond	13,000	30,000			
Interest on capital:					
Clayton	7,733				
Hammond	4,800	12,533			
Shares of residual profit:					
Clayton	12,474				
Hammond	12,473	24,947			
		67,730			67,730

Current account

	Clayton	*Hammond*		*Clayton*	*Hammond*
	£	£		£	£
Drawings	8,000	3,000	Balance b/d	16,850	9,470
Interest on drawings	157	73	Interest on loan	–	250
			Salaries	17,000	13,000
			Interest on capital	7,733	4,800
Balance c/d	45,900	36,920	Shares of residual profit	12,474	12,473
				54,057	39,993
	54,057	39,993	Balance b/d	45,900	36,920

Capital

	Clayton	*Hammond*		*Clayton*	*Hammond*
			Balance b/d	90,000	60,000
Balance c/d	100,000	60,000	Bank	10,000	–
	100,000	60,000		100,000	60,000
			Balance b/d	100,000	60,000

Loan Hammond

	Bank	20,000

25.12 Workings

Interest on loan:

Peace – 5% × £2,000 × $\frac{3}{12}$ = 25

Interest on capital:

Peace –

10% × (£10,000 – £1,000 – £2,000) = £700

10% × £1,000 × $\frac{9}{12}$ = £75

£775

Quiet – 10% × £5,000 = £500

Interest on drawings:

Peace – 8% × £2,200 × $\frac{8}{12}$ = £117

Quiet – 8% × £1,800 × $\frac{4}{12}$ = £48

Peace and Quiet
Statement of profit or loss for the year ended 31 December 20X4

	£	£
Sales revenue		69,830
Less : cost of sales		
Inventory at 1 Jan 20X4	6,630	
Add : purchases	45,620	
	52,250	
Less : inventory at 31 Dec 20X4	5,970	46,280
Gross profit		23,550
Less : expenditure		
Shop assistants' salaries	5,320	
Light and heat (£1,850 + £60)	1,910	
Stationery (£320 – £50)	270	
Bank interest and charges	45	
Depreciation on equipment		
10% × (£8,500 – £1,200)	730	8,275
Profit for the year		15,275

Profit or loss appropriation account 31 December 20X4

	£	£	£
Profit for the year			15,275
Add : Interest on drawings –			
Peace		117	
Quiet		48	165
			15,440
Less : Interest on loan – Peace		25	
Interest on capital – Peace	775		
Quiet	500	1,275	

Salaries –			
Peace	6,200		
Quiet	4,800	11,000	12,300
			3,140
Shares of residual profit –			
Peace			1,570
Quiet			1,570
			3,140

Current accounts

	Peace	Quiet		Peace	Quiet
Drawings	2,200	1,800	Balance	1,280	3,640
Interest on drawings	117	48	Interest on loan	25	–
			Interest on capital	775	500
			Salaries	6,200	4,800
Balance c/d	7,533	8,662	Shares of residual profit	1,570	1,570
	9,850	10,510		9,850	10,510
			Balance b/d	7,533	8,662

Capital accounts

	Peace	Quiet		Peace	Quiet
Loan account	2,000		Balance b/d	10,000	5,000
Balance c/d	8,000	5,000			
	10,000	5,000		10,000	5,000
			Balance b/d	8,000	5,000

Peace and Quiet
Statement of financial position as at 31 December 20X4

ASSETS	£	£	£
Non-current assets	*Cost*	*Agg depn*	*WDV*
Leasehold shop	18,000		18,000
Equipment (£1,200 + £730)	8,500	1,930	6,570
	26,500	1,930	24,570
Current assets			
Inventory			5,970
Stationery			50
Trade receivables			1,210
Bank			3,815
			11,045
Total assets			35,615

EQUITY AND LIABILITIES			
Equity capital	*Peace*	*Quiet*	
Capital accounts	8,000	5,000	13,000
Current accounts	7,533	8,662	16,195
Total equity	15,533	13,662	29,195
Non-current liabilities			
Loan – Peace			2,000
Total non-current liabilities			2,000
Current liabilities			
Trade payables			4,360
Accrued expenses			60
Total current liabilities			4,420
Total liabilities			6,420
Total equity and liabilities			35,615

25.14 Workings – vehicles

	Depreciation on sale	*Depreciation this year*
	£	£
Depreciation on disposal:		
20X2 – 10% × £2,400 × $\frac{9}{12}$	180	
20X3 – 10% × £2,400	240	
20X4 – 10% × £2,400 × $\frac{10}{12}$	200	200
Aggregate depreciation	620	
Book value = £2,400 – £620 = £1,780		
Profit on sale = £1,900 – £1,780 = £120		
Depreciation on remainder:		
10% × (£30,000 – £2,400)		2,760
		2,960

Aggregate depreciation at 31 December 20X4: £18,000 + £2,960 – £620 = £20,340

Simon, Wilson and Dillon
Statement of profit or loss for the year ended 31 December 20X4

	£	£	£
Sales revenue			130,000
Less : returns			400
			129,600
Less : cost of sales			
Inventory at 1 Jan 20X4		34,900	
Add : purchases	64,000		
Less : returns	600	63,400	
		98,300	
Less : inventory at 31 Dec 20X4		31,000	67,300

Gross profit		62,300
Add : investment income (£800 + £320)		1,120
profit on sale of vehicle		120
		63,540
***Less* : expenditure**		
Salesmen's salaries	19,480	
Rates (£12,100 – £160)	11,940	
Motor expenses (£2,800 + £240)	3,040	
Mortgage interest (8% × £40,000)	3,200	
Printing and stationery (£1,100 – £170)	930	
Irrecoverable receivables	2,000	
Allowance for irrecoverable receivables ([2% × (£28,000 – £2,000)] – 400)	120	
Provision for depreciation on Vehicles	2,960	
Tools (£1,200 – £960)	240	
Bank charges	130	44,040
Profit for the year		19,500

Appropriation account 31 December 20X4

	£	£	£
Profit for the year			19,500
Less : salaries			
Simon	15,000		
Dillon	10,000		
		25,000	
Interest on capital			
Simon (10% × £35,000)	3,500		
Wilson (10% × £25,000)	2,500		
Dillon (10% × £10,000)	1,000	7,000	32,000
			(12,500)
Shares of residual loss			
Simon			(5,000)
Wilson			(5,000)
Dillon			(2,500)
			(12,500)

The ledger

Current account

	S	W	D		S	W	D
Balance b/d	–	–	1,800	Balance b/d	5,600	4,800	–
Shares of residual loss	5,000	5,000	2,500	Salaries	15,000	–	10,000
Balance c/d	19,100	2,300	6,700	Interest	3,500	2,500	1,000
	24,100	7,300	11,000		24,100	7,300	11,000
				Balance b/d	19,100	2,300	6,700

Simon, Wilson & Dillon
Statement of financial position as at 31 December 20X4

ASSETS	£	£	£
Non-current assets	*Cost*	*Agg depn*	*WDV*
Freehold land and buildings (£65,000 + £5,000)	70,000	–	70,000
Delivery vehicles (£30,000 – £2,400)	27,600	20,340	7,260
Loose tools	1,200	240	960
	98,800	20,580	78,220
Goodwill			11,000
Unquoted investments			6,720
			95,940
Current assets			
Inventories (£31,000 + £170)			31,170
Prepayments			160
Trade receivables (£28,000 – £2,000)		26,000	
Less: allowance for irrecoverable receivables		520	25,480
Sundry receivable			1,900
Income accrued			320
Bank (£10,100 – £130)			9,970
			69,000
Total assets			164,940
EQUITY AND LIABILITIES			
Equity			
Capital accounts			
Simon		35,000	
Wilson		25,000	
Dillon		10,000	70,000
Current accounts			
Simon		19,100	
Wilson		2,300	
Dillon		6,700	28,100
Total equity			98,100
Non-current liabilities			
8% mortgage on premises			40,000
Total non-current liabilities			40,000
Current liabilities			
Trade payables			25,000
Accruals (£240 + £1,600)			1,840
Total current liabilities			26,840
Total liabilities			66,840
Total equity and liabilities			164,940

Notes

1 It is assumed that the unquoted investments are intended to be kept for more than one accounting year.

2 The capital and current accounts could have been presented in the statement of financial position in columnar form.

26 Changes in Partnerships

26.1 Goodwill

a. The precise nature of goodwill is difficult to define in a theoretically sound manner. However, it is generally recognized that goodwill exists, since a value is normally attached to it when a business is purchased. Goodwill usually arises in the financial statements where another business has been purchased at some time in the past. Its value frequently takes the form of the excess of the purchase price of the other business over the market value of its net assets. The existence of this excess shows that the purchaser of a business is prepared to pay for something in addition to the net assets. Goodwill is the label given to that something.

b. Goodwill arises from a number of attributes that an ongoing business possesses, such as the following:

1 The prestige and reputation attaching to the name of a business or its products and thus the likelihood that present customers will continue to buy from the business in future (e.g. Rolls-Royce, Microsoft).

2 Existing contracts for the supply of goods in the future (e.g. construction, aerospace, defence equipment).

3 The location of the business premises (e.g. a newsagent next to a railway station) and other forms of captive customers (e.g. a milk distributor's clientele).

4 The possession of patents, trademarks, brand names and special technical knowledge arising from previous expenditure on advertising and research and development. However, some of these may be accounted for as separate assets.

5 The existence of known sources of supply of goods and services, including the availability of trade credit.

6 The existing staff, including particular management skills. The costs of recruiting and training present employees give rise to an asset that is not recorded in the statement of financial position but nevertheless represents a valuable resource to the business. Furthermore, these costs would have to be incurred if a business were started from scratch.

7 Other set-up factors. An existing business has the advantage of having collected together the various items of equipment and other assets necessary for its operations. Obtaining and bringing together these assets usually involves delay and expense, and avoiding this is an advantage of an ongoing business.

26.7 Workings

Shares of goodwill	£
Brown $\frac{1}{2}$ × £90,000	45,000
Jones $\frac{1}{2}$ × £90,000	45,000
	90,000
Jones $\frac{3}{5}$ × £90,000	54,000
Smith $\frac{2}{5}$ × £90,000	36,000
	90,000

The ledger

Revaluation account				
Inventory		4,000	Premises	35,000
Allowance for irrecoverable receivables		3,000	Fixtures	8,000
Profit –				
Brown	18,000			
Jones	18,000	36,000		
		43,000		43,000

Capital							
	Brown	*Jones*	*Smith*		*Brown*	*Jones*	*Smith*
Goodwill	–	54,000	36,000	Balance b/d	110,000	87,000	
Cash	173,000	–	–	Cash	–	–	100,000
Balance c/d	–	96,000	64,000	Profit on revaluation	18,000	18,000	–
				Goodwill	45,000	45,000	–
	173,000	150,000	100,000		173,000	150,000	100,000
				Balance b/d	–	96,000	64,000

26.8 Workings

Valuation of goodwill:	£
Net asset value before revaluation (£30,100 – £2,500)	27,600
Less: loss on revaluation (see below)	600
Net asset value after revaluation	27,000
Estimated profit for 20X4	48,750
Less : partners' salaries (3 @ £15,000)	45,000
Earnings/super profit	3,750

$$\text{P/E ratio} = \frac{\text{price}}{\text{earnings}}$$

$\therefore$ Price = earnings $\times$ P/E ratio

Capitalized value of estimated super profits = £3,750 × 8 = £30,000

Goodwill = £30,000 – £27,000 = £3,000

The ledger

Vehicles			
Balance b/d	7,000	Prov for depn	1,800
Revaluation	1,500	Balance c/d	6,700
	8,500		8,500
Balance b/d	6,700		

Inventory			
Balance b/d	9,200	Revaluation	1,200
		Balance c/d	8,000
	9,200		9,200
Balance b/d	8,000		

Allowance for irrecoverable receivables			
		Revaluation	900

Revaluation account				
Inventory	1,200	Vehicles		1,500
Allowance for irrecoverable receivables	900	Loss on revaluation –		
		Capital B	200	
		Capital P	200	
		Capital N	200	600
	2,100			2,100

Capital									
	B	P	N	L		B	P	N	L
Revaluation	200	200	200	–	Balance b/d	10,000	8,000	5,000	–
Loan account	–	–	5,800	–	Bank	–	–	–	6,000
Balance c/d	10,800	8,800	–	6,000	Goodwill	1,000	1,000	1,000	–
	11,000	9,000	6,000	6,000		11,000	9,000	6,000	6,000
					Balance b/d	10,800	8,800	–	6,000

Goodwill			
Capital – Blackburn	1,000		
Capital – Percy	1,000		
Capital – Nelson	1,000	Bal c/d	3,000
	3,000		3,000
Bal b/d	3,000		

Current account – Nelson			
Loan account	1,400	Balance b/d	1,400

Loan – Nelson			
		Capital account	5,800
Bal c/d	7,200	Current account	1,400
	7,200		7,200
		Bal b/d	7,200

27 Partnership Dissolution and Conversion to a Limited Company

27.1 Reasons for dissolving a partnership

However, the phrase '**dissolution** of partnerships' refers to the circumstances where all the partners wish to leave, and thus the activities of the partnership are wound up without a new partnership being created. Partnerships are usually dissolved because either it is unprofitable to carry on trading or the partners no longer wish to be associated with each other for personal reasons.

27.3

Realization account

Non-current assets	3,600	Bank – Trade receivables	3,500
Inventories	4,150	Bank – Non-current assets	2,950
Trade receivables	3,850	Bank – Inventories	4,980
Realisation costs	50	Discount on trade payables	280
Profit on realization –			
Martin	40		
Stephen	20		
	11,710		11,710

Cash account

Balance b/d	250	Trade payables	2,520
Real. – Trade receivables	3,500	Realization expenses	50
Real. – Non-current assets	2,950	Loan account: Martin	1,000
Real. – Inventories	4,980	Capital – Martin	5,190
		Capital – Stephen	2,920
	11,680		11,680

Loan a/c Martin

Cash	1,000	Bal b/d	1,000
	1,000		1,000

Trade payables

Cash	2,520	Bal b/d	2,800
Discount			
Realization	280		
	2,800		2,800

Current account

	Martin	Stephen		Martin	Stephen
	£	£		£	£
Bal b/d		100	Bal b/d	150	
Capital account	150		Capital account		100
	150	100		150	100

Capital account					
	Martin	*Stephen*		*Martin*	*Stephen*
	£	£		£	£
Current account		100	Bal b/d	5,000	3,000
Bank account	5,190	2,920	Current account	150	
			Realization a/c	40	20
	5,190	3,020		5,190	3,020

28 The Nature of Limited Companies and their Capital

28.1 Characteristics of companies limited by shares

The characteristics are as follows:

1 A company is a legal entity that is separate from its shareholders (owners). This means that companies enter into contracts as legal entities in their own right. Thus, creditors and others cannot sue the shareholders of the company but must take legal proceedings against the company.

2 A company has perpetual existence in that the death of one of its shareholders does not result in its dissolution.

3 The liability of a company's shareholders is limited to the nominal value of their shares. Limited liability means that if a company's assets are insufficient to pay its debts, the shareholders cannot be called upon to contribute more than the nominal value of their shares towards paying those debts.

4 The shareholders of a company do not have the right to take part in its management as such. They appoint directors to manage the company. However, a shareholder may also be a director (or other employee).

5 Each voting share carries one vote at general meetings of the company's shareholders (e.g. in the appointment of directors). There may be different classes of shares, each class having different rights and, possibly, some being non-voting.

6 A limited company must have at least two shareholders but there is no maximum number.

28.12

Equity shares	*Preference shares*	*Loan stock debentures*
1 Owners of the company who are normally entitled to vote at general meetings of the company's shareholders (e.g. to elect directors)	1 No voting rights	1 No voting rights
2 Receive a dividend the rate of which is decided annually by the company's directors. It varies each year depending on the profit and is an appropriation of profit	2 Receive a fixed rate of dividend each year that constitutes an appropriation of profit. Have priority over equity dividends	2 Receive a fixed rate of interest that constitutes a charge against income in computing the profit. Have priority over preference dividends
3 Last to be repaid the value of their shares in the event of the company going into liquidation	3 Repaid before the equity shareholders in the event of liquidation	3 Repaid before the equity and preference shareholders in the event of liquidation

4 Non-repayable except on the liquidation of the company	**4** All but one particular type are non-repayable except on liquidation	**4** Normally repayable after a fixed period of time
5 Rights in Articles of Association	**5** Rights in Articles of Association	**5** Rights specified in the terms of issue
6 Dividends non-deductible for tax purposes	**6** Dividends non-deductible for tax purposes	**6** Interest deductible for tax purposes

28.14 Categorizing preference shares as debt or equity instruments

Debt	**Equity**
Cumulative	Non-cumulative
Redeemable	Irredeemable
Non-participating	Participating
Non-convertible	Convertible

29 The Final Financial Statements of Limited Companies

29.19

D. Cooper Ltd
Statement of profit or loss for the year ended 30 September 20X4

	£
Sales revenue	135,250
Cost of sales	(65,520)
Gross profit	69,730
Other income (investment income)	650
Distribution costs	(910)
Administration expenses	(31,080)
Other costs	(1,270)
Finance costs	(4,150)
Profit before taxation	32,970
Income tax	(6,370)
Profit for the year	26,600

D. Cooper Ltd
Statement of financial position as at 30 September 20X4

ASSETS	*Note*	£	£
Non-current assets			
Property, plant and equipment	1		202,700
Goodwill			20,000
			222,700
Current assets			
Inventories			13,480
Trade receivables		11,200	
Less : allowance for irrecoverable receivables		1,120	10,080

Prepayments		1,150
Listed investments		8,000
		32,710
Total assets		255,410
EQUITY AND LIABILITIES		
Equity		
Share capital	2	100,000
Share premium account		35,000
Revaluation reserve		9,860
Revenue reserve		12,700
Retained earnings		23,430
Total equity		180,990
Non-current liabilities		
10% debentures		24,000
50,000 7% preference shares of 50p each		25,000
Total non-current liabilities		49,000
Current liabilities		
Bank overdraft		7,800
Trade payables		8,300
Current tax payable		6,370
Debenture interest (£2,400 – £1,200)		1,200
Preference dividends		1,750
Total current liabilities		25,420
Total liabilities		74,420
Total equity and liabilities		255,410

Statement of changes in equity for the year ended 31 September 20X4

	Share capital £	*Share premium* £	*Revaluation reserve* £	*Revenue reserve* £	*Retained earnings* £	*Total* £
Balance at 1 October 20X3	100,000	35,000	9,860	10,200	2,580	157,640
Changes in equity for 20X4						
Equity dividends paid	–	–	–	–	(3,250)	(3,250)
Total comprehensive income for the period	–	–	–	–	26,600	26,600
Transfer to general reserve	–	–	–	2,500	(2,500)	
Balance at 30 September 20X4	100,000	35,000	9,860	12,700	23,430	180,990

Notes to the financial statements

1 **Property, plant and equipment**

	Cost	*Deprec*	*NBV*
	£	£	£
Leasehold premises	140,000	–	140,000
Plant and machinery	80,000	25,100	54,900
Loose tools	13,000	5,200	7,800
	233,000	30,300	202,700

2 **Share capital**

Authorized, allotted and called-up share capital

	£
100,000 equity shares of £1 each	100,000
50,000 7% preference shares of 50p each	25,000
	125,000

3 **Dividends**

During the year a dividend of £3,250 was paid. At the year end the directors proposed a dividend of 13p per share (£13,000).

Workings

Finance costs

	£
Interest on debentures (10% × £24,000)	2,400
Preference share dividend	1,750
	4,150

Cost of sales

	£	£
Inventory at 1 Oct 20X3	9,400	
Add : purchases	49,700	
	59,100	
Less : inventory at 30 Sep 20X4	13,480	45,620
Plant hire		6,600
Depreciation on plant (15% × £80,000)		12,000
Depreciation on tools (£9,100 – £7,800)		1,300
Total		65,520

Administration

	£
Directors' salaries	22,000
Rates (£4,650 – [$\frac{3}{6}$ × £2,300])	3,500
Light and heat	3,830
Audit fees	1,750
	31,080

Selling and distribution

	£
Allowance for irrecoverable receivables	210
[(10% × £11,200) – £910]	700
Bad debts	910

Other expenses

Preliminary expenses £1,270

Notes

1 Preliminary expenses could have been written off against the balance on the share premium account instead of being charged to the statement of profit or loss.

2 It is assumed that listed investments will be held for less than one accounting year.

3 Aggregate depreciation on plant and machinery = £80,000 – £66,900 + £12,000 = £25,100.

4 Aggregate depreciation on loose tools = £13,000 – £7,800 = £5,200.

29.20

L. Johnson Ltd
Statement of profit or loss for the year ended 31 December 20X5

	£
Sales revenue	129,217
Cost of sales	(80,889)
Gross profit	48,328
Other income (dividends received)	310
Distribution	(14,166)
Administration	(15,112)
Finance costs	(5,500)
Profit before taxation	13,860
Income tax	(2,544)
Profit after taxation	11,316

L. Johnson Ltd
Statement of financial position as at 31 December 20X5

ASSETS	*Note*	£	£
Non-current assets			
Property, plant and equipment	1		185,410
Intangible assets	2		5,940
Goodwill			10,000
			201,350
Current assets			
Inventory			12,456
Trade receivables		11,600	
Less : allowance for irrecoverable receivables		580	11,020

Prepayments		100
Listed investments		4,873
		28,449
Total assets		229,799
TOTAL EQUITY AND LIABILITIES		
Equity		
Share capital	3	80,000
Share premium account		5,350
Revaluation reserve		13,500
Capital redemption reserve		9,000
Revenue reserve		12,400
Retained earnings		10,442
Total equity		130,692
Non-current liabilities		
10% debentures		30,000
5% preference shares		50,000
Total non-current liabilities		80,000
Current liabilities		
Bank overdraft		3,643
Trade payables		8,450
Accruals		220
Debenture interest		3,000
Current tax payable		2,544
Preference dividend (£2,500 – £1,250)		1,250
Total current liabilities		19,107
Total liabilities		99,107
Total equity and reserves		229,799

Statement of changes in equity for the year ended 31 December 20X5

	Share capital	*Share premium*	*Capital redemption*	*Revaluation reserve*	*Revenue reserve*	*Retained earnings*	*Total*
	£	£	£	£	£	£	£
Balance at 1 January 20X5	80,000	5,600	9,000	13,500	8,400	3,126	119,626
Changes in equity for 20X5	–	–	–	–	–	–	–
Equity dividends paid	–	–	–	–	–	–	–
Formation expenses	–	(250)	–	–	–	–	(250)
Total comprehensive income for the period	–	–	–	–	–	11,316	11,316
Transfer to general reserve	–	–	–	–	4,000	(4,000)	–
Balance at 31 December 20X5	80,000	5,350	9,000	13,500	12,400	10,442	130,692

Notes

1 Property, plant and equipment

	Cost	*Deprec*	*NBV*
	£	£	£
Freehold buildings	137,000	–	137,000
Motor vehicles	35,000	12,950	22,050
Plant and machinery	40,000	13,640	26,360
	212,000	26,590	185,410

2 Intangible assets

Development costs	10,000	4,060	5,940
	10,000	4,060	5,940

3 Share capital

	£
Authorized capital	
200,000 equity shares of £1 each	200,000
90,000 5% preference shares of £1 each	90,000
	290,000
Allotted and called-up share capital	
80,000 equity shares of £1 each	80,000
50,000 5% preference shares of £1 each	50,000
	130,000

4. Dividends

The directors have proposed a final dividend of £5,000.

Workings

	£
Sales revenue	
Sales revenue	130,846
Less: returns inwards	1,629
Net sales	129,217
Finance costs	
Debenture interest (10% × £30,000)	3,000
Preference shares (£50,000 × 5%)	2,500
	5,500

Cost of sales	£	£
Less: cost of sales –		
Inventory at 1 Jan 20X5	9,436	
Add: purchases	78,493	
Less: returns outwards	(1,834)	
	86,095	
Less: inventory at 31 Dec 20X5	12,456	73,639

Depreciation on:	
Plant (20% × £32,950)	6,590
Development costs (10% × £6,600)	660
	80,889

Administration	£
Discount received	(396)
Directors' emoluments	13,000
Rates (£596 – £100)	496
Light and heat (£1,028 + £220)	1,248
Audit fee	764
	15,112

Selling and distribution	£
Reduction in allowance for irrecoverable receivables	
(£860 – [5% × £11,600])	(280)
Wages and salaries	5,948
Irrecoverable receivables	656
Discount allowed	492
Depreciation on: Vehicles (25% × 29,400)	7,350
	14,166

Notes

1 It is assumed that the listed investments are to be held for less than one accounting year.

2 Aggregate depreciation on:

Motor vehicles = £35,000 – £29,400 + £7,350 = £12,950

Plant and machinery = £40,000 – £32,950 + £6,590 = £13,640

Development costs = £10,000 – £6,600 + £660 = £4,060

29.21

Oakwood Ltd **Statement of profit or loss for the year ended 30 June 20X4**	
	£
Sales revenue	119,410
Cost of sales	(85,450)
Gross profit	33,960
Other income (interest received)	410
Distribution	(2,640)
Administration costs	(22,950)
Finance costs	(5,000)
Profit before taxation	3,780
Income tax	(1,080)
Profit for the year	2,700

Oakwood Ltd Statement of financial position as at 30 June 20X4			
ASSETS	*Notes*		£
Non-current assets			
Property, plant and equipment	1		207,110
Intangible assets	2		4,050
Goodwill			8,000
			219,160
Current assets			
Inventory (£11,680 + £500)			12,180
Trade receivables (£10,400 – £1,000)		9,400	
Less : allowance for irrecoverable receivables		470	8,930
Prepayments			150
Available for sale investments			
(*listed investments*)			3,250
			24,510
Total assets			243,670
EQUITY AND LIABILITIES			
Equity			
Share capital			125,000
Share premium account			8,800
Revenue reserve			9,100
Retained earnings			5,400
Total equity			148,300
Non-current liabilities			
5% preference shares			60,000
10% debentures			20,000
Total non-current liabilities			80,000
Current liabilities			
Bank overdraft			2,630
Trade payables			7,890
Accruals			270
Current tax payable			1,080
Debenture interest			2,000
Preference dividends (£3,000 – £1,500)			1,500
Total current liabilities			15,370
Total liabilities			95,370
Total equity and liabilities			243,670

Statement of changes in equity for the year ended 30 June 20X4					
	Share capital	*Share premium*	*Revenue reserve*	*Retained earnings*	*Total*
	£	£	£	£	£
Balance at 1 July 20X3	125,000	9,000	6,100	7,700	147,800
Changes in equity for 20X4					
Equity dividends paid	–	–	–	(2,000)	(2,000)
Formation expenses	–	(200)	–	–	(200)
Total comprehensive income for the period	–	–	–	2,700	2,700
Transfer to general reserve	–	–	3,000	(3,000)	–
Balance at 30 June 20X4	125,000	8,800	9,100	5,400	148,300

1. Property, plant and equipment

	Cost	*Deprec*	*NBV*
	£	£	£
Freehold buildings	165,000	–	165,000
Delivery vehicles	28,000	11,170	16,830
Plant and machinery (£34,000 – £300)	33,700	8,420	25,280
	226,700	19,590	207,110

2. Intangible assets

	£	£	£
Development costs	12,000	7,950	4,050
	12,000	7,950	4,050

3. Share capital

Share capital	*Authorized*	*Called-up*
Equity shares of £1 each	150,000	125,000
5% preference shares of £1 each	70,000	60,000
	220,000	185,000

4. Dividends

The company paid a dividend of £2,000 in the year. The directors have proposed a final dividend of £4,000.

Workings

Sales revenue	£
Sales revenue (£120,640 – £1,000)	119,640
Less: returns inwards	230
Net sales	119,410

Finance costs	£
Debenture interest (10% × 20,000)	2,000
Preference dividend (5% × 60,000)	3,000
	5,000

Cost of sales	£	£
Inventory at 1 July 20X3	8,760	
Add : purchases	81,230	
Less : returns outwards	(640)	
Add : carriage inwards	310	
	89,660	
Less : inventory at 30 June 20X4 (£11,680 + £500)	12,180	77,480
Consumable tools		300
Depreciation on –		
Development costs (25% × £5,400)		1,350
Plant (20% × [£31,900 – £300])		6,320
		85,450

Administration	£
Administrative salaries	6,370
Discount received	(440)
Audit fee	390
Directors' remuneration	14,100
Rates (£600 – £150)	450
Light and heat (£940 + £270)	1,210
Postage and telephone	870
	22,950

Selling and distribution	£
Allowance for irrecoverable receivables	
([5% × (£10,400 – £1,000)] – £730)	(260)
Irrecoverable receivables	740
Discount allowed	290
Depreciation on –	
Vehicles (10% × £18,700)	1,870
	2,640

Notes

1 It is assumed that the investments are to be held for less than one accounting year.

2 Aggregate depreciation on:

Development costs = £12,000 – £5,400 + £1,350 = £7,950

Delivery vehicles = £28,000 – £18,700 + £1,870 = £11,170

Plant and machinery = £34,000 – £31,900 + £6,320 = £8,420

30 Statement of Cash Flows

30.15

A Brooks **Statement of cash flows (indirect method) for the year ended 30 June 20X5**		
Cash flows from operating activities	£	£
Loss before taxation	(1,800)	
Adjustments for:		
Depreciation	1,500	
Investment income	(900)	
Finance charges	1,250	
	50	
Decrease in trade and other receivables (£5,400 – £4,100)	1,300	
Increase in inventories (£7,300 – £6,700)	(600)	
Increase in trade and other payables (£6,200 – £4,800)	1,400	
Cash generated from operations		2,150
Cash flows from investing activities		
Interest received	900	
Purchase of property, plant and equipment (£72,000 – £65,000)	(7,000)	
Net cash used in investing activities		(6,100)
Cash flows from financing activities		
Capital introduced	20,000	
Drawings	(7,600)	
Interest paid	(1,250)	
Repayment of bank loan	(5,000)	
Net cash from financial activities		6,150
Net increase in cash and cash equivalents		2,200
Cash and cash equivalents at beginning of period (note 1)		(1,300)
Cash and cash equivalents at end of period (note 1)		900

1 Cash and cash equivalents

	At 1 July 20X4	*Cash flows*	*At 30 June 20X5*
	£	£	£
Cash in hand, at bank	–	900	900
Overdrafts	(1,300)	1,300	–
	(1,300)	2,200	900

30.17 Workings

Accumulated depreciation plant					
20X4		£	*20X4*		£
31 Dec	Plant – depn on disposal (£10,000 – £6,000)	4,000	1 Jan	Balance b/d	7,000
31 Dec	Balance c/d	9,500	31 Dec	P or L a/c	6,500
		13,500			13,500

The charge to the statement of profit or loss in respect of depreciation on plant for the year of £6,500 is the difference between the two sides of the above account.

Plant					
20X4		£	*20X4*		£
1 Jan	Balance b/d	41,000	31 Dec	Bank – disposal	6,400
31 Dec	P or L a/c – profit on sale	400	31 Dec	Dep'n on disposal (10,000 – 6,000)	4,000
31 Dec	Bank – acquisitions	17,000	31 Dec	Balance c/d	48,000
		58,400			58,400

The cost of plant acquired of £17,000 is the difference between the two sides of the above account.

J. Kitchens Ltd
Statement of cash flows for the year ended 31 December 20X4

Cash flows from operating activities	£	£
Profit before taxation	24,000	
Adjustments for:		
Depreciation (£6,500 + (£9,000 – £6,000))	9,500	
Allowance for irrecoverable receivables (£600 – £400)	200	
Profit on sale of non-current assets	(400)	
Finance charges	750	
	34,050	
Decrease in trade and other payables (£19,700 – £17,600)	(2,100)	
Increase in inventories (£22,500 – £14,900)	(7,600)	
Increase in trade and other receivables ((£16,400 + £600) – (£11,300 + £400))	(5,300)	
Cash generated from operations		19,050
Cash flows from investing activities		
Purchase of property, plant and equipment	(17,000)	
Proceeds from sale of property, plant and equipment	6,400	
Net cash used in investing activities		(10,600)

Cash flows from financing activities		
Interest paid	(750)	
Dividends paid	(17,000)	
Net cash from financial activities		(17,750)
Net increase in cash and cash equivalents		(9,300)
Cash and cash equivalents at beginning of period (note 1)		(500)
Cash and cash equivalents at end of period (note 1)		(9,800)

1 Cash and cash equivalents

	At 1 Jan 20X4	*Cash flow*	*At 31 Dec 20X4*
	£	£	£
Overdrafts	(500)	(9,300)	(9,800)

30.18 Workings

Provision for depreciation					
20X5		£	*20X4*		£
31 May	Non-current assets – depn on disposal (£ 12,000 – £7,500)	4,500	31 May	Balance b/d	28,000
			20X5		
31 May	Balance c/d	37,000	31 May	P or L a/c	13,500
		41,500			41,500

The charge to the profit or loss account in respect of depreciation for the year of £13,500 is the difference between the two sides of the above account.

Computation of profit before taxation and dividends		
	£	£
Increase in balance on retained earnings account (£5,200 – £3,400)		1,800
Transfer to reserve (£6,900 – £4,200)		2,700
Equity dividends paid –		
Proposed final 20X4	21,800	
Interim 20X5	6,400	
		28,200
Income tax		7,200
		39,900

L. Tyler Ltd Statement of cash flows for the year ended 31 May 20X5		
Cash flows from operating activities	£	£
Profit before taxation	39,900	
Adjustments for:		
Depreciation	13,500	
Increase in allowance for irrecoverable receivables (£700 – £500)	200	
Profit on sale of non-current assets (£8,100 – £7,500)	(600)	
Investment income	(1,800)	
Finance charges	1,600	
	52,800	
Increase in trade and other receivables (£14,200 – £11,800)	(2,400)	
Decrease in inventories (£21,600 – £19,400)	2,200	
Decrease in trade and other payables (£8,400 – £6,700)	(1,700)	
Cash generated from operations	50,900	
Income tax paid	(5,800)	
Net cash from operating activities		45,100
Cash flows from investing activities		
Purchase of investments (£17,100 – £3,900)	(13,200)	
Proceeds from sale of property, plant and equipment	8,100	
Interest received	1,800	
Net cash used in investing activities		(3,300)
Cash flows from financing activities		
Proceeds from the issue of share capital (£70,000 – £60,000) + (£34,000 – £25,000)	19,000	
Repayment of loan stock (£30,000 – £5,000)	(25,000)	
Interest paid (long term)	(1,600)	
Dividends paid (£19,600 + £6,400)	(26,000)	
Net cash from financial activities		(33,600)
Net increase in cash and cash equivalents		8,200
Cash and cash equivalents at beginning of period (note 1)		4,600
Cash and cash equivalents at end of period (note 1)		12,800

1 Cash and cash equivalents

	At 1 June 20X4	*Cash flow*	*At 31 May 20X5*
	£	£	£
Cash in hand, at bank	4,600	8,200	12,800
Total	4,600	8,200	12,800

—31 The Appraisal of Company Financial Statements using Ratio Analysis—

31.10

When answering questions such as this with apparently open-ended requirements that do not specify which ratios to calculate, it is very important to consider the data carefully in order to decide what ratios should be computed. First, note that these are sole traders not companies. Second, a related point, as in the case of companies where no share price is given, it is not possible to compute the return on investment ratios. Third, there are no non-current liabilities and thus no gearing ratio. Fourth, search the requirements carefully for key words and phrases such as in this question, performance and financial position. The latter is often taken to include solvency, liquidity and the appraisal of working capital. Fifth, the number of ratios you are expected to compute may be influenced by the marks/time allocated to the question.

The ACCA suggested answer contains references to the following accounting ratios (all money values are in 000s):

	White	*Black*
Return on capital employed	$\frac{£48}{£192} \times 100 = 25\%$	$\frac{£48}{£160} \times 100 = 30\%$
Gross profit to sales revenue	$\frac{£150}{£600} \times 100 = 25\%$	$\frac{£176}{£800} \times 100 = 22\%$
Profit for the year to sales revenue	$\frac{£48}{£600} \times 100 = 8\%$	$\frac{£48}{£800} \times 100 = 6\%$
Turnover of capital employed	$\frac{£600}{£192} = 3.125$ times	$\frac{£800}{£160} = 5$ times
Inventory turnover	$\frac{£450}{£56} = 8$ times	$\frac{£624}{£52} = 12$ times
Trade receivables' collection period	$\frac{£75}{£600} \times 52 = 6.5$ weeks	$\frac{£67}{£800} \times 52 = 4.4$ weeks
Trade payables' period of credit	$\frac{£38}{£450} \times 52 = 4.4$ weeks	$\frac{£78}{£624} \times 52 = 6.5$ weeks
Liquidity ratio	$\frac{£75 + £8}{£38} = 2.2$	$\frac{£67}{£78 + £4} = 0.82$

Comparison of ratios

1 Black has a higher ROCE than White, which shows that it is more profitable.

2 Black has a lower GP and profit for the year to sales revenue (profit margin) than White, which suggests either higher unit costs and / or lower selling prices.

3 Black has a higher turnover of capital employed (asset turnover) than White. The lower profit margin and higher asset turnover ratio may be the result of selling large quantities at a lower price. This strategy appears to be resulting in a higher ROCE.

4 Black has a higher inventory turnover ratio and longer period of credit from credit suppliers than White, and a lower trade receivables' collection period. This suggests that Black is more effective and efficient at controlling its working capital.

5 **Black has a considerably lower liquidity ratio than White, which shows that it is stretching itself financially and may encounter liquidity problems.**

Overall impressions

Black's performance is superior to White's. It is more profitable, and has a higher level of activity and better control of working capital. However, Black appears to have a weak liquidity position. This may be the result of overtrading.

Additional information needed

1 **Do either of Black or White work in their businesses? If one does and the other does not the profit is not strictly comparable without a notional salary for the one who does work in the business.**

2 **There is a difference in accounting policy for the depreciation of buildings. Black has a charge of £5,000 whereas White has no depreciation. This distorts comparisons. Are there any other differences in accounting policies?**

31.12

$$\text{Return on capital employed} = \frac{£580{,}000 + £240{,}000}{£5{,}210{,}000} \times 100 = 15.74\%$$

$$\text{Profit margin} = \frac{£580{,}000 + £240{,}000}{£4{,}230{,}000} = 19.39\%$$

$$\text{Asset turnover} = \frac{£4{,}230{,}000}{£5{,}210{,}000} = 0.81$$

$$\text{Working capital ratio} = \frac{£1{,}070{,}000}{£730{,}000} = 1.47$$

$$\text{Liquidity ratio} = \frac{£1{,}070{,}000 - £480{,}000}{£730{,}000} = 0.81$$

$$\text{Inventory turnover ratio} = \frac{£2{,}560{,}000}{£480{,}000} = 5.33$$

$$\text{Trade receivables' collection period} = \frac{£270{,}000}{£4{,}230{,}000} \times 365 = 23 \text{ days}$$

$$\text{Trade payables' collection period} = \frac{£260{,}000}{£2{,}560{,}000} \times 365 = 37 \text{ days}$$

$$\text{Dividend yield} = \frac{£200{,}000}{£500{,}000 \times £5} \times 100 = 8\%$$

$$\text{Dividend cover} = \frac{£310{,}000}{£200{,}000} = 1.55$$

$$\text{Earnings per share} = \frac{£310,000}{£500,000} = £0.62$$

$$\text{Price-earnings ratio} = \frac{£5}{£0.62} = 8.07$$

$$\text{Return on equity} = \frac{£310,000}{£2,210,000} \times 100 = 14.03\%$$

$$\text{Gearing ratio} = \frac{£3,000,000}{£3,000,000 + £2,210,000} = 0.58$$

$$\text{Gearing ratio (market values)} = \frac{30,000 \times £110}{(30,000 \times £110) + (500,000 \times £5)} = 0.57$$

Comments on ratios

1 The return on capital employed and return on equity are reasonable, indicating satisfactory profitability.

2 The asset turnover ratio appears low (but may be because the company is capital intensive).

3 The working capital ratio is a little low and the liquidity ratio is weak indicating a poor liquidity position and possible insolvency.

4 The trade receivables' and trade payables' ratios are very low. See limitations below.

5 The dividend yield is high, which means an above average return on investment.

6 The dividend cover is somewhat low and the gearing ratio is rather high. These make the equity shares a risky investment.

7 The P/E ratio, profit margin and inventory turnover ratio are probably about normal.

Limitations include:

1 The lack of comparative figures for previous years and other companies means generalizations about the results can only be tentative.

2 It is not possible to make judgements about the acceptability of these ratios without knowing the type of industry and the current economic climate.

3 The ratios may be distorted since they are calculated using historical cost data.

4 The calculation of some ratios necessitates the use of surrogate data that may give misleading results. For example, the trade receivables' (and trade payables') collection period appears to be extremely low, which may be because revenue (cost of sales) includes cash sales (purchases).

31.13 The following are points that should be included in a report:

Comparison of ratios

1 The dividend yield of Chips plc is relatively high.

2 The dividend cover of Fish plc is relatively high.

3 The EPS are not really comparable.

4 The P/E ratio of Fish plc is higher; earnings growth may be expected. The P/E ratio of Chips plc is lower; little growth in earnings may be expected.

5 The ROCE suggests that Fish plc has made more profitable use of its assets.

6 The profit margin indicates that Chips plc has higher selling prices and or lower unit costs.

7 The asset turnover suggests that both companies are capital intensive but Fish plc has a higher level of activity.

8 The gearing of Chips plc is high, suggesting greater financial risk.

9 The high gearing ratio of Chips plc has probably resulted in a larger return on equity.

Overall impressions

Fish plc may be a better investment because it has a lower financial risk (i.e. low gearing and high dividend cover), is more profitable (i.e. greater ROCE), and has a higher level of activity (i.e. asset turnover). Also, although Fish plc has a lower dividend yield, it probably offers growth in earnings (and thus dividends) resulting from retained profits (as shown by the high dividend cover and P/E ratio). It appears to be pursuing a policy of low selling prices, high turnover and expansion by internal financing from retained profits.

In contrast, Chips plc provides a higher dividend yield but with greater risk.

31.14 The following are points that should be included in a report:

Comparison of ratios

1 The working capital ratio has improved but the liquidity ratio has worsened. This suggests a possible build-up of inventories.

2 The inventory turnover has slowed, which also points to either an increase in inventories and or a decrease in sales.

3 The trade receivables' ratio shows that credit customers are being allowed to take a considerably longer period of credit.

4 The trade payables' ratio shows that this company is taking longer to pay its debts.

Overall impressions

There is deterioration in liquidity and control of working capital. It appears that there is overstocking, poor inventory control and a relaxation of credit control procedures.

Index

abnormal profit 497
accountability
  definition 6
  public 51–3
accounting, history of 4
accounting concepts 66
accounting entity 73, 122–4
accounting equation
  statement of financial position 124–9
accounting estimates, changes in
  disclosure 81
  IAS 8 *Accounting policies, changes in accounting estimates and errors* 35–6, 81, 585–6
accounting irregularities
  inventory valuation 439–40
  provision for bad debt 283
  using accruals basis of accounting 292–3
  WorldCom 132
accounting period concept 129
accounting policies 78–9
  allowance for irrecoverable receivables 282–3
  changing 35–6, 80, 586
  definition 78
  depreciation 256–7
  disclosure 80–1
  IAS 8 *Accounting policies, changes in accounting estimates and errors* 35–6, 78, 79–81, 585–6
  inventory valuation 414
  selecting 79–80
  SSAP 2 *Disclosure of accounting policies* 66
accounting principles 66
accounting ratios
  acid test 654–5
  asset-turnover ratios 652
  dividend cover 660
  dividend yield 659
  earnings per share 660–1
  gearing ratio 663–6
  inventory turnover ratio 658–9
  limitations 648, 666–8
  liquidity/quick ratio 654–5
  price-earnings ratio 661–2
  profit margin 651–3
  return on capital employed (ROCE) 650–1
  return on equity 662–3
  trade payables' ratio 657–8
  trade receivables' ratio 656–7
  working capital/current ratio 654
accounting records 5–6
  see also documentation
accounting regulation *see* regulatory framework of accounting
accounting software
  advantages and disadvantages of computerized system 144–7
  'free' packages 195–6
  manufacturing accounts 430
accounting standards
  advantages and disadvantages of using global standards 24
  harmonization 33
  tangible assets 250–1
  see also Accounting Standards Board (ASB); Financial Accounting Standards Board (FASB); International Accounting Standards Board (IASB); International Financial Reporting Standards (IFRSs); standard setting
Accounting Standards Advisory Forum (ASAF) 25, 33
Accounting Standards Board (ASB)
  convergence project 30, 33
  FRS 5 *Substance over form* 74
Accounting Standards Committee (ASC) 30
  SSAP 9 *Stocks and long term contracts* 419
  SSAP 16 *Current cost accounting* 74
Accounting Standards Steering Committee (ASSC)
  The Corporate Report 50, 53, 56
  SSAP 2 *Disclosure of accounting policies* 66
accounting system
  computerized 144–7, 195–6, 430
  objectives 5–7
accounting theory 44, 60
  see also conceptual framework of accounting
accounting year 129
accounts
  double-entry bookkeeping 150
  see also financial statements
accruals basis of accounting 68–9
  fraudulent use of 292–3
accruals concept 68–9, 292
accrued expenses
  accounting for 292–4, 296–8
accuracy 103
Act of Parliament
  bodies corporate 542
adjusting events after the reporting period 586–7
adjustments
  drawings and capital introduced 161–2
  extended trial balance 310–16
  post trial balance 310–17
  year-end inventories 298–9
administrative overheads 430
adverse opinion 107
agency costs 108
agency theory 107–8
aggregate/accumulated depreciation 251
aggregation 94–5
allotment of shares 565, 566
allotted share capital
  disclosure 562–3

allowance for irrecoverable/ doubtful receivables 276–84
  accounting manipulation 283
  accounting policy 282–3
  general allowance 276
  specific allowance 276
Altman, E. A. 655–6
analyst-adviser group
  users of annual reports 56
annual general meeting (AGM) 571
  purpose 551–2
annual reports 4, 9, 47
  contents 6–7, 9–10
  see also final financial statements; financial statements; published financial statements; users of annual reports
annual return 551
application for shares 565, 566
appropriation account 12
  partnerships 459–64
appropriation of profit 546
arithmetic errors 370
Articles of Association 544
articles/deed of partnership 456
asset account 160
asset-turnover ratios 652
assets
  definition 8, 124, 250
  separate determination concept 76
  types 8, 250
audit assertions 100
audit plan 102
audit planning memorandum 102
audit report 103–7, 551
  contents 104
  example 104–6
audit risk 102
audit scope 104
auditing
  definition 100
  objective, scope and principles 100–1
  process 102–3
  statutory audit requirement 101–2
auditing by exception 102
Auditing Practices Board (APB)
  Ethical Standards for Auditors 100–1, 113
  see also International Standards on Auditing (ISAs)
auditor ethics 113–14
authorised/nominal share capital 543
  disclosure 562–3
available-for-sale assets
  terminology 8

bad debt 276
  accounting irregularities 283
  accounting policy for allowance for 282–3
  allowance for 276–84
balance brought down 172
balance carried down 172
balance sheet 4, 16
  see also statement of financial position
bank account
  example of closing the statement of financial position account 173–4
  ledger entries 152
bank paying-in book 142
bank reconciliation statement 330–7
  procedures 331–7
bank transactions
  ledger entries 152–5
bankruptcy
  prediction 655–6
bill of exchange 143
bill (of exchange) payable 351
bill (of exchange) payable book 143
bill (of exchange) receivable 351
bill (of exchange) receivable book 143
board of directors *see* corporate governance
bodies corporate 542
bodies sole 542
book value 252
books of account 143–4, 550
books of prime entry 143
  case study of preparation of journals for a limited company 691–8
  case study of preparation of journals for a sole trader 684–9
  credit transactions 188–94
  example entries 190–4
  see also cash book; journal; petty cash book; purchases day book; purchases returns day book; sales day book; sales returns day book
buildings
  depreciation 254
business combinations
  IFRS 3 *Business combinations* 37, 251, 495
business entity 73, 122

Cadbury Report 108
called-up share capital
  disclosure 562–3
calls 549, 565, 566
capital 124, 230
  matching principle 72
capital/non-distributable reserves 570
capital account 164
  example of closing the capital introduced account 174–5
  partnerships 458
capital employed 648
capital expenditure 250, 616
  matching principle 72–3
  versus revenue expenditure 129–32
capital introduced, adjustments for 162
capital introduced account 152
  example of closing the account 174–5
capital maintenance 78, 128
capital redemption reserve (CRR) 545, 570
carriage inwards 155
carriage outwards 161
carrying amount 252
cash
  definition 610
cash account
  ledger entries 152
cash book 143, 202–12
  bank reconciliation 330–7
  examples of entries 203–8
  three-column 202, 209–11
  two-column 202–8
cash discount 138, 203
cash equivalents
  definition 610
cash flow statement *see* statement of cash flows
cash flows
  definition 610
cash flows from financing activities 614
cash flows from investing activities 613–14, 627

cash flows from operating
activities 610–13
cash profit 611
cash transactions
documentation 138–44
ledger entries 152–5
casting 370
Certificate of Incorporation 544
cessation
partnerships 522–33
cheque 140, 142
information provided on 142
unrecorded 331
classification 94–5
clean audit report 104
Combined Code 108–9
companies 15–17
definition 542
legal entity 542
regulation 15, 543–4
statement of cash flows 618–26
statutory books 551, 552
types 542
see also companies limited by
guarantee; companies limited
by shares; limited companies
(Ltd); private companies
(Ltd); public limited
companies (plc)
Companies Act 1967 456
Companies Act 2006 6, 542, 558
formats of published financial
statements 558
companies limited by
guarantee 15, 542
companies limited by shares
characteristics 542
classes of companies 542–3
see also limited companies
(Ltd); public limited
companies (plc)
comparability of financial
information 92–3, 583
accounting standards and
accounting policies 93
comparatives 17, 35, 93, 583
compensating errors 368
competitors
users of annual reports 56
completeness 91, 103
compliance testing 102
comprehensive income
statement *see* statement of
comprehensive income
computerized accounting
system
advantages and
disadvantages 144–7
'free' software packages
195–6
manufacturing accounts 430
conceptual framework of
accounting 44–61
debate 59–60
definition 44–5
IASB *Conceptual framework for
financial reporting* 34, 35,
44–51, 76–8, 88–97
purpose 44–7
qualitative characteristics of
financial information 88–97
confidentiality, client 114
confirmatory value 89
consistency concept 75, 92, 97
consumable tools 298–9
consumables 412
consumption 253
contingency
definition 587
contingent assets
definition 588
disclosure 588
IAS 37 *Provisions, contingent
liabilities and contingent
assets* 37, 588
contingent liabilities
definition 587–8
disclosure 587–8
IAS 37 *Provisions, contingent
liabilities and contingent
assets* 37, 587–8
contra entry 351
control accounts 348–56
alternative systems 355
example 350–2
purpose 352–5
conversion
partnerships into limited
company 526–32
convertible loan stock/
debentures 546–7, 548
corporate bonds 546
corporate failure
prediction 655–6
corporate governance 107–11
agency theory 107–8
Cadbury Report 108
Combined Code 108–9
definition 107
Greenbury Report 108
Hampel Report 108
Smith Report 109
Turnbull Report 109
*UK Corporate Governance
Code* 109, 110–11
corporate governance report
example 109–10
corporate report 47
The Corporate Report 50, 53, 56
corporate social responsibility
(CSR) 56–8
corporation tax 15, 559
accounting for 300–1
correction of errors 371
cost flow assumptions 415–19
cost of goods sold 11
cost of sales 231
cost of services 11
cost-benefit analysis
provision of financial
information 95–6
costs of conversion 414–15,
439
creative accounting 44
depreciation 266–7
credit balance 163
credit card sales 394
credit note 138–40
credit purchases 156
credit sales 156
credit side 150
credit transactions
books of prime entry 188–94
documentation 138–44
ledger entries 155–61
creditors 156–7
users of annual reports 51
see also trade creditors; trade
payable
cumulative preference
shares 545, 548
current accounts
partnerships 458
current assets 234
examples 250
terminology 8–9
current cost 74, 77
current liabilities 234
terminology 9
current value 252
customers
users of annual reports 54

day books *see* purchases day book;
purchases returns day book;
sales day book; sales returns
day book
debenture discount 549

debentures 544, 546–9
advantages and disadvantages of issuing 548
characteristics 547
issue 549–50
types 548
debit balance 163
debit note 138
debit side 150
debt, accounting for 588–91
debt capital 663
debtors 156
see also trade debtors
deductive theories 60
deed of partnership 456
deferred income 72
demand deposits
definition 610
depreciable amount 253
depreciation 253–67
accounting for 257–60
accounting policy 256–7
buildings 254
creative accounting 266–7
definition 253
diminishing/reducing balance method 255–6
methods 254–6
on acquisitions and disposals 262–6
partial year depreciation 262–6
straight line/fixed instalment method 255
sum of the years' digits method 256
versus diminution in value 254
depreciation expense 255
diminishing balance method of depreciation 255–6
diminution in value
versus depreciation 254
direct costs 430
examples 431
direct expenses 432
direct labour 432
direct materials 432
direct method (cash flows from operating activities) 611–12
directors *see* corporate governance
disclosure
accounting policies 80–1
formats 95
discontinued operations
definition 583–4
IFRS 5 *Non-current assets held for sale and discontinued operations* 38, 251, 254, 583–4
discount allowed 202
discount received 202–3
Discussion Paper (DP) 29
dissolution
partnerships 522–5
dividend 544, 550
accounting for 571
dividend cover 660
dividend yield 659
documentation
cash transactions 138–44
credit transactions 138–44
double entry 74, 150
double posting error 368
double-entry bookkeeping 6
case study for a sole trader 684–9
case study of preparation of journals and ledgers for a limited company 691–8
principles 150–2
drawings, adjustments for 161–2
drawings accounts 152
partnerships 458
dual aspect 74, 125, 150
duality concept 74, 125, 150
earnings management 69
earnings per share (EPS) 650, 660–1
earnings yield 662
economic decision-making 7
emphasis of matter paragraph 107
empirical theories 60
employees
users of annual reports 53–4
engagement letter 102
entity concept 73, 122
environmental accounting 58–9
equity 124
terminology 9
equity capital 234
equity shareholders
terminology 9
equity shares 544
characteristics 547
ownership disclosure in financial statements 562–3
error of commission 368
error of omission 368
error of original/prime entry 368
error of principle 368
errors
disclosure 586
IAS 8 *Accounting policies, changes in accounting estimates and errors* 35–6, 585–6
suspense accounts 371–4
that cause trial balance to disagree 370–1
that do not cause trial balance to disagree 368–70
trial balance 183
estimation techniques 75, 79
disclosure 81
ethics 111–14
events after the reporting period
definition 586
disclosure 586–7
IAS 10 *Events after the reporting date* 36, 586–7
exceptional items
disclosure 584
expectations gap 107
expense account 164
expenses
accounting for 559
accruals basis of accounting 68, 292–4, 296–8
terminology 8
Exposure Draft (ED) 29
extended trial balance 310–17
extraction error 370
face value 544
factory cost of completed production 432
factory/production/manufacturing overheads 430
examples 431
fair value
definition in IFRS 3 495
definition in IFRS 5 251
definition in IFRS 13 74
IFRS 13 *Fair value measurement* 74
intangible assets 37
tangible assets 36
terminology 36
fair value accounting 132, 252
faithful representation 60, 90–1
completeness 91
free from error 91
neutrality 91
FASB *see* Financial Accounting Standards Board
final dividend 550
accounting for 571
final financial statements 47, 230

case study of preparation of journals and ledgers for a sole trader 684–9
illustration of preparation 572–7
partnerships 456–68
preparation from extended trial balance 310–16
preparation from trial balance 236–41, 296–8
preparation of limited companies 558–93
sole traders 230–42
finance
accounting for debt 588–91
financial accounting
definition 4–5
functions of 4–5, 7
Financial Accounting Standards Board (FASB)
convergence project 30, 33
financial accounts 47
see also final financial statements; financial statements; published financial statements; users of annual reports
financial assets 251
financial performance 583
measures 650–3
ratio analysis 648–50
financial position
ratio analysis 648–50
financial reporting 47
Financial Reporting Council (FRC)
convergence project 33
ISA (UK and Ireland) 700 *The independent auditors report on financial statements* 100, 103
structure 30–1
UK Stewardship Code 109
Financial Reporting Standards (FRSs) 18, 30
FRS 100 *Application of financial reporting requirements* 31, 32
FRS 101 *Reduced disclosure framework* 32
FRS 102 *Financial reporting standard applicable in the UK and in the Republic of Ireland* 32
see also Accounting Standards Board (ASB)
financial risk 664
measures 659–66
financial statements
commercial versus manufacturing businesses 430
comparatives 17, 93, 583
IAS 1 and UK GAAP compared 16
limitations under IFRS 48–9
manufacturing entities 430–41
notes *see* notes to the financial statements
partnerships 12–13, 14
rules and regulations 17–18
sole traders 11, 12
statements comprising 6, 9–10
see also annual reports; final financial statements; published financial statements
financial year 129
financing activities 614
definition 614
finished goods 412, 430, 432
valuation 414–15, 439–40
first in, first out (FIFO) 415, 416–17
compared with LIFO 419
fixed assets 16
see also non-current assets
fixed charge debentures 546, 548
fixed production overheads 415
Flint, Douglas 109
float 218
floating charge debentures 546, 548
forfeited shares 565, 566
fraud, accounting *see* accounting irregularities
FRC *see* Financial Reporting Council
free from error 91
FRSs *see* Financial Reporting Standards
fungible inventory 415

GAAP *see* Generally Accepted Accounting Practice (UK GAAP); Generally Accepted Accounting Practice (US GAAP); Generally Accepted Accounting Principles
gain on bargain purchase 495
Garner v Murray ruling 495, 522
gearing 663
gearing ratio 663–6
general ledger 143, 150, 348
account balances 163–4, 172–8
example postings 190–4
see also ledger
general purpose financial statements 47
objectives 47–8
see also final financial statements; financial statements; published financial statements; users of annual reports
general reserve 571
Generally Accepted Accounting Practice (UK GAAP)
IAS 1 and UK GAAP compared 16
qualifying entities 31
Generally Accepted Accounting Practice (US GAAP)
convergence with IFRS 33
Generally Accepted Accounting Principles (GAAP) 44
going concern 66–8
goods on sale or return 162–3
goodwill
admission of new partner 498–502
changes in profit-sharing ratio 504–9
definition 495
IFRS 3 *Business combinations* 37, 251
impairment review 497
incoming and outgoing partners 502
outgoing partners 502
partnerships 486, 495–504
purchased 496
recognition in partnership financial statements 496–7
governments
users of annual reports 54
Greenbury Report 108
gross capital employed 651
gross profit 155, 231–4
gross profit ratio 653
guaranteed share of profit 465

Hampel Report 108
held for sale 584
IFRS 5 *Non-current assets held for sale and discontinued operations* 38, 251, 254
Hicks, J. R. 128
historical cost
valuation, approach to 251–2
VAT implications 252
historical cost accounting
strengths and limitations 132–3
historical cost concept 74, 77

IASs *see* International Financial Reporting Standards (IFRSs)
IFRS Advisory Council 28
IFRS for SMEs 26–7
IFRS Foundation
 Accounting Standards Advisory Forum (ASAF) 25, 33
 International Financial Reporting Interpretations Committee (IFRIC) 27–8
 Monitoring Board of Public Capital Market Authorities 25, 27
 support operations 28
 Trustees 27
impairment of assets 252
impairment review
 goodwill 497
impersonal ledger 348
imprest system 218, 221
 advantages 221
income
 separate determination concept 76
income tax, accounting for 300–1, 559
incomplete records 384–96
 case study of preparation of statements of financial position using 690–1
 revenue income and expenditure 384–9
 single entry 384, 389–94
incorporated bodies 542
independence, auditor 112, 113–14
indirect costs 430
 examples 431
indirect method (cash flows from operating activities) 612–13
insolvency
 prediction 655–6
insolvent 653
intangible assets
 examples 251
 IAS 38 *Intangible assets* 37, 251
 terminology 8, 251
integrity, auditor 113
interest on the capital
 sharing partnership profits 457–8
interest on drawings
 sharing partnership profits 457–8
interim dividend 550
 accounting for 571
internal check
 double-entry bookkeeping 6
internal control 5, 348
internally generated goodwill 496
International Accounting Standards (IASs) *see* International Financial Reporting Standards (IFRSs)
International Accounting Standards Board (IASB) 4, 24–5
 Conceptual framework for financial reporting 34, 35, 44–51, 76–8, 88–97
 current work programme 38
 development 26
 harmonization 33
 institutional framework for setting IFRSs 25
 membership 26
 objectives 26
 standard-setting process 28–9
International Accounting Standards Committee (IASC)
 history 26
International Auditing and Assurance Standards Board (IAASB) 100
International Financial Reporting Standards (IFRSs) 18, 25, 26, 34
 IAS 1 *Presentation of financial statements* 9, 15–16, 34, 558, 560
 IAS 2 *Inventories* 35, 70, 413, 419
 IAS 7 *Statement of cash flows* 35, 610–26
 IAS 8 *Accounting policies, changes in accounting estimates and errors* 35–6, 78, 79–81, 585–6
 IAS 10 *Events after the reporting date* 36, 586–7
 IAS 12 *Taxation* 300
 IAS 16 *Property, plant and equipment* 36, 250, 251, 252, 253, 254
 IAS 17 *Leases* 251
 IAS 18 *Revenue* 36–7, 69, 75
 IAS 33 *Earnings per share* 661
 IAS 36 *Impairment of assets* 252
 IAS 37 *Provisions, contingent liabilities and contingent assets* 37, 587–8
 IAS 38 *Intangible assets* 37, 251
 IAS 40 *Investment property* 251, 254
 IFRS 3 *Business combinations* 37, 251, 495
 IFRS 5 *Non-current assets held for sale and discontinued operations* 38, 251, 254, 583–4
 IFRS 13 *Fair value measurement* 74
 institutional framework for standard setting 25
 small and medium-sized entities, standard for 26–7
 UK GAAP and IAS 1 compared 16
International Standards on Auditing (ISAs) 100
 ISA 200 *Overall objectives of the independent auditor and the conduct of an audit in accordance with ISAs* 100
 ISA 210 *Agreeing the terms of audit engagements* 102
 ISA 300 *Planning an audit of financial statements* 102
 ISA 330 *The auditor's responses to assessed risks* 102
 ISA 700 *The independent auditors report on financial statements* 100
inventory 231–3
 accounting for 412
 fungible 415
 IAS 2 *Inventories* 35, 70, 413, 419
 ledger entries 155–7
 matching principle 70, 412
 SSAP 9 *Stocks and long term contracts* 419
 terminology 9
 types 412, 430, 432
 year-end adjustments 298–9
inventory turnover ratio 658–9
inventory valuation 412–21
 accounting irregularities 439–40
 accounting policy 414
 finished goods 414–15, 439–40
 IAS 2 *Inventories* 413, 419
 work in progress 414–15, 439–40
investing activities 613–14
 definition 613
investment property
 IAS 40 *Investment property* 251, 254
investment ratios *see* accounting ratios
investments 251
investments in associates
 terminology 8
investors
 users of annual reports 50
invoice 138
 example layout 140
 information on 141

irrecoverable receivable *see* allowance for irrecoverable/ doubtful receivables; bad debt

Jenkins, Sir Brian 109
journal 143, 189–90
  opening entries 194
  takeovers 194–5

Large and Medium Sized Companies and Group (Accounts and Report) Regulations 2008 558
last in, first out (LIFO) 415, 417–18
  compared with FIFO 419
leased assets
  IAS 17 *Leases* 251
ledger 143, 150
  account balances 163–4, 172–8
  case study of preparation for a limited company 691–8
  case study of preparation for a sole trader 684–9
  cash and bank transactions 152–5
  credit transaction entries 155–61
legal form 75
lenders
  users of annual reports 50
letter of engagement 102
leverage 663
liabilities 124–5
  separate determination concept 76
  terminology 9, 124
liability
  definition 587
limited companies (Ltd)
  accounting for share issues 563–4
  case study of preparation of journals, ledgers and trial balances 691–8
  conversion of partnerships 526–32
  illustration of preparation of final financial statements 572–7
  legal powers and duties 543–4
  preparation of final financial statements 558–93
  types of share and loan capital 544–9
limited liability 15, 542
limited liability partnerships (LLP) 465–6, 526–32
liquidity 648
  measures 653–6
liquidity ratio 654–5
listed companies 15, 543
  statutory audit 101–2
loan creditor 152
loan stock 544, 546–9
  advantages and disadvantages of issuing 548
  characteristics 547
  types 548
loans
  accounting for debt 588–91
long-term liabilities 16
  see also non-current liabilities
loose tools 298–9
loss for the period 9, 234
loss on sale 260

management
  users of annual reports 56
  see also corporate governance
management accounting
  definition 4
management ethics 111–13
manufacturing account 430
  preparation 432–7
  purpose 432
manufacturing entities
  financial statements 430–41
  inventory valuation 412–21
manufacturing profit 437–9
matching concept/principle 70–3, 129
material items
  disclosure 584
material misstatement 102, 107
materiality 89–90
materiality concept 73
measurement 77
  definition 77
measurement bases 77
measurement unit 132
Memorandum of Association 543
modified audit report 107
money measurement concept 74, 132
Monitoring Board of Public Capital Market Authorities 25, 27

negative goodwill 502
negative premium 502
net book value (NBV) 251
net carrying amount 251
net current assets 656
net realizable value (NRV) 67, 413
netting 75–6
neutrality 91
nominal accounts 163–4
nominal ledger 143, 150
nominal value 544
non-adjusting events after the reporting period 587
non-cumulative preference shares 548
non-current assets 234
  depreciation 253–67
  discontinued operations 38, 251, 254, 583–4
  held for sale 38, 251, 254, 584
  IAS 16 *Property, plant and equipment* 36, 250, 251, 252, 253, 254
  IFRS 5 *Non-current assets held for sale and discontinued operations* 38, 251, 254, 583–4
  impairment 252
  journal entry 189
  nature of 250–1
  partial year depreciation 262–6
  profits and losses on disposal 260–2
  terminology 9, 250
  types 250–1
  valuation 251–2
  see also intangible assets; tangible assets
non-current liabilities 234
  terminology 9
non-financial assets 251
non-monetary assets 251
non-purchased goodwill 496
normative theories 60
notes to the financial statements 9, 578–83
  equity share dividends 571

obsolescence through demand changes 253
obsolescence through technological change 253
off-balance-sheet finance 75
offer for sale 564
opening entries
  journal 194
operating activities 610
operating risk 664
ordinary share 544
other comprehensive income 9

other income
terminology 7
overcast 370
overheads 430
owners of shares 9

par value 544
participating preference shares 545, 548
partners' commission 465
Partnership Act 1890 456–7, 458
partnership agreement 12, 456
partnership salary 457–8
partnerships 11–13
admission of new partner 488–95, 498–502
appropriation account 459–64
capital accounts 458
changes 486–510
changes in profit-sharing ratio 504–9
conversion to a limited company 526–32
current accounts 458
definition 456
dissolution 522–5
drawings accounts 458
final financial statements 456–68
Garner v Murray ruling 495, 522
goodwill 486, 495–504
guaranteed share of profit 465
law 456–7
limited liability 465–6, 526–32
retirement of partner 486–8, 492–5, 502
revaluation of assets on changes in partners 492–5
sharing of profits between partners 457–8
statement of cash flows 616–17
statement of changes in equity 13, 14
statement of financial position 12, 14
statement of profit or loss 12, 13
taxation 12, 300
valuation of goodwill 495–8
periodicity concept 129
perpetual inventory system 415
petty cash book 143, 218–22
columnar 218–21
positive goodwill 495
positive theories 60
posting 150
posting errors 370
posting the transaction 150
predictive value 89
preference shares 544–5
accounting for 545–6
advantages and disadvantages of issuing 548
characteristics 547
types 545, 548
preliminary, promotion or formation expenses 544
premium contra 500
prepayments 69
accounting for 294–8
present value 77
price-earnings (P/E) ratio 661–2
prime cost 432
prior period adjustments
disclosure 585–6
IAS 8 *Accounting policies, changes in accounting estimates and errors* 35–6, 80, 585–6
private companies (Ltd) 15, 543
see also limited companies (Ltd)
profit
definition 128, 230
profit and loss account 4, 16
see also statement of profit or loss
profit and loss account credit side 310–16
profit and loss account debit side 310–16
profit or loss for the period 9, 234
profit margin 651–3
profit measurement 128–9
profit on sale 260
profitability 648
property, plant and equipment 8, 16
IAS 16 *Property, plant and equipment* 36, 250, 251, 252, 253, 254
see also non-current assets
prospectus 549–50, 564
provision for, aggregate or accumulated depreciation 260
provision for bad debt *see* allowance for irrecoverable/doubtful receivables
provisions
definition 587
IAS 37 *Provisions, contingent liabilities and contingent assets* 37, 587–8
prudence concept 69–70
the public
users of annual reports 55
public accountability 51–3
public limited companies (plc) 15, 542–3
accounting for share issues 564–70
legal powers and duties 543–4
preparation of final financial statements 558–93
types of share and loan capital 544–9
published financial statements 47, 550–1, 558
appraisal using ratio analysis 648–69
format 558
notes *see* notes to the financial statements
see also final financial statements; financial statements; users of annual reports
purchase of consideration account 528–32
purchase returns 157
purchased goodwill 496
purchases day book 143, 188–9
purchases ledger 189, 348
purchases ledger control account 349
example 349
purchases returns day book 143, 189

qualified audit report 107
qualitative characteristics of financial information 88–97
comparability 92–3, 96–7
conflicting characteristics 96–7
consistency 92, 97
cost-benefit issues 95–6
faithful representation 90–1, 96–7
relevance 89–90, 97
timeliness 94, 95
understandability 94–5, 96–7
uniformity 93
verifiability 93–4, 97

ratio analysis
financial statement appraisal using 648–69
limitations 648, 666–8
see also accounting ratios
raw materials 412, 432
realization concept 69
receipt 142–3
recognition 76–7

record-keeping
small businesses 395
recoverable amount 252
redeemable preference shares 545, 548
reducing balance method of depreciation 255–6
regulatory framework of accounting 17–18
IFRSs 24–9
United Kingdom 30–2
reissued shares 565, 566
relevance of financial information 89–90
materiality 89–90
reporting entity
definition 122
reporting period 129
reserves
accounting for 570
residual profit/loss
partnerships 457
residual value 254
retail entities
inventory types 412
retained earnings 570
transfers to reserve account 571
return 648
return of goods *see* purchase returns; sales returns
return on assets 650
return on capital employed (ROCE) 650–1
return on equity (ROE) 651, 662–3
return on investment
measures 659–66
revaluation reserve 570
revaluations 252
partnerships following changes in partners 492–5
partnerships following changes in partners' profit-sharing ratio 504–9
revenue
matching principle 72
terminology 7
revenue/distributable reserves 570
revenue expenditure 250
example of closing a revenue type account 175–8
versus capital expenditure 129–32
revenue recognition 69
IAS 18 *Revenue* 36–7, 69, 75
matching principle 70–2
Royal Charter
bodies corporate 542
sales day book 143, 188
sales ledger 188, 348
sales ledger control account 348
example 349
sales returns 157
sales returns day book 143, 189
Sarbanes-Oxley Act 2002 109
secured debentures 546
selling and distribution overheads 430
separable/identifiable net assets 495
separate determination concept 75–6
share issue 549–50
share options 108
share premium 549, 570
shareholder participation 552–3
single entry 384, 389–94
single-entry bookkeeping 150
small and medium-sized entities
IFRS standard 26–7
small businesses
record-keeping 395
Small Companies and Groups (Accounts and Directors Report) Regulations 2008 558
SME Implementation Group (SMEIG) 26–7
Smith Report 109
social accounting 58–9
sole traders 10–11
case study of preparation of journals and ledgers for final financial statements 684–9
final financial statements 230–42
financial statements 11, 12
incomplete records 384
statement of cash flows 616–17
statement of financial position 11, 12, 234–6
statement of profit or loss 11, 230–4
taxation 11, 300
trading account 232–3
solvency
measures 653–6
special resolution 544
stakeholders 10, 52–3
standard setting
conceptual framework debate 60
IASB process 28–9
see also accounting standards; Accounting Standards Board (ASB); Financial Accounting Standards Board (FASB); International Accounting Standards Board (IASB); International Financial Reporting Standards (IFRSs)
statement 140
example layout 141
statement of affairs 386–9
statement of cash flows 9, 51, 610–29
advantages 627–8
cash flows from financing activities 614
cash flows from investing activities 613–14
cash flows from operating activities 610–13
classified 628
companies 618–26
IAS 7 *Statement of cash flows* 35, 610–26
limitations 627–8
notes 626
presentation 615
purposes 610, 626–7, 628
relationship with statement of profit and loss and statement of financial position 610
sole traders/partnerships 616–17
uses 626–7, 628
statement of changes in equity 9, 51, 570–1
partnerships 13, 14
statement of comprehensive income 4, 9, 51, 230
companies 15–16
presentation 558–60
statement of financial position 4, 9, 51, 230
accounting for reserves 570
accounting for share issues 563–70
accounts 164
as accounting equation 124–9
case study of preparation 689
companies 16–17
companies versus sole traders/ partnerships 562
example of closing the bank account 173–4
format 560–3
IAS 1 and UK GAAP compared 16
partnerships 12, 14

statement of financial position (*Continued*)
profit reporting 127–32
purpose 234
relationship with statement of cash flows and statement of profit and loss 610
sole traders 11, 12, 234–6
structure 234–6
terminology 8
statement of other comprehensive income 9, 16, 558
statement of profit or loss 4, 9, 234, 558
case study of preparation 689
example of closing a revenue type account 175–8
partnerships 12, 13
purpose 230
relationship with statement of cash flows and statement of financial position 610
sole traders 11, 230–4
terminology 7–8
see also statement of comprehensive income
Statements of Standard Accounting Practice (SSAPs) 30
SSAP 2 *Disclosure of accounting policies* 66
SSAP 16 *Current cost accounting* 74
statutory books 551, 552
stewardship accounting 4, 6
stewardship concept 50
stock *see* inventory
stores ledger 415
straight line/fixed instalment method of depreciation 255
substance of a transaction 75
substance over form concept 74–5
substantive testing 103
sum of the years' digits method of depreciation 256
summary of significant accounting policies 80
super profit 497
suppliers
users of annual reports 51
suspense accounts 371–4

T accounts 151–2
Taffler, R. J. 655–6
takeover bidders
users of annual reports 56
takeovers
journal entry 194–5
tangible assets
accounting standards 250–1
IAS 16 *Property, plant and equipment* 36, 250, 251, 252, 253, 254
terminology 8
tangible fixed assets 16
tangible non-current assets 250
historical cost approach to valuation 251–2
revaluations 252
tax avoidance 123
tax evasion 123–4
taxation
accounting for 300–1
corporation tax 15, 559
partnerships 12, 300
small business record-keeping 395
sole traders 11, 300
terminology
accounting 7–9
IAS 1 and UK GAAP compared 16
three-column cash book 202, 209–11
threshold 90
time interval concept 73–4, 129
time period concept 73–4, 129
timeliness 94, 95
total accounts 349
total equity attributable to owners 570
total factory costs 432
trade creditors 16
see also creditors; trade payable
trade debtors 16
see also trade receivable
trade discount 138, 188
trade payable 156
terminology 9
see also creditors; trade creditors
trade payables' ratio 657–8
trade receivable 156
terminology 9
see also trade debtors
trade receivables' ratio 656–7
trading account 232–3
Trading Certificate 544
transfer price 437
transposed figures 370
trial balance 178–83
case study of preparation for a limited company 691–8
errors 183
errors that cause trial balance to disagree 370–1
errors that do not cause trial balance to disagree 368–70
preparation of 179–82
preparing final financial statements from 236–41, 296–8
purpose 178–9
see also extended trial balance
trial balance credit side 310–16
trial balance debit side 310–16
true and fair view 100
Turnbull Report 109
two-column cash book 202–8

ultra vires 543
undercast 370
understandability of financial information 94–5
uniformity 93
unincorporated bodies 542
unincorporated businesses
member-governed bodies 13, 15
partnerships 11–13
sole traders 10–11
United Kingdom
regulatory framework of accounting 30–2
see also Financial Reporting Council (FRC); Financial Reporting Standards (FRSs); Generally Accepted Accounting Practice (UK GAAP)
United States
Sarbanes-Oxley Act 2002 109
Securities and Exchange Commission (SEC) 33, 109
see also Financial Accounting Standards Board (FASB); Generally Accepted Accounting Practice (US GAAP)
unlimited liability 457
unmodified audit report 104
example 104–6
unpresented cheques 331
unpresented lodgements 331
unqualified audit report 104
unrealized holding gains and losses 492
unrecorded cheques 331
unrecorded lodgements 331
unsecured debentures 546, 548
useful (economic) life 253–4

users of annual reports 10, 47, 48–9
abilities 94
analyst-adviser groups 56
competitors 56
creditors 51
customers 54
employees 53–4
evaluation of performance and financial position 650, 653
governments 54
investors 50
lenders 50
management 56
the public 55
suppliers 51
takeover bidders 56
see also qualitative characteristics of financial information

validity 103
valuation
fair value approach 252
finished goods 414–15, 439–40
goodwill in partnerships 495–8
historical cost approach 251–2
inventory 412–20
non-current assets 251–2
work in progress 414–15, 439–40
valuation model 132
value added tax (VAT)
implications for historical cost 252
variable production overheads 415
veil of incorporation 542
verifiability 93–4

warranties
revenue recognition 72, 252
weighted average method (AVCO) 415, 418–19
window dressing 412–13
work in progress (WIP) 412, 432
valuation 414–15
working capital 648
appraisal 656–9
working capital/current ratio 654
written down value (WDV) 251